The seven types of pasta, 118

A TASTE OF ITALY

Spaghetti al pomodoro al forno (*Spaghetti in Sauce with Baked Tomatoes*), 139

Properly made, fresh pasta shows light and shadow.

GIULIANO BUGIALLI'S

Classic Techniques of
ITALIAN COOKING

by Giuliano Bugialli

Photographs by Paolo Tosi

SIMON AND SCHUSTER • NEW YORK

Thanks to all who have helped on the long road to preparing this book, especially my sister-in-law, Gianna, and "Enrico" Weinberg for his unwavering belief in what I am doing.

Many thanks to the Biblioteca Nazionale and Biblioteca Riccardiana, two libraries in Florence, and the Biblioteca Marciana, a third in Venice, for making available to me the rare sixteenth- and seventeenth-century books referred to in the text.

Special thanks to Kim Honig and Rosalyn T. Badalamenti for their dedication as my editors.

PHOTO CREDITS

FRONT ENDPAPER, LEFT: "Cleopatra's Feast" by Allari and sepia drawing by Michelangelo—Scala, Firenze, Italy. *Fagiano ripieno*—Paolo Tosi.
FRONT ENDPAPER, RIGHT: *Spaghetti al pomodoro*—Photograph by Karen Radkai. Courtesy House & Garden. Copyright © 1981 by Condé Nast Publications Inc. Two pasta photos—Paolo Tosi.
BACK ENDPAPER, LEFT: *Ossobuco alla novese*—Richard Jeffery. *Arrochiato di vitella*—Photograph by Karen Radkai. Courtesy House & Garden. Copyright © 1981 by Condé Nast Publications Inc. *Carciofi in umido o in salsa* and *Polenta alla pistoiese*—Paccione.
BACK ENDPAPER, RIGHT: *Bavarese all' arancia*—Photograph by Karen Radkai. Courtesy House & Garden. Copyright © 1981 by Condé Nast Publications Inc. *Panettone* and *Panforte*—Paolo Tosi, courtesy *Attenzione* magazine. *Pere alla Corrado*—Paccione. *Torta di pere*—Richard Jeffery.

The sixteenth-century prints of herbs by Mattioli throughout the book and those in chapter 1 from Matteo Giegher's *Li Tre Trattati* (1637), Vincenzo Cervio's *Il Trinciante* (1581) and Scappi's *Opera* (1605) are from the collection of the author.

TO LELLA

Contents

FOREWORD 11
HOW TO USE THIS BOOK 15

1. Carving and Presentation: An Historical Perspective 19

   Techniques for: Preparing *Anitra peposa* (Duck with Green Peppercorns);
   Tying Poultry; Carving Stuffed Fowl; Preparing *Fagiano ripieno* (Pheasant
   Stuffed with Fruits); Preparing the Presentation of the "Live" Pheasant

2. Ingredients, Homemade Ingredients, and Basic Preparations 38

   Techniques for: Preparing Ricotta; Preparing Mascarpone; Preparing
   Mascarpone in coppa (Brandied Mascarpone Dessert); Preparing Wine
   Vinegar; Preparing *Sottoaceti* (Italian Pickles); Preserving Aromatic Herbs;
   Preparing *Oca in pignatto* (Goose Preserved in Its Own Fat); Preparing
   Zampone; Preparing *Cotechino*; Cleaning Anchovies in Salt; Grating
   Oranges and Lemons; Preparing *Sciroppo di arancia* (Orange Syrup);
   Preparing *Scorze di arancia candite* (Glacéed Orange Rind); Preparing
   Mostarda di Cremona (Fruit Relish of Cremona); Caramelizing Sugar
   Without a Mold; Cleaning and Cutting White and Black Truffles; Buying
   Fresh and Dried *Porcini* Mushrooms; Preparing Dried *Porcini* Mushrooms
   for Cooking

   Glossary of Basic Ingredients 67

3. Equipment for the Italian Kitchen 70

4. Chopping, Grinding, and Passing 79

   Techniques for: Using the *Mezzaluna* (Half-moon Chopper); Preparing
   Salsa di rognone (Kidney Sauce); Preparing *Torta di noci* (Walnut Cake);
   Grinding Nuts with Mortar and Pestle; Blanching Nuts; Grinding Spices
   with Mortar and Pestle; Grinding Meat with a Machine; Preparing Ravioli;
   Passing Food with a Food Mill

5. *Crespelle*, Batters, *Frittate* 102

   Techniques for: Seasoning a Pan; Preparing *Crespelle*; Sifting Flour;
   Preparing the *Crespelle* Batter; Cooking (Frying) *Crespelle*; Preparing
   "Fazzoletti" ripieni (Stuffed "Handkerchiefs"); Preparing *Frittata*;

6. Fresh Pasta 118

   Techniques for: Preparing Basic Egg Pasta; Preparing and Kneading the
   Dough; Stretching the Dough by Hand with a Rolling Pin; Cutting Pasta
   by Hand; Preparing *Tagliatelle* and *Taglierini*; Stretching the Dough with

a Hand Pasta Machine; Cutting Fresh Pasta Made with a Manually Operated Machine into Different Shapes; Drying Pasta; Storing Fresh Pasta; Cooking Fresh Pasta; Cutting Spaghetti; Preparing Gramigna; Cutting Pasta with a *Chitarra* ("Guitar"); Shaping Pasta for *Pinci*; Cutting Pasta into *Trenette*; Preparing *Pappardelle*; Preparing Pasta with Semolina Flour; Making *Orecchiette*; Cutting and Preparing Pasta for *Cannelloni* and Lasagne; Making *Tortelli*; Preparing *Uova alla fornaia* (Baked Giant *Tortelli*); Preparing *Tortellini*; Preparing *Cappelletti*

7. Dried Pasta   179

Techniques for: Cooking Dried Pasta (to Be Eaten Hot); Preparing *Spaghetti neri* (Spaghetti with the Ink of the Squid); Preparing *Pasticcio di pasta* (Baked Pasta Mold); Cooking Dried Pasta for Pasta Salad

8. *Risotti* and Polenta   199

Techniques for: Preparing *Risotto*; Cutting Polenta for *Crostini*

9. Some Special Methods of Cooking (Meats, Poultry, Fish, and Legumes)   212

Techniques for: Cooking in Clay; Cooking *al cartoccio* (or in a Paper Bag); Preparing *Faraona al cartoccio* (Guinea Hen Cooked in a Paper Bag); Preparing *Pollo al prosciutto* (Chicken wrapped in *Prosciutto*); Preparing *Costine al "Vecchio Molinetto"* (Spareribs "Molinetto" Style); Preparing *Petto di pollo al piatto* (Chicken Breast Cooked on a Plate); Preparing *Pollo al sale* (Chicken Cooked Covered with Salt); Preparing *Stracotto alla parmigiana* (Braised rump of Beef Parma Style); Larding Meat; Cooking on a Range-top Grill (*Gratella*); Tenderizing Fish

10. How to Bone and Stuff Poultry and Meats   233

Techniques for: Boning a Chicken Breast from the Whole Chicken; Boning a Whole Chicken Breast; Butterflying Chicken Breasts; Cutting Chicken into Pieces with Bone; Boning a Turkey, Goose, or Chicken Neck; Tying Meats or Boned Fowl "Like a Salami"; Boning, Stuffing, Cooking, and Pressing a Veal Breast; Boning a Leg of Lamb; Boning a Lamb Shoulder; Boning a Whole Rabbit

11. Veal   268

Techniques for: Cutting and Pounding a Veal Cutlet; Preparing *Tordimatti* ("Mock" Game Birds); Cleaning and Cutting Veal Kidney; Preparing, Rolling, and Tying *Involtini*; Flouring Very Lightly; Butterflying a Veal Loin; Rolling a Veal Loin; Preparing *Vitello tonnato* (Veal with Tuna Flavoring); Cutting Veal Shank into *Ossibuchi*; Preparing *Ossobuco di tacchino* (Turkey *Ossobuco*); Preparing *Fricassea di vitella* (Fricassee of Veal)

12. Mollusks, Seafood, and Fish   299

Techniques for: Filleting Fresh Sardines; Cleaning Cuttlefish (Inksquid) and Squid; Cleaning Shrimp; Cleaning Eels; Filleting a Sole

13. Galantines   313

Techniques for: Scaling and Boning Whole Fish; Assembling the *Galantina;* Boning Whole Large Fish; Boning a Chicken for *Galantina;* Preparing the Farcia and the Stuffing for the *Galantina;* Assembling the Chicken *Galantina*

14. Pasticci   331

Techniques for: Preparing *Pasticcio di lepre (Pasticcio* of Hare); Preparing *Balsamella;*

15. Vegetables and Legumes   341

Techniques for: Cooking Asparagus for a Variety of Dishes; "Steaming" Asparagus Tips; Preparing *Asparagi in salsa* (Asparagus in Egg-Lemon Sauce); Cleaning and Cutting Artichokes; Cleaning and Cutting Cardoons; Boiling Carrots a Special Way; Cleaning and Boiling Cauliflower; Cutting Kale for Cooking; Cutting Savoy Cabbage into Strips with a Mandolin; Cleaning Button Onions; Cleaning String Beans or Green Beans; Cutting Fennel for Cooking; Cutting Eggplant into Different Shapes for a Variety of Dishes; Shredding Potatoes; Cleaning and Cutting Peppers into Different Shapes; Removing the Skin from Tomatoes; Preparing Tomatoes to be Stuffed; Slicing Tomatoes for Tomato Salad; Cleaning Leeks; Cutting Zucchini into Different Shapes for Various Dishes; Preparing Zucchini Flowers for Cooking

16. Yeast Dough   402

Techniques for: Preparing Ice Dough; Improvising a Brick Oven; Preparing *Quaglie nel nido di un pane toscano* (Quail in a Nest of Tuscan Bread); Preparing a Nest with Tuscan Bread; Preparing a Loaf of Tuscan Bread; Preparing *Focaccia farcita* (Stuffed *Focaccia*); Preparing *Bomboloni* or Brioche and *Cotechino in camicia (Cotechino* Sausage Baked in Crust); Preparing *Babà alla Crema* (Babà Layer Cake); Preparing *Rotolo di Natale* (Christmas Fruit and Nut Roll)

17. Molds and Aspics   431

Techniques for: Preparing *Gelatina* (Aspic); Preparing *Petti di pollo allo specchio* (Rolled Chicken Breast in Aspic); Preparing *Sformato di maionese* (Mayonnaise Mold); Preparing *Maionese* (Mayonnaise); Preparing *Budino di pollo* (Chicken Budion); Preparing a *Bagnomaria;* Preparing *Bavarese al Marsala* (Marsala-flavored *Bavarese*); Peeling Fresh Chestnuts

18. Pastries   451

Techniques for: Preparing *Pasta sfoglia* (Puff Pastry); Preparing a Large *Turbante* (or Vol-au-vent); Preparing *Pasta frolla fragile* (Short Pastry Made with Hard-cooked Egg Yolk); Preparing *Marronata* (Chestnut Tart); Preparing *Pasta frolla* (Short Pastry); Preparing *Pasta briciolata* (Pâte Brisée); Preparing *Pasta mezza frolla* (Short Pastry with Milk); Preparing *Bocca di dama* (Italian Sponge Cake); Assembling *Zuccotto;* Preparing *Pasta savoiarda/Savoiardi* (Homemade Italian Ladyfingers); Preparing

Cannoli; Preparing *Pasta soffiata* (Cream Puff Pastry/Pâte à Chou);
Preparing *Pasta genovese* (Genoese Pastry).

19. Creams, Ice Cream, and Ices   489

Techniques for: Preparing *Crema pasticcera* (Custard Cream); Preparing
Zabaione; Whipping Cream by Hand; Folding Whipped Cream In;
Preparing *Gelato di frutta fresca* (Italian Fresh Fruit Ice Cream); Preparing
Granita di limone (Italian Lemon Ice)

A NOTE ON ITALIAN WINES   502
GLOSSARY OF ITALIAN TERMS   504
WEIGHTS AND MEASURES   505
TEMPERATURES   505
APPENDIX I. LIST OF RECIPES   506
APPENDIX II. LIST OF MENUS   512
INDEX   517

Foreword

Italian cooking has a very wide range, from the simplicity of many authentic regional dishes to the complexity of the *alta cucina* (haute cuisine) dishes used for formal dining all over Italy. This book covers the entire range. The simpler dishes are drawn from regions all over Italy and the islands of Sicily and Sardinia, and stress authenticity and genuineness. In order to include the more complex dishes so often neglected in Italian cookbooks written in English, it is really necessary to illustrate many techniques which are called for in making them. Also illustrated are some particularly Italian basic techniques, such as methods of chopping, ways of cooking, etc.

If I stress authenticity, it is because I feel that the authentic versions of dishes are the ones that have stood the test of time, even of centuries. Any personal innovations should stem from knowledge of the authentic traditional version. It is becoming increasingly possible to retain the authenticity of Italian cooking outside of Italy with the greater availability of the proper ingredients and is worth the extra effort to arrive at the traditional dish. After you have prepared and tasted the original recipe, then you can be more creative—what happens next is up to you.

The first chapter of this book documents, with prints from the sixteenth and seventeenth centuries, the development of aspects of formal presentation which spread from Italy to other countries at that time. It is my conviction that Italian cooking reflects the same spirit that gave birth to the Italian arts. *Alta cucina* reflects the aesthetic developments that occur in any high culture, and the simple regional dishes reflect the more stable folk character of the different local traditions.

The arrangement of the whole menu, what foods should properly accompany others to make a balanced ensemble, is most important to an Italian meal. Therefore, I have included in the appendix fifty menus along with a note on Italian wines for the menus. You will be able to choose a menu for any type of occasion, whether simple and homey or very formal. What is most important is to eat well, whatever the occasion.

I did not want to duplicate or repeat the recipes and other information covered in my first book, *The Fine Art of Italian Cooking*; therefore, you will see that I have occasionally referred you back to it, when necessary.

—G.B.

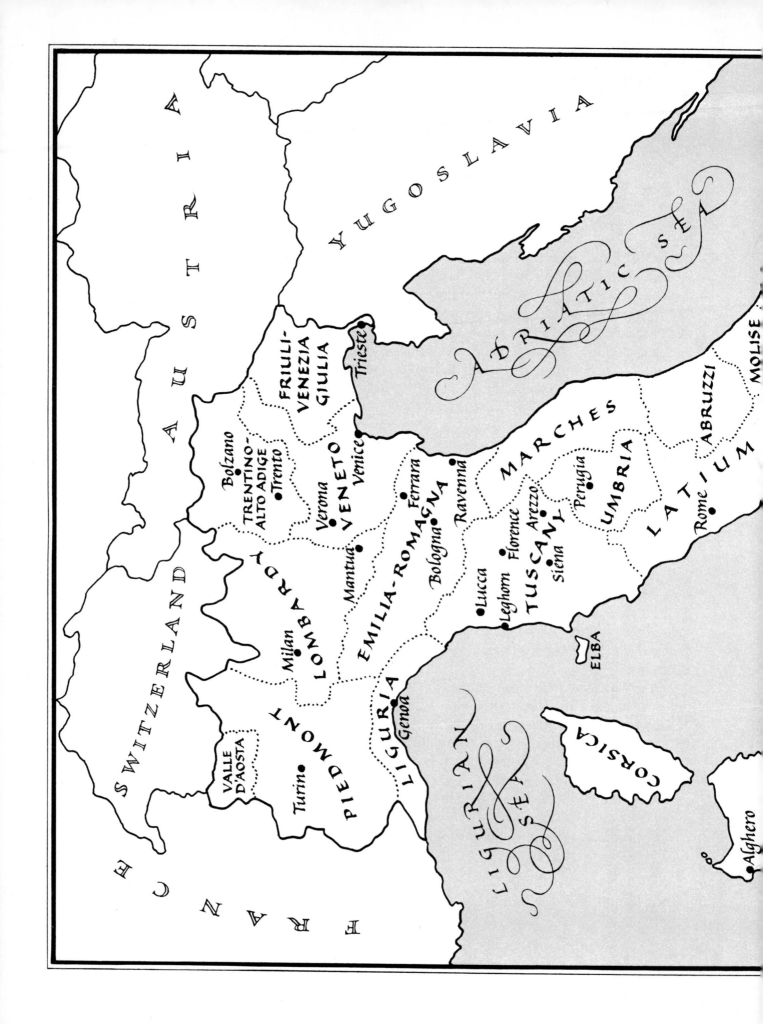

APULIA

Bari

BASILICATA

CAMPANIA

Naples

CALABRIA

IONIAN SEA

Reggio di
Calabria

TYRRHENIAN

SEA

SICILY

Palermo

Marsala

Catania

SARDINIA

Cagliari

MEDITERRANEAN SEA

Miles

0   40   80   120   160   200

Kilometers

0   80   160   240   280

Food
&Wine
Regions
OF
Italy

WONG

How to Use This Book

The main thread of the book's structure is technique. It is mainly organized into chapters logically developing series of related techniques. But I was also deeply concerned that the book follow through on certain themes that were introduced in *The Fine Art of Italian Cooking*, and to expand the representation of dishes from all the regions of Italy.

The book may be used to learn the classic Italian techniques necessary to make a body of more complex dishes that are not often made outside of Italy. (Each chapter title in the Contents is followed by a list of the techniques contained in the chapter.) It may also be used, quite simply, as a recipe and menu cookbook, by consulting the appendix list of recipes organized according to the courses of an Italian meal and the fifty full suggested menus with accompanying wines that come immediately after. Following the menus is a short discussion of the suggested wines. For tips on Italian ingredients, including directions for making some of them yourself, see chapter 2. For descriptions and illustrations of the basic equipment used in an Italian kitchen, see chapter 3. A glossary of Italian terms appears at the back of the book.

Classic Techniques of
ITALIAN COOKING

CHAPTER 1

Carving and Presentation:
An Historical Perspective

The painting by the fascinating Allori, in the color photo section, decorates the Grand Duke's *studiolo* in Florence's Palazzo Vecchio. The subject is "Cleopatra's Feast," presented as a realistic portrait of the last group of courses of a dinner in the painter's own time, the late Renaissance. Allori lived in the atmosphere of that remarkable group of "mannerist" gastronome-painters, all students or followers of the great Michelangelo, who formed the first modern gastronomic society, *Il Paiolo*, in the second half of the sixteenth century.

In this painting, as in his "Last Suppers," Allori details his really first-hand knowledge of food, an expertise which also led him to prepare a manuscript cookbook. A comparison between these paintings and those of feasts by Veronese reveals the difference between one who really knew food and another, certainly greater painter, who was portraying splendor for purely visual purposes.

While Venus and Cupid look on benignly, Cleopatra, Caesar, Antony, and the others are beginning the last round of courses of a Renaissance dinner. The dishes served are absolutely accurate for the so-called fruit *servito*,* as documented in innumerable ceremonial programs and cookbooks of the period. Along with the fresh fruit arranged on the table, including grapes, pears, and peaches, there are prepared vegetables, such as artichokes (in the middle) no longer green after cooking, and the whole eggplant (on the right), which was probably roasted. Though this is not a formal ceremonial feast, but rather an intimate dinner of friends of high rank, this example of how the food was presented is intriguing. The marzipan decorative figures for the table (in the foreground) are clearly shaped by real sculptors, not from stereotyped molds. You will see in the following pages that sculptors also did table decorations in sugar, butter, and ice. On the left there is a beautiful *putto* (or angel) holding a fish, like Michelozzo's bronze "Boy with a Dolphin" in the courtyard of the same palace; another creature, possibly a turtle, standing up (in the extreme right), and Neptune holding a trident while poised on a shell (center). The fruit and *frutti di mare* (seafood), here probably crabs, are served on warmly colored copper. It is unclear what the decorated covered terra-cotta casserole contains, but a pastry-covered *pasticcio* (pâté) on a wooden cutting board ready to be served is instantly recognizable. The relishes or *savori* are in crystal containers

---

* Presentation is the art of preparing to please the eye as well as the palate. A *servito* is one of the five or more servings, each of which contained as many as thirty dishes of the same category.

with silver lids and are being served on trays. Though there are paintings by other artists of the time depicting presentations more designed to impress and astonish, this scene by Allori, showing the connection between artists and chefs, is most charming, authentic, and sincere.

The chefs themselves were considered artists at this time as they developed and refined Italian cuisine to a science and an art, now described as technique in cooking. For example, the pastry crusts in which foods were wrapped reached a new high in variety, subtlety, and luxuriousness. The table was elaborately decorated through the aesthetic shaping of fruit and napkins into flower and animal disguises, and fish and meats were presented to please the eye as well as the palate. The same ingredients and materials were varied by different textural treatments. These special trade secrets developed by the chefs were performed with great virtuosity and guaranteed success to a battery of difficult culinary tasks. Serving was done with a perfected ceremoniousness and with rich and beautiful service and vessels. These chefs were echoing, in their approach, the same aesthetics as the artists of the flowering Manneristic art and its successor, the Baroque. The breathtaking dishes and tables that were developed in court dining of the time were imitated by the wealthier middle class. The artists who collaborated with the chefs on imaginative presentation of the food and the table also designed the room settings and often painted sets for the comedies and operas which were performed between the courses.

Among the chefs who had the highest artistic standing of the century were Messiburgo and Scappi. Scappi, whose most triumphant ceremonial dinner took place in 1536 in honor of Emperor Charles V, had the title of *cuoco segreto* (secret cook) to several popes. It is not certain to what extent *segreto* literally meant "secret" and to what extent it was a title of high honor, for the cooks of this period were sometimes raised to high rank and at least one of them, Cristoforo di Messiburgo, like the composer Orlando di Lasso, was raised to the nobility for his achievements. It must be remembered that Scappi and Messiburgo were really cooks and not simply humanist literary figures who incorporated the recipes of humble servants, as the humanist Platina had published the recipes of the celebrated cook Maestro Martino a century before. Those who were involved in the actual cooking now wrote books with great style, influenced by the fashionable Platonic dialogues.

Sugar and ice sculptures were also developed in this period, and to a level which must have been far beyond anything since, for these sculptures were done by some of the most famous artists of the late Renaissance. At the splendid wedding of Maria de' Medici to the future Henry IV of France in Florence's Pitti Palace, the design for the entire table was supervised by Buontalenti and the sugar sculptures were done by Giambologna and Tacca!* One weeps at the thought of what these artists created in such a perishable material. Buontalenti himself was famous for his ice sculpture. When Henry III of France, son of Caterina de' Medici, visited Venice some years before 1600, not only was the decorative sculpture done with sugar, then a luxury foodstuff imported from the

---

* See "The Marriage Feast of Maria de' Medici," by Giuliano Bugialli, *Gastronome*, Autumn 1981.

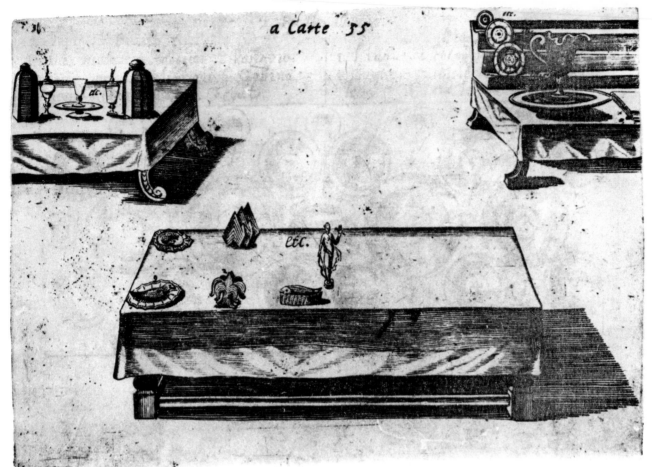

1. A woodcut from the 1605 edition of Scappi's Opera shows the table arrangement for serving.

The two back tables are the credenza and the bottigliaria (in the modern language it is bottiglieria), on the first of which are placed the many previously prepared dishes served at room temperature, such as savory and sweet tarts, fruit preparations, and any other dishes from courses not eaten hot. The second table is for service of the wine. Scarlino's Nuovo Trattato de' Vini lists some fifty-two different Italian wines that were regularly shipped to Rome in the mid-sixteenth century.

The table in front sparks a particular interest. It contains a variety of decorative figures all made with the complicated art of napkin folding. The first of Matteo Giegher's Tre Trattati (Three Treatises) (1637) is devoted to piegature or folding. Giegher, perhaps a maestro di casa or chamberlain, was one of the many south Germans, like the painter Dürer or the composer Heinrich Schutz, whose art was completely formed by their long studies in northern Italy, especially Venice. Giegher had a permanent post close to Venice, at the University of Padua. Two of his three treatises are simply repeats of earlier Italian ones, but the third is our best source for this Manneristic and Baroque form of decoration.

21

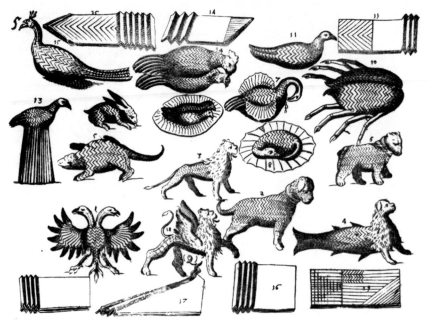

2. *A small sampling of the many fantasy figures made by folding napkins (of linen or cotton), here mostly birds and animals. Along the top and bottom are some technical illustrations of particular folds.*

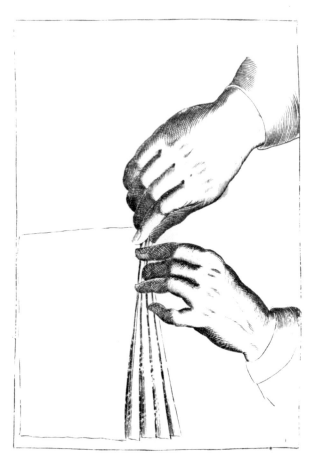

3. *The first folds of the napkin.*

4. *Beginning the herringbone pattern.*

East, but so were even the beautiful tablecloth and napkins (the Venetians were always anxious to impress important visitors with their splendor). Henry III was taken by surprise when he attempted to use a napkin to wipe his mouth and found it was made of sugar. Another favorite mortal material, butter, was used for productions of what probably deserved to be immortal works of art. However clever the decorations in these materials have been in succeeding centuries, it is unlikely that they have ever matched these early examples.

Il Trinciante, or the *Art of Carving*, first printed in Venice in 1580, remains a uniquely important work to this day. It details the carving and boning, the latter especially for rolling and stuffing, of every beast eaten, all carefully illustrated. It also includes decorative carving for presentation of fish and fruit. All subsequent Italian works that deal with these subjects are based on it, and it is safe to say that no work in any language has superseded it. The name of the author, Vincenzo Cervio, may have actually been a pseudonym for the Cavalier Reale Fusoritto de Narni whose name appears on the title page in some early editions. Like all of the books mentioned here, it was printed in Venice because that city was one of the, if not *the* most important center of printing in the century after its invention. (Cervio, however, was not Venetian.)

The carving of fruit for decoration and presentation was a very important part of the Italian meal.

The etiquette of carving was also extremely important in the Renaissance and *Il Trinciante* is, therefore, part of the literature beginning with Castiglione's *Il Cortegiano (The Courtier)* that painted pictures of the genteel life at an ideal court to serve as models for other courts and large households. These works were translated and imitated in France, Elizabethan and Jacobean England, Germany, especially the courts of Vienna and Munich where Italian was the court language, Spain, and as far away as Poland and Hungary. These works probably had a more profound effect in establishing the etiquette of the next centuries than Louis XIV's dicta a century later. The wealthy middle class always imitated the court styles to the extent they could, so that many of these

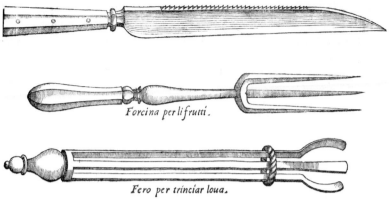

Forcina per li frutti.

Fero per trinciar loua.

6. *Some special implements used for the carving of fruit: a serrated knife, a fork, and a specialized implement for carving.*

7. *The carving of pears. Numbers 2 and 5 show the implements for holding and cutting the pear. Other examples show the decoration with stripes and wedges. Number 2 is the pear made into a decorative container for presentation of something else. The most elaborate carving is Number 7, in which the pear has been made into a swan. There are also some apples, including at least one cored and prepared for stuffing or as a vessel of presentation.*

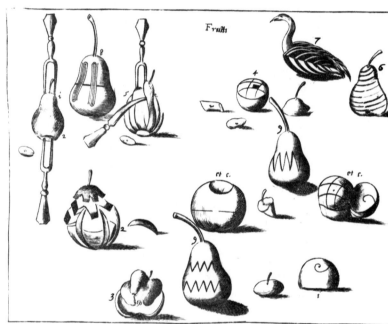

Frutti

8. *The decoration of oranges. The skins were often cut into or were elaborately carved in designs. Some are halved and others prepared as containers for the presentation of other food.*

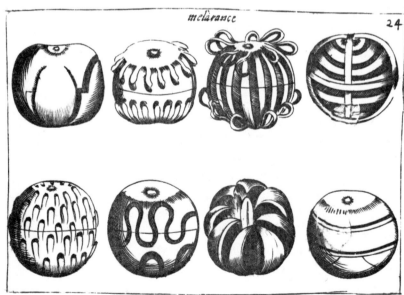

melarance 24

9. *The greatest fantasy is shown in the carving of citrons, which resemble large lemons. The branches and leaves are incorporated in making birds, fish, mythological animals, and flowers.*

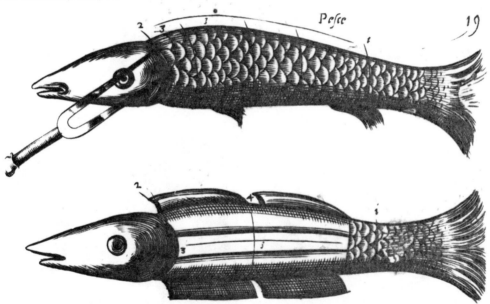

10. *The decorative carving of fish. The drawing in the upper part shows the implement for holding the fish while carving. The lower one gives one example of the decoration for presentation made by cutting away some of the skin, creating designs in the alternation of skin and flesh. This kind of fish presentation has come down to the present almost unchanged.*

These complicated designs carved into food or special techniques required to prepare a dish could not be accomplished without the proper utensils, so an assortment of cooking tools was designed. Each of these utensils performed a specific function. Even as early as the 1400s we know from Martino that there was a trade secret technique of making tubular pasta with a special floured stick. Another fascination of Scappi's Opera lies in its page after page of illustrations of cooking implements, hundreds of specialized devices to aid in the techniques involved in many individual dishes. Among other things, there are illustrations of mortars and setacci (sieves), molds and pastry bags, hundreds of specialized pots and other cooking implements of iron, copper, and terra-cotta, stove types for cooking in a number of different ways, professional arrangement of the kitchen, etc.

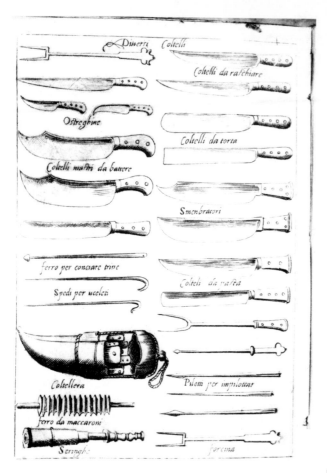

11. A small sampling of the knives and some other implements. Italian cooking then used chef's knives for many things. It had not yet developed the ingenious mezzaluna so that the techniques of chopping, cutting, etc., more resembled the modern French ways than present Italian methods. There are (on the right side of the illustration) special knives for cutting pastry, oysters, and tarts and (on the top left) the coltelli per battere or chopping knives. On the bottom left is a device for cutting maccaroni and a siringa (syringe), probably for pastry and decoration for presentation.

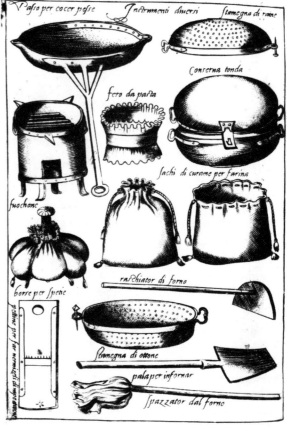

12. On the bottom left is the mandolin-like instrument or "comb" to make not pasta but vermicelli or strips of vegetables. In the upper middle is a fero da pasta (in the modern language it would be ferro per pasta), which was likely a scalloped-edged tortelli cutter.

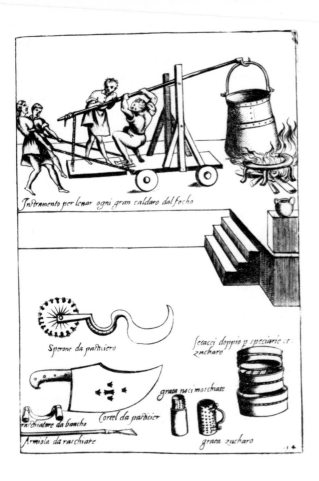

Inftrumento per lenar ogni gran caldaro dal focho

Sperone da paftciero

fetacci doppio p speciarie et zucharo

rafchiatore da bancho

Cortel da paftcier

grata noci mofchiate

Armiola da rafchiate

grata zucharo

13. There is a pastry jagger (left bottom), a special sweet pastry-maker's knife, and graters for nutmeg and sugar. On the bottom right is a double sieve for sugar and spices, probably to obtain the fine texture in confectioners' sugar.

pignatta *butiglia* *mortaro* *trinello*

pignatta grande *cucuma* *fchiumarelo da cucina* *gratta caffio*

Salsoneto per far ona *cuchiari da menestrar*

cazzolo conil manico fburiato *cazzolo cò il manico forato* *foratoro colmanico*

lecarda *ghiottela* *paftrella*

14. On the upper left are two sizes of pignatta, the traditional terra-cotta vessels for storing preserved goose, etc. [See Oca in pignatto (Goose Preserved in Its Own Fat), p. 49.] These vessels were still widely used until recent decades. Notice also the mortaro, a pharmacy type of mortar, for grinding spices. On the middle right is a gratta cascio, a cheese grater similar to a type which also existed until recently.

27

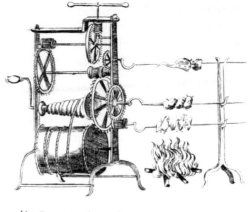

15. *A large spit for roasting meats with three skewers that turn mechanically with a wind-up mechanism exactly like that of the works of a clock.*

Molinello con tre spedi che si uolta dasse per forza de moue con il tempo a foagia di orologio come nella presente figura si dimostra

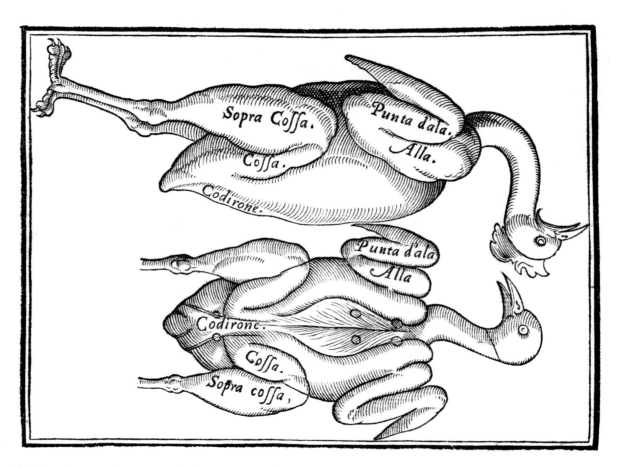

Sopra Coſſa.

Punta d'ala.

Coſſa.

Alla.

Codirone.

Punta d'ala

Alla

Codirone.

Coſſa.

Sopra coſſa,

16. This famous drawing, which appears in both *Scappi* and *Il Trinciante*, shows the fascination of the sixteenth century with the supposed similarity between the newly discovered Turkey or Rooster of India (bottom) and the Peacock (top), that precious bird which from Roman times had been the most prestigious dish to serve at royal and noble feasts. Cooks of this period thought they had found a plentiful supply of what had once been a rare and trea- sured meat. Though the print appears to be just front and side views of the same bird, in the version from Il Trinciante the two are clearly labeled Pavone (pea- cock) and Gallo d'India (rooster of India). The parts crucial for carving are labeled as well, and the text accompanying these illustrations details the carving of these birds. All the other animal illustrations are labeled in the same way with accompanying text.

28

things have passed along to us as standards of table manners and the other types of etiquette.

The etiquette of carving established at that time has remained in Italy to this day. The head of the household, or at a noble court some high-ranking person, had to do the carving himself at the table in the presence of the guests. Skill and elegance in performance at the table was as important as skill on the horse when at the hunt or other ceremonies. In Italy today it is still considered poor taste at a formal dinner for the host not to do his own carving and to perform it with expertise.

Not presented in the literature of that period are the poultry shears, which were developed later. If a fowl such as chicken or turkey has been left unboned, with or without stuffing, the usual Italian way of carving it is into quarters or eighths, cutting through meat and bone with the shears. Americans are surprised when I carve even a large American turkey in this way, not slicing the meat off the bone, but rather serving sections with the bone and all, in the Italian way.

An especially attractive way of carving unboned, densely stuffed fowl in Italy is to cut straight across with the shears, producing rings or slices of meat with the bone and stuffing in the middle. The following recipe for *Anitra peposa* (Duck with Green Peppercorns) illustrates this way of carving and presentation.

PEPE D'INDIA.

17. A 1536 drawing of a pepper plant from Mattioli, Siena.

29

Anitra Peposa

DUCK WITH GREEN PEPPERCORNS

FAMILY RECIPE, POSSIBLY FROM OLD AREZZO IN TUSCANY

The normal pepper plant (*Piper nigrum*) is native to India. The trade in pepper since ancient times would form a full length romance of its own. The berries are first green and then turn red when fully ripe. When dried in the sun with their hull or coating still on, the result is the usual black peppercorn. With the hull removed just before final ripening, or if the sun-dried berry is washed at a later stage, it becomes our white peppercorn. Green and red peppercorns are undried and preserved in some other way, such as in wine vinegar or brine. There has been a great vogue recently of first green and then red peppercorns (including imitation red ones).

This duck recipe has been made in my family as long as I can remember, but I am not sure when it originated, though I am certain it is not recently. It is not only the use of green peppercorns which gives the main spice flavor to the dish, but the contrast of the green ones inside the duck's stuffing with the black peppercorns in the accompanying bed of rice. The relatively small amount of rice in the stuffing does not preclude the more substantial rice accompaniment.

With a stuffing of uncooked sausage, half-cooked rice, and green peppercorns, the duck is sautéed, and then baked in an unusual way. It is placed directly in the baking dish with no rack and the skin is unpricked. The result is very crisp and greaseless, because the very high temperature of the oven seals the skin completely so that the fat dripping off through the duck does not re-enter it while it is cooking.

1 Long Island-type duck, about 5 pounds   SERVES 6

For the stuffing:
½ cup raw rice, preferably Italian Arborio
3 cups boiling water
Coarse-grained salt
2 Italian sweet sausages without fennel seeds (about 6 ounces)
1 tablespoon green peppercorns in brine, drained
Salt and freshly ground black pepper

For cooking:
1 tablespoon sweet butter
¼ cup olive oil
Salt and freshly ground black pepper

To accompany the duck:
1½ cups raw rice, preferably Italian Arborio
9 cups boiling water
Coarse-grained salt
About 15 whole black peppercorns
4 tablespoons sweet butter
About 4 tablespoons duck drippings

Wash the duck well, pulling off any fat left inside cavity.

Prepare the stuffing. Cook the rice, uncovered, in boiling salted water for only 10 minutes. Drain and cool under cold running water. Drain again and put the rice in a bowl.

HOW TO PREPARE ANITRA PEPOSA

1. Remove the skin from the sausages and add them to the bowl with the rice.

2. Add the green peppercorns and salt and pepper to taste.

3. Mix all ingredients thoroughly with a wooden spoon.

4. Transfer the stuffing to the cavity of the duck.

5. Close the cavity with needle and thread.

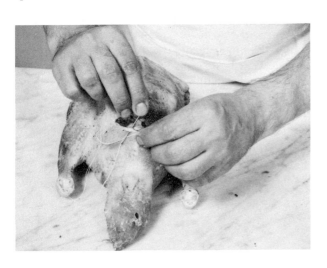

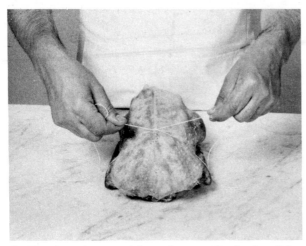

6. Tie the wings and legs close to the body of the duck, by first placing the string under the duck at the level of the wings. Tie a double knot on the breast.

7. Make a double knot again with the two ends of the string at a point corresponding to the middle of the legs.

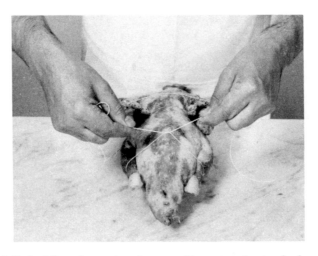

8. Turn the duck over, while holding the two ends of string, and double knot again, keeping the legs in place. Cut off the excess string.

Heat the butter and oil in a large casserole. When the butter is melted, add the duck. Sprinkle with salt and pepper and sauté until lightly golden brown on all sides (about 15 minutes). Preheat the oven to 450 degrees.

Put the browned duck breast side up into a baking dish without a rack. (The duck will not stick to the dish as it emits its own grease.)

Place the baking dish in the oven for 1 hour and 45 minutes, turning the duck two or three times without removing any fat or basting.

Twenty minutes before the duck is done, add the 1½ cups of rice to the boiling water with coarse-grained salt to taste and the black peppercorns.

Prepare a large serving dish with the butter and about 4 tablespoons of duck drippings taken from the baking dish in the oven. Cook the rice for about 18 minutes, drain, keeping the black peppercorns with the rice. Transfer the rice to the prepared serving dish. Mix thoroughly so that the butter and drippings are incorporated into the rice. Cover the dish with aluminum foil to keep the rice warm while you carve the duck.

HOW TO CARVE STUFFED FOWL

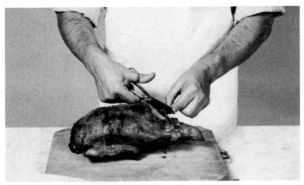

9. Transfer the cooked duck to a cutting board and remove the string.

10. Use a poultry shears to cut off the legs at the joint.

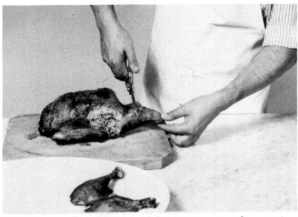

11. To cut the whole duck into rings start by cutting a 2-inch slice off the tail end. Using the poultry shears one can cut straight across through the meat, bone, and stuffing, leaving the slice whole.

12. Cut off a second slice to the end of the wings.

13. Cut off the wings at the joint.
    It is now possible to cut the rest of the duck into slices. With the slices and pieces, reconstruct the shape of the duck on the serving dish.

14. Arrange the previously prepared peppered rice in a ring around the duck slices.

Fagiano Ripieno

PHEASANT STUFFED WITH FRUITS

A striking adjunct to carving is the type of presentation in which the cooked animal is reconstructed into an illusion of the still-live creature. This was a favorite Renaissance presentation, as when a fish was arranged as though it were swimming on an ice brook or a peacock or pheasant with its feathers placed back on was standing in a woodland munching fruit. The following recipe is for a pheasant cooked in and stuffed with fruit which reappears alive again in its bright plumage. This manner of cooking the bird with fruit is authentically Renaissance, but still exists in the region of Lombardy.

1 whole pheasant with feathers on the neck, wings, and tail   SERVES 4
  and uncleaned, about 4 pounds

For the stuffing:
5 medium-sized Delicious apples
3 medium-sized Bosc or Comice pears
20 dried prunes
Salt and freshly grated nutmeg
½-inch piece cinnamon stick
About 5 cups hot beef or chicken broth

For decoration:
Apples, pears, and fruits in season (about 3 pounds of fruit)
About 2 tablespoons vegetable oil

1. The whole pheasant.

2. Holding onto the tail with one hand, use the other hand to pull out the tail feathers one by one, keeping them whole.

3. Once the feathers are out, cut off the tail.

4. Carefully cut off the whole wings at the joint. (This way the feathers will not be broken.)

5. Leaving the feathers intact, cut off the whole neck and set aside with the wings and tail feathers for later use.

Singe the pheasant on the burner (by passing all areas quickly over the flame) and pull out all the small singed feathers from the body.

Core the apples and pears with an apple corer, then peel them carefully and cut vertically into slices almost ½ inch thick. Soak the dried prunes in lukewarm water for about 10 minutes.

6. With a knife make an opening in the bottom of the pheasant and thoroughly clean out the cavity.

7. Wash the pheasant very well and dry it with paper towels.

8. Stuff the cavity of the pheasant with about one third of the sliced fruit and soaked prunes.

9. Sew up the lower opening with thread and needle.

Place a pinch of salt in the neck opening and sew it up as well. Tie body and legs of the pheasant like a duck (page 32, photos 6 through 8). Add half of the remaining fruit to a flameproof casserole, preferably oval shaped with a cover. Place the pheasant on top of the fruit.

10. Then cover the pheasant with the remaining fruit.

Sprinkle with salt and freshly grated nutmeg and add the cinnamon stick. Cover the casserole and cook over medium heat for about 15 minutes. Heat the broth to the boiling point. Turn the pheasant and start adding 1 cup of the hot broth. Cover the casserole and simmer very slowly adding broth as needed and turning the pheasant four or five times. When all the broth has been incorporated, the pheasant should be cooked and tender (about 2 hours). Remove the pheasant from the casserole and let it cool on a board for about 10 minutes.

PREPARING THE PRESENTATION OF THE "LIVE" PHEASANT

Arrange the fruit for decoration around a serving bowl, such as the typical oval-shaped Renaissance bowl pictured below. Lightly brush all the feathers with vegetable oil before replacing them on the pheasant.

11. Place the pheasant breast side down on the fruit. Stick tail feathers into the cooked pheasant in their original position.

12. Lay the wings in their original position.

13. Place the neck and head back in position.

14. Support the head by gently inserting the beak into a piece of fruit. This also creates the pleasant illusion that the live bird is eating the fruit. Transfer the sauce from the casserole to a sauceboat, discarding the pits of the prunes.

To serve the pheasant, remove the feathers and cut it into rings on a chopping board (page 33, photos 10 through 13). Place the rings on a serving dish and serve with some of the sauce.

CHAPTER 2

Ingredients, Homemade Ingredients, and Basic Preparations

In the Glossary of Basic Ingredients (page 67) are listed many ingredients which are necessary for authentic Italian cooking, with some tips about buying, handling, and storing them. Some ingredients are not easily available outside of Italy or a homemade version enhances the quality of dishes so much that it is worth making them yourself. In addition, making them is often just plain fun.

With several of these otherwise unavailable ingredients, it is possible to add dishes to one's repertory that generally can be enjoyed only in Italy. Each ingredient is followed by a recipe using it, whether it be savory or sweet. See the list of menus (page 512) for information about how each of these dishes may be integrated into an entire menu.

Ricotta

FROM ALL OVER ITALY

Ricotta is generally made from the whey which is the liquid left over from the making of cheese. However, it can also be made at home, using whole or skim milk, or a combination of the two. When ricotta is made from whey, more of the same rennet used in making the cheese is added. When making it from milk, in the family style, a similar result comes through adding a combination of yogurt and lemon juice as the activating and coagulating agents. The ricotta which results is really very close to that made with whey and rennet. With either method, what is obtained is not technically a cheese. The whey produces a second curd and the home method yields a result which is still not the same as a fresh cheese. Ricotta is never referred to as a cheese in Italy, but is considered a category in itself.

The whey left from making sheep's milk cheese produces ricotta which is more prized in Italy than that of cow's milk. And the rarest and most delicate of all is the one obtained from the milk of water buffaloes after the making of the true mozzarella. But even in Italy, as elsewhere, the most common is that made from cow's milk.

Ricotta may be preserved, and it is sometimes pressed and salted, as in the Ricotta salata of southern Italy which is available in the United States. This is most often made from sheep's milk and is a good substitute for other sheep's milk cheeses (Pecorino) when they are difficult to obtain. Ricotta may also be pressed and smoked.

3 *quarts whole or part skim milk*
3 *drops lemon juice*
1 *cup (8 ounces) plain yogurt*

YIELD: 2 CUPS

HOW TO PREPARE RICOTTA

1. Pour the milk into a glass or crockery bowl.
   Stir in the lemon juice. Let the mixture stand covered for 36 hours in a cool place or on the lowest shelf in the refrigerator.

2. Add the yogurt and mix with a wooden spoon, until the yogurt is completely incorporated.
   Transfer the contents of the bowl to a large saucepan and bring to a boil, stirring constantly with a wooden spoon. Boil for 1 minute, then remove the pan from the heat.

3. Use a large colander lined with heavy cheesecloth to drain the prepared ricotta.

4. Tie the cheesecloth together at the top with string.

The bag must be tied with a string so that it hangs free above a bowl which will catch any drippings. The easiest solution is to tie the string around a paper towel rack above the kitchen counter. Or, you can tie the string around the faucet of the kitchen sink. Let the bag hang for about 1 hour. The ricotta will then be ready to be used.

5. The finished product. This is the authentically dry unsalted Italian ricotta which is to be used as a binding ingredient. It does not have a rich flavor in itself.

Mascarpone

ORIGINALLY FROM LODI (NEAR MILAN)

Mascarpone is a type of solidified cream, which some consider a cheese, made originally from the especially rich cream of Lombardy. It has the natural sweetness of the cream itself. It originated in the area of Lodi, not far from Milan, and the earliest written reference to it is in 1168, though it may be much older, since that area was highly developed even in Roman times when Milan was briefly the capital of the Roman Empire.

Mascarpone is now made all over Italy, and though it is sometimes eaten as a cheese, it is more often used in combination with pastries, liqueurs, etc., to make rich, cold desserts. Visitors to Italy often regard *mascarpone* as a great discovery and they are disappointed that, being eaten very fresh, its texture changes in traveling, even when refrigerated. For this reason, for *mascarpone* lovers, or those waiting to discover it, we give this quite simple method of making it at home, followed by two typical desserts.

1 quart heavy cream
¼ teaspoon tartaric acid*

YIELD: ½ POUND (8 OUNCES)

* Tartaric acid, one of the most common vegetable acids and similar to cream of tartar but more acidic, is found in berries and the tamarind seed, and is used in making baking powder, effervescent drinks, and homemade wines. It can usually be purchased in pharmacies and is available through Caswell-Massey, 518 Lexington Avenue, New York, N.Y. 10017. (The store telephone number is 212/755-2254; if ordering by mail, call 212/620-0900).

HOW TO PREPARE MASCARPONE

1. Pour the heavy cream into a Pyrex saucepan and improvise a *bagnomaria*.

Place the improvised *bagnomaria* over medium heat and bring the heavy cream to a temperature of 180 degrees. Check carefully with a cooking thermometer. Remove from the heat.

2. Add the tartaric acid.

3. Stir with a wooden spoon for 30 seconds.

Then remove the insert from the *bagnomaria* and keep stirring for 2 minutes more.

4. Line a basket with heavy cheesecloth and pour in the cream mixture. Let the *mascarpone* stand for 12 hours in a cool place or on the lowest shelf of the refrigerator.

Cut four 9-inch squares of heavy cheesecloth. Open one on the table.

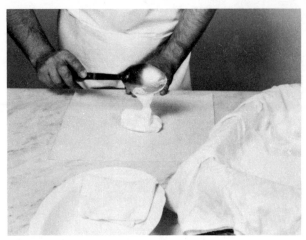

5. With a large spoon transfer one fourth of the *mascarpone* to the center of one of the squares of cheesecloth.

6. Fold one side on top of the *mascarpone*, then fold over the other side.

7. Fold over both ends but do not tie. Put the package of *mascarpone* folded side down on a serving dish.

Prepare the remaining three quarters of the *mascarpone* in the same way. Refrigerate the *mascarpone* for about 12 hours before using.

Mascarpone in Coppa

BRANDIED MASCARPONE DESSERT

FROM LOMBARDY

5 *extra large eggs, separated*
8 *ounces* mascarpone *(page 40)*
16 *amaretti cookies*
⅓ *cup brandy*
7 *tablespoons granulated sugar*

SERVES 8

1. Put the egg yolks and *mascarpone* into a crockery bowl. Mix with a wooden spoon until the yolks are completely incorporated with the *mascarpone*.

2. Meanwhile, soak 8 of the amaretti cookies in the brandy so that the liquid is completely absorbed. Then add the sugar to the bowl with the *mascarpone*-egg mixture and stir until the sugar is incorporated.

3. Add the soaked amaretti cookies, one by one, and mix very well.

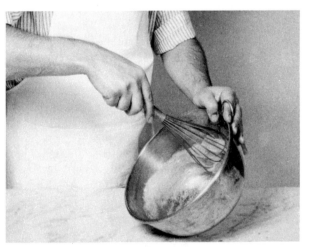

4. In a copper bowl beat the egg whites with a wire whisk until they are stiff.
  Gently fold the whites into the *mascarpone*-egg yolk-sugar-amaretti mixture.

5. Ladle the mixture into 8 individual dessert cups.

6. Place 1 amaretto cookie on top of each cup. Refrigerate for at least 1 hour before serving.

Tiramisù

"LIFT ME UP"

FROM NORTHERN ITALY

8 ounces bittersweet chocolate
24 ladyfingers (page 480)*
2 cups strong espresso coffee, cooled
6 eggs, separated
6 heaping tablespoons granulated sugar
1 pound mascarpone (page 40)

SERVES 12

* If the ladyfingers are not homemade, toast them in a 375-degree oven for about 15 minutes.

Chop the chocolate coarsely or cut it into small pieces. Put the ladyfingers on a plate and lightly soak them with the cold coffee. Arrange half of the ladyfingers in one layer on a rectangular or oval serving dish with sides at least 2 inches high.

While the ladyfingers are soaking, use a wooden spoon to mix the egg yolks together with the sugar in a crockery bowl. Mix until the sugar is completely incorporated and the egg yolks turn a lighter color. Then add the *mascarpone* and stir gently. In a copper bowl beat the egg whites with a wire whisk until they are stiff. Gently fold the whites into the *mascarpone*-egg yolk-sugar mixture.

Use half of this mixture to make a layer on top of the ladyfingers in the serving dish. Sprinkle with half of the chopped chocolate. Repeat the procedure to make another layer of soaked ladyfingers, the *mascarpone* mixture, and the chopped chocolate.

Cover with aluminum foil and refrigerate for at least 1 hour before serving.

NOTE: If you do not make your own *mascarpone*, substitute ½ pound ricotta and 1 cup heavy cream. Even just ricotta (1 pound) will work satisfactorily. Blend in a food processor until a light cream forms.

Wine Vinegar

In Italy we often make good young vinegar by leaving the wine exposed to the air for several weeks. The yeast in the wine is still active and, with the help of enzymes in the air, a "mother" forms and turns the wine to good vinegar.

When trying to make vinegar from Italian wine in the United States, the "mother" does not often form, whether from the absence of enzymes in the air or perhaps because some of the wine might have been pasteurized, killing the active yeast. However, it is easy enough to reintroduce the active yeast, using a centuries-old method. In medieval times, yeast was most often reactivated from old bread. Using this method, put some of the crumb of the bread in the wine; this will reintroduce the yeast, and cause the wine to become good vinegar.

After about 3 weeks, you will notice the first evidence of fermentation: There will be some white powder floating on top of the wine, and the smell will be noticeably that of vinegar. Leave it for at least one more week and a real gelatinous "mother" will form. Once formed, the mother will continue to grow as more wine is added, and pieces of it may be cut off and used to make other barrels or bottles of vinegar.

4 cups dry red wine
1 cup white bread, crusts removed

YIELD: 4 CUPS

HOW TO PREPARE WINE VINEGAR

1. Pour the wine into a jar and add the bread. Place a lid loosely over the jar to allow some air to enter. Let stand for about 4 weeks at which time the "mother" should be formed.

2. The wine vinegar is kept in a small wooden barrel (page 78) and wine is added as needed so there is always a fresh supply of wine vinegar. You may safely add as much as three times the amount of wine as the quantity of wine vinegar left in the barrel. Before adding the new wine, remove enough vinegar to last through the week. With an active "mother," the new wine will turn to good vinegar in less than a week. In the front part of the photo you see the "mother" which looks like dark gelatin.

Sottoaceti

ITALIAN PICKLES

Sottoaceti are Italian pickles, which comprise not only the small pickle cucumbers, called *cornichons* in France, but also small onions, Tuscan peppers, cauliflower flowerets, small carrots, etc.

The vegetables may be prepared separately or in combination—called *giardiniera*—which is often used to accompany a boiled course, such as boiled beef, chicken, or capon. The little pickles are used to garnish a piquant cold dish such as *Vitello tonnato* (Veal with Tuna Flavoring), page 287, and the *giardiniera* is also used as a garnish with *Sformato di maionese* (Mayonnaise Mold), page 438, which is served as an accompaniment to many dishes.

The marinade consists primarily of wine vinegar and a few light aromatic herbs. It is different from most types of pickles known in America as it is not sweet nor does it use dill or some of the other familiar pickling spices for flavoring, as does the *Mostarda di Cremona* (Fruit Relish of Cremona), page 59. This recipe is for the light marinade common in the North, without the garlic often used in the South.

1½ pounds of mixed vegetables (pearl or button onions,
  Tuscan peppers, very small pickle cucumbers, cauliflower
  flowerets, carrots)
3 cups white wine vinegar
2 cups cold water
Coarse-grained salt
2 tablespoons granulated sugar
4 tablespoons olive oil
5 whole white peppercorns
5 whole black peppercorns
5 juniper berries

YIELD: 1 QUART

To prepare the small onions, first remove the thin skins. Then wash the onions and dry them with paper towels. For the small pickles and Tuscan peppers, remove the small stems. Peel the carrots and cut them into small pieces.

HOW TO PREPARE SOTTOACETI

1. Combine 1 cup of the white wine vinegar and the 2 cups water and bring the mixture to a boil. Add the cleaned vegetables and coarse-grained salt. Let boil slowly for about 5 minutes.

2. With a strainer-skimmer, remove the vegetables from the boiling liquid and put them in a mason jar. In a saucepan, bring to a boil the remaining 2 cups of vinegar. Add the sugar and olive oil. Boil for 2 minutes.

3. Pour the hot vinegar mixture over the vegetables, adding the white and black peppercorns and the juniper berries. Let cool for about ½ hour. Close the jar tightly. Store in a cool place. You can use the *sottoaceti* after they have marinated for about 3 weeks.

Preserved Aromatic Herbs

BASIL, SAGE, ROSEMARY, ETC.

FROM TUSCANY

This is the best method for keeping fresh herbs after the growing season and they are more flavorful than dried herbs. The technique of using the coarse-grained salt works successfully to absorb the moisture of the herbs and it does not overpower the taste and smell of the herbs. They will last for about 6 months —until the next growing season.

Remove the leaves from the stems but do not wash them.

1. Make a layer of coarse-grained salt about ½ inch thick in a mason jar.

2. Place a layer of the herb (basil in these photos) over the salt layer.

3. Then add more salt.
   Repeat this procedure until the jar is full.

4. The top layer should be of salt.
   Close the jar tightly and keep it in a cool place for the whole winter.

NOTE: When you use the herbs, wash them off, to remove the excess salt and to clean them. Generally, herbs preserved in salt do not turn dark during the preserving process. However, some herbs, like basil, will lose some of their green color, although none of the flavor, so just remove the leaves from the prepared dish before serving.

Oca in Pignatto

GOOSE PRESERVED IN ITS OWN FAT

FROM VENICE

This conserve of goose was a mainstay of Venice for many centuries. It was given credit for saving the Venetians from famine during many a siege of "the Queen of the Adriatic." Preserving meats in fat has been used for centuries in many regions of Italy. It usually stemmed from the necessity of keeping meats for long periods of scarcity. Another notable example is the sausages preserved in fat from Siena.

The goose is boned before preserving and it reaches the right taste in its aging after 3 months. A *pignatto* (in the modern language *pignatta*) (page 71) is a type of terra-cotta vessel traditionally used for storing the conserve, although it is a rarity to find one these days (a thick glass mason jar can be substituted). Though it has virtually disappeared now, this goose dish was one of the most characteristic elements in the old Venetian cooking, used to flavor other dishes as well as being eaten for itself. See the recipe for *Tagliatelle con sugo di oca conservato* (page 134). If served as a main course, remove meat with only the fat that clings to it. Warm through and serve accompanied by boiled beans or potatoes.

1 goose, about 8 pounds
3 large cloves garlic, peeled
2 or 3 sprigs fresh rosemary,
    or 1 heaping tablespoon preserved rosemary leaves
2 cups olive oil
Salt and freshly ground black pepper
6 or 7 bay leaves

YIELD: 4 CUPS MEAT,
APPROXIMATELY (SERVES 8
AS A DRESSING FOR PASTA;
SERVES 6 AS A MAIN DISH)

HOW TO PREPARE OCA IN PIGNATTO

1. Clean and wash the goose very well and dry with paper towels. Do not remove any fat from the goose. Cut the garlic into small pieces.

49

2. Place the goose in a large casserole and add the garlic and rosemary. Pour 1 cup of olive oil over the goose.

Sprinkle with salt and pepper to taste. Cover the casserole and put it over low heat. Cook very slowly for about 2½ hours, turning the goose once. Then transfer the goose from the casserole to a chopping board. Let the fat in the casserole cool for about 10 minutes, then put 1 ladleful of the fat into a mason jar.

3. With a knife, remove the skin from the breast first.

4. Detach the half of the breast in one boneless piece.

Put it on a plate until needed. Repeat the procedure with the other breast half and the rest of the goose, until all the cooked boneless meat is on the plate. Discard the skin.

5. When the fat in the jar has cooled enough to solidify (about 1 hour), make a layer of meat.

6. Then pour over enough fat to completely cover the meat. This layer of fat from the pan should still be slightly liquefied but cool enough not to melt the fat below.

After the layer of fat is solidified continue to make layers of fat and meat until all the meat and fat are used. Again do not add another layer of meat until the previous layer of fat is solidified. The top layer should be of fat. As the fat cools, each layer takes less time to solidify.

Place the bay leaves over this last layer of fat and then pour over the remaining cup of olive oil.

7. Close the jar tightly and keep it in this way, preferably in the refrigerator, for at least 3 months.

A favored way to use the preserved meat with its flavored fat is as a delectable sauce for fresh *tagliatelle* (page 134).

Zampone

Zampone is the celebrated sausage of Modena and is used throughout Italy, particularly during the Christmas holidays, when it is eaten as a main dish by itself and as an important part of the *Gran bollito misto* (Grand Mixed Boiled Dinner) (see *The Fine Art of Italian Cooking*). It is in the form of a boiled pig's foot that is stuffed with pork. Like all pork products from Italy, it has not been permitted to be shipped into the United States since 1963, so that it's worthwhile to know how to make an authentic one at home. As this recipe contains no preservatives, and is not sealed in fat, the sausage will not last as long as those made commercially. The newly-made *zampone* should age in the refrigerator for about 3 or 4 days before it is cooked. It should then be boiled for about 3 hours in salted water. Because it is not dried like the commercial ones, it does not have to be soaked, nor does it cook as long. If served by itself as a meat course, it is traditional to accompany it with potato purée on the same plate. The pig's foot casing is delicious and should be eaten together with the meat. After boiling, it may also be baked in a crust when cooled, like the *Cotechino in camicia* (*Cotechino* Sausage Baked in Crust), page 422.

About 4 quarts water
1 heaping tablespoon coarse-grained salt
A small pig's foot
1 pound coarsely ground lean pork, approximately
Salt and freshly ground black pepper
5 whole black peppercorns
5 whole cloves

SERVES 6

The first step is to remove the nails from the pig's foot. Bring a saucepan with salted water to a boil. Hold the bottom of the pig's foot (with the nails) in the boiling water for about 2 minutes. Remove and cool under cold running water.

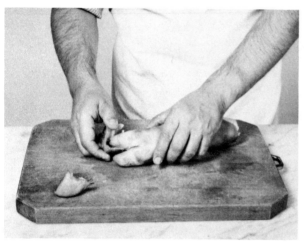

1. Remove the two nails by pushing them off the foot.

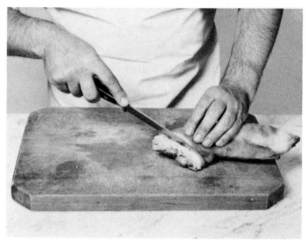

2. At the other end of the foot, insert a knife under the skin and move it all the way around, freeing the skin at the end.

3. Open the skin by cutting all the way down the center of the inner side of the foot.

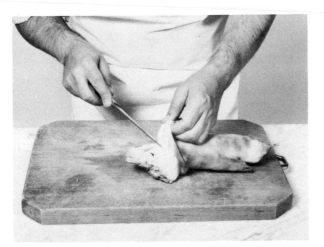 

4 and 5. With a boning knife, detach the skin from the bone a little at a time,

 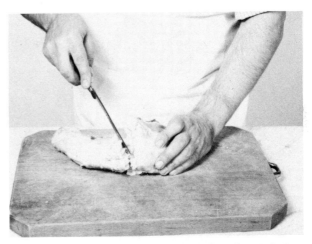

6. until you reach the joint at the bottom part of the foot.

7. Cut that joint apart to free the skin that is being removed.

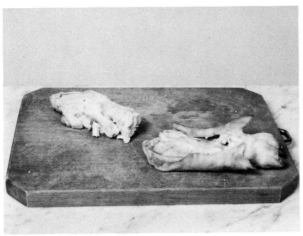 

8. The photo shows the removed bone, and at the right the pig's foot to be sewn and stuffed.

Prepare the stuffing by mixing the ground pork with salt and pepper to taste and whole black peppercorns and cloves.

9. With a very thick needle and strong thread, sew up about three quarters of the length of the foot (from the toe end) and stuff the closed part.

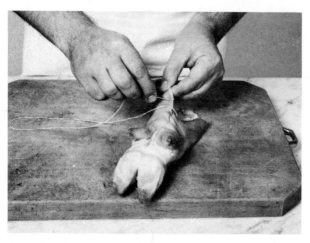

10. Finish sewing up the center, adding the rest of the stuffing.

11. Seal the end by sewing it closed, holding the thread in place,

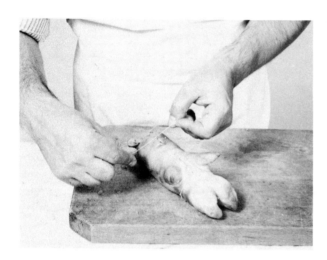

12. and making a strong knot.

HOW TO PREPARE COTECHINO

FROM CENTRAL ITALY

A *cotechino* sausage may be prepared by stuffing a casing about 2 inches in diameter, instead of the boned pig's foot, with the same ground pork and spices.

Soak the casing and dry it. Tie one end and push out the air starting at the tied end. Stuff the casing using a funnel, and tie the other end. It should resemble a salami. (Other regions of Italy have their own variations of the seasonings.) Refer to the Introduction and reicpe for *Cotechino in camicia* (*Cotechino* Sausage Baked in Crust), page 422. Like *zampone*, a homemade *cotechino* should age at least 4 days before being used.

How to Clean Anchovies in Salt

In Italy, the use of anchovies packed in oil is restricted to those dishes which use oil, such as salads. As an ingredient for most cooked dishes, however, anchovies packed in salt are preferred. These are sold either from large barrels or canned. Cans of varying sizes are imported to the United States and may be found in Italian grocery stores.

Salted anchovies should be cleaned under cold running water. In order to show the steps more clearly, these photos were taken without the water. Salted anchovies come with the heads already removed. Already filleted anchovies packed in oil can be used, if the whole salted ones are not available.

1. Open the fish completely starting at the head end (under cold running water) and lift off one complete fillet.

2. Remove the bone and tail from the remaining half. Rinse completely to remove any remaining salt.

A Special Way to Grate Oranges and Lemons

Many Italian recipes require grated orange or lemon rind. Examples are *Rotolo di Natale* (Christmas Fruit and Nut Roll), page 429, and *Torta di zucchini* (Zucchini Tart), page 397. This is a method of grating that saves much labor in cleaning the grater.

1. Place a piece of wax paper over the holes of a hand grater (preferably a curved one).

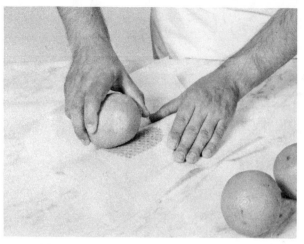

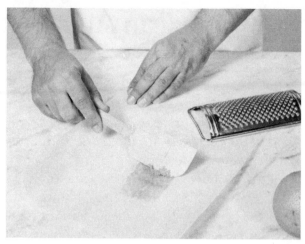

2. Hold the wax paper in place with one hand and move the orange (or lemon) back and forth with the other.

The grated orange peel will cling to the wax paper rather than the surface of the grater. Do not grate continuously on one spot of the wax paper, but change the area so that the paper does not wear through.

3. It is easy to remove the grated rind from the wax paper with a rubber spatula.

Sciroppo e Sugo

SIRUP AND SYRUP

FROM ALL OVER ITALY

Sirups are thin sweet liquids made by boiling sugar with water. They are then generally flavored with fruit juices. The word originally derived from the Arabic word for drinks; from its Latin form it became *sciroppo* in Italian and sirup in English.

The thick type of reduced sirup (which has the consistency of honey and which is not drinkable by itself) is generally referred to as *sugo* in Italian, the same word used for sauce. It is called "syrup" in English, as in maple syrup.

Orange and lemon sirups are the most frequently used traditionally. Generations ago they were sometimes used as beverages, providing us with good examples for the many bad artificial imitations that exist today. In cooking they are still used to moisten a mold for pastries or in dessert aspics. [See *Babà alla crema* (Babà Layer Cake), page 425, and *Gelatina dolce di frutta* (Orange or Lemon Dessert Aspic), page 443.] The recipe which follows for *Albicocche al sugo* (Apricots with Wine Syrup) makes a thick syrup by reducing the wines mixed with sugar and other flavorings.

Sciroppo di Arancia

ORANGE SIRUP

2 juice oranges
12 cubes granulated sugar
4 navel oranges
4 cups cold water
¾ cup granulated sugar

YIELD: ABOUT 4 CUPS

   Wash the oranges very well and dry them with paper towels.

HOW TO PREPARE SCIROPPO

1. Squeeze the juice oranges with a lemon squeezer (or orange juicer). Line a sieve with a piece of filter paper (placing a small bowl underneath) and pass the juice through it. Set the juice aside until needed.

2. Rub one side of each cube of sugar back and forth on the skin of the navel oranges, to thoroughly absorb some orange oil.

3. With a knife scrape off the sugar that has absorbed the orange oil into a small bowl and set it aside until needed.
   Put the water and the granulated sugar in a small saucepan over medium heat. Stir with a wooden spoon until the mixture reaches a boil. Let simmer, stirring occasionally, for 10 minutes. The temperature should not exceed 100 to 105 degrees.
   Remove the saucepan from the heat and add the sugar with the orange oil. Stir with a wooden spoon and return the saucepan to the heat. When the sirup reaches the boiling point again, add the orange juice. Stir with a wooden spoon and simmer for 5 minutes, then remove from the heat. Stir again for 2 or 3 minutes and let stand until cool.

4. Transfer the sirup to a bottle and let cool completely before using. The sirup may be kept in the refrigerator for several months.

VARIATION: Lemon sirup may be made in the same way, using 6 lemons.

Scorze di Arancia Candite

GLACÉED ORANGE RIND

FROM ALL OVER ITALY

4 thick-skinned oranges
1 teaspoon coarse-grained salt
3 cups granulated sugar
Salt

MAKES ABOUT 64 PIECES

Wash the whole oranges and dry them with paper towels. Cut off the tops and bottoms of the oranges. Cut the rind of each orange vertically, from top to bottom, first into fourths, then eighths, then sixteenths. With a paring knife detach each piece of orange rind. Scrape out the white part still attached to the pieces of the orange rind. Soak the pieces of rind in a bowl of cold water for 6 hours, changing the water every hour. Bring 2 quarts of cold water to a boil in an enamel or stainless steel saucepan. Then add the coarse-grained salt. Drain the orange rind pieces and add them to the pan. Simmer for 5 minutes, then drain and put them in a bowl of cold water for 1 hour.

Prepare the syrup. Put 4 cups of water, 2 cups of the sugar, and a pinch of salt over medium heat for about 1 hour, or until a very thin syrup is formed.

Drain the rinds, pat them with paper towels and add to the prepared syrup. Immediately remove the pan from the heat and let stand until cool (about 1 hour). Drain the rinds, put them in a crockery bowl, cover with aluminum foil, and refrigerate until needed.

Place the syrup back over medium heat until the consistency is a thin string when pouring from a spoon (about ½ hour). Remove the bowl from the refrigerator, uncover it, and pour the hot syrup over the cold rinds. Let stand for about 1 hour.

Cover a surface with wax paper and place 3 or 4 racks on the paper. Use tongs to transfer each piece of rind to the prepared racks, placing them completely separate from one another. Let stand for 2 hours. Put the remaining sugar in a small bowl and coat each piece of rind. Transfer the coated rind to a glass jar or a platter.

Albicocche al Sugo

APRICOTS WITH WINE SYRUP

FROM ALL OVER ITALY

SERVES 8

2 pounds ripe, but not overripe, apricots
2 cups dry red wine
¼ cup dry Marsala
¼ cup white rum
¼ cup tawny port
½ cup cold water
Juice of 1 orange
1 piece lemon peel
1 cup granulated sugar
Pinch of ground cinnamon

Preheat the oven to 375 degrees.

Wash the apricots well and put them in a small terra-cotta or enamel casserole. Add the red wine, Marsala, rum, port, water, orange juice, and lemon peel. Sprinkle the sugar over the top. Cover the casserole with aluminum foil. Make several punctures in the foil to allow the alcohol to evaporate. Place in the preheated oven and bake for 1 to 1½ hours, depending on the ripeness of the apricots. (The apricots should retain their shape when cooked.) Use a slotted spoon to transfer the apricots from the casserole to a serving plate to cool. When cool, cover with aluminum foil and refrigerate. Meanwhile, transfer the liquid from the casserole to a small saucepan. Put over low heat for about 1 hour to reduce. At that point, a thick syrup should have formed.

When completely cold, pour the syrup over the fruit. The dish is now ready to be served.

VARIATION: Peaches, whole peeled pears, and whole peeled oranges may be prepared in the same way. With the first two of these fruits, baking time still varies from 1 to 1½ hours, depending on the ripeness of the fruit. Whole peeled oranges require from only 10 to 20 minutes.

Mostarda di Cremona

FRUIT RELISH

FROM CREMONA IN LOMBARDY

Mostarda means a relish, which may or may not contain *senape* or mustard. Not only the mustard seeds, but also mustard greens were widely used in Italy in the Middle Ages, but have gradually declined in popularity. It is strange to think that one fourteenth-century cookbook has as many recipes for mustard greens as for any other vegetable, and yet that cooked green is unknown in Italy today. (It is interesting to note that another vegetable associated with Chinese cooking, snow peas, was a popular puréed accompaniment in eighteenth-century Italy.) It is probable that the mustard-flavored relish transferred its name to the hot powder itself in England. There are many *mostarde*, but the most famous is the ancient one of Cremona, in Lombardy, seventeenth-century home of the great violin makers Stradivarius, Guarneri, etc., and birthplace of that century's greatest composer, Monteverdi.

The cooked unripe fruit is marinated in a syrup flavored with yellow mustard seeds. *Mostarda di Cremona* is available commercially in jars and it can vary slightly from brand to brand as from household to household when made at home. This condiment is used to accompany boiled beef, chicken, veal tongue, *Cima alla genovese* (Stuffed Pressed Veal Breast), page 249, or any other boiled meats or fowl.

YIELD: ABOUT 2 CUPS FOR EACH POUND OF FRUIT

Unripe apples, unripe pears, unripe plums, or any of these in combination (except for oranges, mandarins, lemons, or nectarines).

For each pound of fruit use:
2 cups cold water
½ cup granulated sugar
1 tablespoon lemon juice

Plus:
1 cup granulated sugar
¼ teaspoon red pepper flakes wrapped in heavy cheesecloth
8 whole cloves
3 level teaspoons dark mustard seeds
½ cup cold water

Core and peel the fruit. Cut the fruit into 1-inch cubes, keeping the different kinds of fruit separate.

Have as many saucepans ready as kinds of fruit that you use. Combine the water, sugar and lemon juice in the pans and put them over medium heat. Simmer for about 20 minutes, then add the fruit and cook until the cubes are cooked but still very firm. The cooking time will depend on the hardness of the fruit. As each fruit is ready, remove the pan from the heat and let it stand until cool (about 1 hour). When all the fruit is cool, use a slotted spoon to transfer each fruit to its own dish. Combine all the different cooking juices in a large saucepan.

Prepare the syrup by adding the sugar, the red pepper flakes, and the cloves to the saucepan and placing it over medium heat. Let simmer until a thick syrup forms (the time will depend on the amount of cooking juices in the saucepan).

Preheat the oven to 375 degrees. Transfer all the fruit to a baking sheet and bake for 15 minutes. Remove from the oven and let the fruit stand until the syrup is ready.

When the syrup is ready, combine the mustard seeds with the cold water in a small bowl and add the mixture to the saucepan with the syrup. Stir very well with a wooden spoon, then add all the fruit. Mix gently, coating all the fruit cubes with the syrup. Simmer for 10 minutes longer. Then remove the pan from the heat and transfer the *mostarda* to a crockery bowl. Let stand until cold (about 2 hours). Remove the bag with the red pepper flakes and transfer the *mostarda* to a mason jar. Close the jar tightly and refrigerate overnight to blend the relish.

Serve the *mostarda* cold to accompany a boiled course.

Pere alla Corrado

PEARS CORRADO STYLE

Corrado, the great cook of the eighteenth-century Neapolitan court, gives this dish in his earlier cookbook. Its technique is simple, but the result is unforgettable. The taste of the uncooked white wine laced with caramelized sugar is that of a complex fortified wine or a liqueur. At this time dry Marsala was still being developed by the English in Sicily, which was then ruled by Naples. The dry Marsala probably was not yet available, but as the flavor of this combination so recalls that of Marsala, is it possible that Marsala was developed to resemble it?

This is a unique technique of marinating uncooked fruit in wine with caramelized sugar. To cover a molded dessert such as *Latte alla Portoghese* (Crème Caramel) (see *The Fine Art of Italian Cooking*) with caramelized sugar, the mold itself must be lined with sugar. But in this recipe the sugar is caramelized separately and then added to the main ingredient, fresh pears.

2 pounds ripe Bosc or Comice pears
2 cups dry white wine
1 cup granulated sugar
¼ cup cold water
2 or 3 drops lemon juice

SERVES 8

Peel the pears with a peeler rather than a knife, then cut them lengthwise into quarters or eighths, depending on their size. Remove the cores and put the pieces in a large round, deep serving dish. Pour the wine over them. Let the pears marinate for about 30 minutes.

HOW TO CARAMELIZE SUGAR WITHOUT A MOLD

Heat the sugar in an unlined copper pan with ¼ cup cold water added to facilitate the melting. If an unlined copper pan is not available, enamel may be used, but never use an iron pan in combination with sugar.

1. Place the unlined copper pan containing the sugar and water over medium heat and keep mixing with a wooden spoon until the sugar is completely dissolved. When the mixture starts to bubble, add the lemon juice to keep it from crystallizing. Cook slowly, allowing the thick syrup to melt into a smooth thinner one, until it turns a light brown color. At that moment, the sugar is ready and completely caramelized.

2. Pour the caramelized sugar over the pears marinating in the wine, starting from the center and moving outward in circles

3. until the caramelized sugar is distributed over the entire surface.

Cover and refrigerate the pears for at least 3 hours. During this time the sugar will dissolve completely and flavor the wine in a subtle and unusual way.

4. The pears ready to be served.

Tartufi

WHITE AND BLACK TRUFFLES

White truffles are found in the region of Alba in Piedmont and in small quantities in Tuscany. The main area for Italian black truffles is around Norcia in Umbria.

The white ones are spicy and pungent, while the black ones are nutty in flavor. Italian black truffles have a unique taste somewhat different from the French ones of Périgord.

White truffles are more rare and generally more prized. The best white truffles are knobby on the outside and solid inside. Black truffles are grainy. White truffles are generally added to the dish raw, as their flavor is strongest that way, and are usually thinly sliced.

Black truffles are cooked in order to draw out their flavor, and they are usually chopped or cut into small pieces. Their flavors are quite different and each is appropriate to its own set of dishes without the possibility of interchanging. White truffles are used with lightly cooked dishes, and the black are cooked in dishes that require longer cooking times. See *Uova alla fornaia* (Baked Giant Tortelli), page 172, and *Spaghetti di Scheggino* (Spaghetti with Trout-Black Truffle Sauce), page 141, for recipes using white and black truffles respectively.

18. "TARTUFFI" Tartufi *(Truffles) from a Renaissance drawing.*

1. The white truffles still uncleaned and the truffle cutter.

2. Clean the truffles very carefully with a truffle brush to remove all the sand and soil.

3. Slice the truffles by rubbing them along the sharp blade of the truffle cutter.

4. The truffle cutter has an adjustable blade, so it is possible to slice the truffles as thin as desired.

5. Black truffles are generally cut into small pieces or chopped, using the *mezzaluna* (page 74).

6. One black truffle chopped, the other still whole. Notice its graininess.

Porcini Mushrooms, Fresh and Dried

FROM ALL OVER ITALY

1. The fresh whole mushrooms are on the left in the photo. On the right are the dried ones in pieces; a slice of the cap, the more desirable part, is the most forward piece.

When buying dried mushrooms, the better brands contain many slices from the cap; the poorer ones almost all pieces of the stem. The most celebrated dried mushrooms are the ones shown on the right in the photo.

Porcini, the most popular wild Italian mushrooms, have a distinct, complex flavor and are used extensively in Italian cooking, including many dishes in this book. Though now used, domesticated *champignons* are not traditionally popular in Italy and their flavor does not resemble the rich fragrance of the *porcini*. A member of the *Boletus edulis* genera, *porcini* are available fresh in the spring and fall when there is abundant rain and the sun after the rain is hot. The best mushrooms can be found under the chestnut trees in the Tuscan Apennines and around the village of Borgotaro near La Spezia. Sometimes when the mushrooms grow to great size, the whole tender caps are eaten broiled as a main dish, alone, or in combination with a filetto (filet). The stems are more solid and are cut and used with pasta, in sauces and stews, or deep fried. (When making the *Crema di funghi* soup, page 65, both caps and stems are used.) Fresh *porcini* are

64

traditionally cooked with the fresh herb, *nepitella*, a kind of wild mint related to catnip, which is not well known in the United States. *Nepitella* is also available dried in Italy. When the mushrooms are dried, both the caps and the stems are used. In Borgotaro, the mushrooms are sliced through with the stem and cap in one piece for drying.

Dried *porcini* are available here in most Italian food markets and other specialty food shops. Be careful when purchasing them that you get the genuine Italian mushrooms, which have, even dried, a very prominent white part on the stems and caps. The dark parts of the mushrooms should be dry, but still spongy, and not hard like a rock.

HOW TO PREPARE DRIED PORCINI MUSHROOMS FOR COOKING

Soak the mushrooms in a bowl of lukewarm water (approximately 2 cups of water to each ounce of mushrooms) for about 30 minutes. Then drain the water and be sure that all the sand is removed from the stems.

The water in which the mushrooms were soaked can be substituted for the chicken or beef broth called for in some of the sauces. To remove all sand, strain the mushroom water through filter paper or several layers of paper towels before using.

Crema di Funghi

WILD MUSHROOM SOUP

FROM EMILIA-ROMAGNA

One of the few soups called a *crema* in which the vegetable is not puréed. The word *crema*, when used for Italian soups, refers to a thick, smooth texture, not to the addition of cream. The soup is thickened, not by reduction, but by adding a small amount of flour, because it cannot cook for a long time if the mushroom pieces are to remain intact. In thickening with flour, it is most important to keep the amount small and cook the flour well; then the dish will remain light. I do not agree with those who wish to abolish flour thickening completely. But it is true enough that it has been overused, and often used badly. The tradition is a valid one and is the best technique for some dishes such as this one.

½ pound fresh porcini *mushrooms, or 4 ounces dried*   SERVES 6
2 Italian sweet sausages (6 ounces) without fennel seeds, or 6 ounces ground pork
2 tablespoons olive oil
3 cups beef broth (if using fresh mushrooms), or 6 to 8 cups (if using dried mushrooms),
   depending on the dryness of the mushrooms
1 heaping tablespoon unbleached all-purpose flour
Salt and freshly ground black pepper

If using fresh mushrooms, detach the caps from the stems with a knife. Cut them into 1-inch cubes. If using dried mushrooms, soak them in a bowl of lukewarm water for about 30 minutes, then drain and be sure that all sand is removed from the stems.

Remove the skin from the sausages and break each into 4 or 5 pieces.

Heat the oil in a stockpot. When it is hot, add the

65

sausage pieces and sauté them lightly for about 5 minutes. Then add the fresh or soaked mushrooms and sauté for 5 minutes longer. Bring the broth to a boil in another pot. Sprinkle the flour over the sausages and mushrooms and stir with a wooden spoon to incorporate the flour and to let it cook completely. Gradually add the hot broth to the stockpot, stirring constantly. Simmer the *crema* for about 20 minutes. Taste for salt and pepper. Simmer for 2 minutes longer, remove from the heat, and serve immediately.

Whole Glazed Citron

Citron resembles a large lemon but is a different fruit in that it is larger, shaped rather like a quince, and has a rough thick skin. It is very popular in the Mediterranean and it's mostly used there and elsewhere for making glacéed fruit. In the United States it can be found as an ingredient of the commercially-packaged mixed glacéed fruit. Some recipes in the book using the fruit are *Cannoli* (page 480) and *Rotolo di Natale* (Christmas Fruit and Nut Roll), page 429.

1. A whole glacéed citron.

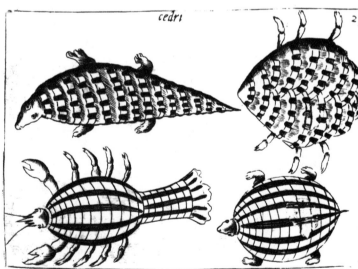

19. A Renaissance print showing citron cut into fantastic animal shapes for presentation and table decoration.

66

GLOSSARY OF BASIC INGREDIENTS

AMARETTI COOKIES The unusual taste of these cookies is derived from mixing both sweet and bitter almonds. Bitter almonds are used extensively in Italian, Hungarian, and other types of cooking, but they are not found in this country. But there is a substitute available, if you desire homemade cookies, in the apricot nut sold as bitter almonds especially in ethnic Hungarian stores. (See *The Fine Art of Italian Cooking* for a recipe.) An imported commercial brand of amaretti cookies can be found in most gourmet shops and food stores.

BALSAMIC VINEGAR The wine vinegar produced in the area of Modena. It is aged for at least 5 to 7 years in wooden barrels with some aromatic herbs and the smell and taste varies a lot from one producer to another. The methods of production are very ancient, very secret, and vary a bit depending on the producer. The spores which are in the air in the Modena area produce the special quality of this vinegar which are essential for achieving the flavor. Balsamic vinegar is used (in very small quantities) to dress salads, on fresh berries as a dessert, and to cook meat. It should not be indiscriminately substituted for normal wine vinegar.

BASIL The common variety of this herb has large leaves and generally grows all over Italy. The basil growing in the Ligurian region has smaller leaves and its taste has some of the aroma of the sea nearby. Only use the leaves, being careful to remove the flowers because their flavor is too strong. The basil plant found in the United States is the same large-leaved type used in Italy.

BAY LEAVES The bay bush is a typical Mediterranean plant and its leaves are used a lot in different cuisines. In Italian cooking they are mostly used to season meats (mainly pork) and to prepare sauces and soups. The California bay leaves available are closer to fresh ones than the dried European imports.

BREAD CRUMBS The homemade unseasoned bread crumbs are the best to use. The bread (preferably homemade or a good quality of packaged commercial white bread) should first be toasted in the oven, then ground in a food processor or blender. Bread crumbs should not be seasoned, not even with salt and pepper.

BROTH (BEEF AND CHICKEN) Broth in Italian cooking is made by boiling beef, veal, or chicken or beef and chicken together with such basic aromatic herbs as carrots, onions, celery, and parsley (sometimes a bay leaf is added). The meat is never browned first. If a darker color is required, this is obtained by adding 1 or 2 tablespoons of dry Marsala.

BUTTER Only sweet (unsalted) butter is used in Italian cooking. Italian butter is lower in fat content than American butter, but that in the United States has a very similar taste. Parma butter is richer and, until recently, the best available was unpasteurized.

CANNELLINI Sometimes called Tuscan beans, these are the dried white kidney beans originally brought from America and which are eaten frequently, particularly in Tuscan cooking.

CAPERS Capers (the bud, not the fruit, of a wild plant which grows in the fissure of stones) are preserved in wine vinegar or salt. If capers in salt are used, soak them in a bowl of cold water, then rinse them in running water to remove any excess salt.

CAUL FAT A fatty membrane resembling a net which is a covering on the intestines of pigs (lamb and veal caul fat also exist but are difficult to find). Caul fat is used to wrap lean meat to keep it from drying out too much while cooking. Caul fat almost completely disappears in the cooking process.

FENNEL SEEDS These are used to give a licorice taste to the food to obtain a sweet-and-sour effect. *Finocchiona* is a kind of Tuscan salami which is seasoned with fennel.

GLACÉED FRUIT See page 476, *Zuccotto*, and page 66, citron.

GORGONZOLA A semi-soft layered cheese made from the very rich milk of Lombardy. Its blue veining occurs because after coagulation a hot layer of curds is placed directly on one which has already cooled. (No mold spores are added.) The town of Gorgonzola is near Milan.

JUNIPER BERRIES These are well known as the basic ingredient for preparing gin. In Italy, juniper berries are used widely to season meat, mostly game, or to give meat a wild game taste.

MINT The kind of mint sold in the United States in fruit and vegetable stores and as plants is spearmint (Lat., *Menta spicata*). It is the most common variety of wild mint in Italy but is also successfully cultivated. *Nepitella*, also called *mentuccia* (see page 306), is another type of wild mint that is usually gathered in Italy but is not found in the United States. It is used most often to flavor wild mushrooms and may not be substituted for *menta* or spearmint.

MORTADELLA   The typical large salami of Bologna made mainly from pork with cubes of fat interspersed throughout. Genuine *mortadella* cannot be imported into this country, but a domestic substitute is available, although its taste and texture are inferior. (American bologna is not the same as *mortadella*, or *Bologna* as it is known, but originally must have been an imitation of it.)

MOZZARELLA   This cheese originated in southern Italy and was made from the milk of the water buffaloes but now is often made of cow's milk. It is a layered cheese made by cutting the curd into strips, tearing the latter into pieces and rolling it up into a ball. It takes its name from *mozzare*, to tear. Mozzarella is eaten rather fresh and should be moist inside and not too densely packed.

NUTMEG   It is always better to use whole nutmeg and grate it freshly as needed, rather than already ground. Special hand nutmeg graters are preferable and are easily available.

OILS (OLIVE, VEGETABLE, AND SOLID VEGETABLE SHORTENING)   The best olive oil is dark green in color with a light and sweet taste. This quality of oil, called "virgin" or "extra-virgin" olive oil, is always produced by the first of the three pressings of the olives. The finest quality olive oil is produced in the central part of Italy in small family-sized vineyards. When choosing a brand of olive oil, be certain that the green color of the oil has not been achieved by the adding of some olive leaves in the pressing process. When the leaves are added, the oil has a very spicy and bitter taste. The taste, color, and lightness of the olive oil is different every year depending on the harvest and the condition of the plants. The olive plant is a very strong plant but vulnerable to many diseases which makes the production of the oil completely variable not only in quantity but mainly in quality. The lightness and sweet taste of the best oil results from the olives being picked by hand and not allowed to fall to the ground. Vegetable oil (*olio di semi*) is the standard light mixed seed oil used mainly for frying in Italy. It may be approximated here by mixing two-thirds corn oil and one-third sunflower oil. Solid vegetable shortening is another good substitute for frying if the dish is to be eaten hot. Olive oil (and others)

purchased in a can should be transferred immediately on opening to a glass or glazed terracotta jar, without a tightly closed lid. Do not refrigerate, but store in a dark place, not exposed to the sun.

ONIONS   The red onion typically used in Italian cooking is the long type, which is different from the so-called Bermuda onion. Even if they resemble each other in color, they are different. If you must use a substitute for the Italian red onion, you should use the Bermuda onion instead of any other type.

OREGANO   The most popular aromatic herb used in southern Italy to season breads, vegetables, meats, etc., and the packaged anchovy paste.

PANCETTA   *Pancetta* is the same cut of pork as bacon, but it is unsmoked and preserved in salt. Never substitute smoked bacon for it, although sometimes a combination of salt pork and boiled ham or just plain boiled ham or *prosciutto* can be substituted (see individual recipes).

PARMIGIANO (REGGIANO)   A "grana" type (generic name for those large forms of aged cheese with a crust developed by the Etruscans over 2,000 years ago. It was the first cheese that could travel and be exported.). Real Parmigiano must be from the areas of Parma and Reggio-Emilia. The English word "Parmesan" is more correctly the translation of the generic term "grana" than of the Italian "Parmigiano." Parmigiano is a hard part-skim milk cheese which is used primarily for grating. It is best to purchase it in a piece, to freshly grate the amount you need and to store the rest in non-recycled brown paper (such as snack bags) with a moistened but squeezed-out cotton towel wrapped around it.

PARSLEY (ITALIAN)   The flat leafed parsley, not the curly variety, which is always used in Italian cooking. It has a more distinctive taste and is more suitable for cooking than the curly parsley. Do not confuse it with the cilantro (coriander) used in Chinese or Mexican cooking.

PECORINO (SHEEP'S MILK CHEESE)   The small forms, called *caciotte*, are eaten after being aged for some months. The large forms, called Pecorino Romano, are aged for several years. All large forms bear this name, no matter where they originate. For example, *Sardo* from Sardinia is really called Pecorino Romano Sardo. It is a hard cheese used for grating and has a dark brown or black rind and piquant taste.

PEPPERCORNS (BLACK, WHITE, GREEN, RED)   See the discussion on page 30 with *Anitra peposa* (Duck with Green Peppercorns).

POTATO STARCH   It is most easily obtained in the United States in the Kosher section of markets.

PROSCIUTTO   An uncooked, unsmoked ham cured in salt. It is eaten as an appetizer, in sandwiches, and is often used for flavoring other dishes. Italy's celebrated *prosciutti*, such as those of Langherano near Parma or Friuli's San Daniele or the saltier Tuscan hams cannot be imported into the United States. All *prosciutti* found in this country are domestic, though they might resemble the Parma or San Daniele type.

RICE (ITALIAN ARBORIO TYPE)   The Po valley, in particular, located in northern Italy, produces a wide-grained rice that has a pearly white spot on it. This rice, called Arborio, is especially suitable for *risotti* (see page 199) because when cooked in this manner it remains *al dente* (firm and chewy). It is preferable to purchase this Italian Arborio rice for such dishes, and it is available in Italian markets as well as gourmet shops in America.

RICOTTA   See page 38.

RICOTTA SALATA   Salted and pressed sheep's milk ricotta from southern Italy. It could be used as a substitute for sheep's milk cheese.

ROSEMARY   If you do not have fresh rosemary or rosemary preserved in salt, it is best to blanch the dried rosemary leaves for a few seconds in boiling water to soften them before using. When blanched, the leaves should be used in the same quantities as the fresh leaves.

SALT (COARSE-GRAINED OR KOSHER)   In Italy, sea salt is used for normal salting of food. Coarse-grained salt is added when cooking with large quantities of liquid, *i.e.*, boiling vegetables or pasta.

SAUSAGE   The sweet Italian sausages are those prepared with pork meat and seasoned with salt, pepper, and black peppercorns. There are many varieties of sausages, depending on the region, such as those seasoned with fennel seeds, red pepper flakes, and other spices. When preparing a dish in which sausages are one of the ingredients, it is better to use sweet sausages without spices, or substitute 3 ounces of ground pork for each sausage.

SAGE   A hardy herb which is best to obtain fresh and then preserve in salt. Avoid dried sage because it is generally made from Balkan sage, a variety that has a different taste from Italian or American sage.

TOMATOES   Fresh tomatoes are eaten cooked or raw as a vegetable or salad. If the tomatoes are used in a sauce, they are generally cooked first and then passed through a food mill to remove the seeds and skin or peeled (by blanching them in boiling water, see page 385) and seeded when raw, and then cooked. When canned tomatoes are used, it is preferable to use the Italian plum or San Marzano variety imported from Italy. The juice must first be drained and then the tomatoes measured. The fresh tomatoes used for sauces and most other dishes can be plum or any tender-skinned variety, such as those from New Jersey.

TOMATO PASTE   Tomato paste is used in Italian cooking, mainly when a light taste of tomatoes is required. It is rarely employed as a base for a sauce. Some imported brands are packaged in tubes so you can use a little at a time and store the remainder in the refrigerator.

CHAPTER 3

Equipment for the Italian Kitchen

The utensils pictured here are used in the recipes and techniques of this book. While many of them are typically Italian and are essential for preparing this cuisine, others are used differently in the techniques of various countries.

BAGNOMARIA   The French term *bain-marie* is a translation of this Italian original, named after the sixteenth-century Florentine lady, Maria de Cleofa, who invented it. A pot or mold holds the food and is placed into a larger pot or baking dish (usually metal) of water (when inserted, the water line should be level with the food in the pot or mold). Add a slice of lemon to the water to prevent mineral deposits from forming. The flame heats the water which then transmits its heat to what is cooking. A *bagnomaria* can be used on top of the stove or in the oven. It can heat anything from *mascarpone* to *Sformato o budino di pollo* (Chicken Budino).

BATTICARNE (MEAT POUNDER)   A typical Italian flat stainless steel meat pounder. The meat is placed between two pieces of wax paper, which have been dampened with cold water so that the meat does not stick to the paper. It is then pounded by hitting and sliding down the meat or poultry carefully (otherwise, you'll hit your knuckles on the table). This process flattens the meat and makes it uniform, while breaking down the grain without pulverizing the meat.

CANNOLI MOLDS   The best cannoli molds are those with a cut in one side so when the shell is cooked it is easier to remove it by pressing the top part like a spring.

CATINO   Typical large terra-cotta bowl used to wash or to soak various ingredients, such as vegetables. This bowl should never be used as a mixing bowl because the spoon or whisk could remove the glazed lining.

CHITARRA (GUITAR)   This is a special pasta cutter used mainly in the regions of Abruzzi and the Marches. A thick layer of pasta sits on this instrument with wide strings (which resemble the strings of a guitar) and is cut into strips (*maccheroni*) by rolling the rolling pin up and down on it. Any strips of pasta caught in the strings are released by strumming your hand across the strings, thus "playing the guitar."

CLAY VESSELS AND POTS   The unglazed terra-cotta vessels are used to cook in the oven. The one on the left in the photo, called a *pignatto* (the modern spelling is *pignatta*), is for *cannellini* beans and the other on the right is for chicken. The special unglazed vessel (front) is used to prepare *Pollo al mattone* (Whole Chicken Cooked Between Terra-cotta) on the top of the stove.

COPPER BOWL (UNLINED) AND WHISK   It is used to beat egg whites stiff (but not to whip cream) and as the insert for a double boiler to prepare pastry cream and *zabaione* because it is a very good heat conductor. The bowl must be cleaned with lemon juice or vinegar and fine salt before it is used, then rinsed and dried. To whip cream, a chilled metal bowl and wire whisk must be used.

DOUBLE BOILER   Instead of using an already prepared double boiler, I prefer to improvise one by placing a heatproof bowl (or insert) on top of a stockpot of boiling water. It is preferable to use a lined or unlined copper bowl because copper is an excellent heat conductor. The boiling water in the stockpot should not touch the bottom part of the insert if it is prepared properly. Only the steam should heat the insert. The photo shows a lined copper bowl with handles and two hooks which allow the bowl to rest on the stockpot.

FISH SCALER   This practically designed scaler, with the serrated edges on the working end and a rolled handle which can be grasped easily, makes the job efficient. The sharp end curves upward so as not to break the skin of the fish and, as the underside is completely open, the scales can be washed through without a problem. The fish scaler is made of stainless steel which also adds to its hygienic features.

FLAMEPROOF CASSEROLE (ENAMEL)   This type of casserole can be used both on top of the stove and in the oven. It usually has a cover.

FLAME-TAMER It is a piece of metal or wire screen placed under a glazed terra-cotta pot in order to spread the heat evenly. Only glazed terra-cotta pots can be used on top of an electric or gas stove—the unglazed terra-cotta pots or molds must be used only in the oven.

FOOD MILL This is used when you want to remove and discard seeds, skin, or the tough part of vegetables (i.e., the inner core of carrots). Only the juice and pulp of the fruit or vegetables (after they have passed through the food mill) are eaten.

GRATELLA (RANGE-TOP GRILL) A shallow iron grill with ridges so that the fat drips off the food being grilled. It is used to grill meats, fowl, and fish directly on top of the stove.

GRATTUGIA (HAND GRATER) The hand grater in the photo is the round one which is used only to grate finely. There are other types of hand graters with four different-sized holes, so it is possible to grate from coarse to fine on them, according to the size of the holes.

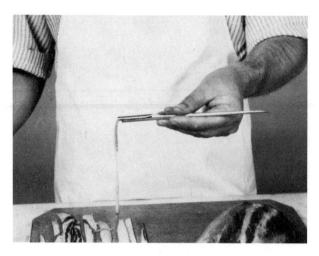

LARDING NEEDLE A strip of fat (i.e., *pancetta*, salt pork, or boiled ham, etc.) is inserted in the hinged end with tooth-like edges of this long and hollow needle. A clasp snaps open for insertion of the fat and then snaps closed. The needle is then inserted into a piece of meat and drawn through, leaving the strip of fat in the body of the meat to give it more flavor and moisture.

MANDOLIN A simple, classic wooden mandolin with an adjustable stainless steel edge (one side is scalloped and the other is straight) for shredding and thinly slicing vegetables.

MEZZALUNA (HALF-MOON CHOPPER) This is the classical Italian knife used to chop a range of ingredients. It makes it possible to achieve various textures from coarsely to finely chopped, even if foods of different textures are combined (i.e., carrots and onions). It is best with a single stainless steel blade rather than a double. A *mezzaluna* can be sharpened like a knife. It is also preferable if the *mezzaluna* has round wooden or plastic handles.

MORTAR AND PESTLE, CHINA (PORCELAIN) OR CERAMIC This is used to grind spices because the mortar is non-porous. The mortar has a round shape and a pouring spout and is usually highly polished (as is the pestle) so that they produce a fine powder. Both can be washed to completely remove the residue of different spices.

MORTAR (MARBLE) AND PESTLE (WOOD) This heavy mortar of unpolished marble (or sometimes stone) gives the best resistance for grinding nuts.

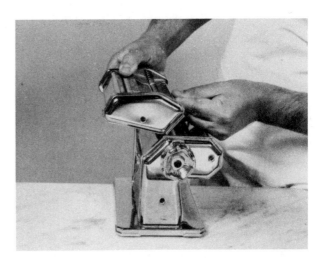

PASTA MACHINE (HAND OPERATED) The hand pasta machine is best for kneading and stretching pasta dough. The dough is inserted into the rollers of the machine and is kneaded and stretched by rotating the handle. The cutting attachment (above right) is then attached to the machine so that the pasta can be cut into strips for *tagliatelle*, *taglierini*, and spaghetti.

PASTRY CUTTER This scalloped wheel (which is best made of brass) is used to cut pastry, squares of pasta for lasagne and *cannelloni*, and small squares for *tortelli*. By cutting the *tortelli* with this pastry cutter (as in the photo), the two layers of pasta are sealed completely and generally do not need to be sealed with egg whites or water.

PASTRY SCRAPER   It is made completely of metal or metal with a wooden handle. The pastry scraper is used to remove dough attached to the pasta or pastry board.

PONZONETTO (UNLINED COPPER PAN)   This pan has a handle and is reserved to prepare génoise pastry, pastry cream, and *zabaione*. It is placed over a stockpot of lukewarm or boiling water. Others like this can also be reserved to cook polenta or to caramelize sugar.

RAVIOLI OR TORTELLI CUTTER   This is used to cut round *tortelli* or ravioli or half-moon *tortelli* or ravioli. By cutting with this pastry cutter, the two layers of pasta are sealed completely and generally do not need to be sealed with egg whites or water.

ROLLING PIN, AMERICAN TYPE   A cylindrical piece of hard wood used to roll out pastry. The two lacquered wooden handles are held by ball bearings which produce a smooth action when stretching dough or pastry in various directions to obtain an even thickness.

ROLLING PIN, ITALIAN TYPE   This is a long piece of rounded wood, even in thickness, with one or two handles, but without ball bearings. It is used mostly to stretch pasta dough.

76

SETACCIO (SIFTER) The best sifter is a large round drum type with a wooden frame and a wire or nylon screen. This sifter makes it possible to sift the flour and incorporate air into it (for batters and cakes), or to "clean" the flour (for pasta) without incorporating air. (See the discussion in the individual recipes for *crespelle*, pasta, doughs, and pastries.) *Setaccio* is the name for both sieves and sifters.

SPIANATOIA AND TAGLIERE (PASTA AND CHOPPING BOARDS) A pasta board is different from a chopping board because it has some very practical features. There is a piece of wood projecting above the upper surface of the pasta board to keep the flour from spilling all over and another piece projecting below the surface of the board which holds it in place on the table. The best chopping board is made of thick wood (like a butcher's block) and has a handle on one side (see the illustration for the mandolin).

TERRA-COTTA CASSEROLE (GLAZED) This is the best pot for cooking vegetables such as artichokes, which have a high percentage of iron so that they remain fresh and do not turn a dark color. It also works well for soups and sauces. Food prepared in such a pot has a soft, integrated taste which is not possible to achieve with most other types of pots.

TRUFFLE CUTTER A flat stainless steel implement with a sharp adjustable blade used to cut truffles. The truffle is slid across the blade to make the slices.

WINE-VINEGAR BARREL   This classic wooden barrel with the half-conical shape is used to keep wine vinegar. The little faucet allows the vinegar to be removed without disturbing the "mother" or the white powder on top. Before using the barrel, you must season it by soaking it in cold salted water for about 12 hours.

ZUCCHINI CORER   A long trough-like stainless steel blade with a rosewood handle, it is used to remove the pulp from eggplant and zucchini in order to stuff them.

CHAPTER 4

Chopping, Grinding, and Passing

CHOPPING

Technique of Using the Mezzaluna (Half-moon Chopper)

The *mezzaluna*, or half-moon chopper, is the all-purpose chopper in Italian cooking, having replaced the battery of chef's knives used in earlier times in Italy (and still used in France). The *mezzaluna* seems to have been developed in the late eighteenth or early nineteenth century. Because it is rarely lifted from the chopping surface, it was welcomed as an ingenious energy saver and because it is manually controlled it allows more flexibility than a machine.

The first four photos illustrate the stages of movement in chopping with the *mezzaluna*. Hold the handles gently and do not press. Without lifting the chopper from the chopping board,

1. rock from extreme left

2. to right

3. and back again,

4. while gradually moving forward.
When you arrive at the front of the board, reverse the direction of the gradual movement.

5. With the *mezzaluna* and one hand, gather in the scattered chopped ingredients (in this case, parsley).

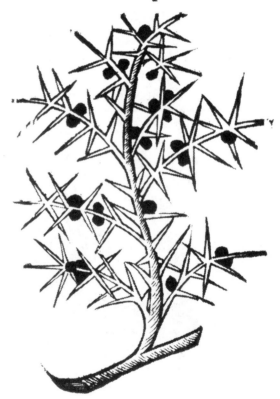

Ginepro.

20. Ginepro (Juniper)

6. Repeat forward and backward motions and the gathering in until ingredients are chopped to the fineness necessary for any particular recipe you are making.

Salsa di Rognone

KIDNEY SAUCE

FROM NAPLES

A versatile thick sauce, almost the consistency of a paste, in which the kidney is flavored with juniper berries, sage, rosemary, and a little wine vinegar. It was a favorite in the eighteenth-century Neapolitan court, where it was used as a sauce for mild meats which blend well with the stronger flavor. This sauce was also called *Rognonata*. I find it most effective when used with slices of roast veal, and on *crostini*, the rustic Tuscan canapés.

SERVES 6

8 ounces veal kidney
4 ounces (1 stick) sweet butter
2 tablespoons olive oil
5 sage leaves, fresh or preserved in salt
1 tablespoon rosemary leaves, fresh or preserved in salt
5 juniper berries
1 small clove garlic, peeled, but left whole
Salt and freshly ground black pepper
1 teaspoon flour
⅓ cup hot chicken or beef broth
1 tablespoon red wine vinegar

Clean the veal kidney following the instructions on page 280. Put the kidney on a board and chop coarsely with a *mezzaluna*.

Heat the butter and oil in a saucepan over medium heat. When the butter is completely melted, add the sage and rosemary leaves, the juniper berries, and the garlic. Sauté lightly for 5 minutes.

HOW TO PREPARE SALSA DI ROGNONE

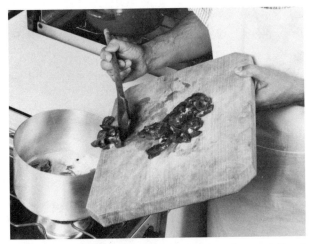

1. Then add the chopped kidney and sauté for 5 minutes longer. Taste for salt and pepper. Use a slotted spoon to transfer the solid ingredients (not the juice) to a chopping board.

2. Finely chop all the ingredients together with a *mezzaluna*.

3. Put the pan with the leftover juice over low heat. Add the flour and stir well for 1 minute. Add the hot broth and mix very well.

4. Add the finely chopped ingredients to the pan and cook for about 5 minutes.

Remove the pan from the heat, add the wine vinegar, and mix all the ingredients together. Transfer the sauce to a sauceboat and serve.

Salsa Rustica

TUSCAN COUNTRY SAUCE

FROM THE CHIANTI AREA

A spicy cold sauce to be used with boiled meats and fowl, on boiled potatoes or even on *crostini*. It is a type of *Salsa verde* (Green Sauce) made from chopped green herbs, such as parsley, like two others that are still popular in the Chianti area and imitated in other parts of Italy—*Salsa verde del Chianti* and *Salsa rossa del Chianti* (see *The Fine Art of Italian Cooking*). In this sauce, the main ingredient, finely chopped hard-boiled eggs, is added to the parsley base and the sauce is flavored with capers and finely chopped anchovies. The beautiful caper plants grow out of the ancient walls of the many villages and castles in Chianti. They flower through the summer, but the bud must be picked for preserving in wine vinegar or salt before the bud opens. Preserved capers are used in a variety of dishes.

3 extra large hard-boiled eggs
4 anchovies in salt, or 8 fillets in oil, drained
10 sprigs Italian parsley, leaves only
3 ounces capers in wine vinegar, drained
3 cloves garlic, peeled
5 slices white bread (to equal 1 cup), crusts removed
5 tablespoons red wine vinegar
Salt and freshly ground black pepper to taste
⅓ cup olive oil

SERVES 6

Shell the eggs. Clean the anchovies if preserved in salt (page 55).

Finely chop the eggs, anchovies, parsley, capers, and garlic together on a board with the *mezzaluna*. Place the chopped ingredients in a crockery bowl and let stand until needed.

Soak the bread in 3 tablespoons of the wine vinegar and ½ cup of cold water for about 20 minutes.

Squeeze out the liquid and add the bread to the bowl with the other ingredients. Taste for salt and pepper, then start adding the oil, little by little, mixing continuously with a wooden spoon. When all the oil is incorporated, add the remaining vinegar, and mix well. The sauce should have a smooth texture. Cover the bowl and refrigerate for about ½ hour before serving.

Torta di Noci

WALNUT CAKE

FROM PARMA

This walnut cake ring from Parma is made completely with finely chopped walnuts (using the *mezzaluna*) with no flour at all. It is a very old recipe, and was almost certainly made originally without the chocolate. When the Austrian Maria Luigia of Hapsburg, the second wife of Napoleon, was made Duchess of Parma after her husband's exile, she brought some rich Austrian tastes to the already rich butter and nut pastries of Parma. So perhaps she was the one responsible for this uncharacteristically Italian chocolate flavoring in the cake. However, the Parmenese have taken it to their hearts, as they did the saucy Maria Luigia.

6 ounces (1½ sticks) sweet butter
6 ounces shelled walnuts
6 ounces (¾ cup) granulated sugar
4 ounces unsweetened cocoa powder
2 or 3 drops vanilla extract
5 extra large eggs
2 ounces glacéed citron, cut into small pieces
3 tablespoons unseasoned bread crumbs, preferably homemade

To place around cake:
About 20 shelled walnut halves

Optional:
1 pint heavy cream
2 tablespoons granulated sugar
1 teaspoon confectioners' sugar

Melt the butter in a small metal bowl improvising a double boiler. Remove the bowl from the heat and let stand until needed.

SERVES 8

Delle Noci.

21. Delle Noci (The Walnuts)

83

1. Put the shelled walnuts and sugar on a chopping board.

2. Chop them together very fine with a *mezzaluna*.

Transfer the nuts and sugar to a large crockery bowl. Add the cocoa powder and vanilla and mix very well with a wooden spoon.

3. One by one, separate the yolks from the egg whites and add the yolks to the bowl. Keep the whites in a crockery or glass bowl to use later.

4. Add the citron and pour over the melted and cooled butter.

Mix thoroughly until the mixture has a thick but smooth texture. Use a whisk to beat the egg whites in an unlined copper bowl until they are stiff. To remove the egg whites left on the whisk, do not bang the whisk against the bowl.

5. But rather gently tap the whisk above the bowl with the side of your hand until all the egg white has dropped into the bowl.

Use a rubber spatula to scrape all the egg whites into the bowl with the nuts. With a wooden spoon, fold the egg whites into the nut mixture (see photos pages 445 and 446) until homogeneous.

Preheat the oven to 375 degrees.

6. Butter a 10-inch (2- to 3-quart) ring mold and line it with bread crumbs.

Shake out any excess bread crumbs and reserve them. Gently spoon the mixture into the prepared mold.

7. Sprinkle over the leftover bread crumbs.

Bake the mold in the preheated oven for about 40 minutes. Remove from the oven, let cool for a few minutes, then unmold and place on a rack until thoroughly cool. Transfer to a serving dish.

8. Circle the cake with the walnut halves.

If you wish to serve the torte with whipped cream, beat the heavy cream and sugars together with a wire whisk in a chilled metal bowl, following the instructions on pages 445 and 446. Fill the center of the torte with the whipped cream.

Panforte

Panforte, a flat cake of chopped dried fruit and nuts, flavored with honey, cinnamon, white pepper, and mace, is the quintessentially medieval taste. It has been made, with slight variation, in Siena since the Middle Ages. *Panforte* is one of the traditional desserts served during Christmas in Italy and this good home-made version, which is eaten more as a confection, is fine to serve all year round. Commercially packaged brands are widely exported as well.

8 ounces blanched almonds (see page 87)
4 ounces blanched walnuts (see page 87)
2 ounces filberts
4 ounces dried figs
4 ounces glacéed citron (see page 66)
1 tablespoon sweetened cocoa powder
1 teaspoon ground cinnamon
Pinch of freshly ground white pepper
Pinch of freshly ground mace
6 ounces honey
3 ounces granulated sugar
Confectioners' wafer papers (found in German or Hungarian specialty stores)
2 tablespoons confectioners' sugar
  (enough to cover an 11-inch circular pan twice)

SERVES 12

With a *mezzaluna*, finely chop the almonds and walnuts, and coarsely chop the filberts and figs. Cut the citron into ¼-inch cubes. Put the ingredients into a large bowl. Add the cocoa powder, ½ teaspoon of the cinnamon, the white pepper, and the mace. Mix with a wooden spoon until all the ingredients are well blended.

Pour the honey into a lined copper or stainless steel saucepan and put it over medium heat. Add the granulated sugar and stir until the honey is completely melted and the sugar incorporated. Do not allow the mixture to boil.

Remove the saucepan from the heat and transfer the contents to the bowl with the nuts, citron, and spices. Using a wooden spoon, mix well but gently, until all the ingredients are well blended. Preheat the oven to 375 degrees.

Line the bottom and sides of an 11-inch layer cake pan (with removable bottom) with the confec-tioners' wafers. Pour in the "batter," smoothing out the mixture in the pan. Cover with another layer of confectioners' wafers, place in the oven and bake for about 35 minutes. Remove from oven and cool in the pan for about 10 minutes. Remove the sides and bottom of the pan and transfer the *panforte* to a rack to cool completely (about 8 hours). Wrap tightly in aluminum foil.

Panforte should be eaten the day after it is baked. Before serving, transfer it to a serving plate and sprinkle it with the remaining cinnamon and then with the confectioners' sugar.

VARIATION: For the white *panforte*, follow the same procedure as for dark *panforte*, but omit the cocoa powder, use only 2 ounces of the dried figs, and increase the citron by 2 ounces.

GRINDING

Grinding Nuts with Mortar and Pestle

In the past centuries, the large rough stone mortars were used for grinding meats with a metal pestle. For cooked meats, nuts, etc., one could use a softer pestle. A stone one was not used as it could splinter against the stone of the mortar. Today, a large marble mortar and a wooden pestle are used to grind nuts (herbs and spices are ground with a smaller marble mortar and a marble pestle). This piece of equipment is also traditionally used to make *Pesto* (Basil Sauce) (see *The Fine Art of Italian Cooking*).

Torta di Mandorle

ALMOND CAKE   FROM LIGURIA AND GENOA

The flat almond cake, almost a huge cookie, is produced in a region where the mortar and pestle is traditionally used to grind the almonds. The ground almonds are mixed with flour and the stiffly beaten egg whites help to lighten a dense, crunchy texture. This is one of the classic almond cake recipes.

12 ounces almonds
6 ounces (1½ sticks) sweet butter
6 extra large eggs, separated
12 ounces granulated sugar
8 ounces unbleached all-purpose flour
Grated rind of 1 lemon
Pinch of ground cinnamon

SERVES 8

HOW TO BLANCH NUTS

Bring a small saucepan of water to a boil, then add the nuts (almonds in this recipe) and boil them for 2 or 3 minutes. Drain well and put the nuts into a bowl of cold water.

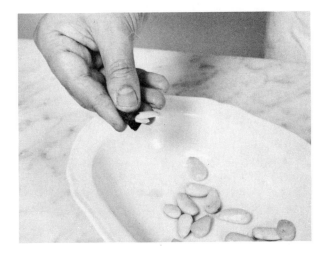

1. Holding each nut between the thumb and first finger, push, and the nut will slip from the skin onto a plate.

Almonds and pistachios are skinned in this way. Walnuts must be peeled little by little.

Preheat the oven to 375 degrees.

2. Place the blanched almonds on a cookie sheet and put it into the preheated oven for about 25 minutes, or until the nuts are lightly golden brown.

Melt the butter in a small saucepan over a pot of boiling water. Let the melted butter stand until cool.

Place the egg yolks in a crockery bowl and add the sugar. Stir with a wooden spoon, always in the same direction, until the sugar is completely incorporated and the egg yolks turn a lighter color. Slowly add the cooled melted butter to the bowl, mixing thoroughly. Then add the flour, stirring constantly until homogeneous.

Grind half of the toasted almonds.

HOW TO GRIND NUTS WITH MORTAR AND PESTLE

3. Put the almonds in a marble mortar and, with a rotating motion of the wooden pestle,

4. grind the nuts by pushing them against the stone surface. Keep rotating until the nuts are uniformly ground into very small pieces but not a powder.

5. Add the ground almonds to the bowl with the other ingredients, then the whole almonds along with the grated lemon rind and cinnamon.

Mix thoroughly with a wooden spoon. Preheat the oven to 375 degrees. Butter a 14-inch diameter pizza plate or a jelly roll pan. Beat the egg whites in an unlined copper bowl with a wire whisk until stiff.

6. Very gently fold the beaten egg whites into the almond mixture (see pages 445 and 446).

7. Pour the mixture into the prepared plate.

8. Spread it out with a spatula and bake for about 30 minutes.

Remove from the oven and transfer to a rack to cool for 1 hour.

9. Cut it and serve directly from the plate.

Ricciarelli

SIENESE ALMOND COOKIES

FROM SIENA

These Sienese almond-shaped almond cookies are traditional for Christmas like *panforte*, and probably equally as ancient. The almond shape is customarily associated with the angel's Annunciation to the Virgin as well as having the more general symbolism of fertility. Packaged commercial *ricciarelli* are available from Siena during the Christmas season, but again there is nothing like the homemade product, ground with mortar and pestle.

8 ounces blanched almonds (page 87)
6 ounces granulated sugar
4 ounces (1 stick) sweet butter
3 extra large eggs
½ teaspoon orange extract
*20 ounces potato starch or cornstarch**
Pinch of salt
About 4 tablespoons confectioners' sugar

YIELD: APPROXIMATELY 2 DOZEN

* Cornstarch may be substituted for the potato starch, but only as a last resort. The texture of the cookies will not be the same as when you use potato starch.

Mix the blanched almonds with 3 ounces of the sugar in a mortar. Finely grind with a pestle until a very smooth paste is formed. Put the butter and the remaining sugar in a small bowl and stir thoroughly until the sugar is completely incorporated and the mixture is creamy. Gradually add the ground almonds and sugar to the butter mixture, mixing with a wooden spoon. Add the eggs, one at a time, making sure to incorporate each one completely. Add the orange extract, potato starch, and salt and continue to stir. Transfer the "dough" to a marble surface heavily spread with potato starch and spread it out to a thickness of ¼ inch with a metal spatula.

With a 3-inch almond-shaped cookie cutter, cut the dough into *ricciarelli.*

Line a cookie sheet with wax paper or parchment paper, and butter the paper. Preheat the oven to 375 degrees.

Using a spatula, transfer the *ricciarelli* to the prepared cookie sheet and bake for about 35 minutes.

Remove from the oven and allow to cool completely in the pan (about 1 hour). Transfer the *ricciarelli* to a serving dish, sprinkle with the confectioners' sugar, and serve.

Marzapane

ALMOND PASTE

FROM SICILY

The almond paste known as *marzipan* now exists in many places throughout the world, and German-speaking countries are particularly fond of it. But medieval Sicily was its place of origin, and the *marzapane* made even today in Sicily and southern Italy is in a special class. That is because it is the place of origin of the fresh almonds and of the skill developed in this oldest *marzipan* tradition. The almond paste lends itself to being shaped into figures, like fruit or little animals. *Marzapane* forms are available in Italy, as are the special kinds of vegetable dyes needed to paint the fruit and animal figures. If you cannot find the forms, it is also common to shape the *marzapane* with your fingers, with cookie cutters, or with small molds, the only limit being that of one's own imagination. If you wish to paint them, you can use any vegetable dye available.

½ pound blanched almonds (see page 87)
6 ounces glucose (available in pharmacies)
2 pounds granulated sugar
Food coloring (vegetable dye)

YIELD: APPROXIMATELY 1½ CUPS

Use a mortar and pestle to grind the almonds very fine. Transfer the ground nuts to a crockery or glass bowl. Add about 4 ounces of the glucose and stir

well with a wooden spoon. Combine the remaining 2 ounces of glucose with the sugar in a saucepan over medium heat. Remove the pan from the heat before the sugar turns light brown and pour the contents over the almond-glucose mixture. Stir well with a wooden spoon, then pour the *marzapane* onto a marble slab to cool. When it is completely cool, wet the *marzapane* with a few drops of cold water, and pass it through the rollers of a manual pasta machine on the first setting (page 127) about five times, or until the mixture is smooth and homogeneous.

At this point you can shape the *marzapane* into the forms you like, using either your fingers or a cookie cutter. Cover with plastic wrap and let the small figures rest for about 24 hours. You can then paint them with any shade of food coloring or in any pattern.

Salsa di Noci

WALNUT SAUCE

FROM GENOA

The famous Genoese walnut sauce is traditionally made with a mortar and pestle (although it can also be prepared with a *mezzaluna*), using ricotta as a binder. It is most often used to dress pasta [see *Tagliatelle con salsa di noci* (*Tagliatelle with Walnut Sauce*) page 136] or with cold boiled meats.

YIELD: APPROXIMATELY 2 CUPS
(SUFFICIENT TO DRESS
FRESH PASTA PREPARED
WITH 2 EGGS)

2 slices white bread
8 ounces shelled walnuts
1 large clove garlic, peeled
15 ounces ricotta
3 tablespoons olive oil
4 tablespoons sweet butter
Salt and freshly ground black pepper

Remove the crusts from the bread and soak the bread in a small bowl of cold water for about 20 minutes.

Meanwhile, blanch the walnuts (page 87) and skin them.

Squeeze the water out of the bread and put it in a mortar. Add the blanched walnuts and the garlic. Finely grind with a pestle until a smooth paste is formed. (You can also use a *mezzaluna* and a chopping board instead of a mortar and pestle.)

Transfer the contents of the mortar to a crockery bowl. Add the ricotta, olive oil, and butter. Season with salt and pepper to taste. Mix very well with a wooden spoon until homogeneous. At this point, the sauce is ready to be used.

Grinding Spices with Mortar and Pestle

Both the mortar and the pestle used for grinding spices are usually made of marble. (When grinding nuts, page 88, a large marble mortar and a wooden pestle are used.) In the earlier centuries, however, when spices were used extensively for pharmaceutical purposes and their food and medicinal purposes overlapped, the pharmacy bronze mortar and pestle were often used for food as well. See *Tagliatelle al peperoncino* (Red Pepper *Tagliatelle*), page 135, for a recipe with ground spices.

1. Gently crush the spice against the bottom of the mortar.

2. Grind fine by moving the crushed spice against the sides of the mortar in a rotating motion.

Grinding Meat with a Machine

The two photos show three textures achieved by grinding meat with a machine. Originally meat was ground in a coarse stone mortar, so that the pestle would push the meat against the coarse cutting surface. For a finer texture, the meat could be pushed through a *setaccio*, or sieve, as well. While this is almost never done anymore we must not pretend that the texture achieved by the machines is the same. The result is simply different, though not necessarily inferior. Generally we have found the substitution desirable because of the enormous saving in labor. Even the different machines produce slightly different results. The food processor, because of its varied controls, can produce very fine textures as well as coarser ones. The photographs illustrate the particular textures produced by fine and coarse grinding by meat grinders, hand and electrically turned. Here the electric grinder was used for coarse grinding, the hand one for fine.

1. The manual grinder is using its fine-grinding attachment, the electric one the coarse grinder. Both are capable of the other texture as well through changing attachments. The side handle is turned by hand and the meat is added little by little to the "mouth" on top. It is pushed by an internal spiral which is rotated by turning the handle, and the pressure then forces the pieces through a disc with holes, through which the meat exits. The discs are interchangeable and come with holes of three different sizes. Speed is controlled manually. The entire machine comes apart for cleaning. The principle is still that of the sieve, but with a mechanical pusher. Though the machine probably dates from the late nineteenth century, the principle appears in one of Leonardo Da Vinci's drawings.

2. The food processor on the right may be controlled to grind from very coarse to very fine. If you compare its coarse grinding of the meat with that of the electric meat grinder on the left it is only slightly different.

Hand chopping produces still a different result. See *Salsa di rognone* (Kidney Sauce), page 81, for a photo of hand chopped kidneys. The snipping used in *Maccheroni alla chitarra* (*Maccheroni* Cut with the "Guitar" in Lamb Sauce), page 143, is still another texture needed when the meat must retain its body. For grinding nuts, the mortar and pestle is best for almonds in the recipe for *Torta di mandorle* (Almond Cake), page 87. The recipe for *Salsicce di Siena* (Siena Sausages), page 96, requires coarsely ground meat, that for *Ravioli di pollo in brodo* (Chicken Ravioli in Broth), page 94, finely ground meat.

Rapa domeſtica

22. *"Rapa domestica" (Round Turnip) whose shape is imitated in the original dumpling-like "rabiole" or ravioli. Rape or broccolirab (in dialect) are the greens of this type of turnip.*

Ravioli or Gnocchi

The names *tortelli* and *ravioli* both now refer to a small basically flat stuffed pasta, which is either square, rectangular, round, or half-moon in shape. Indeed, nowadays, the word *ravioli* is perhaps better known for these than *tortelli*.

In the early cookbooks, however, these stuffed pasta were all called *tortelli*. The word *ravioli* was used for something completely different: shaped dumplings, which were only occasionally wrapped in pasta. The origin of the name is the Latin word *rabiola* which was the word for the round-rooted turnip, now called *rape* (see the old drawing above). It was the shape of this turnip root which was imitated in these dumplings and hence the name *ravioli* evolved. The absolutely incorrect derivation from a Genoese dialect word *(rabiole)* given in *Larousse Gastronomique* is now omnipresent and it is time to correct this mistake. So originally *ravioli* were a lighter type of *gnocchi* or dumpling but of a specific shape.

Ravioli "nudi" alla fiorentina ("Naked" Ravioli Florentine Style) are the only ones of the original type that survive today (see *The Fine Art of Italian Cooking*). However, the cookbooks of the fourteenth through the eighteenth centuries have many, many types of dumplings called *ravioli*, which were eaten with sauces, in soups, and put into composite pies.

It is probable that many of those which survive in present-day Austria and Germany go back to that time.

Ravioli di Pollo in Brodo

CHICKEN RAVIOLI IN BROTH

FROM NAPLES

Ravioli di pollo is a recipe from the eighteenth-century Neapolitan court and is eaten in soup. At that time *pastasciutta* (fresh or dried pasta eaten with a sauce) had not yet been accepted for formal dining, and first courses were usually one of a great variety of flavored soups, no longer used in Italy, which often contained *ravioli* of fish, meat, fowl, cheese and/or herbs.

The meat should be ground into tiny pieces, but not packed together, so that air may enter and the *ravioli* retain their lightness when cooked. This result comes easily from using the fine attachment on a meat grinder, hand or electric.

1 whole chicken breast
2 extra large egg yolks
3 tablespoons plus ½ cup freshly grated Parmigiano
Salt, freshly ground black pepper, and freshly grated nutmeg
Coarse-grained salt
About 9 cups hot chicken or beef broth
1 cup unbleached all-purpose flour

SERVES 6

Bone the chicken breast (page 235) and remove the skin. Use a meat grinder to grind the chicken breast (page 92) finely. Transfer the ground chicken to a crockery bowl.

HOW TO PREPARE RAVIOLI

1. Add the egg yolks, 3 tablespoons of the Parmigiano, and salt, pepper, and nutmeg to taste to the bowl. Mix all the ingredients together with a wooden spoon.

Bring a large pot of cold water to a boil. Add coarse-grained salt to taste. Meanwhile, heat the broth in a different stockpot. When the salted water reaches the boiling point, spread the flour on a piece of aluminum foil on a flat surface.

2. Take 1 tablespoon of the chicken mixture and shape it into a small ball.

3. Lightly flour the ball on the board. Repeat until all the balls are formed. Drop the chicken *ravioli* into the boiling water. When they rise to the surface of the water, cook them for about 1 minute.

Pour the heated broth into a tureen.

4. With a slotted spoon transfer the *ravioli* to the tureen.

5. For each serving, ladle 3 or 4 *ravioli* and about 1¼ cups of broth into each bowl. Sprinkle each serving with some of the ½ cup grated Parmigiano.

Salsicce di Siena

SIENA SAUSAGES

FROM SIENA

The Sienese sausages specifically use the meat of only the pork butt, without the fat of the *pancetta* or any other meat. Unlike the other Tuscan sausages, they are spiced with red pepper flakes as well as the usual black peppercorns. These are among the most celebrated sausages in Italy.

1 large clove garlic, peeled and coarsely chopped
1 tablespoon salt
Pinch of hot pepper flakes
About 5 whole black peppercorns
2 pounds pork butt, coarsely ground
Sausage casing, approximately 40 inches

YIELD: ABOUT 10 SAUSAGES

Add the garlic, salt, hot pepper flakes and peppercorns to the ground meat and mix together thoroughly, using a wooden spoon.

Soak the casing in a small bowl of lukewarm water for 10 minutes, then remove from the water and dry with paper towels. Attach the casing and insert as directed on the description of the sausage machine or insert a funnel into the casings, pushing the meat through it (see *The Fine Art of Italian Cooking*).

When the casing is full, tie a long string to one end. Now, 3 inches from the end where it is tied, draw the long string around, pass it through and knot it tight. Every 3 inches, tie the string around in the same manner, making a long series of sausage links.

Let the sausage hang in a cool room with lots of fresh air. They should turn a reddish color about the third day. Allow them to hang for another 3 or 4 days: The salt will cure the meat in this period. After 6 or 7 days the sausages may be used or refrigerated for up to several weeks.

Salsa di Cervello

BRAIN SAUCE

FROM LOMBARDY

The creamy purée of brains used as a sauce is a classic accompaniment to meats of strong character, such as the lamb and spiced chicken dishes mentioned below. It may be a good introduction to brains for those who are not yet *appassionati* of this favorite of many *buongustai* (gourmets). The creamy texture, achieved through grinding in a food processor, and delicious flavor may be used to enhance a simply cooked meat.

This sauce may be used to pour over the *Coscia di agnello* (Boned Leg of Lamb) in place of the fresh mint sauce (see page 255) or on the *Petti di pollo allo specchio* (Rolled Chicken Breast in Aspic) on page 435, in which case you substitute this sauce for the aspic.

1 veal brain, approximately 1 pound
6 tablespoons sweet butter
2 tablespoons olive oil

SERVES 6

½ bay leaf
1½ cups chicken broth
3 tablespoons unbleached all-purpose flour
Salt, freshly ground black pepper, and freshly grated nutmeg
Pinch of dried thyme
½ cup dry white wine

Blanch the veal brain by placing it in a bowl and pouring over enough boiling water to cover it. Let stand for about 5 minutes, then remove the membranes from the inside part under cold running water. The same method can be used for sweetbreads.

Put 4 tablespoons of the butter and the oil in a small saucepan and heat until the butter is melted. Add the brains and bay leaf and sauté for 2 minutes. Heat the broth in a small pan. Mix the remaining 2 tablespoons of butter with the flour, combining them with a fork on a plate. Add the butter-flour mixture to the brains, stir and immediately add the hot broth. Lower the heat, simmer for 2 minutes, then remove the pan from the heat. Transfer the brains to a food processor, which is best for obtaining the desired texture, and pureé. Return the ground brains to the pan over medium heat. Season with salt, pepper, and nutmeg to taste and the thyme. When the sauce reaches a boil, add the wine and let it evaporate very slowly (about 10 minutes). At this point the sauce should be smooth. Remove from the heat, transfer to a sauceboat, and serve.

PASSING

For many centuries the *setaccio* (in the vernacular "*staccio*") or sieve was the main implement for passing, using the hand itself to push the ingredients through. When the substance was tough, such as raw meat, it was ground first with the stone mortar and metal pestle and passed through the *setaccio* for the fine textures needed for *pasticci, quinquinelle (quenelles)*, etc.

In the late nineteenth-century cookbooks the *setaccio* was still universally referred to. By the early twentieth century, a mechanical device had been invented in which the sieve was fitted inside a metal bowl with a butterfly-shaped metal plate that pushed the food against the sieve as you turned a handle. Jarro, the great turn-of-the-century Florentine chef, in his 1902 writings was already referring to this clever instrument. The advantages of hand control were still retained and the texture changed little. This is the forerunner of the food mill used today.

For a description of use of the food mill with the disc having the finest holes, see the discussion of puréeing cooked fish in the recipe for *Spaghetti con passato di pesce alla genovese* (Genoese Fish Sauce with Spaghetti) on page 184. The photos below demonstrate the coarser disc.

HOW TO PASS FOOD WITH A FOOD MILL

1. It is best to pour the solid cooked materials into the food mill together with the liquid. It will make the passing easier.

2. Begin turning the handle immediately while some liquid still remains unpassed.

3. The turning can be stopped and the job completed when only the tough material, such as the fiber and seeds of a tomato, remain unpassed in the sieve while the pulp and juice have passed through.

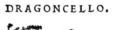

DRAGONCELLO.

23. Dragoncello (Tarragon)

Salsa di Pomodori ai Capperi

CAPER-TOMATO SAUCE

1 pound fresh tomatoes, or 2 cups drained canned
   imported Italian tomatoes
1 medium-sized clove garlic, peeled
2 tablespoons capers in wine vinegar, drained
1 piece lemon peel
4 tablespoons sweet butter
2 tablespoons unbleached all-purpose flour
Salt and freshly ground black pepper
Juice of ½ lemon

MAKES ABOUT 2 CUPS

If the tomatoes are fresh, cut them into quarters; if they are canned, leave them whole. Put the tomatoes, garlic, capers, and lemon peel into a heavy saucepan. Cook over medium heat for about 25 minutes, or until the tomatoes are very soft. Remove from heat and pass the contents of the pan through a food mill.

Melt the butter in a small saucepan. When the butter is completely melted, add the flour. Stir with a wooden spoon until the flour is completely incorporated. Add the strained sauce and taste for salt and pepper. Simmer for about 15 minutes. When the sauce has reduced, add the lemon juice and mix with a wooden spoon. Transfer the sauce to a sauceboat and serve immediately.

Zuppa alla Senese

BEAN SOUP SIENESE STYLE

FROM SIENA IN TUSCANY

This thick soup made from puréed *cannellini* beans reaches its rustic peak in the countryside of Tuscany, where the inhabitants do not shrink from eating it with the slices of raw red onion that go so well with the country bread that is covered with the rich soup. Of the versions I have eaten, perhaps I have enjoyed most those using tarragon rather than thyme, though both herbs are authentic for the dish.

2 cups dried cannellini beans
2 red onions
About 10 sprigs Italian parsley, leaves only
1 large celery stalk
2 cloves garlic, peeled
5 basil leaves, fresh or preserved in salt
1 teaspoon rosemary leaves
Coarse-grained salt
3 fresh tomatoes, or 3 drained canned imported Italian tomatoes
2 ounces pancetta, or 1 ounce boiled ham and 1 ounce salt pork
1 teaspoon fresh thyme leaves, or ½ teaspoon dried thyme or tarragon
Salt and freshly ground black pepper
¼ cup plus 8 teaspoons olive oil
1 small Savoy cabbage, about 2 pounds
8 slices Tuscan bread (page 412)
Sliced red onions (optional)

SERVES 8

Soak the beans overnight in a bowl of cold water. If you wish to accelerate the soaking time by several hours, add 1 tablespoon of flour to the cold water.* The following morning, rinse them very well and put them in a large stockpot.

Coarsely chop one of the onions, the parsley leaves, celery, garlic, basil, and rosemary together on a board. Add everything to the stockpot. Drain the beans and add them to the pot. Pour over about 5 quarts of cold water and add coarse-grained salt to taste. Cover the stockpot and bring it to a boil over medium heat. Simmer for about 1½ hours. At this point, the beans should be cooked but still retain their shape.

Meanwhile, pass the tomatoes through a food mill and finely chop the remaining onion. Cut the *pancetta* into small pieces.

Heat ¼ cup of the oil in a saucepan over medium heat and add the onion and *pancetta*. Sauté lightly for about 10 minutes, then add the tomatoes. Taste for salt and pepper and add the thyme or tarragon. Simmer for about 10 minutes, then remove the saucepan from the heat and set aside until needed.

Clean and wash the cabbage very well. Cut it into quarters and then strips about ½ inch wide. When beans have finished cooking, remove the stockpot from the heat and transfer half of the beans to a bowl with a slotted spoon. Let stand until needed. Pass the remaining beans and all the cooking liquid with the aromatic vegetables through a food mill into a large bowl. Return the bean purée to the stockpot and add enough cold water to make about 4 quarts of liquid. Bring the liquid to a boil. Add the cabbage and simmer until the cabbage is completely cooked (about 25 minutes). Then add the tomatoes and *pancetta* to the stockpot and simmer for 5 minutes longer. Taste for salt and pepper. Preheat the oven to 300 degrees. Toast the slices of bread in the oven for about 25 minutes, or until lightly golden brown on both sides. Put a slice of the toasted bread in each individual soup bowl. Add the cooked whole beans to the stockpot and stir thoroughly. Remove the pot from the flame and let stand covered for 10 minutes.

Ladle the soup over the bread and let stand for 5 minutes longer. Then serve, adding teaspoon of olive oil to each serving. This soup may be eaten after 3 or 4 hours at room temperature or reheated later. Always add the bread and oil just before serving. Raw red onions are often sliced over each serving.

Torta di Castagne

FRESH CHESTNUT TORTE

OLD ITALIAN-JEWISH RECIPE

A unique cake made from puréed fresh chestnuts, flavored with fennel. It does not resemble the *Monte Bianco* (Molded Purée of Fresh Chestnuts) on page 448. Another one of the dishes of the more than thousand year tradition of Italy's ancient Jewish communities, in continuous existence since Roman times. It is important that these still valid recipes do not disappear after being used traditionally for centuries.

2 pounds fresh chestnuts
Coarse-grained salt
½ teaspoon fennel seeds
3 tablespoons sweet butter
7 eggs
½ pound granulated sugar
3 tablespoons confectioners' sugar

SERVES 8

---

* Flour and water produce yeast, which acts as a tenderizer.

Soak the chestnuts overnight in a large bowl of cold water. Bring a large stockpot of salted water to a boil, then add the drained soaked chestnuts and fennel seeds. Boil until the chestnuts are completely cooked (about 2 hours). While they are still hot, remove the shells and skin from the chestnuts and pass them through a food mill into a large bowl.

Melt the butter in the top of a double boiler over hot water and let cool for about 10 minutes. Add the cooled butter to the chestnut purée and mix well with a wooden spoon.

Separate 4 of the eggs placing the whites in a copper bowl and the yolks in a large crockery or glass bowl. Add the remaining 3 whole eggs to the yolks along with the granulated sugar. Stir very well with a wooden spoon until all the sugar is incorporated and the eggs turn a lighter color. Add the egg-sugar mixture to the chestnuts and mix thoroughly. Preheat the oven to 375 degrees.

Using a wire whisk, beat the egg whites until stiff. Butter a 12-inch layer cake pan. Gently fold the stiff egg whites into the chestnut mixture and transfer it to the prepared pan. Place the pan in the oven and bake for about 1 hour. Transfer the torte to a rack to cool completely.

Sprinkle the torte with the confectioners' sugar and serve it, sliced like a pizza.

CHAPTER 5

Crespelle, Batters, Frittate

HOW TO SEASON A PAN

Before making the *crespelle* (crêpes) and the *frittate* (high omelets) recipes that follow, it is important that the pans when new be well-seasoned.

Crêpe pans for the *crespelle* and the omelet pans used for *frittate* may be of iron, aluminum, or stainless steel. Copper is beautiful for serving, but not for making either of the above. Crêpe pans should be reserved only for making *crespelle* or crêpes. It is especially important to *never* use them for eggs or they will be ruined. It is also best to reserve omelet pans for eggs, omelets, and *frittate*. The pans will have to be reseasoned if anything burns or sticks in them, or if in washing they are rubbed with an abrasive material, even a light one. The following photographs illustrate the seasoning of an omelet pan, but the same procedure can be used for the crêpe pan in the photographs on pages 106.

1. Place the pan over medium heat with about 2 tablespoons of salt (not coarse). Add about 1 tablespoon of vegetable oil to the pan.

2. When the oil is warm, but not hot, use a paper towel to rub the salt and oil into first the bottom of the pan

3. and then the sides. Continue rubbing the pan over medium heat for 2 or 3 minutes. Remove the pan from the heat and wipe it out thoroughly with a clean towel. The pan is now ready to use.

Sauté pans may also be seasoned in this way.

102

CRESPELLE

Crespelle, or crêpes, have been made in the past with an extra large amount of egg mixed into the flour, with chestnut flour, and, as we can see from a recipe below, with potato starch. There are many, however, made with a more typical batter using flour, butter, eggs, egg yolks, and milk. Since the amount of the ingredients for the *crespelle* varies from recipe to recipe, they are not listed in the following instructions on how to make *crespelle*. Refer to the individual recipes for the amounts and follow the illustrated steps for the technique.

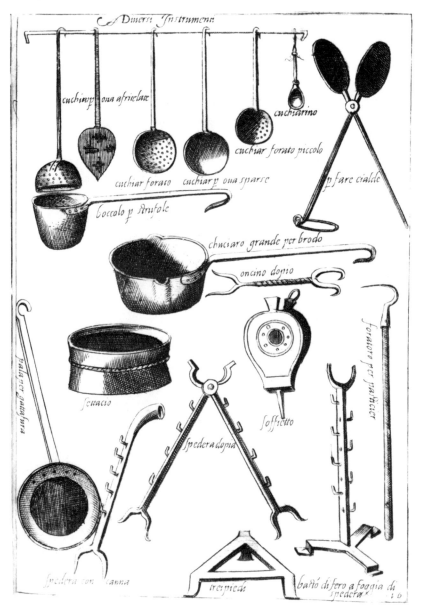

24. *"Per fare cialde"* (to make cialde)
  The cooking utensils illustrated here (many of which are still used today) for making cialde *(and other foods).* Cialde *are thin wafers which are baked, rolled up and used to scoop up whipped cream.*

When the batter is fried into a pancake that is filled and either rolled or folded, it is called *crespella* (crêpe), or the batter may be baked (*cialde*). Both were made as early as the Middle Ages. With *cialde* the batter is baked in the form of paper-thin wafers and then rolled up. In modern times they are also called *cialdoni*. *Cialde* were so popular in fifteenth-century Florence that Lorenzo the Magnificent wrote a poem about them.

Each of the four recipes included is quite different. *"Fazzoletti" ripieni* or Stuffed "Handkerchiefs" are so called because of the way the *crespelle* are folded and placed against one another in the baking dish.

The best known *crespelle* in Italy are *Crespelle alla fiorentina*, the classical Florentine-style crêpes with the spinach-ricotta stuffing which are covered with *balsamella*. They are rolled like *cannelloni*, and in fact are sometimes listed as *cannelloni* on restaurant menus outside of Florence.

The usual potato flour *crespelle* from Parma, *Frittatini ripieni* (Potato Flour Crêpes), may be stuffed with sweetbreads, with vegetables or meat. They are folded like a package and lightly deep fried. Then there is *Merendine del Granduca* (Grand Duke Ferdinand's Snacks), the delicious dessert in which the *crespelle* are stuffed with ricotta and fresh strawberries and covered with sweet liqueur. This dish is named after one of the Grand Dukes Ferdinand (of which there are two), the great seventeenth-century Tuscan rulers, and is associated with the hunting lodge at Artimino. Ferdinand II was lively and gregarious but had to temper his spirit around his puritanical wife and son, so perhaps he needed this "snack" to refresh him periodically.

PREPARING CRESPELLE
HOW TO SIFT THE FLOUR

1. Place the flour in the sifter and lift it off the board.

2. In order to incorporate some air into the flour, shake from side

3. to side.

HOW TO PREPARE THE BATTER

Melt the butter in a *bagnomaria* or in the top of a double boiler over hot water and let stand until cool.

1. Put the flour in a crockery bowl and make a well in the flour. Place the eggs and egg yolks in the well. Stir very carefully, absorbing some flour from the edges of the well.

2. Start adding the cold milk little by little, always stirring with a wooden spoon, until all the flour is incorporated. Then add the cooled butter and salt.

Mix very well. Cover the bowl and place it in a cool, draft-free place to rest for at least 1 hour to allow the gluten to expand.

1. Put the batter into a cup or ladle. When the pan is hot pour the batter into the greased pan.

2. Very quickly swirl the batter around until the bottom of the pan is covered.

3. As the batter sets, shake the pan vigorously to keep the bottom of the *crespella* detached from the pan.

4. Shake the *crespella* onto the edge of the pan so that you can either

5. flip it, by giving the pan a short abrupt movement forward then up, when

6. the *crespella* should turn in the air

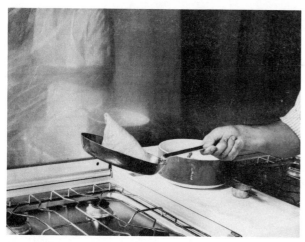

7. and land in the pan on its other side.

8. Or, leaving pan on the stove, hold the *crespelle* with index finger and thumb of both hands and quickly turn it over.

The *crespelle* may be prepared one day in advance and kept in the refrigerator separated by wax paper or paper towels and wrapped in aluminum foil. *Crespelle* may be kept for several days in the refrigerator.

"Fazzoletti" Ripieni

STUFFED "HANDKERCHIEFS"

FROM LUCCA IN TUSCANY

MAKES 24 CRESPELLE
SERVES 8

For the *crespelle*:
8 ounces (2 cups) unbleached all-purpose flour
2 ounces (4 tablespoons) sweet butter
1 egg yolk plus 2 whole eggs
2 cups cold milk
Pinch of salt

For the stuffing:
1 medium-sized clove garlic, peeled
1 celery stalk
1 medium-sized carrot
1 medium-sized red onion
5 or 6 sprigs Italian parsley, leaves only
5 tablespoons olive oil
3 ounces pancetta, or 1½ ounces boiled ham and 1½ ounces salt pork
½ pound ground beef
1 whole, skinned and boned chicken breast, ground
½ pound ground veal shoulder
Salt and freshly ground black pepper
1 cup dry red wine
2 extra large eggs
2 tablespoons freshly grated Parmigiano
Freshly grated nutmeg to taste

For the *balsamella*:
2 tablespoons sweet butter
2 tablespoons unbleached all-purpose flour
2 cups milk
Salt to taste
4 tablespoons freshly grated Parmigiano

For the tomato sauce:
2 cups drained canned imported Italian tomatoes
1 tablespoon olive oil
Salt and freshly ground black pepper

To serve:
2 tablespoons freshly grated Parmigiano

Prepare the *crespelle* with the ingredients listed above, following the directions on pages 104–107. Fry the *crespelle* in a greased 6½-inch crêpe pan, using 2 tablespoons of batter for each *crespella*.

Prepare the stuffing: Finely chop the garlic, celery, carrot, onion, and parsley together on a chopping board with a *mezzaluna*. Heat the oil in a saucepan over medium heat. When the oil is hot, add the chopped ingredients to the saucepan and sauté for 5 minutes, stirring with a wooden spoon.

Coarsely chop the *pancetta* and add it to the saucepan. Sauté for 10 minutes longer. Then add the ground beef, chicken, and veal to the saucepan. Use a fork to combine all the ingredients well. Add salt and freshly ground pepper to taste and sauté for 15 minutes, stirring occasionally.

Pour the wine over the mixture in the pan and let it evaporate by cooking over low heat for about 15 minutes. Remove the pan from the heat and transfer the contents to a large bowl. Let stand in a cool place, but not in the refrigerator, until needed. The eggs, Parmigiano, and nutmeg will be used later when assembling the dish (see below).

Prepare the *balsamella* with the ingredients listed above, following the directions on page 334. Add the 4 tablespoons of grated Parmigiano just before removing the saucepan from the heat. Cover the *balsamella* with buttered wax paper and let stand until cool.

Prepare the tomato sauce. Pass the tomatoes through a food mill to remove the seeds and skin (page 98). Put the strained tomatoes, olive oil, and salt and pepper to taste in a small saucepan. Reduce very slowly, uncovered, for about 20 minutes, then remove the pan from the heat, transfer the sauce to a crockery bowl, and let stand until cold.

To put dish together: Preheat the oven to 400 degrees. Add 1 cup of *balsamella* to the meat stuffing. Combine the tomato sauce and the remaining *balsamella*. Add the eggs, Parmigiano, and nutmeg to the bowl containing the stuffing. Taste for salt and pepper.

1. Pour half of the tomato sauce and *balsamella* mixture into a round 12-inch baking dish. Place all the *crespelle*, which are stacked one on top of another and separated by wax paper or paper towels, on the table. In the middle of each, place 1 heaping tablespoon of the stuffing.

2. Close each *crespella* by holding together its edges,

3. making little sacks.

Stand the sacks together closely and against the side of the baking dish. To do this, hold the sack together and place a second one next to it. Holding the second one together, let go of the first one. Continue in this manner around the edge of the dish. When the entire outside edge of the baking dish is filled, all will support each other and remain closed.

4. Then make a series of inner circles in the same way until the pan is full. Pour the remaining tomato sauce and *balsamella* mixture on top of the *fazzoletti* and place the baking dish in the oven for about 20 minutes. Remove the dish from the oven and allow to cool for 5 minutes. Sprinkle with Parmigiano and serve.

Crespelle alla Fiorentina

CRESPELLE FLORENTINE STYLE

For the *crespelle*:
2 tablespoons sweet butter
8 ounces (2 cups) unbleached all-purpose flour
2 whole extra large eggs plus 1 egg yolk
2 cups cold milk
Pinch of salt

For the filling:
3 pounds fresh spinach
2 pounds fresh Swiss chard
Coarse-grained salt
15 ounces ricotta
3 extra large whole eggs
5 tablespoons freshly grated Parmigiano
Salt and freshly ground black pepper
½ teaspoon freshly grated nutmeg

For the *balsamella*:
2 cups milk
2½ tablespoons sweet butter
2½ tablespoons unbleached all-purpose flour
Salt to taste

For the tomato sauce:
1 cup drained canned imported Italian tomatoes
1 tablespoon olive oil
Salt and freshly ground black pepper
3 or 4 basil leaves, fresh or preserved in salt

Prepare about 24 *crespelle* with the ingredients listed above, following the directions on pages 104–107. Fry the *crespelle* in a greased 6½-inch crêpe pan, using 2 tablespoons of batter for each *crespella*.

Prepare the filling. Rinse the spinach and Swiss chard very well in cold water. Remove the stems from both the spinach and Swiss chard. Bring a large stockpot of salted water to a boil. Add the spinach and Swiss chard and cook for about 12 minutes after the water starts boiling again. Drain and cool under cold running water. Squeeze very dry, then chop finely. Put in a large bowl with the ricotta, eggs, and Parmigiano. Add salt and pepper to taste and the nutmeg. Mix together with a wooden spoon.

Prepare the *balsamella* with the ingredients listed above, following the directions on page 334. Cover the *balsamella* with buttered wax paper and let stand until cool.

Prepare the tomato sauce. Pass the tomatoes through a food mill to remove seeds and skin (page 98). Put the strained tomatoes, olive oil, and salt and pepper to taste in a small saucepan. Reduce very slowly, uncovered, for about 15 minutes. Remove from the heat and add the basil leaves, torn into two or three pieces. Let the sauce stand until cold.

To put dish together: Butter two 13½- x 8¾-inch Pyrex baking dishes. Preheat oven to 375 degrees. Place 2 heaping tablespoons of the filling on one end of each *crespella*. Roll them up and place in the baking dish, one next to the other with the seam on top. Gently pour the *balsamella* over the *crespelle* first, then the tomato sauce. Place the dishes in the oven and bake for about 20 minutes. Remove the dishes from oven and allow the *crespelle* to cool for 1 to 3 minutes, then serve.

Frittatini Ripieni

POTATO FLOUR CRÊPES

FROM PARMA

YIELD: APPROXIMATELY 20
SERVES 6

For the batter:
2 tablespoons sweet butter
1⅓ cups potato starch
Pinch of salt
4 whole extra large eggs
2 cups cold milk

For the stuffing:
There are three different stuffings that can be used:
1. Vegetables alla parmigiana *(a boiled vegetable such as carrots, string beans, spinach, Swiss chard, etc., sautéed with butter and oil and seasoned with salt, white pepper, grated nutmeg and Parmigiano)—1 pound, approximately*
2. *Any thick meat sauce—2 cups, approximately*
3. *Blanched sweetbreads (see page 97), which have been sautéed in butter and seasoned with salt and black pepper—1 pound, approximately*

Plus:
2 pounds solid vegetable shortening
Salt to taste

To serve:
Lemon wedges

Prepare the batter using the ingredients listed above, following the directions on pages 104–107. Do not allow the batter to rest. Prepare the *frittatini (crespelle)* immediately using a well-buttered 9-inch crêpe pan and ¼ cup of the batter for each *crespella*.

Place a heaping tablespoon of the prepared stuffing in the center of the *crespella* and fold it like a package.

Heat the shortening in a deep-fat fryer. Prepare a large serving dish by lining it with paper towels. When the shortening is hot, put in 4 or 5 stuffed *frittatini*, with the folded sides down. Fry until light golden brown (about ½ minute), then turn and let the other side brown for the same length of time. As each is ready, remove the *frittatini* from the pan with a strainer-skimmer and place them on the prepared serving dish. When all the *crespelle* are on the serving dish, remove the paper towels, season the *frittatini* with salt, and serve with lemon wedges.

Merendine del Granduca

GRAND DUKE FERDINAND'S SNACKS

To reproduce the sweet-almond taste of the old Malvasia, the modern Amaretto is the right compromise.

For the *crespelle:*
2 ounces (4 tablespoons) sweet butter
8 ounces (2 cups) unbleached all-purpose flour
1 extra large egg yolk plus 2 whole extra large eggs
2 cups cold milk
Pinch of salt

For the stuffing:
15 ounces ricotta
4 tablespoons granulated sugar
24 fresh strawberries

For the sauce:
1 cup Amaretto liqueur
¼ cup granulated sugar
1 cup cold water

YIELD: APPROXIMATELY 24
SERVES 12

Prepare the *crespelle* with the ingredients listed above, following the directions on pages 104–107. Fry the *crespelle*, in a greased 6½-inch crêpe pan, using 2 tablespoons of batter for each *crespella*. Stack the *crespelle*, placing a piece of paper towel between each two. Let stand until needed.

Prepare the filling. Mix the ricotta and sugar together in a crockery bowl. Refrigerate, covered, until needed.

Put the Amaretto, sugar, and water in a small saucepan and simmer, uncovered, over low heat for about 15 minutes. Remove from the heat and set aside until needed.

Rinse the strawberries and remove the stems. Butter a 13½- x 8¾-inch Pyrex baking dish. Preheat the oven to 375 degrees. Place a tablespoon of the ricotta-sugar mixture in the center of each *crespella*. Put a strawberry on top of the ricotta mixture. Fold the *crespella* like a package and place it in the baking dish with the folded edges *on the top*. When all the *crespelle* are in the baking dish, pour the reduced Amaretto sauce over them and place dish in the oven for 35 minutes. Remove from oven and allow the *crespelle* to cool for 2 to 3 minutes. Then serve with about 1 teaspoon of the sauce on top of each *crespella*.

Salvia Fritta

DEEP-FRIED SAGE LEAVES

This unusual and delicious salted hot appetizer sets off the pungent sage leaves which are dipped in a batter, lightened by folding in the stiff egg whites, that puff up when fried. This dish can also work well with fresh sage leaves preserved in salt (page 48), as they do not dry out when preserved that way.

SERVES 8

For the batter:
1¾ cups unbleached all-purpose flour
½ teaspoon salt
3 tablespoons olive oil
2 extra large eggs, separated
Pinch of granulated sugar
¼ cup pure (grain) alcohol or vodka
1 cup cold water
About 50 sage leaves, fresh or preserved in salt (fresh bay leaves may be substituted)

Plus:
About 2 pounds solid vegetable shortening
Salt to taste

To serve:
1 lemon cut into wedges

Sift the flour into a large bowl. Make a well in the flour, then start adding the salt, olive oil, egg yolks, sugar, alcohol, and water one at a time. After each ingredient is added, mix it thoroughly with a little of the flour before adding the next. When all the ingredients are incorporated, stir with a wooden spoon until the batter is smooth. Let stand, covered, in a cool place for about 2 hours. Set aside the egg whites to incorporate later.

Meanwhile, wash the sage leaves and pat them dry with a paper towel. Heat the vegetable shortening in a deep-fat fryer until very hot. Just before the fat is ready for frying, beat the egg whites in a copper bowl until they are stiff. Fold them into the batter and mix very gently in a rotating motion until they are completely incorporated. Cover a large serving dish with a layer of paper towels.

Dip each sage leaf in the batter and drop it into the fat. Let cook until light golden brown all over and very puffy (about 1 minute). Using a strainer-skimmer, remove the sage leaves as each one is cooked and place them on the paper towel-lined dish. When all the leaves are on the dish, remove the towels, sprinkle with salt, and serve hot with lemon wedges.

NOTE: Fresh bay leaves may also be fried in this manner. For another batter see also *Filetti di sogliola fritti* (Deep-fried Sole Fillets), page 312.

FRITTATE

Frittate are high omelets which incorporate ingredients such as vegetables, herbs, meats, etc., and are rather different from the thin omelets that are stuffed with such ingredients and then rolled, although that kind of omelet, now popular in France and elsewhere, was once also eaten in Italy. In the sixteenth century, it was called *Pesce d'uovo*, or egg fish, as the shape suggested a fish to them. It was a great favorite of the Florentine mannerist painter and *buongustaio*, Pontormo.

After illustrating the basic technique of making the *frittata*, examples of recipes from different parts of Italy follow. *Frittata profumata*, the herb-flavored one made with mixed fresh basil, mint, and parsley is one of the delights of southern Italian cooking. Ricotta is incorporated into the eggs in the *Frittata con la ricotta* of Sicily. Thin omelets are made for the *Frittata trippata* and are cut into strips to resemble tripe. It is then served in the light tomato sauce which is also the sauce used for tripe. And yes, there is even a pasta *frittata*, which is delicious. When made with *penne*, as in the photo on page 116, it is also beautiful when sliced through.

Frittate are served either warm or at room temperature as a main dish or appetizer.

HOW TO PREPARE FRITTATA

Break the eggs into a large crockery bowl. The number of eggs will vary according to the recipe. See the individual recipes below.

If the omelet pan used for the *frittata* is new be sure to season it first (page 102).

1. With a fork, break the yolks of the eggs and beat them lightly so no air bubbles or foam begins to form.

2. Place a 10-inch omelet pan over medium heat. Add 1 scant tablespoon of olive or vegetable oil to the pan. When the oil is hot, add the beaten eggs.

Keep puncturing the bottom with a fork as the eggs set to allow the liquid on top to move through to the bottom. This will help the eggs cook uniformly.

3. When the eggs are well set and the *frittata* is well detached from the bottom of the pan, put a plate, upside down, over the pan.

4. Holding the plate firmly,

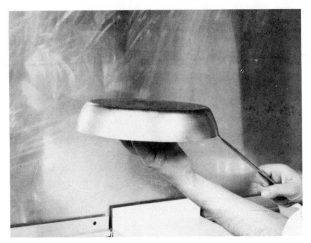

5. reverse the pan and

6. turn the *frittata* out onto the plate.

7. Return the pan to the heat and carefully slide the *frittata* into the pan and cook the other side.

When the eggs are well set on the second side (about 1 minute), reverse the *frittata* onto a serving dish.

Frittata con la Ricotta

FRITTATA WITH RICOTTA

FROM SICILY

SERVES 6

15 ounces ricotta, preferably whole-milk
6 whole extra large eggs
6 tablespoons freshly grated Parmigiano
Salt, freshly ground black pepper, and freshly grated nutmeg
1 scant tablespoon olive oil

Drain the ricotta very well in heavy cheesecloth.

Begin to make the *frittata*, following the directions on page 114, through photo 1. Then add the ricotta, Parmigiano, and salt, pepper, and nutmeg to taste to the eggs. Mix with a wooden spoon until all the ingredients are well blended.

Finish making the *frittata* according to the directions on pages 114–115, photos 2 through 7. Serve hot, slicing the high *frittata* like a cake and seasoning each slice with more freshly ground black pepper. The *frittata* may be accompanied by sliced fresh tomatoes.

Frittata Profumata

FRITTATA WITH MIXED FRESH HERBS

FROM SOUTHERN ITALY

SERVES 6

10 sprigs Italian parsley, leaves only
About 15 fresh basil leaves, torn into thirds
About 15 whole fresh mint leaves
6 extra large eggs
Salt and freshly ground black pepper
1 scant tablespoon olive oil

Wash the parsley, basil, and mint and dry on paper towels. Finely chop the parsley on a board.

Begin to make the *frittata*, following the directions on page 114, through photo 1. Then add the chopped parsley, basil, mint, salt and a little pepper to the beaten eggs. Mix through with a fork. Finish making the *frittata* according to the directions on pages 114–115, photos 2 through 7. Sprinkle with a little more black pepper before serving. The *frittata* may be served hot or at room temperature.

Frittata di Pasta

PASTA FRITTATA

FROM SOUTHERN ITALY

SERVES 6 AS A MAIN COURSE
8 AS AN APPETIZER

1 pound dried pasta, such as penne
Coarse-grained salt
2 ounces (4 tablespoons) sweet butter
5 sprigs Italian parsley, leaves only
9 extra large eggs
⅓ cup freshly grated Parmigiano
10 fresh mint leaves
About 6 or 7 large basil leaves
Salt and freshly ground black pepper
1 scant tablespoon olive oil

Bring a large pot of cold water to a boil. Add coarse-grained salt to taste and cook the pasta according to the directions on page 181 until *al dente*. Drain the pasta and put it in a large bowl together with the butter. Toss very well so that the butter completely coats the cooked pasta. Cover the bowl and let stand for about 20 minutes.

Finely chop the parsley on a board.

In a large bowl beat the eggs with a fork, adding the grated Parmigiano, mint leaves, 3 of the basil leaves torn into small pieces, and the chopped parsley. Taste for salt and pepper. Add the cooled pasta and mix thoroughly.

Place a 10-inch omelet pan over the heat and add the oil. Prepare the *frittata*, following the directions on pages 114–115, photos 2 through 7. When the *frittata* is on the serving platter, spread the remaining whole basil leaves over it and serve.

116

1. Slicing the *frittata*.

Frittata Trippata

FRITTATA MADE IN THE MANNER OF TRIPE

FROM PISTOIA IN TUSCANY

SERVES 6

6 *extra large eggs*
Pinch of salt
1 *tablespoon olive oil*

For the sauce:
1 *pound fresh tomatoes, or 2 cups drained canned imported Italian tomatoes*
1 *clove garlic, peeled but left whole*
4 *tablespoons olive oil*
3 *or 4 basil leaves, fresh or preserved in salt*
¼ *cup freshly grated Parmigiano*
Salt and freshly ground black pepper

Begin to make the *frittata* following the directions on page 114, through photo 1. Then, instead of making one single *frittata*, make two separate thin ones, using half of the eggs for each. Follow the remaining directions for each of the two *frittate*. Add salt to taste and finish making the *frittata*, following the directions on pages 114–115, photos 2 through 7. After finishing second *frittata* allow both to cool completely.

Prepare the sauce. If the tomatoes are fresh, cut them into pieces. Place the tomato pieces or the canned tomatoes in a saucepan over medium heat and cook lightly for about 5 minutes. Add the garlic and cook for 15 minutes longer. Discard the garlic. Pass the tomatoes through a food mill into a bowl and then return the strained tomatoes to the saucepan. Add the olive oil and cook for 15 minutes longer. Taste for salt and pepper.

Wash the basil leaves and dry them on paper towels. Tear each basil leaf into 2 or 3 pieces.

Roll up the two cooled thin *frittate* and cut them into ½-inch-wide strips. Add the strips to the finished sauce, lower the heat and simmer for 3 minutes longer. Remove the pan from the heat and sprinkle the Parmigiano and basil leaves over the top. Serve immediately directly from the pan.

CHAPTER 6

Fresh Pasta

TYPES OF FRESH PASTA

1. The various ingredients (arranged in wells of flour) contained in each of the seven types of pasta, from left to right: red, egg, semolina, without eggs, chocolate, green, egg without oil. (See the photo on the front right.) The equipment used to make pasta is also pictured here in the center of the photo, from top to bottom: sifter, manually-operated pasta machine, pastry cutters, rolling pins, cookie cutters.

It is probable that in ancient times when flour mixed with water was made into pasta to be dried for preservation, some of it must have been eaten immediately when freshly made. The type of flour used was the coarsely ground *puls*, close to our modern semolina. This type of flour and water pasta survives mainly in two forms today. The first, and closest to

the ancient form, is used in southern Italy to make such types as the *orecchiette* of Puglia. The ingredients of this, illustrated by the third well from the left, are semolina flour, almost always mixed in modern times with normally ground flour, water, and a little salt. A second type, probably surviving from the Middle Ages, uses only the more finely milled flour with a little oil added to the water and salt. The *trenette* and *trofie* of Genoa use this type of pasta as does such a Sienese dish as *pinci*. The fourth well from the left contains the ingredients of this type.

Egg pasta is mentioned in the first modern Italian manuscript cookbook, from Florence in about 1300, so it is at least that old. The well on the extreme right

118

shows the simplest form of egg pasta, that made with just flour, eggs, and salt. A variation of this has just a little water added. This type is widely used all over Italy. A fourth basic variant, shown in the second well from the left, is the Tuscan type which employs flour, eggs, salt, and a little oil. This type is often used also in other parts of central Italy.

Fresh pasta of any of the above types must be at least partially kneaded by hand, and the kneading may be completed by a manually-operated machine. The stretching should be either with a rolling pin or a manually-operated machine. I personally am not satisfied with the results of kneading by electric machines, because tactile control is important to me for the flexibility required by the ever-changing conditions of flour and eggs, not to speak of weather and humidity. A type of fresh pasta is made commercially both in Italy and abroad, employing large heavy machines. The dough used for this pasta is of a tougher consistency than for more normally tender fresh pasta. It uses a coarsely ground flour like semolina and often does not contain fresh eggs so that a dough is produced that can resist the heavy machines. The pasta produced and sold in many commercial fresh pasta outlets should not be confused with real handmade or manually-operated machine-made pasta. It is certainly the best substitute if one doesn't have the real thing, but it is not the same. Given the ever-increasing avail-ability of this pasta, we should begin to use a term such as "commercial fresh pasta" to differentiate it from real fresh pasta. In summary, it can be good and is certainly useful at times, but it is not the same.

Green pasta, adding chopped spinach to the ingredients, has long been popular. It is also used in both dried pasta and commercial fresh pasta, but in these latter two, it is clear that some form of green coloring must be substituted for the fresh spinach. When spinach is used, the green color is uneven and has distributed green of varied shadings. The types that are not homemade have a uniform green coloring. The second well from the right contains the ingredients for green pasta.

The well on the extreme left, that of red pasta, contains chopped beets and the other basic ingredients, which is the recipe used in central Italy. In the South, the red color is produced by tomato paste.

A uniquely Tuscan variant is chocolate pasta, of a warm brown color, created by the discreet addition of cocoa powder. Shown in the third well from the right, this pasta must be eaten only with its classic *dolce-forte sauce* (page 136).

Finally, not shown in this photo, we have the very special hot pepper pasta, with its flecks of pink coloring. See *Tagliatelle al peperoncino* (Red Pepper *Tagliatelle*) on page 135.

Basic Egg Pasta

1 cup unbleached all-purpose flour
1 extra large egg
1 teaspoon olive oil or vegetable oil
Pinch of salt

SERVES 2 PEOPLE
FOR PASTA WITH SAUCE,
4 PEOPLE FOR PASTA IN BROTH

To make any of the other six kinds of pasta shown on page 118, use the same technique below for egg pasta, but with these specific ingredients:

Green pasta
3½ cups unbleached all-purpose flour
2 extra large eggs
2 teaspoons olive oil or vegetable oil
1 heaping tablespoon finely chopped boiled spinach (from ½ pound cooked fresh spinach)
Pinch of salt

Red pasta
Use the same ingredients as above, but substituting 1 heaping tablespoon finely chopped boiled beets (from 1 medium-sized beet), or 1 tablespoon tomato paste, for the spinach.

Egg pasta without oil
1 scant cup unbleached all-purpose flour
1 extra large egg
Pinch of salt

Chocolate pasta
See page 136.

Semolina pasta
See page 152.

Pasta without eggs
See pages 147 and 149.

HOW TO PREPARE THE DOUGH AND KNEAD IT

1. Place the flour in a mound on a pasta board. Use a fork to make a well in the center.

2. Put the eggs in the well,

3. then the oil

4. and salt.

120

5. With a fork, first mix together the eggs, oil, and salt,

6. then begin to incorporate the flour from the inner rim of the well, always incorporating fresh flour from the lower part, pushing it under the dough that is forming to keep it from sticking to the board.

7. Remove the pieces of the dough attached to the fork.

8. Put the pieces of the dough together with your hands.

9. Scrape the board with a pastry scraper, gathering together all the unincorporated flour as well as the pieces of dough coated with flour.

10. Place this flour with the pieces of dough in a sifter.

11. Resting the sifter on the board and using one hand, "clean" the flour by moving the sifter back and forth.

The globules of dough will remain in the sifter screen and will not filter through. Discard them because, being already coated with flour, they will not integrate into the wet dough and will cause lumps which make holes when the dough is stretched.

12. Start kneading the dough using the palm of the hand

13. and folding the dough over with the other hand, absorbing the leftover flour from the board. Do not sprinkle the flour over the dough.

Continue kneading, for about 5 minutes, absorbing the flour until the dough is no longer wet and all but 4 or 5 tablespoons have been incorporated (the remaining flour will be used for second kneading of the dough—see below). If you intend to stretch the dough by machine, knead for only 2 to 3 minutes. The amount of flour left over will remain about the same.

14. A ball of elastic and smooth dough should be the result of kneading the dough for this length of time. You can now do the additional kneading and stretching of the dough either by hand or with a pasta machine. See pages 123–125 and 127–129.

HOW TO STRETCH THE DOUGH
BY HAND WITH A ROLLING PIN

Take the ball of dough that has been kneaded for 5 minutes and continue kneading for about 10 minutes longer, incorporating some, but not all, of the flour that remained from before.

The following photos demonstrate the technique of using the long Italian-style rolling pin. The American ball-bearing rolling pin may also be used (see *The Fine Art of Italian Cooking* for the technique of using it).

1. Place the center of the long rolling pin over the ball of dough. Rest the palms of your hands a bit in from the ends (do not grasp the rolling pin by the handles).

2. Gently roll the pin forward

3. then backward. This is the basic motion, and should be repeated until the dough is elastic, that is, until the dough springs back when pulled.

To stretch to an even thickness,

4. fold the edge over the rolling pin

5. and roll up the sheet of dough around the pin, moving the fingers of your hands outward along the edge of the pasta sheet to even the edges out.

6. Move your hands outward almost to the edges of the pin. With a quick jerky movement roll the pin away from you so that the edge of the pasta sheet slaps against the board. This movement stretches the edge of the sheet as thin as the rest.

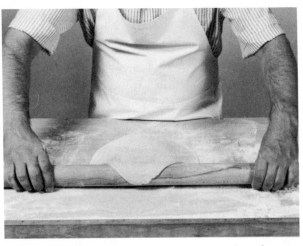

7. Flip the rolling pin over so that the edge of the pasta sheet is facing toward you rather than away from you.

8. Unroll the sheet away from you, so that the underside will now be on top.

To stretch the pasta evenly, it is important to alternate back-and-forth motion with side-to-side motion. This can be accomplished by first,

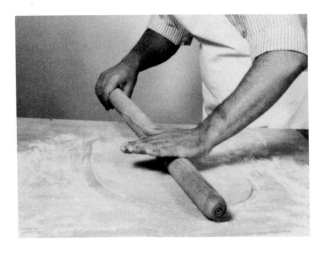

9. turning your body sideways. Let one end of the long rolling pin overlap the end of the pasta board. Loosely hold this end with one hand. Rest the palm of the other hand, as before, on the rolling pin, but closer to the center. With this one hand roll the pin from side to side until the layer of pasta is stretched out to a little less than ⅛ inch thick.

10. Roll up the sheet in order to reverse it again. However, in this position it is not possible to make the slapping movement. Simply flip the pin over and unroll the sheet on the other side.

Keep alternating the two kinds of movements until the pasta is stretched large and less than 1/16 inch thick.

11 and 12. The rolled up sheet of pasta, larger and thinner than before. Again, move the fingers outward along the edge to even out the sheet.

13. The larger sheet of pasta being unrolled and reversed.

14. The pasta stretched evenly to its final thinness, less than 1/16 inch thick.

CUTTING PASTA BY HAND

Both *tagliatelle* and *taglierini*, the names of the two most common cuts of flat pasta, derive from *tagliare*, which means "to cut."

HOW TO PREPARE TAGLIATELLE AND TAGLIERINI

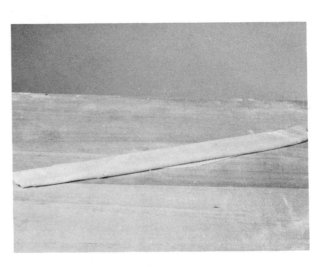

1 and 2. Roll up the sheet of pasta.

3. With a knife cut into *tagliatelle* about ¼ inch wide or into *taglierini* of less than ⅛ inch wide.

4. Unroll the strands of pasta to their full length before allowing them to dry. See the discussion on drying pasta under cutting pasta with a manually-operated machine, page 131.

To cut the hand-rolled sheet of pasta into other shapes, follow the same directions as for cutting machine-rolled pasta (page 129).

Recipes for the different shapes of pasta begin on page 132.

HOW TO STRETCH THE DOUGH WITH A HAND PASTA MACHINE

The machine has two parts (detachable or in one piece), one for rolling and stretching the dough in layers, the other for cutting.

25. *The first part—the base of the machine (attached at the table by a clamp at the bottom, see arrow—not shown here but visible in photo 2 below at the bottom) consists of two rollers. The distance between them can be adjusted by a wheel on the side. On the opposite side there is a detachable handle to turn the rollers. The different brands of pasta machines vary in the number of notches controlling the rollers for stretching. They even vary in the final thinness achieved. On some, the last notch produces such a thin sheet (close to 1/32 inch) that it is impossible to use without breaking the pasta. Get to know your own machine and whether the last or next to the last produces the slightly less than 1/16-inch thickness desirable for most pasta. (The cutting part of this type of machine is detachable and is not shown here, but is visible in photo 2, page 75. In some machine types, the roller and cutter form a single unit.)*

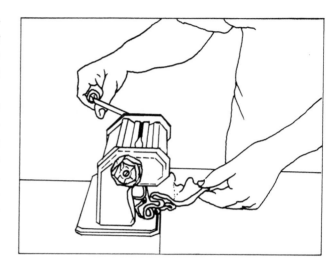

NOTE: If the pasta dough is made with more than 2 eggs, divide the dough into 1-cup portions before you flatten it in preparation for putting it between the rollers.

1. With the palm of your hand, flatten the ball of dough so it can fit between the rollers (about ½ inch thick).

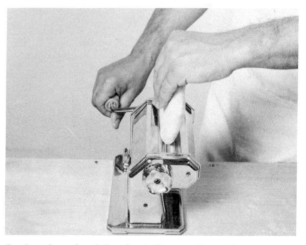

2. Set the wheel for the rollers at the widest setting. Turning the handle, pass the dough through the rollers.

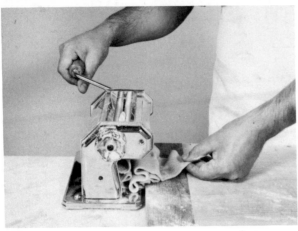

3. With your hand remove the layer of dough from underneath the pasta machine.

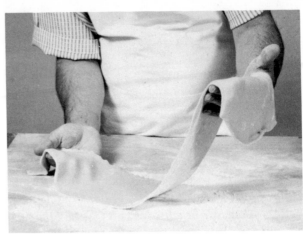

4. Holding the layer of dough with both your hands, gently flour one side of the dough by drawing it across the flour on the board.

5. Fold the dough into thirds and

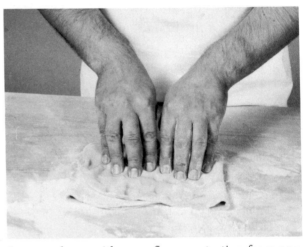

6. press down with your fingers, starting from one open side toward the opposite open side, so that the three layers will be melded together and no air will remain inside between the three layers of dough.

Using the same wide setting of the rollers, insert the open end of the folded layer of dough through the rollers. Repeat the rolling and folding 8 to 10 times, until the dough is very smooth and elastic. It is now ready to be stretched.

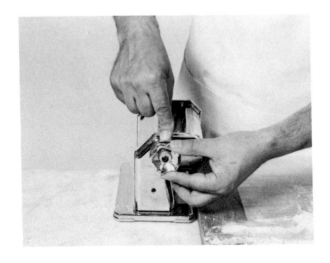

7. To move the rollers to a narrower setting, press down the notch above the wheel on the side in order to release the rollers and with the other hand turn the wheel to the next setting.

8. Flour the layer of pasta on both sides by drawing it across the flour on the board.

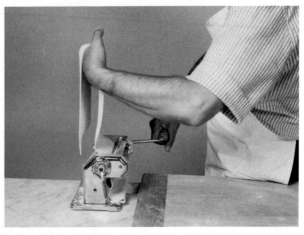

10. Still letting the pasta hang over one hand, pull it out to its full length. It is now ready to be cut into different shapes with the pasta machine.

9. When feeding the layer of pasta into the machine, the position of your body is very important. Stand sideways in relation to the table, holding the handle of the machine with your right hand. Hold the other hand up sideways, keeping the four fingers together and holding the thumb out. Let the sheet of pasta rest over your hand between the first finger and the outstretched thumb.

Pass the dough through the rollers once; do not fold any more. Move the wheel to the next notch, passing the dough through the rollers just once. After passing each time, sprinkle the layer of pasta with a little flour. Each successive notch will produce a thinner layer of pasta. Repeat this procedure until the layer reaches the thickness desired. The specific thickness of each kind of pasta is indicated in the individual recipes.

HOW TO CUT FRESH PASTA MADE WITH A MANUALLY OPERATED MACHINE INTO DIFFERENT SHAPES

The instructions for cutting *tagliatelle* and *taglierini* (the recipes for which follow) serve to illustrate the basic technique for cutting pasta. Each recipe has a note on how to cut that particular pasta, so refer to them for specific instructions. *Tagliatelle* are ¼ inch wide and *taglierini* are ⅛ inch wide.

For *tagliatelle* and *taglierini* stretch the layer of pasta to the last notch of the pasta machine. *Taglierini* may be a little wider when cut by hand. (For a discussion of other cuts, see fresh *spaghetti* and *tortelli* or *ravioli*.)

1. With a pastry cutter, cut the layer of pasta into pieces about 15 inches long. Let the pieces dry for about 15 minutes on a lightly floured pasta board.

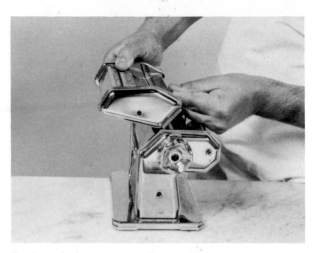

2. Attach the cutter to the machine.

3. For *tagliatelle*, insert the layer of pasta into the wider cutter.

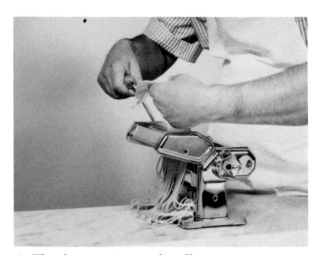

4. The sheet cut into *tagliatelle*.

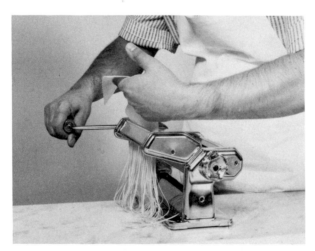

5. For *taglierini*, insert the layer of pasta into the narrower cutter.

6. Place the cut pasta on a lightly floured pasta board to dry.

HOW TO DRY PASTA

If you wish to cook the pasta immediately, you can use it after several minutes. The pasta may be stored for up to an hour, uncovered; on a lightly floured wooden surface or in special drawers (such as I use), or on a drying rack. If you want to use fresh pasta dried longer than 1 hour, but less than 12 hours, lay the pasta between two dry lightly floured cotton dish towels. Pasta must be covered when left to dry for more than an hour. Do not use drawers or racks.

If you want to save the fresh homemade pasta for 3 or 4 days before using it, let the pasta stand, uncovered, for about 2 hours. It will then be dry enough to store.

HOW TO STORE FRESH PASTA

7. Place the already dried pasta in a plastic bag. Tie the bag and keep it at room temperature. Do not refrigerate. Do not keep pasta longer than 4 days.

Real homemade pasta is more delicate than commercial fresh pasta and it's a shame to freeze it, as the pasta will lose some of its delicacy and becomes very breakable. However, if forced to freeze it, pre-cook the pasta for 2 or 3 seconds while it is still fresh. Then transfer it to a bowl of cold water with a little oil (as in precooking *cannelloni* and lasagne, pages 154–155, photos 2–5). Remove from the water and, while still wet, place the pasta in freezer bags and put in freezer. When needed, allow to defrost before cooking. Cooking time will be several seconds longer than for completely fresh pasta.

HOW TO COOK FRESH PASTA

To cook fresh pasta, bring a large pot of water to a boil. Add coarse-grained salt to taste. For most of the fresh pasta recipes, use 4 to 6 quarts (16 to 24 cups) of cold water and 2 tablespoons of coarse-grained salt. Then add the pasta and stir with a wooden spoon to be sure pasta does not stick together. Do not add oil to the boiling water. Cover the pot to bring the water back to a boil as soon as possible (the pasta floats to the top almost immediately). Remove the cover and cook the pasta until done. (The cooking time will be much less than that for dried pasta.) For very fresh (just made) thin pasta, such as *taglierini*, a maximum of 15 seconds after the water returns to a boil is usually enough. For comparably fresh wider *tagliatelle*, up to 30 seconds is required. Slightly thicker forms of *tagliatelle* require a maximum of 1 minute. The thicker spaghetti, *gramigna* and maccaroni require a minimum of 1 minute. The cooking time given in the individual recipes is the minimum one used with the pasta freshly made. With that dried for from 2 hours to 4 days, time should not exceed 1 minute for *taglierni* or *tagliatelle*, 3 minutes for spaghetti, *gramigna*, or maccaroni. The eggless pasta requires less cooking time.

The term *al dente* is not appropriate to the cooking time of fresh pasta; it is only used when speaking of commercial dried pasta. The cooking time of fresh pasta dried for 2 hours increases to a minimum of 1 minute. Even if pasta is stored for up to 4 days, the cooking time is still 1 minute. For frozen pasta, see the note above. For thicker pasta, the cooking time is given in the individual recipes.

Drain the pasta in a large colander. *Absolutely do not rinse pasta in either hot or cold water.* Transfer the pasta to a serving dish or bowl, pour the sauce over the pasta, and toss very well with fork and spoon. If the sauce and pasta are both properly prepared, the pasta should be evenly coated with the sauce, and all the sauce should coat the pasta without any excess sauce remaining on the bottom of the dish. Do not add extra sauce on top.

Never use homemade fresh pasta for a pasta salad, especially not homemade *tortellini* or other stuffed pasta. (For pasta salads, see page 195.)

Tagliatelle al Sugo di Manzo

TAGLIATELLE WITH BEEF SAUCE

This beef sauce is shared both by Livorno and Genoa where it's used on *tagliatelle* and on lasagne in the respective cities. Unlike a *Sugo di carne* which has bits of meat in it, here the beef is cooked for about 5 hours, until its juice is cooked out, and then the sauce is passed through a food mill to remove the last essence. None of the meat itself passes through the medium-sized holes of the strainer. Further cooked down, this reduction has such a rich flavor that it should be used in smaller quantities than a usual meat sauce. It is an altogether unique sauce, probably quite ancient, and because it requires much time to make, it is less used than in the past, though my hope is to spur its revival.

For the sauce: SERVES 8
4 ounces pancetta *sliced, or 2 ounces boiled ham and 2 ounces salt pork*
2 medium-sized red onions, sliced
1 celery stalk, cut into small pieces
1 medium-sized carrot, cut into small pieces
1 pound piece boneless beef chuck
Salt and freshly ground black pepper
¼ cup olive oil
3 tablespoons sweet butter
2 whole cloves
1 cup cold water
2 quarts beef broth

For the pasta:
4 cups unbleached all-purpose flour
4 extra large eggs
4 teaspoons olive oil or vegetable oil
Pinch of salt

To cook the pasta:
Coarse-grained salt

To serve:
½ cup freshly grated Parmigiano

Prepare the sauce. Cover the bottom of a heavy aluminum, stainless steel, or enamel saucepan with the sliced *pancetta*. Make a layer of the sliced onions over the *pancetta*, then add the celery and carrot pieces. Place the beef over the aromatic herbs and sprinkle with salt and pepper. Pour the oil over all and add the butter and the cloves. Cover the pan and cook over medium heat for about 25 minutes. At that time the *pancetta* and onions should be very dark. Add 1 cup of cold water, cover the pan again, let simmer for about 20 minutes.

Heat the broth to a boil. Add all the broth to the pan and simmer, covered, for at least 4 hours.

Remove the meat, and pass all the remaining ingredients through a food mill. Place the strained sauce in a crockery bowl and let it cool for about 1 hour, then refrigerate overnight. The following day, remove the solid fat which will have formed on top of the sauce.

This sauce, when it is reheated completely, could be used to dress the *tagliatelle*, or to prepare *Pasticcio di tortellini* (page 177) or to season *Schiacciata unta alla fiorentina* (page 417).

Prepare the *tagliatelle* with the ingredients listed above, following the directions on pages 120–122 and 127–129. To cut into *tagliatelle*, see page 130, photos 1–4. Let the *tagliatelle* stand on a pasta board, covered with a dish towel, until needed.

Bring a large pot of cold water to a boil. Add coarse-grained salt to taste. When the water reaches the boiling point, add the *tagliatelle* and cook for about 30 seconds after the water has returned to a boil. Drain and toss with the sauce. Sprinkle the Parmigiano over the pasta and serve immediately.

Tagliatelle al Sugo di Asparagi

TAGLIATELLE WITH ASPARAGUS SAUCE

FROM NORTHERN ITALY

This puréed asparagus sauce is different from the one used on page 274 with veal *scaloppine*.

Here all the asparagus are passed through the food mill into a prepared *Salsa bianca* (White Sauce) base of butter, flour, and chicken broth. The sauce is then reduced and used to dress the pasta. There is nothing else added except a little parsley or grated cheese because it would interfere with the clean taste of the fresh asparagus. This is one of a large number of vegetable sauces which are popular in Italy and little known outside the country.

SERVES 4

For the pasta:
2 cups unbleached all-purpose flour
2 extra large eggs
2 teaspoons olive oil or vegetable oil
Pinch of salt

For the sauce:
1 pound asparagus
Coarse-grained salt
1½ cups beef or chicken broth
6 tablespoons sweet butter
1½ tablespoons unbleached all-purpose flour
Salt and freshly ground pepper

To cook the pasta:
Coarse-grained salt

To serve:
About 15 sprigs Italian parsley, leaves only
Salt and freshly ground black pepper
¼ cup freshly grated Parmigiana (optional)

Prepare the *tagliatelle* with the ingredients listed above, following the directions on pages 120–122 and 127–129. To cut into *tagliatelle*, see page 130, photos 1–4. Let the *tagliatelle* stand on a pasta board, covered with a dish towel, until needed.

Prepare the sauce. Boil the asparagus in salted water (page 344). Remove the asparagus from the pot and let rest for a few minutes. Then cut off the tough bottom white part. Pass the green part of the boiled asparagus through a food mill into a small bowl. Transfer passed asparagus to a saucepan and add the broth. Bring to a boil over medium heat.

Meanwhile, melt 4 tablespoons of the butter in a second saucepan over medium heat. When the butter is completely melted, add the flour and stir with a wooden spoon until the flour turns a very light

133

brown color. Add the boiling broth-asparagus mixture all at once and mix very well. Simmer for about 10 minutes. Taste for salt and pepper.

Bring a large pot of cold water to a boil. Add coarse-grained salt to taste.

Coarsely chop the parsley. Melt the remaining butter by putting it in the serving dish and placing the dish over the pot of boiling water. Remove the dish when the butter has melted completely.

Add the *tagliatelle* to the boiling salted water and cook for about 30 seconds after the water has returned to a boil. Drain the pasta and put it in the prepared serving dish. Pour the sauce over the pasta, mix very well, and sprinkle with the parsley and some of the freshly ground black pepper. Serve immediately.

Tagliatelle con Sugo di Oca Conservato

TAGLIATELLE WITH SAUCE OF PRESERVED GOOSE

FROM OLD VENICE

See page 49 for discussion of *Oca in pignatto* (Goose Preserved in Its Own Fat). This fresh pasta dish is the form in which it is most often encountered nowadays. For many centuries it was used in a variety of dishes which have now unfortunately all but disappeared. Even this combination is rare enough, though so delicious that its revival should be encouraged.

For the pasta: SERVES 8
4 cups unbleached all-purpose flour
4 extra large eggs
4 teaspoons olive oil or vegetable oil
Pinch of salt

For the sauce:
2 tablespoons sweet butter
2 cups preserved goose meat and fat (see page 49)

To cook the pasta:
Coarse-grained salt

Prepare the *tagliatelle* with the ingredients listed above, following the directions on pages 120–122 and 127–129. To cut into *tagliatelle*, see page 130, photos 1–4. In order to stretch the pasta to the required thickness for this sauce, a little more than 1/16 of an inch, it is necessary to stop one or two notches before the last on most machines. Let the *tagliatelle* stand on a pasta board, covered with a dish towel, until needed.

Prepare the sauce. Melt the butter in a saucepan over medium heat. When the butter is completely melted, add the meat and the fat from the preserved goose. Let the fat melt very slowly and be sure not to sauté the meat.

Bring a large pot of cold water to a boil. Add coarse-grained salt to taste. When the water reaches the boiling point, add the *tagliatelle* and boil for a maximum of about 1 minute. Drain the pasta and put it in a serving dish. Toss with the sauce and serve immediately. Each serving should consist of pasta, sauce, and a piece or two of the preserved goose.

Tagliatelle al Peperoncino

RED PEPPER TAGLIATELLE

In a country house near Pistoia lives an old man who makes and sells an incredible variety of fresh pastas, many kinds of forgotten pastas that only he remembers from the nineteenth century. This is one of them worth remembering and it requires just the simplest of dressings. (Again, I thank Avv. Fabrizio Vitaletti for his help with this dish.)

For the pasta:
2 teaspoons red pepper flakes
2 cups unbleached all-purpose flour
2 extra large eggs
2 teaspoons olive oil or vegetable oil
Pinch of salt

For the sauce:
About 25 sprigs Italian parsley, leaves only
½ cup olive oil

To cook the pasta:
Coarse-grained salt

SERVES 4

Coarsely grind the red pepper flakes with a marble mortar and pestle.

Prepare the pasta with the ingredients listed above, following the directions on pages 120–122 and 127–129, placing the ground red pepper flakes in the well with the other ingredients. Roll out the pasta with a machine, but do not reach the last notch; the pasta should not be very thin as the red pepper specks would break a very thin sheet. To arrive at the required thickness, a little more than ¹⁄₁₆ of an inch, it is necessary to stop one or more notches before the last on most machines. To cut the *tagliatelle*, see page 130, photos 1–4. Let the *tagliatelle* stand on a pasta board, covered with a dish towel, until needed.

Chop the parsley coarsely and set it aside until needed.

Bring a large pot of cold water to a boil. Add coarse-grained salt to taste. Add the *tagliatelle* to the boiling water and cook for a maximum of 1 minute after the water has returned to a boil. Drain the pasta and put it in a serving dish. Pour the olive oil over the pasta and sprinkle it with the chopped parsley. Toss very well and serve immediately. No cheese should be added.

Tagliatelle con Salsa di Noci

TAGLIATELLE IN WALNUT SAUCE

FROM GENOA

One of Genoa's most famous traditional sauces. See *Salsa di noci* (Walnut Sauce), on page 91, for a further discussion of the sauce. It is used primarily for this dish.

For the pasta: SERVES 4
2 cups unbleached all-purpose flour
2 extra large eggs
2 teaspoons olive oil or vegetable oil
Pinch of salt

For the sauce:
2 slices white bread
8 ounces shelled walnuts
1 large clove garlic, peeled
15 ounces ricotta
3 tablespoons olive oil
4 tablespoons butter
Salt and freshly ground black pepper

To cook the pasta:
Coarse-grained salt

Prepare the *tagliatelle* with the ingredients listed above, following the directions on pages 120–122 and 127–129. To cut into *tagliatelle*, see page 130, photos 1–4. Let the *tagliatelle* stand on a pasta board, covered with a dish towel, until needed.

Prepare the sauce with the ingredients listed above, following the instructions on page 91. Cover the sauce and refrigerate it until needed.

Bring a large pot of cold water to a boil. Add coarse-grained salt to taste. Add the *tagliatelle* to the boiling salted water and cook for about 30 sec-onds after the water has returned to a boil. Drain the pasta and put it in a warm serving dish. Pour the sauce over the pasta, mix very well, and sprinkle with some freshly ground black pepper. Serve immediately.

NOTE: If you use the drier homemade ricotta, reserve 2 or 3 tablespoons of the pasta cooking water to add when mixing the pasta and sauce together.

Pasta al Cioccolato in Dolce-Forte

CHOCOLATE PASTA IN SWEET AND SPICY SAUCE

FROM FLORENCE

Although the very idea of chocolate pasta is startling to most people, it was, indeed, a very well-established and traditional dish for my grandparents' generation. And, once you have seen the warm color that a small amount of unsweetened cocoa powder gives the freshly made pasta, and you have eaten it with one of the sauces that traditionally accompany it, the idea will not seem so outrageous. For me it has been a gratifying experience to watch the skeptical faces of friends who were unacquainted with these dishes change to looks of pleasant surprise as they tasted them.

It is, I must stress, essential to prepare this pasta in one of its traditional forms because it is very difficult to match it with other sauces. For instance, in the sugared dessert version, that also exists, the idea of cocoa is not too difficult to understand and accept. And in the case of *dolce-forte* presented here, the bit of chocolate in the sauce complements the cocoa taste in the pasta itself and makes for a perfect blending of flavors. Chocolate was brought to Italy from the New World through Spain but it didn't become widely popular in Italy until the eighteenth century. Italians, unlike the Austrians and French, have always used chocolate *only* to embellish cakes, never in them. Chocolate cake does not exist in Italy because it is too heavy for the light touch of the Italian culinary tradition. Yet, pasta with chocolate did establish itself as a traditional food. Perhaps it is because cocoa powder does not make pasta any heavier.

For the sauce: SERVES 6
1 medium-sized red onion
3 celery stalks
1 medium-sized clove garlic
2 medium-sized carrots
10 sprigs Italian parsley, leaves only
4 ounces pancetta, or 2 ounces boiled ham and 2 ounces salt pork
½ cup olive oil
1 pound lean ground beef
1 cup dry red wine
1 cup drained canned imported Italian tomatoes
Salt and freshly ground black pepper to taste
½ cup red wine vinegar
4 tablespoons raisins
2 tablespoons pignoli (pine nuts)
1 heaping tablespoon semisweet chocolate chips
1 tablespoon granulated sugar

For the pasta:
3 cups unbleached all-purpose flour
4 extra large eggs
2 teaspoons olive or vegetable oil
Pinch of salt
4 level tablespoons unsweetened cocoa powder

To cook the pasta:
Coarse-grained salt

Prepare the sauce. Finely chop the onion, celery, garlic, carrots, and parsley together on a board. Cut the *pancetta* into small pieces.

Heat the oil in a terra-cotta or enamel saucepan. When the oil is hot, add the chopped ingredients and *pancetta* and sauté slowly over low heat for about 15 minutes, stirring occasionally with a wooden spoon. Then add the ground beef and in-

corporate it into the sautéed ingredients using the wooden spoon. When the meat is no longer reddish, add the wine and let it evaporate (about 5 minutes).

Meanwhile, pass the tomatoes through a food mill and, when the wine has evaporated, add the strained tomatoes to the saucepan. Taste for salt and pepper and simmer slowly for about 25 minutes.

Prepare the *dolce-forte*. Put the wine vinegar, raisins, pignoli, chocolate chips, and sugar into a small bowl and set aside for about 20 minutes.

When the meat sauce is ready, add the contents of the bowl to the saucepan. Stir with a wooden spoon to incorporate all ingredients and simmer for 5 minutes longer.

Prepare the *tagliatelle* with the ingredients listed above, following the directions on pages 120–122 and 127–129. To cut into *tagliatelle*, see page 130, photos 1–4. Let the *tagliatelle* stand on a board, covered with a dish towel, until needed.

Bring a large pot of cold water to a boil. Add coarse-grained salt to taste.

Prepare a serving dish by spreading 1 cup of the sauce over the bottom.

Add the *tagliatelle* to the boiling salted water and cook for about 30 seconds after the water has returned to a boil. Drain the pasta and put it in the prepared serving dish. Pour the remaining sauce over the pasta and toss very well. Serve immediately.

Passato di Ceci con Taglierini

TAGLIERINI IN CHICK-PEA SOUP

FROM UMBRIA

The finely cut fresh pasta, *taglierini*, almost as fine as angel's hair, is appropriate to very delicate sauces and to broths and soups. (Angel hair [*Capelli d'angelo*] is actually used as the name for the thinnest of pastas. It exists only as a dried pasta, and is classically dressed only with the lightest of tomato sauces and a pat of fresh butter.) This chick-pea *passato* (literally "passed through" a sieve or food mill) is different from the classic soup of *cannellini* in that all the ingredients are passed through the food mill together after cooking. It is usually eaten with this fine fresh pasta rather than with dried pasta as in the other version.

Though customarily eaten hot in the winter, it is equally good as a cold summer dish, when allowed to cool after being ladled into the individual bowls.

For the soup:

SERVES 6 TO 8

1 cup dried chick-peas
3 cups plus 5 quarts cold water
2 cloves garlic, peeled but left whole
1 teaspoon rosemary leaves, fresh or preserved in salt
2 ounces pancetta, cut into small pieces
2 tablespoons olive oil
1 medium-sized very ripe tomato, or 2 canned tomatoes, drained
Salt and freshly ground black pepper

For the pasta:
2 cups unbleached all-purpose flour
2 extra large eggs
2 teaspoons olive oil or vegetable oil
Pinch of salt

To cook the pasta:
Coarse-grained salt

To serve:
6 to 8 teaspoons olive oil

138

Soak the chick-peas overnight in the 3 cups of cold water. The next day, drain and rinse the chick-peas and put them in a pot with the 5 quarts cold water. Then add the garlic, rosemary, *pancetta*, olive oil, and tomato. Bring to a boil over medium heat and simmer, covered, for 1 hour. Then add salt to taste, cover again, and simmer for 1 hour longer. At that time, the chick-peas should be tender. Remove all the solid ingredients with a slotted spoon and pass them through a food mill. Return the purée to the pot. Taste for salt and pepper and simmer, covered, for 10 minutes longer.

Prepare the *taglierini* with the ingredients listed above, following the directions on pages 120–122, 127–129, 130 (photos 1, 2 and 5). Let the *taglierini* stand on a pasta board, covered with a dish towel, until needed.

Bring a large pot of cold water to a boil. Add coarse-grained salt to taste. Add the *taglierini* to the boiling salted water and cook for about 30 seconds after the water has returned to a boil. Drain the pasta and add it to the stockpot with the chick-pea purée. Combine very well. Ladle into individual bowls, pour over 1 teaspoon of the olive oil and sprinkle with freshly ground black pepper. Serve immediately.

SPAGHETTI

Spaghetti (little strings) are ⅛ inch wide and, unlike *taglierini*, equally thick. As commercial dried pasta, they are rounded, but this is not essential to their identity. (Linguine are ⅛ inch thick but are cut slightly wider, making a flatter impression.) Though spaghetti cutting attachments do exist, it is easy enough to cut into spaghetti with the *taglierini* cutter by using a thicker layer of pasta. (Linguine cutting attachments also exist.)

When stretching pasta (pages 127–129, photos 1–9), do not reach the last notch on the pasta machine. Continue only up to that notch which stretches the pasta layer to the thickness of about ⅛ inch.

HOW TO CUT SPAGHETTI

1. To cut spaghetti, insert layer of pasta into the *taglierini* cutter (narrower cutter). See also page 130, photo 5.

Spaghetti al Pomodoro al Forno

SPAGHETTI IN SAUCE WITH BAKED TOMATOES

FROM TUSCANY

This marvelous dish is probably a direct descendant of the original recipe (1841) which first combined the best-known ingredients of Italian cuisine: pasta, tomatoes, and olive oil. That basic recipe has evolved into this more delicate version which contains fresh pasta, quickly boiled and then dressed with a sauce of baked sliced tomatoes and anchovies. The sliced tomatoes are placed in the oven with their flavoring (added since the original version) of a little anchovy and red pepper and olive oil (still a basic ingredient), and baked for a short time so that the tomato slices remain whole. Though this version is more refined than the old one, the original spirit remains in the freshness with which the tomato flavor emerges.

For the pasta: SERVES 6
4 cups unbleached all-purpose flour
4 extra large eggs
4 teaspoons olive oil or vegetable oil
Pinch of salt

For the sauce:
2 pounds fresh tomatoes
5 anchovies preserved in salt, or 10 anchovy fillets in oil, drained
Salt and freshly ground black pepper
Pinch of red pepper flakes
1 cup olive oil
15 sprigs Italian parsley, leaves only

To cook the pasta:
Coarse-grained salt

Prepare the fresh spaghetti with the ingredients listed above, following the directions on pages 120–122 and 127–129, photos 1–9. To cut into spaghetti, see page 139. Let the spaghetti stand on a pasta board, covered with a dish towel, until needed.

Prepare the sauce. Slice tomatoes horizontally into thirds. Cover the bottom of an ovenproof baking dish with a layer of the sliced tomatoes. If using anchovies in salt, clean and fillet the anchovies under cold running water (page 55), removing the bones and salt. Then place them on top of the tomato slices. Sprinkle with salt, pepper, and a pinch of red pepper flakes. Place another layer of sliced tomatoes on top and then pour the olive oil over all.

Coarsely chop the parsley and set it aside until needed.

Preheat the oven to 400 degrees and place the baking dish in the oven for about 20 minutes.

Bring a large pot of cold water to a boil. Add coarse-grained salt to taste. Five minutes before the tomatoes are ready, add the fresh spaghetti to the boiling salted water and cook for from 1 to 3 minutes, depending on the dryness of the pasta. Remove the tomatoes from the oven. Drain the spaghetti and put the pasta on top of the baked tomatoes. Sprinkle the chopped parsley over the pasta. Toss very well and serve.

Spaghetti di Scheggino

FRESH SPAGHETTI IN TROUT-BLACK TRUFFLE SAUCE

FROM SCHEGGINO IN UMBRIA

Scheggino in Umbria is blessed in being one of the few places on earth where black truffles are found. And since trout are also plentiful in the region, this unique trout-black truffle sauce emerges. The flavor of the black truffle intensifies with the long cooking time and the trout, usually associated with very short cooking periods, acquires a completely different, rich taste in this reduced sauce. The integration of the two is unexpectedly perfect.

1 black truffle (about 4 ounces) fresh or canned   SERVES 6
2 whole brook trout or 4 fillets
1 teaspoon lemon juice or red wine vinegar
1 medium-sized red onion
1 small clove garlic, peeled
1 teaspoon rosemary leaves, fresh or preserved in salt
1 small celery stalk
5 sprigs Italian parsley, leaves only
½ cup olive oil
2 tablespoons sweet butter
1 tablespoon tomato paste
1 cup dry white wine
1 cup chicken broth
Salt and freshly ground black pepper

For the pasta:
4 cups unbleached all-purpose flour
4 extra large eggs
4 teaspoons olive oil or vegetable oil
Pinch of salt

To cook the pasta:
Coarse-grained salt

Start making the sauce first. If the truffle is fresh, clean it very carefully with a truffle brush to be sure all the clinging soil is removed (page 63), then coarsely chop it on a board. If using whole trout, remove the heads, clean and wash very well in a bowl of cold water with lemon juice or wine vinegar. Then dry with paper towels. Finely chop the onion, garlic, rosemary, celery, and parsley together on a board.

Heat the oil and butter in a saucepan over medium heat. When the butter is completely melted, add the chopped ingredients and sauté for about 10 minutes. Then add the tomato paste and sauté for 5 minutes longer. Add the truffle and the wine to pan and simmer for about 20 minutes. Bring the broth to a boil. Add the whole trout or fillets to the pan and cook for 4 minutes, then add the hot broth and simmer for 5 minutes more.

Remove the pan from the heat and transfer the trout to a board. Remove the bones from trout, then pass the fish and all the contents of the saucepan through a food mill, using the disc with medium-sized holes. Return all the sauce to saucepan and put it over medium heat. Taste for salt and pepper and simmer for about 15 minutes, when a smooth sauce will have formed.

Prepare the fresh spaghetti with the ingredients listed above, following the directions on pages 120–122 and 127–129, photos 1–9. To cut into spaghetti, see page 139. Let the spaghetti stand on a pasta board, covered with a dish towel, until needed.

Bring a large pot of cold water to a boil. Add coarse-grained salt to taste.

When the sauce is ready, add the spaghetti to the boiling salted water and cook for from 1 to 3 minutes, depending on the dryness of the pasta.

Put one ladleful of the sauce into a warm serving dish. Drain the pasta and put it in the dish. Pour the remaining sauce over the pasta, toss very well, and serve immediately. No cheese should be added.

GRAMIGNA

Gramigna are like spaghetti cut into short pieces. When dried, they twist up into dissimilar shapes. The word itself means "weed," suggested by the formless twisting arrangements of a dish of this pasta.

Gramigna ai Quattro Formaggi

GRAMIGNA WITH FOUR CHEESES

FROM NORTHERN AND CENTRAL ITALY

This four-cheese dressing for pasta actually only contains three cheeses, but the butter becomes an honorary cheese. It is probably a recipe less than a century old, recent for Italy.

Using two cheeses from the extreme north (Gorgonzola and Fontina) and one from the south (mozzarella), it has a national rather than a regional character. If one should venture a guess about its origin, it would probably be in the extreme north, as its combination of thick melted cheeses relates to the Fonduta of Piedmont and Lombardy. Fontina and mozzarella have both been the main melting cheeses of their respective areas, but both are mild. It is the touch of Gorgonzola which adds the sharpness to the flavor. The result is a tasty rich creamy sauce which works well with a substantial fresh pasta such as *gramigna* (below) or equally well with dried pasta such as *penne* (page 179). This already extravagant and rich recipe contains an additional indulgence of thirty pistachio nuts.

SERVES 6

For the sauce:
30 unsalted shelled fresh pistachio nuts, for cooking
Coarse-grained salt
4 ounces (1 stick) sweet butter
4 ounces Gorgonzola, preferably the "sweet" type
4 ounces mozzarella
4 ounces Italian Fontina, preferably from the Val d'Aosta area
Salt and freshly ground black pepper

For the pasta:
3 cups unbleached all-purpose flour
3 extra large eggs
3 teaspoons olive oil or vegetable oil
Pinch of salt

To cook the pasta:
Coarse-grained salt

Blanch the pistachio nuts in boiling salted water. (Pistachios require salted water for blanching to preserve their color.) When finished put them aside until needed.

Wrap the butter in a dampened cheesecloth and soften it with your hands. Put the butter and the Gorgonzola in a bowl and mix in a rotary motion with a wooden spoon until the two are well amalgamated and almost whipped.

Prepare the *gramigna* by making fresh spaghetti

with the ingredients listed above, following the directions on pages 120–122 and 127–129, photos 1–9. Cut the strands into 3-inch pieces. Allow the pasta to dry for about 20 minutes. In drying, the pieces will curl up to form the required shape for *gramigna*.

While the pasta is drying, continue preparing the sauce. Cut the mozzarella and Fontina into ½-inch pieces and place them in a terra-cotta or enamel saucepan. Put the saucepan over low heat, stirring constantly, until the two cheeses melt. Then add the pistachios and remove the saucepan from the heat.

Bring a large pot of cold water to a boil. Add coarse-grained salt to taste. Add the pasta and cook for from 1 to 3 minutes, depending on the dryness of the pasta.

Put the saucepan with the melted cheeses over low heat. Drain the cooked pasta well and add it to the saucepan. Mix very well, adding salt and pepper to taste. When all the pasta is completely coated with the melted cheese, remove the pan from the heat. Immediately add the whipped butter and Gorgonzola from the bowl and mix thoroughly. Serve immediately from the terra-cotta saucepan.

HOW TO CUT PASTA WITH A CHITARRA ("GUITAR")

To prepare pasta with the "guitar" for *Maccheroni alla chitarra*, the famous Abruzzese dish, prepare the layer of pasta as you would for making spaghetti (⅛ inch thick). Then cut the layer of pasta into segments about 12 inches long.

1. Place the 12-inch piece of pasta on the guitar, leaving about 2 inches free on each end of the guitar. Roll back

2. and forth with a rolling pin

3. against the strings until pasta is completely cut.

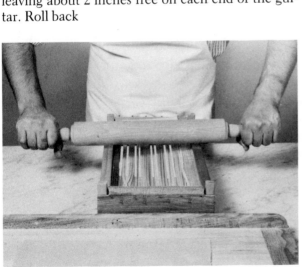

 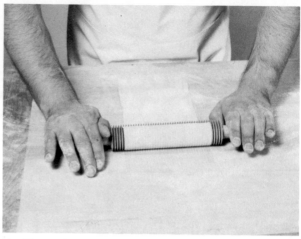

4. "Play" the guitar drawing your thumb across the string until all of the loosened strips fall through on to the tray below. Remove the pasta from the tray and place it on a lightly floured board to dry.

5. Above is an instrument used in other parts of Italy (such as the Marches) which also cuts pasta into *maccheroni*.

Maccheroni alla Chitarra

MACCHERONI CUT WITH THE "GUITAR" IN LAMB SAUCE

FROM ABRUZZI

The old traditional way of cutting pasta in the Abruzzi, a mountainous area east of Rome, is to "play the guitar." This pasta cutter does indeed have strings strung across and the strings are actually tuned in a fixed pattern as in an actual guitar. It is both interesting and mysterious that the folklore surrounding the instrument, such as the reasons why it's tuned in a particular way, has never been passed along with the tradition. The imagination drifts to thoughts of old rituals and cults, but who can tell? There is a different set of strings on each side of the guitar which is separated by a board. By flipping the guitar over, you can change from one set of strings to the other. The more narrowly spaced strings are for cutting pasta used with the traditional Abruzzese lamb broth; those more widely spaced are used in the dish below, with a sauce of lamb and peppers.

In making this sauce, the lamb must be snipped rather than ground or chopped. It also has the special feature in that the sauce is not salted and peppered to taste, but has fixed amounts of salt and pepper which traditionally are not modified. This scant tablespoon of salt and half teaspoon of pepper is spread over the snipped meat, mixed through and then the meat is sautéed. It is very important to allow the sauce to reduce sufficiently so that the liquid from the peppers evaporates enough to make the texture dense and thick.

For the sauce: SERVES 8
1½ pounds lamb shoulder with bone (to give 12 ounces of meat)
1 scant tablespoon salt
½ teaspoon freshly ground black pepper
6 tablespoons olive oil

144

2 medium-sized cloves garlic, peeled
2 bay leaves
¾ cup dry white wine
1 cup drained canned imported Italian tomatoes, passed through a food mill
2 green peppers
¼ cup hot beef broth or water, if necessary

For the pasta:
4 cups unbleached all-purpose flour
4 extra large eggs
4 teaspoons olive oil or vegetable oil
Pinch of salt

To cook the pasta:
Coarse-grained salt

Make the sauce. Use a scissors to snip the lamb meat off the bones into small pieces about ½ inch square. Put the lamb pieces in a small bowl, add the salt and pepper, and mix thoroughly with a wooden spoon.

Heat the oil in medium-sized terra-cotta or enamel saucepan over medium heat. When the oil is hot, add the garlic and the bay leaves. Sauté gently until the garlic is light golden brown. Add the seasoned lamb, raise the heat, and sauté for about 15 minutes, mixing occasionally with a wooden spoon. Add the wine, lower the heat, cover the pan, and cook for about 15 minutes to let the wine evaporate. Then add the tomatoes and cook uncovered for about 10 minutes.

Meanwhile, cut the peppers into long thin strips, removing the seeds and top section with stem. Add the peppers to the pan, cover, and simmer for 1 hour, stirring occasionally. If the sauce gets too thick, add ¼ cup hot broth or water. Remove the bay leaves from the pan and let the sauce stand until needed.

Prepare the pasta with the ingredients listed above, following the directions on pages 120–122 and 127–129, photos 1–9. Roll the dough out into sheets ⅛ inch thick. Cut the layers of pasta 2 inches shorter than the length of the guitar. Cut the sheets of pasta on the *chitarra* (pages 143 and 144), and let the *maccheroni* stand on a pasta board, covered with a dish towel, until needed.

Bring a large pot of cold water to a boil. Add coarse-grained salt to taste. Add the pasta to the boiling salted water and cook for from 1 to 3 minutes, depending on the dryness of the pasta. Drain the pasta and put it in a warm serving dish. Pour the sauce over the pasta, mix very well, and serve immediately. No cheese should be added.

HOW TO SHAPE PASTA FOR PINCI

Pinci are rounded pasta rolled out completely by hand, without a rolling pin, to about 9 inches in length and a little over ⅛ inch in thickness. They are unique to the province of Siena.

Prepare the *pinci* with the ingredients listed in the recipe for *Pinci di Montalcino*, page 147, following the directions on pages 120–122. Form the dough into a ball.

1. Flatten the ball with both hands to a thickness of less than ½ inch.

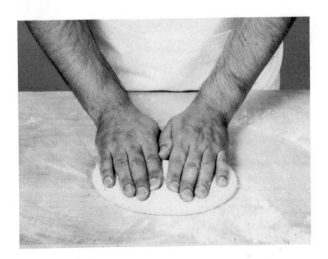

2. Use a knife to cut the thick layer into strips less than ½ inch wide.

3. Then cut across, making the strips into small cubes.

4. Take an individual cube,

5. and, holding it between the thumbs and the first fingers of both hands, "pinch" the cube

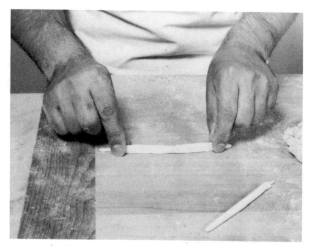

6. so that it extends sideways only into a non-rounded strip about 3 inches long.

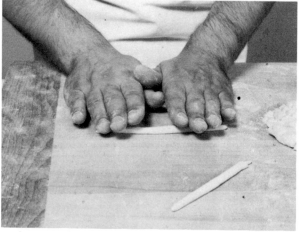

7. With the four fingers of both hands, lightly roll the strip of dough, moving both hands gradually apart from the center

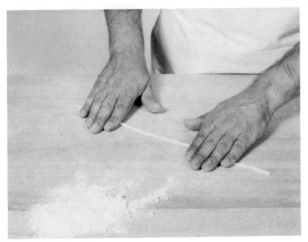 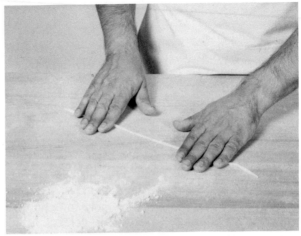

8. to the sides. Keep repeating this motion,

9. until the strip is rounded and about 9 inches long. The thickness will be a little more than ⅛ inch.
Roll out the other cubes of dough in the same manner.

Pinci di Montalcino

PINCI MONTALCINO STYLE

FROM MONTALCINO NEAR SIENA IN TUSCANY

Montalcino, a blessed little town built on a hillside in the province of Siena, produces the famous Brunello wines in its farm-vineyards and has there and in the lovely medieval village also situated on it, some unique and ancient food traditions, based on incomparable sheep's cheese, pork products, and wine. The method of rolling each cube into a single long strand of egg-less pasta is a jealously retained tradition from earlier centuries when character and uniqueness mattered more than time.

SERVES 6

For the sauce:
2 medium-sized red onions
About 20 sprigs Italian parsley, leaves only
4 ounces pancetta (in one piece), or 2 ounces boiled ham and 2 ounces salt pork
½ cup olive oil
3 Italian sweet sausages without fennel seeds (about 9 ounces), or 9 ounces ground pork
1 pound ground pork
1 whole boneless and skinless chicken breast, ground
Salt and freshly ground black pepper
1 cup dry red wine, preferably Brunello di Montalcino
½ pound fresh tomatoes or drained canned imported Italian tomatoes
2 tablespoons tomato paste
2 cups hot beef broth
*½ cup freshly grated Tuscan-type Pecorino (sheep's milk cheese), preferably from Siena**

* If not available, substitute Ricotta salata.

For the pasta:
3 cups unbleached all-purpose flour
3 teaspoons olive oil or vegetable oil
Pinch of salt
1 cup cold water

To cook the pasta:
Coarse-grained salt

Finely chop the onions and parsley together on a board. Cut the *pancetta* into ¼-inch cubes.

Heat the oil in a flameproof casserole over medium heat. When the oil is hot, add the chopped ingredients and sauté until lightly golden brown (about 10 minutes).

Meanwhile, remove the skin from the sausages. Add the sausages, ground pork, and ground chicken breast to the casserole and sprinkle with salt and pepper. Sauté the meat lightly for about 15 minutes, stirring occasionally with a wooden spoon, until the meat has lost its redness. Then add the wine and cook for 10 minutes to let it evaporate.

Pass the tomatoes through a food mill and add them and the tomato paste to the casserole. Simmer for about 20 minutes. Pour 1 cup of the broth into the casserole, cover, and cook for about 1½ hours, adding the remaining broth as needed. Taste for salt and pepper, keeping in mind that the grated cheese to be added later is a little bit saltier than the Parmigiano usually sprinkled on pasta.

Prepare the *pinci* with the ingredients listed above, following the directions on pages 120–122 and 145 and 146.

Bring a large pot of cold water to a boil. Add coarse-grained salt to taste. Add the *pinci* to the boiling salted water and cook for from 45 seconds to 1 minute after the water has returned to a boil, depending on the dryness of the pasta. Drain the pasta and put it in a warm serving dish. Pour the sauce over the *pinci*, toss thoroughly but gently, and serve with the freshly grated cheese.

HOW TO CUT PASTA INTO TRENETTE

For *trenette* (the pasta shape used for *pesto* sauce), prepare the pasta with the ingredients listed in the recipe for *Trenette con salsa di carciofi* (page 149), following the directions on pages 120–122 and 127–129, photos 1–10. Stretch the layer of pasta to a thickness of slightly less than ⅛ inch. *Trenette* are shaped like *tagliatelle* with one scalloped side. They must be cut by hand.

1. With a pastry cutter, cut the layer of pasta into pieces about 15 inches long.

2. Cut one side lengthwise, with the pastry cutter, to a width of about ½ inch,

3. and the other side with a knife. Repeat the above steps on all the layers of pasta.

Trenette con Salsa di Carciofi

TRENETTE WITH ARTICHOKE SAUCE

FROM GENOA

Trenette, the egg-less Genoese pasta, is not only used with *pesto*, but is also traditional with this other classic Genoese sauce, combining artichoke pieces with dried wild mushrooms. The same combination is used in the classic *Torta Pasqualina* (Easter Torte) of the same area. The final touch is dry white wine, making this one of those recipes which disproves the old injunction against combining wine and artichokes (see *The Fine Art of Italian Cooking*).

SERVES 6

For the sauce:
3 large artichokes
1 lemon
1 ounce dried porcini *mushrooms*
About 10 sprigs Italian parsley, leaves only
1 small clove garlic, peeled
1 medium-sized red onion
⅓ cup olive oil
2 tablespoons sweet butter
Salt and freshly ground black pepper
2 tablespoons tomato paste
1½ cups chicken or beef broth
1 tablespoon unbleached all-purpose flour
⅓ cup dry white wine
Salt and freshly ground black pepper

For the pasta:
About 3 cups unbleached all-purpose flour
1 cup cold water
2 teaspoons olive oil or vegetable oil
Pinch of salt

To cook the pasta:
Coarse-grained salt

Put the artichokes in a large bowl of cold water with the juice of the lemon, and the squeezed lemon halves. Soak the artichokes for 1 hour, then remove them one at a time from the water and rub them all over with one of the lemon halves. Clean the artichokes following the directions on pages 350 and 351 and cut them into thin slices (about ⅛ of an inch thick). Return the slices to the cold water with lemon until needed.

Soak the mushrooms in a small bowl of lukewarm water for about 30 minutes. Drain the mushrooms and be sure that no sand remains attached to them. Pat the mushrooms dry with paper towels and chop them finely together with the parsley, garlic, and onion on a board.

Heat the oil and butter in a saucepan over medium heat. When the butter is completely melted, add the chopped ingredients. Sauté for about 10 minutes, then drain the artichokes and add them to the pan. Sprinkle with salt and pepper and cook the artichokes for about 10 minutes.

Meanwhile, dissolve the tomato paste in the broth and add the mixture to the pan. Simmer for about 35 minutes. Put the flour in a small bowl and slowly incorporate the wine. Add the wine-flour mixture to the pan, mix very well, and cook for about 15 minutes to let the wine evaporate. Taste for salt and pepper.

Prepare the *trenette* with the ingredients listed above, following the directions on page 148.

Bring a large pot of cold water to a boil. Add coarse-grained salt to taste. Add the *trenette* to the boiling salted water and cook for 30 to 45 seconds, depending on the dryness of the pasta. Drain the pasta, but not thoroughly, leaving approximately 4 tablespoons of water in with the pasta. Put the pasta in a warm serving dish and pour the sauce over it. Mix well and serve immediately. The texture of this pasta is softer and more adhesive than that of egg pasta, and the proper way to eat it is to cut it with a fork (as you would eat lasagne).

PAPPARDELLE

Pappardelle are different from *trenette*, because both sides are cut with the pastry cutter and the pasta is prepared with flour, eggs, and salt (and optional oil). They are also much wider (1½ inches) than *trenette*. See the instructions for cutting *trenette* (page 148) but cut both sides of the layers of pasta with the pastry cutter.

Pappardelle allo Spezzatino di Coniglio

PAPPARDELLE WITH STEWED RABBIT SAUCE

FROM TUSCANY

Pappardelle, famous in combination with wild hare sauce, are also combined in this dish with what is essentially a rabbit stew. In the sauce, the rabbit liver, vegetables, *pancetta*, broth, butter, and oil bring out the sweet flavor of the rabbit and the touch of tomato does not dominate. The combination of the fresh pasta with the larger pieces of meat on the bone is quite unusual, the only other example coming to mind being *tagliatelle* with duck, eaten in Parma.

SERVES 8

For the sauce:
1 whole rabbit, skinned and cleaned, but with liver (approximately 3 pounds)
1 medium-sized red onion
1 celery stalk
About 20 sprigs Italian parsley, leaves only
1 medium-sized carrot
4 ounces pancetta, or 2 ounces salt pork and 2 ounces boiled ham
7 tablespoons sweet butter
¼ cup olive oil
2 cups (approximately) beef broth
4 tablespoons tomato paste
Salt and freshly ground black pepper

For the pasta:
4 cups unbleached all-purpose flour
4 extra large eggs
4 teaspoons olive oil or vegetable oil
Pinch of salt

To cook the pasta:
Coarse-grained salt

To serve:
½ cup freshly grated Parmigiano

Prepare the sauce. Carefully wash the whole rabbit and dry it with paper towels. Discard the head and then cut the rabbit into 8 pieces. First sever the two hind legs, then cut widthwise through the entire body enough times to divide it into 6 pieces. The virtually meatless front legs remain attached to the front piece.

Finely chop the rabbit liver, onion, celery, parsley, carrot, and *pancetta* together on a board.

Heat 5 tablespoons of the butter and the oil in a large saucepan over medium heat. When the butter is completely melted, add the rabbit pieces and the chopped ingredients. Sauté for about 20 minutes, stirring occasionally.

Heat the broth. Add the tomato paste and 1 cup of the broth to the saucepan. Taste for salt and pepper. Simmer for about 30 minutes, adding additional broth as needed.

NOTE: If the rabbit is larger than 3 pounds, an additional cup of broth and a longer cooking time will be necessary. (A larger rabbit is tougher and is not recommended.)

Prepare the *pappardelle* with the ingredients listed above, following the directions on page 148.

Bring a large pot of cold water to a boil. Add coarse-grained salt to taste.

Transfer the rabbit pieces from the saucepan to a large serving dish, spreading the pieces all around the dish. Then cover the dish with aluminum foil to keep the rabbit warm. At that moment the sauce should be ready. Add the remaining butter, mix very well, and keep the sauce hot until the pasta is cooked.

Add the *pappardelle* to the boiling salted water and cook for 30 seconds after the water has returned to a boil.

Drain the pasta. Remove the aluminum foil from the serving dish. Place the pasta over the rabbit pieces and pour the sauce over everything. Toss very well, sprinkle with the cheese, and serve immediately. Each serving should consist of some *pappardelle* and a piece of the rabbit.

FRESH PASTA MADE WITH SEMOLINA FLOUR

Pasta made with semolina is directly related to the oldest types of pasta. Unlike modern commercial dried pasta, in this early kind of pasta the coarse flour was uncooked when it was mixed with the water and was then dried in the sun. It must have been tougher than any modern pasta, fresh or dried, and required a long cooking time. When dried pasta began to be made by machine for much larger distribution in the nineteenth century, the process changed. Semolina was still used, mixed or unmixed with durum flour, because it was strong enough to resist the machine handling, but in the process it was cooked by steaming before being dried. While it remained resistant it became more tender and required less cooking time. Fresh pasta made with semolina is rare and a regional specialty. Egg pasta is never made with it. There is still a strange misconception outside of Italy that the really authentic fresh pasta should be made with semolina, but this is simply not true for egg pasta or any other of the light types preferred in Italy.

The most popular type of fresh pasta prepared with semolina flour is *orecchiette*.

HOW TO MAKE ORECCHIETTE

Orecchiette means "little ears," and the shaping of the pasta with the thumb is meant to create just this resemblance.

To prepare *orecchiette*, mix semolina flour and unbleached all-purpose flour with water and a pinch of salt (see the recipe for *Orecchiette con cime di rape* on page 153 for the amounts of ingredients) and follow the directions to prepare the pasta. When the ball of dough is prepared, divide it into 3 or 4 pieces. Roll each piece with the same motions shown in photos 7 and 8 of How to Prepare Pinci (pages 146–147). Roll these large pieces of dough into a long cord about ½ inch in diameter.

1. Cut the long cord of dough into ½-inch pieces.

2. Flatten each piece into a small disk

3. by pressing your thumb into it.

4. Make the central depression more round and deep by turning your thumb a bit in place clockwise. (The size of the *orecchiette* in the photos is slightly enlarged to make the shaping clearer.)

Orecchiette con Cime di Rape

ORECCHIETTE WITH BROCCOLIRAB

FROM PUGLIA

Orecchiette from this area of southern Italy is one of the few types of fresh pasta still widely prepared that uses semolina mixed with the durum wheat flour. That is because its cooking time works perfectly with the usual vegetable ingredient in the dish, *cime di rape*, known in America by its southern Italian dialect name *broccolirab* (actually the green leaves and stems of the round turnip). This full-bodied rustic dish is not delicate, so fresh egg pasta would be totally inappropriate. Even normal dried pasta does not combine as well with the *cime di rape*.

For the pasta:
1 cup semolina flour
2 cups unbleached all-purpose flour
Water
Pinch of salt

SERVES 6

For the sauce:
Coarse-grained salt
2 pounds rape *(broccolirab)*
½ cup olive oil
1 large clove garlic, peeled
2 anchovies in salt, or 4 anchovy fillets in oil, drained
Freshly ground black pepper

Prepare the *orecchiette* with the ingredients listed above, following the directions on page 152. Let the pasta dry between two dish towels.

Clean and wash the *rape*, removing the large stems. Bring a large pot of water to a boil. Add coarse-grained salt to taste. When the water reaches the boiling point, add the *rape* and cook for about 11 minutes. Depending on the dryness of the pasta, the *orecchiette* should be added from 5 to 10 minutes before the *rape* finish cooking.

153

Meanwhile, prepare the sauce. Clean the anchovies, removing the bone and excess salt (page 55).

Heat the oil in a small saucepan over medium heat. When the oil is hot, add the clove of garlic and sauté for about 3 minutes. Then discard the garlic. Remove the pan from the heat and add the anchovy fillets. Mash the anchovies with a fork until completely blended with the oil. Drain the *orecchiette* and *rape* and place on a large serving dish. Pour the sauce over, add black pepper, and toss very well. Serve immediately.

HOW TO CUT AND PREPARE PASTA FOR CANNELLONI AND LASAGNE

Cannelloni are rolled stuffed squares of pasta, while lasagne is made of the same squares (but not rolled) alternating with sauces and stuffings. The square pasta are cut from the same sheet of dough that is used for *tagliatelle*, etc.

Make the dough for the *cannelloni* and lasagne, with quantities and ingredients listed following the directions on pages 120–122 and 127–129, and stretch the layer of pasta to the last notch of the pasta machine.

1. With a pastry cutter, cut the layer of pasta into pieces about 6 inches long. Let the pieces dry for about 10 minutes on a lightly floured pasta board.

2. Bring a large pot of water to a boil. Add coarse-grained salt to taste. Put a large bowl of cold water with about 2 tablespoons of oil added next to the pot.

3. When the water reaches the boiling point, put the squares of pasta into the pot, one by one, and cook for about 5 seconds (counting from when the water returns to a boil), then

4. use a slotted spoon to transfer each piece of pasta to the bowl of cold water to cool.

5. Dampen a dish towel and spread it out on a table. Remove each piece of pasta from the bowl and place it

6. on the dampened towel. Allow to rest for about 20 minutes before stuffing. You can let the pieces of pasta rest for several hours before stuffing by covering them with a second dampened towel.

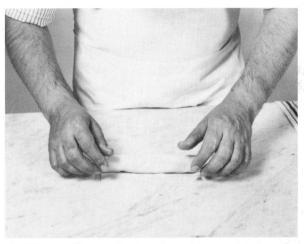

7. To stuff the *cannelloni*, transfer the piece of pasta to a smooth surface. Spread about 3 heaping tablespoons of the stuffing along one of the jagged edges.

8. Then roll, starting at the edge containing the stuffing and

9. ending with the other jagged edge on top. Transfer the *cannelloni* to your buttered or sauced baking dish (depending on the recipe you are preparing), still with the jagged edge on top. In this way the stuffing will remain inside when *cannelloni* are served.

For lasagne also cut the prepared layer of pasta into squares and precook them as you do for *cannelloni*. To assemble the lasagne see the recipe for *Lasagne al pesto* (page 159). For additional discussion of lasagne with photos see *The Fine Art of Italian Cooking*.

CANNELLONI

In the following two recipes for *cannelloni* dishes, two different *balsamella* sauces are employed within each one. A thicker one is used to bind the stuffing mixed with Parmigiano and in *Cannelloni con punte di asparagi* (Cannelloni Stuffed with Asparagus) this *balsamella* is flavored with black pepper and nutmeg, and in *Cannelloni con lingua salmistrata* (Cannelloni Stuffed with Tongue and Chicken) with white pepper. The thinner, simpler *balsamella* in both recipes is used as a topping, so that when baked, the *cannelloni* will not dry out.

The *Cannelloni con punte di asparagi* originates in the town of Mantova (Mantua), which is located near Bassano, the Italian asparagus center. The combination of Parmigiano, butter or *balsamella*, and nutmeg is fundamental for many Italian asparagus dishes but the novelty in this dish is having it all wrapped in fine pasta before baking. A welcome vegetable stuffing for *cannelloni*, it yields a versatile dish that may precede almost anything. Mantua was the seat of the Gonzaga family, whose Renaissance court was excelled only by that of the Medici in Florence. A Gonzaga court painter was Mantegna, whose frescos still bring multitudes to visit the royal palace of Mantua today; a court composer was Monteverdi, who wrote the first great opera *Orfeo* for them. The Hall of Mirrors in the Mantua palace, still intact, was probably Louis XIV's model for that in Versailles.

The stuffing for the second *cannelloni* recipe has a different texture: tender little cubes of contrasting meats (tongue and chicken), one strong, the other mildly flavored, instead of the usual chopped or ground meats. Bound together by *balsamella* and Parmigiano, it is rich and should be followed by a very light second course, possibly of veal or an elaborate vegetable treatment. Even with a stuffing like this, *cannelloni* are always a first course, never a main course. I would advise that you serve only one per person with this recipe.

Cannelloni con Punte di Asparagi

CANNELLONI STUFFED WITH ASPARAGUS

FROM MANTUA

For the pasta:
2 cups unbleached all-purpose flour
2 extra large eggs
2 teaspoons olive oil or vegetable oil
Pinch of salt

To cook the pasta:
Coarse-grained salt
2 tablespoons olive oil or vegetable oil

YIELD: ABOUT 12 CANNELLONI

156

For the stuffing:
2 pounds fresh asparagus
Coarse-grained salt
4 tablespoons sweet butter
2 tablespoons olive oil
Salt, freshly ground black pepper, and freshly grated nutmeg to taste
3 extra large egg yolks
½ cup freshly grated Parmigiano

Balsamella for the stuffing:
6 tablespoons sweet butter
½ cup unbleached all-purpose flour
1½ cups milk
Salt to taste

Balsamella for the topping:
4 tablespoons sweet butter
¼ cup unbleached all-purpose flour
2½ cups of milk
Salt and freshly ground black pepper

Prepare the *cannelloni* with the ingredients listed above, following the directions on page 154. Let the precooked squares of pasta rest between two dampened dish towels until needed.

Soak the asparagus in a bowl of cold water for about 20 minutes, then cut them into 1½-inch pieces, discarding the white part. Do not scrape the asparagus. Bring a large pot of cold water to a boil. Add coarse-grained salt to taste, then add the asparagus and boil for 2 minutes. Drain the asparagus in a colander and cool under cold running water.

Heat 4 tablespoons of butter and the olive oil in a saucepan over medium heat.

When the butter is completely melted, add the asparagus and sauté for 10 minutes. Taste for salt, pepper, and nutmeg. Use a slotted spoon to transfer the asparagus to a bowl. Let them cool for about 20 minutes.

Meanwhile, prepare the *balsamella* for the stuffing with the 6 tablespoons of butter, the flour, milk, and salt, following the directions on page 334. Transfer this *balsamella* to a crockery bowl, pressing a piece of buttered wax paper over the sauce. Let stand until cool.

Prepare the *balsamella* for the topping with ingredients and quantities listed above, following the directions on page 334. Transfer this sauce to a second crockery bowl, pressing a piece of buttered wax paper over the sauce. Let stand until cool.

Place the egg yolks and Parmigiano in the bowl with the cooled *balsamella* for the stuffing and mix very well until all the ingredients are well incorporated. Add the cold asparagus and mix gently. Preheat the oven to 375 degrees.

To stuff the *cannelloni*, place each pasta square on a board and spread about 3 heaping tablespoons of the stuffing along one of the jagged edges. Then roll up, starting at the same edge, ending with the other jagged edge on top. Repeat until all the *cannelloni* are rolled. Then place them, jagged edge up, in one or two well-buttered 13½- x 8¾-inch Pyrex baking dishes. (A maximum of 8 will fit in one dish of this size.) Pour the *balsamella* for the topping over, then bake for about 20 minutes. Allow to cool for 10 minutes, then serve with a large spatula.

157

Cannelloni con Lingua Salmistrata

CANNELLONI STUFFED WITH TONGUE AND CHICKEN

FROM NORTHERN ITALY

YIELD: ABOUT 12 CANNELLONI

For the pasta:
2 cups unbleached all-purpose flour
2 extra large eggs
2 teaspoons olive oil or vegetable oil
Pinch of salt

To cook the pasta:
Coarse-grained salt
2 tablespoons olive oil or vegetable oil

For the stuffing:
8 ounces cooked cured (unsmoked) tongue, in one piece
Coarse-grained salt
1 small red onion
1 medium-sized carrot
1 celery stalk
5 sprigs Italian parsley, leaves only
1 whole chicken breast, boned and skinned
4 tablespoons sweet butter
Salt and freshly ground white pepper
3 extra large egg yolks
5 tablespoons freshly grated Parmigiano

Balsamella for the stuffing:
6 tablespoons sweet butter
½ cup unbleached all-purpose flour
2 cups milk

Balsamella for the topping:
4 tablespoons sweet butter
¼ cup unbleached all-purpose flour
2½ cups milk
Salt to taste
Optional: 1 cup Tomato Sauce (page 447)

Prepare the pasta for the *cannelloni* with ingredients listed above, following the directions on page 154. Let the precooked squares of pasta rest between two dampened cotton dish towels until needed.

Make the stuffing. Cut the tongue into pieces of less than ½ inch square. Bring a small saucepan of salted water to a boil, add the onion, carrot, celery, and parsley. When the water returns to a boil, add the chicken breast and cook for about 15 minutes. Remove the breast and cut it into ½-inch cubes.

Prepare the *balsamella* for the stuffing, using 6 tablespoons of butter, the flour, milk, salt, and pepper, following the directions on page 334. Transfer the sauce to a crockery bowl, pressing a piece of buttered wax paper over the sauce. Let stand until cool.

Melt the 4 tablespoons of butter in a small saucepan and add the cubes of tongue and chicken breast. Sauté for about 5 minutes, then taste for salt and pepper. Transfer to a crockery bowl and let stand until completely cold. Combine the cold *balsamella* and meat. Add the egg yolks, Parmigiano, and salt and pepper to taste. Mix thoroughly with a wooden spoon.

Prepare the *balsamella* for the topping, with ingredients and quantities listed above, following the directions on page 334. Transfer the sauce to a crockery bowl, pressing a piece of buttered wax paper over the sauce. Let stand until cool. Preheat the oven to 375 degrees.

To stuff the *cannelloni*, place each pasta square on a board and spread about 3 heaping tablespoons of the stuffing along one of the jagged edges. Then roll up, starting at the same edge, ending with the other jagged edge on top. Repeat until all the *cannelloni* are rolled. Then place them, jagged edge up, in one or two well-buttered 13½- x 8¾-inch Pyrex baking dishes. (A maximum of 8 will fit in one dish of this size.) Pour the *balsamella* for the topping over and then pour over the tomato sauce. Then bake for about 20 minutes. Allow to cool for 10 minutes, then serve with a large spatula.

LASAGNE

Lasagne dishes usually have layers of pasta alternating with one or more stuffings. Most often the pasta layer is constructed of squares of fresh pasta, but sometimes each of these layers is one long rectangle. (Dried lasagne is generally in the form of these long rectangles.) The following four lasagne dishes come from Genoa, Piedmont, and Sicily.

Lasagne al Pesto

LASAGNE WITH PESTO   FROM GENOA

This first of the two lasagne from Genoa, one type of *Lasagne al pesto*, was popular in Italy earlier in this century. It uses the layers of pasta squares alternating with the *pesto* sauce and a light *balsamella* and is then baked. The current method with this dish in Genoa, as in the following recipe, *Lasagne alla genovese* (Boiled Lasagne with Beef Sauce), is to arrange the boiled pasta squares more informally, then some *pesto* is placed over each square—it is made without using the *balsamella* nor is it baked. For me, the earlier version has more style and is more impressive in presentation. The *pesto* recipe used retains earlier ingredients such as walnuts and pignoli (see *The Fine Art of Italian Cooking* for a detailed discussion of *pesto*). I consider this one to be one of the great lasagne dishes.

For the pasta: SERVES 8 TO 10
4 cups unbleached all-purpose flour
4 extra large eggs
4 teaspoons olive oil or vegetable oil
Pinch of salt

To cook the pasta:
Coarse-grained salt
2 tablespoons olive oil or vegetable oil

For the *balsamella*:
8 tablespoons sweet butter
½ cup unbleached all-purpose flour
3½ cups milk
Salt to taste

For the *pesto* sauce (proportions for the blender or food processor):
1½ cups of olive oil
12 whole walnuts, shelled
2 tablespoons pignoli (pine nuts)
4 ounces pancetta, or 2 ounces boiled ham and 2 ounces salt pork, cut into small pieces
About 3 cups fresh basil leaves
3 heaping tablespoons boiled and chopped spinach
3 cloves garlic, peeled
4 ounces freshly grated Parmigiano
4 ounces freshly grated Sardo or Romano or additional freshly grated Parmigiano cheese
Salt and freshly ground black pepper

Prepare the pasta with the ingredients listed above, following the directions on page 154. Let the precooked squares of pasta rest between two dampened dish towels until needed.

Prepare the *balsamella* with the ingredients listed above, following the directions on page 334. Transfer the sauce to a crockery bowl, pressing a sheet of buttered wax paper over the sauce. Let stand until cool.

To prepare the *pesto* with a blender or food processor place ½ cup of the olive oil and all the other ingredients in the blender or food processor container and grind very fine. Add the remaining olive oil and blend for a few seconds, or until very smooth. For *pesto* prepared with a *mezzaluna* or mortar and pestle, you must use different proportions of ingredients (see *The Fine Art of Italian Cooking*). Preheat the oven to 375 degrees.

To assemble the dish, heavily butter a 13½- x 8¾-inch Pyrex baking dish. Then fit in enough squares of precooked pasta to cover the bottom of the baking dish and to allow about 1 inch to hang out over the edge all around the dish. Cover the layer of pasta on the bottom of the dish *only* with one third of the *balsamella*. Add another layer of pasta just to cover the *balsamella*. (Do not allow any pasta to hang over the edge of the dish.) All the rest of the pasta layers should be done in this way. Then cover this layer with approximately 4 tablespoons of *pesto*. (As *pesto* is an intense sauce, you should apply it sparingly and not attempt to cover the whole layer of pasta. Just be sure that some layers get more sauce toward the ends and some more toward the middle. Make three more alternating layers of pasta and *pesto*. Then begin with another layer of *balsamella*, then four more layers of pasta and *pesto*. After covering the last *pesto* with pasta, make a layer of *balsamella* and cover it with 3 squares of pasta. Take the pasta ends (from the bottom layer) hanging over the edges of the baking dish and fold them in over the top layer of pasta squares. Place the dish in the oven for about 25 minutes; the top layer should be lightly golden brown and crisp. Remove the dish from the oven and allow to cool for 15 minutes. Serve from the baking dish by slicing with a knife and lifting each portion out with a spatula.

Lasagne alla Genovese

BOILED LASAGNE WITH BEEF SAUCE

FROM GENOA

Lasagne alla genovese uses squares of boiled fresh pasta with a little sauce poured over each square. This lasagne dish is eaten immediately and is not baked. The sauce is the same noteworthy, rich reduction of the essence of beef, used for the *tagliatelle* found on page 132. It is also the best sauce to use with this type of lasagne which is so traditional and favored in Genoa. One should experience the particular Genoese treatment of the lasagne pasta and this dish is the most special of its type. It should be followed by a second course which does not have beef and, if sauced, should emphasize a vegetable flavoring, such as in the

Bracioline o scaloppine all' empolese (Veal Scaloppine with Puréed Artichokes), page 271.

For the sauce:
Sugo di manzo (page 132)

For the pasta:
4 cups unbleached all-purpose flour
4 extra large eggs
4 teaspoons olive oil or vegetable oil
Pinch of salt

To cook the pasta:
Coarse-grained salt

To serve:
1 tablespoon sweet butter
½ cup freshly grated Parmigiano

SERVES 8 TO 10

Prepare the sauce first with the ingredients listed on page 132.

Prepare the pasta with the ingredients listed above, following the directions on page 154. Cut the layers of pasta into squares and let dry for at least 10 minutes, or cover with a dish towel until needed.

Bring a large pot of cold water to a boil. Add coarse-grained salt to taste. Warm a large serving dish and spread it with the butter. When the water reaches the boiling point start adding the squares of pasta, 5 or 6 at a time, and cook for from 30 seconds to one minute, depending on the dryness of the pasta.

Reheat the sauce. With a slotted spoon transfer the pasta squares from the pot to the prepared serving platter. Do not flatten the pasta squares out, but let them fall naturally like a fallen handkerchief. With several squares on the serving dish, spoon over about ½ cup of the sauce. (This sauce is very rich so you should not use too much.) Arrange additional squares over the sauce, spoon on another ½ cup of sauce and continue until all the pasta is used. The last layer of the dish should be sauce, not pasta. Sprinkle over the Parmigiano and serve immediately.

NOTE: Midway between the method of Genoese lasagne and that of the normal Baked Lasagne is the famous regional lasagne from Reggio-Emilia called *La Spugnola*. The special wild mushrooms, called *spugnole*, found in that area serve as the basis of the sauce. The layers of boiled pasta are baked with only the *balsamella* between them. The lasagne is cut up into individual portions and only then is the mushroom-based sauce placed over each portion. Though wild mushroom dishes do not employ grated cheese, I was surprised to find that even in Reggio-Emilia, just next to Parma, they still conformed to this, despite the tendency in that area to use Parmigiano (the local product) even in combination with ingredients that do not usually combine well with it. Unfortunately, because the unique *spugnole* are found only there, the dish cannot be exported, despite its fame. Try it when in that part of Italy.

Minestra di Lasagne con Luccio

LASAGNE WITH PIKE

FROM PIEDMONT

This recipe harks back to the days before pasta was usually served as a first course, so that the lasagne was called a *minestra* (like a thick soup) to make it appropriate for the first or *minestra* course. It was most popular from the time of Napoleon to later in the nineteenth century, but today it has virtually disappeared because modern Italians have an almost unshakable prejudice against the combination of fish and cheese. And, indeed, the pasta layers are separated by alternations of pike in a butter sauce with Parmigiano. The combination works here because the fish is a fresh water one and the butter acts as an intermediary. In recent years, a gastronomic society in Italy attempted to revive the dish using perch rather than pike and insisted on replacing the cheese with *balsamella*. It didn't work. Once you taste this dish it will be apparent to you why the original popularity of the dish was justified. This is an example of another classic dish that I hope can be revived.

For the pasta:
4 cups unbleached all-purpose flour
4 extra large eggs
4 teaspoons olive oil or vegetable oil
Pinch of salt

To cook the pasta:
Coarse-grained salt
2 tablespoons olive oil or vegetable oil

For the stuffing:
1 or 2 pike (about 5 pounds total weight)
⅓ cup red wine vinegar
14 cups cold water
Coarse-grained salt
½ cup dry white wine
5 whole black peppercorns
1 bay leaf
2 whole cloves
10 ounces (2½ sticks) sweet butter
Salt and freshly ground black pepper
Freshly grated nutmeg
1½ cups grated Parmigiano

SERVES 8 TO 10

Prepare the pasta with the ingredients listed above, following the directions on page 154. Let the precooked squares of pasta rest between two dampened dish towels until needed.

Clean the fish and wash it in a large bowl of cold water with the red wine vinegar. Discard the liquid.

Pour the 14 cups of cold water into a fish poacher and bring to a boil. Add coarse-grained salt to taste. When the water reaches the boiling point, add the wine, peppercorns, bay leaf, and 2 cloves. Add the pike and cook for about 10 minutes.

Transfer the fish to a chopping board, lift the meat off the bones and discard the skin and bones. Put the meat into a bowl with 7 tablespoons of the butter cut into pieces. Sprinkle with salt, pepper, and nutmeg to taste. Break up the fish pieces and mix thoroughly with a wooden spoon to incorporate the butter into the fish pieces for a uniform texture.

Preheat the oven to 375 degrees. Cut the remaining butter into small pieces.

To put the dish together, butter a 13- x 1¾- x 8¾-inch Pyrex baking dish, then proceed according to directions for *Lasagne al pesto* (page 159), alternating layers of grated Parmigiano and pieces of butter with one of the fish mixture. The layer below the pasta stuffing should be of pieces of butter only. Place the dish in the oven and bake for 30 minutes. Remove from the oven and allow to cool for 15 minutes. Serve from the baking dish by slicing with a knife and lifting each portion out with a spatula.

Lasagne con Melanzane

LASAGNE WITH EGGPLANT

The delicate layers of fresh pasta are alternated with lightly fried thin slices of eggplant with a touch of a simple tomato sauce and a thin *balsamella*. Sicily has several characteristic eggplant and pasta dishes, and this is the most impressive of all. Typically Sicilian flavors, such as capers and oregano, add the finishing touch.

SERVES 8 TO 10

For the pasta:
4 cups unbleached all-purpose flour
4 extra large eggs
4 teaspoons olive oil or vegetable oil
Pinch of salt

To cook the pasta:
Coarse-grained salt
2 tablespoons olive oil or vegetable oil

For the *balsamella*:
8 tablespoons (1 stick) sweet butter
½ cup unbleached all-purpose flour
4 cups milk
Salt and freshly ground black pepper

For the eggplant stuffing:
4 pounds small eggplants with a minimum of seeds
Coarse-grained salt
2½ pounds fresh tomatoes or drained canned imported Italian tomatoes
4 level tablespoons capers in wine vinegar, drained
2 pounds solid vegetable shortening
1 teaspoon dried oregano
1 teaspoon red pepper flakes
Salt and freshly ground black pepper
About ½ cup unseasoned bread crumbs, preferably homemade

Prepare the pasta with the ingredients listed above, following the directions on page 154. Let the precooked squares of pasta rest between two dampened dish towels until needed.

Prepare the *balsamella* using the quantities and ingredients listed above, following the directions on page 334. Transfer the sauce to a crockery bowl, pressing a piece of buttered wax paper over the sauce. Let stand until cool.

Do not peel the eggplants. Cut them lengthwise into ⅜-inch-thick slices. Sprinkle the slices with coarse-grained salt, place them in a dish, cover them with another dish to weight them, and let stand for 30 minutes.

Meanwhile, pass the tomatoes through a food mill into a crockery bowl. Season with the oregano, red pepper flakes and salt and pepper to taste. Wash the capers in cold water, finely chop them on a board, and add them to the bowl. Mix this tomato sauce very well with a wooden spoon.

Rinse off the eggplants in cold water and dry with paper towels. Prepare a serving dish by lining it with paper towels.

Melt the solid vegetable shortening in a frying pan. When it is very hot, deep-fry the eggplant slices, a few at a time, until they are golden brown on both sides. Remove the slices from the pan and drain them on the prepared serving dish. When all the eggplant slices have been transferred to the serving dish, sprinkle them with a little salt and let stand until cool (about 20 minutes).

Preheat the oven to 375 degrees.

To put the dish together, butter a Pyrex baking dish (13½ x 8¾ inches), then proceed according to instructions for *Lasagne al pesto* (page 159), but put one third of the *balsamella* over the first layer of pasta, and substitute layers of eggplant sprinkled with tomato sauce for the pesto. Put one more third of the *balsamella* over the sixth layer of pasta, and the last third on top of the dish. Cover the top *balsamella* with a very thin layer of bread crumbs. Fold over the hanging ends of the pasta squares and bake in the preheated oven for about 25 minutes. Remove from the oven and allow to stand for 15 minutes. Serve from the baking dish by slicing with a knife and lifting each portion out with a spatula.

HOW TO MAKE TORTELLI

Tortelli are squares, rounds, rectangles, or half-moons of two layers of pasta filled with a little stuffing and sealed. They are sometimes called *ravioli*, though that word originally referred to dumplings. Originally, *tortelli* were probably round, as the word itself means "round-shaped." *Tortelli* may vary in size, but I suggest 2-inch squares, 2-inch diameter rounds and half-moons, and 2- x 2½-inch rectangles. *Tortelloni* refers most often to large tortellini, but may also refer to large tortelli.

1. For *tortelli*, stretch the layer of pasta to the last notch of the pasta machine. If the width of the layer of pasta is not narrower than 5 inches, place dots of the filling (see individual recipes for the ingredients of the varied fillings) starting an inch from the top and side edges of the layer of pasta, in two rows lengthwise. The dots of filling should be 2 inches apart. (If pasta is narrow, place dots of filling along the middle and cover with a second sheet of pasta.)

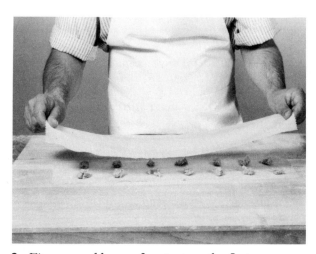

2. Fit a second layer of pasta over the first.

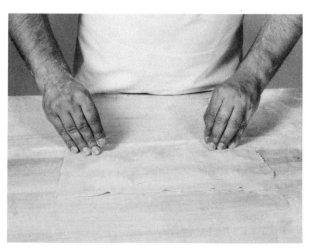

3. With the tips of your fingers, press down the edges and

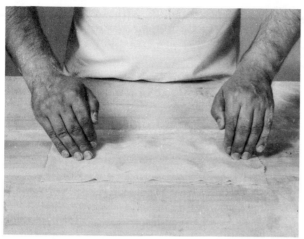

4. along the center of the two overlapped layers of pasta to remove the air.

5. Then, for square- or rectangular-shaped *tortelli*, using a pastry cutter, cut first lengthwise, then across, making sure the dot of filling is in the center of the *tortello*. If you make the *tortelli* immediately after the pasta is prepared, it is still wet enough for the *tortelli* to be sealed simply by cutting them as above. Otherwise, first draw 3 vertical lines with a wet finger, half the length of the pasta, one down each edge and one through the center; then draw lines across, between the dots of filling and along the sides of the pasta. In this way, when cut, the edges of each *tortello* will be moist enough to seal well.

6. Lift out each *tortello* and press the edges all around between the thumb and first finger, to make sure they are completely sealed.

7. If you want round *tortelli*, use a large

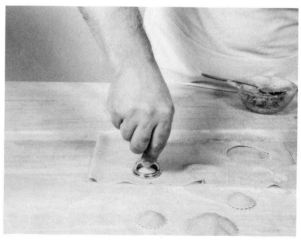

8. or small *ravioli* cutter.

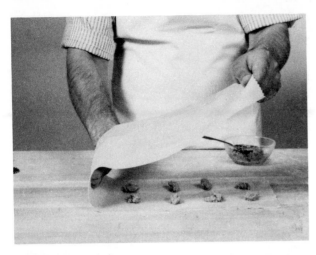

9. You can also prepare *tortelli* by cutting the layer of pasta 30 inches long, placing dots of filling only on half of the layer of pasta and folding over the other half.

If you want to prepare half-moon *tortelli*, stretch the layer of pasta to the last notch of the pasta machine and cut the layer of pasta into pieces about 15 inches long.

10. Starting 1 inch from the edge begin a lengthwise row of dots of filling 2½ inches apart, in the center of the layer of pasta.

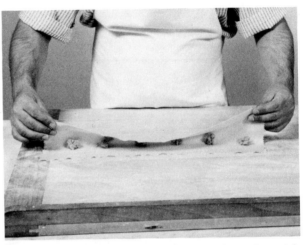

11. Then carefully pick up one of the sides with both hands and fold the sheet lengthwise in half. Press down around the dots of filling.

12. Cut out half-moons or semicircles by placing only half of a round *ravioli* cutter over the area containing the filling. Lift out each half-moon and press the edges on the semicircular side between two fingers, to be sure they are completely sealed.

Tortelli di Michelangelo

TORTELLI OF MICHELANGELO BUONAROTTI

Michelangelo (Buonarotti), one of the supreme artists, is generally thought of as an ascetic man who would not be much concerned with what he ate. But his letters, notebooks, and poems tell a much different story. The food references abound, even as imagery in his poetry. Letters exist thanking people for various delectable culinary gifts, which the givers must have known would please him. Trout, wild mushrooms, and lamb brains are mentioned frequently, perhaps indicating a more than symbolic interest in them.

On the front left endpaper, we see a drawing of Michelangelo's made with the same ink which is used in the recipe for *Spaghetti neri* (Spaghetti with Ink of the Squid), page 187, with its beautiful color "seppia." It is a sketch of his design for the facade of the church of San Lorenzo in Florence, which, alas, was never built, though his tombs for the Medici rulers were carried out in the New Sacristy of the church. A wooden model was built from this, and related drawings were done by Pietro Urbani, Michelangelo's assistant. Another assistant, Urbano, helped the artist on a sculpture and is the same man for whom the menu below was drawn, as he also cooked for the *Maestro*.

The accepted explanation that the great artist drew the menu because his cook couldn't read seems a bit oversimplified and I'm frankly skeptical of it. This recipe for the *tortelli* stuffing comes from one of Michelangelo's letters. It contains his beloved lamb's brains and his favorite *carnesecca* which is another name for *pancetta*. The stuffing has the same combination of sensuality and perfect, though startling, proportion that we find in the master's work.

For the stuffing: SERVES 8

1 small lamb or veal brain (about 8 ounces)
4 ounces boneless veal shoulder
1 whole chicken breast, skinned and boned
4 tablespoons butter
4 ounces mortadella
4 ounces pancetta *or* prosciutto
Salt and freshly ground black pepper
2 extra large egg yolks
½ cup freshly grated Parmigiano
Freshly grated nutmeg to taste

For the pasta:
4 cups unbleached all-purpose flour
4 extra large eggs
4 teaspoons olive oil or vegetable oil
Pinch of salt

For the sauce:
4 to 5 sage leaves, fresh or preserved in salt
6 ounces (1½ sticks) sweet butter
½ cup freshly grated Parmigiano
Freshly ground black pepper

To cook the pasta:
Coarse-grained salt

Blanch the lamb or veal brain following directions on page 97. Cut the brain into small pieces and let stand until needed.

Grind the veal and chicken breast in a meat grinder.

Melt the butter in a saucepan over medium heat. When the butter is completely melted, add the brain pieces and sauté lightly for about 3 minutes. Add the ground veal and chicken breast and sauté for about 5 minutes.

Grind the *mortadella* and *pancetta* in a meat grinder and add to the saucepan. Stir well to amalgamate all ingredients. Taste for salt and pepper. Sauté for 5 minutes longer, then transfer to a crockery bowl and let sit until cold (about 1 hour). Add the egg yolks, Parmigiano, and salt, pepper, and nutmeg to taste, stirring constantly with a wooden spoon.

Prepare the pasta with the ingredients listed above, following the directions on pages 164 or 165. Place 1 heaping teaspoon of the filling on each *tortello*.

Bring a large pot of cold water to a boil. Add coarse-grained salt to taste. Tear the sage leaves into quarters. Melt the butter for the sauce in a serving dish placed over the boiling water in the pot and sprinkle in the sage leaves. When the butter is completely melted, remove the serving dish and add the *tortelli* to the boiling water quickly but gently, being careful not to break them. Cook the *tortelli* in the boiling salted water for from 30 seconds to 2 minutes, depending on the dryness of the pasta. With a strainer-skimmer, remove the *tortelli* from the pot to the prepared serving dish. Sprinkle with Parmigiano and freshly ground black pepper and serve immediately.

Tortelloni alla Casentinese

LARGE TORTELLI CASENTINO STYLE

FROM THE TUSCAN APENNINES

The area of the Casentino range in the Tuscan Apennine mountains produces sweet sausages (as well as the salty but well-aged *prosciutto*) of Tuscany. This basic sausage stuffing comes from there, where it is the custom to even eat the sausages uncooked, as there is no danger in eating them uncooked in Europe. In the United States, however, the sausages should be sautéed a little before they are added to the stuffing for the *tortelli*, so that by the combination of the two cookings they will be done enough, but still retain the taste of the lightly boiled sausages in the original recipe. The light dressing of butter and sage is the perfect complement.

For the stuffing: SERVES 8
4 Italian sweet sausages without fennel seeds (about 12 ounces),
   or 12 ounces ground pork
4 tablespoons olive oil
1 medium-sized clove garlic, peeled
10 sprigs Italian parsley, leaves only
1 tablespoon tomato paste
5 tablespoons freshly grated Parmigiano
3 tablespoons unseasoned bread crumbs, preferably homemade
2 extra large eggs
Pinch of red pepper flakes
Salt, freshly ground black pepper, and freshly grated nutmeg to taste

For the pasta:
4 cups unbleached all-purpose flour
4 extra large eggs
4 teaspoons olive oil or vegetable oil
Pinch of salt

For the sauce:
8 ounces (2 sticks) sweet butter
About 10 sage leaves, fresh or preserved in salt, torn in half
1 cup freshly grated Parmigiano

To cook the pasta:
Coarse-grained salt

Prepare the stuffing. Remove the skin from the sausages.

Heat the oil in a small skillet. When the oil is hot, add the sausages. Break up the sausages with a fork, mixing them into the oil, and sauté until the meat has lost its redness (about 5 minutes). Transfer the contents of the skillet to a crockery bowl and let cool completely (about ½ hour).

Then finely chop the garlic and parsley together on a board and add them to the bowl with the cooled sausage. Add the tomato paste, Parmigiano, bread crumbs, and eggs and mix very well with a wooden spoon. Add the red pepper flakes and salt, pepper, and nutmeg to taste. Mix again until all the ingredients are well amalgamated. Cover the bowl and refrigerate until needed.

Prepare the *tortelli*, using the ingredients listed above, following the directions on pages 164 and 165, photos 1–6. Use 1 tablespoon of the filling for each *tortello* and cut the pasta almost double the size of the usual *tortelli*. (These *tortelloni* are always cut square in shape.)

Bring a large pot of cold water to a boil. Add coarse-grained salt to taste.

Meanwhile, prepare the sauce. Melt the butter in a double boiler, and add the torn sage leaves. When the water boils, add the *tortelloni* quickly and cook them from about 1 minute to 2 minutes, depending on the dryness of pasta.

Pour 3 or 4 tablespoons of the sage-butter sauce in a warm serving dish and, when the *tortelloni* are ready, remove them with strainer-skimmer to the prepared serving dish. Make a layer of *tortelloni*, pour over half of the remaining sage-butter and ½ cup of the Parmigiano, then make a second layer of pasta and pour over the remaining butter and cheese. Sprinkle with freshly ground black pepper and serve immediately.

Tortelli di Piccione

TORTELLI STUFFED WITH SQUAB

FROM MANTOVA (MANTUA)

Here is another example of a dish which exemplifies the great tradition of Mantua. The tradition is also apparent in the old court cities of the Emilia-Romagna region like Ferrara and Parma. The *tortelli* with squab stuffing is a perfect balance of rich but integrated cooking that goes back for centuries. Its flavor should not be covered with a heavy sauce, because butter and Parmigiano (the marvelous cheese originates in nearby Parma) is enough.

SERVES 8

For the stuffing:
2 quarts cold water
Coarse-grained salt
1 medium-sized carrot
1 small red onion
1 celery stalk
5 or 6 sprigs Italian parsley
1 bay leaf
1 squab
4 ounces prosciutto
2 ounces sweet butter
1 extra large egg
4 ounces freshly grated Parmigiano
Salt, freshly ground black pepper, and freshly grated nutmeg to taste

For the tortelli:
4 cups unbleached all-purpose flour
4 extra large eggs
4 teaspoons olive oil or vegetable oil
Pinch of salt

For the sauce:
8 ounces (2 sticks) sweet butter
1 cup freshly grated Parmigiano

To cook the pasta:
Coarse-grained salt

Prepare the stuffing first. Fill a small stockpot with the 2 quarts of cold water and bring to a boil. Add coarse-grained salt to taste. Add the whole carrot, onion, celery, parsley, and bay leaf and return to a boil. Add the squab and let it simmer slowly for about 40 minutes. (Do not cover the stockpot.)

Transfer the squab to a chopping board and strain the broth into a larger stockpot, discarding all the aromatic vegetables and herbs and saving the broth for cooking the pasta.

Bone the squab keeping the meat and skin. Finely chop the meat and skin together with the *prosciutto* on a board.

Melt the butter in a small saucepan over medium heat. When the butter is completely melted, add the chopped meats and sauté gently for about 3 minutes, incorporating all the melted butter. Transfer the contents of the saucepan to a crockery bowl and let stand until completely cool. Then add the egg and Parmigiano and stir until all the ingredients are very well amalgamated. Taste for salt, pepper, and nutmeg.

Prepare the *tortelli* with the ingredients listed above, following the directions on pages 164 or 165. Use a heaping teaspoon of the stuffing for each *tor-tello*. Add enough water to the squab broth to have sufficient liquid to boil the *tortelli*. Bring the broth-water mixture to a boil, then add coarse-grained salt to taste.

Meanwhile, melt the butter in the top of a double boiler or *bagnomaria* and pour 3 or 4 tablespoons of the melted butter into a warm large serving dish. Add the *tortelli* to the boiling liquid quickly but gently, being careful not to break them. Cook the *tortelli* from 30 seconds to 2 minutes, depending on the dryness of pasta. When ready, transfer them with strainer-skimmer onto the prepared serving dish. Make a layer of *tortelli*, pour over half of the remaining melted butter, and sprinkle over ½ cup of Parmigiano. Keep making alternating layers of *tortelli*, butter, and cheese until all have been used. Serve immediately.

Optional sauce: You can also use a very light tomato sauce with this recipe. To prepare it, reduce 1 pound of fresh or imported Italian canned tomatoes in a small saucepan. Pass the tomatoes through a food mill and combine at the last moment with melted butter. Use the sauce instead of the melted butter when making the *tortelli* layers above.

Tortelli di Mele

APPLE TORTELLI FOR CHRISTMAS EVE

In an ancient walled hilltop village near Parma, it has long been the Christmas Eve tradition for each family to prepare a huge terra-cotta pot of these *tortelli* swimming in heavy cream. All the celebrants travel from family to family, keeping the *tortelli* warm in a large *bagnomaria*. By the end of Christmas Eve, all the families have exchanged their warm *tortelli* with the others' in an atmosphere of joyous sharing. In the recipe below for these *tortelli* (to be served immediately as a first course), the amount of heavy cream in the sauce has been reduced. The apple flavoring, as with many savory dishes incorporating fruit, will not result in a sweet taste at all. (Many thanks to Betty Galbreath for whetting my curiosity about this dish.)

SERVES 8

For the stuffing:
1 pound baking apples
8 ounces boiling potatoes
Coarse-grained salt
2 ounces dried porcini *mushrooms*
5 walnuts, shelled but not blanched
1 small red onion
¼ cup olive oil
2 tablespoons dry Marsala
Salt and freshly ground black pepper
4 tablespoons freshly grated Parmigiano
4 tablespoons unseasoned bread crumbs, preferably homemade
Freshly grated nutmeg

For the pasta:
4 cups unbleached all-purpose flour
4 extra large eggs
4 teaspoons olive oil or vegetable oil
Pinch of salt

For the sauce:
10 walnuts, shelled but not blanched
8 ounces (2 sticks) sweet butter
1 pint heavy cream
Salt and freshly ground black pepper

To cook the pasta:
Coarse-grained salt

Prepare the stuffing. Preheat the oven to 375 degrees. Peel the apples, cut them into quarters, and remove the cores. Put the apples in a baking dish and bake for about 25 minutes. Remove from the oven and let cool completely.

Boil the unpeeled potatoes in salted water for about 30 minutes. Then put the potatoes on a board, peel them, and let them stand until cold.

Soak the mushrooms in a small bowl of lukewarm water for about 30 minutes.

Take the 5 walnuts and chop them very fine. Drain the mushrooms and chop them very fine on a board, together with the onion.

Heat the oil in a small casserole. When the oil is hot, add the chopped mushroom-onion mixture. Sauté over medium heat for 3 or 4 minutes, then add the chopped walnuts and Marsala. Let the Marsala evaporate.

Pass the baked apples and boiled potatoes through a potato ricer into a small bowl. After the Marsala has evaporated, add the mashed potato-apple mixture to the saucepan. Taste for salt and pepper, and mix well with a wooden spoon for about 2 minutes to consolidate all the ingredients.

Remove the saucepan from the heat and transfer the contents to a crockery bowl. Let stand until cold (about 30 minutes). Then add the Parmigiano and bread crumbs and incorporate them well with a wooden spoon. Taste for salt, pepper, and nutmeg.

Prepare the *tortelli* with the ingredients above, following the directions on page 164 or 165. Place 1 heaping tablespoon of the filling inside each *tortello*.

Finely chop the 10 walnuts for the sauce. Bring a large stockpot of cold water to a boil. Add coarse-grained salt to taste.

Melt the butter in a skillet placed over this stockpot. When the butter is completely melted, transfer the skillet from the top of the stockpot to a very low flame, and let the water in the stockpot boil. Cook the *tortelli* in the boiling water for from 30 seconds to 2 minutes, depending on the dryness of the pasta.

With a strainer-skimmer, transfer the *tortelli* to the skillet containing the melted butter. Add the heavy cream and stir with wooden spoon. Taste for salt and pepper and sprinkle with the chopped walnuts. When the sauce is mixed through (about 1 minute), transfer to a serving dish, with all the unabsorbed heavy cream. To make individual servings, pile the *tortelli* high in an Italian-style soup bowl. Do not eat *tortelli* one by one as is usually done, but rather cut through the layers of *tortelli* with a fork, the way you would eat lasagne. Each serving should contain unabsorbed cream. Do not add Parmigiano.

Uova alla Fornaia

BAKED GIANT TORTELLI

FROM PARMA

A dish for a celebration, these oversized *tortelli* require careful handling because they are made with a whole egg yolk encased in the thinnest, most breakable pasta. The egg yolks will remain whole if handled carefully and when cooked according to these directions will emerge as soft as in a lightly poached egg. The finished product makes a pretty picture with the green ring of creamy spinach and the yellow yolk plainly visible through the thin pasta. Truffles, though they are optional, will really enhance the flavor of this dish when added and are not an extraneous flourish as when added to some dishes to simply impress.

SERVES 8

For the stuffing:
1 pound fresh spinach
Coarse-grained salt
4 ounces ricotta
2 extra large egg yolks
¼ cup freshly grated Parmigiano
Salt, freshly ground black pepper, and freshly grated nutmeg to taste

Plus:
8 extra large eggs

For the pasta:
3 cups unbleached all-purpose flour
3 extra large eggs
3 teaspoons olive oil or vegetable oil
Pinch of salt

172

To cook the paste:
Coarse-grained salt
2 tablespoons olive oil or vegetable oil

For the sauce:
4 ounces (1 stick) sweet butter
½ cup freshly grated Parmigiano

Optional:
2 small or 1 medium-sized white truffle (about 1 ounce), fresh or canned

Prepare the stuffing first. Remove the large stems from the spinach and wash carefully in several changes of cold water.

Bring a large stockpot of cold water to a boil. Add coarse-grained salt to taste. Then add the spinach and cook for 10 minutes. Drain the spinach and cool under cold running water. Squeeze very dry. Chop the spinach fine and put in a bowl along with the ricotta, 2 egg yolks, Parmigiano, salt, pepper, and nutmeg. Mix together with a wooden spoon until everything is thoroughly combined.

Prepare the pasta, following the directions on pages 120–122 and 127–129. Stretch the layer of pasta to the last notch of the pasta machine. Put the stuffing in a pastry bag with a medium-sized tip.

Meanwhile, bring a large pot of cold water to a boil. Add coarse-grained salt to taste. Fill a large bowl with cold water and 2 tablespoons of olive oil.

HOW TO PREPARE UOVA ALLA FORNAIA

1. Place a jagged-edge cookie cutter 4 inches in diameter on the layer of pasta. With the pastry bag make a ring of the stuffing around the inside edge of the cookie cutter.

2. Separate the 8 egg yolks from the whites, being careful that the yolk remains whole and that all the white is removed. Place an egg yolk inside the ring in the middle of the stuffing.

3. Be sure the egg yolk is in the center. Then sprinkle with salt.

4. Carefully remove the cookie cutter and place a layer of pasta over the prepared *tortelli.*

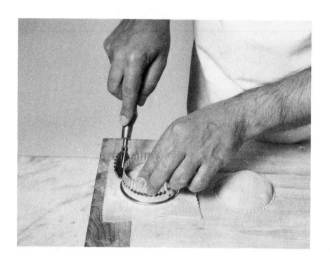

5. Replace the cookie cutter this time upside down (the top part is wider) and cut all around the cookie cutter with a pastry cutter.

Let the *tortelli* rest for about 10 minutes. Do not allow the prepared *tortelli* to dry.

Cut the butter for the sauce into pieces and put them in a baking dish. Melt the butter by fitting the baking dish over the stockpot as a lid. When the water is boiling, carefully put the *tortelli* into the pot one at a time and let them cook for only 5 seconds after the water has returned to a boil. With a large skimmer-strainer, transfer each to the bowl of cold water, put the next *tortello* in to boil, and remove the cooled one from the water to the baking dish with melted butter.

Preheat the oven to 375 degrees. When you add each *tortello* to the baking dish, be sure that they do not touch one another. When all the *tortelli* are in the baking dish, sprinkle Parmigiano over them, cover the dish with a sheet of aluminum foil, and bake for 15 minutes.

Remove from oven and serve immediately, one *tortello* per serving.

6. Sprinkle over a little more Parmigiano or a few shavings of white truffle.

HOW TO PREPARE TORTELLINI

Tortellini are small stuffed rings of pasta, with the stuffing concentrated on one side, and the two ends joined on the other. The name means literally "small tortelli" and they have retained the original meaning of *tortelli* referring to a round shape.

To prepare *tortellini*, make the dough using the ingredients in the following recipe, according to the directions on pages 120–122 and 127–129. Stretch the layer of pasta to the last notch of the pasta machine.

1. Cut the sheet of pasta into circles with a 1½-inch round cookie cutter without jagged edges. A 1-inch cookie cutter may be used for smaller *tortellini* and the 2-inch one to make the larger *tortellini*.

Do not wait for the pasta to dry. As each piece of the dough is rolled out, begin to make *tortellini* immediately.

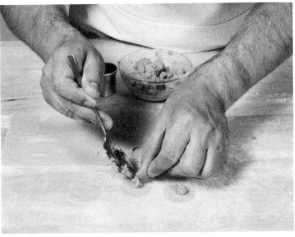

2. Place a scant ½ teaspoon of filling in the center of each circle. (The amount of filling varies according to the size of the *tortellini*.)

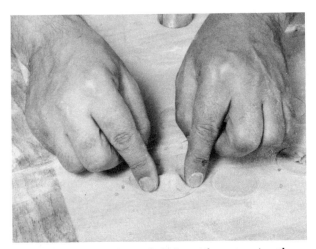

3. Moisten the edges slightly with water (as these small pieces of pasta dry very quickly). Then double over one side of the pasta circle, but not all the way to the other edge; leave a little border arc of the pasta undoubled.

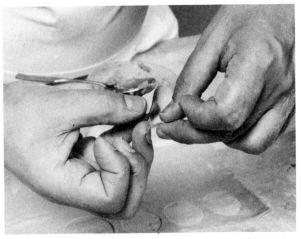

4. Wrap the half-moon around your index finger (or little finger as shown in the photo), the top of the finger reaching only to the top of the filled section.

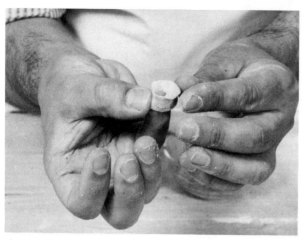

5. With your thumb, connect the two edges of the half-moon.

6. Take the pasta overlapping your fingers and curl it outward.

7. The typical "bolognese" *tortellino*.

HOW TO PREPARE CAPPELLETTI

Cappelletti are shaped differently than *tortellini* and their name means "little hats" which they are thought to resemble. To prepare *cappelletti*, make the dough using the ingredients in the following recipe, according to the directions on pages 120–122 and 127–129. Stretch the layer of pasta to the last notch of the pasta machine.

1. With a pastry cutter, cut the layer of pasta into pieces about 6 inches long. Let the pieces dry for 1 or 2 minutes, then cut into pieces 2 inches square. Do not wait for the pasta to dry. As each piece of the dough is rolled out, begin to make *cappelletti* immediately. Place a scant ½ teaspoon of filling in the center of each square.

176

2. Turn the pasta square so that it resembles a diamond. Moisten the two lower sides of the diamond with a little water, then holding the bottom point, draw the bottom half up over the top, almost but not all the way to the opposite side. (Leave a little border of the pasta undoubled.) The shape should now be triangular. If the dough is very fresh it will still be moist enough to seal when pressed without moistening with water. *Cappelletti* retain their shape better when they are sealed without water.

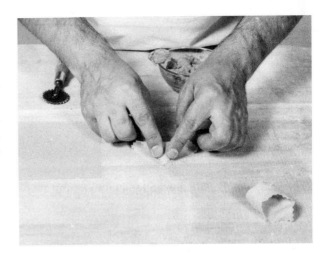

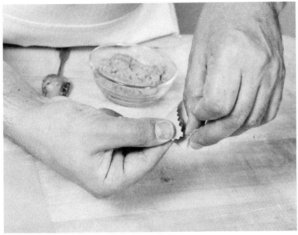

3. Wrap the triangle around your index finger, the top of the finger reaching only to the top of the filled section.

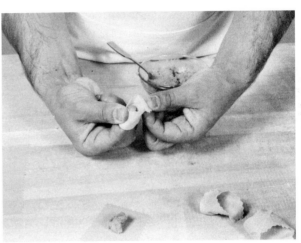

4. With your thumb, connect the two edges of the pasta triangle and curl the overlap of pasta outward. The result should resemble the little hat which gives the *cappelletti* their name.

Pasticcio di Tortellini o Cappelletti alla Bolognese

BAKED TORTELLINI OR CAPPELLETTI BOLOGNESE STYLE

FROM BOLOGNA

Tortellini and *cappelletti* are made all over Italy and in each place its egg pasta reflects the style of the particular region. Making a baked mold of these pastas, however, as in this dish, is a Bolognese usage, widely copied in other places. Hence, a *Pasticcio alla bolognese* may be made in any part of Italy, but the style of its pasta will vary, mainly in whether oil and/or water are added.

We offer below the two most widely used variants: flour, eggs, and salt, or flour, eggs, salt, and oil.

SERVES 8

For the sauce:
Prepare Sugo di manzo *(page 132), using half the amount of the ingredients.*

For *tortellini* or *cappelletti* stuffing:
4 ounces fatty prosciutto
2 ounces mortadella
6 ounces uncooked marrow from the bone of the veal shank
4 ounces freshly grated Parmigiano
1 extra large egg
Freshly grated nutmeg to taste

For pasta (I):
3 cups unbleached all-purpose flour
4 extra large eggs
Pinch of salt

For pasta (II):
4 cups unbleached all-purpose flour
4 extra large eggs
4 teaspoons olive oil
Pinch of salt

For the *balsamella:*
4 tablespoons sweet butter
1/3 cup unbleached all-purpose flour
1½ cups milk
Salt and freshly grated nutmeg to taste

Plus:
2 ounces prosciutto
3 tablespoons sweet butter, cut into pieces

To cook the pasta:
Coarse-grained salt

First prepare the sauce and let it stand until needed. Then make the stuffing for the *tortellini* or *cappelletti.* Finely chop the *prosciutto, mortadella,* and uncooked marrow together on a board. Transfer the chopped ingredients to a crockery bowl and add the Parmigiano, egg, and nutmeg. Mix all the ingredients very well with a wooden spoon. Cover the bowl with aluminum foil and refrigerate until needed.

Prepare the pasta for *tortellini* or *cappelletti* with the ingredients listed above, following instructions on page 175. Stuff each one with 1 scant teaspoon of the stuffing. Let the *tortellini* or *cappelletti* rest between two dish towels until needed.

Prepare the *balsamella* with the ingredients listed above, following the directions on page 334. Transfer the sauce to a crockery bowl, pressing a piece of buttered wax paper over the sauce. Let stand until cool.

Bring a large stockpot of cold water to a boil. Add coarse-grained salt to taste.

Meanwhile, finely chop the *prosciutto* and pour the sauce into a large casserole.

When the water reaches the boiling point, add the *tortellini* and partially cook for only 20 to 30 seconds, depending on the dryness of the pasta. Drain the *tortellini* and transfer them to the casserole with the sauce. Put the casserole over medium heat and sauté for 1 minute longer, gently mixing with a wooden spoon while cooking to incorporate the sauce. Heavily butter a round baking casserole. Preheat the oven to 375 degrees.

Remove the casserole with the *tortellini* from the heat and add the *balsamella* and the chopped *prosciutto.* Mix gently and transfer to the buttered baking casserole. Place the pieces of butter on top. Cover the casserole with aluminum foil and bake for 20 minutes. Remove from the oven, let rest, covered, for 2 minutes, then serve directly from the casserole.

CHAPTER 7

Dried Pasta

1. Some shapes of dried pasta used in the recipes of this chapter: spaghetti, *viti* or *tortiglioni* spirals, and four different types of short tubular pasta (*pasta corta*). All these types of pasta except the spaghetti can be used interchangeably in the recipes for pasta salads and those containing heavier sauces.

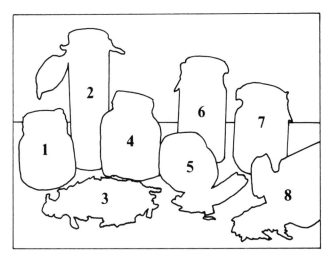

26.
1. penne rigate (*ridged short tubes, with two ends cut diagonally*)
2. *spaghetti (long "strings" of various thicknesses; thinner ones called* spaghettini)
3. *the mounds in front:* viti or tortiglioni (*spirals*)
4. rigatoni *or* denti di cavallo (*like* penne rigate *but with straight-cut edges*)
5. sedanini (*small rigatoni*)
6. rigatoni (*a different-sized rigatoni*)
7. penne (*short tubes, with two ends cut diagonally*)
8. gramigna bucata (*short thick spaghetti with a very narrow hole down the center*)

2. *Chiocciole* or "snails."

NOTE: In the southern Italian recipes using spaghetti, linguine (similar to spaghetti but slightly flattened) may also be used. Linguine is rarely used in the north of Italy.

In ancient and medieval times, when coarsely milled wheat was a basic staple of the Mediterranean diet, the preservation of this flour was critical to survival. It was discovered that by mixing the coarse flour with water and then drying it in the sun, it could be preserved for long periods and travel without spoiling. Egypt, the location of the first Mediterranean granary, was joined by green tree-covered Sicily which was closer to Rome. Food scholars generally feel that dried pasta started its long slow rise to eminence in Italy from Roman Sicily. Flat pasta was joined in the eleventh century by tubular pasta, developed after Roman times by the Arabs in what had been the eastern provinces of the old empire. By 1279, a year or so before Marco Polo's return from the East, a certain Signor Bastone, Genoese, so treasured his "macaronis" that he left a chest of them to his heirs in his will.

Dried pasta is a different category from fresh, not an inferior one. It is appropriate to wholly different dishes and sauces, with just a few overlaps. Within the world of dried pasta it was possible to develop an even greater variety of shapes and textures and these called forth a wide variety of sauces, each pasta and sauce restricted in its appropriate combination. One can easily understand that a tubular shape as opposed to a flat one, ridged surface rather than smooth, fine rather than thick would all accommodate a great variety of sauces of different density, sharpness, and flavor. Italians are rather strict in their traditions of which shape of pasta, whether dried or fresh, belongs to which sauce. This is not a matter of thoughtless conservatism but rather the result of centuries of experience, in particular that of the last 150 years.

It is difficult to believe in these last decades of the twentieth century that dried pasta was not important in the Italian diet even at the beginning of the nineteenth century. So many wonderful dishes have emerged in this short time, such variety, such inventiveness. In the two great compendia of late eighteenth-century Italian cooking as well as in the most famous book of the great Neapolitan Corrado, one searches in vain for dried pasta. And though it became popular with all classes of Neapolitans in the early 1800s, it was not as yet even the "national" dish of Naples itself. It was still eaten with the hands, presumably without sauce, by all classes, as testified by the many popular prints of the time showing Neapolitans on the street and in the home, holding the long cooked strands in their hands with mouths open to receive them.

Only in the last 150 years has pasta come to occupy a central place in Italian cooking. And in this time Italians have arrived at strong ideas of what constitutes well-cooked pasta. We can see from early nineteenth-century books that a variety of cooking methods acceptable then are considered unacceptable for today's more practiced palate.

Most pasta dishes are eaten hot. Cooking instructions continue to evolve toward a higher standard and some older ideas no longer generally accepted in Italy hang on, even in current cookbooks. Among pasta fanciers in Italy now it is not acceptable to add oil to the cooking water nor to rinse the pasta after cooking unless it is being prepared to be eaten in a cold pasta salad. We follow with instructions for cooking pasta for both hot and cold dishes and recipes for a variety of dishes using pasta with eggs and cheese, fresh tomatoes, vegetables, fish, and meat and finally an attractive mold of pasta baked with meat sauce.

HOW TO COOK DRIED PASTA (TO BE EATEN HOT)

1. For 1 pound of dried pasta use 4 to 6 quarts (16 to 24 cups) cold water and 2 tablespoons coarse-grained salt. Bring the water to a boil in a large stockpot. Then add the salt. This is the right proportion of water to salt and will give the bland pasta enough taste to integrate it with the taste of the sauce used. I always start with *cold* water because hot tap water already has its own taste.

2. Add pasta and

3. stir with a wooden spoon, to be sure the pasta does not stick together.

Do not add oil to the boiling water. Cover the stockpot to bring the water back to a boil as quickly as possible. Remove the lid and cook the pasta until *al dente*. *Al dente* means that the pasta still has some resistance to the bite. Cooking time could vary from 7 to 14 minutes (after the water returns to a boil) depending on the enormous range of brands, since the proportions of durum, hard durum, and semolina flours vary from one brand to the other. Atmospheric conditions also play a role. Generally, imported Italian pasta takes about 12 minutes, and domestic United States pastas take less time to cook. However, it is always best to test pasta after 7 minutes to judge how much further cooking time is needed.

4. Drain pasta in a large colander. Absolutely do not rinse pasta in either hot or cold water, unless you are preparing a pasta salad.

5. Transfer the pasta to a serving dish or bowl. Pour the sauce over the pasta and toss very well with a fork and spoon. If both the sauce and pasta are properly prepared, the pasta should be evenly coated with sauce, and all the sauce should stick to the pasta without any excess sauce remaining in the bottom of the bowl. Do not add extra sauce on top.

Maccheroni "all'Ultima Moda 1841" alla Napoletana

PASTA "IN THE LATEST STYLE NAPLES 1841"

In a cookbook of 1841 there are two recipes entitled *Maccheroni alla napoletana*. The first, at that time *the* Neapolitan pasta, was with a meat and classic red wine sauce. The style for the second, "all'ultima moda," that is "in the latest style," is the earliest version I have seen in print of the magical combination of pasta and tomato sauce. I could not believe that this archetypical combination was that new. Looking through the late eighteenth-century sources, tomatoes appeared in the many volumed work of Leonardi, the great cook of Catherine the Great, but as whole tomatoes baked in crust. The great Corrado who introduced the pasta so beloved of the Neapolitan populace to court dining does not yet have this combination as late as the early nineteenth century.

This second recipe may indeed be the very first way in which tomatoes were wedded to pasta. It is different from what we know today. About five pounds of halved San Marzano plum tomatoes are arranged in layers alternating with one pound of dried pasta. No liquid, just a little butter, is added. The instructions are to cook it "between two fires," above and below, which was the nineteenth-century antecedent of our modern oven baking. Having tried the recipe many times, I concluded that though the resulting tomato flavor in the pasta was incomparably good, the best ever, the pasty, gummy consistency of the pasta itself when done this way was unacceptable to modern tastes. Then I found that in some small villages near Naples today, there exists a dish which is *maccheroni* baked in a whole tomato, again with no additional liquid. Watching closely how it is done, I realized that the old recipe had evolved. The dried pasta is soaked in olive oil for a while before it is stuffed into the tomato. Remaking the old recipe after doing this, the pasta had a more modern consistency, completely acceptable. It was fascinating to realize that pasta expertise had gone so far in a rather

182

short time, only one century. The modern stuffed tomato recipe appears on page 387, and here is the earliest *Maccheroni al pomodoro* (Pasta with Tomato Sauce).

¾ cup olive oil
1 pound of any short tubular pasta, preferably imported Italian
3 pounds imported Italian canned tomatoes, including the juice, or 4 pounds very ripe summer tomatoes
Salt and freshly ground black pepper
½ cup freshly grated Parmigiano

SERVES 4 TO 6

Pour the olive oil into a crockery bowl. Add the pasta and mix very well. Let the pasta soak in the oil for about 20 minutes.

Preheat the oven to 400 degrees.

Add the canned tomatoes and all the juice to the bowl along with salt and pepper to taste. Mix very well, then transfer to a Pyrex casserole 14 inches in diameter. Bake for about 45 minutes, mixing two or three times. (If tomatoes are fresh, cut them into ½-inch-thick slices and alternate layers of tomato and pasta with tomatoes as top and bottom layers. Do not mix even while baking.)

Remove the casserole from the oven and sprinkle the cheese over the pasta mixture. Mix very well and then transfer to a serving dish. Serve immediately without adding extra cheese.

Spaghetti con Broccoli

SPAGHETTI WITH BROCCOLI

FROM CALABRIA

This is one of the most classic southern Italian pastas. First the broccoli is cooked, but not overcooked, and then the pasta is cooked in the water of the broccoli. Anchovy and a dash of red pepper flakes add the perfect finish.

Coarse-grained salt
1 bunch fresh broccoli
1 pound dried spaghetti or linguine
5 whole anchovies in salt, or 10 fillets in oil, drained
¾ cup olive oil
Pinch of red pepper flakes
Freshly ground black pepper to taste

SERVES 4 TO 6

Bring a large pot of cold water to a boil. Add coarse-grained salt to taste. Meanwhile, remove and discard the large tough stems from the broccoli and cut the remainder into approximately 3-inch pieces. Soak the broccoli pieces in a bowl of cold water for about 30 minutes. When the water in the pot reaches a boil, add the broccoli and cook for about 10 minutes.

Drain the broccoli and save the cooking water. Transfer the broccoli to a large serving dish and cover the dish with aluminum foil to keep it warm. Pour the broccoli water back into the stockpot and bring it back to a boil. Add the pasta and cook following the directions on page 181.

While the pasta is cooking, prepare the sauce. If using anchovies in salt, fillet them and wash them well (page 55). Drain on paper towels.

Heat the olive oil in a heavy enamel or aluminum saucepan over low heat. When the oil is hot, remove the pan from the heat and quickly add the filleted anchovies and the red pepper flakes. Use a fork to mash them into the oil until amalgamated.

Drain the spaghetti in a colander and place it in the serving dish on top of the broccoli. Pour the anchovy sauce over the pasta. Sprinkle with freshly ground black pepper and toss gently but very well. Serve immediately.

Spaghettini dell' Ortolano

THIN SPAGHETTI WITH AROMATIC HERBS AND VEGETABLES

FROM UMBRIA

The *battuto* (chopped aromatic herbs and vegetables) forms the basis of the majority of sauces. When it is tossed in its vegetable purity with fine *spaghettini*, it is very natural and satisfying. *Ortolano* means "fruit and vegetable man."

1 pound medium-sized carrots
Coarse-grained salt
1 medium-sized red onion
1 celery stalk
1 clove garlic, peeled
15 sprigs Italian parsley, leaves only
Coarse-grained salt
1 pound fine dried pasta, such as spaghettini
4 ounces (1 stick) sweet butter
5 tablespoons olive oil
Salt and freshly ground black pepper

Optional:
4 to 6 tablespoons freshly grated Parmigiano

SERVES 4 TO 6

Boil the carrots according to the directions on page 357. Then coarsely chop them.

Finely chop the onion, celery, garlic, and parsley together on a board.

Bring a large pot of cold water to a boil. Add coarse-grained salt to taste. Add the pasta and cook following the directions on page 181, remembering that for finer pasta, the cooking time will be several minutes less than usual (about 8 minutes) for it to be *al dente*. The pasta will be sautéed later, so do not overcook it.

While the pasta is cooking, put the butter and oil in a saucepan over medium heat. When the butter is completely melted and the pasta is almost cooked, add the carrots to the pan and sauté lightly for 2 minutes. Meanwhile drain the pasta. Add the finely chopped ingredients to the saucepan with the carrots, then add the drained pasta. Sprinkle with salt and pepper to taste and toss very well for about 2 minutes while still over the heat. Transfer the pasta to a serving dish and serve immediately. This dish is usually served without grated Parmigiano, but it may also be served with it.

Spaghetti con Passato di Pesce alla Genovese

GENOESE FISH SAUCE WITH SPAGHETTI

FROM GENOA

In this old Genoese recipe for fish sauce for pasta, the cooked fish is passed through a food mill. For passing a more solid food than tomatoes, the removable disc must be changed to one with slightly larger holes. These discs come with holes of three or four different sizes. Be careful to use the one which is next to the finest, as larger holes might allow bits of skin and small bones to get through. A single passing will leave much of the fish still in the food mill. It will be necessary to return the passed liquid to the top of the mill as many times as necessary to get most of the fish through. However, do not force through the very last bits which will contain some skin and small bones.

Like many a classic recipe evolved over centuries, it is difficult to imagine the final product from the beginning stages of making it. The texture after reduction is less a normal purée than a thick sauce like a bean paste. A pasta like spaghetti will absorb most of the sauce and yield maximum flavor.

Genoese fish dishes are created out of the unique combination of fish from the local waters such as *pesce prete, scorfano rosso, capone gallinella, caviglione,* etc. To preserve the pure fish flavors not even wine or garlic is introduced. This dish or a *Zuppa di pesce* made from these can no more be exactly duplicated outside of Genoa than a real Bouillabaisse outside of Marseilles. Accepting this, we feel that the sauce is so worthwhile in principle that it is worth making with other carefully chosen and well integrated combinations. We offer the following which retains the spirit though not the letter.

1½ pounds of fish pieces with bones but not heads   SERVES 4 TO 6
(Use at least three kinds of ocean fish, such as whiting, porgy, scrod, or sea bass.)
6 cups cold water
1 heaping teaspoon coarse-grained salt
1 medium-sized red onion
⅓ cup olive oil
About 20 sprigs Italian parsley, leaves only
½ tablespoon rosemary leaves, fresh or preserved in salt
Salt and freshly ground black pepper
1 pound dried spaghetti, preferably imported Italian

To cook the pasta:
Coarse-grained salt

Wash the fish pieces well and dry them with paper towels. Put the cold water in a medium-sized saucepan and bring the water to a boil. Add the salt and then the fish and simmer for 2 minutes. Remove the pan from the heat. Use a slotted spoon to transfer the fish pieces to a chopping board. Reserve the fish broth. Cut the onion into thin slices. Heat the oil in a saucepan over medium heat. When it is hot, add the onion slices. Lower the heat and sauté lightly for about 5 minutes. Remove the bones from the fish pieces and add the fish to the saucepan with one quarter of the leaves of parsley and the rosemary. Sauté for about 15 minutes. Add 4 cups of the reserved fish broth and simmer for 25 minutes.

Using the disc described above, pass all the contents of the pan through the food mill, returning the liquid to the top of the mill several times until most of the fish has passed through. Reduce the sauce by simmering it for ½ hour, stirring occasionally. Add salt to taste and a good amount of freshly ground black pepper to the sauce 10 minutes before it is ready. The sauce should be quite peppery.

Coarsely chop the remaining parsley.

Bring a large pot of water to a boil. Add coarse-grained salt to taste. Cook the spaghetti, following the directions on page 181. Pour a little sauce in the bottom of a warm large bowl or serving dish. Drain the pasta and place it in the bowl or dish. Pour the rest of the sauce over and toss very well. Sprinkle the chopped parsley on top and serve immediately.

Spaghetti all'Aragosta
SPAGHETTI WITH LOBSTER

FROM SARDINIA

The Italian Islands—Elba, Giglio, and especially Sardinia—are famous for the quality and quantity of their lobsters, aragosta and leoni di mare, two different Mediterranean types corresponding to the French Hommard and Langouste. In Sardinia it is not unusual to have dishes of both types, prepared differently, at the same meal. Though American lobsters are different, this aragosta recipe adapts nicely to them. The dish is best, of course, with the meat of freshly boiled lobster, if live ones are available in your area. The hot pasta combines well with the cool marinated lobster and sauce, releasing its flavor.

½ pound freshly boiled lobster meat
2 cloves garlic, peeled and cut in half
About 20 sprigs Italian parsley, leaves only, coarsely chopped
1½ cups olive oil
Juice of 1½ lemons
Salt and freshly ground black pepper to taste
1 pound dried spaghetti, preferably imported Italian

To cook the pasta:
Coarse-grained salt

SERVES 4 TO 6

Cut the lobster meat into 1-inch pieces and put them in a crockery bowl. Add the garlic and parsley to the bowl. Pour the oil over the lobster, then add the lemon juice, salt, and pepper. Mix well with a wooden spoon. Cover the bowl and marinate in the refrigerator for at least 3 hours. (Do not reduce the quantity of oil or the dish will not have the proper taste and texture.) When ready to serve, bring a large pot of water to a boil. Add coarse-grained salt to taste. Cook the spaghetti according to the directions on page 181. Drain the pasta and place it in a serving dish. Remove the garlic pieces from the lobster sauce and immediately pour the sauce over the pasta. Toss very well. Top each serving with a grinding of black pepper.

Spaghetti con Caviale di Tonno
SPAGHETTI WITH FRESH FISH ROE

FROM SARDINIA

Along with its two types of lobster, other specialties of Sardinian food are both the milt (soft roe of the male) and the roe of fresh tuna, producing the wonderful appetizer of cubed cooked milt with oil and vinegar and the excellent unusual pasta given below. When in the city of Alghero, do not miss these dishes.

Fresh tuna is available in American waters. It is a deep-water sea fish but approaches the coast in the spring to lay its eggs. So, in that season, fresh roe (and milt) could be available if there were a demand for it. Shad roe is a great delicacy and specialty of North America and works beautifully in this dish. The "caviar" of many fish were used in a variety of dishes in medieval and Renaissance Italy. Sturgeon itself was more plentiful then in northern Italy, particularly in the Po River, and was even found in the Arno. But there are other fresh-water fish with delicate roe, which, unfortunately, are not used as much today.

¾ pound (about 1½ pairs) fresh shad roe, or ¾ pound fresh tuna roe   SERVES 4 TO 6
½ cup olive oil
4 tablespoons (½ stick) sweet butter
Salt and freshly ground black pepper
About 15 sprigs Italian parsley, leaves only
1 pound dried spaghetti, preferably imported Italian

To cook the pasta: *Coarse-grained salt*

Bring a large pot of cold water to a boil.

Meanwhile, begin to prepare the sauce. Remove the inside connecting membrane from the fish roe. Put the oil and butter in a small saucepan over medium heat. When the butter is completely melted, add the fish roe. Sprinkle the roe with salt and pepper to taste. (The roe of the fresh-water shad requires more salt than that of the salt-water tuna.)

Break up the roe with a wooden spoon until it is well blended with the oil and butter. The sauce will be cooked in about 5 minutes. If the sauce is too dense add a tablespoon or two of the boiling water from the pasta. When the water has come to a boil, add coarse-grained salt to taste. Add the pasta and cook following the directions on page 181.

Chop the parsley coarsely. Drain the pasta and transfer to a warmed platter. Pour the roe sauce over it and toss very well. Serve immediately, sprinkling the chopped parsley on each serving.

Spaghetti Neri

SPAGHETTI WITH THE INK OF THE SQUID

FROM TUSCANY

Gastronomy and art sometimes utilize the same ingredients and mediums: those spices and herbs which are used as natural flavorings for dishes can also provide the colors for paintings. For example, the ink of the squid that we eat is the very same that was used for the beautiful brownish-tinged sepia ink drawings of the great masters. (See the drawing by Michelangelo Buonarotti on the front left endpaper.) This ink is used in the traditional *Risotto nero* of Venice as well as in this less-known but equally delicious recipe from Tuscany, which is rich in taste, slightly sweet and sour, and not at all fishy. It is no accident that the areas that were the two great centers of Renaissance painting and drawing have given us these two dishes.

SERVES 4 TO 6

For the sauce:
3 medium-sized cuttlefish (inksquid)
1 medium-sized red onion
1 clove garlic, peeled
⅓ cup olive oil
2 cups dry white wine
½ cup fresh tomatoes or drained canned imported Italian tomatoes
2 cups chicken or beef broth
Salt and freshly ground black pepper
1 pound dried spaghetti, preferably imported Italian
Scant ½ teaspoon red pepper flakes

To cook the pasta: *Coarse-grained salt*

Clean and cut the cuttlefish following the directions on pages 302–303, photos 1 through 8, reserving the whole ink glands. Set the strips aside.

Finely chop the onion and garlic together on a board. Heat the oil in a saucepan and, when it is hot, add the chopped ingredients and sauté until lightly golden brown (about 10 minutes). Add the squid and sauté for 3 minutes longer. Then add the wine and evaporate it very slowly (about 30 minutes).

Pass the tomatoes through a food mill. Heat the broth to the boiling point. Remove the saucepan with the squid from the heat and place a strainer over the pan.

HOW TO PREPARE SPAGHETTI NERI

1. Put the ink glands in the strainer and mash them with a spoon until most of the ink has been squeezed out.

2. Pour 1 cup of the broth through the mashed glands to extract the remaining ink.

Return the saucepan to the heat and add the strained tomatoes. Taste for salt and pepper and simmer uncovered, for about 20 minutes, adding the remaining hot broth as needed. Bring a large pot of water to a boil. Add coarse-grained salt to taste. Add the pasta and cook following the directions on page 181.

At this point the sauce should be reduced and the squid pieces completely tender. Sprinkle the red pepper flakes over the sauce, stir, and simmer for 1 minute longer.

Drain the pasta in a large colander, and transfer it to a large serving dish.

3. Pour the sauce over and toss the pasta well.

4. Serve hot.

Finocchio.

27. Finocchio (Fennel)

Pasta con le Sarde

PASTA WITH FRESH SARDINES

FROM SICILY

The most popular of all pasta dishes in Sicily, *Pasta con le sarde* has a long history and varies slightly from town to town all over the island.

Though fresh sardines are little known in the United States, they swim in northern waters as well as the Mediterranean and are unavailable mainly because there is no demand for them. They can, however, be obtained at some Italian fish markets in the United States, particularly if the proprietors are of Sicilian origin. Just as with other fish, if the sardines are fresh when you purchase them, they should not have a fishy odor. If your fish market does not carry them, encourage the proprietor to stock them so that they will be more easily available than they are now.

Recipes for this dish do circulate in English-language cookbooks, but the ones I have seen are not really authentic. Though there are variations of the dish in Sicily, all agree that wild fennel (*finocchio di montagna* or *finocchiella*) is *the* necessary ingredient. This herb is much closer to dill (*finocchio marino*) than to the leaves of the ordinary "bulb" fennel. Though wild fennel does grow in California, it is not generally available. A substitution of dill produces a result very close to the original, and it is better to include it than to simply ignore a basic ingredient. Wild fennel is also sold in Italy, dried in little bunches. An interesting feature of the recipe is that the wild fennel is cooked in the water in which the pasta will be cooked. It is then removed before the pasta is added, chopped very fine, and combined with the sardine sauce. Because dill is stronger, I suggest using the chopped top leaves of only two of the sprigs to be added. Our version of the recipe is an older one, still in current use, however, without tomatoes or tomato paste. As a simple family version it omits saffron, an ingredient of the more elaborate recipes, both old and modern. We do include the raisins and pignolis, which are used in the old ones and most other versions of the recipe. Some bake the dish after it is cooked and assembled, but we opt for the simpler, lighter version without baking.

SERVES 4 TO 6

1 pound fresh sardines
Coarse-grained salt
3 or 4 sprigs of fresh dill or wild fennel
¼ cup raisins
¼ cup olive oil
Salt and freshly ground black pepper to taste
2 tablespoons red wine vinegar
1 tablespoon pignoli (pine nuts)
1 pound dried pasta, such as spaghetti or short pasta (penne rigate or rigatoni),
preferably imported Italian

To cook the pasta:
Coarse-grained salt

Clean and wash the fresh sardines very well, removing the head and the central bone (page 300). Soak in salted cold water for 10 minutes.

Bring a large pot of cold water to a boil and add coarse-grained salt to taste and the dill or wild fennel. Simmer for about 15 minutes.

Soak the raisins in a bowl of lukewarm water for about 20 minutes.

Heat the oil in a saucepan over medium heat. When the oil is hot, add the cleaned sardines and sauté for 2 to 3 minutes, mashing the fish with a fork. Sprinkle with salt and pepper. Add the wine vinegar and let it evaporate (about 2 minutes).

Meanwhile, remove the dill or fennel from the boiling water to a chopping board and add the pasta. Cook following the directions on page 181.

Drain the raisins and pat them dry. Coarsely chop 2 sprigs of the dill, or all of the fennel. When the wine vinegar has evaporated, add the raisins, chopped dill or fennel, and pignoli and cook the sauce for 1 minute longer. Drain the pasta and transfer it to a large serving dish. Pour the sauce over the pasta and toss very well. Serve immediately.

Penne Trippate

PENNE WITH TRIPE SAUCE

FROM TUSCANY

The sauce is made by cutting the tripe into pasta-like thin strips and cooking it with herbs, broth, and tomatoes. In Italy, where tripe is a favorite dish and made in different styles in various regions, it is possible to buy it completely precooked, so that the sauce takes about half an hour to prepare. In the United States, tripe is only partially precooked, and it may have to simmer for from 2 to 4 hours.

This is the best dish to introduce people to tripe if they are loath to try it. It has been my experience that almost everyone finds it a pleasant discovery once they have eaten it this way.

For the sauce: SERVES 4 TO 6
1 pound cooked fresh tripe
10 sprigs Italian parsley, leaves only
1 large clove garlic, peeled
1 teaspoon rosemary leaves, fresh, preserved in salt or dried and blanched
¼ cup olive oil
1 cup fresh tomatoes or drained canned imported Italian tomatoes
2 tablespoons tomato paste
2 cups beef or chicken broth
Salt and freshly ground black pepper
1 pound dried penne, preferably imported Italian
½ cup freshly grated Parmigiano

To cook the pasta:
Coarse-grained salt

If the tripe is already precooked, soak it in a bowl of cold water for about 1 hour. Cut the tripe into thin strips less than ¼ inch thick and set it aside.

Coarsely chop the parsley and finely chop the garlic and rosemary.

Heat the oil in a saucepan over medium heat. When the oil is hot, add the chopped ingredients and sauté for 2 minutes. Then add the tripe and sauté for 10 minutes longer.

Pass the tomatoes through food mill and combine them with the tomato paste. Add the mixture to the saucepan and simmer for about 10 minutes. Then start adding the hot broth as needed until all the broth is incorporated and the tripe is fully cooked (about 40 minutes).

Remove the pan from the heat. Use a slotted spoon to transfer the tripe from the pan to a chopping board. Coarsely chop the tripe and return it to the pan. Return the pan to medium heat. Taste for salt and pepper, stirring thoroughly with a wooden spoon. The sauce should now be smooth and homogeneous; let it simmer for a few minutes more.

Bring a large pot of water to a boil. Add coarse-grained salt to taste. Cook following the directions on page 181. Drain the pasta and transfer it to a warm serving dish. Pour the sauce over the pasta and mix well. Sprinkle with Parmigiano and serve immediately.

Penne Strascicate al Sugo di Vitella

PENNE STIR-SAUTÉED IN VEAL SAUCE

FROM LIVORNO (LEGHORN)

Penne strascicate, partially cooked *penne* which finishes cooking by being sautéed in a meat sauce (one of the several that can be used), is the most typical dried pasta dish of Tuscany. *Strascicare* means to drag through, as the pasta is constantly stirred through the sauce until it absorbs most of it. In Florence (see *Penne strascicate alla fiorentina* which follows), it is made with the usual meat sauces (also employed in the *Pasticcio di pasta*, page 193), but in Leghorn this unusual veal sauce, so typical of that city, is served. The sauce for this dish should be prepared a day in advance.

SERVES 4 TO 6

For the sauce:
2 ounces dried porcini mushrooms
3 ounces sliced pancetta, or 1½ ounces salt pork and 1½ ounces boiled ham
1 pound boneless veal shoulder, in one piece
1 chicken drumstick
2 medium-sized carrots, diced
1 small red onion, sliced
1 celery stalk, diced
Salt and freshly ground black pepper
¼ cup olive oil
4 tablespoons sweet butter
1 whole clove
½ cup dry white wine
2 tablespoons tomato paste
8 cups beef or chicken broth
1 pound dried pasta, such as penne or penne rigate, preferably imported Italian

To cook the pasta:
Coarse-grained salt

To serve:
½ cup freshly grated Parmigiano

Prepare the sauce first. Soak the mushrooms in a bowl of lukewarm water for about 30 minutes. Drain the mushrooms and be sure that no sand is still attached to the stems. Set them aside until needed.

Cover the bottom of a heavy aluminum, stainless steel, or enamel saucepan with the sliced *pancetta*. Place the veal shoulder and the chicken drumstick on top of the *pancetta*. Distribute the carrots over the meat. Add the sliced onion and the celery. Sprinkle with salt and pepper to taste. Pour the oil over the vegetables and add the butter and the clove. Cover the pan with its lid and cook over medium heat for about 25 minutes. At that time the *pancetta* and meat should be golden brown. Add the wine, reserved mushrooms, and tomato paste. Cover again and let the wine evaporate for about 15 minutes. Bring the broth to a boil in a separate pan. Add the broth to the saucepan with the meat and simmer, covered, for at least 5 hours.

Remove and discard the bones from the chicken drumstick and pass all the meats and the sauce through a food mill into a crockery bowl, trying to extract as much liquid from the meats as possible. Cool the sauce for about 1 hour. Then cover and refrigerate overnight. The following day, remove the solid fat that has formed on top of the sauce.

Bring a large pot of water to a boil. Add coarse-grained salt to taste. Add the pasta and cook it for 9 minutes.

Meanwhile, heat the prepared sauce in a large casserole over medium heat. Drain the pasta and add it to the sauce. Stir with a wooden spoon until the sauce is almost completely absorbed by the pasta and pasta is cooked *al dente* (about 5 minutes). Transfer the pasta to a warmed serving dish. Sprinkle with the Parmigiano and serve immediately.

Penne Strascicate alla Fiorentina

PENNE STIR-SAUTÉED IN MEAT

1 recipe for the meat sauce from the recipe for
    Pasticcio di pasta *(page 193)*
1 pound dried penne, *preferably imported Italian*

SERVES 4 TO 6

To cook the pasta:
Coarse-grained salt

To serve:
½ cup freshly grated Parmigiana

Prepare the meat sauce with the ingredients and procedures given in the recipe.

Cook the pasta following the directions on page 181. Then sauté it in the sauce following the directions given in last paragraph of *Penne strascicate al sugo di vitella* (page 191).

Pasticcio di Pasta

BAKED PASTA MOLD

FROM ALL OVER ITALY

The *Pasticcio di pasta*, an attractive baked mold, is the most formal presentation for a dried pasta dish. The name *pasticcio* here refers to the crust formed in the baking by the pasta, an analogy to the real presentation crust used in the *pasticci* of meat, etc. (see chapter 14). The old traditional meat sauce used in this recipe (a variety of meat sauces are used for the dish depending on the region of Italy) has the meat snipped rather than chopped or ground. In the old Italian dishes called *paste pasticciate* the *maccheroni* were baked without being cooked first. The result was a substantial though somewhat heavy dish. In the modern method of partially precooking the pasta by boiling, the dish is lightened considerably while retaining its rich flavor. This is a delicious and impressive first course using the easily obtainable dried spaghetti.

For the sauce: SERVES 12
1 pound boneless beef sirloin, in one piece
2 Italian sweet sausages without fennel seeds (about 6 ounces), or 6 ounces finely ground pork
4 ounces prosciutto, *in one piece*
1 large carrot
1 medium-sized red onion
1 leek, or 1 medium-sized red onion
1 clove garlic, peeled
10 sprigs Italian parsley, leaves only
1 celery stalk
Small piece of lemon peel
¼ cup olive oil
4 tablespoons sweet butter
1 cup dry red wine
1 pound fresh plum tomatoes, or 2 cups drained canned imported Italian tomatoes
Salt and freshly ground black pepper
About 2 cups hot chicken or beef broth
2 pounds dried spaghetti

Plus:
3 extra large eggs
½ cup freshly grated Parmigiano
Freshly grated nutmeg
About ¼ cup unseasoned bread crumbs, preferably homemade
2 tablespoons sweet butter, cut into pieces

To cook the pasta:
Coarse-grained salt

Prepare the sauce first.

1. Use a scissors to snip the beef sirloin into tiny pieces.

Remove the skin from the sausages and cut the *prosciutto* into small cubes. Finely chop the carrot, onion, leek, garlic, parsley, celery, and lemon peel together on a board. Heat the olive oil and butter in a flameproof casserole, preferably terra-cotta, over medium heat. When the butter is completely melted, add the *prosciutto* and sauté for 2 minutes. Then add the chopped ingredients and sauté, stirring occasionally, until the onion is translucent (about 15 minutes). Add the sausages and beef and sauté for 10 minutes longer. Add the wine and let it evaporate very slowly (about 10 minutes).

Meanwhile, pass the tomatoes through a food mill and add them to casserole. Taste for salt and pepper.

Cover the casserole and simmer for about 2 hours, adding the hot broth as needed.

Transfer the sauce to a large crockery bowl and let it stand until cool (about 1 hour). The cool sauce should be of medium thickness, neither too liquid nor too dense.

Bring a large pot of cold water to a boil. Add coarse-grained salt to taste. Cook the pasta for about 10 minutes (it should be almost *al dente*, but not that tender, because it will be baked later). Drain the pasta in a colander and rinse it under cold running water until it is completely cold. Drain the pasta well and transfer it to a large bowl. Add the eggs and the Parmigiano to the cold pasta and mix very well.

2. Pour the cold meat sauce over the pasta

3. and toss the pasta very well.

Sprinkle a little nutmeg over the pasta.

Butter a 12-inch springform pan and sprinkle it with the bread crumbs.

Preheat the oven to 375 degrees.

4. Transfer the pasta to the prepared springform pan.

5. Distribute the pieces of butter over the top of the pasta.

Place the springform pan in the oven and bake for about 40 minutes. Remove the *pasticcio* from the oven.

6. Open the springform pan and transfer the *pasticcio* to a large serving dish, removing the bottom of the springform pan. Serve immediately, slicing like a cake.

Insalate di Pasta

PASTA SALADS

Cold pasta salads are popular for fresh summer eating all over southern Italy. However, they are never made with *maionese* (mayonnaise): Pasta and *maionese* are never combined in Italy. Some types of so-called *pasta corta* (short pasta), such as *rigatoni*, *penne rigate*, *viti* or spirals, *chiocciole*, or even the large (not the small) elbow macaroni, are used.

When the pasta is to be used cold, it must be cooked in a different way. First, the amount of salt for the cooking should be doubled, as some salt is washed away when the pasta is rinsed. Then a little olive oil is added to the cooking water because it is rinsed, and used cold, with a cold sauce. (Oil should not be used when the pasta is to be eaten hot.) And finally, the pasta is rinsed under cold water. (Pasta should never be rinsed under water, hot or cold, when it is to be eaten hot.)

The salad always includes other ingredients, such as fresh or cooled cooked vegetables, cold fish, and such piquant additions as capers in wine vinegar, peppers in wine vinegar, olives, anchovies, etc. The dressing is always simply good uncooked olive oil or the sauce formed by cooking vegetables in oil and herbs, always with a little lemon juice added at the end.

Following are three pasta salads from different parts of southern Italy. The ingredients, though found all over Italy, are particularly delectable in the South.

The first, from Puglia, is flavored with peppers in wine vinegar, anchovies, capers, and a little fresh tomato. The second, from Sicily, resembles the first, but uses tuna in place of the peppers and anchovies. The third, another from Puglia, has a sauce made with wine and pieces of fresh cold fish.

HOW TO COOK DRIED PASTA FOR PASTA SALAD

Bring a large pot of water to a boil. [Use 4 to 6 quarts (16 to 24 cups) of water and 4 tablespoons of coarse-grained salt (twice the amount used for other dried pasta dishes), for each pound of pasta.] Add coarse-grained salt and 1 tablespoon oil. Add the pasta and stir with a wooden spoon to be sure the pasta does not stick together. Cover the pot to bring the water back to a boil as quickly as possible. When the water is boiling again, remove the lid and cook the pasta until *al dente*. Remove the pot from the heat and place it under cold running water. Keep the water running until the pasta is cold. Drain the pasta in a large colander and transfer it to a serving dish or bowl. Then dress the pasta according to the directions in the individual recipes.

Insalata di Pasta I

PASTA SALAD WITH PEPPERS AND ANCHOVIES

FROM PUGLIA

SERVES 6

3 whole anchovies in salt, or 6 anchovy fillets in oil, drained
3 sweet peppers, red or yellow, in wine vinegar, drained
3 tablespoons capers in wine vinegar, drained
1 cup olive oil
½ teaspoon red pepper flakes
Salt and freshly ground black pepper
1 pound ripe, but not overripe, tomatoes
½ tablespoon lemon juice

To cook the pasta:
About 4 tablespoons coarse-grained salt
1 tablespoon olive oil or vegetable oil
1 pound dried "short" pasta, such as imported Italian rigatoni, penne rigate, chiocciole, *etc.*

If using the anchovies in salt, fillet them under cold running water (page 55). Finely chop the anchovy fillets on a board and put them in a crockery bowl. Cut the peppers into thin strips and add them to the bowl along with the capers, olive oil, red pepper flakes, and salt and pepper to taste. Mix very well and let stand until needed.

Cook the pasta according to the directions on page 196. While the pasta is cooking, cut the tomatoes into 1-inch cubes. Drain the pasta and transfer it to a large bowl. Pour the sauce and the lemon juice over the pasta and toss very well. Transfer the pasta to a large serving dish and distribute the tomato cubes throughout. Toss again and serve, or wrap in foil and refrigerate until needed.

Insalata di Pasta II

PASTA SALAD WITH TUNA

FROM SICILY

SERVES 6

For the sauce:
½ pound large black Greek olives in brine, drained
7 ounces canned tuna in olive oil, drained
4 tablespoons capers in wine vinegar, drained
1 cup olive oil
Salt and freshly ground black pepper
1 pound fresh ripe, but not overripe, tomatoes

For the pasta:
About 4 tablespoons coarse-grained salt
1 tablespoon olive oil or vegetable oil
1 pound dried "short" pasta, such as imported Italian rigatoni, penne rigate, chiocciole,
   etc.
½ tablespoon lemon juice

Pit the olives and cut them into pieces. Break the tuna into pieces. Put the olives, tuna, capers, and olive oil into a small bowl. Sprinkle with salt and pepper to taste. Mix well.

Cook the pasta according to the directions on page 196.

While the pasta is cooking, cut the tomatoes into 1-inch cubes. Drain the pasta and transfer it to a large bowl. Pour the sauce and the lemon juice over the pasta and toss very well. Add the tomato cubes, toss again, and serve, or wrap in foil and refrigerate until needed.

Insalata di Pasta III

PASTA SALAD WITH SWORDFISH

FROM SICILY

SERVES 6

½ pound large black Greek olives in brine, drained
About 40 sprigs Italian parsley, leaves only
3 large cloves garlic, peeled
½ cup olive oil
1½ pounds fresh swordfish, in slices about 1 inch thick
1 cup dry white wine
1 scant teaspoon red pepper flakes
Salt and freshly ground black pepper

For the pasta:

About 4 tablespoons coarse-grained salt

1 tablespoon olive oil or vegetable oil

1 pound dried "short" pasta, such as imported Italian rigatoni, penne, penne rigate, chiocciole, *etc.*

½ tablespoon lemon juice

Pit the olives and cut them into pieces.

Finely chop about half of the parsley and the garlic together on a board.

Heat the oil in a skillet over medium heat. When the oil is hot, add the chopped ingredients. Sauté lightly for 1 minute. Then add the fish slices and sauté for 3 minutes on each side. Add the wine and the olives to the skillet. Sprinkle with the red pepper flakes and salt and pepper to taste. Let the wine evaporate over low heat for 10 minutes.

Remove the skillet from the heat and transfer the fish to a board. Use a fork to break the fish into 1-inch cubes. Discard all the bones and skin and return the fish cubes to the skillet. Taste for salt and pepper. Return to the heat and cook over low heat for 5 minutes longer, then transfer the sauce to a crockery bowl. Let cool completely, then cover the bowl with aluminum foil, and refrigerate for at least 1 hour.

Cook the pasta according to the directions on page 196.

Meanwhile, coarsely chop the remaining parsley. Drain the pasta and transfer it to a large bowl. Pour the cooled sauce and the lemon juice over the pasta and toss very well. Transfer the pasta to a large serving dish, sprinkle with the chopped parsley, and serve, or wrap in foil and refrigerate until needed.

A Variety of Dried Pasta

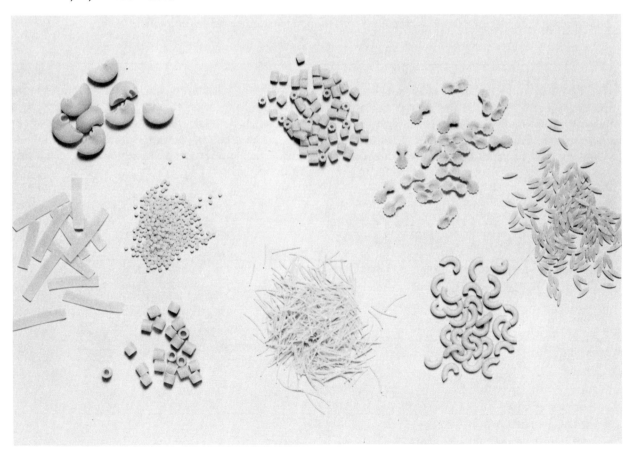

CHAPTER 8

Risotti and Polenta

TECHNIQUES FOR PREPARING RICE AND POLENTA

The type of rice preferred in Italy is the Po valley Arborio type. It is available in the United States at ethnic Italian markets and gourmet shops. There are three different ways of cooking rice in Italy, depending on the dish to be made. In the *risotto* method of cooking, illustrated by the recipe for *Risotto alle quaglie* (Risotto with Quail), on page 200, the raw rice is sautéed and liquid is added in small quantities as needed, until the rice is cooked *al dente*. In a real *risotto*, the grains of rice can be bitten into, while the outside of the rice is very creamy.

Risotto spread from Lombardy and the Veneto throughout all of Italy, but is probably more frequently found in the North. In the following pages are a sampling of the vast number of such dishes, drawing from different regions. From Lucca there is the rosemary-flavored *risotto* using red wine. The rice mold stuffed with squab, from Parma, is made with rice cooked in the *risotto* manner. This differs from the other famous rice mold, the Apennine mountain *Timballo* (or *Bomba*) *di riso*, stuffed with sausages and wild mushrooms, found in my first book, in that the rice in that recipe is cooked in the second classic way, starting in cold water so that the crust will form easier.

In the third manner of cooking, the rice is poured into already boiling water, which absorbs much of the starch and lightens the rice. This is the normal method used for *Riso bollito* (Boiled Rice), for rice salads and *Riso in bianco*, simple boiled rice dressed with oil or butter and cheese. The Abruzzese version of the summer rice salad on page 205 has its own regional combination of ingredients, differing from those of other areas. A variety of summer vegetables, such as zucchini, eggplant, pepper, cucumber, and tomato are used, but not meat or fish.

The method for preparing polenta is illustrated on pages 206–207. Polenta is always a hearty dish, generally eaten in the fall and winter, and usually is combined with full-flavored mushrooms, game, or rich meats. A cornmeal adaptation in recent centuries of the diverse coarse grains that were sustenance for many throughout the history of the Mediterranean, polenta exists today all over Italy. The ancient version with coarse wheat flour or semolina is still used in couscous dishes made today in Livorno and other places.

Barley flour polenta, once eaten, now exists mainly as a hot plaster for treating colds. Of the hundreds of such polenta dishes, included here is one from Pistoia with sausages and quail and another from the mountainous Casentino area in the Apennines.

Instructions for cutting polenta for fried canapés are given on page 209, followed by a delicious wild mushroom paste spread on them.

And finally there is a polenta mixed with ricotta and chocolate in a pudding-like baked dessert cake which can easily become an addiction.

Risotto alle Quaglie

RISOTTO WITH QUAIL

FROM VENICE

SERVES 6

For the sauce:
6 quail
6 ounces pancetta, or 3 ounces boiled ham and 3 ounces salt pork
1 tablespoon rosemary leaves, fresh or preserved in salt
3 tablespoons sweet butter
Salt and freshly ground black pepper
½ cup olive oil
½ cup dry white wine
About 1 cup hot beef or chicken broth

For the *risotto:*
1 medium-sized red onion
About 4 cups beef or chicken broth
2 cups raw rice, preferably Italian Arborio
1 tablespoon sweet butter
3 tablespoons grated Parmigiano
Salt and freshly ground black pepper

Clean the quail very well and dry them with paper towels. Sprinkle a little salt and pepper inside each quail.

Cut the *pancetta* into small pieces and finely chop the rosemary on a board.

Heat the butter and oil in a flameproof casserole over medium heat. When the butter is completely melted, add the prepared ingredients. Sauté very lightly and add the quail. Sprinkle with salt and pepper and sauté on all sides for about 10 minutes. Then add the wine and let it evaporate over very low heat (about 15 minutes). Add the broth, cover the pan and simmer for about 25 minutes, or until the quail are cooked. Let the quail stand covered until needed.

HOW TO PREPARE RISOTTO

Finely chop the onion on a board. Ladle off half of the quail sauce into a second casserole, preferably of terra-cotta or enamel. Put it over medium heat, and, when the sauce is warm, add the chopped onion. Sauté until translucent (about 5 minutes).

Heat the broth to the boiling point in a separate pan. Add the rice to the casserole with the sautéed onion and,

1. sauté for about 4 minutes, stirring constantly with a wooden spoon.

2. Then start adding the hot broth, about ½ cup at a time, always stirring.

Do not add more broth until that previously added is completely absorbed. When all the broth has been incorporated (16 to 18 minutes), the rice should be cooked *al dente*—not soft and mushy.* Heat the quail in the remaining sauce. Remove the casserole with the *risotto* from the heat and stir in the butter with wooden spoon.

* If you double the recipe, add 2 or 3 minutes to the cooking time for the *risotto*.

3. Transfer the *risotto* to a serving dish. (When it is properly prepared, *risotto* should be completely detached from the casserole.)

4. Make a well in the center of the *risotto* and place the quail and the sauce in it. Sprinkle with Parmigiano and serve immediately.

Risotto alla Parmigiana

RISOTTO IN THE STYLE OF PARMA

FROM PARMA

SERVES 6

For the sauce:
1 ounce dried porcini mushrooms
1 large carrot
1 celery stalk
1 medium-sized red onion
10 sprigs Italian parsley, leaves only
4 tablespoons olive oil
8 tablespoons (1 stick) sweet butter
1 cup drained canned imported Italian tomatoes
4 ounces chicken livers
2 Italian sweet sausages without fennel seeds (about 6 ounces),
or 6 ounces ground pork
5 cups hot beef or chicken broth
Salt and freshly ground black pepper

For the *risotto:*
1 celery stalk
1 medium-sized carrot
2 cups raw rice, preferably Italian Arborio
About 3 cups hot beef or chicken broth
Salt and freshly ground black pepper
½ cup freshly grated Parmigiano

Prepare the sauce. Soak the dried mushrooms in a small bowl of lukewarm water for about 30 minutes.

Meanwhile, finely chop the carrot, celery, onion, and parsley together on a board.

Heat the olive oil and butter in a large casserole over medium heat. When butter is completely melted, add the chopped ingredients and sauté until lightly golden (3 to 5 minutes).

Pass the tomatoes through a food mill and add them to the casserole. Cut the chicken livers into 4 pieces each and remove the skin from the sausages. Add the livers and sausages to the casserole along with the hot broth. Simmer for about 40 minutes, stirring occasionally.

Drain the mushrooms and add them to casserole.

Simmer for 40 minutes longer. Taste for salt and pepper. A thick sauce should have formed (about 2 cups).

Prepare the *risotto.* Coarsely chop the celery and carrot together on a board. Add chopped ingredients to the sauce and cook for about 5 minutes. Then add the rice and sauté it in the sauce for 5 minutes longer. Begin to add the hot broth, a small quantity at a time, always stirring. Do not add more broth until the previously added broth is completely absorbed. Taste again for salt and pepper.

When the *risotto* is ready, remove the casserole from the heat and stir in ¼ cup of the Parmigiano with a wooden spoon. Transfer the *risotto* to a serving dish. Sprinkle with the remaining Parmigiano and serve immediately.

28. Rosmarino Domestico (*Domestic Rosemary*)

Risotto al Ramerino

RISOTTO WITH ROSEMARY

FROM LUCCA

SERVES 6

1 *heaping tablespoon rosemary leaves, fresh or preserved in salt*
   or dried and blanched
1 *clove garlic, peeled*
2 *tablespoons sweet butter*
5 *tablespoons olive oil*
4 *cups beef broth*
½ *cup dry red wine*
2 *cups raw rice, preferably Italian Arborio*
Salt and freshly ground black pepper

Finely chop the rosemary and garlic together on a board. Heat the butter and oil in a flameproof casserole over medium heat. When the butter is completely melted, add the chopped ingredients and sauté lightly for about 2 minutes. Meanwhile, heat the broth to boiling point in a separate saucepan. Add the wine to the casserole and let it evaporate for about 5 minutes. Then add the rice and sauté for about 4 minutes.

Start adding the broth a small quantity at a time, each time stirring gently until the rice has absorbed the broth (16 to 18 minutes).* When all the broth has been absorbed, taste for salt and pepper. Transfer the *risotto* to a serving dish and serve immediately with a twist of black pepper over each serving.

* If you double the recipe, add 2 or 3 minutes to the cooking time for the *risotto*.

Timballo (*or* Bomba) di Riso alla Parmigiana

RICE TIMBALLO STUFFED WITH SQUAB

FROM PARMA

SERVES 8

For the stuffing:
2 squab
1 medium-sized carrot
1 medium-sized red onion
4 sage leaves, fresh or preserved in salt
4 ounces (1 stick) sweet butter
1 tablespoon olive oil
Salt and freshly ground black pepper
About 1 cup chicken broth

For the *risotto*:
1 small carrot
1 medium-sized red onion
4 ounces (1 stick) sweet butter
1 tablespoon olive oil
3 cups raw rice, preferably Arborio type
About 6 cups hot chicken or beef broth
Salt and freshly ground black pepper

Plus:
About 1 tablespoon sweet butter (for heavy buttering of pan)
4 tablespoons unseasoned bread crumbs, preferably homemade
4 tablespoons freshly grated Parmigiano
2 extra large egg yolks
Pinch of freshly grated nutmeg

Wash the squab carefully and cut them into quarters. Finely chop the carrot, onion, and sage leaves together on a board. Heat the butter and oil in a flameproof saucepan over medium heat. When the butter is completely melted, add the chopped ingredients and sauté lightly until pale golden brown (about 10 minutes). Add the squab pieces and sprinkle them with salt and pepper. Sauté for about 10 minutes. Then start adding the broth as needed, until the squab is completely cooked (about 20 minutes). Transfer the contents of the saucepan to a bowl and cool completely.

Finely chop the carrot and onion together on a board. Heat the butter and oil in a flameproof casserole over medium heat. When the butter is completely melted, add the chopped ingredients. Sauté gently until the onion is translucent (about 10 minutes), then add the rice. Sauté for 4 minutes, stirring constantly with a wooden spoon. Then start adding the hot broth about ½ cup at a time, stirring constantly. Do not add extra broth until that previously added is completely absorbed. When all the broth has been absorbed (16 to 18 minutes), the rice should be cooked *al dente*, but with a creamy texture.* Taste for salt and pepper. Transfer the rice to a crockery bowl and let stand for 10 minutes.

Preheat oven to 375 degrees. Heavily butter a 13½- x 8¾-inch baking dish with the butter. Coat it with 3 tablespoons of the bread crumbs. Add the grated Parmigiano, egg yolks, and nutmeg to the bowl with the rice and mix thoroughly with a wooden spoon. Cover the bottom of the baking dish with half of the rice and place the squab pieces on top. Pour the sauce over the squab and cover with the remaining rice. Sprinkle the remaining bread crumbs over the rice and bake for about 20 minutes. Serve immediately.

* If you double the recipe, add 2 to 3 minutes to the cooking time.

"Insalata" di Riso Estiva

SUMMER RICE SALAD

Cold rice salads are extremely popular as summer dishes in Italy. This one takes advantage of the fresh vegetables and herbs of the season, set off by a light dressing.

Coarse-grained salt
2 cups raw rice, preferably Italian Arborio
2 lemons
3 medium-sized zucchini
1 medium-sized eggplant
Salt and freshly ground black pepper
6 tablespoons olive oil
1 green medium-sized pepper
1 very small cucumber
2 medium-sized ripe (but not overripe) tomatoes
About 5 large fresh basil leaves

SERVES 8

For the sauce:
1 clove garlic, peeled
1 lemon
5 tablespoons olive oil
Salt and freshly ground black pepper

Bring a large pot of cold water to a boil. Add coarse-grained salt to taste. Add the rice, stir with a wooden spoon, and cook until the rice is *al dente* (about 16 minutes). Drain the rice in a colander and cool it under cold running water. Drain the rice again and put it on a large serving dish. Squeeze the lemon and pour the juice into the rice. Mix well with a wooden spoon. Cover the dish with aluminum foil.

Clean the zucchini, cutting off the ends. Cut each into 1-inch cubes. Boil the zucchini in salted water for about 10 minutes, then drain and place them on a plate until cool.

Cut the eggplant into (do not peel it) 1-inch cubes. Heat the oil in a small saucepan. When the oil is hot, add the eggplant pieces. Sprinkle with a little salt and pepper. Sauté the eggplant until soft (about 20 minutes), stirring occasionally with a wooden spoon. Transfer the eggplant to a small bowl and let it cool.

Singe the green pepper on all sides by leaning it against a pot of water boiling on the stove. When singed, remove the skin, inside seeds, and ribs under cold running water. Cut the pepper into thin strips and add them to the rice without mixing.

Peel and slice the cucumber very thin and add it to the serving dish.

Cut the tomatoes into 1-inch cubes and add them to the serving dish.

Prepare the sauce. Rub a small crockery bowl with the peeled garlic. Squeeze the lemon and add juice to the bowl. Then add the oil and salt and pepper to taste. Mix with a wooden spoon for about 2 minutes, using a rotating motion.

Add the cooled zucchini and eggplant to the serving dish. Pour the sauce over them. Mix gently but very well. Tear the basil leaves into 2 or 3 pieces and sprinkle them over the salad. The dish may be served immediately or refrigerated and served after several hours. If refrigerating it, cover the dish with aluminum foil to prevent it from drying out.

Polenta

A little over 2 quarts cold water
1½ teaspoons coarse-grained salt
½ pound coarse or stone-ground yellow cornmeal
½ pound regular finely ground yellow cornmeal

Bring the cold water to a boil in a large pot. When the water reaches the boiling point, add the salt. Mix the two types of cornmeal together and begin adding the cornmeal to the boiling salted water.

HOW TO PREPARE POLENTA

1. Pour the cornmeal in a very slow stream, simultaneously stirring with a wooden spoon (the flat wooden polenta spoon).

Be sure to pour the cornmeal slowly and steadily and to keep stirring, otherwise the polenta can easily become very lumpy. Stir slowly, without stopping, for about 40 to 50 minutes, from the point when all the cornmeal was added to the pot.

2. If some lumps form, push them against the side of the pot to crush them.

If the polenta is to be used as an appetizer (deep-fried or baked) or to prepare *crostini* (small canapés), prepare a smooth surface of marble by wetting it with cold water (or spread aluminum foil shiny side up over any work surface, and wet that). When the polenta is cooked, taste for salt and leave it over the heat without stirring,

3. but scraping it, with the wooden spoon, from the sides of the pot. In this way some steam will form under the polenta and it will completely detach from the bottom of the pot. After 3 minutes

4. quickly turn the polenta out onto a marble surface, if it is to be deep fried or baked or made into *crostini* (see page 209).

Spread the polenta out with a spatula (wet in cold water first) to a ½-inch thickness (see *Crostini di polenta*, page 210).

If serving the polenta immediately, quickly turn it out into a large serving dish.

Polenta alla Pistoiese

POLENTA WITH SAUSAGES AND QUAIL IN THE STYLE OF PISTOIA

FROM PISTOIA, NEAR FLORENCE IN TUSCANY

SERVES 8

For the sauce:
2 ounces dried porcini *mushrooms*
4 medium-sized leeks, cleaned (see page 388) or 4 medium-sized red onions
1 medium-sized red onion
½ cup olive oil
4 tablespoons sweet butter
8 quail
8 thin slices pancetta *(or substitute boiled ham)*
16 Italian sweet sausages without fennel seeds (about 3 pounds)
½ cup dry red wine
5 tablespoons tomato paste
2 cups drained canned imported Italian tomatoes
Salt and freshly ground black pepper
About 2 cups hot chicken or beef broth

For the polenta:
4 quarts chicken broth
1 pound coarse or stone-ground yellow cornmeal
1 pound regular finely ground yellow cornmeal
Salt to taste

Soak the dried mushrooms in a bowl of lukewarm water for about 30 minutes.

Finely chop the leeks and onion together on a board.

Heat the olive oil and butter in a saucepan. When the butter is completely melted, add the chopped ingredients and sauté over medium heat for about 15 minutes, stirring occasionally with a wooden spoon.

Wrap each quail with a slice of *pancetta* and fasten with a toothpick. Use a fork to prick the sausages in several places on both sides. When the leek-onion mixture is a very light golden brown, add the quail and sausages and sauté over medium heat for about 15 minutes. Then add the wine and let it evaporate (about 10 minutes). Drain the mushrooms and be sure that no sand remains attached to them. Add the mushrooms to the saucepan. Lower the heat and simmer for about 15 minutes longer.

Pass the tomatoes through a food mill, incorporate the tomato paste, and pour the tomato mixture into the saucepan. Simmer for about 25 minutes. Taste for salt and pepper, and add hot broth as needed. The sauce should be thick and smooth. The quail and sausages should then be ready and the sauce reduced. Let the sauce stand until needed.

Prepare the polenta with the broth and the other ingredients listed above, following the directions on pages 206–207.

When the polenta is almost ready, heat the sauce with the sausages and quail. Quickly reverse the pot of polenta onto a large serving dish. Place the sausages and quail on the polenta and pour the sauce over all. Let stand for a few minutes before serving.

Polenta del Casentino

POLENTA FROM CASENTINO

For the sauce:
2 ounces dried porcini mushrooms
2 large leeks, cleaned or 2 large red onions
3 large celery stalks
2 cloves garlic, peeled
½ cup olive oil
6 Italian sweet sausages, preferably without fennel seeds
About ¼ cup unbleached all-purpose flour
1 veal shank with bone and marrow (1½ inches thick)
1 cup dry red wine
2 cups fresh tomatoes or drained canned imported Italian tomatoes
5 tablespoons tomato paste
Salt and freshly ground black pepper
About 1 cup beef or chicken broth

For the polenta:
A little over 2 quarts cold water
1½ teaspoons coarse-grained salt
½ pound coarse or stone-ground yellow cornmeal
½ pound regular finely ground yellow cornmeal

SERVES 6

First prepare the sauce. Soak the dried mushrooms in a bowl of lukewarm water for about 30 minutes. Meanwhile, finely chop the leeks, celery, and garlic together on a board. Heat the olive oil in a saucepan over medium heat. When it is hot, add the chopped ingredients and sauté over medium heat, stirring every so often with a wooden spoon, until lightly golden brown (about 15 minutes). Prick the sausages in several places with a fork and flour the veal shank on both sides. Add the sausages and veal shank to the saucepan and sauté lightly for 3 or 4 minutes. Then add the wine and let it evaporate (about 10 minutes). Pass the tomatoes through a food mill and add them to the saucepan along with the tomato paste. Cook for 5 minutes. Drain the mushrooms and be sure that no sand remains attached to them. Add the mushrooms to the sauce. Taste for salt and pepper and simmer, uncovered, for about 1 hour, adding broth as needed. The texture should be smooth but thick.

Prepare the polenta with the ingredients listed above, following the directions on pages 206–207. When the polenta is ready, turn it out onto a large serving dish. Pour the sauce and sausages over the polenta and serve it hot.

HOW TO CUT POLENTA (for *crostini* as an appetizer)

When the polenta is cold, you can cut it for different uses. (Polenta must be cooled first for at least 3 hours. Cover it with aluminum foil if you wish to refrigerate it and then cut it on another day.) It can be kept covered in the refrigerator for 4 or 5 days.

1. For *crostini:* Use a long knife to cut the polenta into strips ½ inch thick. Then cut the strips into pieces 2½ inches long.

2. To deep-fry or bake, cut polenta into strips ½ inch thick. Then cut the strips into pieces 2½ inches long and 1 inch wide.

Crostini di Polenta

POLENTA CANAPÉS

FROM ROME (DEEP-FRIED)
FROM TUSCAN APENNINES (BAKED)

SERVES 6 TO 8

For the polenta:
2 quarts water
1½ teaspoons coarse-grained salt
½ pound coarse or stone-ground yellow cornmeal
½ pound regular finely ground yellow cornmeal

For the sauce:
4 ounces dried porcini *mushrooms*
1 large red onion
1 small clove garlic
⅓ cup olive oil
½ cup dry red wine
1 tablespoon tomato paste
1 cup hot beef broth
Salt and freshly ground black pepper

Prepare the polenta with the ingredients listed above, following the directions on pages 206–207. Oil or wet a smooth surface of marble and, when the polenta is ready, unmold it on to the surface. Then spread it out with a wet spatula until it is uniformly ½ inch thick. Let the polenta cool at least 3 hours.

Prepare the sauce. Soak the mushrooms in a bowl of lukewarm water for about 30 minutes.

Finely chop the onion and garlic together on a board.

Heat the oil in a saucepan over medium heat. When the oil is hot, add the chopped ingredients and sauté for 10 minutes.

Meanwhile, drain the mushrooms and be sure that no sand remains attached to them.

Finely chop the mushrooms and add them to the saucepan with the onions. Sauté for 5 minutes longer. Add the wine and let it evaporate for about 15 minutes.

Dissolve the tomato paste in the broth and add the mixture to the saucepan. Taste for salt and pepper and simmer for about 25 to 30 minutes, or until a thick, smooth paste is formed. Remove the pan from the heat and let stand until needed.

Cut the polenta into pieces (page 209). Polenta pieces may be shaped into *crostini* and cooked in one of the following ways:

1. They can be deep-fried in olive oil or a mixture of solid vegetable shortening and lard until golden brown. While frying, turn once to brown on both sides.

2. They can be baked in a buttered pan in a 375-degree oven for 20 minutes, topped with pieces of butter or slices of a soft cheese. (At this temperature, the cheese will not brown and turn bitter.)

The sauce should be reheated and spread over the *crostini* at the last moment.

Sformato Dolce di Polenta

POLENTA CHEESECAKE

4½ cups milk
Pinch of salt
¾ cup coarse or stone-ground yellow cornmeal
¾ cup regular finely ground yellow cornmeal
½ cup raisins
15 ounces ricotta
½ cup granulated sugar
Grated rind of 1 lemon
Pinch of ground cinnamon
3 extra large eggs
¼ cup semisweet chocolate chips

SERVES 8

Prepare the polenta with the milk, salt, and cornmeal listed above, following the directions on pages 206–207.

Soak raisins in a bowl of lukewarm water for about 30 minutes.

Combine the ricotta and sugar in a large bowl and mix very well with a wooden spoon. When the polenta is ready, incorporate it immediately into the bowl with the ricotta-sugar mixture. Stir very well so that no lumps form and a very smooth and thick "batter" is formed. Drain the raisins, dry them on a paper towel, and add to the bowl. Add the grated lemon rind and the cinnamon to bowl. Mix well.

Add the eggs, one at a time, mixing thoroughly with a wooden spoon in order to prevent the eggs from coagulating. Then add the chocolate chips to the bowl.

Preheat oven to 375 degrees.

Butter an 8½- x 4½- x 2½-inch loaf pan. Transfer the batter to the pan and place it in the oven. Bake for 1 hour. Remove from the oven, unmold onto a rack and cool for at least ½ hour. Then transfer to a serving plate. This dish can be eaten lukewarm or at room temperature after several hours. (If any leftover cake is refrigerated, let it warm to room temperature before eating.)

CHAPTER 9

Some Special Methods of Cooking
(Meats, Poultry, Fish and Legumes)

COOKING IN CLAY

This ancient method of cooking was known to the Etruscans who were associated with the area near Siena. The "crete," the clay from which the cooking vessels are made, was composed of the famous Siena red soil. In fact, that area is sometimes called "Le crete." Whether these vessels were introduced to the Etruscans from the island of Crete (*Creta* in Italian) is not known, but it seems possible.

The clay vessels are fire-resistant and may originally have been put right into the fire with the food to be cooked inside. Now they are generally placed over the heat, with a flame-tamer, if glazed, or in the oven, if unglazed. Cooking this way seals in the flavor of the food itself and gives what the Italians call "a soft, round" flavor.

The following photographs illustrate the traditional forms of clay vessels used for different foods.

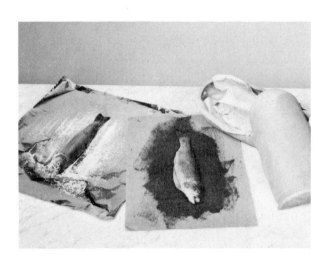

1. The long rounded shape used to cook fish, mainly whole fish. (Trout is used most often.) A sheet of brown paper or aluminum foil is first lightly oiled and then the fish (about 1 pound) is placed on it and sprinkled with salt, pepper, and a few drops of lemon juice. The fish is wrapped up and placed in the vessel, which is then closed tightly. The vessel is placed in a 375-degree oven for 35 minutes.

2. Two clay vessels for cooking chicken. The round one in front is the famous traditional container for making *Pollo al mattone* (Whole Chicken Cooked Between Terra-cotta) which follows. In two pieces, the bottom is a glazed clay plate and the top is an extremely heavy unglazed lid, which is called *mattone* after the word for a heavy brick. First the *mattone* is placed over a flame for a long time until it has absorbed a great deal of heat. While the *mattone* is heating, the whole chicken is split so that it lies flat on the bottom "plate," and is seasoned with coarse-grained salt, pepper, and a sprig of rosemary. Then the *mattone* is placed on top of the chicken, weighting it down. The chicken, sandwiched between the two clay pieces, is placed over medium heat to cook for about 45 minutes. It is turned twice during this time by the *mattone* being lifted off and set aside. After cooking, the chicken is crisp on the outside and very juicy throughout.

The two pieces at the right are the halves of a larger rounded vessel, deeper, but not as long as the one for fish shown above. The chicken is simply sprinkled with salt and pepper and wrapped in a sheet of unoiled brown paper. The wrapped chicken is placed in the vessel which is then closed tightly. The vessel is placed in a 375-degree oven for 1½ hours, for a chicken weighing about 3½ pounds. (Cooking time is 40 minutes a pound.)

In the back, at the left of the photo is the traditional shape of *creta* for baking beans in the oven. It is called a *fagioliera*. The recipe for *Fagioli al forno* (Baked Cannellini Beans) is:

1 pound dried cannellini *beans*
2 ounces pancetta, or 1 ounce boiled ham and 1 ounce
  salt pork cut in small pieces
¼ cup olive oil
2 cloves garlic, peeled
3 or 4 whole black peppercorns
5 or 6 sage leaves, fresh or preserved in salt
Salt and freshly ground black pepper to taste

First soak the dried beans overnight in water to cover to tenderize them. Drain the beans. Preheat oven to 375 degrees. Transfer the beans to the *fagioliera* and add all the seasonings and enough water to cover them. Cover the pot and bake for about 2 hours.

In June, when the fresh beans are in season in Italy, a great treat is to have them in this manner, unsoaked and baked for a maximum of 45 minutes. This serves 6 to 8.

3. The same three vessels, closed and ready for cooking.

AL CARTOCCIO OR COOKING IN A PAPER BAG

One of the basic techniques of cooking a game bird or anything with dry meat or meat that may easily dry out in cooking is to keep the juices in by sealing the meat. The picturesque old method was to oil a brown paper bag and enclose the meat in it, so that the meat would remain juicy. The paper bag has been largely replaced by the invention of aluminum foil, but I have found the result is not quite the same for some dishes.* Guinea hen (and pheasant) are undoubtedly more succulent when cooked in the old way. The guinea hen recipe, *Faraona al cartoccio* (Guinea Hen Cooked in a Paper Bag), also uses caul fat to wrap the bird before it is placed in the oiled paper. (The caul fat prevents the meat from dripping out in the oven and adds moisture.) The same recipe may be used for cooking *fagiano* (pheasant) as well.

The *Pollo al prosciutto* (Chicken Wrapped in Prosciutto) and *Costine al "Vecchio Molinetto"* (the wrapped rolled stuffed spareribs, preserved from old Parma cooking by Anna of Parma's Vecchio Molinetto restaurant) work perfectly well when wrapped in foil. You may be surprised at the long cooking time of the last two Parmenese dishes, but that is the old style of that great gastronomic city, and when done in the *al cartoccio* method, the result is juicy and quite unlike anything else you have tasted.

Faraona al Cartoccio

GUINEA HEN COOKED IN A PAPER BAG

FROM UMBRIA

1 guinea hen, about 3 pounds   SERVES 4
4 ounces pancetta, *sliced, or 2 ounces boiled ham and 2 ounces salt pork, sliced*
2 cloves garlic, peeled but left whole
Salt and freshly ground pepper to taste
15 sage leaves, fresh or preserved in salt
1 large piece caul fat
About 2 tablespoons olive oil

Clean the guinea hen well and dry it with paper towels. Cut 1 ounce of the *pancetta* into small pieces on a board with a *mezzaluna*.

---

* If you cook with the paper bag, be sure to use only a bag that is *not* made from recycled paper.

1. Stuff the hen with the pieces of *pancetta*, the garlic and 5 sage leaves. Sprinkle the cavity with salt and pepper.

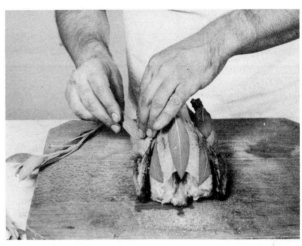

2. Sprinkle the outside of the hen with salt and pepper, and place the remaining sage leaves on top of the hen.

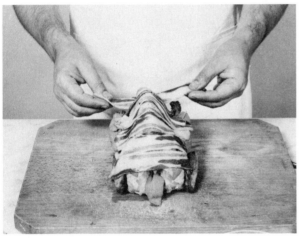

3. Place the remaining slices of *pancetta* over the sage leaves.

4. Put the caul fat in a small saucepan of lukewarm water for 2 or 3 minutes.

5. Transfer the caul fat from the saucepan to a large bowl (catina) of cold water and let stand for about 2 minutes.

6. Remove the caul fat from the bowl and spread it out on the table.

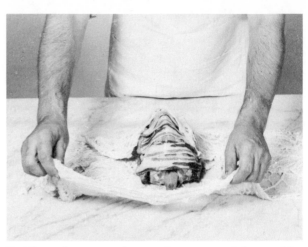

7. Place the guinea hen in the center of the caul fat and

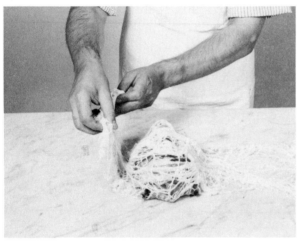

8. wrap the hen completely in the fat. Preheat the oven to 350 degrees.

9. With a brush, oil a non-recycled brown paper bag with the olive oil until it is thoroughly coated.

10. Place the hen inside the bag, and, folding the bag under to close it, transfer it to a baking pan.

Place the pan in the oven and bake for about 1 hour and 10 minutes. Remove from the oven and transfer the bag with the hen to a serving dish.

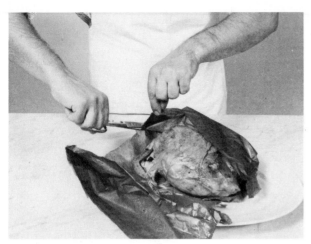

11. Use a scissors to cut the bag open at the table. Cut the hen into quarters with a poultry shears and serve.

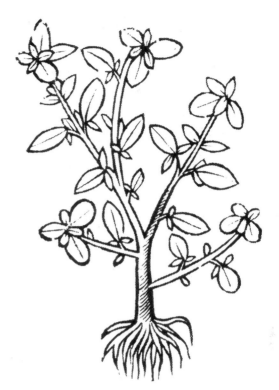

Maggiorana.

29. Maggiorana (*Marjoram*)

Pollo al Prosciutto

CHICKEN WRAPPED IN PROSCIUTTO

FROM PARMA

1 chicken, about 2 pounds
3 tablespoons sweet butter
5 large sage leaves, fresh or preserved in salt
1 teaspoon rosemary leaves, fresh, preserved in salt or dried and blanched
1 teaspoon dried marjoram
1 teaspoon salt
¼ teaspoon freshly ground black pepper
About 1 tablespoon olive oil
8 slices prosciutto (about ½ pound)

SERVES 4

Cut the chicken into 8 pieces (pages 238–240).

Melt the butter in a small saucepan over a pot of boiling water.

Finely chop the sage, rosemary, and marjoram together on a board. Put the chopped ingredients into a small bowl. Add the melted butter and the salt and pepper to the chopped ingredients. Mix very well.

217

HOW TO PREPARE POLLO AL PROSCIUTTO

1. Lay a large sheet of aluminum foil on the table and brush the shiny side with the oil.

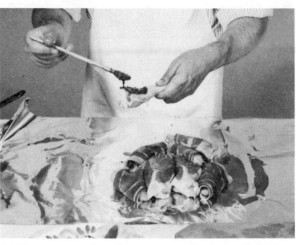

2. Use a pastry brush to coat each piece of chicken with the herb-butter mixture.

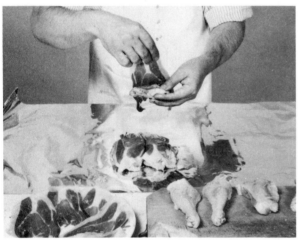

3. Wrap each piece in a slice of *prosciutto*. Place the chicken pieces on the aluminum foil, fitting the whole chicken back together again.

4. Secure the shape by wrapping the chicken the way you make a package.

5. Place the package in a terra-cotta casserole and cover it with its lid.

Place the casserole in a cold oven and turn the oven temperature to 450 degrees. Bake for 1 hour and 45 minutes without opening the casserole. Remove the casserole from the oven and let stand for 5 minutes, then remove the lid.

6. Use a scissors to cut from the center of the foil outward in all four directions, making a cross. Then cut each foil quarter in half.

7. Fold back each of the foil pieces from the center to the side of the casserole,

8. making a flower shape. Serve immediately.

Costine al "Vecchio Molinetto"

SPARERIBS "MOLINETTO" STYLE

FROM PARMA

SERVES 4

4 pounds pork spareribs
4 slices white bread, trimmed of crusts
1 cup cold whole milk
2 Italian sweet sausages (6 ounces) without fennel seeds, or 6 ounces ground pork
1 heaping tablespoon rosemary leaves, fresh or preserved in salt or dried and blanched
Salt and freshly ground black pepper
1 cup heavy cream

Have the butcher cut a 4-pound piece from the front end of the ribs. It is the front end that has a layer of meat on the other side of the bone, which can be used like a pocket for stuffing.

Soak the bread in milk for about 20 minutes.

HOW TO PREPARE COSTINE AL "VECCHIO MOLINETTO"

1. To form a pocket, cut a layer of meat on the underside away from the bone,

2. leaving it attached only at the end. In this position, the layer of spareribs is ready to be stuffed.

To make the stuffing, first remove the skin from the sausages. Squeeze the milk out of the bread and put the bread in a small bowl along with the sausage meat, rosemary, and salt and pepper to taste. Add ½ cup of the cream to the bowl and mix all ingredients together thoroughly with a wooden spoon.

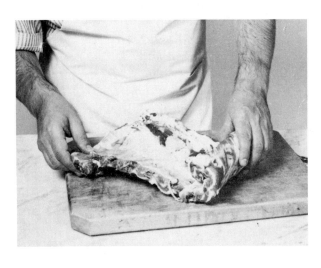

3. Arrange all the stuffing over the spareribs,

4. then fold the layer of meat back in place over the stuffing.

5. Starting from one end, roll up the spareribs

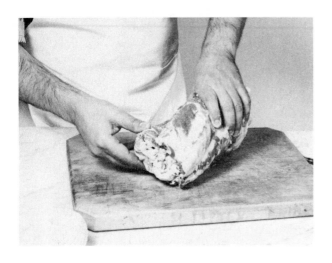

6. to resemble a jelly roll.

Then tie the rolled spareribs like a salami (pages 247–249). Preheat the oven to 400 degrees. Place a large sheet of aluminum foil on a flat surface with the shiny side facing up. Sprinkle the foil with salt and pepper and then place the rolled spareribs on it.

Pour the remaining heavy cream over the meat and bring foil up around the meat,

7. making a closed package.

Place the package in a baking dish. Bake for 2 hours.

8. Remove from the oven, unwrap, and transfer to platter. Let it cool for a few minutes.

Remove the string and cut through at every second rib to make individual servings.

Quaglie in Foglie

QUAIL WRAPPED IN GRAPE LEAVES

FROM TUSCANY

In Italy the hunting season and the harvest of grapes coincide. The result is this marvelous dish in which the quail are cooked wrapped in fresh vine leaves. It is possible to make it using the vine leaves preserved in brine that are widely available at Greek and other stores, but one must be careful to remove the excess salt from the leaves. Even in this form, the dish recalls the autumn feeling when in Italy you simply go into the fields and gather the fresh leaves, obtain your quail from the hunters and make this unforgettable dish.

8 grape leaves, fresh or preserved in brine, stems removed
8 quail, cleaned but left whole
8 sage leaves, fresh or preserved in salt
Salt and freshly ground black pepper
8 slices pancetta, *¹⁄₁₆ inch thick*
2 small red onions
½ cup olive oil
1 cup dry white wine
1 cup hot chicken or beef broth

Whether fresh or preserved in brine, soak the grape leaves in cold water for about 30 minutes, changing the water every 5 minutes. If the leaves are of a brand that is especially briny, you can remove the salt more effectively by blanching them in boiling water for 30 seconds instead of soaking. Pat each leaf dry with paper towels to remove any excess moisture.

Stuff each quail with a sage leaf and put a pinch of salt and pepper in the cavity. Wrap each quail in a grape leaf, and then wrap it in a slice of *pancetta.* Tie each bird up with string like a package.

Coarsely chop the onion. Heat the oil in a large saucepan. When the oil is hot, add the onions and sauté until they are translucent (about 5 minutes). Place the quail in the saucepan and sprinkle each one with a pinch of salt and pepper. Cook, turning occasionally, until the *pancetta* is light golden brown all over. Add the wine, cover the saucepan and simmer until the wine has evaporated (about 15 minutes). Start adding the broth a little at a time, replacing the cover after each addition. When all of the broth has been incorporated (about 25 minutes), the quail should be tender. Remove the string from the birds, place them on a serving dish, and pour all the sauce over them. Serve immediately. Each serving should consist of two quail with *pancetta* and grape leaves.

STEAMING CHICKEN (OR FISH) ON A PLATE

Petto di Pollo al Piatto

CHICKEN BREAST COOKED ON A PLATE

FROM FLORENCE

The method of steaming on a covered plate put over a boiling pot works just as well for a delicate chicken breast as for trout fillets. The zucchini is very slowly steamed together with the chicken, both because the combination is delicious and also because the cooking times are the same. This is a delightful, light one-dish meal. Do not make arbitrary substitutions. Trout fillets (cooking time 16 to 18 minutes) and the chicken breast-zucchini combination are the two classic dishes using this technique. Steamers for vegetables are not popular in Italy (see discussion page 341).

3 teaspoons olive oil
1 6- to 8-ounce chicken breast, cut in half
1 lemon
¼ cup dry white wine
Salt and freshly ground white pepper
3 small thin zucchini
About 5 sprigs Italian parsley

HOW TO PREPARE PETTO DI POLLO AL PIATTO

1. Pour 1 teaspoon of the oil on a china or oven-proof dish.

Place the chicken breast on the plate. Squeeze the lemon and add the wine to the lemon juice (in the squeezer container). Add salt and freshly ground white pepper to taste to the lemon-wine mixture.

Clean the zucchini, removing the ends, and cut them into quarters. Then cut each quarter into pieces 1½ inches long (see pages 393–394).

2. Arrange the zucchini pieces all around the chicken breast and place the parsley on top of it.

3. Mix the lemon juice and wine together very well in the squeezer and spoon the mixture over the chicken and zucchini.

Put a large quantity of water in a large saucepan and bring it to a boil. Wrap the dish with the chicken and zucchini completely in aluminum foil and

4. place it on top of the saucepan. Let the chicken breast steam for about 40 minutes.

5. Remove the dish from the saucepan and carefully unwrap the foil.

6. Let cool for 2 minutes and serve.

Pollo al Sale

CHICKEN COOKED COVERED WITH SALT

FROM ALL OVER ITALY

It would appear that cooking a chicken with 2 pounds of salt would defy all established gastronomic and health criteria. I use this dish in my classes to initially horrify the sodium-free faddists, who usually find it a pleasant surprise. Everyone expects this dish to be very salty and they are pleasantly surprised to find that the coarse salt solidifies into a crust and does not penetrate the chicken, but seals in its flavor, imparting a unique taste without excessive saltiness. This ancient cooking method must have originated in Calabria, the seat of salt production. It is found in the small villages there today and, with the government tax on salt, it could only have been used in such quantities where there exists a free and easy source.

1 clove garlic, unpeeled
1 sprig fresh rosemary, or 1 tablespoon rosemary leaves preserved in salt, or dried and
  blanched
1 chicken, about 3 pounds
About 2 pounds coarse-grained salt

SERVES 4

Place the garlic and rosemary in the cavity of the chicken.

HOW TO PREPARE POLLO AL SALE

1. Make a 1-inch layer of coarse-grained salt on the bottom of a terra-cotta casserole. Place the chicken on the salt.
  Preheat the oven to 300 degrees.

2. Pour the remaining salt over the chicken so that chicken is completely covered.
  Cover the casserole with its lid and place it in the oven. Bake for 10 minutes, then raise the oven temperature to 400 degrees and bake for about 1½ hours longer.
  Remove the casserole from the oven. Uncover the casserole and let the chicken rest for 2 minutes.

3. A solid white crust should have formed. Crack the crust with a wooden meat pounder or a heavy wooden spoon.

4. Transfer the chicken to a serving dish.
  The chicken should be golden and the skin very crisp. Brush off any loose salt and serve immediately.

BRAISING MEAT

When braising a large piece of meat, there are a number of ways it can be treated so that the result will be juicy and flavorful. *Stracotto alla parmigiana* (Braised Rump of Beef, Parma Style) illustrates how the flavoring may be inserted so that it penetrates the meat and does not remain just on the outside. In this dish, the pot is first sealed with wax paper to keep the moisture in before the lid is put on.

Stufato di Milano (Braised Rump of Beef, Milan Style) illustrates how to lard meat so that it does not dry out. It is also perhaps the best-known example in Italian cooking of meat being marinated before it is braised. Because it is larded, unlike many marinated meat dishes, it remains juicy.

Carne ai sette sapori (Beef with Seven Flavors) is a fascinating recipe, for it contains an unusual mixture of ingredients which integrate perfectly. This is another dish which requires larding.

Stracotto alla Parmigiana

BRAISED RUMP OF BEEF, PARMA STYLE

FROM PARMA

SERVES 6 TO 8

3½ pounds rump roast of beef
2 cloves garlic, peeled
½ tablespoon salt
1 teaspoon freshly ground black pepper
3 medium-sized carrots
2 medium-sized red onions
10 ounces (1¼ sticks) sweet butter
1 tablespoon olive oil
2 cups dry white wine
4 tablespoons tomato paste
Salt and freshly ground black pepper
About 1 cup of hot beef or chicken broth, if necessary

Tie the meat like a salami (pages 247–249). Cut the cloves of garlic into small pieces and put them in a small bowl. Add the salt and pepper and mix very well in order to completely coat the garlic pieces.

HOW TO PREPARE STRACOTTO ALLA PARMIGIANA

1. Using a knife, first make a puncture, then turn the knife all the way around to make a hole.

Make about 10 such holes all over the meat.

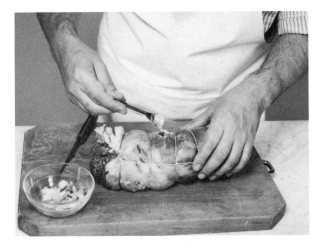

2. Place some of the garlic-salt-pepper mixture in each hole.

Coarsely chop the carrots and onions together on a board. Put 8 ounces of the butter and the oil in a casserole over medium heat. When the butter is completely melted, add the chopped ingredients and sauté lightly, or until onion is translucent (about 10 minutes). Add the meat to the casserole and sauté gently, turning the meat occasionally, for about 15 minutes. Combine the wine and tomato paste and add the mixture to the casserole.

3. Place a sheet of wax paper on top of the casserole, then cover with the lid.

Simmer for about 1 hour, turning the meat twice. Taste for salt and pepper. Add the remaining butter (and broth, if needed) and cover again. Simmer again for almost 1 hour longer.

Transfer the meat to a chopping board and remove the string. Cut the meat into 1-inch-thick slices. Arrange the slices on a serving dish, pour the sauce over it, and serve.

Stufato di Milano

BRAISED RUMP OF BEEF, MILAN STYLE

FROM LOMBARDY

This dish is even better if prepared one day in advance and served cold with only the sauce reheated just before serving.

4 ounces of pancetta, or 2 ounces boiled ham and 2 ounces salt pork   SERVES 6 TO 8
3 pounds rump roast of beef or yearling
4 cups dry full-bodied red wine from northern Italy, such as Barolo, Barbera,
    or Gattinara
2 bay leaves
2 whole cloves
1 medium-sized red onion
1 medium-sized carrot
1 celery stalk
1 clove garlic, peeled
Salt, freshly ground black pepper, and freshly grated nutmeg
About ½ cup unbleached all-purpose flour
4 ounces (1 stick) sweet butter
2 tablespoons olive oil

HOW TO LARD MEAT

1. Cut half the *pancetta* into long strips.

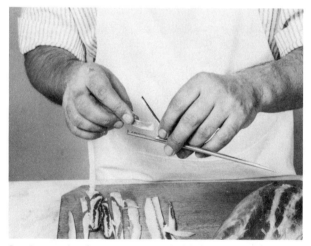

2. Open the bottom part of the larding needle on the unpointed end and insert one strip of *pancetta*.

228

 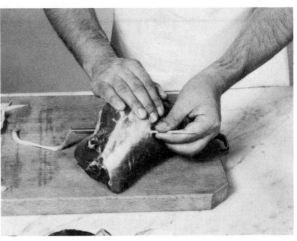

3. Close the open part of the needle, leaving the attached strip hanging from the end, and

4. lard the meat by inserting the pointed end of the needle, pushing needle through, and leaving the strip of fat inside the meat. Detach the needle.

Tie the meat like a salami (pages 247–249). Place the tied meat in a small crockery bowl and pour the wine over it. Add 1 bay leaf and the cloves to the bowl.

Then coarsely cut over the meat half of the red onion, the carrot, celery stalk, and garlic. Sprinkle with a little salt, pepper, and nutmeg. Let the meat marinate for about 5 hours in a cool place (not the refrigerator).

Finely cut the remaining *pancetta* into small pieces, then finely chop it together with the onion on a board.

Remove the meat from the bowl and dry it with paper towels. Lightly flour the meat, by placing it in a large colander, sprinkling the flour over it, and shaking the colander to remove any excess flour. Put the butter and oil in a casserole, preferably of terra-cotta, over medium heat. When the butter is completely melted, add the finely chopped ingredients and sauté for about 5 minutes. Then place the meat in the casserole, raise the heat, and sauté until the meat is lightly golden brown all over (about 10 minutes). Strain the marinade and discard all the vegetables and aromatic herbs. Add the marinade to the casserole along with the remaining bay leaf. Cover and simmer for about 4 hours, turning the meat over every hour. Transfer the meat to chopping board, remove the string, and cut it into 1-inch-thick slices.

5. Arrange the slices on a platter and pour the sauce over them.

229

Carne ai Sette Sapori

BEEF WITH SEVEN FLAVORS

FROM LOMBARDY

3 ounces pancetta or prosciutto
3 pounds rump roast of beef
1 medium-sized red onion
1 clove garlic, peeled
3 tablespoons capers in wine vinegar, drained
2 tablespoons olive oil
1½ cups cold milk
1 teaspoon anchovy paste
Salt and freshly ground black pepper
1 cup hot beef or chicken broth
2 tablespoons red wine vinegar

SERVES 6

Cut the *pancetta* into thin strips. With a larding needle, lard the meat in several parts (pages 228–229).

Finely chop the onion, garlic, and capers together on a chopping board.

Combine the oil and milk in a small crockery bowl, and mix in the anchovy paste until it dissolves.

Tie the rump roast (pages 247–249) and place it in a small oval casserole with a lid. Pour the oil, milk, and anchovy paste mixture over the meat and add the chopped vegetables to the casserole. Sprinkle with a little salt and pepper.

Cover the casserole and cook over medium heat for about 2 hours, turning the meat several times. If more liquid is needed, add some hot broth but only a very small quantity at a time. Ten minutes before the meat is ready, add the wine vinegar and let it evaporate (about 2 minutes).

Remove the casserole from the heat and transfer the meat to a cutting board. Slice the meat and serve it with some of the sauce remaining in the casserole.

This dish can be prepared in advance. Slice the meat at the last moment and serve it with the re-heated sauce.

Spezzatino alle Carote

CUBES OF BEEF SHANK IN CARROT-WINE SAUCE

FROM FRIULI

This is a noteworthy *spezzatino* (cut up meat or fowl), having the extraordinary flavor of the abundant carrots, with clove, bay leaf and sage, and a rich sauce produced by the beef shank's own gelatin without adding any thickening. As this dish originates from the mountainous northern area of Friuli, which is renowned for its fine red wines as well as the famous whites, you'll note that wine is integral to this recipe. The combination of clove, bay leaf and sage is unusual.

2 pounds beef shank
5 medium-sized carrots
2 large cloves garlic, peeled
1 bay leaf
About 5 sage leaves, fresh or preserved in salt

SERVES 4

3 tablespoons sweet butter
¼ cup olive oil
1 cup dry red wine
2 whole cloves
4 tablespoons tomato paste
2 cups cold chicken broth
Salt and freshly ground black pepper

Cut the beef shank into 1-inch-square pieces.

Cut the carrots into ½-inch pieces. Coarsely chop the garlic on a board.

Put the carrots and meat into a terra-cotta or enamel casserole. Sprinkle over the garlic and add the bay leaf and sage. Cut the butter into pieces and place them over the meat, then pour the oil over the meat. Put casserole over medium heat and cook without stirring for about 15 minutes. Stir, add the wine and let it evaporate (about 15 minutes). Add the cloves, tomato paste, and the cold broth. Cover the casserole and simmer for 1 hour, then taste for salt and pepper. Stir, cover the pan again, and simmer for 1 hour longer. At that time the meat should be tender and juicy.

Transfer the meat to a serving dish. Discard the cloves and reduce the sauce if necessary before serving. Whole boiled potatoes may accompany the *spezzatino*.

COOKING ON A RANGE-TOP GRILL (GRATELLA)

1. The heavy iron *gratella*, or range-top grill, is often used to grill chops, such as the *lombatina* or veal chop, or steaks, or small chickens or squab, which have been split in half (see page 213, photo 2).

It is also a delicious way to cook fish which are not too lean. Whole small fish, such as sole or trout, or slices of large meaty fish, such as fresh cod, are the best. Thin fillets of sole or other similar fish are not appropriate for this method of cooking.

Once it has been seasoned (see page 102), the ridged grill can generally be used without any additional grease, with just some coarse salt sprinkled over it. The outside of the meat or fish is seared, producing a taste not far from that which comes from cooking over an open wood or charcoal fire. The ridges allow the fat to drain from the meat so that it is not cooking in its own grease. Salt the grill and then let it get very hot before placing the meat on it.

GRILLED VEAL CHOP (about 1 inch thick)
Cook for about 3 minutes on each side. The inside will remain pink and juicy. Pour a few drops of olive oil over the chop and serve it with lemon wedges.

GRILLED LAMB CHOP (about 1 inch thick)
After cooking 3 minutes on each side, the lamb chop will be well done as the Italians prefer it. (Lamb is never marinated before cooking in Italy.) If you prefer your lamb pink, cook 1 minute less on each side. Do not add olive oil. Serve with lemon wedges.

Veal Liver

Cut the liver very thin (about ⅓ inch thick) and cook for 30 seconds on each side. Serve with or without drops of olive oil but with the lemon.

Fish

Whole trout may be cooked for 4 minutes on each side. Slices of fish with bone, about 1 inch thick, such as swordfish, should be cooked 4 to 5 minutes on each side. (It is best to cook only slices of a slightly oily fish in this manner.) Sprinkle the grilled fish with freshly ground pepper and serve with lemon wedges.

Chicken Breast

Cook the boned half breast with a sprig of fresh rosemary, if it is in season, pushed inside the meat, for 4 to 5 minutes on each side. If fresh rosemary is not available, you can substitute 1 teaspoon rosemary leaves preserved in salt (page 48). Make a hole in the chicken breast and push the leaves in. Serve with lemon wedges.

Pesce ai Capperi

FISH WITH CAPERS

FROM ROME

The unusual feature of this preparation is the marinating of the fish in milk in order to tenderize it. The capers are combined with the juice of the fish in a small saucepan to integrate them. This is quite different from using the classic *Salsa di capperi* (Caper Sauce) which exists independently.

Only fish is marinated in milk in Italy. Pork is sometimes cooked in milk, but never marinated.

SERVES 4

4 slices (about 2 pounds) of a large fish, such as haddock,
*   halibut, striped bass, or fresh cod*
1 cup cold milk
1 cup unbleached all-purpose flour
5 tablespoons sweet butter
¼ cup olive oil
Salt and freshly ground black pepper
2 tablespoons capers in wine vinegar, drained and
*   coarsely chopped*

To serve:
About 10 sprigs Italian parsley, leaves only, plus 4 whole sprigs

Soak the fish slices in cold milk for about 30 minutes. Remove the fish slices from the milk and pat them dry with paper towels.

Lightly flour the fish slices and let them sit for 5 minutes on paper towels.

Heat 2 tablespoons of butter and all the olive oil in a large frying pan. When the butter is completely melted, sauté the fish slices for about 5 minutes on each side, sprinkling them with salt and freshly ground pepper as they cook.

Remove the pan from the heat and transfer the fish slices to a serving dish. Pour the fat remaining in the frying pan into a small saucepan. Put the saucepan over medium heat and add the remaining 3 tablespoons of butter. When the butter is completely melted, remove the pan from the heat and add the chopped capers. Stir the sauce very well with wooden spoon and pour it over the fish slices. Sprinkle with chopped parsley and place one sprig on each fish slice. Serve immediately.

CHAPTER 10

How to Bone and Stuff Poultry and Meats

CHICKEN

HOW TO BONE A CHICKEN BREAST FROM THE WHOLE CHICKEN

Since it is often more convenient and economical to buy the whole chicken and then divide it for various purposes, the illustrations below show the boning of the breast from the whole chicken. The most delicate part in removing a chicken breast whole is in detaching the thin part along the breastbone so that the two halves of the breast remain together. For most boneless breast of chicken dishes, however, it is not necessary to go to this bother, since the breast is halved, or even cut into smaller pieces. The simplest way is to first cut along the middle of the breast, then each boneless breast can be detached. Of course, the same technique is even easier with the whole breast already separated by the butcher, which can then be boned (see pages 235–236, photos 1 through 7). These boneless half chicken breasts are used in *Petto di pollo al piatto* (Chicken Breast Steamed on a Plate) on pages 222–224, and many other dishes.

1. First remove the skin from the chicken's breast. Pull the leg aside from the breast, finding the line where the skin of the breast attaches to the leg.

233

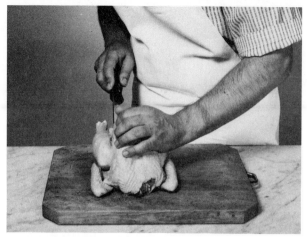

2. Cut along that line, separating the skin along the side of the breast.

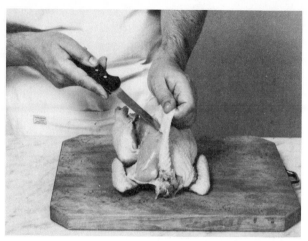

3. Scrape underneath the skin to remove it from the breast and continue until it is detached up to the breastbone. Then pull it aside.

4. Cut all the way down the line of the breastbone, separating the breast into two halves.

5. Scrape the meat free from the bone, moving from the breastbone back toward the leg.

6. Cut along the side connecting the breast with the leg, freeing the half breast entirely.

Repeat the procedure for the other half of the breast.

Sometimes half breasts are butterflied to make thinner fillets (see page 237, photos 8 through 11).

Boning and Butterflying Whole Chicken Breasts

To make a rolled stuffed chicken breast dish such as *Petto di pollo allo specchio* (Rolled Chicken Breast in Aspic), page 435, it is necessary to bone the chicken breast keeping both halves attached to each other, in one whole piece, and then to butterfly it. The technique of doing this is illustrated below.

HOW TO BONE A WHOLE CHICKEN BREAST

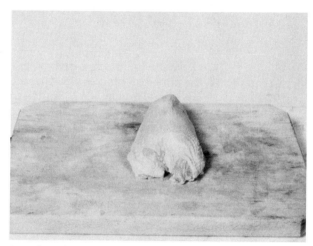

1. The whole chicken breast.

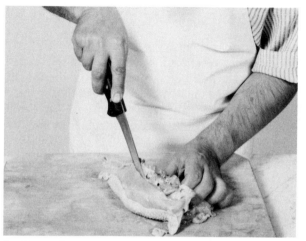

2. Turn the breast over. The butcher has already removed the back, leaving an opening between the left and right parts of the breast. On the open side of the left part, insert a boning knife between the meat and the rib bones and cut all along the bone, freezing the meat, but leaving it attached on the left where it meets the breastbone.

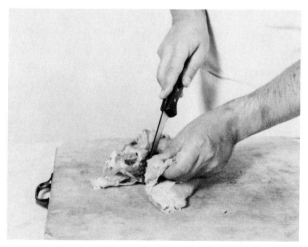

3 and 4. Repeat the procedure from the open side of the right part. The two parts of the breast are still attached to each other only along the breastbone.

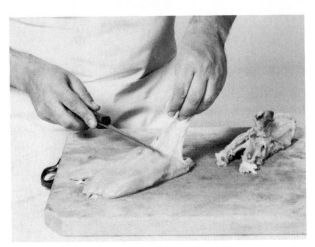

5. Turn the breast over. The whole breast is free of the bone at its lower end, below the breastbone. Lift up the loosened meat, and carefully scrape the meat free from the breastbone, being sure to leave both sides of the breast completely attached to one another.

6. On the right side we see the whole carcass of the breast, on the left the boned whole breast. Using the knife just to hold the meat in place pull off the skin, with any attached fat.

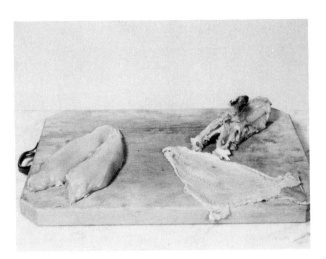

7. Skinless whole breast (on the left), the skin in one piece (center), and the carcass (right). This whole piece of skin can be used as the casing for a type of forcemeat sausage for boiling.

The whole breast may be grilled this way, or it may be butterflied, stuffed, and rolled.

HOW TO BUTTERFLY CHICKEN BREASTS

The photos below show the slicing and opening technique used in butterflying chicken breast halves, but the procedure is the same for a whole breast.

8. Chicken breast halves. It is easier to obtain these by cutting the meat down the breastbone before removing it from the bone as shown in the photos on page 234, where the half breasts are removed from the whole chicken. Naturally the same procedure may be used here with the whole chicken breast only (see below).

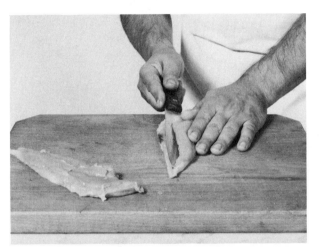

9. To butterfly the breast half, slice through the thinner side which was close to the breastbone, opening the breast to slightly less than 1 inch from the end.

10. With the knife, open it out.

11. Draw the flat side of the knife over the breast, evening it out.

The opened, butterflied half breast is ready to be grilled, deep-fried, or sautéed. The whole butterflied breast can be stuffed and rolled as for *Petto di pollo specchio* (pages 435–437).

To butterfly the whole chicken breast, each side of it is opened from the middle; this part of the breast was attached to the breastbone and is quite thin. On each side, about 1 inch from the middle, where the meat thickens, insert the knife and slice most of the way through. Open it, and flatten it out.

CUTTING CHICKEN INTO PIECES WITH BONE

The traditional method of cutting chicken into 8 or more pieces is used in a variety of dishes including *spezzatini*, such as the four which follow or in *Fricassea di pollo* (Chicken Fricassee) or *Pollo affinocchiato* (Fenneled Chicken). (See *The Fine Art of Italian Cooking*.) In Italy, when chickens are cut into 8, 10, or 18 pieces, the pieces are usually not boned. It is felt that cooking small pieces with the bone enhances the flavor.

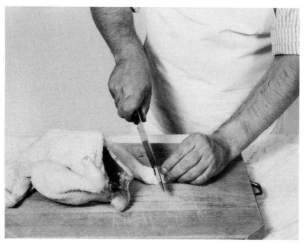

1. If the butcher has left the tops of the feet attached, first cut them off from the bottoms of the legs.

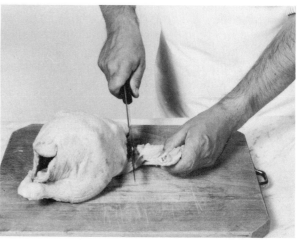

2. Cut the wings off at the joints with the breast. Remove the tips of the wings at the middle joint and discard them.

3. Cut off the leg where it joins the thigh.

4. At the bottom part of the back, there is the joint which connects it with the thigh. Cut at that point.

238

5. With the breast up, insert the knife into the openings left by the removed thighs and cut open the skin where it is attached at the tail end.

6. Turn the chicken on its side with the bony back facing you and cut through the spine where the back joins the breast. This one cut will separate the back, which, having bones but no meat, may be discarded.

7. Holding the remainder of the chicken breast side down, insert the knife and cut down the central breastbone separating the breast side into halves.

8. Turn chicken over and cut through the backbone completely, freeing the two halves from each other. The entire breast is now in two large pieces.

9. The chicken cut into its classic 8 pieces, unequal in size. When an Italian recipe calls for a chicken cut in 8, this is the procedure to use.

10. When an Italian recipe requires a chicken cut into 10 pieces, the two large breast pieces are each halved. First cut through the flesh and then chop through the bone with a knife.

In any recipe for *spezzatino* the pieces are even smaller. The wings are left as they are. All the other pieces are cut into two by cutting through the flesh, and then chopping through the bone with a knife, making 18 pieces in all. Sometimes the bones are soft enough to break.

Pollo ai Peperoni

BAKED MARINATED CHICKEN WITH PEPPERS

FROM LUCANIA

An interesting and simple preparation from southern Italy with no tomato sauce, nor even wine, which brings out the flavors of the two featured ingredients: chicken and peppers. The chicken is cut into 8 pieces, marinated in oil, lemon juice, and parsley and baked, while the peppers are sautéed in the marinade. The sautéed peppers (with their sauce) are then combined with the baked chicken.

1 chicken, about 3 to 3½ pounds
2 lemons
About 10 sprigs Italian parsley, leaves only
¾ cup olive oil
Salt and freshly ground black pepper
3 green peppers

SERVES 4

Clean and wash the chicken carefully. Cut it into 8 pieces (pages 238–240) and put the pieces into a crockery bowl.

Squeeze the lemons and add the juice to the bowl with the chicken. Coarsely chop parsley and add it to the bowl along with ½ cup of the oil. Sprinkle with salt and pepper. Mix together all the ingredients in the bowl with a wooden spoon and then let the chicken marinate for 1 hour, turning the pieces over after ½ hour.

Clean the peppers, removing the stems and the ribs and seeds from the inside. Cut the peppers into rings less than ½-inch thick (page 383).

Preheat the oven to 400 degrees. Use tongs to transfer the chicken pieces with some of the chopped parsley clinging to them from the bowl to a baking dish. Pour the remaining ¼ cup of oil over the chicken. Place the dish in the oven and bake for 35 minutes.

Meanwhile, transfer the marinade to a saucepan and heat it over medium heat. When the marinade is hot, add the peppers and sauté for about 20 minutes. At that moment they should be cooked but still firm. Taste for salt and pepper.

Remove the baking dish from the oven and transfer the chicken pieces to a serving dish. Arrange the peppers and sauce in a ring around the chicken. Serve immediately.

Pollo alla Toscana

CHICKEN SAUTÉED WITH MUSHROOMS

FROM TUSCANY

The chicken is once again cut into 8 pieces, sautéed in a rich combination of oil and butter, wine, broth, and tomatoes and flavored with sage and wild mushrooms. The sauce is thickened through the minimal flour that clings to the chicken pieces.

1 chicken, 3 to 3½ pounds
¼ cup unbleached all-purpose flour
1 ounce dried porcini *mushrooms*
1 cup lukewarm chicken broth
4 tablespoons sweet butter
4 tablespoons olive oil
4 sage leaves, fresh or preserved in salt
½ cup dry red wine
1 cup fresh tomatoes, or drained canned imported tomatoes
Salt and freshly ground black pepper

SERVES 4

Cut the chicken into 8 pieces. Lightly flour the pieces by placing them in a colander with the flour and shaking through the excess flour.

Soak the mushrooms in the lukewarm broth for about 30 minutes. Heat the butter and oil in a casserole. When the butter is completely melted, add the chicken pieces and sauté gently until light golden brown (about 15 minutes). Add the sage leaves and the wine and let the wine evaporate very slowly (for about 10 minutes). Remove the mushrooms from their broth bath and be sure they are completely free of sand. Then pass the broth itself through heavy cheesecloth to remove any sand deposited by the mushrooms. Add the mushrooms and broth to the casserole. Pass the tomatoes through a food mill and when the broth is half reduced (about 20 minutes), add the tomatoes to the casserole and simmer for about 15 minutes longer. Taste for salt and pepper. Mix very well and cook for 1 minute longer. At this point, the chicken should be cooked and ready to be served.

Pollo in Forno

OREGANO CHICKEN BAKED WITH POTATOES AND TOMATOES

FROM CALABRIA

The chicken is cut into 18 pieces and laid on slices of potato and covered with slices of tomato. Its pungent flavor comes from oregano, red pepper flakes, and garlic. The spicy chicken in combination with the baked vegetables is a satisfying main dish. The lemon juice has been absorbed into the potatoes, and adds the final touch.

1 chicken, 3 to 3½ pounds

SERVES 4

1 pound potatoes
1 lemon
1 pound fresh tomatoes, ripe but not overripe
Salt and freshly ground black pepper
1 clove garlic, peeled
½ cup olive oil
½ teaspoon red pepper flakes
½ teaspoon dried oregano

Clean and wash the chicken carefully and cut it into 18 pieces (pages 238–240).

Peel the potatoes and cut them into slices ¼ inch thick. Put the slices in a bowl of cold water until needed.

Squeeze the lemon and reserve the juice.

Cut the fresh tomatoes horizontally into slices less than ½ inch thick. Remove the seeds from the tomatoes.

Lightly oil a 13- x 8¾-inch Pyrex baking dish. Preheat the oven to 400 degrees.

Layer the potatoes over the bottom of the prepared baking dish. Sprinkle the potato slices with salt and pepper, then pour the lemon juice over them. Make a layer of chicken pieces over the potatoes. Put a tomato slice over each piece of chicken.

Finely chop the garlic. Pour the oil into a small crockery bowl, then add the garlic, red pepper flakes, oregano, and salt to taste. Mix very well with a wooden spoon. Pour the sauce over the tomato layer in the baking dish. Place dish in the oven and bake for about 40 minutes.

Remove from oven, let stand for 2 minutes, then serve directly from the dish.

Pollo all'Aceto

CHICKEN WITH VINEGAR SAUCE

FROM LOMBARDY

The chicken is cut into 18 pieces, sautéed, and then simmered in broth while the garlic and rosemary marinate in the red wine vinegar. The vinegar is added over a very high heat and evaporates, leaving all its flavor in the chicken. This dish is related to *Pollo alla cacciatora* in some of its versions (without the tomatoes), but with wine vinegar instead of wine. Notice that red rather than white wine vinegar is used for the chicken, its full-bodied flavor combining better with the garlic and rosemary.

SERVES 4

2 cloves garlic, peeled
1 tablespoon rosemary leaves, fresh or preserved in salt
½ cup red wine vinegar
1 chicken, 3 to 3½ pounds
½ cup olive oil
½ cup chicken broth
Salt and freshly ground black pepper

Chop the garlic and rosemary leaves very fine. Put the wine vinegar and chopped ingredients into a crockery bowl. Let marinate for 1 hour. Clean and wash the chicken carefully, then cut it into 18 pieces (pages 238–240). Heat the oil in a skillet. When the oil is hot, add the chicken pieces and sauté over high heat until golden brown all over (about 15 minutes).

Meanwhile, bring the broth to a boil. When the chicken pieces are thoroughly sautéed, add the boiling broth to them, lower the heat, and simmer, uncovered, until almost cooked (about 15 minutes). Pour the marinated vinegar mixture over the chicken pieces, raise the heat, and let the wine vinegar evaporate. Taste for salt and pepper. When ready, transfer the chicken pieces to a serving dish. Pour the sauce over them and serve immediately.

Cosce di Pollo Ripiene

STUFFED CHICKEN DRUMSTICKS

FROM NORTHERN ITALY

The method of boning the drumsticks, leaving the skin on, is illustrated below. Then the boneless dark meat is stuffed with a little of a light and tasty mixture, sewn up, and sautéed, using both wine and broth. This truly wonderful, though simple, dish is always a great success when I serve it. Two legs per serving should be enough, but sometimes a third is hard to resist.

NOTE: You may find that you have a little stuffing left over after you have prepared the drumsticks. Please do not try to adjust the recipe; this much stuffing must be made to retain the proper proportions.

12 chicken drumsticks (from chickens weighing 3 to 3½ pounds)   SERVES 4 TO 6
4 ounces boiled ham
10 sprigs Italian parsley, leaves only
2 medium-sized cloves garlic, peeled
2 extra large eggs
4 tablespoons freshly grated Parmigiano
Salt and freshly ground black pepper
10 tablespoons olive oil
2 tablespoons sweet butter
½ cup dry white wine
About 1 cup hot chicken or beef broth

1. Cut the two tendons at the end of the leg (some fowl have more than two).

2. Scrape back the meat with a knife, to detach it from the bone. Be careful not to make any holes in the skin.

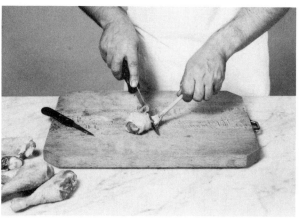

3. When you reach the point where the meat is attached to the other end of the bone, and the meat has been completely turned inside out, cut around the cartilage at the end to detach it completely.

4. Use a needle and thread to sew the skin together at the larger opening.

Finely chop the boiled ham, parsley, and garlic together on a board and put them into a small bowl. Add the eggs and Parmigiano. Mix very well with a wooden spoon. Taste for salt and pepper.

5. Stuff each leg with about 1 tablespoon of the stuffing.

6. Sew up the other opening.

When all the legs are ready, heat the oil and butter in a flameproof casserole over medium heat. When the butter is completely melted, add the stuffed legs and sauté very gently until lightly golden brown (about 15 minutes). Sprinkle with salt and pepper and add the wine. Let it evaporate slowly (about 10 minutes). Then start adding the broth, a little at a time, turning the legs occasionally until they are cooked (about 25 minutes).

Remove the casserole from the heat and transfer the legs to a board. Remove the threads and arrange the legs on a serving dish. Pour the sauce over the chicken and serve immediately. You can also serve the sliced drumsticks at room temperature with the reheated sauce poured over them.

Collo di Tacchino Ripieno

STUFFED TURKEY NECK

FROM FLORENCE

The neck of the turkey or goose (or chicken) is boned and then sliced and eaten as a main dish or *antipasto*. Its stuffing, which contains nuts (as well as meat and liver) is an ancient one. Stuffing the long neck of a goose, turkey, or even a peacock and eating it as a type of sausage has been popular since medieval times. This dish is always eaten cold accompanied by a green sauce of fresh herbs or a mint sauce (see pages 255 and 257).

SERVES 6 AS APPETIZER
4 AS A MAIN DISH

1 turkey neck (about 8½ inches long),
or 2 goose necks or 3 chicken necks, plucked

For the stuffing:
5 shelled walnuts
1 slice white bread, trimmed of crust
½ cup cold milk
2 chicken livers, or 1 turkey or goose liver
4 ounces ground beef
2 tablespoons unseasoned bread crumbs, preferably homemade
2 extra large eggs
1 tablespoon freshly grated Parmigiano
Salt, freshly ground black pepper, and freshly grated nutmeg

For cooking:
Coarse-grained salt
1 medium-sized red onion
1 medium-sized carrot
1 celery stalk
5 sprigs Italian parsley

First prepare the stuffing. Blanch the walnuts in a small saucepan of boiling water for 5 minutes. Then remove the skins under cold running water. Soak the bread in cold milk for about 10 minutes.

Put the walnuts and chicken livers on a board and chop them together very fine.

Squeeze the milk out of the bread and put the bread into a bowl. Add the chopped ingredients, ground beef, bread crumbs, eggs, and Parmigiano to the bowl. Mix very well with wooden spoon. Then add salt, pepper, and nutmeg to taste. Mix thoroughly. Let the stuffing stand until needed.

HOW TO BONE A TURKEY, GOOSE, OR CHICKEN NECK

1. Cut off the head of the turkey where the neck begins.

2. To remove the skin, start at the bottom end of the neck and pull back the skin of the neck all around.

3. With a knife begin to cut the membranes connecting the skin to the neck. The skin must be detached in one piece and without any holes.

4. Continue pulling back skin as you cut.

When the last connections are cut, the whole skin will be inside out. Be sure to remove the esophagus and crop which is attached to the inside of the skin. Reverse so that the original side is out.

5. Sew up one end with needle and thread.

6. Stuff the turkey neck with the prepared stuffing. Be careful not to add too much stuffing, otherwise the neck will split while cooking.

7. When the neck is full, sew up the other opening. Prick the stuffed neck with a fork in two places.

8. Wrap the stuffed neck in a heavy cheesecloth. Tuck ends of the cheesecloth under.

HOW TO TIE MEATS OR BONED FOWL "LIKE A SALAMI"

To tie meats or boned fowl, the string used is ordinary twine, thicker than sewing thread. The general rule about the length of string is to make it six times the length of meat to be tied.

9. Place string under the tucked ends of the cheesecloth (about 1½ inches from the end), leaving only enough string on one side to pull over and knot the first ring in the center.

10. Bring the long end of the string down another 1½ inches, and hold the string in place with a finger. With the other hand, pull the string under and around again

11. to the point where the string is being held by your finger. Pass the end of the string over, then under.

12. Remove your finger, hold the short end of the string with one hand and pull other end tight with the other hand.

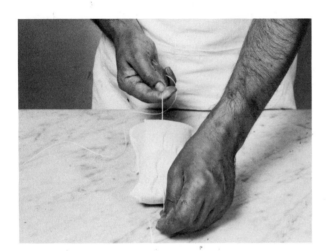

13. Stand the neck on its bottom end and put the remaining string over the top end to the underside of neck.

As the end of the string intersects with each ring of string wrapped around the neck, pull under and over, fastening in the same way as was done on the other side (there is no longer any need to hold with your finger or to pull tight on this side). After the last intersection,

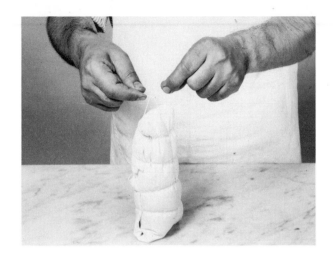

14. tie a knot using the two ends of the string.

With this classic method of tying using only two knots, the string can be easily removed by cutting it in only one place.

Bring a large pot of water to a boil. When the water reaches the boiling point add coarse-grained salt to taste. Then add the vegetables and the neck. Simmer very slowly for about 1 hour, then remove the neck and put it on a platter. Place a flat board on top of the neck with a weight (about 4 pounds). Let the stuffed neck cool. [See *Cima alla genovese* (Stuffed Pressed Veal Breast), page 253, photo 15.] Then refrigerate the turkey neck with the weight on it for about 6 hours. Remove from the refrigerator, and remove the string. Unwrap and slice the neck like a large sausage and serve.

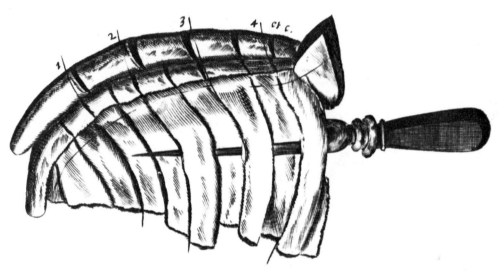

30. Il Petto di Vitella *(The Breast of Veal).*
Drawing from Il Trinciante *(1580).*

VEAL

Cima alla Genovese

STUFFED PRESSED VEAL BREAST

FROM GENOA

Cima alla genovese is one of the glories of Italian cooking. Having its origins in the Renaissance elaborate boiled courses, it is mentioned in Panonto's famous Florentine cookbook of the mid-sixteenth century. It is a dish that one never sees in a restaurant, and even though it is rarely made now in the home, it would be nothing less than a tragedy if it should disappear, especially since the finished dish is worth the effort.

The varied combinations of ingredients in the stuffing make for one of the most interesting forcemeat textures that I know, and it has great subtlety of flavor. In short, it is a real *alta cucina* dish worth the trouble it takes to make it. It is eaten cold as a main dish or as an appetizer for a special meal.

*1 breast of veal, about 7 pounds with rib bones
(about 4 pounds without bones)*

SERVES 18

*For the stuffing:
6 ounces veal spinal marrow, sweetbreads, or brains
6 ounces pancetta, or 6 ounces very fatty ground pork
6 slices white bread
1 cup cold milk
About 15 raw pistachio nuts (for cooking)
8 extra large eggs
About 10 leaves fresh spinach, washed and drained
8 ounces ground lean pork
8 ounces ground veal
2 ounces freshly grated Parmigiano
2 tablespoons fresh marjoram, or 1½ tablespoons dried marjoram
Salt, freshly ground black pepper, and freshly grated nutmeg*

*For cooking:
Coarse-grained salt (approximately 2 tablespoons)
1 large red onion
2 medium-sized carrots
1 large celery stalk
10 whole black peppercorns
1 bay leaf*

HOW TO BONE A VEAL BREAST

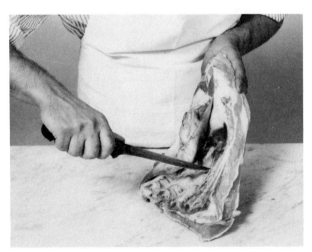

1. The rib bones must be removed one by one. Hold the meat with the unattached ends of the bones up. Make slits on both sides for the entire length of the bones. Do not cut any deeper than the thickness of the bone.

2. Starting at the free end of the bone, detach the bone by cutting underneath.

3. Cut the bone off at the other end.

Repeat the procedure until all the ribs are removed.

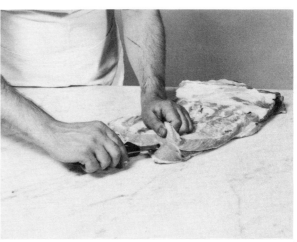

4. Remove the extra fat at the bottom end.

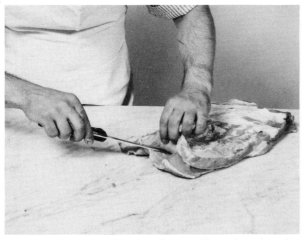

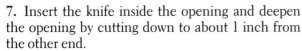

5. To make a pocket for the stuffing, first lay the meat flat, then insert the knife at the top end on one side, precisely in the center of the thickness.

6. As you cut across the meat, be careful to keep the knife in the middle of the meat all the way through. The opening should be in the middle not close to either side.

7. Insert the knife inside the opening and deepen the opening by cutting down to about 1 inch from the other end.

Check to be sure that there are no holes in the meat. If there should be any, sew them up with a needle and thread before stuffing.

Prepare the stuffing. Blanch the spinal marrow, following the instructions for brains on page 168. Cut the *pancetta* into small pieces, then coarsely chop them.

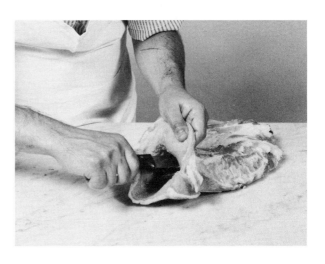

8. Cut the blanched spinal marrow into small pieces on a board.

Remove the crusts from the bread and soak the bread in the milk for about 10 minutes.

Blanch the pistachio nuts (page 87), adding salt to the boiling water. Hard cook 4 of the eggs and shell them. Remove the large stems from the spinach and cut the leaves into strips. Squeeze the milk out of the bread.

Combine the *pancetta*, spinal marrow, soaked bread, pistachios, spinach, ground pork, ground veal, Parmigiano, and the remaining 4 eggs. Add the marjoram and salt, pepper, and nutmeg to taste. Mix well but gently with a wooden spoon until all the ingredients are well amalgamated.

9. Place half of the stuffing in the veal pocket,

10. then place the 4 hard-cooked eggs lengthwise on the stuffing inside, in a row down the center.

Place the remaining stuffing over the hard-cooked eggs and along the sides, being careful to keep the eggs in place.

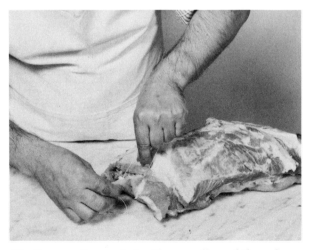

11. Sew up the pocket with a needle and thread.

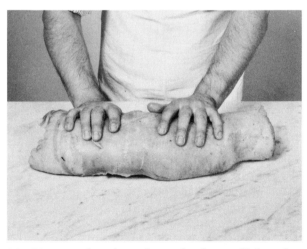

12. Use your hands to shape the flat stuffed pocket by rolling it until it resembles a large loaf of bread.

252

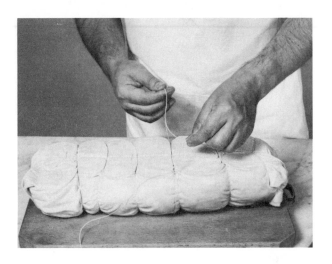

13. Wrap the stuffed breast in heavy cheesecloth and tie the way you would a turkey or goose neck (pages 247–249, photos 9 through 15).

Bring a large pot or fish poacher full of cold water to a boil. Add the coarse-grained salt. When the water reaches the boiling point, add the onion, carrots, celery, peppercorns, and bay leaf. Let the water simmer for 5 minutes.

14. Add the meat to the pot, and simmer, covered, for about 2½ hours.

When cooked, remove the veal breast and

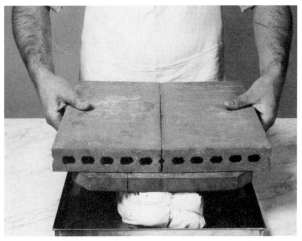

15. place it on a cookie sheet with a weight of about 10 pounds on top.

Let it cool for about 6 hours, then transfer it, with the weight on, to the refrigerator for at least 12 hours.

16. Unwrap the *cima* on a chopping board.

17. Slice the *cima* into slices ¼ inch thick, and arrange them on a large serving platter.

18. Serve the meat accompanied by a sauceboat full of basil or parsley sauce, such as *Salsa verde*, *Salsa verde del Chianti*, etc. (see *The Fine Art of Italian Cooking*).

31. Pistacchi (*Pistachios*)

LAMB

The lamb available in Italy (usually genuine baby lamb) is considerably smaller than that in the United States. The following two recipes illustrate the techniques for boning the Italian cuts of lamb. The first uses the leg of lamb (with a shank attached) and the other the lamb shoulder (with the shank and part of the spine attached). If you are cooking with the American cut of lamb (which doesn't include these parts) simply eliminate the steps illustrating how to remove them.

Coscia di Agnello in Salsa di Menta

BONED LEG OF LAMB WITH FRESH MINT SAUCE

FROM UMBRIA

Leg of lamb is often accompanied by a mint-flavored sauce. Here the leg of the young lamb has a sauce made from fresh mint leaves, lemon juice, wine vinegar, and just a little sugar. It is not really sweet, but just enough to bring out the minty flavor. The sauce blends well with the clove and garlic flavoring imbedded in the lamb.

1 leg of lamb, about 5 pounds
About 6 cloves garlic, peeled
1 teaspoon salt
¼ teaspoon freshly ground black pepper
10 whole cloves
¼ cup olive oil
Salt and freshly ground black pepper

SERVES 6

For the sauce:
1 cup fresh mint leaves
Juice of 1 lemon
2 tablespoons superfine granulated sugar
⅓ cup red wine vinegar
Salt to taste

HOW TO BONE A LEG OF LAMB

Most Italian butchers sell the leg of lamb with the shank attached so unless they bone it for you, here's the boning method. The leg of a small Italian lamb weighs about 5 pounds with bones. It is a classic ¾ leg cut, with the sirloin section at the top removed. It contains the main body of the leg with the leg bone connected by the knee-cap bone to the shank and its bone.

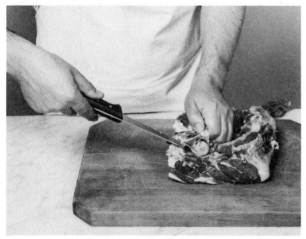

1. With boning knife, starting at the meaty top end, first expose the top of the knob of the leg bone,

2. and then cut along the bone down the inside part of the leg down to the knee.

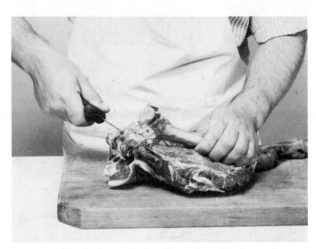

3. Free the bone by cutting away the meat all around and then,

4. completely free the knob so that the bone is now attached only at the other end, at the joint with the kneecap.

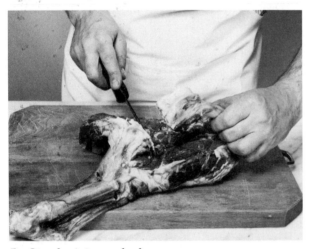

5. Cut the joint at the kneecap.

6. Holding the kneecap at its free end, cut its joint with the shank.

7. Just where the shank bone begins, cut across, separating the shank, meat, and bone. Lay it aside to use for some other purpose.

Cut the garlic into small pieces. Mix the salt and pepper together. Preheat the oven to 375 degrees.

256

8. Open the meat out and sprinkle the inside with the garlic, the salt-pepper mixture, and the cloves. Close and tie the meat like a salami (pages 247–249).

9. Place the meat in the baking dish with the oil. Sprinkle it with salt and pepper to taste.

Bake for about 1 hour, depending on the thickness of the meat, rather than the weight. Italians do not like lamb meat rare, but, at most, slightly pink so you may want to cook the meat until it's medium.

Meanwhile, prepare the sauce. Tear the mint leaves into thirds and put them in a sauceboat. Add the freshly squeezed lemon juice, then the wine vinegar, sugar, and a pinch of salt. Use a wooden spoon to mix the sauce well in the sauceboat. Refrigerate until needed, as the sauce is eaten cold with the hot meat.

10. Slice the meat and arrange it on a plate. Serve with the mint sauce on the side.

This leg of lamb may also be sliced cold and eaten with the *Salsa di cervello* (Brain Sauce) on page 96. The slices should be arranged on a serving dish and the hot brain sauce should be poured over before serving.

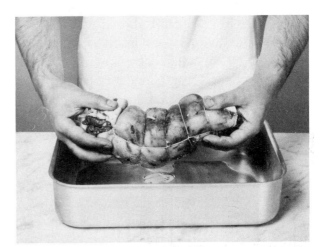

Agnello Ripieno

STUFFED LAMB SHOULDER

Lamb shoulder is usually used cut up for *spezzatino* or snipped as for *Maccheroni alla chitarra* (page 144). This is a unique dish in which the shoulder is boned and stuffed.

When purchasing an Italian shoulder of lamb (which is cut from one of the forequarters), the shank and a piece of the spine are considered part of the shoulder. In order to bone the whole lamb shoulder of the small Italian lamb the joint connected to the bone of the front leg (the shank) and a piece of the spine are usually cut off. But the American lamb shoulder is larger, and is also cut in pieces, so that in the United States it is easy to buy a 3-pound or so piece of lamb shoulder cut from the top of the shoulder (without the spine or shank piece). The following instructions still apply in a slightly simpler form. When small baby lambs are available you may want to try the meat cut in the Italian way. Since it may not be possible to have a butcher bone it for you, this is the way to bone the meat yourself.

3 to 3½ pounds lamb shoulder, from the top in one piece,   SERVES 4
   unboned (or about 1 pound boned)
About 10 sprigs Italian parsley, leaves only
3 sage leaves, fresh or preserved in salt
½ tablespoon rosemary leaves, fresh, preserved in salt, or dried and blanched
3 or 4 basil leaves, fresh or preserved in salt
½ small carrot
½ small red onion
1 Italian sweet sausage without fennel seeds, or 3 ounces ground pork
Salt and freshly ground black pepper to taste
1 tablespoon olive oil
6 tablespoons sweet butter
1 cup dry white wine
About 1 cup chicken or beef broth

HOW TO BONE A LAMB SHOULDER

1. The small Italian lamb shoulder with the shank and piece of the spine attached. With a boning knife, cut off the lower part of the leg bone at the joint.

258

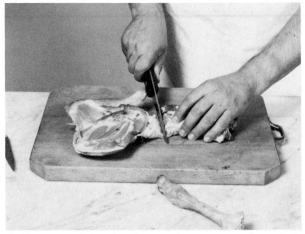

2. Remove the spine by cutting across where it is attached to the shoulder.

There are three different bones left: the upper part of the leg bone, the flat shoulder bone (or blade), and the bone connecting the two with knobs on either end.

3. At the end of the shoulder bone there are no tendons so that the meat is attached directly to the flat bone. Insert the knife between the bone and the meat attached to it, cutting

4. up the joint and freeing the bone.

5. Detach the meat along the length of the connecting bone, on both sides, up the other knob.

6. Cut around the knob, freeing it. Then cut the joint of the knob with the leg bone.

259

7. On the left you see the top of the leg, with the knife held above and parallel to the length of the leg bone. The meat is attached to the two sides; the top and the bottom of the bone have only a membrane holding it in place. Cut along both sides of the bone.

8. The meat is still attached at the lower and upper ends of the bone. At the lower end, insert the knife under the meat and cut through.

9. At the upper end, cut the bone free from the cartilage to which it is still attached.

Wet two pieces of wax paper in cold water. Put the boned shoulder between the pieces of dampened wax paper and pound it flat (page 266). Finely chop the parsley, sage, rosemary, basil, carrot, and onion together on a board. Remove the skin from the sausage.

10. Spoon the chopped ingredients over the flattened meat, then tear off pieces of the sausage and distribute them all over. Sprinkle with salt and pepper.

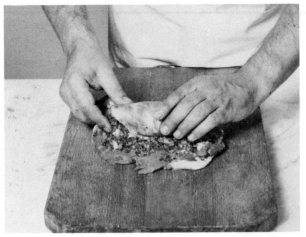

11. Roll up the stuffed meat, and tie it like a salami (pages 247–249).

Heat the oil and butter in a casserole over medium heat. When the butter is completely melted, add the meat and sauté all over for about 10 minutes. Add the wine and let it evaporate (about 15 minutes). Meanwhile, heat the broth. When the wine has evaporated, add about ¼ cup of the broth. Cover the casserole with its lid, and simmer for about 45 minutes, adding the remaining broth as needed. The meat should be slightly pink on the inside, but not completely rare, as Italians do not like lamb that way.

Transfer the meat to a board and remove the string.

12. Slice the meat. It may be served warm with or without its own sauce. Or, wait until it has cooled completely, slice it thinly, and serve either with its sauce, reheated, or without. The slices make an attractive presentation arranged on a plate.

RABBIT

If possible, buy the fresh rabbit with its pelt and have the butcher skin and clean it. Large old rabbits (sometimes mistakenly called hares in the United States) may be tough, so obtain a smaller rabbit of approximately 3 pounds.

Coniglio Ripieno Arrocchiato

BONED WHOLE RABBIT, ROLLED AND STUFFED

FROM PISA

The rabbit is opened down the center and completely boned, but left in one piece. The boning technique is somewhere between *Pollo disossato ripieno* (Boned Whole Stuffed Chicken), which is left unopened when boned, and the *Galantina di pollo* (Chicken in Galantine), which, like this dish, is opened, but only the skin is left in one piece. The illustrations show the steps for boning, flattening, stuffing, and rolling the whole rabbit. The rolled rabbit is sliced through and served warm or cold. It is an impressive main dish, light but full-flavored.

1 whole rabbit (about 3 pounds), skinned and cleaned   SERVES 6 TO 8

For the *frittata:*
3 extra large eggs
Salt to taste
2 tablespoons freshly grated Parmigiano
½ tablespoon olive oil
4 ounces mortadella, sliced thin

For the stuffing:
1 medium-sized clove garlic
5 sage leaves, fresh or preserved in salt, torn into pieces
About 1 tablespoon of rosemary leaves, fresh or preserved in salt
1 tablespoon olive oil
Salt and freshly ground black pepper

HOW TO BONE A WHOLE RABBIT

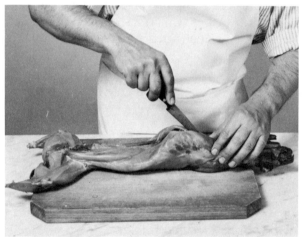

1. With a knife, cut all the way down the line where the left and right rib bones meet, opening the stomach completely.

2. Cut off the head where it joins the neck.

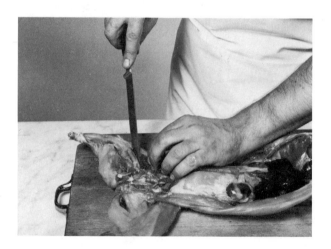

3. The back legs have two bones joined together. Find the joint where the top leg bone is attached to the back and cut it.

4. Pass the knife along the length on both sides of the top bone, up to the other joint, to detach the meat from the bone.

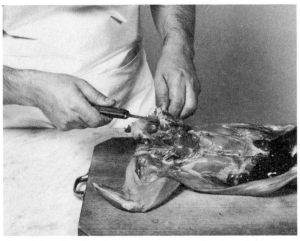

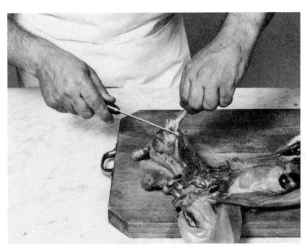

5 and 6. Cut the joint connecting the two bones.

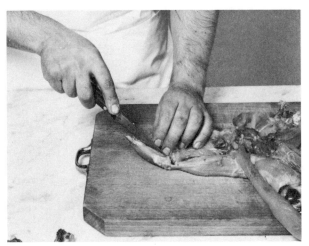

7. As this bone has meat on only one side, simply cut the bone off the meat.

Repeat the procedure for the other back leg.

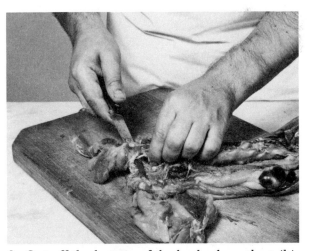

8. Cut off the bottom of the back where the tail is attached to the rest of the back.

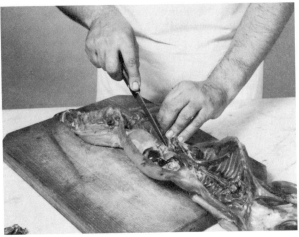

9. With the knife, detach the meat from both sides of the spine until you reach the ribs. The spine bone is still attached to the skin along the back. Since there is no meat on the back or breast, it is a delicate operation to detach the individual vertebrae without breaking the skin.

10. Starting at the bottom end, with the knife

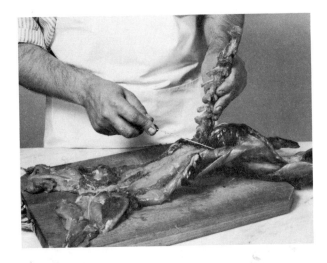

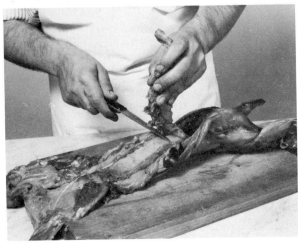

11 and 12. gently follow the undulating pattern of alternating vertebrae and joints. Do not try to cut in a straight line. The meat will be detached from its many connections to the individual vertebrae. Cut off the spine at the beginning of the ribs.

13. The individual rib bones are attached at one end to the spine and at the other end to the skin of the breast. It is necessary to loosen and detach each individual rib from the skin.

14. The ribs are attached to the outer skin by a thin membrane which covers them. This membrane must be cut for each rib.

When all the ribs on both sides are freed,

15. the rest of the spine may be detached in the same way as the first part (see photos 11 and 12).

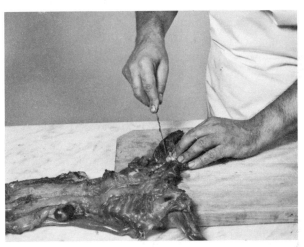

16. The front legs also have two bones joined together. Detach the first leg bone at the top at the joint connecting with the carcass.

17. Cut off the entire lower part of the leg at the joint of the two bones. Discard it as it has no meat. Now the top bone is completely free. Repeat with the other front leg.

Wet a large piece of wax paper in cold water.

265

18. Spread out the boned rabbit at one end of the wet paper and fold over the other half of the paper.

19. Use a meat pounder to flatten the rabbit.

Prepare the *frittata* in a 10-inch omelette pan with the eggs, salt, Parmigiano, and oil (page 114). Cut the *frittata* in half and let it cool for a few minutes.

20. Spread the rabbit open on the table and cover it with the two *frittata* halves.

Finely chop garlic on a board. Arrange the *mortadella* slices over the *frittata*. Then sprinkle with the garlic, sage, 1 heaping tablespoon of the rosemary, and salt and pepper.

Preheat the oven to 375 degrees.

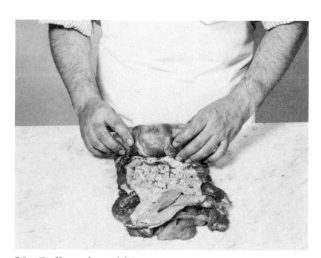

21. Roll up the rabbit.

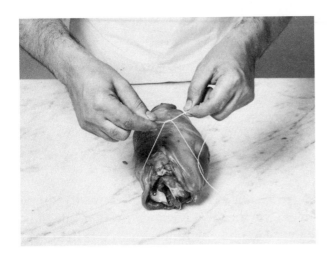

22. Tie the rolled rabbit like the stuffed turkey neck (pages 247–249).

Oil a large sheet of aluminum foil on the shiny side and sprinkle over salt, pepper, and the remaining rosemary leaves. (The shiny side of the foil should always be facing the food as it is less likely to stick. Also, when wrapped up and facing inward, it will not create reflection in the oven, thereby affecting the heat level.)

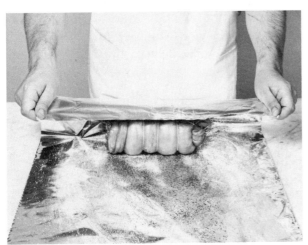

23. Place the rabbit on the foil and roll it up.

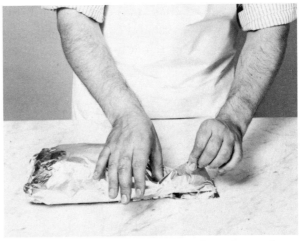

24. Close tightly like a package. Place the package in a baking dish and bake for 1½ hours.

Remove from oven and allow to cool for about 1 hour. Then refrigerate until completely cold (about 2 hours). (The rolled rabbit may also be eaten warm. It may be sliced about an hour after it is removed from the oven.) Unwrap, setting aside the juice, then, remove the string, and

25. slice.

The attractive slices of rabbit roll make a nice presentation when arranged on a serving dish. Pour the reserved juice over the slices. Rosemary sprigs make a fine decoration because rosemary is part of the dish (and is not merely ornamental).

CHAPTER 11

Veal (*Vitella* and *Vitello*)

Veal in Italy is different than in America and generally of better quality; that is because the breeds used are different, and the meat is younger. The white milk-fed veal is called *vitella* and it is difficult to find anything comparable here. The slightly older *vitello*, which has already progressed to eating grass, is still, nonetheless, younger than most pink veal found here. The American categories of veal and calf do not adequately correspond to *vitella* and *vitello*. (Even beef is eaten younger in Italy and probably corresponds to a "yearling" in the United States.)

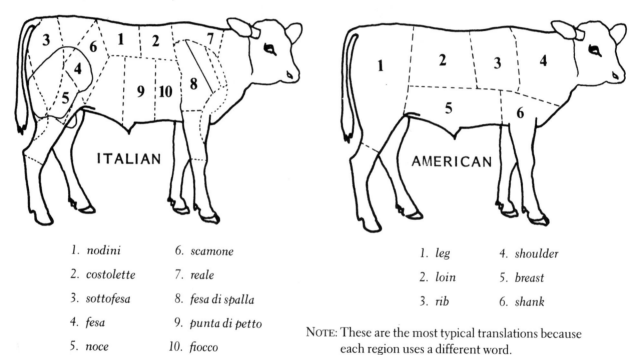

ITALIAN

1. *nodini*
2. *costolette*
3. *sottofesa*
4. *fesa*
5. *noce*
6. *scamone*
7. *reale*
8. *fesa di spalla*
9. *punta di petto*
10. *fiocco*

AMERICAN

1. *leg*
2. *loin*
3. *rib*
4. *shoulder*
5. *breast*
6. *shank*

NOTE: These are the most typical translations because each region uses a different word.

The Italian way of cutting veal is also different. The drawings in illustrations 32–33 demonstrate the correspondences. The tender muscle meat or veal cutlets used for *scaloppine* or *involtini* (stuffed and rolled *scaloppine*) may come from a number of different cuts, mainly the sirloin upper leg sections both front and back (in Italian, the *sottofesa*, *codone*—the *fesa* sections of the front and back sirloins—and *noce*). The rib or *costola* (or *costolette*) meat may also be used. Ten of the recipes included here use the *scaloppine* cut, although it may not necessarily be called *scaloppine* in the recipe's title. Often words such as *involtini*, *piccatine* (the expression used in Veneto), *bracioline* (a slang word meaning small slices of veal, beef or pork), or *tordimatti* (mock veal birds) are used, but they all require *scaloppine*.

   Ossibuchi are cut from the veal shank. (Included is also a turkey imitation of *ossobuco*, which is really quite good.)

   The loin section *(contrafiletto)* is often divided into the whole fillet and the whole contrafillet, of which either may be used for the three dishes, *Arrocchiato di vitella* (Roast Loin of Veal Laced with Green Peppercorns and Sage), *Vitello tonnato* (Veal with Tuna Flavoring), and *Vitella all'aceto balsamico* (Veal in Balsamic Vinegar). The shoulder and breast sections *(spalla* and *petto)* yield the veal cubes or small pieces for the *spezzatini*. A veal *spezzatino* included here is the *Fricassea di vitella* (Fricassee of Veal).

   At the end of the chapter is a section on the specialty cuts of the animal, such as the brains and sweetbreads, which are particularly delicate. The veal kidney is used in the *Involtini ripieni di rognone* (Rolled Veal Scaloppine Stuffed with Kidney). Brains are deep fried or sautéed [see *Cervello al limone* (Veal Brains in Lemon Sauce), page 298]. Sweetbreads are used in the rich filling of the puff pastry *turbante* [*Turbante ripieno* ("Stuffed" *Turbante*), page 458]. Both brains and sweetbreads are often used as a binding ingredient as in *Cima alla genovese* in chapter 10, which is boned, stuffed, and pressed breast of veal.

HOW TO CUT AND POUND A VEAL CUTLET

(Applied to all veal cutlets, whether the dish is called *scaloppine*, *bracioline*, *piccatine*, *tordimatti*, or *involtini*.)

1. With one hand, hold the muscle cut of meat firmly, while cutting a slice no more than ¼ inch thick with a knife held in your other hand.

2. Trim the slice on all sides.

3. Lay the meat between two sheets of wax paper which have been dampened with cold water so that the meat does not stick to the paper.

Notice that the meat and paper are held down by one hand at the end away from the body. The other hand should hold the pounder with the handle off the surface of the table so that you do not hit the table with your knuckles when pounding. The classic movement for pounding is first to strike the meat with the flat pounder, and, in a continuing movement, to

4. draw the pounder over the surface of the meat, toward you. Continue pounding until the meat is as thin as you wish.

5. Another type of meat pounder, a non-Italian one, of wood. Notice the ridged side which may be used to tenderize meat. This type is not popular with Italians because they do not like to tenderize meat artificially.

Bracioline o Scaloppine all'Empolese

VEAL SCALOPPINE WITH PURÉED ARTICHOKE SAUCE

FROM EMPOLI IN TUSCANY

Empoli, in the Arno valley near Florence, is famous for the musician Busoni, for its excellent glass (including the celebrated flasks) and for the large artichokes called *mamme* first developed there in the eighteenth century. Until that time, all artichokes were small. It was the great interest in developing agriculture and new plant species at that time that brought Thomas Jefferson to Tuscany to learn what he could, taking back the knowledge with him to Virginia. Most *all'empolese* dishes include artichokes, but this puréed artichoke sauce is unusual and different from the famous Genoese one using artichoke pieces (page 149).

1 large or 2 medium-sized artichokes
2 lemons
1 clove garlic, peeled
About 15 sprigs Italian parsley, leaves only
½ cup olive oil
Salt and freshly ground black pepper
1 cup hot chicken or beef broth
6 veal scaloppine (about 1½ pounds), pounded
About ½ cup unbleached all-purpose flour
2 tablespoons sweet butter

SERVES 6

Soak the artichoke in a bowl of cold water with the juice and the 2 halves of a lemon for 30 minutes. Clean the artichoke following the directions on page 350, and cut it into 16 pieces by cutting each cleaned quarter first vertically, then separating the stem from the leaf part. Put the artichoke pieces back in the cold water with the lemon.

Finely chop the garlic and two thirds of the parsley together on a board.

Heat ¼ cup of the oil in a saucepan over medium heat. When the oil is hot, add the chopped ingredients along with the drained artichokes. Sauté for about 5 minutes and sprinkle with salt and pepper. Pour in the broth, cover the pan, and simmer for about 25 minutes. At that time the artichokes should be tender. Remove the pan from the heat and pass the contents through a food mill. Let the sauce stand until needed.

Coarsely chop the remaining parsley and squeeze the remaining lemon.

Lightly flour the *scaloppine*. Heat the remaining oil and the butter in a large skillet. When the butter is completely melted, add the *scaloppine* and sauté them for 2 minutes on each side. Pour the strained sauce over the veal, taste for salt and pepper, and cook for about 5 minutes, when the *scaloppine* should be tender and the sauce very creamy. Pour the lemon juice over the *scaloppine* and immediately remove the skillet from the heat. Transfer the veal to a warm serving dish. Pour the sauce over the *scaloppine* and sprinkle them with the remaining chopped parsley. Serve immediately.

Scaloppine alla Senese

VEAL SCALOPPINE WITH TARRAGON SIENA STYLE

Tarragon has been Siena's most characteristic herb since at least medieval times. And, as the Maremma near the city is the main area for water buffalo north of Naples, their cheese, mozzarella, is also used more in Siena than in other northern areas. Naturally, it is to be expected that *scaloppine* in the Siena style would use these two characteristic ingredients.

1 pound fresh tomatoes or drained canned imported Italian tomatoes   SERVES 6
4 ounces mozzarella
6 veal scaloppine (about 1½ pounds), pounded
¼ cup olive oil
2 tablespoons sweet butter
Salt and freshly ground black pepper
½ teaspoon fresh tarragon leaves, or a scant ½ teaspoon dried

Pass the tomatoes through a food mill to remove the seeds and skin.

Cut the mozzarella into ¼-inch slices and then into very thin strips.

Heat the oil and butter in a skillet over medium heat. When the butter is completely melted, add the cutlets. Sauté for 2 minutes on both sides, sprinkle with salt and pepper, and add the strained tomatoes and the tarragon. Simmer for about 5 minutes. Sprinkle over the strips of mozzarella and cook until the cheese starts to melt. Remove the skillet from the heat and transfer the meat and sauce to a warm serving dish. Serve immediately.

Scaloppine di Vitella alla Salvia

VEAL SCALOPPINE WITH SAGE

This dish is another from Siena, but it is the simplest of treatments. The floured veal is sautéed in olive oil seasoned with pungent sage. The alternating unsqueezed lemon slices impart the slightest hint of their perfume.

About ½ cup unbleached all-purpose flour   SERVES 6
6 veal scaloppine (about 1½ pounds), pounded
⅓ cup olive oil
6 large sage leaves, fresh or preserved in salt
Salt and freshly ground black pepper
1 lemon, sliced

Place the flour on a piece of aluminum foil and flour both sides of the veal very lightly.

Heat the oil in a skillet over medium heat. When the oil is hot, add the sage leaves and sauté for a few seconds. Then add 3 or 4 *scaloppine*, sprinkle with salt and pepper, and sauté for 2 minutes on each side.

Remove the *scaloppine* from the pan and place them in a warm serving dish in an overlapping row, alternating each piece with a slice of lemon. Repeat until all the *scaloppine* are cooked. Pour the remaining juice from the skillet over the veal and serve immediately.

Scaloppine ai Funghi Porcini

SCALOPPINE WITH WILD MUSHROOMS

FROM NORTHERN ITALY

This favorite of central and northern Italy is a dish that travels well, because it is better made with the more flavorful dried *porcini* mushrooms than with the fresh ones. This is one of the rare veal dishes made with red rather than white wine, but the rich mushroom flavor requires it.

2 ounces dried porcini *mushrooms*
About 20 sprigs Italian parsley, leaves only
1 clove garlic, peeled
¼ cup olive oil
2 tablespoons sweet butter
About ½ cup unbleached all-purpose flour
6 veal scaloppine (about 1½ pounds), pounded
Salt and freshly ground black pepper
½ cup dry red wine
1 tablespoon tomato paste

SERVES 6

Soak the mushrooms in a bowl of lukewarm water for about 30 minutes.

Finely chop the parsley and garlic together on a board.

Heat the oil and butter in a skillet over medium heat.

Meanwhile, lightly flour the *scaloppine*. When the butter is completely melted, add the chopped ingredients and then the veal. Sauté for 2 minutes on each side, sprinkle with salt and pepper, and transfer the *scaloppine* to a dish. Add the wine and tomato paste to the skillet and let the wine evaporate very slowly (about 15 minutes). Drain the mushrooms and be sure no sand is still attached to them. Pass the soaking water of the mushrooms through very heavy cheesecloth to remove the sand completely. Add 1 cup of the strained water to the skillet along with the mushrooms. Simmer for about 15 minutes to reduce the sauce. Taste for salt and pepper and return the *scaloppine* to the skillet. Cook about 10 minutes.

Coarsely chop the remaining parsley. Remove the skillet from the heat and transfer the *scaloppine* to a warm serving dish. Pour the sauce over the meat, sprinkle with the chopped parsley, and serve immediately.

Scaloppine al Vin Santo

SCALOPPINE WITH VIN SANTO

FROM THE CHIANTI AREA

All *Chianti* vineyards produce a special intense amber-colored wine called Vin Santo. It ranges from dry to sweet in taste and is used for aperitifs and to accompany desserts.

Choice white wine grapes are allowed to dry a bit in the sun on beds of straw. This increases the sweetness of the grapes and, therefore, the alcohol content of the wine. The aging process is unique. Stored in small oak barrels directly under the terra-cotta roofs, the wine should pass through four yearly cycles of hot and cold, after which it may be bottled. This unique wine, produced in small quantities, is greatly prized in Tuscany and invariably by visitors who become acquainted with it and wonder why it is not more widely available. There should be no reason why the *Chianti* producers who ship their normal wines cannot include some cases of Vin Santo if we request it.

Since Vin Santo is much more ancient than Marsala, which dates only from the eighteenth century, it is possible that this dish precedes the more famous *Scaloppine al Marsala*. It is special enough to include here even though the wine may be difficult to obtain.* Perhaps this splendid recipe will help to create the demand for Vin Santo, making it more available. Until then on your next visit to Italy why not bring back some bottles of the rare Vin Santo rather than some other items more available here.

8 tablespoons sweet butter
6 slices Tuscan bread
About ½ cup unbleached all-purpose flour
6 veal scaloppine (about 1½ pounds), pounded
8 tablespoons olive oil
Salt and freshly ground black pepper
1 cup dry Vin Santo, dry Sherry, or dry Marsala†
About 1 cup beef broth

SERVES 6

Melt 4 tablespoons of the butter in a skillet over low heat. When butter is completely melted, add the bread and sauté until very lightly golden brown on both sides (about 2 minutes on each side). Transfer the bread from the skillet to a serving dish, making a single layer which completely covers the bottom of the dish.

Lightly flour the *scaloppine* on both sides. Return the skillet to medium heat and add the remaining butter and the oil. When butter is completely melted, add the veal, sprinkle with salt and pepper, and sauté for about 2 minutes on each side. Add the

Vin Santo and let the wine evaporate very slowly (about 15 minutes). At that time *scaloppine* should be tender and a creamy sauce should have formed.

Use tongs to transfer the *scaloppine* from the skillet to a warm serving dish, placing each one on top of a slice of bread. Cover the serving dish with aluminum foil to keep it warm.

Immediately add the broth to the skillet, raise the heat, and reduce the sauce as quickly as possible. Taste for salt and pepper. Remove the foil from the serving dish, pour the reduced sauce over the veal, and serve immediately.

Scaloppine agli Asparagi

SCALOPPINE WITH ASPARAGUS SAUCE

FROM NORTHERN ITALY

There are two traditional uses for this refreshing sauce of puréed asparagus which is eaten with pasta and may also be used to cover veal *scaloppine*. Thinly sliced veal is the appropriate meat to be sauced by it, and an excellent combination it is. The dish can also be prepared by substituting the tender parts of three large artichokes for the asparagus.

* It is beginning to be more available.

† Preparing the dish with Sherry or Marsala will not only destroy the authenticity of the dish but will also alter its taste completely.

1 pound asparagus
Coarse-grained salt
1½ cups beef or chicken broth
8 tablespoons (1 stick) sweet butter
About 1 cup unbleached all-purpose flour
Salt and freshly ground black pepper
¼ cup olive oil
6 veal scaloppine (about 1½ pounds), pounded
About 15 sprigs Italian parsley, leaves only
1 lemon, sliced

SERVES 6

Prepare the sauce. Boil the asparagus following the directions on page 344. Remove the asparagus from the pot and let stand for a few minutes on a board. Cut off the asparagus tips and set aside. Pass the asparagus stalk through a food mill into a small bowl. Transfer the passed asparagus to a saucepan and add the broth. Bring to a boil over medium heat.

Meanwhile, melt 4 tablespoons of the butter in a second saucepan over medium heat. When the butter is completely melted, add 1½ tablespoons of the flour and stir with a wooden spoon until the flour turns a very light brown. Add the boiling asparagus-broth mixture all at once, mix very well, and simmer for about 10 minutes. Taste for salt and pepper.

Heat the remaining butter and the oil in a large skillet over medium heat. Lightly flour the *scaloppine*. When the butter is completely melted, add the veal and sauté for 2 minutes on each side, sprinkling each side with salt and pepper. Transfer the cutlets to a warm serving dish and cover with aluminum foil to keep the meat warm. Add the sauce and the asparagus pieces to the skillet, taste for salt and pepper, and simmer for 5 minutes longer.

Coarsely chop the parsley on a board.

When the sauce is reduced, pour it over the *scaloppine*, and sprinkle with parsley. Serve immediately with the lemon slices.

Piccatine in Carpione

COLD VEAL SCALOPPINE IN PIQUANT SAUCE   FROM LOMBARDY

Carpione is a type of pink or salmon trout native to Lake Garda. There is a traditional way of cooking and marinating it with wine vinegar, onions, garlic, spices, and herbs. The technique of cooking *in carpione* became so popular that it was applied to other fish and even to veal *scaloppine*. These dishes are always served cold and may be eaten as an appetizer all year long, or as a main dish in the summer. *Piccatine* is the expression used for *scaloppine* in this area of Italy.

2 extra large eggs
6 veal scaloppine (about 1½ pounds), pounded
Salt and freshly ground black pepper
About ½ cup unseasoned bread crumbs, preferably homemade
8 tablespoons sweet butter
About 10 sprigs Italian parsley, leaves only
2 cloves garlic, peeled
2 tablespoons pignoli (pine nuts)
2 tablespoons raisins
1 medium-sized red onion
¼ cup olive oil
About 6 whole black peppercorns
1 bay leaf
½ cup red wine vinegar
½ cup cold water

SERVES 6

Beat the egg with a fork in a small bowl. Add salt to taste and a little pepper. Add the cutlets to the bowl, mix very well, and marinate for at least 1 hour, mixing occasionally.

Lay a sheet of aluminum foil on a board and spread the bread crumbs out on the foil. Remove one cutlet at a time from the egg and bread it on both sides (page 277). Press the *scaloppine* all over with the palm of your hand to make sure that both sides are coated uniformly.

Melt the butter in a large skillet over medium heat. When butter is completely melted, add the cutlets and sauté for 2 minutes on each side. Sprinkle with salt and pepper.

Finely chop the parsley and garlic together on a board. Transfer the cooked meat to a serving dish. (Do not pat with paper towels.) Arrange the cutlets in a row overlapping half of each with the following one. Sprinkle the chopped ingredients over the cutlets along with the pignoli and raisins.

Finely chop the onion on a board.

Heat the oil in a small saucepan over medium heat. When the oil is hot, add the chopped onion. Sauté lightly for about 10 minutes, or until the onion is translucent. Add the whole black peppercorns, bay leaf, wine vinegar, and water to the pan. Let the vinegar evaporate very slowly (for about 15 minutes). During this time the liquid should be reduced by half. Remove the pan from the heat and discard the bay leaf. Pour the sauce over the veal on the serving dish. Let the sauce cool for about 30 minutes, then wrap the dish with aluminum foil and refrigerate for at least 3 hours before serving.

Tordimatti

"MOCK" GAME BIRDS

FROM SIENA

Tordimatti is a humorous name which means literally "crazy *tordi*," the latter being a kind of small bird much prized by Italians for eating. They are "mock" game birds not only because of their shape, like the "veal birds" in English, but more specifically because they are prepared in the same manner and with the seasonings used to cook that delicacy. Once stuffed, they are seasoned with juniper berries and sage, classic elements of game cookery in Italy, and then wrapped in caul fat, which is necessary for game birds because of their dryness. The caul fat imparts its flavor to the veal, bringing it close in taste to the original dish.

SERVES 6

2 extra large eggs
6 veal scaloppine *(about 1½ pounds), pounded*
Pinch of salt

For the stuffing:
8 ounces prosciutto *or* pancetta
9 large sage leaves, fresh or preserved in salt
12 juniper berries
4 slices white bread
2 extra large eggs
6 tablespoons freshly grated Parmigiano
Salt and freshly ground black pepper
1 large piece of caul fat (or substitute 1 piece pancetta *for each cutlet)*
About 1 cup unseasoned bread crumbs, preferably homemade
1 pound potatoes
About ⅓ cup olive oil

Beat 2 of the eggs in a bowl with a pinch of salt. Put the cutlets in the eggs to marinate for about 1 hour.

Prepare the stuffing. Coarsely chop the *prosciutto*, 4 sage leaves, and the juniper berries together on a board and transfer to a second bowl.

Remove the crusts from the bread and add the bread to the second bowl. Then add the eggs, Parmigiano, and salt and pepper to taste. Mix everything together with a wooden spoon until homogeneous. Soak the caul fat in a small bowl of lukewarm water for about 15 minutes. Meanwhile, spread the bread crumbs on a sheet of aluminum foil.

HOW TO PREPARE TORDIMATTI

1. Take the marinated cutlets, one by one, out of the bowl (reserve the egg marinade for later use) and bread them. Press the *scaloppine* all over with the palm of your hand to make sure that both sides are coated uniformly.

2. Turn the cutlet over and repeat the procedure with the other side.

Add the leftover egg marinade to the second bowl with the stuffing ingredients and incorporate it with a wooden spoon.

Transfer the caul fat from the lukewarm water to a large bowl of cold water and let soak for a few minutes. Spread the caul fat out on a table.

3. Place the breaded cutlets on the caul fat well separated from one another.

Divide the stuffing into six parts and put a portion

4. on each piece of meat.

5. Use a scissors to cut the caul fat around each cutlet, leaving a margin of about 1 inch of caul fat around the edges of the meat.

6. Roll up each cutlet in its caul fat, turning in the sides of the fat to

7. make sure that caul fat covers the entire roll.

8. The rolls should look like wrapped *involtini.* Tie the "*involtini*" with string (page 282).

9. Place the rolled cutlets on a skewer with a leaf of sage between each two. (You may find it easier to turn the "*involtini*" if you run two skewers parallel through them.)

Preheat the oven to 375 degrees. Peel the potatoes and cut them into ½-inch-square cubes. Place the potatoes in a baking dish.

10. Place the skewer over the edges of the baking dish. Brush the *"involtini"* with oil and pour the remaining oil over the potatoes.

Place the baking dish in the oven and bake for about 45 minutes, turning the skewer over and stirring the potatoes every 10 minutes. Remove from oven. Sprinkle the potatoes with salt, mix very well, and transfer the potatoes to a warm serving dish.

11. Remove the *"involtini"* from the skewer

12. and arrange them on the serving dish with the potatoes.

Involtini Ripieni di Rognone

ROLLED VEAL SCALOPPINE STUFFED WITH KIDNEY

FROM THE EIGHTEENTH-CENTURY COURT OF NAPLES

Until recently it was possible to obtain veal loin roasts with the kidney left inside, which was a great favorite with many. But there is a marvelous eighteenth-century court dish of Naples which provides a similar combination of flavors. It is a picturesque dish, suitable for a more ambitious formal dinner. The kidneys are sliced and rolled inside the veal *scaloppine* and sautéed with a white wine sauce. When the dish is served, the veal is sliced through, revealing the interesting pattern inside with the contrasting color of the kidney in the center. It is, undoubtedly, a preordained combination of tastes, because veal and veal kidneys are also eaten together in a variety of dishes in different countries.

½ pound veal kidney
4 veal scaloppine *(about 1 pound), pounded*
About 1 cup coarse-grained salt
4 slices pancetta (about 4 ounces)
1 cup unbleached all-purpose flour
6 tablespoons sweet butter
About 1 cup dry white wine
Salt and freshly ground black pepper

SERVES 4

HOW TO CLEAN AND CUT VEAL KIDNEY

1. Insert a knife near the center of the kidney about 1 inch from the edge where the fat is joined to the meat. Move the knife around,

2. cutting the connections between the fat and the meat, on the sides.

3. Cut the connections underneath and pull the fat out in one piece.

4. Place whole kidney top side up in a crockery bowl. Start sprinkling with coarse-grained salt

5. until the entire top side is covered by about 1 cup of salt. The salt will absorb the bitter liquid from the kidney.

Leave the kidney this way for 2 hours. Wash off the salt in a large bowl of cold water and dry the kidney with paper towels. (This is the Italian method of preparing the kidney for cooking.)

6. Cut the kidney in half lengthwise, then slice each half into slices, following the instructions in the individual recipes.

281

1. Slice the kidney into ¼-inch-thick slices. The cross-sectioned kidney will make an attractive pattern when the finished *involtini* are sliced.

2. Place a slice of *pancetta* on each cutlet. Then arrange the kidney slices on top, overlapping slightly, in a row down the center of the cutlet.

3. Fold both sides of the cutlets to partially cover the kidney slices. Then roll up the cutlet.

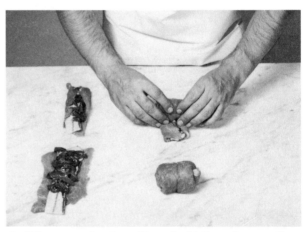

4. When you begin rolling, hold the edges so they do not re-open.

5. Use a thin string or twine, about three times the length of the *involtino*. Slide the string under the *involtino*, to its center. Then pull the ends of the string over and cross them without knotting.

6. Turn the *involtino* over and slide it around 90 degrees. Make a knot in the center.

HOW TO FLOUR VERY LIGHTLY

(This technique may be used to lightly flour anything.)

Place 2 *involtini* in a large colander, pour the flour over the *involtini* all at once, and shake vigorously, using both hands until all the flour passes through the colander.

Using this technique, only the thinnest film of flour clings to the meat, because the meat has not been pressed into the flour.

7. Flour the other two *involtini* the same way.

Melt the butter in a flameproof casserole over medium heat. When the butter is completely melted,

8. add the *involtini* to the casserole.

Sauté lightly for about 10 minutes, turning the *involtini* several times so that they are lightly browned on all sides. Add the wine, sprinkle with salt and pepper, cover, and let the wine evaporate (about 15 minutes) so a thick sauce is formed. At that time the meat should be tender and the kidneys not overcooked.

Transfer each *involtino* to the serving dish, removing the string.

9. To remove string, hold the *involtino* in place with a fork and use a scissors to make one cut in the string.

10. Hold one end of the string with the scissors and pull the entire string off in one piece.

11. Arrange the *involtini* on a warm serving dish and pour the sauce over them. (You may find it necessary to reduce the sauce.)

12. Or before adding the sauce, you may allow the *involtini* to cool for about 1 hour so they may be easily cut into slices from ¼ to ½ inch thick. The attractive slices may be arranged on a serving dish, with the sauce reheated and served in a sauceboat.

Involtini di Vitella

ROLLED VEAL SCALOPPINE STUFFED WITH SAUSAGE

FROM TUSCANY

The surprise stuffing inside the *involtino* is a sausage half. The sauce is a hearty tomato one which is permeated with the rich flavor of aromatic vegetables and sage (also placed inside the cutlet). The unusual feature of the dish is the combination of tomatoes with white rather than red wine.

4 *veal* scaloppine *(about 1 pound), pounded*   SERVES 4
2 *Italian sweet sausages without fennel seeds (6 ounces),*
   or about 6 ounces ground pork
4 *large sage leaves, fresh or preserved in salt*
1 *small red onion*
1 *small clove garlic, peeled*
1 *celery stalk*
1 *medium-sized carrot*
Scant ½ cup olive oil
1 *cup dry white wine*
Salt and freshly ground black pepper
1 *pound fresh tomatoes or drained canned imported Italian tomatoes*

284

Place the cutlets on a board. Remove the skin from the sausages. Cut the sausages in half and place a half on each cutlet with 1 whole sage leaf. Roll up the veal cutlets and tie with string to form *involtini* (page 282).

Finely chop the onion, garlic, celery, and carrot together on a board.

Heat the oil in a casserole over medium heat. When the oil is hot, add the chopped ingredients. Sauté for about 5 minutes, then add the *involtini* and cook for 5 minutes longer. Sprinkle with salt and pepper. Add the wine and let it evaporate for 5 minutes.

Transfer the *involtini* to a bowl. Cover with aluminum foil.

Cut the tomatoes into pieces and add them or the whole canned tomatoes to the casserole and cook for about 25 minutes. Taste for salt and pepper. Pass the sauce through a food mill. Return the strained sauce to the casserole and bring it to a simmer. Then add the half-cooked *involtini*. Cover the casserole and simmer for 15 minutes. At that time the meat should be tender and a smooth sauce should have formed. Transfer the *involtini* to a warm serving dish, removing the string. Pour the sauce over the *involtini* and serve immediately.

Arrocchiato di Vitella

ROAST LOIN OF VEAL LACED WITH GREEN PEPPERCORNS AND SAGE

FROM MILAN

How to butterfly, stuff and roll a tender cut of veal for roasting to pink perfection is illustrated below. When sliced through, it makes an attractive presentation, and the striking flavor of the green peppercorns and sage will have penetrated throughout the meat.

To prepare this veal roast, you or your butcher must cut the loin in the Italian manner: the loin is in two parts, comparable to the fillet and contrafillet of beef, joined by bones. These two sections are called by many names, among them "eye of the loin" as opposed to the "top-loin." The two parts may be separated, leaving the bones attached to the "eye," and then removing the bones. A 4-pound boneless piece of either "eye" or "top-loin" may be used for the *arrocchiato*. In Italy they are called *nodini* and are used mainly for boneless roasts. It is not difficult to instruct your butcher to cut the loin in this way or to do it yourself. See also page 249, *Cima alla genovese* (Stuffed Pressed Veal Breast).

4 pounds veal top loin or 4 pounds veal "eye of the loin"
3 tablespoons green peppercorns, drained
10 large sage leaves, fresh or preserved in salt
Salt and freshly ground black pepper

To prepare the meat for the *arrocchiato*, place the boneless whole fillet or contrafillet on a side that makes it wider than it is high.

HOW TO BUTTERFLY A TOP LOIN OF VEAL

1. Open the meat by cutting lengthwise through the middle,

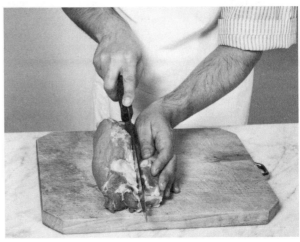

2. with the knife inserted two thirds of the way in.

3. Then spread it flat like a large *braciola*.
   Wet two large sheets of wax paper with cold water and place the opened meat between them.

4. Flatten with a meat pounder.
   Remove the top layer of wax paper and sprinkle the green peppercorns over the meat.
   Place the sage leaves all over and sprinkle with salt and black pepper.

5. Pick up one end of the meat with both hands and roll it up removing the bottom layer of wax paper as you roll.

Tie up the roll with string. Preheat the oven to 375 degrees.

Place the rolled up veal on the shiny side of a piece of aluminum foil. Sprinkle the outside of the meat with salt and pepper. Wrap the foil around it and place it in a baking dish. To get the veal to the proper pinkness, bake for about 45 to 55 minutes, depending on the thickness of the meat roll. Then remove from the oven and cool for 5 minutes.

Unwrap the aluminum foil and

6. slice the rolled veal like a loaf, removing the string from each piece.

Vitello Tonnato (Original version)

VEAL WITH TUNA FLAVORING

FROM PIEDMONT AND LOMBARDY

One of the most famous of all Italian dishes, *Vitello tonnato* in recent decades has been converted into an easier dish in which a tuna flavored *maionese* is placed over slices of veal (usually roasted). The original recipe, probably no older than the nineteenth century, is, however, quite different, more interesting and more delicious. A very tender cut, such as the veal fillet, is braised together with the tuna and other flavorings. All of the tastes enter into the veal itself, rather than just being added as a piquant sauce. And there is no *maionese* in any of the older recipes. In Italy, this version is still thought of as the authentic way of making the dish, though the *maionese* version, particularly with prepared *maionese*, is such a quick and easy way to use leftover veal roast that, unfortunately, it has become more widespread than the original, and one finds it even in Italian-language cookbooks. Once you try the original, I think you will appreciate its superiority and greater subtlety.

About 2 pounds veal "eye of the loin"   SERVES 10 TO 12
12 ounces canned tuna fish in oil (about two 7-ounce cans)
4 whole anchovies in salt, or 8 anchovy fillets in oil, drained
1 medium-sized red onion
2 cups dry white wine
1 bay leaf
½ cup olive oil
¼ cup capers in wine vinegar, drained
Salt and freshly ground black pepper
½ cup cold water

To serve:
2 lemons, sliced
¼ cup capers in wine vinegar, drained
About 25 cetriolini *(very small pickled cucumbers) in wine vinegar (see page 46)*

HOW TO PREPARE VITELLO TONNATO

1. Cut off the eye of the loin or have your butcher cut the loin in this particular way for you.

2. Completely remove the fat all around. Tie the meat like a salami (pages 247–249).

Drain the oil from the tuna fish and coarsely chop it on a board. Clean the anchovies if in salt (page 55).

Put the veal into a small oval casserole, then cut the onion into small pieces over the meat. Add the wine, half of the anchovy fillets, the bay leaf, half the oil, half the capers, and salt and pepper to taste. Bring to a boil over medium heat. When boiling, add the cold water. Cover the pan and simmer for about 2 hours or until the meat is cooked and tender. Let the meat cool in its sauce (about 1 hour).

Transfer the meat to a chopping board. Discard the bay leaf.

Pour the sauce from the casserole into a blender or food processor and add the remaining capers, anchovies, and oil. Blend until the sauce is homogeneous. If it is too thick, thin it with a little lemon juice. Cut the lemons in half, then cut each half into thin slices. Remove the string from the meat.

3. Cut the meat (making sure to cut across the grain) into thin slices. Arrange the slices on a serving dish, half overlapping.

4. Place thin slices of lemon between the slices of meat. Pour the sauce over the meat and arrange the remaining slices of lemon and capers and the pickles all around the edge of the serving dish.

Wrap the dish in aluminum foil or plastic wrap and refrigerate until needed. Serve cold.

Vitella all'Aceto Balsamico

VEAL IN BALSAMIC VINEGAR

FROM MODENA

A tender veal cut, cooked in the aromatic special "balsamic" vinegar of Modena. This celebrated vinegar has such a distinctive flavor that it should not be used interchangeably with normal wine vinegar. Used in a dish from its own region, it is incomparable. It is said in Italy that families in Modena leave the pedigreed "mothers" of their vinegar to heirs in their wills.

About 2 pounds of "eye of the loin" veal
1 clove garlic, peeled
2 medium-sized carrots
2 celery stalks
2 whole cloves
1 bay leaf
3 cups cold water
½ cup balsamic vinegar
2 tablespoons olive oil
Salt and freshly ground black pepper
Pinch of ground cinnamon

For the sauce (optional):
The juice of 1 lemon
½ cup olive oil

SERVES 8

Completely remove the fat from all around the veal. Tie the meat like a salami (pages 247–249).

Coarsely chop the garlic, carrots, and celery together on a board. Put the meat in a small oval casserole, then add the chopped ingredients, cloves, and bay leaf. Pour the cold water, vinegar, and olive oil over the meat. Sprinkle the meat with salt, pepper, and a pinch of cinnamon. Cover the casserole and simmer over medium heat for about 2 hours, turning the meat three or four times, skimming off the foam which rises to the top. Then let the meat cool in its sauce for about 1 hour.

Cut the meat into thin slices and arrange them on a serving dish.

The meat may be eaten with its sauce or with a cold dressing of lemon mixed with oil. If you use the sauce from the meat, it may have to be reduced. Then pass it through a food mill, reheat it, and pour over the veal.

Ossobuco

Two of the many recipes for making ossibuchi, slices of veal shank with the bone and marrow in the center, are included here. For the first, I have researched in the authoritative nineteenth-century cookbooks to get as close to the original as possible, as the dish is now so popular that it has many slight variants. One version that probably is no older than the nineteenth century is the traditional treatment in which each ossobuco is tied to keep its shape while cooking. The center piece of bone with its marrow is considered the pearl in the oyster, though an edible one. The flavoring of tomato and tomato paste is authentic to the dish, another indication that it is probably no more than 150 years old. (Tomato paste or as more accurately translated from Italian, tomato concentrate, has been unjustly maligned. It did not develop as a convenience substitute for tomatoes, but rather as a totally different thing, a concentrate. It has a different taste from cooked tomatoes, being heavily reduced, and is still often made and put up in jars in many Italian homes. Its misuse should not blind us to its legitimate uses.)

The second, a marvelous recipe without tomato sauce, is the ossobuco from the area of Novara in Piedmont, which, despite its famous red wine production, uses white wine in the recipe. The herb sauce is a mixture of chopped sage, rosemary, capers, olives, and lemon peel that achieves such a perfect integration that one does not immediately recognize its component parts.

I also include the mock "ossobuco" of turkey leg, which is still tied with string and, of course, there's no marrow to be eaten. Carrots and marjoram bring out the particular flavor of the turkey leg, which must simmer in broth and wine for a longer time than the veal. But the result is succulent and a very valid dish.

6 ossibuchi (veal shank cut into 1½ inch slices, bone marrow in center)*   SERVES 6
1 medium-sized red onion
1 medium-sized carrot
1 celery stalk
1 small piece lemon peel
2½ cups drained canned imported Italian tomatoes
3 tablespoons tomato paste
⅓ cup plus ¼ cup olive oil
5 tablespoons sweet butter
Salt and freshly ground black pepper
About ½ cup unbleached all-purpose flour
1½ cups dry white wine
1 clove garlic, peeled but left whole
About 20 sprigs Italian parsley, leaves only

Optional:
2 cups rice, preferably Italian Arborio
Coarse-grained salt
Scant ½ teaspoon saffron, ground

---

* Use 1 or 2 shanks depending on size and amount of meat and only the section which has meat surrounding the bone on all sides.

1. Saw off the end of the shank which has only a little meat.

2. With a knife, starting at the narrower end, cut the meat all around the bone every 1½ inches.

3. Finish separating the ossibuchi at the thicker end by sawing through the bone at each point where the meat has been cut. (Notice the butcher's saw for the meat.)

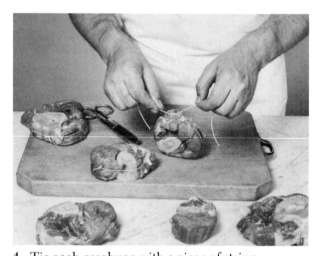

4. Tie each ossobuco with a piece of string.

Finely chop the onion, carrot, celery, and lemon peel together on a board. Pass the tomatoes through a food mill and mix with the tomato paste.

Heat ⅓ cup olive oil and 2 tablespoons of the butter in a saucepan over medium heat. When the butter is completely melted, add the chopped ingredients and sauté lightly for about 10 minutes. Then add the tomato-tomato paste mixture. Taste for salt and pepper and simmer for about 20 minutes.

Meanwhile, lightly flour the ossibuchi on both sides but not on the edges. Heat the remaining oil and butter in a flameproof casserole over medium heat. When the butter is completely melted, add the meat and sauté until golden brown on both sides (about 3 minutes each side). Add the wine and let it evaporate over very low heat for about 20 minutes.

Pass all the ingredients of the saucepan through a food mill and pour over the meat. Add the garlic. Cover the casserole and simmer for about 40 minutes. Then turn the ossibuchi on the other side, discard the garlic, and taste for salt and pepper. Cover again and simmer for about 35 minutes longer. Coarsely chop the parsley on a board.

5. Transfer the ossibuchi to a warm serving dish and remove the string. Pour the sauce over the veal. Sprinkle with the parsley and serve.

Everyone should have a small fork in addition to the normal one in order to eat the marrow, which is considered the choicest part of the ossobuco.

If the ossobuco is to be served accompanied by rice, prepare the rice while the meat is cooking. Twenty minutes before ossibuchi are ready, bring a large pot of water to a boil. Add coarse-grained salt to taste and add the rice and saffron. Stir with a wooden spoon and let the rice cook until *al dente* (about 16 minutes). Drain the rice and arrange it on a warm serving dish. Place the already cooked ossibuchi on top of the rice; then pour over all the remaining sauce from the casserole. Sprinkle with parsley and serve immediately.

Ossobuco alla Novese

OSSOBUCO FROM NOVARA

FROM PIEDMONT

SERVES 6

6 ossibuchi (veal shank cut into 1½ inch slices,
*   with bone and marrow in center)*
About 15 green olives in brine, drained
1 tablespoon rosemary leaves, fresh or preserved in salt
6 sage leaves, fresh or preserved in salt
2 tablespoons capers in wine vinegar, drained
1 small clove garlic, peeled
1 small piece of lemon peel
2 cups dry white wine
4 tablespoons olive oil
2 tablespoons sweet butter
About ½ cup flour
Salt and freshly ground black pepper

Plus:
Coarse-grained salt
2 cups rice, preferably Italian Arborio type

Tie the ossibuchi (page 292).

Pit the olives. Finely chop pitted olives, rosemary, sage, capers, garlic, and lemon peel together on a board. Transfer the chopped ingredients to a crockery bowl and add the wine. Stir very well.

Heat the oil and butter in a flameproof casserole over medium heat. Lightly flour the ossibuchi on both sides but not the edges. When the butter is completely melted, add the meat and sauté until golden brown on both sides (about 3 minutes to a side). Add the wine with all the chopped ingredients, cover the casserole, and simmer for about 50 minutes. Then turn the ossibuchi over, taste for salt and pepper, cover again, and simmer for 25 minutes longer.

Meanwhile, bring a large pot of water to a boil. Add coarse-grained salt to taste and add the rice. Stir with a wooden spoon and let the rice cook until *al dente* (about 16 minutes). Drain the rice and arrange it on a warm serving platter. Remove the string from the cooked ossibuchi and place meat over the rice. Then pour over all the remaining sauce from the casserole and serve immediately.

"Ossobuco" di Tacchino

TURKEY "OSSOBUCO"

FROM PIEDMONT

4 turkey drumsticks (from turkeys weighing about 15 pounds)   SERVES 4
1 medium-sized clove garlic, peeled
1 medium-sized carrot
1 medium-sized red onion
About ⅓ cup unbleached all-purpose flour
¼ cup olive oil
6 tablespoons sweet butter
¼ cup dry white wine
2 teaspoons rosemary leaves, fresh, preserved in salt, or dried and blanched
About 2 cups hot chicken or beef broth
1 teaspoon dried marjoram
Salt and freshly ground black pepper
About 10 sprigs Italian parsley, leaves only

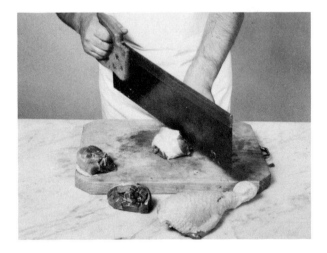

1. Cut the turkey drumsticks into ossibuchi using only the thicker top parts of the leg (about 5 inches long).

Tie these tall turkey ossibuchi with string as in photo for classical ossibuchi (page 292).

Finely chop the garlic, carrot, and onion together on a board. Lightly flour the ossibuchi on both sides but not at the sides.

Heat the oil and butter in a flameproof casserole over medium heat. When the butter is completely melted, add the ossibuchi. Watch the turkey ossibuchi during cooking to be sure they remain standing and do not tilt to one side. Sauté until golden brown on both sides (about 2 minutes each side). Add the chopped ingredients, sauté for 2 minutes, then add the wine and let it evaporate very slowly (for about 5 minutes).

Meanwhile, put the rosemary leaves in a small piece of cheesecloth and tie it like a bag. Add half of the broth, the marjoram, and the bag with the rosemary leaves to the casserole. Cover the casserole and simmer for about 1 hour. Taste for salt and pepper, turn the ossibuchi, and add more broth if needed. Cover again and simmer for about 30 minutes longer. At that time the ossibuchi should be tender and a sauce should have formed.

Coarsely chop the parsley. Transfer the "ossibuchi" from the casserole to a board. Free the meat from the bone, removing any tough tendons. Meanwhile, reduce the sauce over high heat until (about 15 minutes). Transfer the meat to a warm serving dish, pour the hot sauce over it, and sprinkle with the chopped parsley. Serve immediately.

FRICASSEA

Fricassea in Italian means a *spezzatino* of veal, chicken, or lamb, made with a sauce of egg yolks and lemon juice. This is different from the American "fricassee." Even the Italian dictionary assumes that the origin of the term is the French "fricassée." But at the risk of sounding chauvinistic, I must point to a recipe in a 1556 Italian cookbook, almost 150 years before De la Varenne was translated into Italian with his recipes for fricassées. The recipe is called *Pottaccio di vitello in fracasso*. *Fracassare* in Italian has a similar meaning to *spezzare*, but implies only a bit more violence while breaking the thing into pieces. The meaning of *fracassare*, to break the meat into small pieces, would apply to all fricassees, even the American ones. And the 1556 recipe is for a *spezzatino* of veal. I believe we have here another example of movement back and forth from Italy to France and then back again that we see so often in the sixteenth and seventeenth centuries in the joint development of "cuisine" and "cucina." In any case, the *Fricassea di vitella* is a delicious *spezzatino* and a long established favorite in Italy.

Fricassea di Vitella

FRICASSEE OF VEAL

FROM ALL OVER ITALY

SERVES 6

¾ ounce dried porcini mushrooms
1½ pounds veal shoulder or breast
1 medium-sized carrot
1 celery stalk
½ medium-sized red onion
5 or 6 sprigs Italian parsley
5 or 6 basil leaves, fresh or preserved in salt
12 tablespoons (1½ sticks) sweet butter
1 tablespoon unbleached all-purpose flour
1 cup hot beef or chicken broth
Salt and freshly ground white pepper
2 tablespoons lemon juice
2 extra large egg yolks

Soak the mushrooms in a small bowl of lukewarm water for 30 minutes.

HOW TO PREPARE FRICASSEA DI VITELLA

Cut the veal into 1-inch cubes.

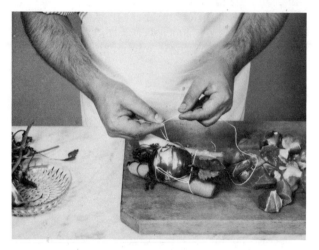

1. Tie together the carrot, celery, onion, parsley, and basil with a string so they can be removed all together.

Heat 8 tablespoons of the butter in a casserole over medium heat. When the butter is completely melted, add the flour and stir very well until it is completely incorporated. Then add the tied vegetables and hot broth. Simmer for 2 minutes and add the meat. Sprinkle with salt and white pepper.

2. Place a sheet of wax paper or parchment paper over the casserole, then

3. cover the casserole with its lid.

Simmer for 15 minutes over low heat. Meanwhile, drain the mushrooms and be sure that no sand remains attached to them. Coarsely chop the mushrooms on a board.

4. Remove the tied vegetables and add chopped mushrooms. Cover again with the wax paper and lid and simmer for about 15 minutes longer. At that moment the meat should be tender.

5. Combine the lemon juice with the egg yolks, stirring with a wooden spoon in a rotating motion (like a *maionese*) until well amalgamated.

Remove the casserole from the heat, and add the egg yolks-lemon juice mixture. Cut the remaining butter into small pieces over the *fricassea* and mix thoroughly. Transfer to a warm serving dish.

6. and serve immediately.

ANIMELLE, SCHIENALI E CERVELLO

(Sweetbreads, Spinal Marrow, and Brains)

1. On the left is the sweetbreads or *animelle*, which consist of the pancreas (shown here), and in younger animals also the thymus. The thymus, which is not visible in the photo, takes its name from the herb thyme, whose leaf it resembles in shape. These two glands are sometimes differentiated for culinary purposes as stomach sweetbreads and throat or neck sweetbreads. Sweetbreads are used as

a binder. In the center we see the spinal marrow or *schienali*, used extensively in Italian cooking for pasta stuffings and as a binder in forcemeats. (See *Cima alla genovese* [Stuffed Pressed Veal Breast], page 249.) This is more difficult to obtain from American butchers than the more commonly used sweetbreads. On the right are veal brains. Even more delicate and highly prized are the brains of very young lambs, though they are obtainable for only a very short period of the year.

Considered a delicacy since Renaissance times in Italy are the unusual sausages made of fresh brains, which, of course, must be cooked and eaten immediately.

Cervello al Limone

VEAL BRAINS IN LEMON SAUCE

FROM NORTHERN ITALY

The delicate veal brains are blanched, lightly sautéed in butter, and then simmered in broth. Then lemon juice and peel are added with fresh parsley to complete the sauce.

2 veal brains
About ½ cup unbleached all-purpose flour
8 tablespoons (1 stick) sweet butter
About 1 cup chicken broth
Salt and freshly ground black pepper
1 lemon
About 15 sprigs Italian parsley, leaves only

SERVES 4

Blanch the brains following the directions on page 168. Remove only the inside membrane. Cut the brain into 2-inch pieces.

Put 2 level tablespoons of the flour on a plate. With a fork incorporate 4 tablespoons of the butter into the flour. Heat the broth in a small saucepan. Lightly flour the brains with the remaining flour.

Heat the remaining butter in a casserole over medium heat. When the butter is completely melted, add the floured brains. Sauté for 2 minutes, taste for salt and pepper, and add the butter-flour mixture.

Stir with a wooden spoon and add the hot broth. Lower the heat, cover the pan, and simmer for about 10 minutes.

Grate the lemon rind and squeeze the lemon. Mix the lemon juice and the grated rind together. Finely chop the parsley on a board. Warm a serving dish.

Remove the pan with the brains from the heat. Add the juice and rind and mix gently, but very well. Transfer the brains with all the sauce to the prepared dish. Sprinkle the parsley over the brains and serve immediately.

CHAPTER 12

Mollusks, Seafood, and Fish

SARDINE E ACCIUGHE (FRESH SARDINES AND ANCHOVIES)

1. The slightly larger fish in the upper part of the photo are sardines. Fresh sardines are silver with blue tints and are a member of the herring family. Sardines are called *sardine* in Italian. In the dialect of some regions this is shortened to *sarde*, as in the Sicilian dish *Pasta con le sarde* (Pasta with Fresh Sardines), page 189. Sardines, of course, are used extensively on their namesake island, Sardinia, as, for example, in the following recipe for *Sardine di Alghero* (Sardines in the Style of Alghero).

Fresh sardines are used a great deal in Italy and a variety can be found on both the Atlantic and Pacific coasts of the United States for a good part of the year. Italian fish markets in America often have them in season and they could be more generally available if there was more of a demand for them.

The smaller fish in the lower part of the photo are anchovies, *acciughe* in classic Italian and *alici* in many dialects. This is strictly a Mediterranean fish, bluish on the back and white on the stomach. Of the many ways in Italy of preparing fresh anchovies, some especially worth trying are boned anchovies freshly marinated in olive oil and lemon juice or wine vinegar, and anchovies boned, stuffed, and deep-fried. Fresh anchovies are not salty as they are when they are dried and preserved in salt or oil.

1. Use a knife to open the stomach. Then remove the insides.

2. Cut off the head and tail and discard them.

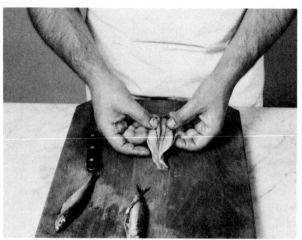

3. You should now be able to open out the fish like a book.

4. With your fingers, grasp the bone at one end and pull it out.

Sardine di Alghero

SARDINES IN THE STYLE OF ALGHERO

FROM SARDINIA

Alghero, on the west coast of Sardinia facing toward the Balearics, was the seat of Spanish rule in the late Middle Ages. Its language is still thirteenth-century Catalan, and one Spanish fortress houses a memorable restaurant. In parts of the interior of Sardinia, Latin is still spoken. In the following popular treatment, the boneless small fresh fish are baked with seasonings for only 10 minutes. The tomatoes are a latecomer to the dish (they were not part of the original recipe), but they work very well.

12 fresh small sardines
Coarse-grained salt
2 medium-sized cloves garlic, peeled
About 20 sprigs Italian parsley, leaves only
1 pound fresh tomatoes, or 2 cups drained canned imported Italian tomatoes
¼ cup olive oil
Salt and freshly ground black pepper

Prepare the sardines, following the directions on page 300. Soak the sardines in cold salted water for ½ hour. Then rinse them and pat them dry with paper towels.

Finely chop the garlic and coarsely chop the parsley on a board. Preheat the oven to 400 degrees.

Pass the tomatoes through a food mill. Put the puréed tomatoes in a small bowl and add the chopped ingredients and the oil. Taste for salt and pepper. Mix all the ingredients together with a wooden spoon to dissolve the salt completely.

Lightly oil an ovenproof terrine or baking dish. Arrange the sardines on their sides in the bottom of the terrine. Pour the sauce over the fish and place the terrine in the oven. Bake for 10 minutes. Remove from oven and serve immediately from the terrine.

CALAMARI, SEPPIE E POLPI [SQUID, CUTTLEFISH (INKSQUID), AND OCTOPUS]

1. Left to right: two squid, a cuttlefish, and an octopus. These three mollusks, though not very appealing in appearance, are delicious when properly prepared.

Notice the long thin shape of the squid with the two side "wings," clearly visible on the upper part of the left-most squid, and 8 tentacles on the lower part. The recipe for *Crostini caldi di mare* (Rustic Seafood Canapés) contains squid as does *"Insalata" di seppie, calamari e gamberi* (Salad of Cuttlefish, Squid, and Shrimp). The best, most tender are the small ones about 1 inch wide with a stomach about 3 inches long.

The more rounded cuttlefish, of darker hue, has shorter tentacles and a large ink sac, which is used to make several unusual sauces. It is the same celebrated brownish ink known as "sepia" (from the Italian word for cuttlefish, *seppia*), the pigment used by many old masters, such as Michelangelo, for their drawings (see the illustration on the front left endpaper). The cuttlefish is also eaten by itself as in *Seppie in umido* (Inksquid Leghorn Style). The tender small ones are about 3 inches in diameter.

On the right is an 8-tentacled mollusk or octopus, called *polpo* in Italian and poulp or polyp in English. Those of this small size are a greatly favored seafood in Mediterranean countries. The best and most tender *polpi* are those which have double rows of suckers on the tentacles.

HOW TO CLEAN CUTTLEFISH (INKSQUID)

NOTE: Squid may be cleaned in the same way as cuttlefish with the differences indicated in the steps. (For photos of cleaning squid, see *The Fine Art of Italian Cooking*.)

1. Pull out the large white bone in the stomach or casing. (Squid have a long translucent bone which must also be removed.)

2. Use a knife to cut open the stomach or casing on the side where the bone was. The cut must be on that side, so as not to break the delicate ink sac located on the other side.

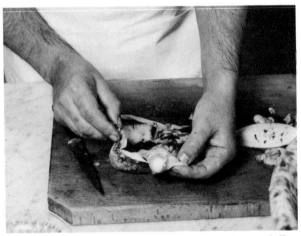

3. Holding the edges of the cut stomach carefully, open the stomach. Grasp the membranes around the sac, without touching the sac itself, and pull, detaching both from the stomach.

4. Gently squeeze the membranes, pushing the sac out into a small bowl. (The tiny sac of the squid will come off with the membrane and, not being usable, should be discarded with the membrane.)
  Detach the head from the stomach by pulling. Cut off the head below the eyes and discard, leaving the tentacles attached to the lower part of the head.

5. The tough dark outer skin of the stomach must be pulled off in cold water.

6. Turn the lower part upside down. The tentacles will now hang over the sides and the inside of the lower head will be pulled open to reveal a black spot which is the mouth. Pull it out.

7. Cut the tentacles into pieces about 2 inches long.

8. Slice the open stomach into thin strips about ¼ inch wide, cutting on the diagonal.

Seppie in Umido

CUTTLEFISH LEGHORN STYLE

FROM LEGHORN

Cuttlefish cooked in a spicy sauce in the style of Livorno (Leghorn). This port was created by the Tuscan Grand Duke Cosimo I in the sixteenth century to replace Pisa, from which the sea had retreated, leaving the city inland. In that century, fraught with religious wars, Livorno (Leghorn) was guaranteed absolute freedom of religion, making it a haven and, incidentally, giving it a large population in only a few years. The Livornese style, traditionally associated with hot and spicy dishes, is used with all kinds of fish and shellfish and is popular all over Italy.

8 cuttlefish (inksquid)
Coarse-grained salt
2 cloves garlic, peeled
About 20 sprigs Italian parsley, leaves only
¾ cup olive oil
1 cup dry white wine
1 pound fresh tomatoes or drained canned imported Italian tomatoes
Salt and freshly ground black pepper
1 scant teaspoon red pepper flakes

SERVES 4

Clean the cuttlefish following the directions on page 302, photos 1 through 8.

Put the squid in a bowl of cold water with coarse-grained salt. Soak for about 30 minutes.

Finely chop the garlic and coarsely chop half of the parsley leaves. Heat the oil in a casserole, preferably of terra-cotta or enamel, over medium heat. When oil is hot, add the chopped ingredients and sauté for 2 minutes. Then use a slotted spoon to transfer the squid strips from the bowl to the casserole. Sauté for about 5 minutes. Add the wine and let it evaporate for 10 minutes. Pass the tomatoes through a food mill and add them to casserole. Sprinkle with salt and pepper and add the red pepper flakes. Cover the casserole and simmer for about 45 minutes, stirring occasionally, and adding hot water if additional liquid is needed.

Coarsely chop the remaining parsley. Remove the casserole from the heat and transfer the contents to a serving dish. Sprinkle with the chopped parsley and serve immediately.

Crostini Caldi di Mare

RUSTIC SEAFOOD CANAPÉS

FROM THE VERSILIA AREA ON THE TUSCAN COAST

It is worth making the Tuscan bread on page 412, if only to have these seafood canapés. Because the bread contributes so much to their character, I wouldn't recommend using any other bread for these canapés. What could be a more refreshing summer appetite whetter than these briny canapés accompanied by a bottle of cold white wine?

1 medium-sized squid
¼ pound shrimp

SERVES 6

304

Coarse-grained salt
1 lemon
About 10 sprigs Italian parsley, leaves only
1 clove garlic
1 egg yolk
Salt and freshly ground black pepper
6 tablespoons olive oil
18 2-inch-square pieces Tuscan bread, cut 1-inch thick (see page 412)

To serve:
1 lemon, cut into wedges

Clean the squid following the directions on page 302, photos 1 through 8. Shell the shrimp following the directions below, photos 1 through 3. Put the squid and the shrimp in a bowl of cold water with coarse-grained salt. Squeeze the lemon and add juice to the bowl. Soak for ½ hour. Drain the squid and shrimp.

Finely chop the squid, shrimp, parsley, and garlic together on a board with a *mezzaluna,* or use a food processor. (This is one of the cases in which a food processor produces as good a result as the *mezzaluna,* but be sure to stop the machine when the result is finely chopped, but not reduced to a paste.)

Put the chopped ingredients in a small bowl. Add the egg yolk, salt and pepper to taste, and 2 tablespoons of the oil. Mix the sauce very well with a wooden spoon.

Preheat the oven to 400 degrees. Lightly oil a baking dish. Spread about 1 heaping tablespoon of the sauce on each *crostino* and place it in the prepared baking dish. When all the *crostini* are in the dish, pour 3 or 4 drops of the remaining oil over each one. Place the dish in the oven and bake for about 20 minutes. Remove from oven, transfer to serving dish, and serve immediately with the lemon wedges.

HOW TO CLEAN SHRIMP

In the photos below, I used *mezzancolle,* a large type of Mediterranean shrimp, but the basic procedure is the same for American shrimp.

1. In the rare case that the shrimp should still have their heads, gently pull them off.

2. Cut off the tail and squeeze the shrimp at the tail end. The whole shrimp should slip out of the shell.

3. Remove the vein with a knife.

305

34. Menta (*Mint*)
Renaissance drawing of fresh mint.

"Insalata" di Seppie, Calamari e Gamberi

SALAD OF CUTTLEFISH, SQUID, AND SHRIMP

FROM THE CARRARA AREA

Carrara, which is a unique combination of sea and mountain, gives us this mixed seafood salad. There are contrasting flavors and textures created by the small pieces of cuttlefish and squid, the shrimp, and the cubes of potato. The basil and fresh mint combined with wine vinegar adds a special taste, again appropriate for a summer appetizer, or even a first course.

SERVES 6

1 pound cuttlefish, uncleaned
1 pound squid, uncleaned
½ pound small shrimp, uncleaned
Coarse-grained salt
1 cup plus 1 tablespoon red wine vinegar
1 pound boiling potatoes (but not new potatoes)

For the sauce:
2 large cloves garlic, peeled
About 20 sprigs Italian parsley, leaves only
1 cup olive oil
Salt and freshly ground black pepper
About 10 basil leaves, fresh or preserved in salt
About 15 fresh mint leaves
1 lemon
1 tablespoon wine vinegar

Clean and cut the cuttlefish and squid following the directions on page 302, photos 1 through 8. (For the techniques of cleaning squid, where the stomach is left whole for stuffing, see *The Fine Art of Italian Cooking.*) Clean the shrimp following the directions on page 305, photos 1 through 3 and leave the shrimp whole.

Put the cuttlefish and squid together in a bowl. Put the shrimp in another bowl. Cover all the fish with cold water to which coarse-grained salt has been added. Soak for 30 minutes.

Bring a large pot of cold water to a boil. Add coarse-grained salt to taste. Then add 1 tablespoon of wine vinegar. Drain the strips of cuttlefish and squid and add to the boiling water. Cover the pot and cook for about 20 minutes.

Bring a small saucepan of water to a boil. Add coarse-grained salt to taste. Drain the shrimp and add them to the boiling water. Cover the pan and cook for about 6 minutes. When the fish are cooked, drain them and transfer them to bowls to cool (about 1 hour).

Meanwhile, peel the potatoes and cut them into 1-inch cubes. Put the cubes in a bowl of cold water and let them stand until needed. Bring a third pot of water to a boil. Add coarse-grained salt to taste. Then add 1 cup of wine vinegar and when the water returns to a boil, add the potato cubes. Cook for about 15 minutes. Drain the potatoes and put them in a large bowl to cool completely (about 1 hour).

Prepare the sauce. Finely chop the garlic and coarsely chop the parsley. Put the chopped ingredients into a small bowl and add the oil and salt and pepper to taste. Tear the basil and mint leaves into three or four pieces and add them to the bowl. Squeeze the lemon and add the juice to the bowl with the tablespoon of wine vinegar. Mix all the ingredients together well.

Add cooled fish to the bowl with the cooled potatoes. Pour the sauce over the potatoes and fish and toss gently but very well. Cover the bowl and refrigerate for at least 3 hours before serving.

HOW TO CLEAN AND FILLET EELS

Eels are eaten, both fresh and preserved, all over Italy. The sweetest are found in fresh water lakes. Each region has its particular recipes for eel. The large eels of Rome (*capitoni*) are traditionally eaten on Christmas Eve.

While cleaning eels always protect your hands by wearing rubber or plastic gloves, because the secretion from the raw eel could irritate your skin.

See the recipe for *Torta di anguille* (Eel Tart), page 474, which uses the fillets made from the eel demonstrated below.

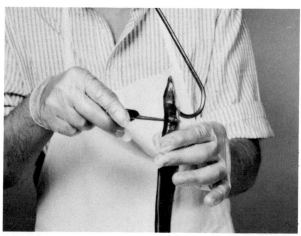

1. Hang a fish hook from something rigid, such as a pot rack. Hook the eel just under the head. With a knife, cut just the skin (not the flesh) all around under the head.

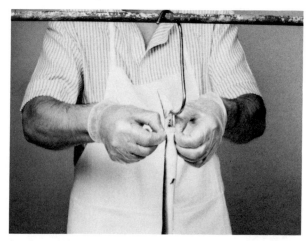

2. Grasp the skin at the cut with the thumb and first finger of both hands, and pull down the skin a little bit.

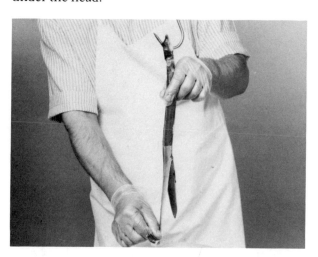

3. Then holding the top of the eel with one hand, pull off the whole skin with the other hand.

307

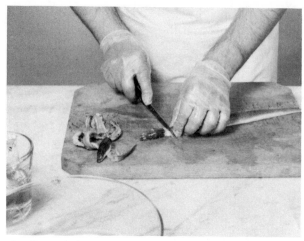

4. Place the eel on a chopping board and cut off and discard the head.

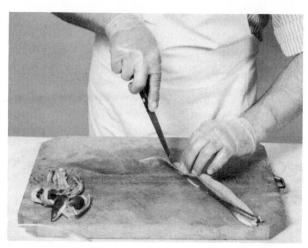

5. Open the eel by cutting lengthwise on the stomach side and clean it completely.

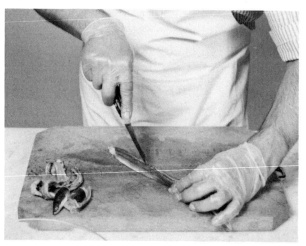

6. Then open the entire length of the back side of the eel in the same way.

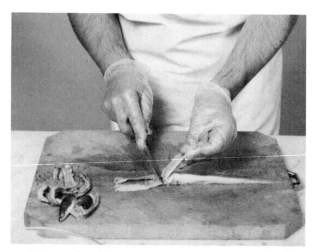

7. Make one fillet by scraping with a knife where the meat is attached to the spine while pulling the meat free with the other hand.

Fillet the other side in the same way.

HOW TO FILLET A SOLE

While it is easy to purchase sole already filleted, it is good to know the filleting technique which is unique to this fish.

1. Place the sole on a board with darker side up. Use a boning knife to cut off the tail.

When the tail has been removed, it will be easy to detach the dark skin completely with a paring knife.

2. Insert the knife at one end and

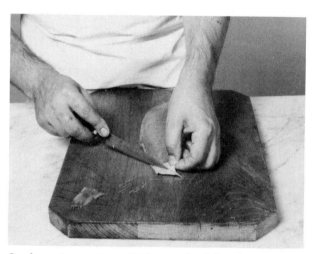

3. draw it across until that end of the skin is completely free.

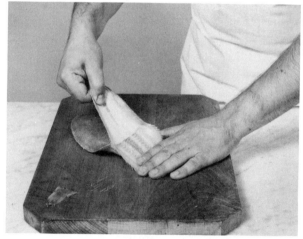

4. Holding the free end firmly with one hand, and holding the fish with the other, pull off the dark skin in one piece.

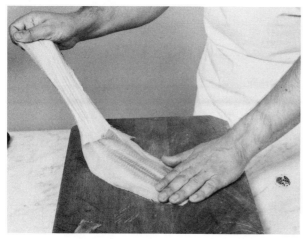

5. It will detach easily at the other end where it is attached to the head.

Once the skin is off you will notice a line on each side separating the flesh of the fillet from the bony side fins.

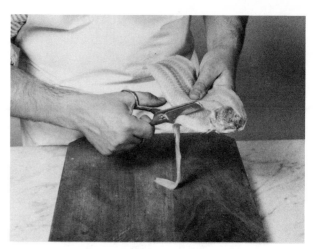

6. With a scissors, cut along that line to free the fillet from one side,

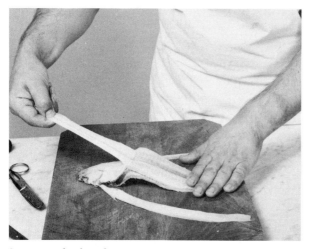

7. then from the other, leaving the side strips still attached to the head.

8. Turn the fish over with the white skin up, then pull that skin free

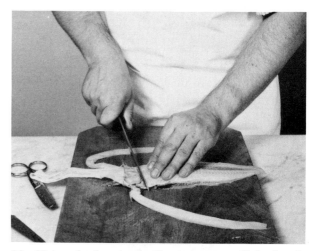

9. up to the head.

10. Using the boning knife again, cut off the head. This removes both bony side fins and also the white skin.

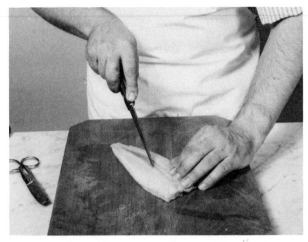

11. Cut along the central line separating the two fillets of the top side from each other.

12. With the knife, free the fillets from the spine and its attached bones.

13. After one fillet has been freed, repeat procedure with the other, then

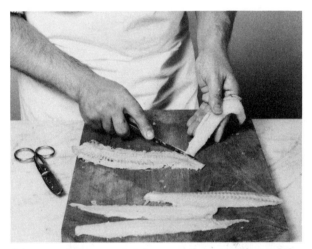

14. turn fish over and remove the two fillets of the other side. Here we see a fish cut into its four fillets.

Filetti di Sogliola Fritti

DEEP-FRIED SOLE FILLETS

FROM LEGHORN

Thin, delicate sole fillets are coated with this light batter, which is fluffed up by its beaten egg whites when fried.

2 whole sole, about 2 pounds, or 8 fillets
Coarse-grained salt

SERVES 4

For the batter:
1 cup unbleached all-purpose flour
Pinch of salt
3 tablespoons olive oil
¾ cup cold water
3 extra large egg whites
1 pound solid vegetable shortening

To serve:
Salt
Lemon wedges

If whole, fillet the sole following the directions on pages 309–311, photos 1 through 14. Put the fillets in a bowl of cold water with some coarse-grained salt.

Prepare the batter. Sift the flour (see How to Make *Crespelle*, pages 104–105, photos 1 to 3) and put it in a large bowl. Add a pinch of salt to the flour and mix with a wooden spoon. Make a well in the flour and add the oil. Start mixing with a wooden spoon incorporating some of the flour. Then add the water a little at a time to prevent lumps from forming. When all the water is incorporated, let the batter rest for at least 1 hour in a cool place.

Line a serving dish with paper towels. Beat the egg whites until stiff in a copper bowl. Gently fold the whites into the batter always incorporating them in a rotating motion. Heat the solid shortening in a deep fat fryer. When the shortening is hot, remove the fillets from the water and pat them dry with paper towels. Dip each fillet in the batter and put it in the fryer. Cook for 1 minute on each side, remove from pan, and place on the serving dish. When all the fillets are cooked, remove the paper towels, sprinkle the fillets with a little salt, and serve hot with lemon wedges.

CHAPTER 13

Galantines

The Italian galantine appears to have originated in Naples. De la Varenne has galantines in his seventeenth-century cookbook which was translated into Italian, but whether or not the dish developed first in France, it has always been made differently in Italy, with strips and cubes rather than forcemeat. There is no doubt that the Italian galantine reflects the court tradition of Naples, in that it is made with a technique that is similar to the way provolone and mozzarella have been made for centuries, perhaps millennia, in Campagnia. In making the authentic version of these cheeses, the curd is cut into strips which are then pressed together to form layers. The Italian galantines are simply the combination of strips and cubes of the ingredients, which are then pressed to form layers. The Neapolitan court *galantina* is the one still made all over Italy.

The most common one is that of chicken. In making the chicken galantine, the bird is opened down the back before it is boned. The *Pollo disossato ripieno* (Boned Whole Stuffed Chicken), from my first book, is not a galantine, as some have suggested, as the chicken is left whole while boning, not opened, and uses *only* a special type of *farcia* (forcemeat).

The layering of the classic Italian fish galantine is different from the ground stuffing of de la Varenne's version. A variety of fish and shellfish of different sizes and shapes is used. When cooking, the fish forms its own gelatin to hold the galantine together, unlike chicken which must be cooked together with a calf's foot to form the gelatin binder.

Pesce farcito, the stuffed carp recipe used by Italian Jews, is still made in the old way, which is clearly derived from the fish galantine. The fish is opened, boned, and the inside meat removed and, in this instance, ground, but the fish is otherwise left whole, put back together again, brought to the table whole, usually in the clarified fish aspic, and sliced through at the table. Each serving is a slice of galantine with or without a cold sauce and/or aspic. It may be used as either a main dish or an appetizer, and is particularly fine for buffets.

In recent times, these dishes have been made less often than in the preceding two centuries, but they are perfect for many a dinner needing a more elaborate presentation. The chicken galantine is very common still, in a more commercial version, of which slices may be obtained at local *salumerie* (gourmet shops). But there is nothing like the fresh homemade version.

Pesce in Galantina

FISH GALANTINE

FROM THE EIGHTEENTH-CENTURY COURT OF NAPLES

SERVES 8

1 whole striped bass, about 3½ pounds
2 sole, about 2 pounds with bone (to make 8 fillets)
10 fresh sardines or smelts
1 pound medium-sized shrimp
Salt and freshly ground white pepper

For the poaching broth:
1 bay leaf
1 celery stalk
1 medium-sized carrot
1 clove garlic, peeled
5 or 6 sprigs Italian parsley
½ teaspoon dried thyme
½ cup dry white wine
1 tablespoon coarse-grained salt

To serve:
15 sprigs Italian parsley

HOW TO SCALE AND BONE WHOLE FISH

1. Holding the bass at the tail end, scrape off the scales with the fish scaler, always starting at the tail end.

2. Move in repeated long strokes from tail to head.

3. Use a scissors to cut off the large back fin,

4. and the four small ones (two around the gills and two on the underside).

5. Use a boning knife to open the stomach and remove the insides.

6. Starting at the bottom of the head, make a shallow slit all the way down the back.

7. Insert the knife into the slit, cut along the side of the backbone all the way through. Then draw the knife along the backbone

8. down to the tail, detaching the end of the top side from the tail.

315

9. Fold the free top side over the head and with a knife cut off the tail.

10. At the head end, slip the knife under the exposed backbone and slide it along the bone all the way to the tail end.

11. Open out both sides of the fish and detach the backbone from the head with the knife. Reserve the backbone for poaching the fish.

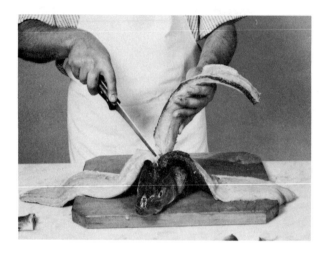

Fillet the soles following the directions on pages 309–311, photos 1 through 14. Then fillet the sardines following the directions on page 300, photos 1 through 4. Clean the shrimp following the directions on page 305, photos 1 through 3.

HOW TO ASSEMBLE THE GALANTINA

12. Place the bass on a large piece of heavy cheesecloth and pull top side over the head. On the bottom side make a layer of sole, using 4 of the 8 fillets. Sprinkle them with salt and pepper.

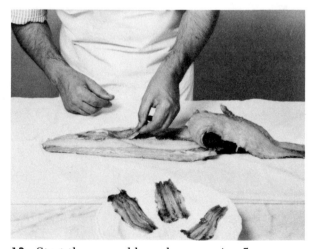

13. Start the second layer by arranging 5 open sardines lengthwise in a row down the center of the fish, then arrange the shrimp all over

316

14. the sole-sardine layer.

15. Make another layer of sole on top of the shrimp

16. and of sardines. Sprinkle with salt and pepper. Lay the top side of the bass back into place, covering all the layers.

17. Wrap both sides of the cheesecloth around the fish. Tuck the ends under and tie it like a salami (pages 247–249).

18. Put the fish on a rack in a fish poacher. Add the bay leaf, celery, carrot, garlic, parsley sprigs, and the thyme. Pour the wine over the fish and add coarse-grained salt. Then pour in enough water to cover the fish.

Finally, add the heads of the sardines and the bones of the bass. Cover the poacher and put it over low heat (across two burners). When the water comes to a boil, simmer for about 50 minutes. Remove the poacher from the heat and let the fish cool in the poacher for about 1 hour.

Remove the fish from the poacher and transfer it to a board to cool completely (about 2 hours). Then wrap it in aluminum foil and refrigerate it for at least 3 hours. As the fish produces its own gelatin, the *galantina* should remain together when cold. With fish, it is also unnecessary to use a weight to press it together.

Carefully untie and unwrap the fish.

19. Put the fish on an oval serving platter with the parsley.

20. In order to slice the fish for serving, it is best to transfer the fish from the platter to a cutting board. First cut fish in half through center so the different layers of *galantina* may be seen. Then cut each half into slices 1 inch thick and arrange the slices on the serving dish.

Pesce Farcito

STUFFED WHOLE CARP WITH ASPIC

NINETEENTH-CENTURY ITALIAN JEWISH

1 whole carp, about 4 pounds
About 1 pound of boneless hake or whiting meat
4 slices white bread
2 small red onions
2 extra large egg yolks
1 teaspoon salt
½ teaspoon freshly ground black pepper
½ teaspoon granulated sugar

For poaching the fish:
2 medium-sized carrots, cut into large pieces
2 small red onions, cut into large pieces
About 2 quarts water
Plus: 4 extra large egg whites to clarify the gelatin

SERVES 8

318

HOW TO BONE WHOLE LARGE FISH

If the fish needs to be scaled, follow the directions on page 314, photos 1 and 2.

1. Use a boning knife to open the stomach and remove the insides. Clean very well and wash under cold running water. (The roe may be saved for use later.)

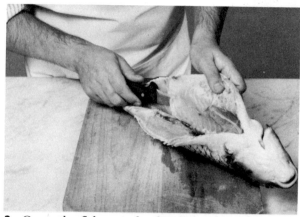

2. Open the fish completely, then insert the knife, sharp edge up, from the tail end, between the ribs and the flesh. Slide the knife upward along the ribs, freeing all the rib bones from the flesh along the whole length of the fish up to the head.

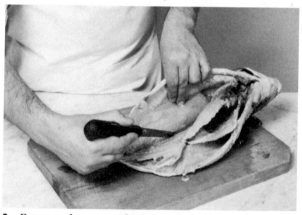

3. Repeat the procedure on the other side of the fish.

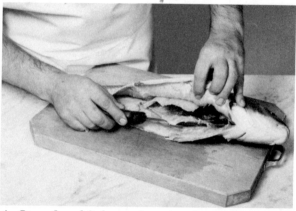

4. Steps 2 and 3 shown from another angle to illustrate clearly how the knife is held as close to the bones as possible in order not to lose any of the flesh.

5. Insert the knife where the backbone meets the tail,

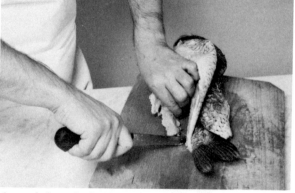

6. and detach the bone without making any holes in the flesh.

7. Starting from the freed tail end, carefully scrape away the backbone from the skin, without making any holes in the skin.*

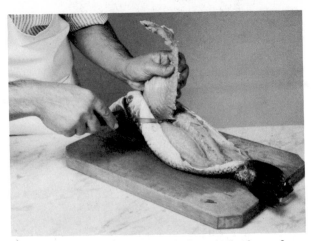

8. When you reach the head, detach the bone from the head, by cutting with the knife. Reserve the bone to poach with the fish.

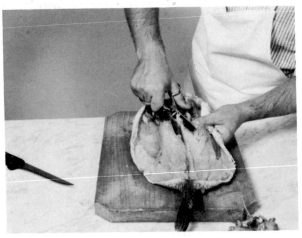

9. Use a scissors to search out and cut away any little bones that may remain.

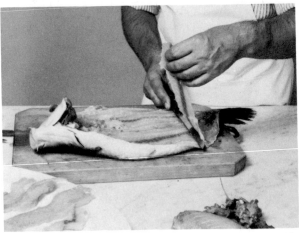

10. Cut off the flesh in thin slices along the length of the fish.

    The meat of the carp is very delicate and difficult to slice. Be specially careful not to try to cut off the slices too close to the skin, but remove as much of the fish as possible.

11. Close the fish and use a scissors to trim the tail.

* On your first attempts, if you should make a hole in the skin, try to sew it up as invisibly as possible. Of course, mastering the technique is to achieve it without holes.

12. Cut the flesh of the carp, hake, or whiting, and the bread and onions into pieces.

Use a meat grinder, with the coarse attachment, to grind together the fish, bread, and onions. (A coarsely-ground texture is desired.) Put all the ground ingredients into a crockery bowl. Add the egg yolks, salt, pepper, and sugar. Mix very well with a wooden spoon.

13. Open the fish and spoon about half of the stuffing along the length of the opening. Then begin to sew up the opening from the tail end with a needle and thread.

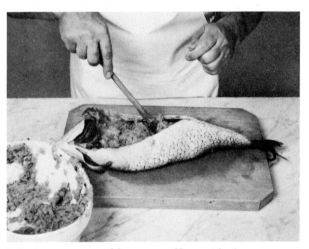

14. As you sew, add more stuffing with the spoon to the closed part.

15. Use all the stuffing and close the fish completely. Tie off the thread with a knot.

Wrap the fish in heavy cheesecloth, then tie it like a salami (pages 247–249, photos 10 through 15).

16. Lay the fish on a rack in a fish poacher. Add the fish bones and the carrots and onions. Pour in enough lukewarm water (about 2 quarts) to cover the fish completely. Add coarse-grained salt to taste. (If you wish to use the roe, shape it into small balls and place them in the poacher.)

Cover the poacher and put it over medium heat (across two burners) and when water just reaches the boiling point, simmer for about 50 minutes. Then remove from the heat and let the fish cool in its broth for about 1 hour. Transfer the fish to serving platter until completely cold (about 2 hours). Cover with aluminum foil and refrigerate it for at least 3 hours. Meanwhile, strain the broth through a cheesecloth and let it cool completely (about 2 hours). Prepare the fish gelatin following the directions on pages 432–434. The fish gelatin may have to be clarified twice. Pour the clarified gelatin on a long fish serving dish and refrigerate until it is solidified (about 6 hours). Unwrap the fish

17. and place it on a bed of the solidified gelatin. If there is roe, arrange the little balls on both sides of the fish.

18. To serve the fish, put it on a cutting board. Cut it in half and slice it into 1-inch-thick slices. Cut the gelatin into cubes. Each portion should be accompanied by some of the cubed gelatin (and roe).

Galantina di Pollo

CHICKEN IN GALANTINE

1 chicken, about 3 pounds (with the liver)

For the *farcia* (forcemeat):
8 ounces lean veal, in one piece
12 ounces lean pork, in one piece
1 small black truffle, fresh or canned (about 1 ounce)
2 whole extra large eggs
1 tablespoon sweet butter
Pinch of dried thyme
2 tablespoons dry Marsala
About 10 raw pistachio nuts (for cooking)
Salt and freshly ground black pepper

For the stuffing:
4 ounces prosciutto, *in one piece*
4 ounces cooked cured tongue, in one piece
4 ounces pancetta (*or* prosciutto *or boiled ham*)

For cooking the galantine:
1 medium-sized red onion
1 medium-sized carrot
1 celery stalk
1 small calf's foot
1 bay leaf
3 whole cloves
Coarse-grained salt
Plus: 3 extra large egg whites to clarify the gelatin
1 to 3 tablespoons dry Marsala

First bone the chicken, setting aside the chicken liver.

HOW TO BONE A CHICKEN FOR GALANTINA

There are several ways to bone a whole chicken. For *Pollo disossato ripieno* (Boned Whole Stuffed Chicken), page 307 in *The Fine Art of Italian Cooking*, the bones are removed from the cavity and the chicken remains whole. For the *galantina*, the back of the chicken is opened and then the chicken is boned. After boning, the meat is removed and cut.

1. Using a boning knife, cut through the skin at the end of the leg (around the joint). Then cut through again to sever the tendons, detaching the meat from the bone.

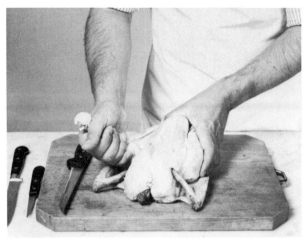

2. Free the entire leg from the thigh bone by twisting it around, and pushing out a little bit. (There is nothing to cut here.)

3. Pull out the freed leg bone.
Repeat the procedure for the other leg.

4. Turn the chicken down slightly on its side. Use a boning knife to begin cutting through the skin and meat attached to the spine,

5. cutting all the way down the back

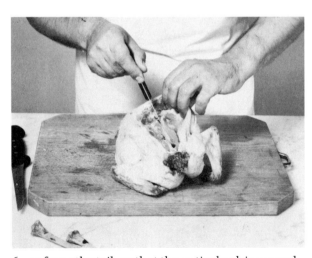

6. as far as the tail, so that the entire back is opened.

7. Cut the tendons connecting the upper part of the thigh to the spine and cartilage.

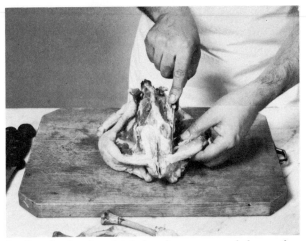

8. At the other end of the thigh the bone is still attached to a piece of cartilage left after the removal of the leg bone. Cut the bone free from this cartilage.

Repeat the procedure with the other thigh.

9. On the back, which has been opened down the center, starting at the tail end, begin to free the meat on both sides from the carcass. Continue to free all meat around to the breast side. Be sure that all the meat including the breast is completely detached, being careful to make no holes in the skin.

10. The meat remains attached now only at the tail end. Insert the knife sharp side up between the meat and the end of the carcass just above the tail and cut through. The tail will come off with it.

11. Take the carcass at the tail end and lift it off the meat. It's now attached only at the end of the breast.

12. The meat is to one side and the carcass to the other. Cut all along the end of the breast completely detaching the meat in one piece.

Reserve the carcass for cooking with the prepared chicken.

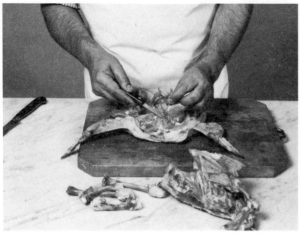

13. Open out the whole chicken. Remove the wishbone at the top of the breast.

14. The wing is divided into three sections. First, detach the bone connecting the whole wing to the shoulder by cutting into the joint. Then detach it at the other end where it connects to the double bone of the second section of the wing, and remove it.

15. Cut off the third section, the tip of the wing, and discard it.

16. Scrape the meat off the double bone of the second section of the wing,

17. and cut off the bone from the attached cartilage. Reserve all these bones for cooking with the chicken.

18. Separate the meat of the leg and thigh from the breast meat.

Use a paring knife to carefully detach the membranes connecting the meat to the skin. Do not make any holes in the skin. The meat will then pull off rather easily, leaving the skin in one piece. The chicken is now completely boned.

The whole chicken is re-formed by stuffing the intact chicken skin with two different textures of meat. The first, called *farcia*, consists of cubes of the dark meat of the chicken, veal, pork, chopped chicken liver, the black truffle cut into pieces and whole blanched pistachio nuts. The stuffing is made of strips of the white meat of the chicken, *prosciutto*, *pancetta*, and tongue.

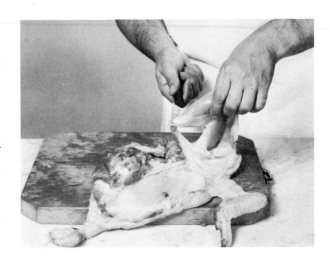

HOW TO PREPARE THE FARCIA AND THE STUFFING

Start by cutting the dark meat of the chicken into cubes of less than ½ inch square.

1. Cut the veal into cubes the same size as the dark chicken meat. Cut the pork in cubes the same size as the veal.

Cut the black truffle into small pieces.

2. Cut the *prosciutto* into strips about ⅛ inch thick.

3. Then cut the tongue into strips of the same thickness.

Slice the *pancetta* about ⅛ inch thick and then lengthwise in ¼-inch pieces, if the supplier has not already done so. If the *pancetta* purchased is rolled, unroll each slice into a long strip and cut it lengthwise into about ¼-inch pieces.

4. Finally, cut the reserved chicken breast into strips ¼ inch thick.

5. Finely chop the chicken liver on a board with a *mezzaluna*.

6. Put the cubes of the dark chicken meat, veal, and pork in a bowl and add the eggs.

Reserve the strips of different meat for assembling the *galantina* (see below). Add the butter, thyme, Marsala, pistachio nuts, and the truffle pieces. Taste for salt and pepper. Mix all these ingredients for the *farcia* together until they are well blended.

HOW TO ASSEMBLE THE GALANTINA

1. Lay the whole chicken skin out flat, with the outside skin facing up. Where the tail has been removed the two sides of the skin are not connected. Sew them together with a needle and thread.

2. Turn the skin over and flatten it out again. Spread all of the *farcia* to cover its entire surface.

3. Arrange all of the strips of different meats lengthwise at random.

4. Carefully roll up the skin with all its stuffing in the form of a large *braciola* or jelly roll.

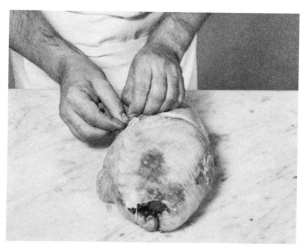

5. Close the *galantina* by sewing up the end of the skin with a needle and thread

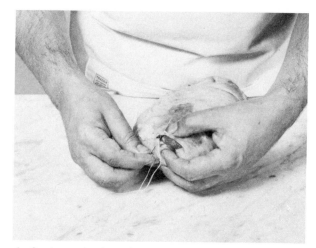

6. for its entire length.

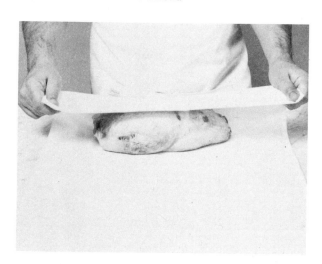

7. Wrap the *galantina* in a heavy cheesecloth. Tie it like a salami (pages 247–249).

8. Place the *galantina* in a large oval casserole with just enough cold water to cover it.

Then add the onion, carrot, celery stalk, the bones of the chicken, the calf's foot, bay leaf, cloves, and coarse-grained salt to taste. The calf's foot and the chicken bones are cooked together with the *galantina* so that the *gelatina* (gelatin) they make will also help the *galantina* to hold together.

Put the casserole over medium heat and let simmer for 1 hour and 45 minutes. Then remove the pan from the heat and let *galantina* cool in the gelatinous broth for about 3 hours. Transfer the *galantina* to a flat serving dish, place weights on top (see page 253), and refrigerate for 24 hours.

Meanwhile, strain and clarify the liquid gelatin in the casserole, and color it to the shade that you prefer (see How to Prepare *Gelatina*, pages 432–434), then refrigerate. When the *galantina* and *gelatina* are ready, unwrap the *galantina*. Slice it and arrange overlapping slices on a serving dish.

9. Cut the *gelatina* into cubes and arrange them around the slices of *galantina*. In these photos the gelatin has been darkly colored with dry Marsala to contrast with the lighter colors of the meat.

10. The final product ready to serve.

CHAPTER 14

Pasticci

The *pasticcio* (or Italian pâté in crust) is even older than the French pâté. The word *pasticcio* is a dialect form of the vulgar Latin *pasticium*, the same word from which the Italian and French words *pasta* and pâté later derived.

The word pâté, itself, referred to the crust in which the forcemeat was wrapped, so it is clear that all pâtés were originally like *pasticci*. The Italians have remained true to the older usage in which the emphasis is placed on the crust, and, therefore, the dish is preferably eaten still warm, when the crust is at its best.

As the French began to emphasize the cold pâté as an appetizer, the crust suffered and often disappeared, belying the name of the dish. Though *pasticci* are excellent at room temperature and very much resemble their French counterparts, Italians still regard a *pasticcio* as primarily a hot dish, and, therefore, appropriate as both a main course and an appetizer. In Italy the shape is always round.

Because *pasticci* belonged to the court tradition, the recipes are very well documented in cookbooks throughout the centuries. The tradition reached such a peak in eighteenth- and nineteenth-century *alta cucina* that the inevitable twentieth-century reaction to their richness followed. There are always a few dishes in the *haute cuisine* of a culture that set the standard for that cuisine. *Pasticci* are the dishes which keep Italian *alta cucina* alive and it would be

35. Lepre *(Hare)*
Renaissance drawing of a kitchen courtyard where the hares are hanging to age and live fish are swimming in tubs of water.

disastrous if they should disappear. The three examples here, which are but a sampling of this large area of Italian cooking so popular in the past, have three different crusts, as each type of *pasticcio* has a crust subtly appropriate only to itself. All the crusts, however, contain alcohol in some form to ensure crispness.

While the two crusts used with the meat *pasticcio* call for pure alcohol, the *Pasticcio di magro* (Fish-Vegetable *Pasticcio*) employs Marsala. Throughout the eighteenth and nineteenth centuries, Marsala gradually replaced the numerous sweet white wines that were used for cooking and drinking throughout Italy. But Marsala is also used in the two other recipes: for marinating the meat in *Pasticcio di lepre* (*Pasticcio* of Hare) and as an ingredient of the stuffing for *Pasticcio di anitra* (Duck *Pasticcio*). In addition to the flour, the variable ingredients of the crusts are butter, eggs, lemon juice, water, and salt (although one crust uses a little sugar instead). *Balsamella* is used as the binder for the stuffing in two of the recipes included.

Pasticci may be eaten either warm or at room temperature. Though when warm, the crust is at its best; when cool, the filling may be tastier, but the crust suffers. *Pasticci* should never be reheated.

Pasticcio di Lepre

PASTICCIO OF HARE

FROM THE OLD ITALIAN COURTS

This hare *pasticcio* alternates hare fillets marinated in Marsala and herbs with a forcemeat of the remaining hare meat, veal, and aromatic vegetables, with thin slices and cubes of *prosciutto*. The texture is interesting and varied.

For the crust:
6 tablespoons (¾ stick) sweet butter
4 cups unbleached all-purpose flour
2 extra large egg yolks
2 tablespoons pure grain alcohol or Vodka
About 5 drops lemon juice
¼ cup cold water
½ teaspoon salt

SERVES 8 TO 10

For the stuffing:
½ hare, about 3 pounds
1 small red onion, cut in half
½ celery stalk
½ medium-sized carrot
About 5 sprigs Italian parsley
2 bay leaves
1½ cups dry Marsala
Salt and freshly ground black pepper
6 ounces prosciutto *(2 ounces in one piece and 4 ounces thinly sliced)*
8 tablespoons (1 stick) sweet butter
8 ounces ground veal

2 cups hot chicken or beef broth
2 extra large eggs

For the *balsamella*:
9 tablespoons sweet butter
1 cup unbleached all-purpose flour
4 cups milk
Pinch of salt

Prepare the crust first. Melt the butter in a bowl or small saucepan over a pot of boiling water and set it aside until cool.

Arrange the flour in a mound on a pasta board. Make a well in the center and put in the egg yolks, alcohol, lemon juice, cooled melted butter, water, and salt. Use a fork to mix together the ingredients in the well. Then begin to incorporate the flour from the inner rim of the well until almost all of the flour has been absorbed. Knead the dough, always using the palms of your hands, until the dough is smooth and elastic (10 to 15 minutes). Leave enough flour on the board to knead the dough later. (For kneading technique, see page 410, photo 13.) Wrap the dough in a slightly dampened dish towel and let it rest in a cool place for about 4 hours while you prepare the stuffing. (This crust must rest for a long time.)

Prepare the stuffing. Put the half hare on a chopping board.

1. Cut the meaty parts of the hare, both fore and hind sections, into thin fillets. Put the fillets into a crockery bowl.

2. Cut the rest of the hare, meat and bones, into about 6 pieces.

Put the hare pieces over the fillets in the bowl. Lay the onion, celery, carrot, parsley, and bay leaves on top of the pieces of hare.

3. Pour 1 cup of the Marsala over the hare. Sprinkle with salt and pepper, cover, and marinate for 3 hours in a cool place.

Cut the 2-ounce piece of *prosciutto* into ¼-inch cubes.

Melt 6 tablespoons of the butter in a large saucepan. When the butter is completely melted use tongs to add the marinated vegetables, hare pieces, and fillets to the saucepan. Sauté over medium heat for about 15 minutes. Then add the Marsala marinade and the remaining ½ cup Marsala. Let the wine evaporate slowly (about 15 minutes). Meanwhile, prepare the *balsamella*.

4. Melt the butter in a heavy saucepan, preferably copper or enamel, over low heat.

5. When the butter reaches the frothing point, add the flour all at once. Mix very well with a wooden spoon.

Then cook until the flour is completely incorporated (1 to 3 minutes, depending on the quantities). If any lumps form, dissolve them by crushing them against the side of the pan with a wooden spoon. Remove the pan from the heat and let stand for 10 to 15 minutes. Allowing the half-cooked flour to stand will eliminate its uncooked taste.

While the butter-flour mixture is standing, heat the milk in another pan until it is very close to the boiling point.

6. Put the saucepan with the butter-flour mixture over low heat and add all of the hot milk at once. In this way you avoid having lumps form. Stir until the sauce is smooth.

When the sauce reaches the boiling point, add the salt and continue to stir gently while the sauce cooks slowly for about 10 minutes longer. Remove from the heat and transfer the sauce to a crockery bowl pressing a piece of buttered wax paper over the sauce to prevent a skin from forming. Let the sauce cool completely.

When the Marsala has evaporated, add the ground veal to the saucepan, and start adding the broth, a little at a time, as needed until the hare is cooked (about 1½ hours). Taste for salt and pepper. Remove the saucepan from the heat and discard the bay leaves. Transfer all the hare pieces to a chopping board and

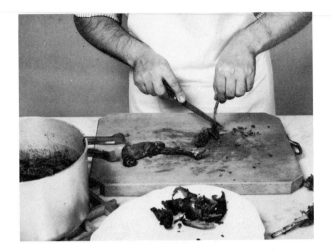

7. remove the meat from the bones.
Place all the hare fillets on a plate.

Finely chop all the vegetables from the pan along with the meat removed from the bones together on a board. Put the chopped ingredients back into the saucepan with the leftover sauce, add the remaining 2 tablespoons of butter and cook over medium heat for about 10 minutes, or until the chopped ingredients have blended into the sauce. Transfer the contents of the saucepan to a large bowl and cool completely. When cool, add the 2 ounces of reserved *prosciutto* cubes. Then add the cooled *balsamella* and the whole eggs to bowl. Mix thoroughly and taste for salt and pepper.

Butter a 10-inch springform pan. Unwrap the dough and knead it with the remaining flour for 5 minutes. Cut off one third of the dough and set it aside. Make a ball of the remaining two thirds of the dough and roll it out (page 462, photos 10 and 11), into a round layer about 17 inches in diameter and not thicker than ⅛ inch.

HOW TO ASSEMBLE PASTICCIO

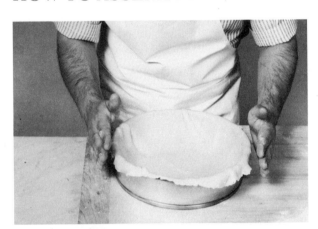

8. Line the inside of the buttered springform pan with the dough, and lightly press the dough down along the edges of the pan with the palm of your hand.

9. Spread half of the stuffing on the bottom layer of pastry.

10. Then make a layer of the hare fillets.

335

11. Make a third layer with the remaining half of the stuffing.

13. Roll out the smaller piece of dough into a round layer about 11 inches in diameter and place it over the springform pan.

Gently press the two layers of dough together at the edge of the pan.

15. The top layer of the pastry will drop a little to the level of the filling.

Place the springform pan in the oven and bake for about 40 minutes.

16. Remove the *pasticcio* from the oven and cool for a few minutes. Then open the springform pan and transfer the *pasticcio* to a large serving platter. Slice like a cake to serve.

336

12. Then arrange the *prosciutto* slices over everything.

Preheat the oven to 400 degrees.

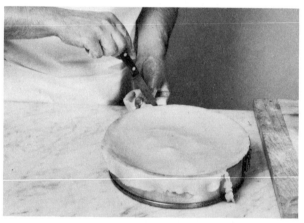

14. Cut off the overlapping dough of both the bottom and top crusts by running a knife around the rim of the springform pan.

With the thumb and first finger of both hands, move around the rim of the springform pan, pressing together the two layers of dough, but not pressing the dough against the side of the springform pan.

Pasticcio di Anitra

DUCK PASTICCIO

FROM NORTHERN ITALY

The forcemeat in this duck *pasticcio* is flavored with *prosciutto*, wild mushrooms, and Marsala. The crust contains a small amount of sugar, a traditional usage to blend with the slight sweetness of the meat. The duck leftover from *Lasagne all' Anitra* all'Aretina (see *The Fine Art of Italian Cooking*) or any roast duck, may be used to make this *pasticcio*.

For the crust:
2 tablespoons sweet butter
2 cups unbleached all-purpose flour
2 extra large egg yolks
2 teaspoons pure grain alcohol or vodka
1 teaspoon granulated sugar
1 teaspoon lemon juice
2 tablespoons cold water
Pinch of salt

SERVES 8 TO 10

For the *balsamella*:
3 tablespoons sweet butter
¼ cup unbleached all-purpose flour
1 cup milk
Salt, freshly ground black pepper, and freshly grated nutmeg

For the duck stuffing:
2 ounces dried porcini *mushrooms*
1 small red onion
1 small carrot
5 or 6 sprigs Italian parsley, leaves only
1 celery stalk
1 cup dry Marsala
1 duck (about 5 pounds), already roasted
2 bay leaves
Salt and freshly ground black pepper to taste
¼ cup olive oil
2 tablespoons sweet butter
1 cup beef broth

Plus:
2 whole extra large eggs
¼ cup freshly grated Parmigiano
Freshly ground nutmeg to taste
4 ounces prosciutto, *sliced*

Prepare the crust first. Melt the butter in a bowl or small saucepan over a pot of boiling water and set aside until cool.

Arrange the flour in a mound on pasta board. Make a well in the center and put in the cooled melted butter, egg yolks, alcohol, sugar, lemon juice, cold water, and salt.

Use a fork to mix together the ingredients in the well. Then begin to incorporate the flour from the inner rim of the well until almost all the flour has been absorbed. Knead the dough, always using the palms of your hands until all the flour is incorporated and the dough is smooth and elastic (10 to 15 minutes). For kneading technique see page 410, photo 13.

Wrap the dough in a slightly dampened cotton towel and let it rest in a cool place until the stuffing is ready.

Prepare the stuffing: Make the *balsamella*, using the quantities listed above and following the instructions on page 334. Transfer the sauce to a crockery bowl pressing a piece of buttered wax paper over the sauce to prevent a skin from forming. Let stand until cool.

Soak the mushrooms in a small bowl of lukewarm water for about 30 minutes.

Coarsely chop the onion, carrot, parsley, and celery together on a board and put them in a crockery bowl with ½ cup of the Marsala. Then remove the meat of the roasted duck from the bones (discard the skin) and add it to the bowl with the chopped vegetables and Marsala. Add the bay leaves to the bowl. Sprinkle the mixture with salt and pepper and let stand for about 20 minutes.

Heat the olive oil and butter in a flameproof casserole. Using a slotted spoon, transfer the chopped ingredients, duck pieces, and bay leaves to the casserole, leaving the Marsala in the bowl. Sauté the duckmeat mixture over medium heat for about 10 minutes, stirring occasionally. Then add the Marsala marinade and let it evaporate very slowly (about 15 minutes). Drain the mushrooms and be sure that all the sand is removed from them. Add the mushrooms to the casserole.

Heat the broth in a small saucepan. When it is hot, begin adding it to the casserole a little at a time. Do not add more broth until that previously added is completely absorbed. Continue adding broth until all the broth is incorporated (about 15 minutes). Remove the casserole from the heat. Use a slotted spoon to transfer the solid ingredients from the casserole to a chopping board. Discard the bay leaves. Chop all the ingredients together until they are very fine. Return them to the casserole and add the remaining ½ cup Marsala. Put the casserole over low heat. Stir with a wooden spoon and let the wine evaporate (about 10 minutes). Taste for salt and pepper. Then transfer the contents of the casserole to a bowl and cool completely.

Butter a 10-inch springform pan. Unwrap the dough, and cut off one third of the dough and set it aside. Make a ball of the remaining two thirds of the dough and roll it out with the remaining flour (see page 462, photos 10 and 11) into a round layer about 17 inches in diameter and not thicker than ⅜ inch. Place the sheet of dough over the prepared springform pan and gently line it, letting the excess dough hang over the sides of the pan.

Combine the duck stuffing and *balsamella*, stirring thoroughly. Then add the eggs and Parmigiano, blending all ingredients well. Taste for salt, pepper, and nutmeg.

Preheat the oven to 400 degrees. Transfer half of the mixture from the bowl to the lined springform pan and spread it evenly with a spatula. Cover with a layer of *prosciutto* slices, then add the remaining stuffing and spread it out evenly.

Roll out the remaining dough into a round layer about 11 inches in diameter and not thicker than ⅛ inch and place it over the springform pan, letting the sides overlap. Gently press the two layers of dough together at the edge of the pan and cut off all the overlapping parts with a knife.

With the thumb and first finger of both hands, move around the rim of the springform pan, pressing together the two layers of dough, but not pressing the dough against the side of the springform pan.

Place the springform pan in the oven and bake for about 40 minutes. Remove the *pasticcio* from the oven and cool for about 10 minutes. Then open the springform pan and transfer the *pasticcio* to a large serving dish. Slice like a cake to serve.

Pasticcio di Magro

FISH-VEGETABLE PASTICCIO

FROM NORTHERN ITALY

This fish and vegetable *pasticcio* alternates layers of several vegetables (artichokes, peas, and mushrooms) with thin fillets of fish and a mixture of rice, cheese, and eggs. A meatless dish with the most complex layering of the three *pasticci* here, it combines a various array of food and, when cut through, has the beautiful alternating pattern of a *galantina*, to which it is related in spirit.

For the crust:
6 tablespoons (¾ stick) sweet butter
2½ cups unbleached all-purpose flour
2 whole extra large eggs
2 tablespoons dry Marsala
Pinch of salt

For the stuffing:

Pot 1: Coarse-grained salt
1 cup raw rice, preferably Italian Arborio
5 tablespoons freshly grated Parmigiano
2 whole extra large eggs
Salt and freshly ground black pepper

Pot 2: 1 medium-sized red onion
2 tablespoons olive oil
2 tablespoons sweet butter
Salt and freshly ground black pepper

Pot 3: 2 ounces dried porcini *mushrooms*
2 small artichokes, or 1 large artichoke
1 lemon
About 5 sprigs Italian parsley, leaves only
1 celery stalk
6 tablespoons olive oil
1½ cups shelled fresh peas
Salt and freshly ground black pepper
5 tablespoons freshly grated Parmigiano

Pot 4: 4 whole sole (about 4 pounds with bone),
*   or 16 sole fillet quarters, filleted Italian style*
About 5 sprigs Italian parsley, leaves only
1 clove garlic, peeled
6 tablespoons olive oil
Salt and freshly ground black pepper
2 tablespoons pignoli (pine nuts)

Prepare the crust first. Melt the butter in a bowl or small saucepan over a pot of boiling water and set aside until cool.

Arrange the flour in a mound on pasta board. Make a well in the center and put in the cooled melted butter, eggs, Marsala, and salt. Use a fork to mix together the ingredients in the well. Then begin to incorporate the flour from the inner rim of the well until almost all the flour has been absorbed. Knead the dough always using the palms of your hands, until it is smooth and elastic (10 to 15 minutes). (For kneading technique, see page 410, photo 13.) Wrap the dough in a slightly dampened dish towel and let it rest in a cool place until the stuffing is ready.

Meanwhile, make the stuffing which is prepared in four different pots for the four separate layers in the mold.

Pot 1: Bring a large pot of water to a boil. Add coarse-grained salt to taste. Then add the rice, stir, and cook for about 16 minutes. Drain the rice and cool under cold running water. Drain again and transfer rice to a bowl. Add the Parmigiano, eggs, and salt and pepper to taste. Mix very well and let stand until needed.

Pot 2: Slice the onion into very thin rings. Heat the oil and butter in a saucepan over medium heat. When butter is completely melted, add the onion rings and sauté them until transparent (about 10 minutes). Taste for salt and pepper. Remove the pan from the heat and cool the onion completely.

Pot 3: Soak the mushrooms in a bowl of lukewarm water for about 30 minutes. Soak and clean the artichokes and cut them into quarters following the directions on page 350, photos 1 through 7. Then cut the quarters into four or five pieces. Place the pieces in a bowl of cold water with the lemon cut into halves and squeezed.

Coarsely chop the parsley and celery together on a board. Heat the oil in a saucepan over medium heat. When the oil is hot, add the chopped ingredients along with the artichoke pieces. Sauté for 5 minutes and add the peas. Sprinkle with salt and pepper and mix all the ingredients together with a wooden spoon. Cook for 15 minutes longer. Drain the mushrooms and be sure that all the sand is removed from them. Add the mushrooms to the saucepan. Add some hot water if additional liquid is needed. Cook for 10 minutes longer, then remove the pan from the heat and pour the vegetable mixture into a crockery bowl. Let stand until cool (about 30 minutes). Once cooled, add the cheese and mix very well.

Pot 4: Fillet the sole if the fish is whole (pages 309–311). Coarsely chop the parsley and finely chop the garlic. Heat the oil in a small skillet over medium heat. When the oil is hot, add the chopped ingredients. Sauté for 1 minute, then start adding 2 fillets at a time, sautéing 1 minute each side and sprinkling with salt and pepper. With a spatula transfer the fillets to a serving dish. When all the fillets have been cooked, add the pignoli to the pan and mix quickly so that the pignoli absorb the juice. Pour the contents of the pan over the fillets on the serving dish.

To put the dish together: Butter a 10-inch springform pan. Unwrap the dough, and cut off one third of the dough and set it aside. Make a ball of two thirds of the dough and roll it out (see page 410, photo 13) into a round layer 17 inches in diameter and about ⅛ inch thick. Place the sheet of dough over the prepared springform pan and gently line it, letting the excess dough hang over the sides of the pan.

Cover the bottom layer of pastry with half of the rice mixture as the first layer. Then scatter half of the onions over it as a second layer. The third layer will be formed with half of the artichoke and pea mixture. The last layer (in the center) will be with all the sole fillets and their sauce. Then repeat the other layers in reverse order. The top layer should be of the remaining rice.

Preheat the oven to 400 degrees. Roll out the remaining dough into a round layer about 11 inches in diameter and not thicker than ⅛ inch thick and place it over the springform pan, letting the sides overlap. Gently press the two layers of dough together at the edge of the pan and cut off all the overlapping parts with a knife.

With the thumb and first finger of both hands, move around the rim of the springform pan, pressing together the two layers of dough, but not pressing the dough against the side of the springform pan.

Place the springform pan in the oven and bake for about 40 minutes. Remove from the oven and cool for about 10 minutes. Then open the springform pan and transfer the *pasticcio* to a large serving dish. Slice like a cake to serve.

CHAPTER 15

Vegetables and Legumes

Vegetables have an important place in Italian cooking, traditionally more so than in northern European or American cookery. Therefore, it follows that the portions of meat in Italy would be smaller than in English-speaking countries and perhaps even in France. It is clear from studying the history and development of cooking in Italy that this is as much a matter of choice as of economics. In the past, countries bordering on the Mediterranean had more vegetables available to them, because of the warm climate, than the northern countries did.

While it was Taillevant who made the breakthrough for vegetables in France, Italian cookbook manuscripts dating to about a century before have many vegetable recipes and indicate that vegetables played a major role in Italian cooking much earlier, in the medieval period. It is also clear from cookbooks of the Renaissance that there was an early conscious interest in the health aspect of foods. This probably spurred the increased use of vegetables in proportion to the entire diet, even in the face of the growing "conspicuous consumption" of heavy meats with increased European prosperity.

The emphasis on the vegetable part of a modern Italian meal is evident even in the manner in which it is served. Rarely is a vegetable placed on the same dish with the meat course. The only examples of this are dishes in which the vegetable is cooked together with the meat, such as pork chops with kale, flavored with fennel seeds, or those classic pairings in which the vegetable is an integral accompaniment to the dish, such as *Arista* (Roasted Pork Loin) with *rape*.

The usual way of serving a vegetable is on a separate plate. If the vegetable is served at the same time as the meat, it is usually on a half-moon shaped plate which exists especially for that purpose. A full dinner service for Italian cooking should include these half-moon plates. If the vegetable has a sauce, it should be served with a main course that either has no sauce or a sauce that does not conflict with the vegetable in any way. If there are two sauces, one should also be careful that they are not too similar.

Sometimes a vegetable is so important that it is served separately and called a *piatto di mezzo* or an in-between course. A *sformato* (related to the technique of the soufflé), containing whole pieces of the vegetable, is an example of this kind of course.

Finally, one should mention the very common southern Italian composite dish of pasta with vegetables, such as eggplant or broccoli. Even here, there is a balance of the two so that the vegetable is not merely a flavoring.

In recent years, Japanese and Chinese cooking have created a new taste in the United States and in French Nouvelle Cuisine for crunchy half-cooked vegetables as a reaction to overcooking and puréeing so prevalent before.

Italy has not accepted this Oriental influence and it is interesting to speculate why.

Salads and uncooked vegetables, as we know them, are really not an integral part of Japanese and Chinese cooking, but in Italy both uncooked salads and cooked vegetables have been important parts of the diet. In Italy, the ideal cooking time for a vegetable is one that removes the rawness completely but allows the vegetable to retain its shape and unique flavor. If it is firm, but can be cut with the fork alone, it is probably cooked to the Italian taste. Anyone who has eaten cauliflower or broccoli in Rome is aware that all the intrinsic flavor of the vegetable is still present after cooking, though the vegetable is completely cooked. Italians have always avoided mushy, waterlogged overcooking or that which brings out strong cabbage-family smells, and, indeed, until recently Italian cooking times for vegetables were the shortest in the Occident.

After centuries of this tradition, Italians are puzzled by vegetables which are for them neither raw nor cooked. They can enjoy it when they eat Oriental cuisines, because it works in these since they have no salad. They do not feel that it works in their *cucina*, which has its own balance.

DIFFERENT VEGETABLES

1. Assorted vegetables (eggplant, zucchini, zucchini blossoms, peppers, tomatoes, celery) used extensively in Italian cooking, cut into different shapes for a variety of preparations.

Tegamaccio di Verdure

COMPOTE OF BAKED VEGETABLES

FROM ABRUZZI AND MOLISE

Each region of Italy has its own characteristic colorful combination of vegetables for its typical compote or *tegamaccio*. This one from Abruzzi is among the most interesting because it uses such a large variety and it's unusual in that it is baked. *Tegamaccio* is a jocular name, meaning a "sloppy" saucepan, because the combination and proportion is completely informal. This dish may be used as an accompaniment to boiled meat or fowl if 2 tablespoons of wine vinegar are added and it is allowed to become completely cold.

1 pound boiling potatoes (but not new potatoes)
2 pounds fresh or drained canned plum tomatoes, preferably imported
*   Italian*
3 large green peppers
2 medium-sized eggplants
3 large red onions
About ¾ cup olive oil
Salt and freshly ground black pepper
About 1½ teaspoons dried oregano

SERVES 8

Peel the potatoes and cut them into slices about ¼ inch thick. Put the slices into a bowl of cold water until needed. If fresh, slice tomatoes like the potatoes (if canned leave them whole). Clean the peppers by removing the stems, ribs, and seeds (page 383) and cut them into strips ½ inch thick. Do not peel the eggplants, but prepare them by removing the stems and cutting them into slices ½ inch thick (page 373). Preheat the oven to 375 degrees.

Lightly oil the bottom of a square or rectangular baking dish with high sides. Place half of the tomatoes on the bottom of dish, sprinkle with salt, pepper, oregano, and a little oil. Then arrange all the potatoes in the next layer. Then make a layer of the peppers, one of the eggplant, and, finally, one of the onions. Sprinkle each layer with salt, pepper, oregano, and oil. Lay the other half of the tomatoes over the onions. Cover the dish with aluminum foil and bake for 2½ hours. Remove, stir all the vegetables together, transfer to a serving dish and serve.

ASPARAGI (ASPARAGUS)

Thinner asparagus are best to use in Italian cooking because they are considered to have more flavor. (The Italians do not care for the very large thick asparagus.) Medium-sized ones are used here. It is not necessary to peel them, but just cut off the tough ends. When asparagus are used in most Italian recipes they are precooked by only partially submerging them in water so that the bottoms are boiled but the tips are steamed. This protects their delicacy, and they are left quite crisp. For many recipes, such as *Asparagi alla fiorentina* (see *The Fine Art of Italian Cooking*), the very thinnest asparagus are preferred by Italians, even thinner than those shown here.

TO COOK ASPARAGUS FOR A VARIETY OF DISHES

1. The medium-sized asparagus in the photo above are green almost to the bottom. If your bunch has a tough white part at the bottom, peel the very tough ends.

2. Arrange all the asparagus in one bunch, with tips even. Wrap a piece of string around toward the bottom, and make a knot to tie the asparagus together securely.

3. With a knife, even off the ends. In this way the whole bunch of asparagus can be made to stand evenly.

4. The asparagus are cooked, standing with tips up, in a tall stockpot.

344

"Steamed" Asparagus Tips

Bring to a boil enough cold water to cover only the white parts of the asparagus and add coarse-grained salt. When the water is boiling, add the tied asparagus, cover the pot and cook over low heat for about 20 minutes, without removing the lid, or until the stalks are tender yet still crisp. This method of cooking asparagus will steam the thin tips and cook the stalks.

At this point, the asparagus could be removed and eaten with a simple dressing of olive oil, salt, and freshly ground black pepper, or sautéed in butter and sprinkled with grated Parmigiano. Generally, Italians eat the tips and leave much of the stalk when they are cooked in this manner.

Asparagi in Salsa

ASPARAGUS IN EGG-LEMON SAUCE

ANCIENT ITALIAN JEWISH, TUSCANY

This recipe for Asparagus in Egg-Lemon Sauce probably predates the arrival of the Sephardim from Spain and belongs to the older Jewish communities in continuous residence in Italy from Roman times. It could not have been derived from the Greek egg-lemon sauces as the Sephardic Jews fled simultaneously to Turkish-ruled Greece and to Italy. (Remember, Jews had not been allowed in Greece under Byzantine rule.) This is still another recipe in which the sauce is exceptionally suited to the particular vegetable with which it is used and would not work well with others. Here the asparagus are sautéed, rather than steamed.

Asparagi in salsa may accompany any dish without a sauce.

2 pounds medium-sized asparagus
½ cup olive oil
1 large clove garlic, peeled but left whole
Salt and freshly ground black pepper
2 lemons
2 extra large eggs
Pinch of salt
1 teaspoon unbleached all-purpose flour

SERVES 4

Cut off the white part of the asparagus, but do not scrape the remaining green part. Place the asparagus in a large bowl of cold water for about 30 minutes. Cut the asparagus into 1½-inch pieces and let them soak in cold water for 5 minutes longer.

Heat the oil in a flameproof casserole, preferably terra-cotta. When the oil is hot, add the garlic and sauté for about 1 minute. Drain the asparagus and add them to the casserole. Sprinkle with salt and pepper, mix very well, and sauté for about 2 min-

utes. Squeeze the lemons. Remove the garlic and add the lemon juice to the casserole. Mix very well and cover the casserole. Simmer for about 15 minutes. At that time the asparagus should be cooked but still firm.

Put the eggs in a small bowl and add a pinch of salt. Beat well with a fork. Mix the flour in slowly, being careful to prevent lumps from forming. Use a slotted spoon to transfer the asparagus from the casserole to a serving dish.

HOW TO PREPARE EGG-LEMON SAUCE

1. Stir the beaten eggs into the leftover juice from the asparagus in the casserole. Stir slowly, until the sauce has reduced by half (about 5 minutes).

2. Pour the sauce over the asparagus and serve immediately.

Asparagi alla Cornaro

ASPARAGUS "CORNARO"

FROM BASSANO IN VENETO

This dish is traditionally made with white asparagus, which in Italy are associated with Bassano near Venice. This area is also the home of beautiful cream-colored pottery dishes, both antique and modern. White asparagus were probably developed by the Dutch in recent centuries and spread to Italy almost immediately, as well as to other European countries. Lately, imported fresh ones have begun to appear in American markets. The white color is developed artificially by burying the asparagus at a certain point during their growth. It is naturally Bassano which has the classic Italian recipes for white asparagus. The one included here is named after a heroine of the great days of Venice, Caterina Cornaro, about whom Donizetti wrote an opera. Though the result would be slightly different, the dish is also valid when made with delicate green asparagus if you cannot find the white ones.

2 pounds medium-thick asparagus (white, if possible)
4 tablespoons sweet butter
4 shelled walnuts
1 teaspoon finely grated orange rind (see pages 55–56)
Coarse-grained salt
3 egg yolks
Salt and freshly ground black pepper

SERVES 4

Wash the asparagus well, then cut them into pieces 2 inches long, discarding the bottom white part. Soak the asparagus pieces in a large bowl of cold water for 30 minutes.

346

Melt the butter in the top of a double boiler and let stand until cool (about 30 minutes).

Finely chop the walnuts and combine them with the grated orange rind.

Bring a large pot of cold water to a boil. Add coarse-grained salt to taste. When the water reaches the boiling point, add the asparagus and cook for about 10 minutes. The asparagus should be tender but not overcooked.

Meanwhile, put the egg yolks into a crockery bowl and mix by stirring, slowly but steadily, with a wooden spoon. When the egg yolks are almost whipped, start adding the cooled melted butter, still mixing with the wooden spoon. When all the butter is incorporated, add the walnut-orange rind mixture, salt and pepper to taste, and mix thoroughly.

Drain the asparagus and put them in a serving dish. Quickly pour the sauce over the hot asparagus and toss very well. Serve immediately.

36. Bietola, ò Herbetta (*Swiss Chard*)

BIETOLE (SWISS CHARD)

Swiss chard is a most unsatisfactory name, as the vegetable is not particularly Swiss and the word chard does not indicate its relationship to the beet. In Italian it is called *bietola* and a beet is *barbabietola*, or the root of the *bietola*, which is exactly what it is.

Beets and Swiss chard are two varieties of the same plant, one of which has developed the root, the other the stems and the leaves. Italians prepare boiled beets for inclusion in *Insalata composta*, but otherwise rarely use the vegetable. In contrast, Swiss chard is widely used in Italy, as much as in any other country. The leaves are cooked like spinach or in combination with spinach. In Parma, the famous *erbette* filling for *tortelli* is made from this combination. The *gambi* (stems) are used separately to make completely different dishes. In the recipe included here, the chard stems are first parboiled and then sautéed. The leaves may be used for a different dish such as *Bietole saltate* ("Stir-sautéed" Swiss Chard) or *Bietole all'Agro* (Boiled Swiss Chard with Olive Oil and Lemon) (see *The Fine Art of Italian Cooking*).

347

Gambi di Bietola in Padella

SAUTÉED STEMS OF CHARD

4 pounds Swiss chard with large white stems
Coarse-grained salt
1 medium-sized clove garlic, peeled
¼ cup olive oil
Salt and freshly ground black pepper

SERVES 4

HOW TO PREPARE BIETOLA

1. Cut off the large white stems and cut them into pieces 2 inches long. Reserve the leaves for another dish.

Soak the stems in a large bowl of cold water for 30 minutes.

Bring a large pot of water to a boil. Add coarse-grained salt to taste. Add the Swiss chard stems and boil for about 10 minutes. Drain the stems and cool them under cold running water.

Cut the garlic into small pieces.

Heat the oil in a skillet over medium heat. When the oil is hot, add the garlic and sauté for 1 minute. Then add the chard. Sprinkle with salt and pepper and sauté for about 2 minutes longer. Cover the skillet and simmer for about 5 minutes. Meanwhile, warm a platter.

Mix the Swiss chard very well, transfer to the warmed platter, and serve immediately.

BROCCOLI

Broccoli appears to be a vegetable of Roman or Etruscan origin and the name *brocco*, derived from the word for "sprout," is an original Italian word. Even today the area around Rome is famous for its broccoli dishes. Romans tend to use the word also to connote other vegetables which have a hard flower on top, such as cauliflower, purple cauliflower, and as *broccoletti*, a diminutive for turnip greens which are properly called *cime di rape* (known here as broccolirab). When you see broccoli on the menu in Rome and some other Italian cities, what arrives at the table may be a surprise. These vegetables are most often eaten cooked but cold in Rome, in a mixed vegetable *antipasto*, dressed with oil and wine vinegar and sometimes with anchovies.

Broccoli, used extensively in Chinese cooking, arrived in China from the West. When purchasing broccoli be sure it is very green, as it yellows with age, with firm stems and unbruised flowerets.

Broccoli alla Romana

BROCCOLI ROMAN STYLE

FROM ROME

This cold spicily dressed Roman-style broccoli is usually eaten as an appetizer. It is not common to use wine vinegar with the olive oil for a cooked vegetable in other parts of Italy.

1 bunch broccoli
Coarse-grained salt
¼ cup olive oil
1 clove garlic, peeled
2 teaspoons red wine vinegar
½ teaspoon red pepper flakes
Salt and freshly ground pepper

SERVES 4 AS AN APPETIZER

Soak the broccoli in a large bowl of cold water for 30 minutes.

Bring a large pot of water to a boil. Add coarse-grained salt to taste.

Remove the woody ends of the broccoli. Cut the flowerets from the large stems and keep them separate. Then cut the stems into strips about 2 inches long and ½ inch thick and add them to the boiling water. Cook for about 5 minutes, before adding the flowerets. Cook both for 5 minutes longer. Both the stems and flowerets should emerge *al dente*, but cooked.

Coarsely chop the garlic on a board and put it in a small bowl. Add oil, wine vinegar, red pepper flakes, and salt and pepper to taste. Mix very well. Let stand until needed.

Drain the broccoli and transfer it to a crockery bowl. Sprinkle the sauce over the broccoli immediately. Do not mix. Cover the bowl and refrigerate for at least 1 hour. Remove from the refrigerator, mix, and serve.

Broccoli al Vino Bianco

BROCCOLI IN WHITE WINE SAUCE

FROM MANTUA

Broccoli in white wine sauce is another simple treatment. When cooking, the stems are placed below, the flowerets on top, because the latter are more tender and should cook less.

This dish may accompany any dish which does not have a wine sauce.

1 bunch broccoli
3 tablespoons olive oil
1 clove garlic, peeled but left whole
Salt and freshly ground black pepper
1 cup dry white wine, approximately

Optional:
1 teaspoon red wine vinegar

SERVES 4

Remove the woody ends of the broccoli and discard them. Cut the remainder into pieces approximately 1½ inches long. Put the stems and the flowerets into two different bowls with cold water. Let soak for about 30 minutes.

Heat the oil in a flameproof casserole, preferably of terra-cotta or enamel. When the oil is hot, add the garlic and sauté very lightly over medium heat for 3 minutes. Discard the garlic. Drain the broccoli stems and flowerets, still keeping them separated. Add the stems to the casserole; then place the flow-erets on top. Sprinkle with salt and pepper and cook for 5 minutes without stirring.

Add ½ cup wine, cover the pan, and simmer for 10 minutes.

Uncover the pan and add the remaining wine, mix very well, and let the wine evaporate over high heat (about 5 minutes). At that time, the broccoli should be cooked, tender but not completely soft.

Serve hot, as they are, or cold, by adding 1 teaspoon of wine vinegar before serving, if desired.

CARCIOFI (ARTICHOKES)

When you buy artichokes be sure they are firm, and the outer leaves completely green and unspotted. The bottom of the stem of a fresh artichoke shows the two shades of green of the inner and outer layers and that should not have turned dark. The best pot to cook artichokes is glazed terra-cotta, then enamel. Aluminum or cast iron will darken the color of the bright green leaves and change the pale yellow of the heart to black.

HOW TO CLEAN ARTICHOKES

After they have soaked in water and lemon juice (see the following two recipes) so that they do not turn dark, the artichokes need to be prepared for cooking.

1. Artichokes with long stems and leaves on.

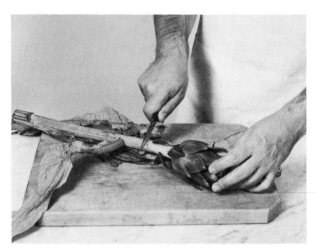

2. Cut off a portion of the stem, leaving about 3 inches.

3. Trim off all of the darker outer ring. The inner core is the best part because it has the real taste of the artichoke.

4. Remove as many rows of the outer leaves as necessary to arrive at those tender inner rows where you can clearly see the separation between the green at the top and the light yellow at the bottom.

5. Then remove the top green part. Press your thumb on the bottom of each leaf, the white part to hold it in place and with the other hand tear off the top green part. As each new row is uncovered, the tender yellow part of the leaves will be bigger.

When you reach the rows in which only the very tips of the leaves are green, cut off all the tips together with a knife.

The artichoke may then be cut in pieces or left whole, depending on the recipe. But in either case, the choke must be removed.

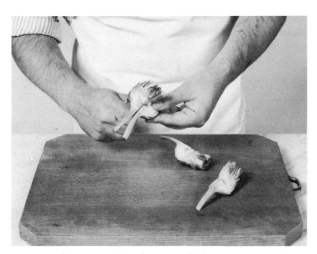

6. It is best to cut the artichokes into quarters lengthwise, in order to remove the choke, even if the artichokes are then to be cut into smaller pieces.

7. Then cut out the inside choke and hair.

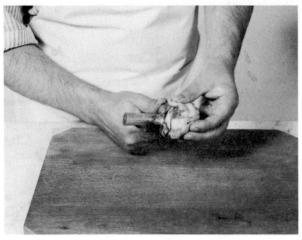

8. If you wish to stuff the artichokes whole, first cut off the stems.

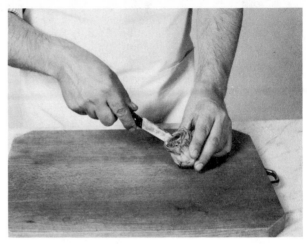

9. To remove the hair, fibers, and the choke, use a knife or a long teaspoon,

10. cutting all around the inside of the choke and scooping it out.

Carciofi alla Fiorentina

ARTICHOKES STUFFED WITH SPINACH AND CHARD

FROM FLORENCE

Stuffed whole artichokes can form a substantial course by themselves. *Carciofi ritti* (Stuffed Artichokes), stuffed with the stem of the artichoke itself, may be an appetizer, and the *Carciofi alla fiorentina* presented here is even more substantial, and should be served as a *piatto di mezzo* or a course in between the *primo* and *secondo*. This is one of the few spinach stuffed dishes that the Florentines themselves call *alla fiorentina*. (In French cooking even a leaf of spinach can cause "Florentine" to be added to the name of the dish.) As is done so often in Florence, the spinach is mixed with Swiss chard to soften its taste.

Artichokes, like cardoons and celery, are sometimes blanched while boiling by adding a little flour to the water. This lightens the color of the vegetables.

This technique is used in this recipe. Artichokes and cardoons should not be cooked in aluminum or cast iron as this darkens them. Use glazed terra-cotta or enamel.

4 large artichokes
1 lemon
Coarse-grained salt
1 tablespoon unbleached all-purpose flour
½ cup cold water
1 pound fresh Swiss chard
1 pound fresh spinach
2 tablespoons sweet butter
Salt, freshly ground black pepper, and freshly grated nutmeg
4 tablespoons freshly grated Parmigiano
¼ cup olive oil

For the *balsamella:*
3 tablespoons sweet butter
2 tablespoons unbleached all-purpose flour
1½ cups milk
Salt to taste

Soak the artichokes in a large bowl of cold water with the lemon, cut into halves, for 30 minutes.

Fill a terra-cotta or enamel saucepan with cold water. Dissolve the flour in the cold water and add the mixture to the saucepan, mixing thoroughly, and bring to a boil. Add coarse-grained salt to taste.

Meanwhile, clean the artichokes following the directions on pages 350–352, but leave them whole. When the water reaches a boil, add the artichokes and cook for about 10 minutes. The artichokes should still be very firm. Drain the artichokes and place them in a dish to cool.

Clean the spinach and Swiss chard well in cold water, removing the heavier stems. If they are very sandy, first rinse them once in lukewarm, not hot, water to loosen the sand, and then use cold water. Boil them in a large quantity of salted water for 10 minutes. Drain, then place under cold running water to cool. When the spinach and Swiss chard are cool, squeeze them very dry and chop them together coarsely on a board.

Melt the butter in a frying pan over medium heat. When the butter is completely melted, add the chopped spinach and chard to the pan. Sprinkle with salt, pepper, and nutmeg to taste. Mix thoroughly, using a fork, then cook over medium heat for 5 to 6 minutes. Transfer the greens to a bowl to cool completely.

Make the *balsamella* using the ingredients listed above, following the directions on page 334.

To stuff the artichokes first cut off the stems and coarsely chop them. Add the chopped stems to the bowl with the cooled spinach and Swiss chard and mix well. Stuff the artichokes with the mixture in the bowl and sprinkle with grated Parmigiano. Stand the artichokes in a flameproof casserole, preferably terra-cotta. Add the olive oil and ¼ cup cold water to the casserole. Sprinkle with a little salt and pepper. Cover the top part of each artichoke completely with the *balsamella.* Cover the casserole and simmer slowly over medium heat for about 35 minutes.

Carefully transfer the whole artichokes to a serving dish. Pour some of the juice from the casserole over each artichoke and serve at once.

Carciofi in Umido o in Salsa

ARTICHOKES IN PARSLEY SAUCE

Artichokes and carrots are the two vegetables whose flavors are especially accented by parsley. The parsley sauce used with artichokes contains lemon, which does not usually combine well with parsley but which works beautifully in this dish because of its special affinity for artichokes. Also, because of the chewy texture of the artichokes, it is necessary to add some chopped raw parsley at the end to make the transition between the cooked parsley and the artichokes. See *Carote al prezzemolo* (Carrots in Parsley Sauce), page 358, for the other sauce.

2 lemons plus the juice of ½ lemon
8 medium-sized artichokes
1 heaping tablespoon unbleached all purpose flour
1 cup cold water
Coarse-grained salt
½ cup olive oil
1 clove garlic, peeled but left whole
About 20 sprigs Italian parsley, leaves only
About ½ cup hot chicken or beef broth

SERVES 8

Cut the 2 lemons into halves and squeeze them into a large crockery bowl of cold water. Add the lemon halves to the water. Place the whole artichokes in the bowl and soak them for about 30 minutes. Then remove one artichoke at a time from the water and clean it, removing the dark green part of the stem and the outside leaves. Cut it into quarters. Remove the choke and put the artichoke pieces back into the bowl (pages 350–352).

Bring a large pot of water to boil, then dissolve the flour in about 1 cup of cold water and pour the mixture into the pot. Add coarse salt to taste. When the water reaches the boiling point again, add the artichoke pieces and lemon halves. Simmer for about 10 minutes. Remove the pot from the heat and let the artichokes stand in the pot for about 15 minutes. Remove the artichokes from the pot with a strainer-skimmer and put them in a large bowl of cold water until needed.

Heat the oil in a flameproof casserole, preferably terra-cotta or enamel. When the oil is hot, add the garlic and sauté very lightly over medium heat for about 2 minutes. Meanwhile finely chop half the parsley and coarsely chop the remaining parsley on a board. Add the finely chopped parsley to the casserole and sauté for about 1 minute. Drain the artichokes and add them to the pan, stirring to coat them with the parsley. Start adding the hot broth a little at a time, as needed. Taste for salt and pepper, and simmer for about 10 minutes. By then the artichoke pieces should be cooked but not overcooked. Pour the lemon juice over them and mix thoroughly. Transfer the artichokes to a serving dish, sprinkle with the remaining parsley, and serve hot.

CARDI (CARDOONS)

The cardoon is the large stem of one variety of the plant *Cynara cardunculus*. The flowers of another variety are artichokes. The flavor of the cardoon is, of course, related to that of the artichoke but is slightly more bitter. Cardoons are most tender if picked after they have experienced some very cold weather. Otherwise, they may be tough and bitter. Sometimes the inside stalks, comparable to celery hearts, become very white and tender and may be eaten raw, *in pinzimonio* (dipped in Tuscan olive oil, salt, and pepper), or *bagna cauda* (dipped in a Piedmontese warm sauce). Cardoons are available at Italian fruit and vegetable stores in the United States.

HOW TO CLEAN CARDOONS

1. Notice that cardoons have large stems like celery. Unlike artichokes, this variety does not have highly developed flowers. Mature cardoons are tough when raw. They are generally boiled first before being cooked in other ways.

Separate the individual stems for boiling by cutting off the end.

2. Remove and discard hard outside stems. Cut each stem into pieces, the length varying according to the different dishes. To prevent discoloring, either rub each piece with lemon before placing in a bowl of cold water to soak or else soak with the lemon juice already in the water.

Cardi al Forno

BAKED CARDOONS

Cardoons are always boiled with a small amount of flour added to the water in order to blanch them before proceeding further with the preparation. The flour lightens their color. Some dishes deep-fry the cardoons after boiling, and others bake them. *Cardi al forno* is an elaborate baked cardoon dish using one of the classic meat sauces, made with wild *porcini* mushrooms.

It may be eaten as a substantial *piatto di mezzo* or as a light main course.

**SERVES 6 AS A PIATTO DI MEZZO
OR 4 AS A MAIN COURSE**

4 pounds cardoons (before cleaning)
1 lemon
Coarse-grained salt
1 tablespoon flour
1 cup cold water

For the sauce:
2 ounces dried porcini *mushrooms*
1 small red onion
4 tablespoons olive oil
8 ounces ground beef
Salt and freshly ground black pepper
2 cups canned drained imported Italian tomatoes
1 cup hot beef or chicken broth

Plus:
1 pound solid vegetable shortening
2 extra large eggs
1 cup unbleached all-purpose flour
Pinch of salt
8 ounces Fontina cheese, cut into thin slices
½ cup grated Parmigiano

Clean the cardoons, removing the hard outside stems. Cut the soft inside stems into pieces about 3 inches long. Soak the pieces in cold water with lemon juice for about 30 minutes.

Bring a large pot of water to a boil. Add coarse-grained salt to taste.

Dissolve the flour in the cold water and add it to the boiling water, stirring with a long spoon. When water starts to boil again, add the cardoon pieces and simmer for about 30 minutes. Then remove the cardoons from the boiling water with strainer-skimmer and let them cool on paper towels.

Prepare the sauce. Soak the *porcini* mushrooms in a small bowl of lukewarm water for 30 minutes.

Finely chop the onion on a board. Heat the oil in a saucepan. When the oil is hot, add the chopped onion and sauté until it is golden brown, about 10 minutes.

Add the ground beef and salt and pepper to taste. Sauté for about 15 minutes, stirring occasionally.

Drain the mushrooms and be sure that all the sand is removed from them.

Pass the tomatoes through a food mill to remove the skin and the seeds. Add the strained tomatoes to the saucepan. Simmer very slowly for about 15 minutes. Then add the hot broth and mushrooms and simmer very slowly, until all ingredients are completely amalgamated and the sauce has thickened (about 30 minutes). Transfer the sauce to a crockery bowl and let stand until cool.

To assemble the dish: Melt the solid shortening in a frying pan. Beat the eggs and a pinch of salt together in a small bowl. Lightly flour the cardoon pieces. When the shortening is completely melted and hot, dip the floured cardoon pieces in the beaten egg and place them in the frying pan. Fry until golden brown on both sides, then put them on paper towels to drain.

Preheat the oven to 300 degrees.

Spread one quarter of the sauce over the bottom of a terra-cotta casserole, then make a layer of one quarter of the cardoons. Lay some slices of Fontina cheese on top of the cardoons, and sprinkle with a little grated Parmigiano, and salt and pepper. Repeat the layers of sauce, cardoons, and cheeses until all the ingredients are used. (The top layer should be of sauce.) Cover the casserole and bake for 35 minutes.

Remove the casserole from the oven and cool for 5 minutes before serving.

CAROTE (CARROTS)

The earliest Italian recipe for carrots uses them as part of a vegetable compote. This is probably the ancestor of the modern *Insalata composta* ("Composed" Salad), which often utilizes cold boiled carrots together with other boiled vegetables. Nowadays, carrots are eaten raw, thinly shredded, either as part of the *Insalata mista* (Mixed Salad), or marinated in lemon juice; they are generally not eaten raw with dips in Italy. Many cooked carrot dishes are first parboiled. The sweet full-flavored quality of Italian carrot dishes comes from the way in which the vegetable is boiled with its skin.

A Special Way to Boil Carrots

Soak carrots in a bowl of cold water for about 30 minutes before cooking. Then cut off both ends of the carrots. Bring a large pot of water to a boil. Add coarse-grained salt and the carrots and cook for 15 to 20 minutes, depending on the thickness of the carrots.

1. When carrots are cooked, cool them in a bowl of cold water, then starting at the thinner bottom end, gently push off the outer skin; it will come off easily and whole. At this point, the carrots may be prepared in different ways.

Carote alla Crema

CARROTS IN CREAM SAUCE

FROM TUSCANY

Carrots in heavy cream is simple, using only essential ingredients. It is typical of the old Tuscan cookery in that both ingredients, the butter and the cream, retain their individual flavors, and Parmigiano is not used at all, as it would completely mask these delicate flavors. Tuscan cooking has its buttery and creamy dishes, but when these ingredients are used, they are not embellishments but dominate the whole. Here, heavy cream is used because it is one of the best ways to bring out the intrinsic flavor of carrots. It is rarely used with other vegetables.

1 pound medium-sized carrots
Coarse-grained salt
2 tablespoons sweet butter
Salt and freshly ground white pepper
½ cup heavy cream

SERVES 4

Boil and peel the carrots following the directions on page 357, photo 1. Cut the carrots into small slices (about ⅛ inch thick).

Melt the butter in a saucepan. When the butter is completely melted, add the carrots and sauté over low heat for about 5 minutes. Taste for salt and white pepper. Then start adding the heavy cream a tablespoon at a time, stirring slowly until the cream is absorbed. Do not add more cream until the previous addition has been absorbed. After all the cream is absorbed, the carrots will be ready to be served.

Carote al Prezzemolo

CARROTS IN PARSLEY SAUCE

FROM NAPLES

The broth-based parsley sauce used in this recipe is a rare example of an herb sauce used with carrots. It is very versatile and works well also with parboiled celery.

1 pound medium-sized carrots
Coarse-grained salt
About 15 sprigs Italian parsley, leaves only
4 tablespoons sweet butter
2 tablespoons olive oil
1 tablespoon unbleached all-purpose flour
About 1 cup hot chicken or beef broth
Salt and freshly ground black pepper

SERVES 4

Boil and peel the carrots following the directions on page 357, photo 1. Cut the carrots into ½-inch-thick slices.

Coarsely chop parsley and put it in a flameproof casserole with the butter and oil. Put the casserole over medium heat and cook until the butter is melted and the parsley is lightly sautéed (about 4 minutes). Add the carrots, stir with a wooden spoon, and sprinkle the flour over the carrots. Stir until the flour is thoroughly incorporated, then add the hot broth, stirring constantly. Taste for salt and pepper. Cook for about 15 minutes more, stirring occasionally. At that time the carrots should be cooked, half of the broth evaporated, and a rich smooth sauce formed. Transfer carrots with the sauce to a warm serving dish, sprinkle over a little black pepper, and serve immediately.

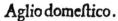

Aglio domeſtico.

CAVOLFIORE (CAULIFLOWER)

Cauliflower is closely related to broccoli and indeed is sometimes called broccoli, particularly in Rome. Both vegetables are associated with Italy more than with any other country and perhaps Italians know how to bring out their flavors best.

The white cauliflower that we find easily in America is sometimes called the "Milan" variety. The Italian preparation of it stresses the visual presentation of either the entire head, with a few tender green leaves left on, or the separate little flowerets, detached from the discarded stem. Green cauliflower, typical of Rome, is not found in America as yet, but it is especially good as a cold *antipasto* with anchovy sauce. Purple cauliflower from Sicily is available in some Italian markets in America. It turns green when cooked and works well with the same recipes as the green.

The main idea behind Italian cauliflower presentation is not to cover this vegetable with any sauce heavy enough to hide the beauty of its shape. Italians prefer to give a piquant dressing to this vegetable rather than a milk or cheese-based one, which they feel also creates heaviness. It is important not to overcook cauliflower or broccoli or let them get water-logged, as this makes them heavier, less tasty, and brings out the cabbage family smell. For this reason, these vegetables are not usually the main ingredients in soups in Italy.

HOW TO CLEAN AND BOIL CAULIFLOWER

Cauliflower can be boiled whole or in flowerets and served plain with olive oil, salt, and pepper or an anchovy sauce (see *The Fine Art of Italian Cooking*). The flowerets are also used for a variety of dishes, such as *Cavolfiore Affogato* (Cauliflower Steamed in Wine) which follows.

1. Before boiling the cauliflower either whole or in flowerets, it must first be cleaned. Remove only the bottom knob and the attached outer leaves with a knife, leaving the smaller tender leaves attached.

2. To cut into single flowerets, detach each at its end from the stem.

3. The flowerets ready for deep-frying, "steaming" (see below), or boiling.

To boil cauliflower, bring a large pot of cold water to a boil. Add coarse-grained salt to taste. Then add the whole vegetable or flowerets and boil until cooked but still firm.

Cavolfiore Affogato

CAULIFLOWER "STEAMED" IN WINE

FROM BARI

In this recipe for *cavolfiore affogato* the cauliflower steams in white wine and when baked in the oven, most of the liquid evaporates. The vegetable retains its crunchiness and lightness. The flavor of the wine overcomes any cabbage smell with its own pungent liveliness.

2 large heads cauliflower
2 cloves garlic, peeled
2 lemons
2 cups dry white wine
1½ tablespoons salt
½ teaspoon freshly ground black pepper
6 tablespoons olive oil

SERVES 8

Remove all the leaves from cauliflower; then turn them bottom side up. Detach the flowerets at the stem from the central stem (page 360). Leave the smaller flowerets whole (not more than 2 inches in length and thickness). Cut the larger flowerets into pieces the same size.

Soak the flowerets in a bowl of cold water for about 30 minutes. Finely chop the garlic and squeeze the lemons. Put the chopped garlic and the lemon juice in a crockery bowl along with the wine, salt, pepper, and oil. Mix all the ingredients together with a wooden spoon, making certain the salt and pepper are thoroughly dissolved.

Preheat the oven to 400 degrees. Drain the cauliflower pieces and put them in a large terra-cotta or enamel saucepan, one piece next to the other, with all the stems facing down and the flowerets standing up. Pour the contents of the bowl over the flowerets, cover the pan, and bake for about 50 minutes. Remove from the oven and let cool for a few minutes. Sprinkle with freshly ground black pepper, then serve directly from the same pan.

CAVOLO NERO (KALE)

In Italy it is the Florentines who are the great kale eaters, and they have created the characteristic *Zuppa di cavolo nero*, the fennel seed-flavored pork chops with kale, as well as the favorite *Cavolo nero in umido* given here. Kale is also an ingredient in many versions of *minestrone*.

A misunderstanding has arisen in the meaning of *cavolo nero* in the English language. It is sometimes translated literally as black cabbage and, hence, is thought to be unavailable here, but it is actually the curly leafed kale, a vegetable that is fairly common. Kale is a member of the cabbage family in the same sense that broccoli and cauliflower are, but it is not a head of cabbage and red cabbage should never be substituted for it.

Kale, as with cardoons, is a product of the winter, and is tender only if the plant has experienced a very cold winter. Unfortunately, sometimes it is on the market too early when it is not yet ready.

Very often the vegetable is tough and stringy not because it is old, but because it was *not* left long enough in the fields to experience sufficient cold weather. When purchasing, avoid kale whose leaves are very hard and resistant. Color is not affected. (Naturally, when very old, the large veins in the leaves become tough again, but I have rarely experienced this on the market.)

361

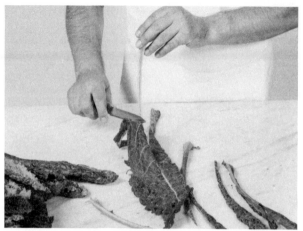

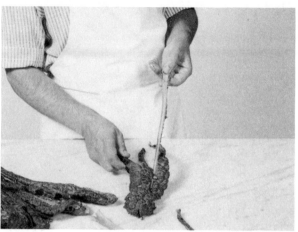

1. To remove the large tough stems of the kale, hold the end of the stem with one hand, and with the other, pass a knife along the entire length of the stem separating half of the leaf from the stem.

2. Repeat the procedure along the other side of the leaf.

Cavolo Nero in Umido

KALE SIMMERED IN BROTH

FROM UMBRIA

The thin strips of kale are simmered in broth. The combination of *prosciutto* or *pancetta* with the butter is unusual for Umbria, a region that produces olive oil and not butter.

3 bunches kale, about 3 pounds
1 medium-sized red onion
4 ounces prosciutto *or* pancetta
6 tablespoons sweet butter
2 tablespoons olive oil
2 cups beef or chicken broth
Salt and freshly ground black pepper

SERVES 4

Wash the kale carefully, in a colander under cold running water, and remove the large stems (photos, above). Cut the leaves into 1-inch strips and soak them in a large bowl of cold water for about 30 minutes.

Finely chop onion and cut the *prosciutto* into small pieces.

Heat 3 tablespoons of the butter and the oil in a casserole over medium heat. When the butter is completely melted, add the prepared ingredients. Sauté for about 5 minutes, or until the onion is translucent.

Meanwhile, bring the broth to a boil. When the onion is translucent, add the broth to the casserole. Simmer for about 15 minutes. Taste for salt and pepper.

Pass the contents of the casserole through food mill and return the passed sauce to the same pot. Put the casserole over medium heat and add the kale. Cook for about 20 minutes. At that time the kale should be cooked and tender. Remove the casserole from the heat and incorporate the remaining butter by mixing it in with a wooden spoon. Serve immediately.

CAVOLO VERZOTTO OR VERZA (SAVOY CABBAGE)

Of the types of head cabbage, Savoy cabbage, crinkled and delicate, is preferred by Italians for many cabbage dishes and even in *minestre* and *minestroni*. Though cabbage was not native to Italy, it was there that many varieties were developed. Blanched cabbage leaves are used to wrap meats, such as whole chicken breast or ground beef. Stuffed cabbage dishes exist in many countries and though they are not usually associated with Italy, one finds them in Italian cookbooks dating back to the Renaissance.

HOW TO CUT SAVOY CABBAGE INTO STRIPS WITH A MANDOLIN

Remove the large outer leaves of the cabbage. Cut the cabbage into halves, then each half into quarters.

1. With a mandolin, shred the cabbage into strips.
   The mandolin is made of wood, and has two horizontal blades, one straight, the other jagged, each adjustable to produce varying thicknesses. This is the traditional Italian instrument for shredding vegetables.

Verza e Patate

CABBAGE-POTATO STEW

FROM FRIULI

This hearty winter dish comes from the mountainous area bordering on Austria and Yugoslavia and would not be out of place in those countries as well.

It best accompanies heavier meats such as pork or beef *spezzatino*, or any boiled meat.

It should not be used with anything fried or made with tomato sauce. It can be served at room temperature in the summer as an appetizer, by adding a tablespoon of wine vinegar to the cooled cabbage.

1 medium-sized Savoy cabbage (3 pounds, approximately)   SERVES 8
Coarse-grained salt
1½ pounds boiling potatoes (but not new potatoes)
1 clove garlic
4 ounces pancetta, or 2 ounces boiled ham and 2 ounces salt pork
½ cup olive oil
1 scant teaspoon red pepper flakes
Salt and freshly ground black pepper

Remove the large outer leaves of the cabbage. Wash the cabbage carefully, then cut it into quarters and cut each quarter into strips using a mandolin (page 363). Put the strips of cabbage in a bowl of cold water and let soak for about 30 minutes.

Bring two large pots of water to a boil. Add coarse-grained salt to taste. When the water reaches the boiling point, add the cabbage to one pot and the whole potatoes with skins to the other. Let the cabbage boil for 10 minutes, then drain and cool under cold running water. Let the cabbage stand until needed. Boil the potatoes for about 35 minutes, or until they are tender. Remove them from the pot and peel them.

Pass the potatoes through a potato ricer. Combine the potatoes and cabbage in a large bowl.

Finely chop the garlic and coarsely cut the *pancetta* on a board.

Heat the oil in a casserole over medium heat. When the oil is hot, add the garlic and *pancetta* and sauté for about 10 minutes. Then add the potato-cabbage mixture. Sprinkle with the red pepper flakes and the salt and pepper to taste. Cook, mixing all the ingredients together, for about 15 minutes. At that point dish should be hot. Remove from the heat and transfer to a serving dish. Serve immediately.

Verza con Salsicce

SAVOY CABBAGE WITH SAUSAGES

FROM MANTUA

This dish has a fascinating history. It has been traced to the ancient Jewish community of Mantua, which has been an important center since the days when the great Roman poet Virgil was born there.

The original version used chicken fat in place of the *pancetta* and sausages made of beef. At some point in its more than a thousand-year history, the dish was adapted in this form by the general population of northern Italy.

1 Savoy medium-sized cabbage, about 3 pounds   SERVES 6
1 large red onion
4 ounces pancetta, or 2 ounces boiled ham and 2 ounces salt pork
3 tablespoons olive oil
2 Italian sweet sausages (6 ounces) without fennel seeds, or 6 ounces ground pork
4 tablespoons red wine vinegar
Salt and freshly ground black pepper
About ½ cup chicken or beef broth

Remove the large outer leaves from the cabbage. Slice it into ½-inch-thick slices and rinse very well. Place the strips of cabbage in a bowl of cold water and soak for about 30 minutes.

Finely chop the onion and cut the *pancetta* into small pieces on a board.

Heat the oil in a terra-cotta or enamel casserole over medium heat. When the oil is hot, add the onion and *pancetta* and sauté for about 5 minutes.

Prick the sausages with a fork. Drain the sliced cabbage and add it to the pan, then add the sausages and wine vinegar. Cover the pan and cook over low heat for about 15 minutes. Then stir, taste for salt and pepper, and add a little broth if needed. Cover again and cook for 25 minutes longer.

Transfer the cabbage to a serving dish, cut each sausage into 3 pieces, and serve immediately.

Cavolo alla Sarda

SAVOY CABBAGE SARDINIA STYLE

FROM SARDINIA

The unusual flavoring of this Sardinian recipe comes from bay leaf and parsley, rarely used in combination with cabbage.

1 medium-sized Savoy cabbage, about 3 pounds
4 ounces pancetta, or 2 ounces boiled ham and 2 ounces salt pork
2 cloves garlic, peeled
About 10 sprigs Italian parsley, leaves only
⅓ cup olive oil
1 large bay leaf
Salt and freshly ground black pepper
½ cup cold water

SERVES 6

Wash the cabbage carefully, then cut it into quarters. Use a mandolin (page 363) to cut the cabbage into thin strips. Soak the strips of cabbage in a bowl of cold water for about 30 minutes.

Cut the *pancetta* into small pieces and finely chop the garlic and parsley together on a board.

Heat the oil in a casserole, preferably of terra-cotta or enamel, over medium heat. When the oil is hot, add the chopped ingredients and sauté for 2

minutes. Then drain the cabbage and add it to casserole along with the bay leaf. Sprinkle with salt and pepper, cover the casserole, and cook for about 10 minutes. Stir, add ½ cup of cold water, cover again, and cook for about 30 minutes longer, stirring occasionally. Remove from the heat, discard the bay leaf, and transfer the cabbage to a serving dish. Sprinkle a little pepper over the cabbage and serve immediately.

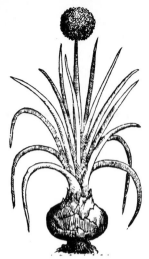

CIPOLLINE (BUTTON ONIONS)

These small onions take their name from the flatness of their shape. They are the ones generally used for a pungent vegetable accompaniment as in *Cipolline in agrodolce* (Sweet-and-Sour Button Onions), below, or as part of *Sottoaceti* (Pickled Vegetables), pages 46–47.

Small pearl onions may also be used for the same recipes and they are cleaned in the same way.

37. Delle cipolle
(Onions)

HOW TO CLEAN BUTTON ONIONS

1. The flat medium-sized button onions. Before cooking, clean them by cutting off the top and bottom knobs and removing the skin.

Cipolline in Agrodolce

SWEET-AND-SOUR BUTTON ONIONS

FROM TUSCANY

The small onions are first parboiled and then sautéed with sugar which becomes almost caramelized. The wine vinegar is added and allowed to evaporate leaving the onions coated with a sweet-and-sour sauce.

1 pound button onions or pearl onions
Coarse-grained salt
½ cup granulated sugar
1½ cups cold water
1 tablespoon unbleached all-purpose flour
⅓ cup red wine vinegar

SERVES 4

Clean and wash the onions very carefully and soak them in a bowl of cold water for about 30 minutes.

Bring a large quantity of water to a boil. Add coarse-grained salt to taste. When the water reaches the boiling point again, add the onions and boil for about 5 minutes. Drain the onions and put them on paper towels to remove any excess liquid.

Put the sugar and ½ cup of cold water in a saucepan over medium heat. Simmer for about 15 minutes, or until a white syrup is formed. Add the flour, mix very well, and simmer until the syrup turns a reddish color (about 5 minutes).

Combine the wine vinegar with the remaining 1 cup of cold water in a bowl. Add this mixture to the syrup and mix very well with a wooden spoon. Simmer for about 10 minutes in order to remove any lumps of flour that might have formed. Add the onions and coat them with the sauce by just shaking the pan (do not use a spoon or fork). When the onions are completely coated (about 2 minutes), transfer them and the sauce to a warmed serving dish and serve immediately.

FAGIOLINI (STRING BEANS OR GREEN BEANS)

Small, young string beans do not have the tough "strings" on either side, which give them their English name. These strings develop when the vegetable is no longer very young. In Italy, string beans are almost always picked before they develop the strings. Since in America they are usually picked when more mature, the strings should be removed before the vegetable is cooked.

HOW TO CLEAN STRING BEANS OR GREEN BEANS

1. First break off one end of the string beans with your fingers. The string will remain attached to the removed end. Just pull it off the entire length of the bean and repeat the procedure with the string on the other side.

If you are lucky enough to find the small string beans, it is only necessary to break off the two ends when preparing them.

Fagiolini alle Nocciole

STRING BEANS WITH A CREAM-HAZELNUT SAUCE

This string bean recipe has a unique flavor, derived from the combination of chopped hazelnuts, lemon juice, and heavy cream. An old, old traditional Parma dish, it reflects the rich taste of the Parma court days. But it is the only dish I know of in which the heavy cream is uncooked, a necessary thing so that it will not curdle in this singular combination with lemon juice.

1 pound string beans
Coarse-grained salt
1 lemon
2 ounces shelled hazelnuts
⅓ cup heavy cream
Salt and freshly ground black pepper

SERVES 6 AS APPETIZER

Clean the string beans following the directions on page 367 and soak them in a large bowl of cold water for 30 minutes.

Bring a large pot of water to a boil. Add coarse-grained salt to taste. Then add the beans and cook for about 12 minutes if beans are thin and young. Often the beans are picked so large that it requires 20 to 25 minutes to cook them. Squeeze the lemon. Drain the beans and cool them under cold running water.

Transfer the beans to a serving dish. Pour the lemon juice over the beans. Finely chop 1 ounce of the nuts and coarsely chop the other ounce.

Pour the heavy cream into a cold crockery bowl and add the chopped nuts and salt and pepper to taste. Pour this over the beans, mix very well with two wooden spoons, cover, and refrigerate for at least 15 minutes before serving.

Fagiolini alla Genovese

STRING BEANS, GENOESE STYLE

The Genoese anchovy-raisin combination is also traditional with string beans, but because they are chewier than spinach, and contain small beans, the pignoli are felt to be out of place.

2 pounds string beans
Coarse-grained salt
3 whole anchovies in salt, or 6 anchovy fillets in oil, drained
1 small clove garlic, peeled
About 15 sprigs Italian parsley, leaves only
⅓ cup olive oil
2 tablespoons sweet butter
Salt and freshly ground black pepper

SERVES 6

Remove the ends of the string beans as well as the coarse string that runs along the side (page 367). Soak the beans in a bowl of cold water for 30 minutes.

Bring a large pot of water to a boil. Add coarse-grained salt to taste. When the water reaches the boiling point again, add the string beans and cook for 12 to 25 minutes, depending on the size of the beans. Drain the beans and cool them under cold running water.

If whole, clean the anchovies in cold water (page 55) to remove the bone and excess salt.

Finely chop the garlic, and coarsely chop the parsley and the anchovy fillets together on a board.

Heat the oil and butter in a flameproof casserole over medium heat. When the butter is completely melted, add the chopped ingredients and sauté for 1 minute. Then add the boiled string beans and stir very well. Taste for salt and pepper and sauté very slowly until the sauce completely coats the beans (about 5 minutes). Serve immediately.

FINOCCHI (FENNEL "BULBS")

The *dulce* (sweet) variety of fennel, *Foeniculum vulgare*, the common type eaten in Italy is often called Florence fennel or sweet fennel. Waverley Root points out that its "bulb" is really a bulbous swollen base of the stems. In the Middle Ages, the flowers were eaten frequently in Florence and throughout Italy and the leaves are still eaten as an ingredient in soups in Friuli. But it is the "bulb" which is most used, and it's among the most popular, versatile vegetables eaten in Italy. People enjoy its faint hint of sweetness and anise-like flavor.

Fennel appears to have originated in the Mediterranean, probably in Italy, and, as with broccoli, was taken to the East and was adopted there as a foodstuff. The seeds are used as an aromatic herb, particularly in Indian curries, and as a basic Chinese spice. Also see discussion of wild fennel, another variety under *Pasta con le sarde* (Pasta with Fresh Sardines), page 189.

In Italy, fennel is eaten raw in salads but more often as a cooked vegetable. It is now available in the United States not only in Italian fruit and vegetable stores but even in supermarkets. When freshest, it is firm and white, without brown spots, and fortunately when less fresh, the outer layer may be stripped off and the rest is still usable.

HOW TO CUT FENNEL FOR COOKING

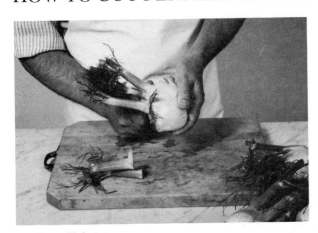

1. Cut off the stems.

2. Cut off the small knob at the bottom.

369

3. Then remove the stringy outer layer.

4. Starting at the bottom end, cut the bulb in half.

5. Then cut each half into quarters. This is the best cut for boiling the fennel, or sautéing it (after it is boiled).

6. You can also cut fennel halves into slices, for when you have to arrange them in layers on a baking dish.

Finocchi alla Parmigiana con Salsicce

FENNEL "BULBS" PARMA STYLE

FROM PARMA

This is one of the two versions of cooked fennel that are popular in Parma. As with most dishes in the style of that region, it employs Parmigiano, along with butter, and is flavored with a little bit of sausage. Although Parmese cooking is very rich, I find its dishes are perhaps the most integrated in their complexity among the style of the Emilia-Romagna region. Its culinary tradition, along with its cheese, goes back two thousand years. This dish may be used as a normal vegetable course, but perhaps works best as a separate *piatto di mezzo* (in-between course) before the main dish.

370

4 large fennel "bulbs"
Coarse-grained salt
2 Italian sweet sausages without fennel seeds (about 6 ounces), or 6 ounces ground
  pork
5 tablespoons sweet butter
¾ cup freshly grated Parmigiano
Salt and freshly ground black pepper

SERVES 4 TO 6

Cut the fennel into quarters vertically (page 370). Remove the small knob at the bottom and cut out the hard inner part at the bottom, which is a continuation of the knob. Place the fennel in a large bowl of cold water and soak for 30 minutes.

Bring a large pot of cold water to a boil. Add coarse-grained salt to taste. When the water reaches the boiling point again, add the fennel and boil for about 10 minutes. Drain the fennel, then place it on paper towels to absorb any excess liquid.

Remove the skin from the sausages and cut them into 5 or 6 pieces each.

Melt 2 tablespoons of the butter in a frying pan. When it is completely melted, add the sausage pieces and sauté for about 5 minutes. Transfer the sausage pieces to a small bowl and let them cool. Preheat the oven to 375 degrees.

Grease the bottom and sides of a 10- x 4- x ¾-inch Pyrex dish with 1 tablespoon of the remaining butter. Cut the remaining 2 tablespoons of butter into small pieces. Cover the bottom of the prepared dish with three quarters of the fennel, sprinkle over half of the Parmigiano, half of the sausage pieces, and half of the butter pieces, then salt and pepper to taste. Make one more layer of fennel with the remaining sausage and Parmigiano, the remaining pieces of butter, salt and pepper. Bake for about 25 minutes. Serve immediately.

Finocchi con Salsa di Capperi e Acciughe

FENNEL WITH CAPER-ANCHOVY SAUCE

FROM TUSCANY

First the fennel is parboiled and then baked with the sauce. The unusual blending of the piquant caper-anchovy flavor with the sweetness and anise-like taste of the fennel makes a unique kind of sweet-and-sour combination. This dish is used mainly as an appetizer or as a vegetable to accompany boiled meat or fowl.

SERVES 4 TO 6

4 large fennel "bulbs"
Coarse-grained salt
2 anchovies in salt, or 4 anchovy fillets in oil, drained
4 tablespoons capers in wine vinegar, drained
½ cup olive oil
Salt and freshly ground black pepper

CAPPARO.

38. Capparo *or* cappero *(Caper Bush)*

371

Wash off and then clean the fennel "bulbs" following the instructions on pages 369–370. Cut the fennel into slices and soak in a bowl of cold water for about 30 minutes.

Bring a large pot of water to a boil. Add coarse-grained salt to taste. When the water reaches the boiling point again, add the fennel and boil for 5 minutes. Drain the fennel and cool under cold running water being careful not to break the slices. Place the fennel slices on paper towels to remove any excess liquid. If whole, clean the anchovies, removing the bone and excess salt (page 55). Finely chop the anchovies and capers together on a board.

Pour all but 1 tablespoon of the oil into a small crockery bowl and add the chopped ingredients. Mix well with a wooden spoon, adding a pinch of salt and pepper to taste. Preheat the oven to 375 degrees.

Heavily oil a 10- x 4- x ¾-inch Pyrex dish with the remaining oil and arrange half of the fennel slices on the bottom. Pour half the sauce from the bowl over the slices of fennel. Then make another layer with the remaining slices and add the remaining sauce. Place the pan in the oven and bake for 25 minutes. Serve immediately.

LATTVCA CRESPA.

39. *"Lattuca crespa"*
("Boston" type lettuce)

LATTUGA (LETTUCE)

In Italy, "Boston" and "Romaine" (Roman style) lettuce are common. "Iceberg" and "Bibb" types are unknown there. Cooked lettuce is sometimes used as a vegetable in Italy. When sautéed, as in the following recipe for lettuce soup, it reveals a complexity of flavor that might not be suspected by those who have tasted it only as a salad green.

Minestra di Lattuga

LETTUCE SOUP

FROM PIEDMONT

For this soup, the lettuce first is sautéed in butter and then placed in a tureen. Lukewarm broth with dissolved egg yolk is added. When the hot broth is finally put in, it is important to stir continuously so that the eggs will not curdle and the soup will have the proper texture.

1 head Boston lettuce
4 tablespoons sweet butter
Salt to taste
4½ cups beef broth
2 extra large egg yolks
8 tablespoons "croutons" (piccoli crostini fritti), *deep-fried in olive oil*
4 tablespoons grated Parmigiano

SERVES 4

Use a mandolin to cut the Boston lettuce into thin strips (page 363). Wash the lettuce carefully and soak in a bowl of cold water for about 30 minutes.

Melt the butter in a flameproof casserole over medium heat. When butter is completely melted, add the lettuce, sprinkle with salt, and cover the casserole. Cook for about 15 minutes, stirring occasion-ally with a wooden spoon. Heat ½ cup of the broth until lukewarm.

Put the egg yolks in a small bowl with the lukewarm broth and dissolve them with a fork.

Transfer the cooked lettuce to a terrine, cover, and let it cool (about 1 hour).

About 15 minutes before the lettuce is ready, heat

the remaining 4 cups of broth to a boil. When lettuce is cool, add the dissolved egg yolks to the terrine and stir very well. Cover the lettuce in the terrine with the deep-fried "croutons" (see *Piccoli crostini* *fritti* in *The Fine Art of Italian Cooking*) and immediately pour in the boiling broth. Stir continuously to prevent curdling. Sprinkle with Parmigiano and serve immediately in warmed soup bowls.

MELANZANE (EGGPLANT)

Though it came from the East and Middle East, the eggplant found its main European home in Italy, both in the northern and the southern regions of the country. There are hundreds of Italian eggplant dishes: marinated, with cheese and tomatoes, in combination with other vegetables, in batter, stuffed in a variety of ways, as preserves, in combination with both dried and fresh pasta, sautéed, fried, baked, and grilled.

In addition to the two eggplant recipes in the pasta chapters, we include here two eggplant *caponata* preserves, one of the vegetable with an unusual meatless stuffing, combining sheep's milk cheese and black olives, and eggplant slices baked in batter with marjoram. Eggplant combines especially well with such vegetables as tomatoes (of course), peppers, onions, potatoes, and celery in a variety of vegetable compotes, such as the *Tegamaccio* (page 343).

HOW TO CUT EGGPLANT INTO DIFFERENT SHAPES FOR A VARIETY OF DISHES

Eggplants are used both peeled and unpeeled. Long eggplants are preferred in Italy. When peeled eggplants are needed:

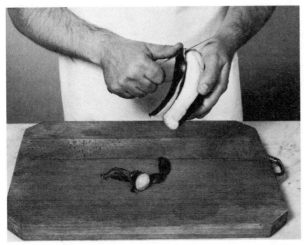

1. First cut off the stem, and cut off the skin in lengthwise strips,

2. then cut the eggplant into rings. The thickness will depend on the dish to be prepared. In this photo, the eggplant is being sliced for deep-frying.

When unpeeled eggplants are needed:

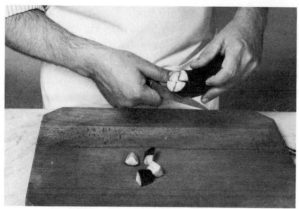

3. Cut the eggplant into quarters vertically. Then, holding the eggplant together, cut into slices each of which will fall off into 4 pieces. This is the cut used for the *Caponata* from Tuscany.

4. Cut lengthwise into slices ¼ inch thick. This is the cut for *Melanzane marinate* (Marinated Eggplants) (see *The Fine Art of Italian Cooking*).

5. To hollow out eggplants for stuffing, use the long so-called eggplant or zucchini corer to remove the pulp.

6. The hollowed out vegetable resembles a boat and it is ready to be stuffed or to be parboiled before stuffing.

Melanzane Ripiene

STUFFED EGGPLANT, PUGLIA STYLE

FROM PUGLIA

6 thin eggplants, about 8 inches long
Coarse-grained salt
3 slices white bread, crusts removed
1 cup cold milk
6 ounces black olives in brine, drained and pitted
4 tablespoons capers in wine vinegar, drained
10 sprigs Italian parsley, leaves only
4 tablespoons grated Pecorino or Ricotta salata
3 tablespoons unseasoned bread crumbs
½ cup olive oil
Salt and freshly ground black pepper

SERVES 6

374

Prepare the eggplants to be stuffed by slicing off ½ inch along the length. Scoop out and save the pulp. Bring a large pot of cold water to a boil. Add coarse-grained salt to taste then add the hollowed-out eggplants and their pulp. Boil for 1 minute, then transfer them to a bowl of cold water. Let stand for 1 minute, then place them on paper towels and pat them dry.

Finely chop the olives, capers, parsley, and eggplant pulp on a board. Soak the bread in the milk and squeeze the milk out after 10 minutes. Place the chopped ingredients and the squeezed bread in a small bowl. Add salt and pepper to taste. Heat ¼ cup of the oil in a small saucepan. When the oil is hot,

add the contents of the bowl. Sauté for about 10 minutes to amalgamate all the ingredients. Transfer the stuffing to a crockery bowl and let stand until cool (about 30 minutes). Preheat the oven to 375 degrees.

Add the cheese to the stuffing and mix well. Stuff each eggplant with the cooled stuffing and sprinkle over a little bread crumbs. Pour the remaining oil into a 13½- x 8¾-inch baking dish and arrange the stuffed eggplant in it. Place the dish in the oven and bake for about 35 minutes. Remove from the oven, transfer the eggplants to a serving dish, and serve immediately.

CAPONATA

There are so many variants of the Sicilian dish *caponata* that one wonders what they all have in common; what is the essential element that links them all. (They usually are associated with eggplant, but not all versions contain it.) After some searching, it becomes clear that the sources never mention anything about the origins of the dish or even what the word, itself, means.

A crucial connection came to me when I discovered that a lost alternate spelling of the word was *capponata*. This second "p" is perhaps not such an astonishing difference to someone who speaks English, but in Italian a single or double consonant often means the difference in the etymology and origin of a word, and a very different meaning. The second "p" enabled me to connect *capponata* with *cappone*, which commonly means the fowl "capon" but again obscurely meant a group of very old dishes, all made with an *agrodolce* or sweet-and-sour flavoring, such as the combination of wine vinegar and sugar. Three specific *cappone* dishes are documented and, in addition to their sweet-and-sour taste, they have a common ingredient, sea biscuit (a very hard cracker which was a mainstay of the seaboard diet in previous centuries). Two of the dishes are specifically built around sea biscuit soaked in wine vinegar and sugar. This clearly suggests that these dishes were made on ships as sailors' food, with the sweet-and-sour marinade possibly used to help preserve the food at sea.

The two most common forms of *caponata* are seafood *caponata* and the famous Palermo style one from Sicily, both of which are marinated with wine vinegar and sugar. It becomes evident that *caponata* derives from *cappone*, and that it must have been carried to port cities by the sailors. Included here is the Palermo *caponata* recipe, as well as a Tuscan variant of it. The simpler seafood *caponata* is omitted in favor of a still more famous seafood version, *Cappon magro*, which originated far from Sicily at the other end of the Italian peninsula, in the great old port of Genoa.

Sicilian or Palermo *caponata* appears in many variants. The essential ingredients seem to be eggplant, celery, onions, tomatoes, olive oil, olives, capers, and, of course, wine vinegar and sugar. Pignoli (pine nuts), which appear in many versions, do not seem to be essential. One recent recipe which adds canned tuna fish is an interesting and possibly unconscious combination of the Palermo style and the simple seafood *caponata*. Tuscans have their own adaptation of eggplant *caponata*. They do not use pignoli. (As nuts were used extensively in medieval and Renaissance Italy, this may suggest that the dish arrived in Tuscany late.) Rather than fresh or canned tomatoes, they use a little tomato paste. Perhaps the most characteristic difference is that Tuscans do not peel the eggplants, and for this reason they must be of the small, long variety so that the skins are very tender. But the strangest part is that while in Sicily eggplant *caponata* is an appetizer, in Tuscany though it may be used as an appetizer it has become mainly a relish accompaniment for dishes of the boiled course. (In Tuscany, all full-course meals at one time had a boiled course, accompanied by a variety of sauces, *savori* or Renaissance relishes, and mustards.)

Caponata

FROM SICILY

SERVES 8

5 small, long eggplants (about 2 pounds), with stems removed
Coarse-grained salt
3 medium-sized red onions
5 celery stalks
¼ pound black olives in brine, drained
¼ pound green olives in brine, drained
1 cup olive oil
1 pound fresh tomatoes, or canned plum, preferably imported Italian, drained
4 tablespoons capers in wine vinegar, drained
2 tablespoons raisins
2 tablespoons pignoli (pine nuts)
Salt and freshly ground black pepper
½ cup red wine vinegar
1 teaspoon granulated sugar

Wash the eggplants carefully, peel them, and cut into 1-inch-square cubes. Put the eggplant cubes in a bowl and sprinkle them with 2 tablespoons coarse-grained salt. Place a dish as a weight on the eggplants to help squeeze out their dark bitter liquid and let stand for about 30 minutes.

Slice the onions very thin and soak them in cold water for about 30 minutes.

Meanwhile, bring a large pot of water to a boil. Add coarse-grained salt to taste.

Cut the celery stalks lengthwise into 3 strips, then cut the strips into ½-inch-long pieces. When the water reaches a boil, add coarse-grained salt to taste and the celery. Parboil for 5 or 6 minutes. Drain the celery and let it dry on paper towels until needed.

Pit the olives. Drain onions and pat them dry with paper towels.

Heat ½ cup of the oil in a skillet over medium heat. When the oil is hot, add the onions and sauté for about 10 minutes.

Pass the tomatoes through a food mill. Add the strained tomatoes to the skillet, then add the pitted olives, capers, raisins, and pignoli. Cover the skillet and simmer for about 15 minutes. Let stand covered until needed.

Wash the eggplants carefully in cold water to remove the salt and pat them dry on paper towels.

Heat the remaining oil in a different skillet. When the oil is hot, add the eggplant cubes and sauté for about 15 minutes. (The eggplant should be cooked but still firm.) Sprinkle with salt and pepper.

Prepare a serving dish by lining it with paper towels. Transfer the cooked eggplant to the dish with a slotted spoon.

Add the parboiled celery to the skillet and sauté for about 10 minutes. Sprinkle with salt and pepper. Add the drained eggplant cubes to the skillet first with the sauce and simmer for about 10 minutes. Transfer the sautéed celery to the skillet with the eggplant. Add the wine vinegar and sugar and let the vinegar evaporate (about 10 minutes). Taste for salt and pepper and mix very well. Remove the pan from the heat and let stand for a few minutes. Then transfer the *caponata* to a serving dish and let cool completely before serving. It can be eaten at room temperature, cold, or reheated.

Caponata

5 *small, long eggplants*
  (about 2 pounds), with stems removed
2 *tablespoons coarse-grained salt*
1 *cup olive oil*
Salt and freshly ground black pepper
4 *medium-sized celery stalks*
1 *medium-sized red onion*
2 *tablespoons tomato paste*
1 *tablespoon granulated sugar*
½ *cup red wine vinegar*
½ *cup cold water*
½ *pound black Greek olives in brine, drained*

SERVES 6 AS VEGETABLE ACCOMPANIMENT
AND 8 AS APPETIZER

Wash the eggplants carefully and cut them into 1-inch-square cubes. (Do not peel the eggplants.) Put the eggplant cubes in a bowl and sprinkle them with the coarse-grained salt. Place a dish as a weight on the eggplants to help squeeze out their dark bitter liquid and let stand for about 1 hour.

Heat the oil in a saucepan. When it is hot, add the eggplant cubes and sauté over medium heat for about 20 minutes, turning often. Sprinkle with salt and pepper to taste.

Cut the celery stalks lengthwise into 3 strips, then cut the strips into ½-inch-long pieces. Chop the onion coarsely.

Use a slotted spoon to transfer eggplant from the saucepan to a bowl, so that the oil remains in the saucepan. Add the celery and onion to the saucepan and sauté for about 20 minutes, stirring often with a wooden spoon. Sprinkle with salt and pepper. Combine the tomato paste, sugar, wine vinegar, and cold water in a small crockery bowl. Blend well.

Use a slotted spoon to remove the onions and celery from the saucepan and add them to eggplant. Pour the vinegar mixture into the saucepan and simmer for 5 minutes.

Pit the olives and cut them into small pieces. Add the olives to the saucepan. Simmer for 20 minutes and return the vegetables to the pan. Stir with a wooden spoon until all ingredients are well amalgamated (about 15 minutes). *Taste for salt and peppers.* Transfer the *caponata* to serving dish.

Although this dish may be served warm, it is better if it is allowed to marinate covered for several hours in the refrigerator. It may be eaten at room temperature or reheated. It may also be kept for a day or two in the refrigerator and served cold. Many prefer the *caponata* served in this manner as the taste is even more striking.

Cappon Magro

CAPONATA GENOESE VERSION

Cappon magro may be served as appetizer, first course, or main course.

SERVES 8 TO 12

For the "base" of the dish:
About 30 sea biscuits or oyster crackers
1 *cup red wine vinegar*

For the sauce:
3 slices white bread
1 cup red wine vinegar
¼ pound green olives in brine, drained
¼ pound black olives in brine, drained
3 anchovies in salt, or 6 anchovy fillets packed in oil, drained
3 hard-cooked eggs
2 heaping tablespoons pignoli (pine nuts)
1 tablespoon capers in wine vinegar, drained
2 medium-sized cloves garlic, peeled
About 15 sprigs Italian parsley, leaves only
1 tablespoon granulated sugar
1 cup olive oil
Salt and freshly ground black pepper

The vegetables:
Coarse-grained salt
1 small cauliflower
1 handful of string beans (about ¼ pound)
4 celery stalks
4 medium-sized carrots
2 large (about 1 pound) boiling potatoes (but not new potatoes)
Salt and freshly ground black pepper

The fish:
Coarse-grained salt
*2 pounds firm-flesh fish, such as sea-bass, striped bass, or red snapper, or other in slices
   with bone*
Juice of 3 lemons
8 large shrimp
1 pound medium-sized shrimp

Plus:
1 cup olive oil
Salt and freshly ground black pepper
8 hard-cooked eggs

Optional:
1 cooked lobster (size optional)

Make a layer of the sea biscuits on a large, round serving dish. Sprinkle the vinegar over the biscuits and cover the dish with aluminum foil. Set aside until needed.

Prepare the sauce. Remove the crust from the bread and soak the bread in a small crockery bowl with the wine vinegar for about 20 minutes.

Pit the olives and clean the anchovies if in salt (page 55). Squeeze the wine vinegar out of the bread. Then put the bread, egg yolks (discarding the whites), olives, pignoli, capers, anchovies, garlic, parsley, and sugar in a mortar or food processor. Grind very well until all the ingredients are well amalgamated and a smooth paste is formed.

Transfer the sauce to a crockery bowl. Add the oil a little at a time, mixing with a wooden spoon in a rotating movement, until all the oil is incorporated. Taste for salt and pepper. Cover the bowl with aluminum foil and refrigerate until needed. Prepare the vegetables. Clean and boil in individual pots, whole cauliflower (page 360), string beans (page 367), celery stalks (page 391), carrots (page 357), and potatoes (page 364). Cool all the vegetables separately. Once cool, separate the cauliflower into flowerets and cut the remaining vegetables into 1-inch pieces. Poach the fish slices in salted boiling water for 4 or 5 minutes, then transfer them to a serving dish. Pour a little lemon juice over them (using about three quarters of the juice) and let stand until cold.

Shell and devein the large and medium-sized shrimp (page 305). Boil the shrimp in salted water from 3 to 5 minutes, according to the size of the shrimp. Drain and transfer to a platter. Pour the remaining lemon juice over them, separating the large shrimp from the medium-sized ones.

Pour some of the 1 cup of olive oil over the individual dishes of cooked vegetables, fish, and shellfish, and sprinkle with salt and pepper as well.

To assemble the dish, first cut the hard-cooked eggs into halves. Remove the aluminum foil from the serving dish and make a ring of the eggs face up around the edge of the biscuit "base." Inside this ring, make a layer of potatoes. Over the potatoes make a layer of carrots, then the slices of fish, then the string beans, the medium-sized shrimp, the celery, and, finally, the cauliflower. Shape the layers of different ingredients like a cone. If using the whole cooked lobster, place it on top. Then stand all the large shrimp around the side of the cone. Pour the prepared sauce from the refrigerator over the cone. Cover the dish with aluminum foil and refrigerate for at least 1 hour before serving.

Melanzane al Forno

EGGPLANT BAKED IN BATTER

FROM FERRARA

How refreshing to have an eggplant dish without tomatoes and/or Parmigiano. This old recipe, antedating the use of tomatoes in Italy, is a welcome rediscovery. Marjoram is the dominant flavor, restoring that herb to its original high place in Italian cooking. *Melanzane al forno* is an important dish that should be served as a separate course (*piatto di mezzo*).

4 medium-sized eggplants, about 2 pounds
2 tablespoons coarse-grained salt
1 cup unbleached all-purpose flour, approximately
1 pound solid shortening
Salt
4 ounces pancetta *or* prosciutto*
10 sprigs Italian parsley, leaves only
1 scant teaspoon dried marjoram, or 4 or 5 sprigs fresh or preserved in salt
6 extra large eggs
2 tablespoons cold milk
Freshly ground black pepper

SERVES 8

Cut off the top part of the eggplants and peel them. Slice the eggplants crossways into slices less than ¼ inch thick. Put the slices in a large bowl, sprinkling them with coarse-grained salt. Place a dish as a weight on the eggplants to help squeeze out their dark bitter liquid and let stand for about 20 minutes. Wash the eggplant slices carefully in cold water to remove the salt and pat them dry with paper towels.

Prepare a serving dish by lining it with paper towels. Lightly flour the eggplant slices.

Heat the solid shortening in a frying pan. When the fat is very hot, deep fry the eggplant slices, a few at a time, until they are lightly golden brown on both sides (about 3 minutes). Remove the fried slices from the pan and put them in the prepared serving dish to drain. When all the slices are in the serving dish, sprinkle them with a little salt. Preheat oven to 375 degrees.

Cut the *pancetta* into small pieces and coarsely chop the parsley and marjoram together on a board. Transfer the prepared ingredients to a large bowl and add the eggs and milk. Mix all the ingredients together with a fork and add a pinch of salt and pepper to taste.

Butter a 13½- x 8¾- x 1¾-inch Pyrex dish. Make layers of fried eggplant slices in the baking dish. Pour the contents of the bowl over the eggplant slices and bake for about 30 minutes. Serve immediately from the baking dish by slicing with a knife and lifting each portion out with a spatula.

* This is an exception to the usual substitution.

PATATE (POTATOES)

Since only one vegetable dish generally accompanies or follows an Italian main course, potatoes may be that vegetable which combines perfectly with a particular dish. They are so rarely used, however, compared with American or northern European cooking, that Italians are not particularly concerned about avoiding pasta in the same menu, because the imbalance in a single meal is overcome by their very high overall consumption of green vegetables.

HOW TO SHRED POTATOES

1. With a mandolin, use the jagged blade to shred the already peeled potatoes soaking in a bowl of cold water.

2. The shredded potatoes.

Patate all'olio o con Maionese

ESCALLOPED POTATO SALAD

FROM TUSCANY

This delicate potato dish uses potatoes thinly cut with the mandolin. Most notable is the method of boiling them with wine vinegar in the water, so that they emerge crisp and firm on the outside and even when dressed, do not lose their shape. This method of cooking is always used when potatoes have a dressing which could cause them to lose their firmness and form.

If *maionese* is used, we strongly suggest making it fresh, as the dish loses all character with the commercial variety. If time is short, it is better to use only the olive oil.

2 pounds boiling potatoes (but not new potatoes)   SERVES 6 TO 8
10 cups cold water
Coarse-grained salt
¾ cup red wine vinegar

¾ cup olive oil or maionese (prepared with 2 egg yolks, 2 cups olive oil, 1 tablespoon
   lemon juice, and salt to taste
Salt and freshly ground black pepper

Peel and shred the potatoes with a mandolin, page 380, and put them in a bowl of cold water.

Bring the 10 cups of cold water to a boil. Add coarse-grained salt to taste and the wine vinegar. Drain the potatoes and add to the boiling water and boil for about 6 minutes. At this point, the potatoes should be cooked but still firm. Drain the potatoes and cool them under cold running water.

Transfer the potatoes to serving dish and pour the oil over them. Sprinkle the potatoes with salt and pepper to taste and toss very well with two wooden spoons.   Or, if you wish to use maionese, make it with the ingredients listed above, following the instructions on pages 438–439. Sprinkle the potatoes with salt and pepper to taste and toss very well.

Patate con Alloro

POTATOES WITH BAY LEAVES

FROM THE APENNINE REGION

The fragrant perfume and taste of bay leaves (laurel) as a dominant flavor is much exploited in Italy because laurel bushes are so plentiful that they are often used as the hedges around gardens and parks, filling the air with their special fragrance. Some California bay leaves, in jars, retain the moisture and taste of fresh bay leaves, but because the herb is sautéed in this dish, even the dried leaves, domestic or imported, produce a more than satisfactory result. The dish is eaten at room temperature, and it may be served as an appetizer as well as a side dish.

2 pounds boiling potatoes (but not new potatoes)   SERVES 6 TO 8
10 cups cold water
Coarse-grained salt
¾ cup red wine vinegar
3 medium-sized cloves garlic, peeled
4 bay leaves, fresh, preserved in salt, or dried
¾ cup olive oil
5 sprigs Italian parsley, leaves only
Salt and freshly ground black pepper

Peel the potatoes, leaving them whole, and put them in a bowl of cold water.

Bring the 10 cups of cold water to a boil. Add coarse-grained salt to taste and the wine vinegar. Add the potatoes and simmer for about 20 minutes, depending on the size of the potatoes, or until they are cooked but still firm. Transfer the potatoes to a serving dish and let them cool completely, or cover the dish with aluminum foil and refrigerate until needed. Once cold, cut the potatoes into 1-inch cubes.

Coarsely chop the garlic. Wash the fresh bay leaves carefully and tear them into 4 or 5 pieces.

Heat the oil in a small saucepan over low heat. When the oil is hot, add the chopped garlic and pieces of bay leaf and sauté slowly for about 5 minutes.

Coarsely chop the parsley on a board.

When the garlic and bay leaf are lightly golden, remove the pan from the heat and pour the sauce over potatoes. Sprinkle with salt and pepper and mix together with two wooden spoons. Sprinkle with the chopped parsley and serve.

Patate "Ragante"

OREGANO POTATOES

The attractive alternating slices of potato, tomato, and red onion are flavored with oregano and grated sheep's milk cheese. Southern Italy shares the taste for oregano with Greece; it is little used in northern Italy. For grating, the aged Romano or Romano Sardo cheese or Ricotta salata may be used since all are made from sheep's milk. The local cheeses of Calabria are generally not available in other areas of the world.

Centuries ago, cheese was used as a binder in many dishes, and, if grated, was used inside the dish. The practice of sprinkling cheese on top was an imitation of topping with bread crumbs. This recipe shows an interesting stage in which the cheese was mixed with its model, the bread crumbs.

1½ pounds ripe tomatoes
2 pounds boiling potatoes (but not new potatoes)
1 pound red onions
About ½ cup olive oil
Salt and freshly ground black pepper
5 tablespoons unseasoned bread crumbs, preferably homemade
5 tablespoons grated Pecorino or Ricotta salata
1 teaspoon dried oregano

SERVES 6 TO 8

Peel the tomatoes (page 385) and cut them into slices less than ½ inch thick. Peel the potatoes and onions and cut them in slices the same thickness as the tomatoes. Preheat the oven to 375 degrees.

Pour 2 tablespoons of the oil into a 13½- x 8¾-inch baking dish. Make a layer of the sliced potatoes on the bottom of the dish. Sprinkle with salt and pepper. Keep adding layers of tomatoes and onions alternating with the potatoes, sprinkling each layer with salt, pepper, and about 1 tablespoon of oil. Finish the oil with the top layer.

Mix together the bread crumbs and the grated Pecorino in a small bowl, and sprinkle the top layer in the baking dish with the mixture. Sprinkle the oregano over the bread crumbs and bake for 1½ hours. Remove from oven, mix thoroughly, and serve immediately.

PEPERONI (PEPPERS)

Plants of the *capsicum annuum* family, native to Brazil, produce a variety of sweet and hot fruit, of many beautiful colors: yellow, orange, red, green. When these fruits were introduced to Europe, they very quickly became an important ingredient of Italian cooking. Italians like to make dishes with multicolored peppers, sautéed, baked, grilled, or stuffed whole.

The green peppers are best known in America, but it is good to see that orange and red ones are beginning to appear, and it would be splendid to have the whole range of colors available. Generally, the orange and yellow peppers are more delicate in flavor than the green and are desirable for that reason as well. Though the red ones of the same size and shape resemble pimientos in appearance, and may be sweet, an occasional one may have spicy seeds, since this family also contains the smaller hot red peppers whose seeds are dried and used as red pepper flakes. (This is not the place to go into the complexities and overlappings of the names pepper, pimiento, cayenne, chilies, etc., but the matter awaits a clear and detailed treatment.)

HOW TO CLEAN AND CUT PEPPERS INTO DIFFERENT SHAPES

To clean peppers for stuffing:

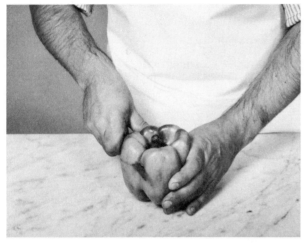

1. Cut off a slice about 1 inch from the top of the pepper.

2. With a knife, cut all around the inside part to loosen the ribs and seeds.

3. Pull and the whole inside part will come off in one piece.

If the dish calls for pepper rings, once they are cleaned

4. cut the pepper into rings about ½ inch thick. The thickness will depend on the dish to be prepared.

Peperoni Ripieni

PEPPERS STUFFED WITH VEAL AND RICOTTA

FROM FRIULI

In this stuffing from Friuli, the veal is first sautéed with the chopped pepper tops, cooled and mixed with the ricotta, cheese, and eggs. The peppers are softened by par-cooking them in boiling water off the heat. The stuffed peppers are then baked in a light tomato-butter sauce. The successful blending of the veal and ricotta is achieved with the help of the other ingredients.

6 large green peppers   SERVES 6
Coarse-grained salt
6 tablespoons sweet butter
¼ cup olive oil
1 pound ground veal
Salt and freshly ground black pepper
1 pound fresh tomatoes or drained canned imported Italian tomatoes
8 ounces ricotta
1 extra large egg yolk
½ cup freshly grated Parmigiano
Freshly grated nutmeg
About ½ cup unseasoned bread crumbs, preferably homemade

Wash the peppers well, then cut off the tops, and set them aside for use later. Remove the ribs and seeds from the peppers (page 383).

Bring a large pot of water to a boil. Add coarse-grained salt to taste. Remove the pot from the heat and add the peppers. Soak them until the water is almost cold (about 1 hour).

Meanwhile, prepare the stuffing. Finely chop the pepper tops on a board, discarding the stems.

Heat 4 tablespoons of the butter and the oil in a saucepan over medium heat. When the butter is completely melted, add the ground veal and the chopped peppers. Sauté for about 5 minutes and taste for salt and pepper. Remove from the heat and transfer the mixture to a crockery bowl. Let stand until cool (about 30 minutes). Pass the tomatoes through a food mill.

When the stuffing is cold, add the ricotta, egg yolk, and Parmigiano. Taste for salt, pepper, and nutmeg. Mix all the ingredients together with a wooden spoon until homogeneous. Remove the peppers from the water and pat them dry with paper towels. Preheat the oven to 375 degrees.

Stuff the peppers and sprinkle the bread crumbs over the stuffing. Pour the strained tomatoes into a baking dish with sides as high as the peppers. Cut the remaining butter into little pieces and distribute them on top of the tomato sauce. Sprinkle with salt and pepper. Arrange the peppers in the baking dish, cover the dish with aluminum foil, and bake for 1 hour. During this time add hot water if the sauce reduces too quickly. Remove from the oven, allow to cool for a few minutes, and serve. The peppers are good even served at room temperature after several hours.

POMODORI (TOMATOES)

(See discussion under ingredients, page 69, and in the introduction to *Pasta "all'ultima moda 1841,"* page 182.)

HOW TO REMOVE THE SKIN FROM TOMATOES

Bring a large pot of cold water to a boil. Add coarse-grained salt and the whole tomatoes and boil for 30 seconds (or 1 minute for large tomatoes). The salt will help the tomatoes to retain their color. Meanwhile, prepare a bowl of cold water. Use a slotted spoon to transfer the tomatoes from the boiling water to the bowl of cold water. Let the tomatoes sit in the cold water for a few minutes before you begin to peel them.

1. Remove the small stem.

2. Then use a paring knife to remove the skin, starting at the point where the stem was removed.

HOW TO PREPARE TOMATOES TO BE STUFFED

1. Slice off the top and save it. (It will be placed on top of the tomato after it is stuffed.)

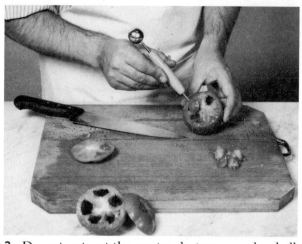 

2. Do not cut out the center, but use a melon-ball cutter to remove the seeds and juice from each section

3. until only the inner pulp remains. This is the modern Italian method for preparing tomatoes to be stuffed.

HOW TO SLICE TOMATOES FOR TOMATO SALAD

1. Slice the tomato horizontally into ½-inch-thick slices.

Insalata di Pomodori

NEAPOLITAN TOMATO SALAD

FROM CAMPANIA

This Neapolitan way of serving sliced tomatoes uses a paste made of hard-cooked egg yolk, anchovies, and capers spread over the slices. The basil leaves used in the more common *Pomodori in insalata* are joined here by a dash of oregano.

2 extra large eggs, at room temperature
2 anchovies in salt, or 4 anchovy fillets in oil, drained
1 heaping tablespoon capers in wine vinegar, drained
Salt and freshly ground black pepper
1 pound tomatoes, ripe but not overripe

SERVES 4

386

About 5 fresh basil leaves
¼ cup olive oil
Scant ½ teaspoon dried oregano

Hard boil the eggs in salted water for about 7 minutes. Shell them and separate the yolks from the whites. Discard the whites.

Clean the anchovies if in salt (page 55). Finely chop the anchovy fillets and capers together on a board. Transfer the chopped ingredients to a small bowl. Add the cooled egg yolks and salt and pepper to taste. Use a fork to mix all the ingredients together in order to incorporate the egg yolks.

Slice the tomatoes (page 386). Spread 1 teaspoon of the mixture on the top side of each slice. Tear the basil leaves into thirds.

Arrange the prepared slices of tomatoes, overlapping, in a row on a serving platter. In a small bowl, mix the oil with the oregano. Pour the dressing over the tomatoes, sprinkle with the basil, and serve.

Pomodori Ripieni di Pasta

TOMATOES STUFFED WITH MACARONI

FROM CALABRIA

Whole tomatoes are stuffed with uncooked pasta which are then baked, allowing the pasta to cook while absorbing the liquid of the tomato. This dish is closely connected with the earliest tomato sauce pasta *Maccheroni "all'ultima moda 1841" alla napoletana* on page 182. It is clearly a descendant of that dish.

This is substantial enough to be served as an *antipasto* and followed by a light broth instead of pasta as a first course, or as a first course itself.

4 large tomatoes   SERVES 4
½ pound of dried short pasta, such as elbow macaroni, preferably imported Italian
¾ cup olive oil
4 large black Greek olives in brine, drained
2 cloves garlic, peeled
Salt and freshly ground black pepper
5 basil leaves, fresh or preserved in salt
½ teaspoon dried oregano
¼ cup cold water

Wash the tomatoes very carefully, then slice off the tops and put them aside to be used later. Remove the seeds and the pulp of the tomatoes using a melon-ball cutter (page 386). Pass the pulp through a food mill into a small bowl.

Put the pasta in a second bowl with ½ cup of the olive oil and soak for ½ hour.

Pit the olives. Finely chop the olives and garlic together on a board and add to the bowl with the strained tomato pulp. Sprinkle with salt and pepper. Preheat the oven to 375 degrees.

Pour the tomato mixture into the bowl with the pasta and mix well.

Tear the basil leaves into pieces and add to the pasta with the oregano. Taste for salt and pepper. Stuff each tomato two-thirds full with the pasta mixture, then cover each tomato with its top.

Place the tomatoes in an 8½-inch-square Pyrex baking dish. Pour the remaining oil and ¼ cup cold water over the tomatoes and sprinkle them with a little salt and pepper. Place the dish in the oven and bake for about 65 minutes. Remove from the oven and allow to cool for 5 minutes before serving.

PORRI (LEEKS)

Like onions, leeks keep very well and one rarely has a problem about their freshness. Just be sure when purchasing them that they are not so old that they have become soft.

In Italy leeks are used both as a vegetable in their own right and as a flavoring for such sauces as the meat sauce for polenta. But they are not used to flavor soups, as is done in other countries.

In addition to the ancient Porrata leek pie, there is a popular leek-potato torte which is included here. Leeks served as a vegetable often have a meat flavoring, such as the pork sauce used in the second recipe which follows.

HOW TO CLEAN LEEKS

40. Porro (*Leek*)

First, rinse the leeks in cold water.

1. Slice off the end with the attached roots.

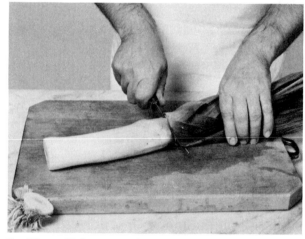

2. Slice off the green leaves at the point where the white stem turns green.

3. Slice the remaining white stem into rings about ½ inch thick.

Then put the rings in a bowl of cold water and let them soak for 30 minutes, or until all the sand is removed. Drain and rinse carefully under cold running water.

Torta di Porri

LEEK-POTATO TORTE

FROM LUCCA

SERVES 8

4 pounds leeks
Coarse-grained salt
1 pound boiling potatoes (but not new potatoes)
8 tablespoons (1 stick) sweet butter
1 cup milk
Salt, freshly ground black pepper, and freshly grated nutmeg to taste
1 tablespoon olive oil
2 whole extra large eggs
1 extra large egg yolk
5 tablespoons grated Parmigiano
About 5 tablespoons unseasoned bread crumbs, preferably homemade

Wash, clean, and cut the leeks, following the directions on page 388. Put the leeks in a bowl of cold water and soak for 30 minutes.

Bring a large pot of water to a boil. Add coarse-grained salt. Peel the potatoes and put them into the boiling water. Cook for about 35 minutes, or longer if potatoes are large. When completely cooked, drain the potatoes and, while they are still hot, pass them through a potato ricer.

Melt 3 tablespoons of the butter in a saucepan over low heat. Add the mashed potatoes and stir constantly until the butter is completely incorporated into the potatoes.

Meanwhile, heat the milk. Add it to the mashed potatoes and stir with a wooden spoon to incorporate them completely (about 5 minutes). Taste for salt, pepper, and nutmeg. Transfer the mashed potatoes to a crockery bowl and let them cool completely (about 1 hour).

Heat the remaining butter and the oil in a saucepan over medium heat. Rinse the leeks. Be sure no sand remains attached to the rings. Drain the leeks. When the butter is completely melted, add the leeks to pan. Sprinkle with salt and pepper and cook for about 35 minutes. At that time the leeks should be tender. Transfer them to a crockery bowl to cool completely.

When potatoes and leeks are cold, mix two thirds of the leeks with the mashed potatoes. Add the eggs, egg yolk, and Parmigiano and taste for salt, pepper, and nutmeg. Mix all ingredients together very well. Lightly butter and bread crumb a 9-inch pie plate. Preheat the oven to 375 degrees.

Spread the potato-leek mixture in the prepared pie plate and scatter the remaining leeks over the top. Bake for 40 minutes. Remove from the oven and let stand for 2 or 3 minutes. Then put a serving plate upside down over the torte. Turn the plate right side up and remove the pie plate. Put another serving plate over the torte and turn it over so that it is top side up. Grind some black pepper over it and serve by slicing like a cake.

The torte may also be eaten at room temperature, after several hours. It may be served as an appetizer or a *piatto di mezzo* before the main course.

389

Porri al Sugo di Maiale

LEEKS IN PORK SAUCE

FROM TUSCANY

SERVES 4

8 medium-sized leeks, about 2 pounds
Coarse-grained salt
1 small clove garlic, peeled
1 medium-sized carrot
1 small celery stalk
About 10 sprigs Italian parsley, leaves only
4 tablespoons sweet butter
⅓ cup olive oil
8 ounces ground pork
½ cup dry red wine
About 2 cups chicken or beef broth
2 tablespoons tomato paste
Salt and freshly ground black pepper

Wash, clean, and cut the leeks, following the directions on page 388. Put the leeks in a bowl of cold water and soak for at least 30 minutes. Rinse the leeks, making sure that no sand remains attached to the rings. Drain the leeks.

Bring a large pot of water to a boil. Add coarse-grained salt to taste. Then add the leeks and blanch for 1 minute. Drain and cool the leeks under cold running water. Transfer them to paper towels to dry.

Prepare the sauce. Finely chop the garlic, carrot, celery, and parsley together on a board.

Heat the butter and oil in a saucepan over medium heat. When the butter is completely melted, add the chopped ingredients and sauté for about 5 minutes. Add the ground pork, mix with a wooden spoon, and cook for about 10 minutes. Add the wine and let it evaporate for about 10 minutes.

Meanwhile, heat the broth to a boil. Add the tomato paste and about ¼ cup of the hot broth to the sautéed pork. Mix well. Taste for salt and pepper. Keep adding hot broth as needed until the sauce is ready (about 35 minutes). At that moment a thick sauce should be formed. Add the cold leeks to the saucepan and cook for about 2 minutes. Stir with a wooden spoon, taste for salt and pepper, and cook for 10 minutes longer. Transfer the leeks to a warmed serving dish and serve immediately.

SEDANO (CELERY)

By Italian standards, celery is a relative newcomer. When the Byzantines brought it with them to Italy in the period following the fall of Constantinople, the Italians were afraid the vegetable might be poisonous. The Medici Pope Clement VII, though he had made many mistakes such as refusing to grant the divorce to Henry VIII of England, made the right choice in this instance, when he backed the Greek Kirgiu who was encouraging people to eat celery. Celery is indispensable to the *battuto*, the group of aromatic vegetables and herbs used as the basis for so many Italian dishes. Italians eat raw celery, as do Americans, but in Italy it is also eaten as a cooked vegetable course.

Sedani Saltati

"STIR-SAUTÉED" CELERY

FROM FLORENCE

To prepare celery as a cooked vegetable in Italy, the preferred method is sautéing rather than braising.

1 bunch celery
Coarse-grained salt
1½ large cloves garlic
¼ cup olive oil
Salt and freshly ground black pepper

SERVES 4 TO 6

Remove the outer stalks and stringy parts from the celery, then cut the remaining stalks into 2-inch-long pieces. Put the pieces in a large bowl of cold water and soak for 30 minutes.

Bring a large pot of water to a boil. Add coarse-grained salt to taste. When the water reaches the boiling point again, add the celery and boil until it is cooked but still firm (about 10 to 15 minutes). Drain the celery and transfer the pieces to a large bowl of cold water to cool (about 15 minutes). When cooled, drain again and transfer the celery to a crockery bowl.

Cut the garlic into small pieces and put it in a frying pan with the oil. Sauté over medium heat until the garlic is lightly golden brown (about 5 minutes). Add the celery pieces and sprinkle with salt and pepper to taste. Use a fork to mix the celery thoroughly then let cook over medium heat for about 10 minutes. Transfer the celery to a serving dish and serve immediately.

SPINACI (SPINACH)

Florentines should know their spinach, and they feel that if it is not well cooked in abundant salted water, it remains heavy with an excess of iron. This is a perfect example of Italian resistance to confusion of salad and cooked vegetable. Italians never use spinach as a salad, nor is it ever half-cooked.

Polpettine di Spinaci

DEEP-FRIED SPINACH CROQUETTES

FROM A NINETEENTH-CENTURY FLORENTINE COOKBOOK

These deep-fried spinach croquettes are related to the *Ravioli nudi* (Naked Ravioli) of spinach and cheese, a survivor of the poached type; it is the only modern dish to retain its original name. But these croquettes differ from the *Ravioli nudi* not only in the way they are cooked, but also in that they contain no ricotta. *Ravioli* or *quinquinelle* (related to the French term quenelles) were the original names for all types of little round dumplings, or *gnocchi*, back in the early cookbook manuscripts. There were many, many types of dumplings in Italy in the Middle Ages and Renaissance (as many or more than in modern

German cooking), made of vegetables and herbs, meat, cheese, fish, and flours. They were both poached and deep-fried. *Polpettine di spinaci* should be used to accompany a fried main course only, or may be served as an appetizer.

SERVES 4 AS VEGETABLE,
6 AS APPETIZER

3 pounds fresh spinach
Coarse-grained salt
2 tablespoons sweet butter
Salt and freshly ground black pepper
2 slices white bread
1 cup cold milk
3 tablespoons unseasoned bread crumbs, preferably homemade
3 tablespoons freshly grated Parmigiano
2 extra large whole eggs
2 extra large egg yolks
1 pound solid shortening

To serve:
1 lemon cut into wedges

Clean the spinach well, removing the heavier stems. Soak the spinach in a bowl of cold water for about 30 minutes. Bring a large pot of cold water to a boil. Add coarse-grained salt to taste, then add the spinach and boil the spinach for about 10 minutes. Drain the spinach and cool it under cold running water. When the spinach is cool, squeeze it very dry and chop it coarsely on a board.

Melt the butter in a flameproof casserole and add the chopped spinach. Sprinkle with salt and pepper. Mix the spinach thoroughly, then cook it over medium heat for 4 or 5 minutes. Transfer the spinach to a bowl to cool (about 20 minutes).

Meanwhile, remove the crusts from the bread and soak the bread in the cold milk for about 20 minutes. Squeeze the bread dry and add it to the spinach,

along with the bread crumbs, Parmigiano, eggs, and egg yolks. Taste for salt and pepper and mix thoroughly.

Heat the vegetable shortening in a deep-fat fryer; prepare a serving dish by lining it with paper towels.

When the shortening is hot, shape heaping tablespoons of the spinach mixture into little balls by rolling them between the palms of your hands. Add the croquettes to the hot shortening one at a time, keeping them separate. Cook the croquettes until they are light golden brown on both sides. Then remove to the prepared serving dish to drain.

When all the croquettes are cooked and drained, remove the paper towels. Sprinkle the croquettes with a little salt and serve hot with lemon wedges.

NOCE MOSCADE.

41. Noce Moscade *(Nutmeg)*

Spinaci alla Genovese

SPINACH GENOESE STYLE

Another old Genoese dish, retaining the taste and complex flavor, with the sweet and salty combination of raisins, pignoli, and anchovies. This dish has made a great comeback in recent years after a long period of neglect, and is now served surprisingly often in restaurants and homes.

¼ cup raisins
4 pounds fresh spinach
Coarse-grained salt
3 anchovies in salt, or 6 anchovy fillets in oil, drained
About 20 sprigs Italian parsley, leaves only
¼ cup olive oil
¼ cup pignoli (pine nuts)
Salt, freshly ground black pepper, and freshly grated nutmeg

SERVES 4 TO 6

Soak the raisins in a bowl of lukewarm water for about 20 minutes.

Clean the spinach well, removing the heavier stems. Soak the spinach in a bowl of cold water for about 30 minutes. Bring a large pot of cold water to a boil. Add coarse-grained salt to taste, then add the spinach and boil the spinach for about 10 minutes. Drain the spinach and cool it under cold running water. When the spinach is cool, squeeze it very dry and chop it coarsely on a board.

Clean the anchovies, removing the bone if they are preserved in salt (page 55). Finely chop them together with the parsley on a board.

Heat the oil in a flameproof casserole over medium heat. When the oil is hot, add the chopped ingredients and sauté lightly for about 5 minutes, then add the spinach and pignoli. Lower the heat and simmer for about 5 minutes, mixing with a wooden spoon. Taste for salt, pepper, and nutmeg. Drain the raisins, pat dry with paper towels, and add them to the casserole. Sauté for 5 minutes longer, then transfer to a warmed serving dish and serve immediately.

ZUCCHINI

HOW TO CUT ZUCCHINI INTO DIFFERENT SHAPES FOR VARIOUS DISHES

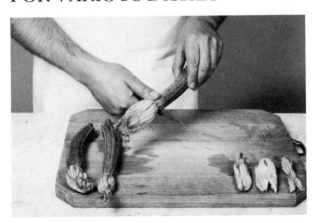

1. The zucchini squash on the left is the stem of the female flower. On the right are the edible blossoms of the male zucchini removed from their thin undeveloped stems. (The female zucchini squash also has a flower attached to its edible stem, but this flower is not good for eating and must be removed.) Cut off both ends of the zucchini squash.

Zucchini are cut into a variety of shapes for different dishes:

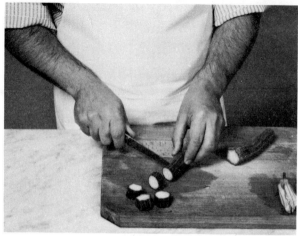

2. sliced width-wise into discs,

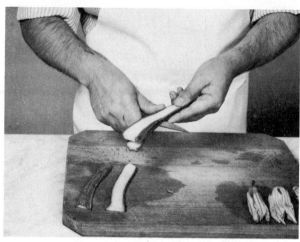

3. sliced through lengthwise,

4. or sliced lengthwise into quarters

5. and then cut into 2-inch pieces, mainly for frying.

6. For stuffed zucchini, one thin slice is removed from one side of the length of the zucchini and saved. Then the vegetable is hollowed out with a zucchini corer

7. until it resembles a little boat.

Shown in the following photos are the round zucchini found in Italy but not generally available in America. In Italy this is the kind used most often for stuffing.

8. To prepare for stuffing, the top is first sliced off and saved,

9. uncovering the white pulp of the inside.

10. Use a melon-ball cutter to scoop out the pulp. The round zucchini may now be stuffed, covered with their tops, and baked.

Zucchini alla Pancetta

ZUCCHINI WITH PANCETTA

FROM GARFAGNANA IN TUSCANY

This is one of the most flavorful zucchini preparations, because the sautéed *pancetta* gives it its special character.

SERVES 8 TO 10

16 medium-sized zucchini
2 tablespoons coarse-grained salt, approximately
4 ounces of pancetta or prosciutto
1 pound fresh tomatoes, or drained canned imported Italian tomatoes
1 medium-sized red onion
About 15 sprigs Italian parsley, leaves only
1 large clove garlic, peeled
¼ cup olive oil
1 tablespoon sweet butter
Salt and freshly ground black pepper

Cut the zucchini horizontally into ½-inch-thick slices (page 394) and place them on a large platter. Sprinkle the zucchini with coarse-grained salt and place a dish as a weight on top of the zucchini. Let it stand for about 1 hour in order to absorb some of the juices. (This is generally not done with zucchini as it is with eggplant, but this recipe uses a large amount of *pancetta* so this step is necessary.)

Cut the *pancetta* into small pieces and set it aside until needed. Pass the tomatoes through a food mill to remove the skin and seeds. Slice the onion very thin. Coarsely chop the parsley and finely chop the garlic. Keep all these ingredients separate until needed.

Heat the oil and butter in a flameproof casserole over medium heat. When the butter is completely melted, add the *pancetta* and the onion and sauté for about 10 minutes.

Meanwhile, wash the sliced zucchini carefully to completely remove the salt. Pat them dry with paper towels.

Add the chopped parsley and garlic to the casserole, and sauté over medium heat for 5 minutes. Then add the strained tomatoes and make a layer of all the zucchini on top of the tomatoes and cook for about 5 minutes. Taste for salt and pepper. Then thoroughly mix all the ingredients in the casserole together and simmer for about 15 minutes longer. At that moment the zucchini should be cooked but still firm.

Transfer to serving dish, sprinkle with freshly ground black pepper and serve immediately.

Zucchini Ripieni in Sugo di Vitella

STUFFED ZUCCHINI IN VEAL SAUCE

FROM TUSCANY

A lighter meat stuffing for zucchini than the usual one with beef, made even more special by a sauce which does not contain tomatoes. Also unusual is the flavoring of nutmeg used with the meat, but here it is just the right touch to bring together the veal and zucchini flavors. The stuffing is prepared by chopping sautéed veal cutlets and mixing them with bread, egg yolks, and Parmigiano. The sauce is formed from the reduced chopped vegetables, *pancetta*, butter, oil, and broth in which the veal has been sautéed.

This is to be eaten hot as a main dish.

6 long or round zucchini
Coarse-grained salt
4 ounces pancetta, or 2 ounces boiled ham and 2 ounces salt pork
1 small red onion
1 medium-sized carrot
1 celery stalk
2 tablespoons sweet butter
⅓ cup olive oil
3 veal cutlets (about ¾ pound)
Salt and freshly ground black pepper
2 slices white bread
1 cup milk
2 cups beef or chicken broth
2 extra large egg yolks
¼ cup freshly grated Parmigiano
Freshly grated nutmeg to taste

SERVES 6

Soak the zucchini in a bowl of cold water for about 30 minutes, then drain and remove the stems. If zucchini are the long type, slice off the top ¼ inch lengthwise; if you find the preferable round zucchini, slice off the tops (page 394). Put the tops aside to be used later. Scoop out the pulp using a zucchini

396

corer if long (page 394) or a melon-ball cutter if round. Discard the pulp. Put the zucchini in a bowl of salted cold water and soak for about 30 minutes.

Cut the *pancetta* into small pieces and then finely chop it together with onion, carrot, and celery together on a board.

Heat the butter and oil in a saucepan over medium heat. When the butter is completely melted, add the chopped ingredients and sauté for about 5 minutes. Add the cutlets and cook for 3 minutes on each side. Taste for salt and pepper.

Meanwhile, soak the bread in the milk and bring the broth to a boil. Add ¼ cup of the broth to the pan with the cutlets and simmer for 5 minutes longer. Remove the cutlets from the pan and chop them finely on a board. Add the remaining broth to the pan and simmer for about 30 minutes.

Squeeze the milk out of the bread and put the bread in a small bowl. Add the chopped veal, egg yolks, and Parmigiano. Sprinkle with salt, pepper, and nutmeg to taste. Add 3 tablespoons of the sauce in which the veal was cooked to the bowl and mix all the ingredients together with a wooden spoon. Remove the sauce from the heat and let stand until needed.

Remove the zucchini from the cold water and pat them dry with paper towels. Stuff the zucchini with the veal mixture and place the tops of the zucchini back on as lids. Preheat the oven to 375 degrees.

Arrange the zucchini in a 13½- x 8¾-inch baking dish. Pour the sauce over the zucchini and place the dish in the oven. Bake for about 40 minutes. Remove from the oven, transfer the zucchini and sauce to a serving dish, and serve immediately.

Torta di Zucchini

ZUCCHINI TORTE

FROM SARDINIA

This subtle and complex torte uses a combination of grated and thinly sliced zucchini so that the two cook to different degrees: the grated one soft and the sliced still crunchy. The lemon rind combines with the vegetable to produce a unique and remarkable blend.

This versatile dish may be used warm or at room temperature as an appetizer, first course or *piatto di mezzo*, before the main dish. It has too much character to be served as a vegetable accompaniment. The simplicity of the preparation does not lead one to expect the sophistication of the result.

For me this dish is the apotheosis of Italy's homespun but beloved *zucchino*.

2 pounds small zucchini
1 lemon
4 extra large eggs
¼ cup freshly grated Parmigiano
½ cup very fine unseasoned bread crumbs, preferably homemade
Salt and freshly ground black pepper

SERVES 6 TO 8

Wash the zucchini very well and soak them in a bowl of cold water for 30 minutes. Remove both ends from the zucchini. Thinly slice 1 pound of the zucchini and coarsely grate those remaining into a small bowl with a hand grater, using the side of the grater with the large holes. Then finely grate the lemon rind. Mix the eggs and Parmigiano together in a second bowl. Then add the grated lemon rind, ¼ cup of the bread crumbs, salt and pepper to taste. Preheat the oven to 375 degrees.

Add the sliced and grated zucchini to the egg mixture, mixing with a wooden spoon and incorporating them very well.

Butter a 10-inch-diameter pie plate and coat it with some bread crumbs. Pour in the zucchini mixture. Sprinkle the remaining bread crumbs over the top and place the plate in the oven. Bake for about 35 minutes. Remove from oven and allow to cool for a few minutes. Then put a serving plate upside down over the torte. Turn the plate right side up and remove the pie plate. Put another serving plate over the torte and turn it over so that it is top side up. Sprinkle with freshly ground black pepper and serve, slicing like a cake.

FIORI DI ZUCCA (ZUCCHINI FLOWERS OR ZUCCHINI BLOSSOMS)

Zucchini flowers last for only a few days so they can just be used only when they are very fresh and, of course, in season. Every part of Italy has its own little touches in preparing them. Most often they are fried in batter, but occasionally they are baked. The flower on the end of the squash is not good for eating. The flowers (from the male plant), which are edible, are sold separately.

HOW TO PREPARE ZUCCHINI FLOWERS FOR COOKING

1. Open up the flower by spreading out the petals.

2. Remove the pistils from the inside.

Fiori di Zucca Ripieni

STUFFED ZUCCHINI BLOSSOMS

FROM CAMPANIA

In contrast to the simple unadorned Tuscan method of frying zucchini flowers, the traditional treatment in Campania is to stuff them.

In this recipe, the garlic, caper, and parsley flavoring is held together with a little bit of bread crumbs and mashed potato. The result is different, less light, but delicious.

12 large zucchini blossoms
1 medium-sized potato
Coarse-grained salt
1 small clove garlic, peeled

SERVES 4

5 sprigs Italian parsley, leaves only
1 tablespoon capers in wine vinegar, drained
2 tablespoons unseasoned bread crumbs, preferably homemade
4 extra large eggs
Salt and freshly ground black pepper
About 1 cup unbleached all-purpose flour
1 pound solid shortening
1 lemon cut into wedges

Wash and remove stems and pistils from the flowers (page 398). Pat the flowers dry with paper towels.

Bring a pan of cold water to a boil. Add coarse-grained salt to taste, then add the whole potato. Cook until tender (about 25 minutes). Peel the potato and, while it is still hot, pass it through a potato ricer into a small bowl.

Finely chop the garlic, parsley, and capers together on a board. Add the chopped ingredients to the potato along with the bread crumbs, 1 egg, and salt and pepper to taste. Mix very well until all ingredients are well amalgamated. Stuff each blossom with about 1 tablespoon of the stuffing and press the ends of the blossoms together to close them.

Mix the flour with 1 teaspoon of black pepper. (It is unusual in Italian classical cooking to season flour for deep frying.)

Use a fork to beat the remaining eggs with a little salt in a small bowl.

Heat the solid shortening in a deep-fat fryer. Prepare a serving dish by lining it with paper towels. When the shortening is hot, lightly flour each stuffed blossom, dip it in the beaten eggs, and place it gently in the hot shortening. Cook for about 1 minute on each side, or until lightly golden brown. Then remove with a strainer-skimmer and place on the prepared serving dish. When all the blossoms are cooked and on the serving dish, remove the paper towels, sprinkle a little salt over the flowers, and serve immediately with lemon wedges.

LEGUMI (LEGUMES)

1. *Front left:* lentils; *front right:* chick-peas; *back:* cannellini beans (also in jar).

Cecina

CHICK-PEA "PIZZA"

Chick-peas (and lentils) are among man's oldest foodstuffs. It is known that they were eaten by Stone Age man, and recipes are found in the oldest cookbooks such as that of the Roman Apicius. With the varieties of beans imported to Europe after the discovery of the New World, the consumption of these two legumes decreased. *Cecina*, the *schiacciata* or *pizza* made of mashed chick-peas, appears in the earliest Italian cookbook manuscripts around 1300 and remained popular for a long time. Even a few decades ago it was widespread on the Tuscan coast, in Livorno (Leghorn), Carrara, and Massa. It was popular then to eat this as thin inner pizza placed inside a slice of bread dough or *schiacciata*. This is still found in one or two places in Carrara. It is delicious, however, unadorned and eaten simply for itself as a sliced pizza.

1½ cups dried chick-peas
Coarse-grained salt
3 tablespoons olive oil
1 tablespoon rosemary leaves, fresh, preserved in salt, or dried and blanched
Salt and freshly ground black pepper

SERVES 8

Soak the chick-peas in a large bowl of cold water overnight.

Next morning rinse the peas well and put them in a large pot of water. Bring to a boil over medium heat and add coarse-grained salt to taste. Cook for about 1½ hours, or until the peas are soft. Drain the chick-peas, saving the cooking liquid, and, while they are still hot, pass them through a food mill into a bowl. Add enough cooking liquid (about 1 cup) to obtain a creamy texture. Add 2 tablespoons of the oil and salt to taste. Preheat the oven to 375 degrees.

Heavily oil a 14-inch pizza pan and pour in the batter. Scatter the rosemary leaves, the remaining oil, and the black pepper over the top. Bake for about 35 minutes. Remove from the oven and slice the *cecina* while it is still hot. Serve immediately.

Lenticchie in Umido

LENTILS IN ROSEMARY-SAGE SAUCE

Lentils were used a great deal in Roman and medieval Italy, but their use decreased substantially when the white *cannellini* beans were introduced from America in the sixteenth century. Before the Second World War, lentils were still eaten regularly in a variety of dishes. During the war years, when food was difficult to obtain, many subsisted largely on lentils with the result that after the war people refused to eat them. At present, they retain their place in Italian *cucina* as a New Year's charm to bring luck for the following year. They are thought to have the specific power to bring money.

In Tuscany, this recipe is used, and, in Lombardy, sage is used without rosemary, and onions are added. This dish is generally served to accompany the large boiled sausages, *zampone* or *cotechino*, for the holidays.

1 pound dried lentils

4 ounces pancetta, or 2 ounces boiled ham and 2 ounces salt pork

4 or 5 sage leaves, fresh or preserved in salt

1 teaspoon of rosemary, fresh or preserved in salt

2 tablespoons olive oil

Salt and freshly ground black pepper

SERVES 6

Soak the dried lentils overnight in a large bowl of cold water. (The water should cover the lentils by 2 inches.) If you wish to accelerate the soaking time by several hours, add 1 tablespoon of flour to the cold water.* Next morning drain the water and rinse the lentils in cold running water.

Cut the *pancetta* into small pieces, then together with the sage and rosemary on a board.

Heat the oil in a glazed terra-cotta or enamel saucepan over medium heat. When the oil is hot, add the chopped ingredients and sauté very lightly for about 5 minutes. Then add the drained lentils, salt and pepper to taste, and enough water to cover the lentils completely. Cover the saucepan and simmer very slowly for about 40 to 45 minutes. At that time the water should all be absorbed and the lentils tender. Taste for salt and pepper, mix, and serve hot.

Fagioli con Sedano e Carote

CANNELLINI BEANS WITH CELERY AND CARROTS

FROM SARDINIA

This rustic Sardinian bean dish is made with *cannellini*, the white kidney beans introduced to Italy from America in the sixteenth century, and the most popular of Italian beans because of their relative lightness. Carrots and celery are also an important part of the dish. It may be eaten over a country bread as a *zuppa* and sprinkled with raw red onion, or the liquid may be removed and the beans and the vegetables served as an accompaniment to a hearty main dish.

2 cups dried cannellini *beans*

4 ounces pancetta, or 2 ounces boiled ham and 2 ounces salt pork

¼ cup olive oil

2 celery stalks

2 medium-sized carrots

Salt and freshly ground black pepper

SERVES 6

Optional:

1 red onion

Soak the beans overnight in a bowl with enough cold water to cover the beans completely. Next morning rinse the beans well.

Cut the *pancetta* coarsely. Put the *pancetta* and oil in a terra-cotta or enamel casserole over medium heat. Sauté lightly for about 5 minutes.

Cut the celery into three strips lengthwise. Then cut the strips into ½-inch pieces. Be sure to scrape the carrots well and cut them into pieces the same size as the celery. Add the beans, celery, and carrots to the casserole. Then add enough warm water to cover all the ingredients completely. Sprinkle with salt and pepper. Cover and simmer for about 1 hour. At that time beans should be cooked and much of the water incorporated into the beans. Serve hot directly from the casserole.

The authentic way to eat the beans is to cut the red onion into thin rings and to use it as a topping.

As a *minestra* or thick soup, the dish should be poured over a slice of toasted bread, preferably homemade crusty bread, such as Tuscan.

As a vegetable, it should be served without the liquid to accompany boiled or roasted meat or as a *piatto di mezzo* (see also *Fagioli al Forno*, page 213).

* Flour and water produce yeast, which acts as a tenderizer.

CHAPTER 16

Yeast Dough

Yeast doughs are used for both breads and desserts. With unbleached all-purpose flour, fresh compressed yeast or active dry yeast, and lukewarm or hot water (depending on which yeast is used and which rising), you have the basis for all of these. The first rising is called the "sponge" and the method for making it is described in each individual recipe as are the other rising or risings. The unique *Pane Ferrarese* (Bread from Ferrara) has no sponge. Kneading is also discussed in the individual recipes.

The recipe for *Quaglie nel nido di un pane toscano* (Quail in the Nest of Tuscan Bread), page 412, also contains the recipe for a basic crusty country loaf made in an improvised brick oven.

When making just the Tuscan bread, do not place the dough in the springform pan, but put it directly on preheated unglazed terra-cotta tiles in the oven. Bake for about 55 minutes. (Do not open the oven door until at least the first 25 minutes of the baking time have passed.)

If you line the middle shelf (or the bottom shelf, depending on the thickness of the bricks) of the oven with unglazed terra-cotta bricks ½ inch to 1 inch thick (use Italian or French tiles, as the Mexican tiles are baked at too low a temperature and may crack), you will then achieve the crustiness associated with baking in a brick oven. (The dough is placed directly on the tiles without flouring, wetting, or oiling them.) Naturally, in those recipes where the dough is baked in a mold or pan the bread will not be as crusty.

When baking yeast doughs, remember not to open the oven door for the first 25 minutes of the baking time.

BREADS

Pane Ferrarese

BREAD FROM FERRARA

The technique for making this bread is fascinating. First of all, seemingly contrary to all the rules, ice is mixed in when the yeast is prepared, and then when the unusual risen dough is ready, it is stretched through a pasta machine. It is also a recipe in which an electric mixer produces perhaps the best result for making the dough. The famous *cilindrati* (rolled-out) or layered rolls are generally thought of when one says Ferrarese bread, but unlayered *cazzottini* (small rolls) are also found in Ferrara. The steps for both kinds are illustrated below. The bread goes best with dishes from the Emilia-Romagna region.

1¾ cups cold water
5½ cups plus ½ unbleached all-purpose flour
½ cup olive oil or vegetable oil
1 teaspoon salt
2 ounces (2 cakes) fresh compressed yeast, or 4 packages active dry yeast

MAKES ABOUT 15 ROLLS

In order to have precisely ½ cup of the water as ice, several hours before you begin to make the bread, pour exactly ½ cup of the water into an ice-cube tray to freeze. When the ice is ready, begin to make the dough.

HOW TO PREPARE ICE DOUGH

1. Using an electric mixer with the dough hook, put the 5½ cups of flour in its bowl, then the oil and salt.

2. Crumble the yeast onto the flour,

3. then add the ice cubes and the remaining 1¼ cups of cold water.

Start mixing on medium speed for 20 minutes, then change to high speed for 10 minutes longer. The result will be softer and more elastic than a normal bread dough.

Spread out the remaining flour (½ cup) on a pasta board.

4. Remove the dough from the bowl with a spatula and place it on the board.

5. Start hand kneading, incorporating more of the flour on the board as needed.

Use a rolling pin to roll out the dough to a layer about ½ inch thick.

6. With a 3-inch cookie cutter, cut out about 15 discs of the dough. At this point you can prepare either the layered *cilindrati* Ferrarese rolls or unlayered *cazzottini* which are much simpler to prepare.

For the *cilindrati* rolls:

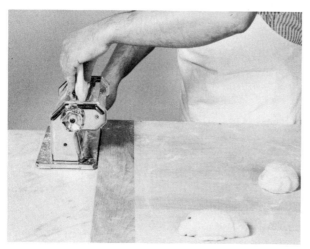

7. Using a manually-operated pasta machine, pass the discs of dough through several times, using the widest setting (see directions for using a pasta machine on page 127, photo 2).

8. Passing through the pasta machine, the discs stretch out into an oval-shaped layer of dough about ¼ inch thick.

9. Shaping the layered rolls requires several different kinds of distinct hand movements. First, hold the near end of the oval-shaped dough in place with your left hand, then with the palm of your right hand, fingers pointing away from you, roll the other end toward you. (If you are left handed, you may reverse the function of the two hands.)

Begin by rolling up two layers in this manner. Then as you roll up the third layer, with a single motion, turn your hand outward to the right as you roll. (This outward movement stretches the edge of the dough.)

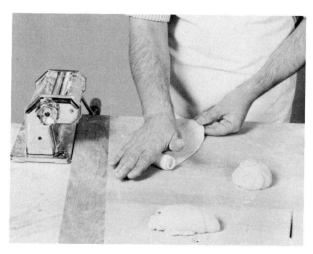

10. For the fourth layer use the same kind of movement, but turn your hand outward to the left this time. With these alternating motions from right to left finish layering the oval until it is all rolled up. With the left hand keeping the other end of the oval from moving, with each pull, the dough at that end stretches a bit so that the layers get gradually both thinner and narrower as they approach the outside. We can see the finished shape in the two rolls up front in the photo. Toward the front of the photo we see a layered *cilindrato* bent into a crescent or *cornetto* shape. This shape is a traditional alternative. It is simply made by bending the two ends of the roll inward to make a "half-moon" shape (see rear of photo 14).

Cover the *cilindrati* rolls with cotton towels and let them rest in a warm place until doubled in size (about 1 hour). If you are preparing the simpler *cazzottini* shape (in the rear of photos 9 and 10):

11. after photo 6, immediately cover the separated discs of dough with dish towels and let them rest in a warm place until double in size (about 1 hour).

HOW TO IMPROVISE A BRICK OVEN

Improvise a brick oven by placing unglazed terra-cotta tiles on the bottom shelf of your oven and preheat to 375 degrees.

Be sure to allow extra time for the tiles to reach the temperature of the oven.*

12. When the dough discs *for the cazzottini* have doubled in size,

13. use a metal spatula to place them in the oven. Bake the unlayered *cazzottini* for about 40 minutes. (Do not open the oven door until at least the first 25 minutes of the baking time have passed.)

14. To finish the rolled *cilindrati* after they have doubled in size, make a shallow cut down the center of the top surface with a sharp knife before placing them in the oven to bake for the same amount of time as the *cazzottini*. However, do not make this cut when the *cilindrati* have been bent into the crescent shape.

15. A basket of the baked Ferrarese rolls, *cazzottini*, *cilindrati*, and *cornetti cilindrati*.

* Before using them for the first time, soak the tiles in cold water for 24 hours and dry them in a 300-degree oven for about 1 hour.

406

Quaglie nel Nido di un Pane Toscano

QUAIL IN A NEST OF TUSCAN BREAD

With the Tuscan bread dough, you shape a "nest" for the quail by building up the sides of a springform pan so the bread will be high and round, the same as making *panettone*. The bread is partially cooked, then most of the soft inner portion is removed and the sautéed quail are placed in the "nest" and covered with a pâté of ground pork liver, veal, and sausages, accented by the game flavoring of juniper berries and sage. The bread, filled with the birds and the pâté, is returned to the oven to finish baking. The hunters of the Maremma, near Siena, like the nutty flavor of the pork liver in the pâté, so they prefer another version which has more liver and less of the other meats, but this milder version is also authentic, and probably more easily understood outside its native habitat. Though a rustic dish, it is sufficiently impressive in presentation to be served at either an informal or a more formal occasion. Each serving includes quail covered with pâté, and a piece of torn off bread which has absorbed all the flavors. The steps for making the dough and the filling are illustrated below.

SERVES 6

For the sponge:
3 ounces (6 cakes) fresh compressed yeast, or 6 packages active dry yeast
1 cup lukewarm or hot water, depending on the yeast
1½ cups unbleached all-purpose flour

For the dough:
12 cups unbleached all-purpose flour
Pinch of salt
3½ cups lukewarm or hot water, depending on the yeast

For the stuffing:
12 quail
3 sweet Italian sausages without fennel seeds (about 9 ounces),
*   or 9 ounces ground pork*
10 large sage leaves, fresh or preserved in salt
16 tablespoons (1 cup) olive oil
Salt and freshly ground black pepper
3 cloves garlic, peeled but left whole
1 bay leaf
About 10 juniper berries
4 tablespoons sweet butter
½ pound pork liver
¾ pound ground veal
¾ pound ground pork
1 cup dry red wine
1½ cups hot beef broth

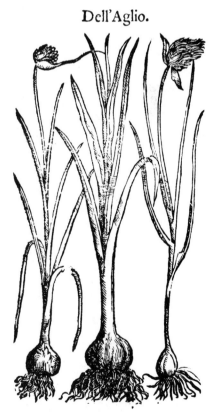

Dell'Aglio.

42. Dell'Aglio (Garlic)

HOW TO PREPARE A NEST WITH TUSCAN BREAD

Prepare the sponge (for first rising) first. Dissolve the yeast in the water in a small bowl, stirring with a wooden spoon.

1. Place all the flour less 2 tablespoons in a larger bowl, make a well in the flour, and add the dissolved yeast. Mix with the wooden spoon until all the flour is incorporated.

2. Sprinkle the 2 tablespoons of flour over the sponge mixture.

The flour uniformly sprinkled over the surface of the sponge will separate into unconnected patches when the sponge has doubled in size. This will help you to recognize when the sponge is ready. Cover the bowl with a dish towel and put it in a warm place away from any drafts. Let the sponge stand until it has doubled in size (about 1 hour).

3. When the sponge has doubled in size,

4. arrange the 12 cups of flour in a mound on a pasta board. Then make a large well in the center.

408

5. Pour the sponge into the well

6. and the water to the well.

7. Add the pinch of salt. Use a wooden spoon to start mixing together all the ingredients inside the well.

8. With your fingers break up all undissolved lumps of sponge in the well.

9. Start mixing with your hands, absorbing the flour from the inside rim of the well little by little.

10. Keep mixing until all but about 3 cups of the flour are incorporated (about 15 minutes) into a mound of dough.

11. Clean the flour by shaking it through a sifter,

12. moving the sifter vigorously back and forth on the surface of the board without lifting it.

13. Start kneading the dough with the palm of your hand, in a folding motion, until it is homogeneous and smooth (about 20 minutes), incorporating the remaining flour.

14. Shape dough into a ball.
Tear off a piece of heavy duty aluminum foil about 3½ feet long.

15. Use a scissors to cut the width down to 10 inches. Fit the foil all around the inside of a 12-inch diameter springform pan. Fold over and staple together the overlapping ends in several places.
Sprinkle a little bit of flour around the bottom of the springform pan and put the dough in the pan.

410

16. Cover with a dish towel and put in a warm place away from drafts. Let the dough rest until doubled in size (about 1 hour). Preheat the oven to 400 degrees.

17. When the dough has doubled in size, remove the towel and immediately place the springform pan in the oven.

Bake the bread for 40 minutes. (Do not open the oven door until at least the first 25 minutes of the baking time have passed.) It should emerge very light brown and half-cooked. Remove the pan from the oven and allow it to cool for 5 minutes. Then open the pan, free the bread, and transfer it to a rack to cool for about 15 minutes.

18. Use a bread knife to gently cut off the top part of the bread (about 1 inch deep) and save it.

19. Insert a knife halfway into the bread, ½ inch from the edge, and cut all the way around in order to loosen the soft inner portion.

411

20. With two spoons, remove the half-cooked dough from the inside of the bread, being careful not to break the outside crust. Save 1 cup of the dough for use later. Leave a shell of about ½ inch of dough on the sides and bottom.

21. In this way you will form the "nest."

HOW TO PREPARE A LOAF OF TUSCAN BREAD

For the sponge (first rising):   MAKES 1 LOAF
1 ounce (2 cakes) compressed fresh yeast or 2 packages active dry yeast
½ cup lukewarm or hot water, depending on the yeast
½ cup plus 1 tablespoon unbleached all-purpose flour

For the dough (second rising):
5 cups unbleached all-purpose flour
1¾ cups lukewarm water
Pinch of salt

When making just a loaf of Tuscan bread, follow from beginning through photo 13 of "How to prepare a nest of Tuscan bread." Then shape dough into a long or round loaf and wrap in a floured dish towel to rise until it has doubled in size. Improvise a brick oven (see p. 688). Preheat the oven to 400 degrees.

To transfer the dough to the brick oven: When the dough is ready, open the towel. With both hands lift the two ends of one side of the towel over to meet the ends of the other. Holding the two ends together with both hands, lay the towel with the dough directly on the hot tiles. Let the two ends of the inner side of the towel fall and, grasping the two ends of the outer side, pull over the towel, letting the dough itself fall onto the tiles. Bake for about 55 minutes to

obtain a crusty loaf. If when the loaf is tapped, it produces a hollow sound, the bread is ready.

Prepare the stuffing for the "nest": Clean the quail very well and dry them with paper towels.

Remove the skin from the sausages and cut them each into 4 pieces. Stuff each quail with 1 piece of sausage and half a sage leaf.

Heat 6 tablespoons of the oil in a large flameproof casserole. When the oil is hot, add quail and sauté over medium heat until they are golden brown all over and half cooked (about 10 minutes). Sprinkle with salt and pepper. Use a slotted spoon to transfer the quail to serving dish. Cover the dish with aluminum foil and let the quail stand until needed.

Pour the remaining 10 tablespoons of oil into the

412

casserole in which the quail were sautéed. Add the remaining sage leaves, garlic, bay leaf, juniper berries, and the butter.

Meanwhile, coarsely chop the pork liver on a board. When the butter is completely melted add the pork liver, ground veal, and ground pork to the casserole and sauté, stirring with a wooden spoon, for about 10 minutes, or until the meat has lost its reddish color. Taste for salt and pepper. Remove the pan from the heat and discard the bay leaf.

Use a slotted spoon to transfer all the solids to a chopping board. Finely chop all the ingredients together.

Return the casserole with the leftover juice to medium heat and add the chopped ingredients. Add the wine and let it evaporate for 5 minutes. Then add the hot broth and simmer for about 10 minutes, stirring occasionally with a wooden spoon. Taste for salt and pepper. Remove the casserole from the heat. Add 1 cup of the dough removed from the bread and stir very well until all the ingredients are well incorporated and smooth. Preheat the oven to 375 degrees.

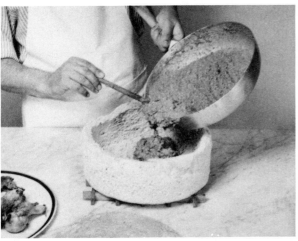

22. Place half of the stuffing in the bottom of the "nest."

23. Arrange the quail on top of the stuffing and

24. pour the remaining stuffing over the quail. (The quail should be completely covered with the stuffing.)

Cover the nest completely with a piece of aluminum foil and bake for 1 hour.

25. Remove from the oven and remove the aluminum foil from the top of the bread. Cover the bread with its own lid (the top part of the bread cut off) and return to the oven for 20 minutes longer.

Remove from the oven and place on a serving dish. Remove the lid to serve. Each serving should consist of 2 quail and some of the stuffing.

413

Pane alla Salvia

SAGE BREAD

A Tuscan sage loaf made with a dough containing sage sautéed in olive oil and also flavored with wine. The baking time is a little longer than that of normal Tuscan bread. It is delicious as a snack or may be used with any dish that blends well with the flavor of sage, such as poultry or game flavored with rosemary.

For the sponge: MAKES 1 LOAF
1 ounce (2 cakes) compressed fresh yeast, or 2 packages dry active yeast
1 cup lukewarm or hot water, depending on the yeast
1½ cups plus ½ cup unbleached all-purpose flour

For the dough:
4 tablespoons olive oil
15 large sage leaves, fresh or preserved in salt
4 cups unbleached all-purpose flour
½ cup dry white wine
1 teaspoon salt
¼ teaspoon freshly ground black pepper
½ cup lukewarm water

Dissolve the yeast in the water in a small bowl, stirring with a wooden spoon. Put the 1½ cups of flour in a larger bowl and add the dissolved yeast. Mix with the wooden spoon until all the flour is incorporated and a small ball of dough has formed.

Sprinkle the additional ½ cup of flour over the ball of dough, then cover the bowl with a dish towel and put it in a warm place away from drafts. Let stand until the sponge has doubled in size (about 1 hour).

Heat the olive oil in a small saucepan over medium heat. When the oil is lukewarm, add the sage leaves, which have been torn into 2 or 3 pieces. Sauté for 1 minute, then remove the pan from the heat and let the oil-sage mixture cool until lukewarm.

Arrange the 4 cups of flour in a mound on a pasta board. Make a well in the flour. Place the sponge in the well, along with the wine, salt, pepper, and the oil-sage mixture. Use a wooden spoon to carefully mix together all the ingredients in the well. Then add the ½ cup of lukewarm water and start mixing with your hands, absorbing the flour from the inside rim of the well little by little. Keep mixing until all

but 7 or 8 tablespoons of the flour is incorporated. Knead the dough with the palm of your hand, in a folding motion, until homogeneous and smooth (about 15 minutes).

Shape the dough into a long or a round loaf (whichever you prefer), and place it on a floured dish towel. Wrap the dough in the towel and put it in a warm place away from drafts, and let stand until doubled in size (about 1 hour).

Line the middle or bottom shelf of the oven with ovenproof terra-cotta tiles. Preheat the oven to 400 degrees.

When the dough of the second rising has doubled in size, quickly remove it from the towel and immediately place it in the oven, directly on the tiles.

Bake the bread for about 75 minutes. (Do not open the oven door until at least the first 25 minutes of the baking time have passed.) The bread is fully baked when the crust is thick and the inside airy so that the bread feels very light in weight.

Remove the bread from the oven and place it on a pasta board, standing it on one of its sides, not lying flat. The bread must cool for at least 3 hours before it is eaten.

Panzarotti

BREAD PILLOWS

In the countryside surrounding Tuscany, where the *Chianti* wine and virgin olive oil are produced, when the crusty Tuscan bread is baked in the brick ovens, often some extra bread dough is put aside to make the beloved *panzarotti*. It is a favorite of all the villa people and the Marchese, and the farm workers who love to eat it hot and freshly prepared, as a snack. The etiquette-conscious Florentines will even relax for these and eat them with their fingers.

For the sponge: YIELD: 20 PANZAROTTI
1 ounce (2 cakes) compressed fresh yeast, or 2 packages active dry yeast
½ cup lukewarm water or hot water, depending on the yeast
¾ cup plus 1 tablespoon unbleached all-purpose flour

For the dough:
2¾ cups unbleached all-purpose flour
Pinch of salt
½ cup lukewarm water

For the choices of fillings:
No. 1—*2 medium-sized ripe fresh tomatoes, or 5 drained canned imported Italian*
   tomatoes, cut into 20 pieces
   4 ounces mozzarella, cut into 20 pieces 1- x 2- x ½-inch thick
   20 basil leaves, fresh or preserved in salt
No. 2—*2 medium-sized ripe fresh tomatoes, or 5 drained canned imported Italian*
   tomatoes, cut into 20 pieces
   10 anchovy fillets in oil, cut in half and drained
No. 3—*2 medium-sized ripe fresh tomatoes, or 5 drained canned imported Italian*
   tomatoes, cut into 20 pieces
   20 basil leaves, fresh or preserved in salt
No. 4—*4 ounces mozzarella, cut into 20 pieces 1- x 2- x ½-inch thick*
   20 basil leaves, fresh or preserved in salt
   1 pound solid vegetable shortening
   Salt

Dissolve the yeast in a small bowl of water, stirring with a wooden spoon. Put ¾ cup flour in a larger bowl and add the dissolved yeast. Mix together with the wooden spoon until all the flour is incorporated. Sprinkle the 1 tablespoon of flour over the sponge. Cover the bowl with a dish towel and put it in a warm place away from drafts. Let stand until the dough has doubled in size (about 1 hour).

Arrange the 2¾ cups of flour in a mound on a pasta board, then make a well. Place the sponge from the first rising in the well, along with the salt and lukewarm water. Use a wooden spoon to carefully mix together all the ingredients in the well.

Then start mixing with your hands, absorbing the flour from the inside rim of the well little by little. Keep mixing until all but 4 or 5 tablespoons of the flour are incorporated. Knead the dough with the palm of your hand, in a folding motion, until it is homogeneous and smooth (about 10 minutes). Form the dough into a ball, cover with a dish towel and allow to double in size again in a warm place away from drafts.

When the dough has doubled, roll it out with a rolling pin into a sheet 3/16 inch thick. Use one of the fillings listed above. Lay out the sheet of dough. Starting 2 inches from the top and side edges, begin a horizontal row of portions of the filling, each one 2 inches from its neighbor. Each portion contains 1 piece of each ingredient of its filling. Carefully pick up the top end of the dough sheet and fold it over the row of filling. Quickly press down around each filling. Cut into squares using a pastry wheel. Repeat the procedure until 20 *panzarotti* are formed. This should use the entire sheet. Lay the *panzarotti* on a floured dish towel, cover with another towel, and allow to rise again (about 1 hour).

Heat the solid shortening in a deep-fat fryer. Pre-pare a serving dish by lining it with paper towels. When the shortening is hot, add the *panzarotti*, a few at a time, and cook until golden brown on both sides (about 1 minute a side). Remove the *panzarotti* with a strainer-skimmer and place them on the prepared serving dish to drain. Repeat the procedure until all the *panzarotti* are cooked and on the dish. Then remove the paper towels from the bottom of the dish and sprinkle each *panzarotto* with just a pinch of salt. Serve hot.

Schiacciata al Sale Grosso

SCHIACCIATA WITH COARSE-GRAINED SALT

FROM PISTOIA

This variation of the pizza-like flat bread is sprinkled with coarse salt. Often eaten as a snack, it may also accompany appropriate courses of a meal, generally the main course. Because the dough itself is virtually salt-free, the result is no saltier than a normally salted bread.

SERVES 8

For the sponge:
1 cup plus 1 tablespoon unbleached all-purpose flour
1 ounce (2 cakes) fresh compressed yeast, or 2 packages active dry yeast
½ cup lukewarm or hot water, depending on the yeast

For the dough:
3¼ cups unbleached all-purpose flour
1 tablespoon olive oil
Pinch of salt
1 cup lukewarm water

Plus:
2 tablespoons olive oil
About ½ tablespoon coarse-grained salt

Put 1 cup of flour in a bowl and make a well. Dissolve the yeast in the ½ cup lukewarm water and pour into the well. Mix the dissolved yeast with a wooden spoon, incorporating about half the flour in the bowl. Sprinkle the 1 tablespoon of flour over the sponge. Cover the bowl with a dish towel and put it in a warm place away from drafts. Let stand until the sponge has doubled in size (about 1 hour).

Arrange the 3¼ cups of flour in a mound on a pasta board, then make a well. Place the sponge and the leftover flour from the bowl in the well, along with the olive oil, salt, and water. Use a wooden spoon to carefully mix all the ingredients in the well. Then start mixing with your hands, absorbing the flour from the inside rim of the well little by little. Keep mixing until all but about 5 tablespoons of the flour are incorporated. Knead the dough with the palm of your hand, incorporating the remaining flour in a folding motion, until the dough is homogeneous and smooth (about 10 minutes). Oil a 14-inch-diameter pizza pan and place the dough on it. Spread the dough with your fingers until it covers the bottom. Because this dough is sticky, cover it with wax paper oiled on the inner side to keep it from sticking before covering the pan with a dish towel. Let rest until the dough has risen again to almost double in size (about 1 hour).

Preheat the oven to 375 degrees. When the dough has doubled, remove the towel, sprinkle the 2 tablespoons of olive oil and the coarse-grained salt over the dough. Place it in the oven and bake for about 1 hour, or until crisp and light golden brown. (Do not open the oven door until at least the first 25 minutes of the baking time have passed.) Remove from the oven. Serve from the pan, slicing like a pizza.

Schiacciata Unta alla Fiorentina

BEEF-FLAVORED SCHIACCIATA

FROM FLORENCE

The rich reduced passed beef sauce which is so delicious with pasta (see *Sugo di manzo*, page 132) adds a marvelous flavor to the pizza-like flat bread so popular in Florence. It is one of the traditional uses of the sauce, so that if you have a little of it left over from the previous day's pasta, it is just the opportunity to make this special *schiacciata*. The flavoring is different when combined with the yeastiness of the dough.

SERVES 8

For the sponge:
1½ cups plus 1 tablespoon unbleached all-purpose flour
2 ounces (4 cakes) fresh compressed yeast, or 4 packages of active dry yeast
1 cup lukewarm or hot water, depending on yeast
Pinch of salt

For the dough:
4 cups unbleached all-purpose flour
1 cup beef sauce (page 132)

Plus:
½ tablespoon olive oil
Coarse-grained salt

Put the 1½ cups of flour in a bowl and make a well. Dissolve the yeast in the lukewarm water and pour it into the well. Mix the dissolved yeast with a wooden spoon, incorporating the flour. Sprinkle the 1 tablespoon of flour over the sponge. Cover the bowl with a dish towel and place it in a warm place away from drafts. Let stand until the sponge has doubled in size (about 1 hour).

Arrange the 4 cups of flour in a mound on a pasta board, then make a well in the flour. Heat the beef sauce. Place the sponge in the well and add the lukewarm sauce. Start mixing with your hands, absorbing the flour from the inside rim of the well little by little. Keep mixing until all but about 5 tablespoons of the flour is incorporated. Knead the dough with the palm of your hand in a folding motion, until it is homogeneous and smooth (about 10 minutes).

Oil a 14-inch-diameter pizza pan and place the dough on it. Spread the dough with your fingers until it covers the bottom. Sprinkle over the ½ tablespoon of oil and 1 teaspoon of coarse salt. Cover the pan with wax paper, then cover with a dish towel and let rest until the dough has again risen to double in size (about 1 hour).

Preheat the oven to 375 degrees. When the dough is ready, remove the paper and the towel and place the pan in the oven and bake for 55 minutes. (Do not open the oven door until at least the first 25 minutes of the baking time have passed.) Remove from the oven, transfer the *schiacciata* to a rack, and serve, slicing like a pizza. This *schiacciata* is good even at room temperature after several hours.

417

Pizza al Formaggio *or Crescia*

CHEESE DOUGH PIZZA

One of the trademarks of this region, this bread is the great exception to the usual Italian practice of not allowing cheese to get browned in the oven. Here the cheese that is incorporated throughout the dough achieves a particular slightly bitter flavor which is appropriate in a bread, where its dominating flavor does not conflict with other tastes. It may be eaten as a snack or appetizer or to accompany a bland main dish without cheese. The complex combination of three cheeses and the interesting texture of the alternation of cubes with grated cheese makes it a noteworthy dish. (The dialect name comes from the word *crescere*, "to grow," which also means "to rise" as a river rises.)

SERVES 8

For the sponge:
1½ cups plus 1 tablespoon unbleached all-purpose flour
2 ounces (4 cakes) fresh compressed yeast, or 4 packages active dry yeast
1 cup lukewarm or hot water, depending on the yeast
Pinch of salt

For the dough:
4 whole extra large eggs
¼ cup freshly grated Parmigiano
¼ cup Parmigiano, cut into tiny cubes
2 tablespoons grated Switzerland Swiss cheese
1 tablespoon Switzerland Swiss cheese, cut into tiny cubes
2 tablespoons grated Caciocavallo or Provolone
1 tablespoon Caciocavallo or Provolone, cut into tiny cubes
1 tablespoon olive oil
3½ cups unbleached all-purpose flour

Put the 1½ cups of flour in a bowl and make a well. Dissolve the yeast in the lukewarm water and pour it into the well. Add the salt. Mix the dissolved yeast with a wooden spoon, incorporating the flour little by little. Sprinkle the 1 tablespoon of flour over the sponge. Then cover the bowl with a dish towel and place it in a warm place away from drafts. Let stand until the sponge has doubled in size (about 1 hour).

Put the eggs, the grated cheeses, the cheeses in cubes, and the olive oil in a small bowl. Mix very well with a wooden spoon to amalgamate all the ingredients.

Arrange the 3½ cups of flour in a mound on pasta board. Then make a well in the flour. Pour the sponge into the well, then the contents of the bowl. Start mixing with your hands, absorbing the flour from the inside rim of the well little by little. Keep mixing until all the flour is incorporated. Knead the dough with the palm of your hand in a folding motion, until it is homogeneous and smooth (about 5 minutes).

Oil a 14-inch-diameter pizza pan and place the dough on it. Spread the dough with your fingers until it covers the bottom. Cover the pan with a dish towel and rest in a cool place away from drafts until the dough has again doubled in size (about 1 hour).

Preheat the oven to 375 degrees. When dough is ready, remove the towel and place the pan in the oven and bake for about 45 minutes. (Do not open the oven door until at least the first 25 minutes of the baking time have passed.) Remove from the oven and transfer the pizza to a rack to cool for several hours. Serve at room temperature, cutting it into slices.

Focaccia Farcita (Sfingione di San Vito)

STUFFED FOCACCIA OR PIZZA

FROM PALERMO

Two thin layers of pizza dough are prepared and the stuffing of ground beef and cheese, as well as many flavorings including fennel seeds, is placed between them. The top is then brushed with egg yolk and sprinkled with bread crumbs. It is a substantial dish, not just a bread, and may be eaten as a first course or appetizer. The steps are illustrated below.

For the filling:

SERVES 8

¾ pound ground beef
1 tablespoon sweet butter
4 tablespoons olive oil
Salt and freshly ground black pepper
1 large red onion
½ pound Caciocavallo

For the crust:
1 cup fresh tomatoes or drained canned imported Italian tomatoes
2 ounces (4 cakes) fresh compressed yeast, or 4 packages dry active yeast
½ cup lukewarm or hot water, depending on the yeast
1½ pounds unbleached all-purpose flour
2 extra large eggs
½ cup olive oil
Pinch of salt

Plus:
½ tablespoon fennel seeds
About 10 sprigs Italian parsley
1 extra large egg yolk
3 tablespoons unseasoned bread crumbs, preferably homemade

HOW TO PREPARE FOCACCIA FARCITA

Prepare the filling. Put ground beef and the butter in a small bowl and incorporate the butter with a wooden spoon.

Heat 2 tablespoons of the olive oil in a small saucepan over medium heat. When the oil is hot, add the ground beef. Sprinkle meat with salt and pepper and sauté until it loses its reddish color. Use a slotted spoon to transfer the meat to a small bowl and let it stand until needed.

Cut the onion into rings ⅛ inch thick. Add the remaining 2 tablespoons of olive oil to the saucepan in which the beef was sautéed and put the pan over medium heat. Add the onion and sprinkle with salt and pepper. Sauté until translucent (about 10 minutes). Use a slotted spoon to remove the onion from the pan and transfer it to a small bowl. Cut the *Caciocavallo* into ½-inch cubes. Pass the tomatoes through a food mill into a small bowl.

Prepare the crust: Dissolve the yeast in lukewarm or hot water, depending on the yeast, in a small bowl. Put the flour in a mound on a pasta board.

1. Make a well in the center and put in the dissolved yeast, eggs, olive oil, and salt.

Use a wooden spoon to first mix together all the ingredients in the well. Then start incorporating the flour from the edges of the well, always pushing the fresh flour under the dough to keep it detached. When almost all of the flour has been absorbed, start kneading, using the palm of your hand only. Knead the dough until it is smooth and elastic (about 10 minutes).

2. Use a knife to cut off one third of the dough. Set it aside. Oil a 14-inch diameter pizza pan.

3. With your hands, begin to stretch the larger piece of dough and place it on the pizza pan.

4. Continue to spread out the dough, using the tips of your fingers, until the bottom of the pizza pan is completely covered and the dough overlaps the sides slightly.

5. Cover the dough with the sautéed meat.

Scatter the onions and then pour the tomato purée over the meat. Sprinkle on the fennel seeds.

Spread the *Caciocavallo* over the top and arrange the parsley on top of the cheese.

6. With rolling pin, stretch the remaining dough into a round shape the same diameter as the pan.

7. Put this layer of dough on top of all the stuffing.

8. With your fingers, carefully press together the edges of the two layers of dough to close the *focaccia*.

Cover the pan with a dish towel and let rest until the dough has doubled in size (about 1 hour).

Preheat the oven to 375 degrees. When the *focaccia* is ready, beat the egg yolk with a fork.

9. Brush the top of the *focaccia* with beaten egg yolk.

Sprinkle the bread crumbs over the top and bake for about 45 minutes. (Do not open the oven door until at least the first 25 minutes of the baking time have passed.)

10. Remove from the oven and allow to cool for a few minutes. Slice like a pizza to serve.

Cotechino in Camicia

COTECHINO SAUSAGE BAKED IN CRUST

Cotechino outwardly resembles a salami but it is always eaten cooked and its texture is grainier than that of a salami. It is made from coarsely ground lean pork flavored with cloves, salt, and black pepper. The *cotechino* sausage is first boiled and then baked in a pastry crust so it is a marvelous opening course. It is sometimes eaten cold, like "saucisson en croute," but, with the Italian emphasis on the crust, it is more often eaten warm when the crust is fresh. This dish deserves to be better known outside of Italy.

SERVES 6

1 cotechino *sausage, about 1 pound* *
Coarse-grained salt

For the *bomboloni* or brioche pastry:
The sponge:
1 ounce (2 cakes) fresh compressed yeast, or 2 packages active dry yeast
½ cup lukewarm or hot milk, depending on the yeast
¾ cup plus 1 tablespoon unbleached all-purpose flour
Pinch of salt

The dough:
6 tablespoons sweet butter
4 extra large egg yolks
1 tablespoon granulated sugar
½ cup lukewarm milk
2½ cups unbleached all-purpose flour

If commercial *cotechino* is used, put it in a large bowl of cold water and soak for 2 or 3 hours. (This is not necessary if you make your own.) After soaking, make several punctures in the sausage with a large needle or fork, then wrap completely in a dish towel and tie both ends with string.

Put the sausage in a large pot of cold water and bring to a boil over medium heat. Meanwhile, put enough water to cover the sausage in a large fish poacher, add coarse-grained salt to taste, and bring to a boil. When the water containing the sausage reaches the boiling point, it will have absorbed some of the excess fat in the sausage. Remove the pot from the heat, transfer the sausage to a board and unwrap it. Transfer the unwrapped *cotechino* to the boiling water in the fish poacher. Lower the heat and simmer for about 2 hours, or until cooked. Remove the *cotechino* to a board and let it cool completely (about 1 hour).

* *Cotechino* made with a slightly different seasoning may also be purchased at ethnic Italian markets.

HOW TO PREPARE THE *BOMBOLONI* OR BRIOCHE PASTRY

To prepare the sponge, dissolve the yeast in the lukewarm milk. Place the flour in a bowl and make a small well in it. Then add the dissolved yeast and the salt. Mix together the ingredients of the well, then incorporate the flour and mix very well. Sprinkle the 1 tablespoon of flour over the sponge. Cover the bowl with a dish towel and let stand in a warm place away from drafts, until the sponge has doubled in size (about 1 hour).

Prepare the dough. Melt the butter in a large bowl over a pot of boiling water. Let the butter cool. Put the egg yolks in a small bowl. When the sponge is ready,

1. start adding the egg yolks one at a time to the cooled melted butter, mixing with a wooden spoon in a rotary movement. When all the egg yolks are incorporated,

2. add the sponge, sugar, and lukewarm milk.

Keep stirring until all the ingredients are well amalgamated. Then add 2¼ cups of the flour, a little at a time, stirring constantly.

3. When all the flour is incorporated, continue to stir until the dough is very elastic and smooth.

Cover the bowl with a dish towel and let it rest in a warm place away from drafts, until doubled in size (about 1 hour).

When the dough is ready, sprinkle the remaining flour on a board and put the dough on the board.

4. Roll out gently with a rolling pin to make a sheet about ¼ inch thick.

If necessary, remove the string at both ends of the *cotechino*.

 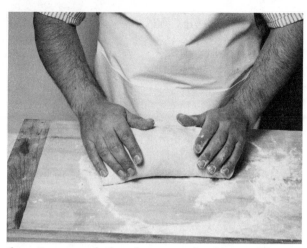

5. Place the boiled and cooled *cotechino* on the dough, and start wrapping the dough around the sausage,

6. using enough dough to completely cover the *cotechino*. Discard any extra dough.

Butter a loaf pan and

7. place the wrapped *cotechino* in the pan, with the seam of the pastry on top, so that once the pastry is cooked it opens like a shirt.

Cover the pan with a dish towel and let rest in a warm place away from drafts, until the pastry doubles in size (about 1 hour).

Preheat the oven to 375 degrees. When dough is ready, place the pan in the oven and bake for about 40 minutes. (Do not open the oven door until at least the first 25 minutes of the baking time have passed.) Remove the pan from the oven and transfer the *Cotechino in camicia* onto serving dish.

8. Before serving, cut it into two pieces, so the sausage covered with its "shirt" of pastry can be seen.

424

DESSERTS

Babà alla Crema

BABA LAYER CAKE

FROM ALL OVER ITALY

The name *babà* is supposed to derive from Polish, but the origin of the pastry itself is uncertain although it has long been a part of Italian cooking. A fresh homemade *babà*, with its delicious light yeast dough cake (which includes raisins), cut in half, with pastry cream between the layers, is quite a different thing from the usual commercial product. Before serving, rum-flavored syrup is traditionally poured over it, creating an extremely moist, flavorful cake.

8 ounces raisins
16 ounces (4 cups) unbleached all-purpose flour
2 ounces (4 cakes) fresh compressed yeast, or 4 packages active dry yeast
⅔ cup lukewarm or hot water, depending on the yeast
8 ounces (2 sticks) sweet butter
6 extra large eggs
2 tablespoons granulated sugar

SERVES 8 TO 10

For the pastry cream:
4 extra large egg yolks
6 tablespoons granulated sugar
3 teaspoons potato starch or cornstarch
1 cup cold milk
Small piece of orange peel

For the syrup:
1 cup water
½ cup granulated sugar
1 cup light rum

Plus:
About 2 tablespoons orange or lemon sirup (see page 57)

HOW TO PREPARE BABÀ ALLA CREMA

Soak the raisins in a small bowl of lukewarm water for about 30 minutes. Sift the flour and put 6 ounces (1½ cups) of the sifted flour in a crockery bowl.

Make a well in the flour. Dissolve the yeast in a small bowl with the lukewarm water. Place the dissolved yeast in the well.

1. Start mixing with a wooden spoon until all the flour is incorporated. Sprinkle 1 tablespoon of the remaining flour over the sponge. Cover the bowl with a dish towel and let stand in a warm place away from drafts until the sponge has doubled in size (about 1 hour).

Melt the butter in the top of a double boiler and let it cool. Drain the water from the raisins and dry them on paper towels. Break the eggs into a bowl. When the sponge has doubled in size, start adding the sugar, stirring constantly with a wooden spoon always in the same direction.

2. Then add the eggs, one by one, and then the cooled melted butter.

Add the remaining flour, a little at a time, until all the flour is incorporated and a very smooth thick batter is formed. Add the raisins and mix carefully. Butter a 3-quart ring mold or tube pan, 10 inches in diameter.

3. Pour the contents of the bowl into the mold. Cover the ring mold with a dish towel and let rest in a warm place away from drafts until doubled in size (about 1 hour).

Prepare the pastry cream with the ingredients listed above, following the directions on page 489. Transfer the pastry cream to a crockery bowl and let cool (about ½ hour). Then cover the bowl with buttered wax paper and refrigerate the custard to cool completely. Preheat the oven to 400 degrees.

Prepare the syrup. Put the water and sugar in a heavy saucepan over low heat. Simmer for about 35 minutes, or until the syrup is formed. (If it is not to be used immediately, the syrup may be stored in the refrigerator.) Add the rum and mix thoroughly.

4. When the dough has doubled in size, remove the towel and place the mold in the oven for about 40 minutes. (Do not open the oven door until at least the first 25 minutes of the baking time have passed.) If the crust becomes too brown, put a piece of aluminum foil over the mold.

Remove from the oven and cool for about 20 minutes.

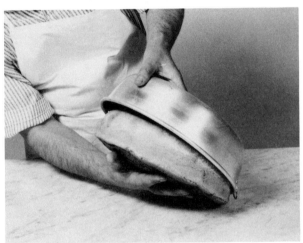

5. Unmold and transfer to a rack to cool.

6. With a slicing knife cut the cake in half horizontally. Moisten the mold with the orange or lemon sirup. Fit the top half of the cake back into the mold

7. and spread the cold pastry cream over the top.

8. Then fit the other half of the *babà* over it. This cake may be served immediately or, if it is not to be used for several hours, place aluminum foil over the ring mold and let stand until needed.

427

9. When ready to serve, carefully unmold the whole cake onto a large serving platter.

10. Spoon the sirup over the cake.

11. The final product.

428

Rotolo di Natale

CHRISTMAS FRUIT AND NUT ROLL

One of the attractive Christmas cakes from the Naples area, it is stuffed with walnuts, pignoli, and raisins and flavored with orange and lemon rind and rum. Like some other older recipes, at a certain point within the last two centuries, a little chocolate flavoring was added to it.

4 ounces (8 cakes) fresh compressed yeast, or 8 packages active dry yeast   SERVES 12
2 cups lukewarm or hot milk, depending on the yeast
1½ pounds (6 cups) unbleached all-purpose flour
8 ounces raisins
8 ounces walnuts
4 ounces pignoli (pine nuts)
8 ounces (2 cups) granulated sugar
Grated rind of 2 oranges
Grated rind of 2 lemons
1 ounce (3 tablespoons) unsweetened cocoa powder
4 ounces (1 stick) plus about 5 pieces sweet butter
2 extra large eggs, separated
½ cup light rum
Pinch of salt

Dissolve the yeast in 1 cup of the lukewarm milk. Put the flour in a large bowl and make a well in it. Pour the dissolved yeast into the well and mix with a wooden spoon until about one fourth of the flour has been incorporated into the yeast mixture. Cover the bowl with a dish towel and let stand in a warm place away from drafts, until the sponge has doubled in size (about 1 hour).

Prepare the stuffing. Soak the raisins in the remaining cup of lukewarm milk for about 30 minutes. Coarsely chop the walnuts and put them in a bowl. Add the pignoli, 4 ounces of the sugar, half of the grated orange and lemon rinds, and the cocoa powder. Mix thoroughly with a wooden spoon. Drain the raisins and dry them on paper towels. Add them to the bowl with the walnuts and other ingredients. Mix gently but thoroughly.

When the sponge has doubled in size, melt the 4 ounces of butter in the top of a double-boiler and let stand until needed.

Pour the remaining sugar over the sponge. Then add the egg yolks, rum, the remaining grated orange and lemon rinds, and the salt. Stir everything into the sponge with a wooden spoon. Then add the cooled melted butter and incorporate all but 5 or 6 tablespoons of the unmixed flour. Transfer the dough to a pasta board and knead until the remaining flour is almost all incorporated and the dough is smooth (about 15 minutes).

With a rolling pin, roll out the dough to a thickness of ½ inch, making the shape of a rectangle not larger than 9 inches wide.

Beat the egg whites until stiff and spread them on top of the sheet of dough with a spatula. Scatter the stuffing in the bowl over the egg whites, and place the pieces of butter on top of the stuffing. Roll up the sheet of dough lengthwise.

Butter a 14-inch-diameter pizza pan. Transfer the rolled and stuffed dough to the pan and make it into a ring. Cover the pan with a dish towel and let rise in a warm place away from drafts until doubled in size (about 2 hours).

Preheat the oven to 400 degrees. When the ring has risen, bake in the oven for about 40 minutes, or until the top is golden brown. (Do not open the oven door until at least the first 25 minutes of the baking time have passed.) Remove from the oven and transfer the *rotolo* to a rack to cool.

Panettone

The most famous of all Italian Christmas cakes, it was once known only in the Milan area (and the chefs of this region, Lombardy, were celebrated in the Renaissance), but is now traditionally served all over Italy in that season. Unfortunately, most of the *panettoni* available are commercial ones packaged in Milan. Of course, they do not compare to a fresh homemade version. The shape of the cake is standard: It is always high and round, and usually made in a springform pan with the sides built up, nowadays most conveniently with aluminum foil (like *Quaglie nel Nido di un pane toscano,* page 407). It is never made in any other shape, and the top is brushed with egg and has a cross cut into it, both to place the butter inside, and probably also for symbolic reasons.

2 ounces raisins
2 cups lukewarm or hot milk, depending on the yeast
3 ounces (6 tablespoons) plus 1 piece sweet butter
4 ounces glacéed citron
2 ounces glacéed orange rind
1 thick-skinned lemon
1½ pounds (6 cups) unbleached all-purpose flour
3 ounces (6 cakes) compressed fresh yeast, or 6 packages active dry yeast
6 extra large egg yolks
4 ounces (½ cup) granulated sugar
Pinch of salt

SERVES 12 TO 16

Soak the raisins in 1 cup of the lukewarm milk for about 30 minutes. Melt 3 ounces of the butter in the top of a double-boiler and set aside to cool. Cut the citron and the orange rind into small pieces. Grate the rind of the lemon.

Arrange the flour in a mound on a pasta board and make a well. Drain the raisins and pat them dry with paper towels. Dissolve the yeast in the remaining cup of milk. Place 5 of the egg yolks, the sugar, salt, and the dissolved yeast in the well, and stir them with a wooden spoon. Add the melted butter a little at a time, gradually incorporating the flour. When almost all the flour has been incorporated with the other ingredients, add the raisins, citron, orange rind, and grated lemon rind. Knead the dough very gently for about 10 minutes, then shape it into a ball. Line an 8-inch springform pan with a piece of wax paper or aluminum foil about 9 inches high (see page 410). Sprinkle the form with a little flour and place the dough in the pan. Cover it with a dish towel. Let rest for about 2 hours in a warm place away from drafts, or until doubled in size.

Preheat the oven to 400 degrees. When the dough has risen, beat the remaining yolk and brush the top with it. Cut a cross into the top, place the piece of butter in the center and bake for about 45 or 50 minutes, or until the top is golden brown. (Do not open the oven door until at least the first 25 minutes of the baking time have passed.) Remove from the oven and let stand for about 10 minutes. Then remove from the springform pan and cool the *panettone* completely on a rack. (If you used wax paper, it might stick to the cake. If this happens, do not attempt to remove it until the *panettone* is completely cold.)

CHAPTER 17

Molds and Aspics

In Italy a visit to a cookware store, or to many antique shops and flea markets, reveals a display of molds in copper, enameled terra-cotta, etc., both shiningly new and romantically antique, in many sizes and shapes. Some are formed to produce fluting or other elaborate decoration in the finished mold of meat, vegetable, or dessert. The most common term for these dishes is *sformati*, meaning literally "unmolded." *Budino* is another much used term, often applied to mousse-like dishes. This array of molds is also featured in most Italian cookbooks from the Renaissance through the nineteenth century, reflecting the preference of Italians for beautiful forms in food as well as for dishes that may be eaten easily without breaches of the elaborate code of Italian table manners. With the nineteenth century, the Romantic movement's emphasis on genuineness and the rediscovery of the simplicity of the "folk," came a new appreciation of the natural look in food. There was a de-emphasis on molds, mousses, and soufflé-like dishes which destroyed the original shape and texture. But this was only a change in frequency of usage. For these presentations had really been overused in the eighteenth and nineteenth centuries. It was possible to dine too tastefully, having dishes in which no animal or fish had a bone, nor did any vegetable or fruit resemble its natural form. But, used in moderation and for more formal occasions, this type of presentation is still an important part of cooking in Italy, and a neat molded form, such as the *Sformato di maionese* (Mayonnaise Mold) on page 438, may dress up an otherwise simple meal and make it more festive.

For the aspics, I believe it important to keep alive the genuine product made from calf's foot and pig's foot, because, though some dishes lend themselves well to packaged unflavored gelatin, in others it produces an inferior result. For the *Petti di pollo allo specchio* (Rolled Chicken Breast in Aspic), for example, a fresh aspic made with real meat is the difference between an ordinary and an exceptional dish.

And a great revelation is the original fruit *gelatina* (*Gelatina dolce di frutta*) dessert made with fresh fruit juice and with the gelatin from a calf's foot. This ancestor of the banal and lowly artificially-flavored gelatin so omnipresent today is quite a different matter. Try the original and you will understand better why this dish was taken seriously by our ancestors.

On the other hand, dessert cream molds are better with the unflavored product. The best and most traditional type of gelatin for this kind of dessert, such as the *Bavaresi*, is the fish gelatin or isinglass, available in sheets, which dissolves without boiling liquid. These are now usually imported from Germany, and their availability should be encouraged, as they produce a lighter result than the packaged unflavored powder. These fish gelatin sheets can usually be obtained in ethnic German specialty shops.

Colla di Pesce
ISINGLASS OR FISH GELATIN

1. For light molded desserts like *Bavaresi*, these sheets of gelatin made from the dried bladder of certain fish, particularly sturgeon, are used in Italy. They produce a very smooth and light mold without graininess. Fish gelatin dissolves easily, and most important, it dissolves evenly and smoothly by first soaking the sheets in cold water, then squeezing them and adding them to the hot, but not necessarily boiling, liquid. Packaged gelatin powder, more available here, requires careful attention to dissolve it smoothly. It is best to first put the powder in a small bowl and pour 2 tablespoons of cold water (for each tablespoon of gelatin powder) over it. Do not stir the water into the gelatin, but allow it to swell. Then the swollen gelatin can be added to the boiling liquid. (I owe this method of dissolving the packaged gelatin to Helen McCully.) At that point, the gelatin should be well stirred to dissolve completely and to avoid graininess.

Both of these gelatins must be allowed to cool before mixing them with such cold ingredients as

whipped cream or pastry cream. Neither, however, takes the place of the *gelatina* made from calf's foot that is used for aspic. Fish gelatin is also useful when you need to put *gelatina* into a custard or *zabaione* which must not reach a boil.

HOW TO PREPARE GELATINA (ASPIC)

Here are illustrations of the steps in making an aspic using the ingredients for a good broth using a calf's foot, pig's foot, and chicken neck to produce the gelatin. Following this are the steps for clarifying and coloring it. The aspic is used in two of the following recipes, as well as to "veil" the mold in a third. The recipe is for a beef-flavored aspic included here but chicken, pork, and fish are also used for dishes appropriate to them.

10 cups cold water
2 pounds beef (any cut good for boiling)
1 medium-sized calf's foot
1 pig's foot
1 chicken neck
1 medium-sized carrot
1 celery stalk
1 small red onion
1½ tablespoons coarse-grained salt
¼ pound lean boneless veal, chopped (optional)
3 extra large egg whites
From 1 to 3 tablespoons dry Marsala

YIELD: 3 CUPS APPROXIMATELY

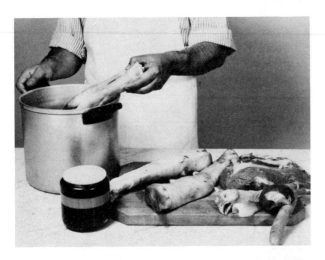

1. Put the water, beef, calf's foot, pig's foot, chicken neck, carrot, celery, and onion into a large stockpot. Bring to a boil over medium heat, then add the salt and simmer half covered for about 4½ hours.

Strain the broth through a heavy cheesecloth into a large bowl and let it cool (1 to 2 hours). Then cover the bowl and refrigerate it for 4 to 6 hours, or until it solidifies.

2. With a spatula remove all the fat on top of the *gelatina*. (Remove last bits with a paper towel.) To clarify the aspic, begin by adding the egg whites to the cold *gelatina*

3. and mix the two together with a wire whisk. Add the veal if used.

4. Transfer the *gelatina* to a saucepan, and add the amount of Marsala you need to get the desired color. (This is an alternate way to coloring with the caramelized sugar.)

5. Place the pan at the edge of the burner, bring to the simmering stage, half cover, and simmer for about 10 minutes, or until eggs with impurities rise to the top and broth becomes transparent.

433

Wet a cheesecloth and put it in the freezer.

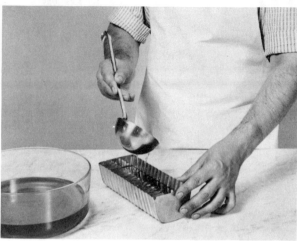

6. Line a colander with heavy cheesecloth and put the colander into a large bowl. Ladle the contents of the pan through the cloth. The liquid *gelatina* passing through will be absolutely transparent and the solid part of the cooked egg whites, with all the impurities, will remain in the cloth. Wet the molds with cold water.

7. Pour the liquid *gelatina* into whichever molds you are using for the particular dish to be made.

Refrigerate the molds for at least 6 hours, or until firm. When the *gelatina* is ready, hold a serving dish upside down tightly over the mold and reverse the plate and mold together.

8. Wet a towel with hot water and squeeze it out. Place the hot towel over the reversed mold. Repeat the procedure with the hot towel until the *gelatina* detaches itself from the mold.

9. Lift off the mold.

10. Two molds of *gelatina* with different shades of color (containing different quantities of Marsala).

434

Petti di Pollo allo Specchio

ROLLED CHICKEN BREAST IN ASPIC

FROM NORTHERN ITALY

This dish, literally translated as "chicken in the looking glass," gets its name from the slices of rolled stuffed chicken breast placed under a clear reflecting aspic. The mold may be a large one of arranged slices or there may be small individual molds of single slices. It can be served as a refreshing summer main course.

1 whole chicken breast (from a 3½-pound chicken)   SERVES 2

For the stuffing:
1 Italian sweet sausage without fennel seeds (about 3 ounces), or about 3 ounces of
  ground pork
4 ounces ground veal shoulder
1 ounce prosciutto or boiled ham
1 sage leaf, fresh or preserved in salt
2 whole extra large eggs
2 tablespoons freshly grated Parmigiano
Salt, freshly ground black pepper, and freshly grated nutmeg

For poaching:
10 cups cold water
1 medium-sized carrot
1 small red onion
1 celery stalk
5 sprigs Italian parsley
1 bay leaf
1 whole clove
Coarse-grained salt

Plus:
1½ cups cold liquid homemade gelatina (see page 432)

Bone and skin the chicken breast, dividing it into two individual halves. Butterfly and open them like *braciola* (page 237).

Prepare the stuffing. Remove the skin from the sausage and put the sausage in a bowl with the ground veal. Finely chop the *prosciutto* together with the sage leaf on a board. Add the chopped ingredients to the bowl along with the eggs and Parmigiano. Mix very well, adding salt, pepper, and nutmeg to taste.

1. Place half of the stuffing on each piece of chicken breast.

2. Roll up the two half breasts. Wrap each individual roll in cheesecloth and tie it like a salami (page 245).

Prepare the cooking broth. Pour the cold water into a stockpot. Add the carrot, onion, celery, parsley, bay leaf, and clove to the water. Bring to a boil and add coarse-grained salt to taste. Then add the chicken breast rolls. Cover and simmer for about 30 minutes. Remove the rolls from the broth and let them cool (about 2 hours). Unwrap the rolls and

3. cut them into slices about 1 inch thick. Place the slices on a serving dish, if you are making one large mold. (For individual molds, see photo 6 below.)

4. Ladle enough *gelatina* (still in the liquid stage) over the slices to cover them and refrigerate the serving dish for about 6 hours.

5. Remove the serving dish from refrigerator and serve. The clarified *gelatina* is so transparent that it almost doesn't show up in the photo.

If you want small molds for individual servings, wet the molds with cold water and

6. make a layer of *gelatina* less than 1 inch thick. Refrigerate the molds for about 2 hours to set.

7. Place a slice of the chicken breast rolls on top of the solid *gelatina* in each mold,

8. then add more liquid *gelatina* to cover the chicken. Return to the refrigerator to completely solidify (about 2 hours more).

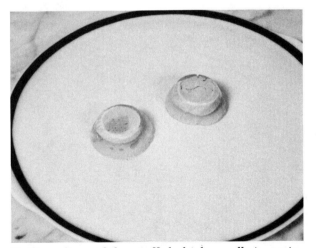

9. Two slices of the stuffed chicken rolls in aspic, unmolded.

NOTE: The chicken breasts could also be eaten hot, accompanied by a warm sauce, such as Brain Sauce (page 96) or Tomato Sauce (page 447).

437

Sformato di Maionese

MAYONNAISE MOLD

FROM NORTHERN ITALY

The combination of a mold of freshly made *maionese*, rich with green virgin olive oil, mixed with homemade aspic, changes a simple dish, such as poached fish or boiled meat, into something elegant.

2 extra large egg yolks, very fresh, at room temperature   SERVES 8
Scant 2 cups virgin olive oil
1 tablespoon freshly squeezed lemon juice
Salt to taste
1 cup cold liquid homemade gelatina *(page 432)*

To serve:
About 30 small pickle sottoaceti *(page 436)*

HOW TO PREPARE MAIONESE

1. Place the egg yolks in a crockery bowl. Use a wooden spoon to mix them slowly, always stirring in the same direction, in a smooth rotation.

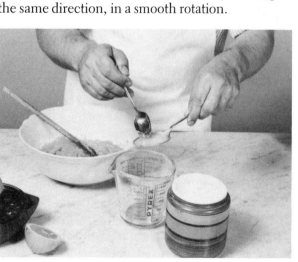

2. When the yolks are well mixed, add the first drop of olive oil and stir slowly until it is absorbed.

Continue to stir slowly, always in the same direction, adding more oil, a few drops at a time, and only adding oil when that already present is well absorbed.

As the emulsion begins to thicken, add more oil a few drops at a time. Be careful not to add too much, too soon. At this point it should begin to resist as you stir, and the mixture should be quite thick. When all the oil is added and the emulsion is perfect,

3. dissolve the salt in a tablespoon full of lemon juice, with a smaller spoon.

438

4. Slowly add the salted lemon juice to the *maionese* while stirring thoroughly. When the *maionese* is finished, moisten a scalloped mold with cold water.

5. Slowly add the liquid *gelatina* to the *maionese*, stirring continuously

6. and homogenizing the *gelatina* with the *maionese*. Pour the *maionese-gelatina* mixture into the mold and refrigerate it for at least 6 hours.

7. Unmold the *sformato* onto a serving dish

8. and arrange the *sottoaceti* all over the mold. Serve immediately as an accompaniment to poached fish or meat.

Sformato or Budino di Pollo

CHICKEN BUDINO

FROM VENICE

A mousse-like *budino*, beautiful, rich, and still faithful to the taste of its main ingredient. It molds without gelatin and can be further elaborated by making a thin "veil" or glaze of aspic over it, though it is perfectly fine without it. Any meat or fish *budino* may be made with a "veil" both for an elegant presentation and to keep it fresh. The technique of "veiling" a mold is shown below.

SERVES 8 AS A MAIN COURSE,
12 AS AN APPETIZER

1 small red onion
1 small carrot
5 sage leaves, fresh or preserved in salt
1 tablespoon rosemary leaves, fresh, preserved in salt or dried, blanched
1 chicken, about 3 pounds
¼ cup olive oil
6 ounces (1½ sticks) sweet butter
½ cup dry red wine
Salt and freshly ground black pepper
1 cup unbleached all-purpose flour
4 cups milk
1 cup chicken or beef broth
5 extra large eggs
5 tablespoons freshly grated Parmigiano
6 tablespoons unseasoned bread crumbs, preferably homemade
Freshly grated nutmeg

Optional (for "veil"):
2 tablespoons cold liquid homemade gelatina (see page 432)

Finely chop the onion, carrot, sage, and rosemary together on a board. Wash the chicken carefully and dry it with paper towels.

Heat the oil and 3 tablespoons of the butter in a saucepan over medium heat. When the butter is completely melted, add the chopped ingredients and sauté for 5 minutes. Add the chicken and sauté until lightly golden brown all over (about 15 minutes). Pour in the wine and let it evaporate (about 10 minutes). Taste for salt and pepper.

Meanwhile, prepare the *balsamella* with the re-maining butter, the flour and the milk, following the directions on page 334. Season the *balsamella* with a pinch of salt. Transfer the sauce to a crockery bowl, pressing a piece of buttered wax paper over the sauce to prevent a skin from forming. Let the sauce cool completely (about 1 hour).

Heat the broth and add it to the chicken. Simmer for about 25 minutes. Transfer the chicken to a board. Save the cooking juice from the chicken for use later.

1. Use a fork and knife to remove all the meat from the bones.

2. Using the disc with large holes, coarsely grind the meat directly into the saucepan with all the left-over juice from the chicken. Add the eggs, Parmigiano, and bread crumbs to the cooled *balsamella* and mix very well. Incorporate all the sauce in the saucepan into the ground chicken, then add the *balsamella* mixture. Mix very well with a wooden spoon. Taste for salt, pepper, and nutmeg.

3. Butter a 3-quart tin-lined copper Turk's Head mold, or a 3-quart ring mold.

HOW TO PREPARE A BAGNOMARIA

Preheat the oven to 375 degrees and prepare a large ovenproof casserole with lukewarm water to make a *bagnomaria* for the mold. (If you use an aluminum casserole, put a slice of lemon in the water to prevent the pan from discoloring.) Pour the contents of the bowl into the mold and place the

4. mold in the *bagnomaria*. Bake in this slow moist heat for about 1 hour and 45 minutes. Remove from the oven and cool completely (for several hours) before unmolding onto a platter.

If you wish, serve the dish cold and veil it (that is, cover the mold with a very thin coating of aspic): First, unmold the cold *budino* onto a serving platter and refrigerate it, covered, until needed. Then moisten the cleaned and empty mold with cold water.

5. Put about 1 tablespoon of the cold liquid gelatin into the mold.

6. Roll the *gelatina* all over the inside of the mold so it is completely lined. Refrigerate the mold for about 2 hours. Again put another tablespoon of cold liquid *gelatina* in the mold, and completely line it. Refrigerate once more for 2 hours. Then gently return the *budino* to the mold and refrigerate it again for at least 6 hours.

7. Gently remove and unmold onto a serving dish as you would unmold a *gelatina* (page 434, photos 8 and 9).

8. A thin veil of aspic is covering the entire *budino*.

Gelatina Dolce di Frutta

ORANGE OR LEMON DESSERT ASPIC

FROM ALL OVER ITALY

This fruit-flavored aspic or gelatin is prepared the way it was originally made before the days of fast pre-packaged mixes. You may be skeptical of going to all this trouble to produce what may appear at first glance to be the result of a gelatin mix, but be assured that this is even further removed from its plebeian commercial descendant than homemade ice cream is from its imitation, or a crusty loaf from packaged white bread. Try it.

8 juice oranges
12 cups water
1 calf's foot
1 cup granulated sugar
2 drops vanilla extract
3 extra large egg whites

SERVES 12

One day in advance, squeeze 6 of the oranges and let the juice drip through a coffee filter. This is a very slow drop-by-drop process, sometimes taking many hours. Let the juice rest, covered, in the refrigerator. The following day, prepare the *gelatina* by putting the water, calf's foot, sugar, and vanilla into a stockpot. Simmer for about 5 hours. Then strain, cool, and clarify the gelatin, following the directions on page 432, adding the filtered orange juice with the egg whites (page 432). Pour the *gelatina* into moistened individual round molds and let it solidify. Slice the remaining oranges into slices 1 inch thick (about 12 slices).

1. Unmold the individual servings of *gelatina* on top of each of the 12 orange slices and serve.

HOW TO PREPARE BAVARESE

Bavarese, which means "Bavarian," is more probably the discovery of Italian and French chefs than of Bavarian ones, though these non-German chefs may have been working in the Bavarian court where Italian was the court language for a long time. This category of dish is so widely used in Italy that, whatever its origin, it has long been an integral part of Italian cooking. Although used more often for desserts, included here is also a non-sweet vegetable example. The custard cream base and the folding in of the whipped cream relate it to various types of ice cream, but instead it is molded with a little gelatin, and chilled but not frozen. The most popular of all *bavaresi* is the one flavored with orange cream. A *bavarese* should not be fluffy, but a tender though firm mold. Sometimes a light pastry is placed on the bottom, particularly when it is to be cut into small pieces for little coffee-time pastries.

The vegetable *bavarese* may be used as a *piatto di mezzo*. The green pepper produces a pastel green color with some little streaks of white from the folded-in whipped cream breaking the homogeneity. A red sauce, produced from either puréed red peppers or from tomatoes, is preferred as a color contrast. Both flavors combine well with that of the *bavarese* itself.

Bavarese al Marsala

(MARSALA-FLAVORED BAVARESE)

FROM TUSCANY

SERVES 8 TO 10

*About 12 sheets (about ⅔ ounce) fish gelatin (isinglass),
    or 2 packages unflavored gelatin (2 tablespoons)*
6 extra large egg yolks
10 tablespoons granulated sugar
1 cup dry Marsala
1 pint heavy cream
1 heaping tablespoon confectioners' sugar

Plus:
2 pints strawberries

1. Place the sheets of fish gelatin in a bowl of cold water and soak for about 5 minutes. (If using powdered gelatin, see page 432.)

Prepare the *zabaione* with the egg yolks, 6 tablespoons of the sugar, and the Marsala, following the directions on page 492. Stir the mixture continuously in the copper bowl on the double boiler until it is lukewarm.

2. Remove the sheets of gelatin from the soaking water, squeeze them, and add them to the insert. Keep stirring constantly, with a wooden spoon, always in the same direction. The gelatin will be completely dissolved in a few seconds. Just before it comes to a boil, the *zabaione* should be thick enough to stick to the spoon. Do not let it boil. Immediately remove the top part of the double boiler from the heat and stir the contents for 2 or 3 minutes longer. Then transfer the *zabaione* to a crockery bowl, cover and let cool completely (about 1 hour).

Prepare the whipped cream. Place a metal bowl and a wire whisk in the refrigerator until cold. Then whip the heavy cream with the remaining 4 tablespoons of granulated sugar and the confectioners' sugar until very firm.

3. When the *zabaione* is cool, add the whipped cream, gently folding it in with a wooden spoon in a rotating movement,

4. also rotating the spoon itself while turning.

When the *zabaione* and whipped cream are well amalgamated, wet a 2-quart loaf pan with a few drops of Marsala and pour the contents of the bowl into the mold. Refrigerate the mold for at least 6 hours, or until completely firm.

5. Unmold the *bavarese* onto a serving platter. Arrange the strawberries around the base and on top of the *bavarese* and serve.

Bavarese all' Arancia

ORANGE CREAM *BAVARESE*

FROM ALL OVER ITALY

SERVES 8 TO 10

4 cups plus 4 tablespoons milk
About 18 sheets (almost 1 ounce) fish gelatin (isinglass),
*   or 3 packages unflavored gelatin (3 tablespoons)**
1 piece orange peel
6 extra large egg yolks
11 tablespoons (½ cup plus 3 tablespoons) granulated sugar
Grated rind of 1 small orange
4 or 5 drops vanilla extract
1 pint heavy cream
1 heaping tablespoon confectioners' sugar

Pour the quart of milk into a saucepan. Add the orange peel. Bring the milk just to a boil, stirring with a wooden spoon. Simmer for 3 or 4 minutes. Then remove the saucepan from the heat and let the milk cool (about 1 hour).

When the milk is cool, begin to make the custard cream by putting the egg yolks, 8 tablespoons of the sugar, the grated orange rind, and vanilla in a crockery bowl. Stir with a wooden spoon in the same direction, until the egg yolks are soft and the color is much lighter (about 10 minutes).

If you use fish gelatin, pour the 4 tablespoons of milk in a bowl of cold water and use the mixture to soak the sheets of gelatin. Then follow the directions on page 432. If you use the packaged unflavored gelatin, pour the 4 tablespoons of cold milk on top of the gelatin in a large crockery bowl to swell it.

Cook the cream, following the directions on page 489, adding the squeezed gelatin sheets when the cream is lukewarm, or pouring the already prepared custard cream on the swollen gelatin. Stir very well, then let stand until cold (about 1 hour).

Prepare the whipped cream. Place a metal bowl and a wire whisk in the refrigerator until cold. Then

* The fish gelatin should equal the weight of the unflavored gelatin.

446

whip the heavy cream with the remaining granulated sugar and confectioners' sugar until very firm.

Wet the inside of a 2-quart loaf pan completely with cold water. Gently fold the pastry cream into the whipped cream, using a wooden spoon, amalgamating all ingredients carefully but very well. Gently pour the contents of the bowl into the mold and refrigerate it for about 6 hours.

To unmold the *bavarese*, place the mold in a large pan of lukewarm water for 2 minutes, then unmold by putting an inverted serving platter on top of the mold and turning both upside down. Slice the *bavarese* like a cake to serve.

Bavarese di Peperoni

GREEN PEPPER BAVARESE

FROM FERRARA

SERVES 8 AS VEGETABLE,
14 AS APPETIZER

For the tomato-butter sauce:
3 cups canned plum tomatoes with juice,
preferably imported Italian tomatoes
4 tablespoons sweet butter
Salt and freshly ground black pepper

For the *bavarese*:
Coarse-grained salt
3 green peppers
2 tablespoons sweet butter
Salt and freshly ground black pepper
4 extra large egg yolks
½ cup cold milk
About 12 sheets (⅔ ounce) fish gelatin (isinglass),
or 2 packages unflavored gelatin (2 tablespoons)
½ pint of heavy cream

Prepare the sauce. Pass the tomatoes and the juice through food mill and pour the sauce into a small saucepan. Add the butter to the pan and heat over medium heat. Simmer for about 30 minutes. Taste for salt and pepper. Then transfer the sauce to a crockery bowl and let stand until cool. Cover and refrigerate until needed.

Prepare the *bavarese*. Bring large pot of water to a boil. Add coarse-grained salt to taste. Wash the peppers and add them to the boiling water. Cook for 25 minutes. Remove the peppers from the pot and cool them under cold running water. Remove the skin, stems, ribs, and seeds and cut the peppers into small pieces. Pass the peppers through a food mill, using the disc with small holes. Pour the purée into a small saucepan. Add the butter and heat the purée over low heat. Taste for salt and pepper and simmer for about 15 minutes. At that point a very smooth cream should have formed. Transfer the pepper cream to a crockery bowl and let it stand until completely cold (about 30 minutes).

Put the egg yolks in a crockery bowl, add a pinch of salt, and mix with a wooden spoon until they turn a lighter color. Add the cold milk slowly, mixing steadily. Then add the cooled pepper purée and mix very well. Prepare the pepper custard, incorporating the fish or powdered gelatin, following the directions on page 432. Let the custard cool for about 40 minutes, but do not refrigerate.

Prepare the whipped cream. Place a metal bowl and a wire whisk in the refrigerator until cold. Then whip the heavy cream.

447

Lightly oil a 2-quart loaf pan or 8 individual small molds.

Fold the whipped cream into the custard with a wooden spoon, using a rotating movement, until the mixture is homogeneous. Pour the custard into the pan or molds and refrigerate until completely set (about 3 hours). Unmold onto a large serving platter or onto 8 individual dinner plates. Make a ring around the *bavarese* of the cold tomato sauce and serve.

For the alternate Sweet Red Pepper Sauce:
4 large sweet red peppers (not pimientos)
Coarse-grained salt
4 tablespoons sweet butter
Salt and freshly ground black pepper

Clean the red peppers, removing the stems and seeds. Cut the peppers into strips. Bring a large pot of water to a boil. Add the peppers and coarse-grained salt to taste. Boil for about 15 minutes. Remove the peppers and cool them under cold running water. Then follow the instructions given above for the sauce, substituting the boiled peppers for the canned tomatoes. The sweet red pepper sauce may also be used as the sauce for fresh *tagliatelle* or for a light dried pasta, such as *spaghettini*.

Monte Bianco

MOLDED PURÉE OF FRESH CHESTNUTS

FLORENTINE VERSION

In Italy, a *Monte Bianco* is always made with fresh chestnuts. Chestnut trees grow plentifully there, and Italy exports many of the chestnuts used in other countries. Canned chestnut purée is neither necessary nor popular there and it makes sense to restrict this dish to the fall and winter seasons when fresh chestnuts are available. In any case, recipes using them are more appropriate at that time. The popular Florentine form of the *Monte Bianco* is molded, making a more imposing presentation than the riced chestnut purée in individual servings which is used in some areas.

4 pounds fresh chestnuts, the large Italian type, with shell
Coarse-grained salt
5 cups milk
Pinch of salt
About 5 drops vanilla extract
½ cup light rum
2 tablespoons unsweetened cocoa powder
1 pound (4 cups) plus 4 tablespoons granulated sugar
3 tablespoons sweet butter
2 cups heavy cream
2 teaspoons confectioners' sugar

SERVES 12

Soak the chestnuts overnight in a large bowl of cold water. Bring a large pot of water to a boil. Then add coarse-grained salt to taste and the soaked chestnuts. Boil until the chestnuts are completely cooked (about 2 hours). Drain the chestnuts and peel them while they are still hot.

1. With a paring knife make a cut at the flat bottom side of the chestnut.

2. Use a knife to lift off all the sections of the shell.

3. A shelled chestnut.

4. Remove the inside peel attached to the nut.

Put the milk in a large saucepan and add a pinch of salt and the peeled chestnuts. Place the pan over medium heat and simmer for about 25 minutes, stirring occasionally to be sure chestnuts do not stick to the bottom. Remove from the heat and pass the chestnuts and milk through a food mill into a large casserole. Add the vanilla extract, rum, cocoa powder, and 1 pound of granulated sugar to casserole. Bring to a simmer over low heat, stirring constantly with a wooden spoon, mixing all the ingredients together well. Then add the butter, still stirring, until a thick paste is formed. Remove the casserole from the heat and let it cool for at least 2 hours.

Lightly butter a 3-quart ring mold and pour in the chestnut paste. Smooth the surface with a rubber spatula. Then wrap the mold in aluminum foil and refrigerate for at least 4 hours. Also chill a metal bowl and whisk to be used for whipping the cream by placing them in the refrigerator.

When the mold is to be removed from the refrigerator, whip the heavy cream using the chilled metal bowl and wire whisk, adding the remaining granulated and confectioners' sugars. Unmold the *Monte Bianco* onto a large serving platter. Arrange whipped cream over the ring like a snow-capped mountain.

5. The final product.

CHAPTER 18

Pastries

PUFF PASTRY *(Pasta Sfoglia* or *Sfogliata)*

Following are illustrations of the Italian method of making puff pastry, including the *giri* (see page 454) so often mentioned in Italian cookbooks. In Florence, its place of origin, the pastry is used extensively for both "salted" (savory) and sweet dishes, that is for *antipasti*, main dishes, and desserts. Most often when used for a main dish it is in the form of a *turbante* or "vol-au-vent." I have found that this method was developed in Renaissance Florence (during the period of great scientific discoveries—it is documented as early as the fourteenth century) as a more efficient way of making thin flaky pastry like the phylo dough used by the Byzantines, and still used in areas that were touched by their culture. Certainly it is ingenious to have the layers separate in this way, rather than rolling each one individually to paper-thinness. (The method was so successful that it was adopted first in France and then all over western Europe.) With all its butter, it is a very rich pastry and, when used as a *turbante* it often has a rich filling, so portions need not be large. Certainly the filling for *Turbante ripieno* included here with kidneys, brains, liver, and mushrooms is a very concentrated one, but quite typical.

Puff pastry may also be made into tarts with fillings of a rich cheese, etc., to be eaten as *antipasti*, and, of course, with fruit for dessert pastries (usually eaten at coffee time in midmorning or late afternoon, rather than after dinner).

Perhaps the most splendid *turbante* I have had was completely filled with large fresh *porcini* mushrooms gathered when the hot sun came out after a rain, and flavored with fresh *nepitella*, that herb which is a wild mint cousin of catnip. It was served as a first course, but after that who would notice what the other courses were!

Pasta Sfoglia *or* Sfogliata

PUFF PASTRY

ORIGINALLY FROM FLORENCE C. 14TH CENTURY
NOW USED ALL OVER ITALY

Though it requires a long time to prepare, puff pastry is essential for certain classic dishes. It is also one of the great challenges to the cook and, when the layering causes the pastry to puff up in the oven, the satisfaction makes up for the several hours of preparation time required. A successful *pasta sfoglia* is extremely rich with butter but it is very light and flaky.

12 ounces (3 sticks) sweet butter   YIELD: 1 10-INCH TURBANTE
12 ounces unbleached all-purpose flour
½ cup cold water
3 or 4 drops lemon juice

Plus:
½ cup flour for rolling out dough
1 extra large egg

HOW TO PREPARE PASTA SFOGLIA

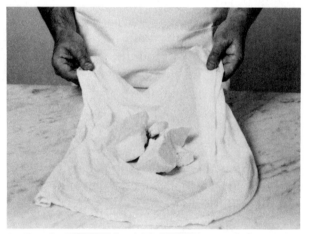

1. Put the butter in a dampened cotton dish towel.

2. Wrap it up and soften by working it with your hands. Let it rest while you make the first dough with water and lemon juice.

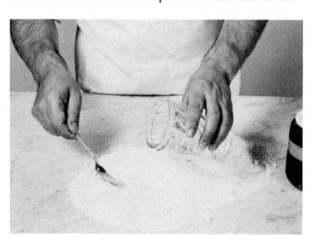

3. Place the flour in a mound on a marble surface and make a well. Pour in the water and the lemon juice. Mix with a fork, incorporating as much of the water as the flour will absorb to make a soft dough. Leave this first dough to rest. Less than 1 cup of flour should be left unabsorbed.

4. Sift this remaining flour (as in the photo) to make the second dough.

5. Unwrap the softened butter and place it on the sifted flour.

6. With a metal pastry scraper start mixing the butter into the flour.

7. Rapidly finish incorporating the butter into the flour with your hands,

8. until the texture is homogeneous. Form the dough into an almost rectangular shape.

9. The two doughs, one with water and the other with butter, should match in softness and elasticity.
Wrap the butter dough in wax paper and refrigerate it for about 25 minutes.

10. With a heavy rolling pin, roll out the water dough

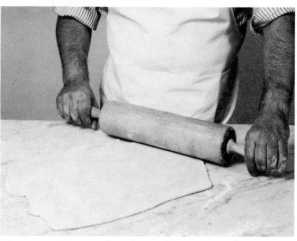

11. to a rectangular shape large enough to completely wrap the butter dough in.

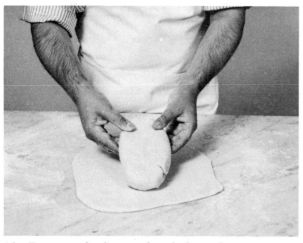

12. Remove the butter dough from the wax paper and place the butter dough vertically in the center of the water dough.

13. Fold over the sides of the larger rectangle,

14. so that one side slightly overlaps the other.

15. Fold over the two ends to enclose the smaller rectangle completely.

454

16. Use the rolling pin to gently stretch the "package" lengthwise until it is one-third longer.

Be sure that no holes develop in the dough and that the butter dough remains completely sealed inside the other and no butter shows through. It is necessary to lightly flour the table continually so that the moist dough does not stick to the table.

17. Fold the layer of dough lengthwise into thirds, first folding over the third on the far side of you,

18. then folding over the near side.

Wrap the dough in wax paper. (At this point in the classical Italian technique, you make a *giro* or turn of 90 degrees so that an open end is facing you. These 90-degree turns are the famous *giri* so often stressed in the Italian discussion of *pasta sfogliata*. But nowadays, we interrupt the classical movement to refrigerate the dough instead of leaving it in place to rest.) Refrigerate the dough for about 25 minutes, then return it to its former position.

19. Take the dough from the refrigerator and remove the wax paper. Put the dough back on the marble surface, with an open end facing you.

20. Roll out, again lengthening the dough by one third.

Repeat steps 17 through 20 four more times, each time turning the dough by 90 degrees and refrigerating it for 25 minutes before each repetition.

21. After the fifth *giro* gently roll out the dough until the dough is stretched to an even thickness of slightly less than ½ inch for the entire rectangle.

HOW TO PREPARE A LARGE TURBANTE (OR VOL-AU-VENT)

22. Using a pastry cutter cut out two equal circles of the size required. The diameter varies according to the size desired.

23. Cut a smaller circle out of the inside of the second disc, lift it out, and discard it.

The proportion of the diameter of this second disc varies depending on the type of *turbante*. (For example, with a fruit filling, the border should be thinner than with a savory filling.)

Fit the pastry ring obtained onto the first (large) pastry disc, and place them on a buttered cookie sheet.

24. Brush the *turbante* all over with beaten egg and refrigerate for about 10 minutes.

Preheat the oven to 400 degrees. Place the cookie sheet in the oven and bake for about 20 minutes. The very cold pastry will puff up when it reacts to the intense heat of the oven. The height should triple and the pastry slightly resemble an open accordion as a result of the partial separation of layers.

25. Remove from the oven immediately. Carefully insert a knife about halfway into the bottom pastry along the inside of the ring. Cut all the way around and a disc of pastry will lift out easily, leaving the bottom pastry inside the ring about one half as thick, and the opening above it deeper.

Transfer the *turbante* to a rack and let it cool. It can then be filled with something exotic, such as wild mushrooms, or rich and concentrated, such as the recipe which follows.

Miniature *turbanti*, as dessert, may be filled with wine-poached fruit or fresh berries with or without pastry cream. In classical Italian cooking it is rare to find dishes wrapped and cooked in puff pastry as in Austria or France. The *turbante* presentation below is the usual one.

26. The stuffed *turbante*.

27. The inside pastry discarded from the second disc of the pastry may be cut into small pieces, and prepared the same way as in steps 22 through 25 above. Bake them for about 15 minutes.

28. After the pastries are baked and cooled they can be salted and served as appetizers with *aperitivi*. (They are not filled.) These little pastries are probably close to the earliest recorded puff pastry eaten with soups at the fourteenth-century Florentine court.

Turbante Ripieno

"STUFFED" TURBANTE

FROM FLORENCE

SERVES 6

For the *pasta sfoglia* pastry:
12 ounces (3 sticks) sweet butter
12 ounces unbleached all-purpose flour
½ cup cold water
3 or 4 drops lemon juice

Plus:
½ cup flour for rolling out dough
1 extra large egg

For the stuffing:
2 ounces dried porcini mushrooms
About 8 ounces veal kidney
1 small veal brain, about ¾ pound
6 chicken livers
1 small red onion
5 sprigs Italian parsley, leaves only
2 sage leaves, fresh or preserved in salt
2 juniper berries
1 clove garlic, peeled
4 tablespoons sweet butter
2 tablespoons olive oil
1 cup dry red wine
1 cup beef or hot chicken broth
Juice of ½ lemon

Prepare the pastry first, using the ingredients listed above, following the directions on page 452. Cut the disc to a 10-inch diameter. Cut out a smaller disc from the center about 6 inches in diameter, leaving a 2-inch ring of the second disc as a border.

Prepare the stuffing. Soak the mushrooms in a bowl of lukewarm water for about 30 minutes.

Clean the veal kidney (page 280) and cut it into thin slices (about ⅛ inch thick). Blanch the brain, following the directions on page 168, and cut it into 1-inch cubes. Cut the chicken livers into quarters.

Finely chop the onion and parsley together on a board. Wrap the sage leaves, juniper berries, and garlic in a small piece of cheesecloth and tie it with string like a package.

Heat the butter and oil in a small saucepan over medium heat. When the butter is completely melted, add the chopped ingredients and sauté lightly for about 5 minutes. Add the kidney and sauté for 5 minutes longer. Then add the wine and the aromatic herbs tied in cheesecloth. Let the wine evaporate very slowly (about 10 minutes). Drain the mushrooms and be sure that no sand remains attached to them. Add the mushrooms and the hot broth to the pan and simmer for 2 minutes. Then add the chicken livers and simmer for 3 minutes. Add the brains and taste for salt and pepper. Simmer for about 10 minutes longer. At this point, the stuffing should be ready. Remove the pan from the heat and discard the cheesecloth package. Add the lemon juice, mix well, and spoon the stuffing into the *turbante*. Serve immediately.

NOTE: The stuffing could be prepared in advance up to the point when you add the lemon juice. When ready to serve, reheat the stuffing and add the lemon juice.

Pasta Frolla Fragile

SHORT PASTRY MADE WITH HARD-COOKED EGG YOLKS

Of the versions of *pasta frolla*, short pastry, as used in Italy, this one is unique in that it uses hard-cooked egg yolks and a little water, in addition to the usual flour, shortening, sugar, and the more unusual variant ingredients. It is called *fragile* and is indeed more difficult to handle than other types. The pastry is then used, without being prebaked first, as a crust for a tart to be filled with attractive whole fresh chestnuts and pastry cream, the *marronata*. The pastry may also be used (without prebaking) to make a vegetable or meat tart.

YIELD: MAKES ENOUGH
CRUST TO COVER THE
BOTTOM OF A 14- x 1¼-INCH
PIE OR PIZZA PLATE, A
14- x 1-INCH TART PAN, OR
A 14-INCH LAYER CAKE PAN
WITH REMOVABLE BOTTOM

16 ounces unbleached all-purpose flour
6 ounces (1½ sticks) sweet butter
6 ounces granulated sugar
1 extra large egg
Grated rind of 1 orange
Pinch of salt
5 hard-cooked extra large eggs
About ½ cup cold water

Arrange the flour in a mound and make a well in it.

Cut the butter into about 6 pieces.

HOW TO PREPARE PASTA FROLLA FRAGILE

1. Put the butter, sugar, the whole egg, grated orange rind, and salt into the well.

Remove and discard the whites from the eggs.

2. Add the hard-cooked egg yolks, one by one, mashing them with a fork (or passing them through a sieve) and mixing them together with the other ingredients in the well.

When all egg yolks have been added the well will be filled in.

3. Mix the contents of the well together with your hands until most of the flour is amalgamated with the other ingredients.

Make a new well in the center of the amalgamated ingredients.

4. Pour the water into the well

5. and mix in almost all the remaining flour with the already amalgamated ingredients, kneading until

6. a ball of dough is formed (about 5 minutes).

7. There should be just a small amount of flour left unincorporated.

461

8. With a scraper loosen the pastry from the board and

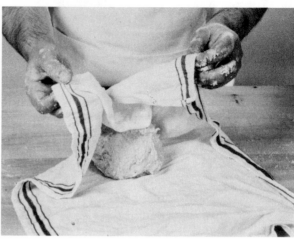

9. place it in a dampened cotton towel.
   Wrap up the towel and let the pastry rest for about 1 hour in a cool place (do not refrigerate). Lightly flour a piece of wax paper. Unwrap the dough and place it on the wax paper.

10. Lightly flour the rolling pin, and roll the dough out

11. into a round sheet of pastry less than ½ inch thick and about 16 inches in diameter.
    Butter the type of pan desired.

12. Holding the wax paper at one end, flip it over with its attached pastry

13. onto the prepared pan.

14. Remove the wax paper from the pastry by lifting it off, and gently fit the pastry into the pan. It is now ready to be filled.

Marronata

CHESTNUT TART

FROM SIENA

SERVES 8 TO 10

For the *pasta frolla fragile:*
16 ounces unbleached all-purpose flour
6 ounces (1½ sticks) sweet butter
6 ounces granulated sugar
1 extra large egg
Grated rind of 1 orange
Pinch of salt
5 hard-cooked extra large eggs
About ½ cup cold water

For the pastry cream:
4 extra large egg yolks
6 tablespoons granulated sugar
2 heaping teaspoons potato starch or cornstarch
1 cup cold milk
Small piece of orange peel

Plus:
1 pound large Italian chestnuts, boiled, peeled, and left whole (page 448)
¼ cup unsweetened cocoa powder
¼ cup granulated sugar

Prepare the crust with the ingredients listed above, following the directions on page 459.

Prepare the pastry cream with the ingredients listed above, following the directions on page 489.

463

HOW TO PREPARE MARRONATA

1. Make a layer of the peeled chestnuts on the pastry lining the bottom of the pan to be used. Preheat the oven to 375 degrees.

2. Sprinkle the cocoa powder and then the sugar over the chestnuts.

3. Use a spoon to cover the chestnuts with the cooled pastry cream.

4. With a pastry cutter, cut off the overhanging pastry flush with the rim all around the pan.

Place the pan in the oven and bake for about 45 minutes. Check the *marronata* after 15 minutes; if chestnuts are getting brown and dried, cover the top with aluminum foil.

5. Remove the pan from the oven, then transfer the *marronata* to a rack, and let it cool for a few minutes.

6. Transfer the *marronata* to a serving dish and slice like a pizza or cake to serve.

Pasta Frolla

SHORT PASTRY

Fruit tarts generally require a fully or partially prebaked crust. The tart recipe that follows uses a type of short pastry crust (*pasta frolla*) that does not call for hard-cooked egg yolks and which must be prebaked.

8 ounces unbleached all-purpose flour
4 ounces (1 stick) sweet butter
1 tablespoon granulated sugar
Pinch of salt
1 to 2 tablespoons cold water

YIELD: ENOUGH CRUST TO COVER THE BOTTOM OF A 10- x 1¼-INCH PIE PLATE, AN 11 x 1-INCH TART PAN, OR A 10-INCH LAYER CAKE PAN WITH REMOVABLE BOTTOM

Melt the butter in the top of a double boiler and let it cool.

Put the flour in a mound on a pasta board and make a well in it. Put the sugar, salt, and the cooled butter into the well. Add the water and mix very well with a fork. Then incorporate the adjacent flour until only 2 or 3 tablespoons of flour remain. Knead for only 1 minute, just enough to make the pastry into a ball. Put the dough in a floured dish towel and let it rest in a cool place or on the bottom shelf of the refrigerator for 2 hours. Preheat the oven to 375 degrees.

Butter the pan. With a rolling pin roll out the *pasta frolla* between two pieces of wax paper to a thickness of less than ¼ inch and about 16 inches in diameter. Remove the wax paper from the top of the pastry and, holding the wax paper at one end, flip it over with its attached pastry onto the pan. Lift the wax paper from the pastry and gently fit the pastry into the pan. Use a knife to cut off any overhanging pastry at the top of the pan. Fit a sheet of wax paper or aluminum foil (shiny side down) loosely over the pastry, then put the dried beans on the wax paper to keep the shape of the shell while it bakes. Bake for about 45 minutes. Once the crust is baked, remove the wax paper with the beans and return the crust to the oven for about 15 minutes, or until even the inside part of the crust is a light golden brown. Let the crust stand until needed.

Torta di Pesche alla Crema

STUFFED PEACH TART

FROM MILAN

This tart is filled with fresh peaches that are stuffed with a paste made from ground almonds, pistachios, and Marsala, and then covered with a pastry cream custard and fruit syrup. A good finale for an ambitious dinner.

Use a 10- x 1¼-inch pie plate, an 11- x 1-inch tart pan, or a 10-inch layer cake pan with a removable bottom.

For the *pasta frolla* crust:
8 ounces unbleached all-purpose flour
4 ounces (1 stick) sweet butter
1 tablespoon granulated sugar
Pinch of salt
1 to 2 tablespoons cold water
About 2 pounds dried beans (for weighting down crust)

SERVES 6

For the stuffing:
6 freestone peaches, medium or large, ripe but not overripe
1 cup dry white wine
1 cup granulated sugar
1 small piece orange peel
About 12 small amaretti cookies
2 ounces unblanched almonds
1 tablespoon dry Marsala

For the pastry cream:
4 extra large egg yolks
6 tablespoons granulated sugar
3 teaspoons potato starch or cornstarch
1 cup cold milk
1 small piece orange peel

Plus:
About 5 fresh pistachio nuts

Prepare the crust with the ingredients listed above, following directions on page 465.

Prepare the stuffing. Wash the peaches carefully. Place the whole peaches in a saucepan and pour in the wine and enough cold water to cover them. Sprinkle with the sugar and add the orange peel. Put the saucepan over medium heat and bring the wine-water mixture to a boil. Cook until the peaches are tender but still firm (15 to 20 minutes). Remove the peaches from the boiling liquid and place them in a bowl of cold water. Return the saucepan containing the liquid from the cooked peaches to medium heat and simmer until a syrup is formed (about 1 hour). Then pour the syrup into a crockery bowl and let it cool completely. Discard the orange peel.

Peel the peaches carefully and cut them into halves, removing the pits. Dry the peaches on paper towels.

Meanwhile, prepare the pastry cream with the ingredients listed above, following the directions on page 489.

Blanch the almonds in boiling water (page 87) and blanch the pistachio nuts in boiling salted water in separate pans. Put the amaretti cookies and the blanched almonds *only* in the container of a blender or food processor and grind them finely. Transfer the ground mixture to a small bowl and incorporate the Marsala to form a paste.

Take each cooked peach and fill in the cavity left by the pit with the prepared paste. Make a layer of peach halves on the bottom of the cooled crust. Fit another peach half over each one already in place on the crust so that they resemble whole peaches. Pour the pastry cream, then the syrup, on top of each "rebuilt" peach. Coarsely chop the pistachio nuts on a board and sprinkle them over the peaches. Refrigerate the tart for about 30 minutes, then serve, cutting into six slices.

Pastiera

NEAPOLITAN EASTER CAKE

This Easter cake has its texture punctuated by the soft spring wheat kernels that are so appropriate to the season and the earth's return to fertility. So many of its ingredients, such as rose water, link it through the long centuries to a more primal joy in that season. The *pastiera* is adored by the Neapolitans who, for all the work involved in making it, keep the tradition tenaciously alive at Easter. However, it cannot be completely appreciated in the traditional way without a very thin and delicate *pasta frolla* covering, and absolutely *with* the wheat kernels, which are the core of its meaning. Many have tasted commercial travesties, but I have never seen anyone disappointed with the real thing. It's a magnificent survival of Naples' culinary traditions.

SERVES 8

For the stuffing:
4 ounces soft wheat kernels (from a health-food store)
10 cups cold milk
2 tablespoons plus ½ cup granulated sugar
2 tablespoons sweet butter
1 small piece lemon peel
2 or 3 drops vanilla extract
15 ounces ricotta
2 extra large eggs, separated
1 tablespoon rose water
2 teaspoons orange extract
¾ cup mixed glacéed citron and orange peel, cut into small pieces
Pinch of ground cinnamon

For the pastry cream:
3 extra large egg yolks
3 heaping tablespoons granulated sugar
2 teaspoons potato starch or cornstarch
1 small piece lemon peel
1 cup cold milk

For the *pasta frolla*:
3 ounces (6 tablespoons) sweet butter
7 ounces unbleached all-purpose flour
2 ounces granulated sugar
3 extra large egg yolks

Plus:
About ¼ cup confectioners' sugar

Prepare the stuffing. Soak the wheat kernels overnight in a large crockery bowl with cold water to cover. Next morning, rinse the wheat with cold running water. Drain well and let stand until needed. Put the milk, 2 tablespoons of the sugar, butter, lemon peel, and vanilla into a stockpot over medium heat. When the milk reaches the boiling point, add the soaked wheat and simmer for about 4 hours. At that time almost all the milk should be incorporated and the wheat kernels completely opened. Transfer the contents of the pot to a crockery bowl and cool completely (about 1 hour).

Meanwhile, prepare the pastry cream with the ingredients listed above, following the directions on page 489.

Prepare the crust with the ingredients and quantities listed above, following the directions on page 465. Wrap the dough in wax paper and place it in the lower part of the refrigerator for about ½ hour.

Put the ricotta, egg yolks, the remaining ½ cup sugar, rose water, orange extract, and the drained opened wheat kernels into a large crockery bowl. Mix thoroughly with a wooden spoon. Add the glacéed fruit, cinnamon, and the cooled pastry cream and stir well.

Preheat the oven to 350 degrees. Butter a 10-inch springform pan and roll out the dough on a piece of wax paper to a round layer about ⅛ inch thick.

Holding the wax paper at one end, flip the dough over the top of the springform pan and carefully line the inside of the form allowing the extra dough to overlap the edges.

Use a wire whisk and copper bowl to beat the egg whites until stiff. Then use a wooden spoon to carefully fold them into the stuffing. Pour the mixture into the dough-lined springform pan. Use a pastry cutter to cut off the dough at the level of the stuffing. Roll out the remaining pieces of dough, cut into strips (½ to ¾ inch wide), and make several vertical and horizontal lines with them over the filling. Place the pan in the oven and bake for 2 hours. Remove from the oven and sprinkle with confectioners' sugar. Let stand until cold (about 2 hours). Open the springform, transfer the *pastiera* to a large platter and serve. The dessert is even better if prepared one day ahead.

Pasta Briciolata

PÂTE BRISÉE

Pasta briciolata is the Italian counterpart to pâte brisée (the tender, buttery crust used for quiches and tarts), and may have originally entered Italy from France, as it appears first in the late seventeenth and eighteenth centuries, when French and Italian influence were most reciprocal. But the traditional Italian way of making it is a little different. We handle this dough quite a bit, and some, who are more familiar with methods that touch the dough less, are quite surprised that the result turns out well.

YIELD: ENOUGH CRUST TO COVER THE BOTTOM OF A 10- x 1¼-INCH PIE PLATE OR AN 11- x 1-INCH TART PAN OR A 10-INCH LAYER CAKE PAN WITH REMOVABLE BOTTOM

8 ounces unbleached all-purpose flour
4 ounces (1 stick) sweet butter
1 tablespoon granulated sugar
Pinch of salt
4 to 5 tablespoons cold water
About 2 pounds dried beans (for
*   weighting down the crust)*

HOW TO PREPARE PASTA BRICIOLATA

1. Sift the flour onto a board and arrange it in a mound. Cut the butter into pieces and place them over the mound. Let rest for ½ hour until the butter softens.

2. Start mixing the flour into the butter with your fingers.

3. Rub the flour and butter between your palms.

4. Then make a well and put in the sugar and salt. Add 2 tablespoons of water, mix with a fork, and keep adding the water until it is all absorbed.

5. Remove the paste that has stuck to the fork

6. and begin to form a ball with your hands.

7. Knead gently until a very smooth and elastic ball of dough is formed (about 2 minutes).

Slightly dampen a dish towel and wrap the ball of dough in it. Let it rest in a cool place or on the bottom shelf of the refrigerator for at least 1 hour.

Preheat the oven to 375 degrees. Butter the pan. Dust a board with flour. Unwrap the dough and knead it for 1 minute on the board.

Flour the board, then using a rolling pin, roll out the dough

8. into a layer less than ¼ inch thick and about 16 inches in diameter.

9. Roll the layer of dough on the rolling pin and unroll it over the buttered pan.

Gently press down the layer of dough into the bottom of the plate.

10. Cut off the dough around the top with a knife to remove any overhanging pastry. If using a tart pan, move the rolling pin over the pan in order to cut off the overhanging pastry.

11. Use a fork to make punctures in the pastry.

12. Fit a sheet of wax paper or aluminum foil (shiny side down) loosely over the pastry, then put the dried beans on the wax paper to keep the shape of the shell while baking.

13. Using a scissors, cut off the excess wax paper or aluminum foil all around. Then bake for about 40 minutes.

Remove from the oven and lift out the paper containing the beans.

14. Let the crust stand for about 15 minutes before using.

Torta di Pere

PEAR TART

This pear tart is unusual in that the pastry cream layer is placed over the poached pears and syrup and is then baked with them. The wine-colored pears are covered with a golden layer of custard when removed from the oven to cool.

For the *pasta briciolata*:
8 ounces unbleached all-purpose flour
4 ounces (1 stick) sweet butter
1 tablespoon granulated sugar
Pinch of salt
4 to 5 tablespoons cold water
About 2 pounds of beans (for weighting down crust)

For the stuffing:
4 to 5 Bosc pears, ripe but not overripe
3 cups dry red wine
¼ cup tawny port
½ cup granulated sugar
Small piece of lemon peel
Pinch of ground cinnamon

For the pastry cream:
3 extra large egg yolks
5 tablespoons granulated sugar
2½ teaspoons potato starch or cornstarch
¾ cup cold milk
Small piece of lemon peel

SERVES 8

Prepare and bake the pastry with the ingredients listed above, following the directions on page 474.

Prepare the stuffing. Peel the pears and cut them into eighths, removing the core. Place them in a bowl of cold water until needed. Put the wine, port, sugar, and lemon peel into a saucepan over medium heat. When the wine reaches the boiling point, drain the pears and add them to the saucepan. Sprinkle the cinnamon over the pears. Simmer for 15 to 25 minutes, depending on the ripeness of the pears. Then transfer the pears with a slotted spoon from the pan to a crockery bowl and let cool completely. Reduce the wine mixture until a syrup is formed (about 1 hour), then transfer the syrup to a second crockery bowl and let it cool completely. Discard the lemon peel.

Prepare the pastry cream with the ingredients listed above, following the directions on page 489.

Make a layer of the cooled poached pears and pour over them all but 1 tablespoon of the syrup and the pastry cream. Pour the remaining syrup in a thin stream over the pastry cream. Return the tart to the oven for 15 minutes longer, or until the pastry is firm. Remove from the oven and let rest for a few minutes, then transfer to a rack to cool. Transfer the tart to a round serving platter and serve, slicing like a pie.

Torta al Formaggio

CHEESE TART

This cheese-filled pastry is a useful dish for a meatless meal and contains both mozzarella and Parmigiano, bound together with eggs and *balsamella*. The crust (*pasta briciolata*) is a simple one of just butter, flour, and a little water, which complements the substantial filling.

For the *pasta briciolata*:   SERVES 8
8 ounces unbleached all-purpose flour
4 ounces (1 stick) sweet butter
Pinch of salt
4 to 5 tablespoons cold water
About 2 pounds dried beans (for weighting down crust)

For the stuffing:
8 ounces mozzarella
1 cup milk
4 ounces freshly grated Parmigiano
2 extra large eggs
Salt, freshly ground black pepper, and freshly ground nutmeg

For the *balsamella*:
4 tablespoons sweet butter
3 tablespoons unbleached all-purpose flour
2 cups milk

Prepare and bake the pastry with the ingredients listed above, following the directions on page 469.

While the dough is resting, prepare the stuffing. Cut the mozzarella into ½-inch cubes. Put the cubes in a small crockery bowl, pour the milk over them, and soak for about 1 hour.

Prepare the *balsamella* with the ingredients listed above, following the directions on page 334. Transfer the *balsamella* to a crockery bowl, pressing a piece of buttered wax paper over the sauce. Let cool for about 1 hour.

Drain the mozzarella and combine it with the cooled *balsamella*. Then add the Parmigiano, eggs, and salt, pepper, and nutmeg and mix very well with a wooden spoon so that all ingredients are well incorporated. Pour the contents of the bowl into the baked crust. Return the *torta* to the oven and bake for 20 minutes longer. Remove from the oven, transfer to a serving dish, and serve, slicing like a pie.

Pasta Mezza Frolla

SHORT PASTRY WITH MILK

This short pastry called pasta mezza frolla is a more flexible short pastry with some milk in the dough. This pastry can also be used for a variety of tarts, such as one filled with wild mushrooms.

4 ounces (1 stick) sweet butter
1 pound unbleached all-purpose flour
2 tablespoons olive oil
1 extra large egg
½ cup cold milk
Pinch of salt

HOW TO PREPARE PASTA MEZZA FROLLA

Prepare the crust with the ingredients listed above, following the directions below.

Arrange the flour in a mound and then make a well in the center. Put the olive oil and the egg in the well. Then start adding the cooled melted butter, then the milk and salt. Carefully mix together all the ingredients in the well with a fork, then start absorbing the flour from the rim of the well, little by little. Keep incorporating the flour until a smooth ball of dough is formed. Knead (page 410) until the dough is homogeneous and all but about 4 tablespoons of the flour are incorporated (about 15 minutes).

1. Wrap the dough in a dish towel and let rest for about 2 hours in a cool place (do not refrigerate).

Prepare the stuffing. Clean and fillet the eels (page 307). Then wash the fillets and cut them into 2-inch-long pieces. Put the eel pieces in a crockery or glass bowl. Squeeze the lemon with a lemon squeezer. Add the lemon juice, wine, thyme, and olive oil to the bowl with the eel pieces. Sprinkle salt and black pepper over the eel. Let the eels marinate for 1 hour.

Preheat the oven to 375 degrees. Butter a 14-inch-diameter and 1½ inches deep pizza pan.

Unwrap the dough and roll it out into a round layer about 17 inches in diameter and not thicker than ⅛ inch.

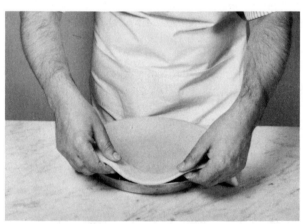

2. Line the inside of the buttered pan with the dough and lightly press down at the bottom of the pie plate. Do not cut off the overhanging dough at the top of the plate. At this point, proceed with the recipe (page 475).

Torta di Anguille

EEL TART

After the eels have been cleaned and filleted they are marinated and then the pieces are arranged in the crust.

The flavorful and delicate eels call for just this crust. The dish is a good introduction to the subtle flavor of eels for those who have been loath to try them. This eel tart is eaten hot as a main course or as an appetizer.

For the *pasta mezza frolla*:
4 ounces (1 stick) sweet butter
16 ounces unbleached all-purpose flour
2 tablespoons olive oil
1 extra large egg
½ cup cold milk
Pinch of salt

SERVES 6 AS MAIN DISH,
8 TO 10 AS AN APPETIZER

For the stuffing:
6 eels (about 2 pounds)
1 lemon
1 cup dry white wine
1 scant teaspoon dried thyme
2 tablespoons olive oil
Salt and freshly ground black pepper to taste

1. Use a slotted spoon to transfer the eel pieces from the bowl to the lined plate.

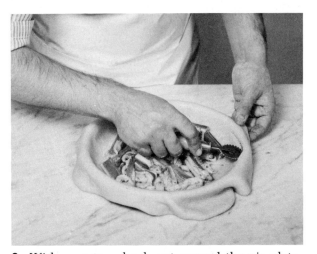

2. With a pastry wheel, cut around the pie plate, just less than ½ inch below the rim of the plate.

3. Ladle about 6 tablespoons of the marinade over the eel pieces.

Place the plate in the oven and bake for about 50 minutes.

Remove from the oven and allow to cool for a few minutes. Then transfer the tart to a serving dish.

4. Slice the tart and serve.

Bocca di Dama

ITALIAN SPONGE CAKE

This is one of the basic Italian sponge cakes used in the preparation of different desserts.

6 extra large eggs, separated
8 ounces granulated sugar
2 ounces unbleached all purpose flour
Grated rind of 1 lemon

HOW TO PREPARE BOCCA DI DAMA

Put the egg yolks in a crockery bowl. Add the sugar and mix with a wooden spoon for about 15 minutes, until the sugar is completely incorporated and the color of the egg yolks lightens. Add the grated lemon rind and mix well. Pour in the potato starch and the flour, little by little, in a light shower, mixing continuously with a wooden spoon.

Butter a round 10-inch-diameter cake pan. Preheat the oven to 375 degrees.

Beat the egg whites with a wire whisk in a copper bowl until stiff, then fold them into the batter gently. Pour the contents of the bowl into the pan and bake for about 45 minutes. Turn off the oven and let the baked sponge cake rest in the oven for 5 minutes before removing.

1. The baked *bocca di dama*. Let it rest until cool, then unmold it and let cool completely on a rack (about 3 hours).

This dessert (zuccotto) is even better if the *bocca di dama* is prepared one day in advance.

Prepare the stuffing. Coarsely grate the chocolate and cut the citron into small pieces. Mix the citron and the whole cherries together in a small bowl.

Put the butter, cocoa powder, 4 tablespoons of the sugar, and the water in a small saucepan. Holding the pan at the edge of the burner, stir with a wooden spoon until all the ingredients are amalgamated. Simmer for about 10 minutes; at that time a syrup should be formed. Remove from the heat and let cool.

Whip the heavy cream in a chilled metal bowl with the remaining 2 tablespoons of granulated sugar and the confectioners' sugar. Refrigerate the whipped cream until needed.

Zuccotto

HOMEMADE ZUCCOTTO

Zuccotto literally means "large pumpkin" in Italian and its vertical ribbing may refer to that, but Florentines prefer to think that this cake recalls the dome of their great cathedral. It is prepared by lining a mold with the light *Bocca di dama* or homemade spongecake with its brown crust left on to make the lines of the ribbing. (Do not substitute pound cake.) The filling consists of fresh whipped cream embellished with bits of chocolate and good glacéed fruit. Be sure the glacéed citron and cherries are of very high quality. (You can find a piece of a whole citron and unpackaged cherries in specialty stores.) Some commercial versions of *zuccotto* add nuts, which are not really part of the traditional recipe, and freeze the cream so that it may be packaged for a long life (not necessary when homemade). A true homemade version, which follows, does not have the mechanical straight lines in the ribbing as do the machine-cut commercial ones. (These latter are also lined evenly so that restaurants may easily cut them into portions.)

For the *bocca di dama* (Italian sponge cake):
6 extra large eggs, separated
8 ounces granulated sugar
Grated rind of 1 lemon
2 ounces potato starch
2 ounces unbleached all-purpose flour

SERVES 8

For the stuffing:
4 ounces sweet chocolate
4 ounces glacéed citron
4 ounces glacéed cherries
2 tablespoons sweet butter
1 tablespoon unsweetened cocoa powder
6 tablespoons granulated sugar
3 cups heavy cream
3 tablespoons cold water
1 teaspoon confectioners' sugar
½ cup light rum
¼ cup Maraschino (an Italian liqueur in which cherries are soaked to make the real maraschino cherries. It is available in the United States.)

HOW TO ASSEMBLE THE ZUCCOTTO

Cut the completely cold *bocca di dama* into slices ¼ inch thick and cut the slices in half. Lay the slices on a large serving dish (or two) and pour the rum and Maraschino over them.

Line a 10-cup *zuccotto* mold (nowadays a translucent plastic dome-shaped bowl of about 10 inches in diameter with plastic lid) with slices of the sponge cake, placed side by side vertically, so that the darker crust of the slices makes vertical ribs. Begin with the longer slices from the center of the round cake, which are long enough to line the mold from its center to the top of one side. The first ones may be too long and may have to be cut down to size. You should have enough of these large slices to completely line both sides of the mold. Then after filling it in, the shorter pieces may be used, as in photo 5.

Remove the whipped cream from the refrigerator and add the cooled syrup. Mix very well and

1. pour one third of the contents of the bowl into the *zuccotto* mold.

2. Place some of the cherries and citron over this and sprinkle with half the grated chocolate.

478

3. Keep making layers of whipped cream and

4. glacéed fruit with grated chocolate until the mold is almost full.

5. Cover the top of the mold with the remaining slices of soaked sponge cake which, when unmolded, will be on the bottom.

6. Cover the mold with its lid or wrap the mold completely with aluminum foil and refrigerate, *placing the mold upside down on the refrigerator shelf*, for about 5 hours.

7. Unmold the *zuccotto* onto a serving dish and serve.

Pasta Savoiarda/Savoiardi

HOMEMADE ITALIAN LADYFINGERS

Ladyfingers are a type of pastry which is shared by both French and Italian cooking. Their Italian name *savoiardi* reflects this, since Savoia is an area which has been part of both Italy and France, and was the place of origin of the former Piedmontese royal family of Italy. The Italian version achieves the lightness in the flour by mixing it with potato starch rather than the French method of sifting and using special cake flour. The oven temperature should not be too high or the pastries will dry out. They should emerge having risen a bit in the oven, but crisp. *Savoiardi* are used to make quite a number of Italian desserts, such as *Tiramisú*, page 44. *Pasta savoiarda* can also be used to make cakes.

6 extra large, separated eggs
8 ounces (1 cup) granulated sugar
4 ounces (1 cup) unbleached all-purpose flour
3 ounces potato starch (½ cup approximately)
Grated rind of 1 orange
Pinch of salt

Plus:
1 tablespoon granulated sugar

YIELD: ABOUT 50

Put the yolks and the whites into two separate large crockery bowls. Add the sugar and stir with a wooden spoon in a rotating motion until all the sugar is completely incorporated and the egg yolks are a very light color (about 15 minutes).

Mix the flour and the potato starch together and start adding the mixture to the beaten yolks in a slow steady stream, stirring continuously with a wooden spoon. Add the grated orange rind and stir very well.

Butter and lightly flour 2 cookie sheets with potato starch. Preheat the oven to 300 degrees.

Use a wire whisk to beat the egg whites stiff in a copper bowl, adding the pinch of salt. Gently fold the stiff egg whites into the batter. Scoop some of the batter into a pastry bag without a tip. Squeeze the batter out of the bag to form strips of batter about 3 inches long.

Sprinkle the tablespoon of sugar over the prepared strips of batter and let them rest for about 5 minutes before placing them on the middle shelf in the oven. Bake for 20 to 25 minutes, or until they are lightly golden brown. Remove from the oven, detach them with a spatula and transfer them to a rack to cool completely.

Cannoli

Perhaps the best known southern Italian pastry, *cannoli* is too often encountered in commercial versions that don't do it justice. With crisp freshly made shells, filled in the authentically Neapolitan way with cinnamon, rose water, and glacéed fruit flavoring the enriched ricotta, you will get the pastry at its best. There are many different sizes of *cannoli* molds on the market and they are often found in ethnic Italian specialty shops or most kitchen equipment stores.

For the stuffing:
1½ cups cold water
3½ tablespoons confectioners' sugar
15 ounces ricotta
1 tablespoon superfine sugar
Pinch of ground cinnamon
3 ounces glacéed citron
3 ounces glacéed orange peel
1 tablespoon rose water

For the *cannoli* pastry shell:
12 ounces unbleached all-purpose flour
3 extra large eggs
4 tablespoons sweet butter
About ½ cup dry Marsala

Plus:
About 1 quart vegetable oil (⅔ corn oil plus ⅓ sunflower oil)
4 tablespoons sweet butter
About ⅓ cup confectioners' sugar

Prepare the stuffing first. Put the water and 3 tablespoons confectioners' sugar into a heavy saucepan and simmer until a heavy syrup is formed (about 30 minutes).

Put the ricotta in a crockery bowl and, when the syrup is ready, add it to the bowl and mix together very well with a wooden spoon. Add the remaining confectioners' sugar and the cinnamon and mix well. Cover the bowl and refrigerate it for about 2 hours.

Cut the citron and orange peel into small pieces.

Remove the ricotta mixture from the refrigerator and strain it through a strainer into a bowl. Add the superfine sugar, rose water, and the glacéed fruit and mix very well. Cover again and refrigerate until needed.

Meanwhile prepare the shells. Arrange the flour in a mound on a pasta board and make a well in the flour. Separate 2 of the eggs. Place the 2 egg yolks and 1 whole egg and the butter in the well and add the Marsala. Save the egg whites for use later. Mix all the ingredients in the well with a fork until they are homogeneous. Incorporate almost all the flour little by little. Then start kneading the dough (page 410), until it is elastic and smooth (about 10 minutes). Let the dough rest, wrapped in a dish towel, for about 30 minutes in a cool place, or on the bottom shelf of the refrigerator.

1. Use a rolling pin to roll out a layer of dough into a square or rectangle on a floured pasta board. The thickness of the layer should not be more than ⅛ inch.

2. Cut the layer of pastry into strips with a jagged pastry cutter. The width of the strips should be a little less than the length of the *cannoli* mold.

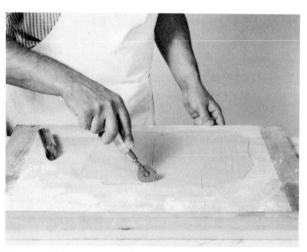

3. Cut the strips of the pastry layer into squares. Beat the remaining egg whites with a fork in a small bowl for 1 minute.

4. Turn a pastry square diagonally to resemble a diamond. Place the *cannoli* mold at one point and roll it

5. on the mold, being careful not to press the pastry with your fingers. Brush the opposite end of the diamond with beaten egg whites to seal the pastry together.

Heat the oil and butter in a deep-fat fryer over medium heat. When the butter is completely melted and the oil is heated to about 375 degrees, which is not quite as hot as for normal deep-frying, put in 3 or 4 *cannoli*.

6. Let the *cannoli* fry slowly until golden brown all over (2 to 3 minutes).

Prepare a serving dish by lining it with paper towels.

7. With a large strainer-skimmer, transfer the *cannoli* from the pan to the prepared serving dish and let cool completely (about 20 minutes).

8. To remove the *cannoli* from the mold, contract the mold by gently pressing it together at one end where the metal is not covered with pastry. The contracted mold will detach from the pastry and can be slid out.

Let the shells sit on paper towels to be sure all the grease is drained off.

9. Using a small spoon or pastry bag without a tip, fill each *cannolo* by inserting the stuffing into both open sides.

Transfer the *cannoli* to a serving dish and sprinkle the confectioners' sugar over them with a strainer.

10. The *cannoli* on serving dish with confectioners' sugar on top.

Pasta Soffiata

CREAM PUFF PASTRY/PÂTE À CHOU

This is one more of the techniques that moved *from* Italy to France.

2 cups cold water
Pinch of salt
1 heaping tablespoon granulated sugar
10 tablespoons (1¼ sticks) sweet butter
1 small piece orange peel
1¾ cups unbleached all-purpose flour
6 extra large eggs

HOW TO PREPARE PASTA SOFFIATA

Put the water, salt, sugar, butter, and orange peel in a heavy pan over low heat. When the water reaches a boil and the butter is completely melted,

1. remove the pan from the heat. Add the flour all at once

2. and mix thoroughly with a wooden spoon until all the flour is incorporated. Remove the orange peel.

3. Place pan back on the heat and cook, mixing without stopping, for a few minutes.

The result will be a ball of smooth dough. (Some think this resembles a cabbage, hence pâte à chou in French.)

4. Remove from the heat, transfer pastry to a bowl and cool for about 15 minutes.

5. Add the eggs, one at a time, mixing very well. Do not add another egg until the previous one is completely incorporated.

When all the eggs are incorporated, the pastry should be very smooth and homogeneous. Lightly butter a tin cookie sheet. Preheat the oven to 400 degrees.

6. Fill a pastry bag with the pastry.

7. Holding the pastry bag with one hand and squeezing the bag from the top part with the other hand, form the desired pastries.

Shape the pastries with about 1 tablespoon of the batter. Be sure to leave enough space between them. As you lift the pastry bag away after forming each pastry, a little tip of dough is left standing up. Push down that tip in order to have a uniform level to the top.

Place the cookie sheet in the oven for about 15 to 20 minutes. Do not open the oven for the first 10 minutes. The baking time is variable because oven temperatures fluctuate, and the temperature throughout the oven may be uneven. For this reason, the whole baking time may reach to an extreme of 1 hour. Reduce the oven temperature to 350 degrees and bake the pastries until they are lightly golden brown and crisp and dry inside. Turn off the oven and open the oven door partially. Let the pastries cool in the oven for about 50 minutes.

8. The pastries should be light, with a crisp crust outside, and dry on the inside.

Bongo

CHOCOLATE CREAM PUFF MOUND

FROM FLORENCE

Small cream puffs filled with pastry cream are arranged in rows into a mound on top of whipped cream which is then heavily covered with chocolate. A latter day "baroque" dessert, it nonetheless presently enjoys wide enthusiasm and popularity in this otherwise reserved city. For those who think Italian desserts are not rich enough, this confection will convince all skeptics otherwise. The making and filling of the cream puffs is illustrated below as well as the arrangement of the ensemble.

For the pasta *soffiata*:
2 cups cold water
Pinch of salt
1 heaping tablespoon granulated sugar
10 tablespoons (1¼ sticks) sweet butter
1 small piece orange peel
1¾ cups unbleached all-purpose flour
6 extra large eggs

For the pastry cream:
6 extra large eggs
8 tablespoons granulated sugar
1 heaping tablespoon potato or cornstarch
1½ cups milk
Small piece of orange peel

For the chocolate topping:
8 ounces semisweet baking chocolate
About ¼ cup milk

Plus:
1 cup heavy cream
1 tablespoon granulated sugar
3 teaspoons confectioners' sugar

SERVES 8

486

First prepare the cream puff pastry.

Meanwhile, prepare the pastry cream using the ingredients listed above, following the directions on page 490.

Bring some water to a boil in the bottom of the double boiler. Cut the baking chocolate into small pieces. Put the pieces and the milk in the top of a double boiler. When the water reaches the boiling point, put the insert in. Stir the chocolate and milk with a wooden spoon until the chocolate is completely melted. Transfer to a crockery bowl, cover, and let stand until cool.

Chill a metal bowl and wire whisk.

Transfer the baked pastries to a rack and let stand for about 15 minutes to cool completely.

Whip the heavy cream in the chilled bowl with the granulated and confectioners' sugar. Use a syringe to fill each pastry with the pastry cream. Arrange the filled pastries in a ring on a round serving dish. Fill the center of the ring with all the whipped cream and arrange the remaining pastries on the whipped cream to resemble a mound. Pour the cooled chocolate over the mound, cover the dish with aluminum foil, and refrigerate for about 2 hours before serving.

Pasta Genovese

GENOESE PASTRY

It may come as a surprise to some that "génoise" (a light sponge cake made of butter, sugar, eggs, and flour) means *Genoese*. In Genoa it is used to make both the simple *Torta genovese* molded cake, which is illustrated below (Italian cakes generally do not have icing). It is also cut into thin layers to make layer cakes. It is not traditional to roll it up into a log shape in Italy. *Pasta genovese* is more often eaten with midmorning coffee or with a sweet wine for afternoon guests than at the end of a meal.

3 ounces (¾ stick) sweet butter
6 ounces granulated sugar
4 whole extra large eggs
4 ounces unbleached all-purpose flour
Pinch of salt

YIELD: 1 SINGLE-LAYER CAKE

Preheat the oven to 350 degrees. Butter a round 9-inch cake pan or a large jellyroll pan and fit a piece of wax paper in the bottom. Butter the wax paper. (The cake pan is used generally when you wish to prepare a cake, the jellyroll pan when you wish to have several discs of the pastry. Baking time will change according to the thickness of the batter in the mold. Even preparing the same dessert, you will find a difference in texture between the pastry pre-

pared as a single cake and then sliced, and the one prepared as individual layers.)

Melt the butter in the top of a double boiler and let it cool.

Put a deep stockpot over medium heat with about 5 cups of cold water. There should be about 5 inches between the water and the bottom of the copper pan.

1. Fit the unlined round copper pan (*ponzonetto*) onto the stockpot. Add the eggs and the sugar.

2. Start mixing and beating with a wire whisk until the eggs are completely incorporated into the sugar and a very light foam is formed.

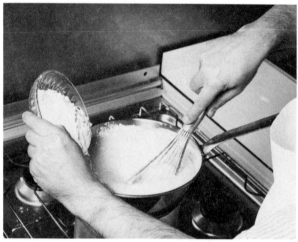

3. Add the flour a little at a time, always beating with the whisk

4. until a long ribbon is formed. Be sure that the insert is never more than lukewarm and that the water never reaches the boiling point.

Remove the insert from the stockpot, add the melted butter to the insert, and mix it through.

5. Transfer the batter from the insert to the prepared mold and bake from 15 to 35 minutes, depending on the thickness of the pastry.

Remove and cool. The simple unglazed cake is just sliced and served.

If the pastry is baked in a layer cake pan, it can be used to make filled cakes.

CHAPTER 19

Creams, Ice Creams, and Ices

PASTRY CREAM

The basic custard-like *crema pasticcera* forms the foundation for many desserts, from the pastry fillings which give it its name to sauces for fruit and the famous Italian ice cream *(gelato)*. It is made with egg yolks, sugar, and milk and is lightly thickened, preferably with potato starch or flour (both lighter and less starchy than cornstarch), by cooking over the steam of a double boiler. The insert with the pastry cream should not touch the boiling water but should only be heated by the steam. The technique of making the pastry cream is the same no matter what the amounts of the ingredients given in the individual recipes.

Coppe di crema zabaione alla parmigiana (Dessert Cups of *Crema Zabaione*, Parma Style) is a variant of *zabaione*, which is made with a similar technique in the double boiler. It may be used as a filling for pastry, or served as it is in the recipes included here, in dessert cups mixed with whipped cream.

A thinner cream mixed with a nectar made of fresh fruit makes a delicious sauce for poached fruit. The recipe here is for fresh figs or a number of other fruits.

Crema Pasticceria

CUSTARD CREAM

4 extra large egg yolks at room temperature
6 scant tablespoons granulated sugar
3 teaspoons potato starch, or flour, or cornstarch
1 cup cold milk
Small piece orange or lemon peel, or few drops vanilla extract

YIELD: 1½ CUPS

HOW TO PREPARE CREMA PASTICCERIA

Bring some water to a boil in the bottom of a double boiler.

1. Put the egg yolks into a crockery or glass bowl and add the sugar and potato starch. Stir with a wooden spoon, always in the same direction,

2. until the sugar and the potato starch are completely incorporated and the egg yolks turn a lighter color.

Slowly add the milk, then the orange peel, mixing steadily.

3. Transfer the contents of the bowl to the top part of the double boiler.

When the water in the bottom of the double boiler is boiling, insert the top part.

4. Stir constantly with a wooden spoon, always in the same direction. Just before it boils, the cream

5. should be thick enough to coat the spoon. That is the moment it is ready. Absolutely do not allow it to boil.

Immediately remove the top part of the double boiler from the heat, and continue to stir the contents for 2 or 3 minutes longer. Then remove the orange peel.

6. Transfer the *crema pasticceria* to a crockery bowl to cool (about 1 hour).

Crema pasticceria could be prepared several hours in advance and kept, covered in the refrigerator until needed.

VARIATION: To prepare a cream custard, follow the same recipe for pastry cream omitting the potato starch or cornstarch. It is served chilled in individual tea cups.

Coppe di Crema Zabaione alla Parmigiana

DESSERT CUPS OF CREMA ZABAIONE, PARMA STYLE

FROM PARMA

You will notice that an improvised double boiler is used in these photos: a round bottom copper utensil, lined or unlined, placed in a saucepan, is warmed by steam, not water. There are also commercial double boilers available made of stainless steel or other materials, but the advantage of this copper insert is that its bottom distributes the heat evenly. If you prefer a "normal" *zabaione*, without whipped cream, use 3 extra large egg yolks, 3 tablespoons of granulated sugar, and ½ cup dry Marsala and prepare it according to the directions below.

5 extra large egg yolks
5 heaping tablespoons granulated sugar
½ cup dry Marsala
¼ cup light rum

For the whipped cream:
1 pint heavy cream
2½ tablespoons granulated sugar
1 teaspoon confectioners' sugar

SERVES 8

491

HOW TO PREPARE ZABAIONE

Bring some water to a boil in the bottom of a double boiler.

Put the egg yolks in a crockery or glass bowl and add the sugar. Stir with a wooden spoon, always in the same direction, until the sugar is completely incorporated and the egg yolks turn a light yellow color. Then add the Marsala and rum slowly, mixing steadily. Transfer the contents of the bowl to the top part of the double boiler. When the water in the bottom part is boiling,

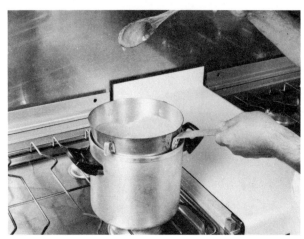

1. insert the top part. Stir constantly with a wooden spoon, always in the same direction.

2. Just before it boils the *zabaione* should be thick enough to coat the wooden spoon.

That is the moment it is ready. Absolutely do not allow it to boil. Immediately remove the top part of the double boiler from the heat and stir the contents for 2 or 3 minutes longer. Transfer the *zabaione* to a crockery bowl to cool (about ½ hour). Cover the bowl with aluminum foil and place in the refrigerator to cool completely. *Zabaione* may be left in the refrigerator up to several hours before mixing with the whipped cream.

Chill a metal bowl (stainless steel, not copper) and a wire whisk for preparing the whipped cream, as well as 8 individual dessert cups in the refrigerator for 1 hour.

HOW TO WHIP CREAM BY HAND

Pour the heavy cream into the chilled bowl. (You can also improvise a cold "double boiler" by placing the bowl with the cream in a larger bowl full of ice.)

3. Whip the cream with the whisk, using a continuous rotary motion from bottom to top, so that it's whipped evenly, until the cream is no longer liquid (about 1 minute).

At this point, to avoid any danger of the heavy cream turning to butter, add about 1 tablespoon of granulated sugar. Then continue whipping, adding the remaining granulated sugar and the confectioners' sugar, until the cream is quite thick (almost solid), but soft. Remove the *zabaione* from the refrigerator, and gently fold it into the whipped cream.

HOW TO FOLD WHIPPED CREAM IN

4. With a wooden spoon gently incorporate the *zabaione* in a slow rotating motion starting at the outside and

5. also rotating the spoon while

6. moving toward the center. Do not overmix.

When homogeneous, ladle the cream *zabaione* into a pastry bag with the tip of your choice. Refrigerate the bag for about 20 minutes. Remove the bag and cups from the refrigerator.

7. Holding the pastry bag with both hands, squeeze with the top hand.

8. Fill the cups by moving the pastry bag in a circular motion, moving from the sides toward the center.

Serve immediately or return to the refrigerator until ready to serve.

Fichi Giulebbati con Crema di Fichi

FIGS "NECTARED" WITH FIG-FLAVORED PASTRY CREAM

FROM NORTHERN ITALY

15 fresh figs, ripe but not overripe
2 cups dry red wine
½ cup tawny port
¼ cup light rum
¼ cup granulated sugar
2 or 3 pieces lemon peel

SERVES 6

For the pastry cream:
4 extra large egg yolks
4 tablespoons granulated sugar
1½ tablespoons potato starch or cornstarch
1 cup cold milk

Preheat the oven to 375 degrees.

Wash the figs carefully, but do not peel them, and put them in a small casserole, preferably of terracotta. Pour the wine, port, and rum over the figs. Sprinkle the figs with the sugar and add the lemon peel. Cover the casserole with aluminum foil. Make several punctures in the foil to allow the alcohol to evaporate. Place the casserole in the oven and bake for 25 minutes. Then transfer 3 of the figs to a dish and set aside, leaving the others in the casserole. Cover again, and bake for about 20 minutes longer, or until the figs are cooked but still retain their shape (baking time varies depending on the ripeness of the figs).

Remove the casserole from the oven and let stand, covered, for about 1 hour. Use a slotted spoon to transfer the figs to serving dish. Cover the dish with aluminum foil and allow the figs to cool completely. Pour the juice from the casserole into a small saucepan and cook over low heat until the wine mixture is reduced to a thick syrup (about 1 hour).

Meanwhile, prepare the fig pastry cream. Remove the skin from the 3 reserved figs and pass them

494

through a food mill. Be sure there are no seeds in the strained figs (use the fine strainer of the food mill). Prepare the pastry cream, following the directions on page 490, adding the strained figs to the egg-sugar-starch mixture just before adding the cold milk. Transfer the pastry cream to a crockery bowl, cover, and let it cool completely. When the syrup is reduced transfer it to a sauceboat.

Prepare individual servings by placing 2 figs in each dessert bowl with a ring of pastry cream around them and 1 tablespoon of the syrup poured over the figs.

VARIATION: This dish may be prepared with some other types of fruit. Always reserve about 6 ounces (approximately 3 plums, 3 or 4 apricots, 2 peaches, 1 pear), after partially cooking, to flavor the pastry cream. Listed below are the fruits which work well and their poaching times:

15 large plums: Use the same time as for the figs.
10 peaches or 15 to 18 apricots (if quite ripe): Use the same time as for the figs.
5 pears: Cook for 30 minutes, then remove 1 pear, and cook for an additional 35 minutes.

GELATI (ITALIAN ICE CREAMS)

The history of ice cream is a long and complicated one, but we can say with certainty that, again, it emerged in its present form in sixteenth-century Florence and was taken to France in that century during the time of Caterina de' Medici. Local tradition often connects the beginnings of production on a commercial scale with the figure of Buontalenti, the artist also famous for his ice sculpture. It was Procopio Coltelli (not Francisco [sic] Procopio, as incorrectly stated in *Larousse Gastronomique*), who created the fashion for both coffee and ice cream (or *sorbetti*) in Paris, when in 1672 he opened the first café for both of these novelties across from the Comédie Française Theatre. *Larousse* also mistakenly calls him a Sicilian rather than a Florentine.

We can trace more primitive forms of frozen drinks, mostly sweet, from the Arabic and Turkish sources of the word *sorbetto* and from references in eleventh- and twelfth-century Sicily. But the full picture is far from clear.* It is most likely that primitive forms of ice cream (in the form of frozen drinks) were brought to Sicily with the eleventh-century invaders from North Africa, following the time-honored routes of the Phoenicians and Carthaginians millennia before. The word *sorbetto*, however, probably entered the Italian language through the Venetians from the Turkish and the word was taken to France to become "sorbet" in the sixteenth and seventeenth centuries.

Basic ice cream or *gelato*, in such flavors as cream, chocolate, *zabaione*, nut, etc., is made with egg yolks and milk, much as a loose pastry cream, and is then placed in an ice-cream maker to churn. This differs from homemade American ice cream, which has no eggs and employs both milk and cream.

Fruit ice cream is traditionally made by starting with a sugar-water sirup mixed with pieces of fresh fruit made into a pulp. What I believe to be the trade secret of the best fruit ice creams is that they also use the pastry cream base instead of the traditional sirup. The fresh fruits most popular for Italian fruit ice creams are strawberries, especially wild ones, raspberries, blueberries, blackberries,

---

* *Larousse Gastronomique*, unlike most sources, mentions a Chinese origin without giving supporting evidence.

peaches, apricots, and melon. The very popular orange and lemon flavors are made with the juice of the fresh fruit, like American sherbets.

A third category is made without a machine, using whipped cream which is then frozen. They are variously called *semi-freddi* or *perfetti* (like the French "parfait").

The word *sorbetto* was originally a generic term meaning any kind of frozen dish, sweet or non-sweet. There exists a famous eighteenth-century treatise, *De' Sorbetti* by the Neapolitan physician Baldini, which includes many non-sweet types, along with a detailed discussion of the uses of these dishes for health purposes. The good and bad effects of iced dishes is still a serious topic of discussion among Italians, and, to this day, ice cream is served in small quantities, so that it can be eaten very slowly in order not to have a bad effect on digestion. Nowadays *sorbetto* is considered a category of *gelato* which is not too sweet, and which, in addition to the base of fruit or pastry cream, may contain whipped cream, liqueur, and egg white, and is frozen with or without using a machine. It is really a type of frozen mousse or *spuma*. A few non-sweet *sorbetti* remain, such as the one of Parmigiano. The final recipe is for *granita*, the Italian lemon "water" ice so popular in the summer.

Gelato di Frutta Fresca

ITALIAN FRESH FRUIT ICE CREAM

FROM ALL OVER ITALY

For the custard cream: SERVES 8
3 extra large egg yolks
6 tablespoons granulated sugar
½ cup milk

For the *gelato*:
About 12 ounces of fresh fruit, such as peaches, apricots, strawberries (small wild ones are best, if available), raspberries, blueberries, blackberries, figs, bananas, pears, cantaloupe, and watermelon
1 teaspoon confectioners' sugar
2 cups heavy cream
About 2 pounds rock salt

Prepare the custard cream with the ingredients listed above, following the directions on page 491. Let the cream rest, covered, until cold (about 1 hour).

Peel the fruit and cut it into small pieces no larger than ½ inch long or wide. Small berries, such as blueberries, raspberries, or wild strawberries, should be used whole. Larger berries should be halved.

Add the fruit to the cold custard cream. Then add the confectioners' sugar and the heavy cream. Mix all the ingredients together well.

HOW TO PREPARE GELATO

1. Pour the contents of the bowl into the insert of the ice-cream maker. [The ice-cream maker shown here (White Mountain) has a wooden canister with a metal can insert for the ingredients. The can must be surrounded by crushed ice and rock salt. Though the cream is churned electrically with a churn called a "dasher," the process and its result remain very close to that of the old-style hand-churned ice-cream maker.] Put the dasher into the center of the can and fit the opening of the lid onto the top of the dasher.

2. Put the can into the wooden canister, fitting it in place in the bottom cavity.

3. Fit the motor onto the frame-button holder on one side of the top of the canister and the latch on the other side.

4. Fill the space between the insert and the canister with ice.

5. Then, fill the spaces with rock salt,

6. and cover the top completely with it.

Start the motor and let run for about 45 minutes.

When turned off, detach the motor, lift off, and remove the insert. If the ice cream is not to be used immediately, place the insert in freezer. When ready to serve, remove the lid and

7. lift the dasher out. All the ice cream will be clinging to it.

8. Scrape the ice cream off the dasher with a wooden spoon and place in a bowl for serving.

498

Gelato di Riso

RICE ICE CREAM

FROM FLORENCE

½ cup raw rice, preferably Italian Arborio
3 cups milk
3 tablespoons granulated sugar
A small piece of vanilla bean
Pinch of salt

SERVES 8

For the custard cream:
3 extra large egg yolks
6 tablespoons granulated sugar
½ cup milk

Plus:
2 cups heavy cream
3 teaspoons confectioners' sugar
About 2 pounds of rock salt

Put the rice in a saucepan. Add the milk, vanilla bean, sugar, and salt and bring to a boil over medium heat, stirring constantly. Then simmer for about 12 minutes. Remove from the heat and let the rice cool completely (about 2 hours).

Pour the contents of the pan through a colander and drain off the excess liquid. Let the rice sit in the colander for about 30 minutes.

Meanwhile, prepare the custard cream with the ingredients listed above, following the directions on page 490.

Transfer the rice to a large bowl and remove the vanilla bean. Then add the cooled custard cream to the rice and combine well. Add the heavy cream and confectioners' sugar and mix again.

Prepare the *gelato*, following directions on page 497, placing the contents of the bowl in the metal insert of the ice-cream maker. The rice is quite crunchy and gives an interesting texture to the *gelato*. This ice cream is very popular in Italy now.

Sorbetto di Parmigiano

SORBET OF PARMIGIANO CHEESE

FROM PARMA

Sorbetti became very popular in the eighteenth century, and the category included many non-sweet dishes. There is a famous treatise on *sorbetti* by a physician of the time, telling of the many therapeutic uses for these iced dishes. This one, of Parmigiano, is typical of the non-sweet examples, and perhaps the easiest to understand for the modern palate. It should be eaten in place of the cheese course, either instead of dessert or before it. The dish has an established place in the old Parma cooking and is *not* an experiment.

1 cup finely grated Parmigiano-Reggiano
3 cups skimmed milk
3 egg yolks
Pinch of salt
1 pint heavy cream

Plus:
About 2 pounds of rock salt

Soak the grated Parmigiano in a small crockery bowl with 1 cup of the milk for 1 hour. Heat the remaining milk in a flameproof casserole and, when the milk reaches the boiling point, add the soaked Parmigiano and the milk. Stir with a wooden spoon to keep the cheese from sticking to the bottom of the casserole. Simmer for 2 minutes. Line a small strainer with a heavy cheesecloth or paper towels and place it over a crockery bowl. Pour the contents of the casserole through the cheesecloth and let stand for about 1 hour to drain completely. Discard the gummy residue of the cheese remaining in the strainer. (This residue will have lost the flavor of years of aging and will resemble the bland fresh curd of Parmigiano. The flavor, of course, will have been absorbed by the milk.)

Be sure the liquid in the bowl has no cheese grains in it. Then prepare a "custard cream" using this liquid and 3 egg yolks and salt, following the directions on page 490. Transfer the cream to a crockery bowl and let stand until completely cool. Prepare the *Sorbetto di Parmigiano*, following the directions for *gelato* on page 497, placing the contents of the bowl and the heavy cream into the metal insert of the ice-cream maker.

Granita di Limone

ITALIAN LEMON ICE

4 lemons
½ cup granulated sugar
1 cup cold water

Optional:
½ pint heavy cream
1 tablespoon granulated sugar
½ teaspoon confectioners' sugar

HOW TO PREPARE GRANITA

1. Begin making the *granita* the night before by first squeezing the lemons and then straining the lemon juice through a coffee filter into a small bowl containing the water. This is a slow drop-by-drop process and takes a long time.

2. The next morning, add the sugar and mix very well with a wooden spoon, until the sugar is completely dissolved.

3. Pour the contents of the bowl into a tin or aluminum pan and place it in the freezer. Let the pan rest in the freezer for about 5 hours. Every hour break up the solid layer of ice that has formed.

If desired, prepare the whipped cream with the ingredients listed above, following the instructions on page 493.

4. Remove the pan from the freezer and cut the ice into pieces with a knife.

5. At this point you can proceed in one of two different ways: Place the ice pieces in a blender at low speed or use an ice crusher. The ice should form a smooth consistent texture of imperceptible grains, almost like ice cream. There shouldn't be large grains or pieces, though be careful to stop blending before any liquefying takes place.

6. Transfer the *granita* to individual glasses and top with whipped cream, if desired.

A Note on Italian Wines Used in the Menus

The fifty wines selected to accompany the menus were chosen with a combination of criteria: what is imported into the U.S.; the greatest wines along with a representative sampling of others from all over Italy, and of course the wines that are appropriate to the dishes, chiefly the main course in each menu. Since Italians do not like to drink more than one or two different wines in a meal, they generally match the wine with the main course. (Often the soup or pasta course is eaten without wine.) I have not been strict about matching the region of the wine with that of the dish, because the menus generally make an ensemble which combines dishes from several different regions.

The availability of a variety of Italian wines outside of Italy has improved greatly in recent years. Fine vintages are now more available in the Bordeaux type of bottles which are better for long aging than the old charming straw covered flasks, once a great step forward in keeping wines. Though nonvintage wines in demijohns cannot be sampled far from their localities, it is important to mention that for most wine lovers in wine countries, that is the normal wine, and it so often goes best of all with the food of that area. Anyone who has ever drunk a fine Chianti at the vineyard, accompanied by the sheep's cheese Pecorino of the vineyard and its *prosciutto* and salami with crusty home baked bread will ponder no more about the perfect pairing of food and wine. But this experience must not necessarily be a restricted one.

We will survey the wines chosen according to their regions. In Piedmont we begin with Barolo and Barbaresco, both produced from the Nebbiolo grape, which is said to mature best in the fog of the Alba area. The limited hilly area of Barolo includes its place-name and several other localities, while Barbaresco is produced just in its own locality. The wines are astringent at first but arrive at a soft, velvety maturity. After 3 years, they may be called Barolo and Barbaresco, but many producers age them 4 or 5 years to produce the riserva. Dolcetto, despite its name, is a dry red produced from the grape of the same name and is interesting as the original native Piedmont wine before the great Barolo was developed. Nebbiolo is of course produced from the grape of the same name in different localities than Barolo and Barbaresco, and Gattinara, also called Spanna, is from that grape as well, but comes from the northern part of the province at Gattinara. Barbera also comes from its own grape. All of the Piedmont reds are rather full-bodied, not all as smooth as Barolo, and are appropriate to roasts and richer meat dishes. The excellent whites of Piedmont, made mostly from the Cortese grape, are best in the Gavi area in the southeast near Lombardy. They have as much character, and are less light than most of the dry northern Italian finer whites.

In the Veneto, the Verona area has particularly felicitous wines, the greatest one of which is Amarone Recioto della Valpolicella, perhaps one of the finest wines of Italy and even the world. It is dry in character though made from grapes which are allowed to dry partially before being made into wine. The vines are also pruned in a special way. A very rich wine, it is at its best with game and variety meat dishes. The white Soave is also from the Verona area, and to best understand its special quality, should be drunk fresh in its locality (like the central Italian white Orvieto) but it retains character when bottled by a good producer. Two other distinguished Veneto wines are the red Venegazzù and Prosecco di Conegliano which comes in white as well as red. These two reds are paired with stuffed veal and lamb dishes respectively. The northeast areas of Italy* also produce pleasant whites from grapes not restricted to Italy. Among the best are some Pinot Bianco and Tocai wines.

In Lombardy, it is the mountainous pre-Alpine Valtellina area which produces reds: Inferno, Sassella, and Grumello among others. They have been

* Veneto, Friuli, Oltrepo

502

paired with roast chicken and grilled veal on these menus.

If one wishes to taste the effervescent wines of Emilia-Romagna at their best, it is important to note that the label says "fermentazione naturale" meaning that the sparkle is naturally rather than artificially induced. These bottles are quite a cut above the other wines of this region such as Lambrusco and Albana, and when these wines are at their best, they are the most appropriate accompaniment to the rich, creamy food of the same region.

If I recommend so many Tuscan wines, it is not only because I am Tuscan, but because Chianti and other types of this area are so very versatile. It was mainly the Etruscans who developed wine making in Italy, and their center was Tuscany, so it is not surprising that there is such a concentration of vineyards. Chianti is made from four grapes: Sangiovese and Canaiolo red vine types and Trebbiano and Malvasia white vine types. They are planted in percentages controlled by law and the resultant wine is dry and slightly tannic, a bit effervescent at first but gradually ages to greater harmony and softness. The various zones of Chianti produce a variation in fullness and in flowery flavor such as that of the violet, iris and cherry. Because of its complexity, it can accompany many foods, from light to more full-bodied, meat, fish, fowl, and even game. There is great variation in character of Chiantis from the lightness of those which may be matched with light chicken (or even fish) dishes to those fuller riserve, more appropriate to roasts or to game. Very recently Carmignano near Florence has again started to produce its old type of all red grape wine, with fine results, and Antinori has developed a really distinguished new wine called Tignanello with new vinification methods in the Chianti area. The two other great reds of Tuscany are Brunello di Montalcino, from the Brunello grape, which in recent decades has been catapulted onto the heights of the world's most celebrated wines. Montalcino is small, and demand is greater than production capacity, so that prices are getting very high. Vino Nobile di Montepulciano, made from Sangiovese rosso, its own special grape, has not been discovered in the same way, though thirty years ago, it was perhaps better known than Brunello. Both wines are big and Brunello especially is capable of very long aging. The younger sibling of Brunello is Brusco, and it is a fine young wine, though now it is also getting expensive.

The Chiana valley has a traditional Tuscan white, made from the same white grapes as those in Chianti (technically, there is no such thing as a white Chianti), which is called Bianco Vergine. It is young, fruity and unpretentious, but very drinkable. With the change in post-World War II vinification methods for Chianti, there is less white put into the mixture, so that Tuscany has leftover white grapes and has been developing more white wines. Again, they are drinkable, pleasantly acidic and unpretentious. Among them are a number called simply Bianco toscano and a most successful recent one called Galestro. The distinguished Vernaccia di San Gimignano has a long tradition, though this originally Ligurian grape has died out in its place of origin. Pomino's vineyards are unusually high for Tuscany, and it is a more full-bodied white.

In the areas of Umbria and Latium, we have the home of the long-famous Orvieto and Est! Est!! Est!!! from Montefiascone.

The Trebbiano of Abruzzo, across from Rome, has become available and perhaps is the best wine of that area.

The reds and whites of Sardinia are very respectable wines, with unique character. They are full-bodied, strong (which is typical of the southern wines) and have refinement. Torbato provides a good sampling of this wine. Greco di Tufo from Campania is made from the Greco grape which was once widely used in the centuries when white wines were all sweet. It retains a very slight sweetness which is appropriate to a dish with a sweet and sour sauce. Lacryma Christi del Vesuvio, the plentiful wines in both red and white from Vesuvio is probably the most famous name from Campania, but the red Taurasi, especially the 4 year old riserva, is probably the best wine of the area. Some of the best Sicilian wines are not yet exported, but the white Tudia available here is representative.

Looking over the pairings of the wines with the main dishes on the menus will give a general idea of the type of dish appropriate to each wine.

For additional reference, consult *The Pocket Encyclopedia of Italian Wines* by Burton Anderson. NOTE: The map of Italy (pages 12–13) provides the location of the regions and major cities where most of the wines are found.

Glossary of Italian Terms

AL DENTE Italian term for pasta, cooked so that when you bite it you can feel the "body" of the pasta itself, which is not soft and overcooked. It is applied only to dried commercial pasta, not to freshly made.

BAGNA CAUDA A Piedmontese warm creamy sauce used as a dip for raw vegetables eaten as an antipasto.

BALSAMELLA (Bechamel) A type of white sauce made with butter, flour and milk.

BATTUTO It is the term for the chopped vegetables and aromatic herbs such as onion, garlic, celery, carrots and parsley used as the starting point for a large variety of meat sauces. Recipes written in Italian do not specify the individual ingredients because that is understood. If an additional vegetable or aromatic herb is added, or one of the above is removed, this is indicated in a particular recipe.

BRACIOLA A slice of beef of any size eaten either flat or rolled and stuffed. When the term is used for other meats, unlike the usage with the normal *braciola*, the veal or pork is usually specified in the name such as *braciola di vitella* or *braciola di maiale*. In the U.S. the term is most heard as the dialect word "bragiol," usually referring to a rolled and stuffed beef slice.

BUONGUSTAI (SINGULAR BUONGUSTAIO) One who has refined taste, especially a fine palate for food and wine.

CARNESECCA Tuscan vernacular for *pancetta*.

CROSTINI Rustic canapés the base of which is made from thinly sliced hearty country bread with the crusts left on.

ERBETTE Dialect word used in Parma and Genoa for a mixture of chard and some other greens characteristic of those places. These greens are the typical filling for *tortelli* and ravioli in those areas.

IN PINZIMONIO A Tuscan term describing the manner of eating raw vegetables dipped in olive oil, salt and pepper. It means literally to use the fingers like pincers to hold the vegetables. This is the only dish for which it is acceptable to Italians to use their hands for eating.

INVOLTINI Small scaloppine (of veal or beef) rolled and stuffed.

MINESTRA Meat or vegetable soup with or without pasta or rice. Once used to refer to any first course.

PAIOLO (II) Unlined copper pot used to prepare polenta. The word is also used as the name of the oldest gastronomic society in Italy, formed by the circle of Michelangelo's disciples in the sixteenth century and still in existence.

PASTA CORTA Short pasta, solid such as *farfalle* ("bow-ties") or butterflies or with a tubular shape such as *penne, penne rigate, rigatoni, chiocciole*, etc.

PIATTO DI MEZZO In-between dish. Generally it is a complex vegetable dish, bridging the abrupt contrast in level of spiciness and difference in texture between the first course and main course.

SALSA BIANCA White sauce made with butter, flour, and broth.

SALSA VERDE A group of green sauces made with fresh green herbs, olive oil, and other ingredients. The most common modern version is based on parsley, oil and garlic.

SAVORI (SINGULAR SAVORE) A class of relishes and thick sauces used in Medieval and Renaissance cooking.

SCALOPPINE A thin cutlet from one of the tender muscle meats, usually of veal but sometimes of young beef.

SETACCI (SINGULAR SETACCIO) Sieve or sifter. In French, it is called "tamis."

SPEZZATINO Cubes or small pieces of boneless meat or small pieces of chicken with bone.

SCALCO Originally in Medieval times the man in charge of the ceremony of carving the meat at court, later the high nobleman who runs the Pope's personal household.

SPUGNOLA (LA) A type of lasagne which is a local specialty of the area of Modena, employing the large meaty mushrooms common to that area called *spugnole*.

PASTASCIUTTA Flat or tubular pasta, fresh or dried, eaten with sauce rather than with broth.

VERMICELLI A type of dried pasta popular in Southern Italy, flatter than spaghetti and very close in texture to linguine.

WEIGHTS AND MEASURES

It is best to measure most ingredients such as flour and sugar by weight when preparing doughs, pastries and cakes as it's more accurate. But since many people prefer to measure these ingredients in cups or they do not have a scale, a conversion chart is provided below. These cup measurements are based on U.S. standard measuring cups such as Foley. (Make sure all measurements are level.)

Conversion to Metric System

1 cup all-purpose flour (unsifted)	= about 4 ounces	= about 112 grams
1 cup granulated sugar	= about 8 ounces	= about 224 grams
8 tablespoons butter	= 4 ounces (1 stick)	= 125 grams
1 ounce (solid)		= about 28 grams
1 pound (solid)	= 16 ounces	= about 448 grams (1 kilogram = 1000 grams)
3 teaspoons	= 1 tablespoon	
16 tablespoons	= 1 cup = 8 ounces (liquid) = ½ pint	
4 cups	= 2 pints = 1 quart (liquid) = almost 1 liter	

TEMPERATURES
(Conversion to Metric System)

$$\text{Fahrenheit} = \frac{\text{Celsius} \times 9}{5} + 32$$

$$\text{Celsius} = \frac{(\text{Fahrenheit} - 32) \times 5}{9}$$

Fahrenheit	Celsius	Fahrenheit	Celsius
75°F	24°C	275°F	135°C
80°F	27°C	300°F	150°C
85°F	29°C	320°F	160°C
100°F	38°C	325°F	163°C
110°F	43°C	330°F	165°C
115°F	46°C	335°F	168°C
120°F	49°C	340°F	170°C
130°F	54°C	350°F	175°C
140°F	60°C	360°F	180°C
150°F	66°C	365°F	185°C
160°F	71°C	370°F	188°C
165°F	74°C	375°F	190°C
170°F	77°C	380°F	193°C
180°F	82°C	400°F	205°C
190°F	88°C	425°F	220°C
200°F	95°C	450°F	230°C
205°F	96°C	475°F	245°C
212°F	100°C	500°F	260°C
225°F	110°C	550°F	290°C
250°F	120°C		

APPENDIX I
List of Recipes

BASIC INGREDIENTS

Almond Paste (*Marzapane*), 90
Cotechino, 54
Fruit Relish of Cremona (*Mostarda di Cremona*), 59
Glacéed Orange Rind (*Scorze di arancia candite*), 58
Goose Preserved in Its Own Fat (*Oca in pignatto*), 49
Italian Pickles (*Sottoaceti*), 46
Mascarpone, 40
Orange Sirup (*Sciroppo di arancia*), 57
Preserved Aromatic Herbs, 48
Ricotta, 38
Siena Sausages (*Salsicce di Siena*), 96
Wine Vinegar, 45
Zampone, 51

BREADS AND PIZZAS

Beef-flavored *Schiacciata* (*Schiacciata unta alla fiorentina*), 417
Bread from Ferrara (*Pane ferrarese*), 402
Cheese Dough Pizza (*Pizza al formaggio* or *Crescia*), 418
Chick-pea "Pizza" (*Cecina*), 400
Sage Bread (*Pane alla salvia*), 414
Schiacciata with Coarse-grained Salt (*Schiacciata al sale grosso*), 416
Stuffed *Focaccia* or Pizza (*Focaccia farcita*), 419
Tuscan Bread (*Pane toscano*), 412

SAUCES

Basil Sauce (*Pesto*), 159
Béchamel (*Balsamella*), 334
Beef Sauce (*Sugo di manzo*), 132
Brain Sauce (*Salsa di cervello*), 96
Caper-Tomato Sauce (*Salsa di pomodori ai capperi*), 49
Fresh Mint Sauce (*Salsa di menta*), 255
Fruit Relish of Cremona (*Mostarda di Cremona*), 59
Kidney Sauce (*Salsa di rognone*), 81
Mayonnaise (*Maionese*), 438
Sweet and Spicy Sauce (*Salsa dolce-forte*), 136
Sweet Red Pepper Sauce (*Salsa di peperoni*), 448
Tomato-Butter Sauce (*Salsa di pomodoro*), 447
Tomato-Butter Sauce (*Salsa di pomodoro con balsamella*), 110
Tuscan Country Sauce (*Salsa rustica*), 82
Walnut Sauce (*Salsa di noci*), 91

ANTIPASTI

Beef-flavored *Schiacciata* (*Schiacciata unta alla fiorentina*), 417
Bread Pillows (*Panzarotti*), 415
Broccoli Roman Style (*Broccoli alla romana*), 349
Caponata Genoese Version (*Cappon magro*), 377
Caponata Sicilian Style, 376
Caponata Tuscan Version, 377
Carrots in Parsley Sauce (*Carote al prezzemolo*), 358
Cheese Dough Pizza (*Pizza al formaggio* or *Crescia*), 418
Cheese Tart (*Torta al formaggio*), 473
Chicken in Galantine (*Galantina di pollo*), 323
Cold *Scaloppine* in Piquant Sauce (*Piccatine in carpione*), 275
Deep-fried Sage Leaves (*Salvia fritta*), 112
Deep-fried Spinach Croquettes (*Polpettine di spinaci*), 391
Eel Tart (*Torta di anguille*), 475
Eggplant Baked in Batter (*Melanzane al forno*), 375
Escalloped Potato Salad (*Patate all'olio o con maionese*), 380
Fish Galantine (*Pesce in galantina*), 314
Frittata Made in the Manner of Tripe (*Frittata trippata*), 117
Frittata with Mixed Fresh Herbs (*Frittata profumata*), 116
Frittata with Ricotta (*Frittata con la ricotta*), 115
Green Pepper *Bavarese* (*Bavarese di peperoni*), 447
Leek-Potato Tart (*Torta di porri*), 389
Mayonnaise Mold (*Sformato di maionese*), 438
Neapolitan Tomato Salad (*Insalata di pomodori*), 386

Peppers Stuffed with Veal and Ricotta (*Peperoni ripieni*), 384

Polenta Canapés (*Crostini di polenta*), 210

Potato Flour Crêpes (*Frittatini ripieni*), 111

Potatoes with Bay Leaves (*Patate con alloro*), 381

Rolled Chicken Breast in Aspic (*Petti di pollo allo specchio*), 435

Rustic Seafood Canapés (*Crostini caldi di mare*), 304

Salad of Cuttlefish, Squid, and Shrimp ("*Insalata*" *di seppie, calamari e gamberi*), 306

Sardines in the Style of Alghero (*Sardine di Alghero*), 300

Schiacciata with Coarse-grained Salt (*Schiacciata al sale grosso*), 416

String Beans with a Cream-Hazelnut Sauce (*Fagiolini alle nocciole*), 368

Stuffed *Focaccia* or Pizza (*Focaccia farcita*), 419

Stuffed Pressed Veal Breast (*Cima alla genovese*), 249

Stuffed Turkey Neck (*Collo di tacchino ripieno*), 245

Stuffed Zucchini Blossoms (*Fiori di zucca ripieni*), 398

Stuffed Zucchini in Veal Sauce (*Zucchini ripieni in sugo di vitella*), 396

Summer Rice Salad ("*Insalata*" *di riso estiva*), 205

Tomatoes Stuffed with Macaroni (*Pomodori ripieni di pasta*), 387

Veal with Tuna Flavoring (*Vitello tonnato*), 287

White Asparagus Cornaro (*Asparagi alla Cornaro*), 346

Zucchini Torte (*Torta di zucchini*), 397

FIRST COURSES (*Primi Piatti*)

Soups

Bean Soup Sienese Style (*Zuppa alla senese*), 99

Cannellini Beans with Celery and Carrots (*Fagioli con sedano e carote*), 401

Chicken Ravioli in Broth (*Ravioli di pollo in brodo*), 94

Lettuce Soup (*Minestra di lattuga*), 372

Taglierini in Chick-pea Soup (*Passato di ceci con taglierini*), 138

Wild Mushroom Soup (*Crema di funghi*), 65

Fresh Pasta

Chocolate Pasta in Sweet and Spicy Sauce (*Pasta al cioccolato in dolce-forte*), 136

Gramigna with Four Cheeses (*Gramigna ai quattro formaggi*), 142

Maccheroni Cut with the "Guitar" in Lamb Sauce (*Maccheroni alla chitarra*), 144

Orecchiette with Broccolirab (*Orecchiette con cime di rape*), 153

Pappardelle with Stewed Rabbit Sauce (*Pappardelle allo spezzatino di coniglio*), 150

Pinci Montalcino Style (*Pinci di Montalcino*), 147

Red Pepper *Tagliatelle* (*Tagliatelle al peperoncino*), 135

Spaghetti in Sauce with Baked Tomatoes (*Spaghetti al pomodoro al forno*), 139

Spaghetti in Trout-Black Truffle Sauce (*Spaghetti di Scheggino*), 140

Tagliatelle with Asparagus Sauce (*Tagliatelle al sugo di asparagi*), 133

Tagliatelle with Beef Sauce (*Tagliatelle al sugo di manzo*), 132

Tagliatelle with Sauce of Preserved Goose (*Tagliatelle con sugo di oca conservato*), 134

Tagliatelle with Walnut Sauce (*Tagliatelle con salsa di noci*), 136

Trenette with Artichoke Sauce (*Trenette con salsa di carciofi*), 149

Stuffed Fresh Pasta

Apple *Tortelli* for Christmas Eve (*Tortelli di mele*), 171

Baked Giant *Tortelli* (*Uova alla fornaia*), 172

Cannelloni Stuffed with Asparagus (*Cannelloni con punte di asparagi*), 156

Cannelloni Stuffed with Tongue and Chicken (*Cannelloni con lingua salmistrata*), 158

Large *Tortelli* Casentino Style (*Tortelloni alla casentinese*), 168

Tortelli of Michelangelo Buonarotti (*Tortelli di Michelangelo*), 167

Tortelli Stuffed with Squab (*Tortelli di piccione*), 169

Large Stuffed Pasta

Boiled Lasagne with Beef Sauce (*Lasagne alla genovese*), 160

Lasagne with Eggplant (*Lasagne con melanzane*), 163

Lasagne with *Pesto* (*Lasagne al pesto*), 159

Lasagne with Pike (*Minestra di lasagna con luccio*), 161

Timballo Dishes

Baked *Tortellini* or *Cappelletti* Bolognese Style

(Pasticcio di tortellini o cappelletti alla
bolognese), 177
Rice *Timballo* Stuffed with Squab (*Timballo di riso
alla parmigiana*), 204

Dried Pasta

Baked Pasta Mold (*Pasticcio di pasta*), 193
Genoese Fish Sauce with Spaghetti (*Spaghetti con
passato di pesce alla genovese*), 184
Pasta *Frittata* (*Frittata di pasta*), 116
Pasta "In the Latest Style Naples 1841" (*Maccheroni
"all' Ultima Moda 1841" alla napoletana*), 182
Pasta with Fresh Sardines (*Pasta con le sarde*), 189
Penne Stir-Sautéed in Meat Sauce (*Penne
strascicate alla fiorentina*), 192
Penne Stir-Sautéed in Veal Sauce (*Penne
strascicate al sugo di vitella*), 191
Penne with Tripe Sauce (*Penne trippate*), 190
Spaghetti with Broccoli (*Spaghetti con broccoli*),
183
Spaghetti with Fresh Fish Roe (*Spaghetti con
caviale di tonno*), 186
Spaghetti with Lobster (*Spaghetti all' aragosta*), 186
Spaghetti with the Ink of the Squid (*Spaghetti
neri*), 187
Thin Spaghetti with Aromatic Herbs and
Vegetables (*Spaghettini dell' ortolano*), 184
Tomatoes Stuffed with Macaroni (*Pomodori ripieni
di pasta*), 387

Pasta Salads

Pasta Salad with Peppers and Anchovies (*Insalata
di pasta I*), 196
Pasta Salad with Swordfish (*Insalata di pasta III*),
197
Pasta Salad with Tuna (*Insalata di pasta II*), 197

Risotti

Rice *Timballo* Stuffed with Squab (*Timballo di riso
alla parmigiana*), 104
Risotto in the Style of Parma (*Risotto alla
parmigiana*), 202
Risotto with Quail (*Risotto alle quaglie*), 200
Risotto with Rosemary (*Risotto al ramerino*), 203

Polenta

Polenta from Casentino (*Polenta del Casentino*),
208
Polenta with Sausages and Quail (*Polenta alla
pistoiese*), 207

Miscellaneous First Courses

Bread Pillows (*Panzarotti*), 415
Caponata Genoese Version (*Cappon magro*), 378
Cheese Tart (*Torta al formaggio*), 473
Crespelle Florentine Style (*Crespelle alla
fiorentina*), 110
Mayonnaise Mold (*Sformato di maionese*), 438
Polenta Canapés (*Crostini di polenta*), 210
Potato Flour Crêpes (*Frittatini ripieni*), 111
Stuffed "Handkerchiefs" ("*Fazzoletti*" ripieni), 107
"Stuffed" *Turbante* (*Turbante ripieno*), 458
Summer Rice Salad ("*Insalata*" *di riso estiva*), 205

SECOND COURSES (*Secondi Piatti*)

Fish and Shellfish

Cuttlefish Leghorn Style (*Seppie in umido*), 304
Deep-fried Sole Fillets (*Filetti di sogliola fritti*),
312
Eel Tart (*Torta di anguille*), 475
Fish Cooked on a Range-top Grill (*Pesce alla
griglia*), 232
Fish Galantine (*Pesce in galantina*), 314
Fish-Vegetable *Pasticcio* (*Pasticcio di magro*), 337
Fish with Capers (*Pesce ai capperi*), 232
Salad of Cuttlefish, Squid, and Shrimp ("*Insalata*"
di seppie, calamari e gamberi), 306
Sardines in the Style of Alghero (*Sardine di
Alghero*), 300
Stuffed Whole Carp in Aspic (*Pesce farcito*), 318
Whole Fish Baked in Clay (*Pesce in creta*), 212

Eggs

Frittata Made in the Manner of Tripe (*Frittata
trippata*), 117
Frittata with Mixed Fresh Herbs (*Frittata
profumata*), 116
Frittata with Ricotta (*Frittata con la ricotta*), 115
Pasta *Frittata* (*Frittata di pasta*), 116

Poultry and Game

Baked Marinated Chicken with Peppers (*Pollo ai
peperoni*), 240
Boned Whole Rabbit, Rolled and Stuffed (*Coniglio
ripieno arrocchiato*), 261
Chicken Breast Cooked on a Plate (*Petto di pollo al
piatto*), 222
Chicken Breast Cooked on a Range-top Grill (*Petto
di pollo alla griglia*), 232

Chicken *Budino* (*Sformato o budino di pollo*), 440
Chicken Cooked Covered with Salt (*Pollo al sale*), 224
Chicken in Galantine (*Galantina di pollo*), 323
Chicken Sautéed with Mushrooms (*Pollo alla toscana*), 241
Chicken with Vinegar Sauce (*Pollo all' aceto*), 242
Chicken Wrapped in *Prosciutto* (*Pollo al prosciutto*), 217
Duck *Pasticcio* (*Pasticcio di anitra*), 339
Duck with Green Peppercorns (*Anitra peposa*), 30
Goose Preserved in Its Own Fat (*Oca in pignatto*), 49
Guinea Hen Cooked in a Paper Bag (*Faraona al cartoccio*), 214
Oregano Chicken Baked with Potatoes and Tomatoes (*Pollo in forno*), 242
Pasticcio of Hare (*Pasticcio di lepre*), 332
Pheasant Stuffed with Fruits (*Fagiano ripieno*), 34
Quail in a Nest of Tuscan Bread (*Quaglie nel nido di un pane toscano*), 407
Quail Wrapped in Grape Leaves (*Quaglie in foglie*), 221
Rolled Chicken Breast in Aspic (*Petti di pollo allo specchio*), 435
Stuffed Chicken Drumsticks (*Cosce di pollo ripiene*), 243
Stuffed Turkey Neck (*Collo di tacchino ripieno*), 245
Turkey Ossobuco (*Ossobuco di tacchino*), 294
Whole Chicken Baked in Clay (*Pollo in creta*), 213
Whole Chicken Cooked Between Terra-cotta (*Pollo al mattone*), 213

Veal

Cold Veal *Scaloppine* in Piquant Sauce (*Piccatine in carpione*), 275
Fricassee of Veal (*Fricassea di vitella*), 295
"Mock" Game Birds (*Tordimatti*), 276
Ossobuco, 290
Ossobuco from Novara (*Ossobuco alla novese*), 293
Potato Flour Crêpes (*Frittatini ripieni*), 111
Roast Loin of Veal Laced with Green Peppercorns and Sage (*Arrocchiato di vitella*), 285
Rolled Veal *Scaloppine* Stuffed with Kidney (*Involtini ripieni di rognone*), 280
Rolled Veal *Scaloppine* Stuffed with Sausages (*Involtini di vitella*), 284
Stuffed Pressed Veal Breast (*Cima alla genovese*), 249
Veal Brains in Lemon Sauce (*Cervello al limone*), 298

Veal Chops Cooked on a Range-top Grill (*Lombatina di vitella alla griglia*), 231
Veal in Balsamic Vinegar (*Vitella all' aceto balsamico*), 290
Veal Liver Cooked on a Range-top Grill (*Fegato alla griglia*), 232
Veal *Scaloppine* with Asparagus Sauce (*Scaloppine agli asparagi*), 274
Veal *Scaloppine* with Puréed Artichokes (*Bracioline o scaloppine all' empolese*), 271
Veal *Scaloppine* with Sage (*Scaloppine di vitella alla salvia*), 272
Veal *Scaloppine* with Tarragon Siena Style (*Scaloppine alla senese*), 272
Veal *Scaloppine* with Vin Santo (*Scaloppine al Vin Santo*), 273
Veal *Scaloppine* with Wild Mushrooms (*Scaloppine ai funghi porcini*), 273
Veal with Tuna Flavoring (*Vitello tonnato*), 287

Beef

Beef with Seven Flavors (*Carne ai sette sapori*), 230
Braised Rump of Beef Milano Style (*Stufato di Milano*), 228
Braised Rump of Beef Parma Style (*Stracotto alla parmigiana*), 226
Cubes of Beef Shank in Carrot-Wine Sauce (*Spezzatino alle carote*), 230

Lamb

Boned Leg of Lamb with Fresh Mint Sauce (*Coscia di agnello in salsa di menta*), 255
Lamb Chops Cooked on a Range-top Grill (*Scottadido alla griglia*), 231
Stuffed Lamb Shoulder (*Agnello ripieno*), 258

Pork

Cotechino, 54
Cotechino Sausage Baked in Crust (*Cotechino in camicia*), 422
Siena Sausages (*Salsicce di Siena*), 96
Spareribs "Molinetto" Style (*Costine al "Vecchio Molinetto"*), 219
Zampone, 51

Miscellaneous Second Courses

Caponata Genoese Version (*Cappon magro*), 378
Cheese Tart (*Torta al Formaggio*), 473
Frittata Made in the Manner of Tripe (*Frittata trippata*), 117

Frittata with Mixed Fresh Herbs (*Frittata profumata*), 116
Frittata with Ricotta (*Frittata con la ricotta*), 115
Polenta from Casentino (*Polenta del Casentino*), 208
Potato Flour Crêpes (*Frittatini ripieni*), 111
Rice *Timballo* Stuffed with Squab (*Timballo di riso alla parmigiana*), 104
"Stuffed" *Turbante* (*Turbante ripieno*), 458
Tomatoes Stuffed with Macaroni (*Pomodori ripieni di pasta*), 387

VEGETABLES AND SALADS

Artichokes in Parsley Sauce (*Carciofi in umido o in salsa*), 354
Artichokes Stuffed with Spinach and Chard (*Carciofi alla fiorentina*), 352
Asparagus "Cornaro" (*Asparagi alla Cornaro*), 346
Asparagus in Egg-Lemon Sauce (*Asparagi in salsa*), 345
Baked Cannellini Beans (*Fagioli al forno*), 213
Baked Cardoons (*Cardi al forno*), 356
Broccoli in White Wine Sauce (*Broccoli al vino bianco*), 349
Broccoli Roman Style (*Broccoli alla romana*), 349
Cabbage-Potato Stew (*Verza e patate*), 363
Cannellini Beans with Celery and Carrots (*Fagioli con sedano e carote*), 401
Caponata Genoese Version (*Cappon magro*), 377
Caponata Sicilian Style, 376
Caponata Tuscan Version, 377
Carrots in Cream Sauce (*Carote alla crema*), 358
Carrots in Parsley Sauce (*Carote al prezzemolo*), 358
Cauliflower Steamed in Wine (*Cavolfiore affogato*), 360
Chick-pea "Pizza" (*Cecina*), 400
Compote of Baked Vegetables (*Tegamaccio di verdure*), 343
Deep-fried Spinach Croquettes (*Polpettine di spinaci*), 391
Eggplant Baked in Batter (*Melanzane al forno*), 379
Escalloped Potato Salad (*Patate all' olio o con maionese*), 380
Fennel "Bulbs" Parma Style (*Finocchi alla parmigiana con salsicce*), 370
Fennel "Bulbs" with Caper-Anchovy Sauce (*Finocchi con salsa di capperi e acciughe*), 371
Green Pepper *Bavarese* (*Bavarese di peperoni*), 447
Kale Simmered in Broth (*Cavolo nero in umido*), 362
Leeks in Pork Sauce (*Porri al sugo di maiale*), 390

Leek-Potato Tart (*Torta di porri*), 389
Lentils in Rosemary-Sage Sauce (*Lenticchie in umido*), 400
Neapolitan Tomato Salad (*Insalata di pomodori*), 386
Oregano Potatoes (*Patate "raganate"*), 382
Peppers Stuffed with Veal and Ricotta (*Peperoni ripieni*), 384
Potatoes with Bay Leaves (*Patate con alloro*), 381
Sautéed Stems of Chard (*Gambi di bietola in padella*), 348
Savoy Cabbage Sardinia Style (*Cavolo alla sarda*), 365
Savoy Cabbage with Sausages (*Verza con salsicce*), 364
Spinach Genoese Style (*Spinaci alla genovese*), 393
"Stir-Sautéed" Celery (*Sedani Saltati*), 391
String Beans Genoese Style (*Fagiolini alla genovese*), 368
String Beans with a Cream-Hazelnut Sauce (*Fagiolini alle nocciole*), 368
Stuffed Eggplant Puglia Style (*Melanzane ripiene*), 374
Stuffed Zucchini Blossoms (*Fiori di zucca ripieni*), 398
Stuffed Zucchini in Veal Sauce (*Zucchini ripieni in sugo di vitella*), 396
Sweet-and-Sour Button Onions (*Cipolline in agrodolce*), 366
Tomatoes Stuffed with Macaroni (*Pomodori ripieni di pasta*), 387
Zucchini Tart (*Torta di zucchini*), 397
Zucchini with *Pancetta* (*Zucchini alla pancetta*), 395

DESSERTS

Almond Cake (*Torta di mandorle*), 87
Almond Paste (*Marzapane*), 90
Apricots with Wine Syrup (*Albicocche al sugo*), 59
Babà Layer Cake (*Babà alla crema*), 425
Brandied *Mascarpone* Dessert (*Mascarpone in coppa*), 43
Cannoli, 481
Chestnut Tart (*Marronata*), 463
Chocolate Cream Puff Mound (*Bongo*), 486
Christmas Fruit and Nut Roll (*Rotolo di Natale*), 429
Cream Puff Pastry (*Pasta soffiata*), 484
Custard Cream (*Crema pasticceria*), 489
Dessert Cups of *Crema Zabaione* Parma Style (*Coppe di crema zabaione alla parmigiana*), 491
Figs "Nectared" with Fig-flavored Pastry Cream (*Fichi giulebbati con crema di fichi*), 494

Fresh Chestnut Torte (*Torta di castagne*), 100
Genoese Pastry (*Pasta genovese*), 487
Grand Duke Ferdinand's Snacks (*Merendine del Granduca*), 112
Homemade Italian Ladyfingers (*Savoiardi*), 480
Homemade *Zuccotto* (*Zuccotto*), 477
Italian Fresh Fruit Ice Cream (*Gelato di frutta fresca*), 496
Italian Lemon Ice (*Granita di limone*), 500
Italian Sponge Cake (*Bocca di dama*), 476
"Lift Me Up" (*Tiramisù*), 44
Marsala-flavored *Bavarese* (*Bavarese al marsala*), 444
Molded Purée of Fresh Chestnuts (*Monte Bianco*), 448
Neapolitan Easter Cake (*Pastiera*), 467
Orange Cream *Bavarese* (*Bavarese all' arancia*), 446
Orange or Lemon Dessert Aspic (*Gelatina dolce di frutta*), 443

Panettone, 430
Panforte, 86
Patê Brisée (*Pasta briciolata*), 468
Pears Corrado Style (*Pere alla Corrado*), 61
Pear Tart (*Torta di pere*), 472
Polenta Cheesecake (*Sformato dolce di polenta*), 211
Puff Pastry (*Pasta sfoglia* or *sfogliata*), 452
Rice Ice Cream (*Gelato di riso*), 499
Sienese Almond Cookies (*Ricciarelli*), 89
Short Pastry (*Pasta frolla*), 465
Short Pastry made with Hard-cooked Egg Yolks (*Pasta frolla fragile*), 459
Short Pastry with Milk (*Pasta mezza frolla*), 474
Sorbet of Parmigiano Cheese (*Sorbetto di parmigiano*), 499
Stuffed Peach Tart (*Torta di pesche alla crema*), 465
Walnut Cake (*Torta di noci*), 83

APPENDIX II
Menus

Tagliatelle al sugo di manzo
(*Tagliatelle* with Beef Sauce), 132
Cosce di pollo ripiene
(Stuffed Chicken Drumsticks), 243
Carciofi in umido o in salsa
(Artichokes in Parsley Sauce), 354
Mascarpone in coppa
(Brandied *Mascarpone* Dessert), 43
WINE: Villa Cerna - Chianti Classico

———————

Polpettine di spinaci
(Deep-fried Spinach Croquettes), 391
Lasagne al pesto (Lasagne with *Pesto*), 159
"Insalata" di seppie, calamari e gamberi
(Salad of Cuttlefish, Squid, and Shrimp), 306
Fresh Fruit
WINE: Angoris - Pinot Grigio

———————

Tagliatelle al peperoncino
(Red Pepper *Tagliatelle*), 132
Pollo al prosciutto
(Chicken Wrapped in *Prosciutto*), 217
Sedani saltati ("Stir-Sautéed" Celery), 391
Tiramisù ("Lift Me Up"), 44
WINE: Chianti Classico - Fattoria Casa Sola

———————

Risotto al ramerino (*Risotto* with Rosemary), 203
Pollo alla toscana
(Chicken Sautéed with Mushrooms), 241
Gambi di bietola in padella
(Sautéed Stems of Chard), 348
Albicocche al sugo (Apricots with Wine Syrup), 59
WINE: Carmignano - Tenuta di Capezzana

———————

Tagliatelle al sugo di asparagi
(*Tagliatelle* with Asparagus Sauce), 133
Quaglie in foglie
(Quail Wrapped in Grape Leaves), 211
Carote alla crema (Carrots in Cream Sauce), 358
Torta di noci (Walnut Cake), 83
WINE: Calissano - Barbera d'Asti

Schiacciata al sale grosso
(*Schiacciata* with Coarse-grained Salt), 416
Passato di ceci con taglierini
(*Taglierini* in Chick-pea Soup), 138
Pollo ai peperoni
(Baked Marinated Chicken with Peppers), 240
Fichi giulebbati con crema di fichi (Figs "Nectared"
with Fig-flavored Pastry Cream), 494
WINE: Cecchi - Chianti Classico

———————

Minestra di lasagna con luccio
(Lasagne with Pike), 161
Scaloppine di vitella alla salvia
(Veal *Scaloppine* with Sage), 272
Carote al prezzemolo
(Carrots in Parsley Sauce), 358
Pere alla Corrado (Pears Corrado Style), 61
WINE: Pomino - Frescobaldi

———————

Salvia fritta (Deep-fried Sage Leaves), 112
Crema di funghi (Wild Mushroom Soup), 65
Faraona al cartoccio
(Guinea Hen Cooked in a Paper Bag), 214
Verza e patate (Cabbage-Potato Stew), 363
Granita di limone (Italian Lemon Ice), 500
WINE: Tignanello - Antinori

———————

Tortelli di Michelangelo
(*Tortelli* of Michelangelo Buonarotti), 167
Involtini di vitella
(Rolled Veal *Scaloppine* Stuffed with Sausages),
284
Carciofi alla fiorentina
(Artichokes Stuffed with Spinach and Chard), 352
Gelato di riso (Rice Ice Cream), 499
WINE: Vino Nobile di Montepulciano - "Fassati"

———————

Collo di tacchino ripieno
(Stuffed Turkey Neck), 245
Salsa rustica (Tuscan Country Sauce), 82
Ravioli di pollo in brodo
(Chicken Ravioli in Broth), 94

Pesce al capperi (Fish with Capers), 233
Torta di pere (Pear Tart), 472
WINE: Antinori - Castello della Sala -
Orvieto Secco

Tagliatelle con salsa di noci
(*Tagliatelle* with Walnut Sauce), 136
Pollo al mattone
(Whole Chicken Cooked Between Terra-cotta), 213
Patate con alloro (Potatoes with Bay Leaves), 381
Torta di pesche alla crema (Stuffed Peach Tart), 465
WINE: Castello di Verrazzano - Chianti Classico

Crostini di polenta (Polenta Canapés), 210
Zuppa alla senese (Bean Soup Sienese Style), 99
Stracotto alla parmigiana
(Braised Rump of Beef Parma Style), 226
Whole Boiled Potatoes
Bavarese al Marsala
(Marsala-flavored *Bavarese*), 444
WINE: Gattinara - Antoniolo

Crespelle alla fiorentina
(*Crespelle* Florentine Style), 110
Coniglio ripieno arrocchiato
(Boned Whole Rabbit, Rolled and Stuffed), 261
Cavolo alla sarda
(Savoy Cabbage Sardinia Style), 365
Fresh Fruit
WINE: Granduca - Nebbiolo d'Alba

Torta di zucchini (Zucchini Tart), 397
Polenta alla pistoiese
(Polenta with Sausages and Quail), 207
Bavarese (Orange Cream *Bavarese*), 446
WINE: Villa Antinori - Chianti Classico

Pinci di Montalcino (*Pinci* Montalcino Style), 147
Pollo al sale
(Chicken Cooked Covered with Salt), 224
Cardi al forno (Baked Cardoons), 356
Panforte, 86
WINE: Brusco dei Barbi

Torta al formaggio (Cheese Tart), 473
Cappon magro (*Caponata* Genoese Version), 377
Bongo (Chocolate Cream Puff Mound), 486
WINE: Gavi - La Giustiniana

Crostini caldi di mare
(Rustic Seafood Canapés), 304
Minestra di lattuga (Lettuce Soup), 372
Stufato di Milano
(Braised Rump of Beef Milano Style), 228
Whole Boiled Potatoes
Coppe di crema zabaione alla parmigiana
(Dessert Cups of *Crema Zabaione* Parma Style),
249
WINE: Contratto - Barbaresco

Spaghetti con passato di pesce alla genovese
(Genoese Fish Sauce with Spaghetti), 184
Pollo in forno
(Oregano Chicken Baked with Potatoes
and Tomatoes), 242
Green Salad
Torta di mandorle (Almond Cake), 87
WINE: Rainoldi - Valtellina Superiore - Inferno

Bavarese di peperoni (Green Pepper *Bavarese*), 447
Uova alla fornaia (Baked Giant *Tortelli*), 172
Petti di pollo allo specchio
(Rolled Chicken Breast in Aspic), 435
Cipolline in agrodolce
(Sweet-and-Sour Button Onions), 366
Fresh Fruit
WINE: Lugana - Visconti

Lasagne alla genovese
(Boiled Lasagne with Beef Sauce), 160
Fricassea di vitella (Fricassee of Veal), 295
Broccoli al vino blanco
(Broccoli in White Wine Sauce), 349
Gelato di frutta fresca
(Italian Fresh Fruit Ice Cream), 496
WINE: Brolio Bianco

Tagliatelle con sugo di oca conservato
(*Tagliatelle* with Sauce of Preserved Goose), 134
Zucchini ripieni in sugo di vitella
(Stuffed Zucchini in Veal Sauce), 396
Schiacciata unta alla fiorentina
(Beef-flavored *Schiacciata*), 417
Fresh Fruit
WINE: Venegazzù Riserva della Casa

Spaghetti neri
(Spaghetti with the Ink of the Squid), 187
Frittatini ripieni
(Potato Flour Crêpes Stuffed with Meat), 111
Cavolfiore affogato
(Cauliflower Steamed in Wine), 360
Gelatina dolce di fruitta
(Orange or Lemon Dessert Aspic), 443
WINE: Fiano di Avellino - Mastroberardino

———————

Gramigna ai quattro formaggi
(*Gramigna* with Four Cheeses), 142
Scaloppine ai funghi porcini
(Veal *Scaloppine* with Wild Mushrooms), 273
Asparagi alla Cornaro (Asparagus "Cornaro"), 346
Cannoli, 481
WINE: Nebbiolo d'Alba - Vignaveja

———————

Fagiolini alle nocciole
(String Beans with a Cream-Hazelnut Sauce), 368
Anitra peposa (Duck with Green Peppercorns), 30
Green Salad
Merendine del Granduca
(Grand Duke Ferdinand's Snacks), 112
WINE: Chianti Classico - Isole e Olena

———————

Spaghettini dell' ortolano (Thin Spaghetti with
Aromatic Herbs and Vegetables), 184
Ossobuco di tacchino (Turkey *Ossobuco*), 294
Asparagi in salsa
(Asparagus in Egg-Lemon Sauce), 345
Fresh Fruit
WINE: Illuminati - Trebbiano d'Abruzzo

———————

Pasticcio di pasta (Pasta *Pasticcio*), 193
Scaloppine agli asparagi
(Veal *Scaloppine* with Asparagus Sauce), 274
Carote al prezzemolo
(Carrots in Parsley Sauce), 358
Sformato dolce di polenta
(Polenta Cheesecake), 211
WINE: Spalletti -
Bianco Vergine della Val di Chiana

———————

Spaghetti all'aragosta (Spaghetti with Lobster), 186
Filetti di sogliola fritti
(Deep-fried Sole Fillets), 312
Green Salad
Marronata (Chestnut Tart), 463
WINE: Mastroberardino - Taurasi DOC

———————

Torta di porri (Leek-Potato Tart), 389
Cima alla genovese
(Stuffed Pressed Veal Breast), 249
Salsa di noci (Walnut Sauce), 91
Mostarda di Cremona
(Fruit Relish of Cremona), 59
Gelato di frutta fresca
(Italian Fresh Fruit Ice Cream), 496
WINE: Bruzzone - Gavi

———————

Sformato di maionese (Mayonnaise Mold), 438
Tortelli di mele
(Apple *Tortelli* for Christmas Eve), 171
Arrocchiato di vitella (Roast Loin of Veal
Laced with Green Peppercorns and Sage), 285
Green Salad
Monte Bianco (Molded Purée of Fresh Chestnuts),
448
WINE: Collio - Tocai Friulano - Livio Felluga

———————

Broccoli alla romana (Broccoli Roman Style), 349
Spaghetti con caviale di tonno
(Spaghetti with Fresh Fish Roe), 186
Peperoni ripieni
(Peppers Stuffed with Veal and Ricotta), 384
Fresh Fruit
WINE: Mastroberardino -
Lacryma Christi del Vesuvio Bianco

———————

Insalata di pomodori
(Neapolitan Tomato Salad), 386
Timballo di riso alla parmigiana
(Rice *Timballo* Stuffed with Squab), 204
Melanzane al forno (Eggplant Baked in Batter), 375
Fresh Fruit
WINE: Bertani - Amarone della Valpolicella Recioto

———————

Sardine di Alghero
(Sardines in the Style of Alghero), 300
Torta di anguille (Eel Tart), 475
Fagiolini alla genovese
(String Beans Genoese Style), 368
Gelato di frutta fresca
(Italian Fresh Fruit Ice Cream), 496
WINE: Galestro - Ruffino

———————

Lasagne con melanzane
(Lasagne with Eggplant), 163
Lombatina di vitella alla griglia

514

(Veal Chops Cooked on a Range-top Grill), 231
Green Salad
Zuccotto (Homemade *Zuccotto*), 477
WINE: Rainoldi - Valtellina Superiore - Grumello

Frittata profumata
(*Frittata* with Mixed Fresh Herbs), 116
Polenta del Casentino
(Polenta from Casentino), 207
Sedani saltati ("Stir-Sautéed" Celery), 391
Fresh Fruit
WINE: Montevertine - Chianti Classico

Pomodori ripieni di pasta
(Tomatoes Stuffed with Macaroni), 387
Spezzatino alle carote
(Cubes of Beef Shank in Carrot-Wine Sauce), 230
Whole Boiled Potatoes
Granita di limone (Italian Lemon Ice), 500
WINE: Bersano - Barbaresco

Spaghetti al pomodoro al forno
(Spaghetti in Sauce with Baked Tomatoes), 139
Seppie in umido (Cuttlefish Leghorn Style), 304
Patate all'olio o con maionese
(Escalloped Potato Salad), 380
Fresh Fruit
WINE: Regaleali Bianco

Fiori di zucca ripieni
(Stuffed Zucchini Blossoms), 398
Galantina di pollo (Chicken in Galantine), 323
Maionese (Mayonnaise), 438
Salsa rustica (Tuscan Country Sauce), 82
Pastiera (Neapolitan Easter Cake), 467
WINE: La Scolca - Gavi di Gavi

Tegamaccio di verdure
(Compote of Baked Vegetables), 343
Ossobuco alla novese (*Ossobuco* from Novara), 293
Green Salad
Torta di castagne (Fresh Chestnut Torte), 100
WINE: Dessilani - Barbera del Piemonte

"Fazzoletti" ripieni (Stuffed "Handkerchiefs"), 107
Scaloppine alla senese
(Veal *Scaloppine* with Tarragon Siena Style), 272
Finocchi alla parmigiana con salsicce

(Fennel "Bulbs" Parma Style), 370
Fresh Fruit
WINE: Monsanto -
Chianti Classico Riserva "Il Poggio"

Cannelloni con punte di asparagi
(*Cannelloni* Stuffed with Asparagus), 156
Coscia di agnello in salsa di menta
(Boned Leg of Lamb with Fresh Mint Sauce), 255
Pere alla Corrado (Pears Corrado Style), 61
WINE: Frescobaldi - Chianti -
Castello di Nipozzano

Maccheroni alla chitarra
(*Maccheroni* Cut with the "Guitar" in
Lamb Sauce), 144
Carne ai sette sapori (Beef with Seven Flavors), 230
Gambi di bietola in padella
(Sautéed Stems of Chard), 348
Gelatina dolce di fruitta
(Orange or Lemon Dessert Aspic), 433
WINE: Bertani - Soave

Risotto alla parmigiana
(*Risotto* in the Style of Parma), 202
Vitella all'aceto balsamico
(Veal in Balsamic Vinegar), 290
Polpettine di spinaci
(Deep-fried Spinach Croquettes), 391
Fresh Fruit
WINE: Riuniti - Lambrusco Reggiano DOC

Fagioli con sedano e carote
(Cannellini Beans with Celery and Carrots), 401
Scaloppine al Vin Santo
(Veal *Scaloppine* with Vin Santo), 273
Porri al sugo di maiale (Leeks in Pork Sauce), 390
Fichi giulebbati con crema di fichi
(Figs "Nectared" with Fig-flavored Pastry Cream),
494
WINE: Ponte a Rondolino -
Vernaccia di San Gimignano

Spaghetti di Scheggino
(Spaghetti in Trout-Black Truffle Sauce), 140
Pesce in creta (Whole Fish Baked in Clay), 212
Patate "raganate" (Oregano Potatoes), 382
Babà alla crema (Babà layer cake), 475
WINE: Le Velette - Orvieto Classico Secco

Caponata (Sicilian Style), 376
Insalata di pasta III
(Pasta Salad with Swordfish), 197
Finocchi con salsa di capperi e acciughe
(Fennel "Bulbs" with Caper-Anchovy Sauce), 371
Fresh Fruit
WINE: Antinori - Est! Est!! Est!!!

———————

Panzarotti (Bread Pillows), 415
Spaghetti con broccoli
(Spaghetti with Broccoli), 183
Piccatine in carpione
(Cold Veal *Scaloppine* in Piquant Sauce), 275
Fresh Fruit
WINE: Mastroberardino - Greco di Tufo

———————

Ravioli di pollo in brodo
(Chicken Ravioli in Broth), 94
Turbante ripieno ("Stuffed" *Turbante*), 458
Carciofi in umido o in salsa
(Artichokes in Parsley Sauce), 354
Bavarese al marsala
(Marsala-flavored *Bavarese*), 444
WINE: Lamberti - Recioto della Valpolicella -
Amarone

———————

Broccoli alla romana (Broccoli Roman Style), 349
Quaglie nel nido di un pane toscano
(Quail in a Nest of Tuscan Bread), 407
Green Salad
Gelato di frutta fresca
(Italian Fresh Fruit Ice Cream), 496
WINE: Fattoria dei Barbi - Brunello di Montalcino

———————

Pappardelle allo spezzatino di coniglio
(*Pappardelle* with Stewed Rabbit Sauce), 150
Cervello al limone
(Veal Brains in Lemon Sauce), 298
Zucchini alla pancetta
(Zucchini with *Pancetta*), 395
Fresh Fruit
WINE: Pinot Grigio - Cavit

———————

Trenette con salsa di carciofi
(*Trenette* with Artichoke Sauce), 149
Agnello ripieno (Stuffed Lamb Shoulder), 258
Whole Boiled Potatoes
Fresh Fruit
WINE: Verdicchio - Fazi Battaglia

Index

acciughe, 299
agnello ripieno, 258–61
albicocche al sugo, 56, 59
alici, 299
Allori, 19–20
almonds:
　amaretti cookies, 67
　bitter vs. sweet, 67
　blanching of, 87–88
　cake, 87–89, 93
　cookies, 89–90
　paste, 90–91
aluminum pots, 350, 353
amaretti cookies, 67
anchovies, 299
　pasta salad with peppers and, 196–197
　salted, cleaning procedures for, 55
animelle, 297
anitra:
　pasticcio di, 332, 337–38
　peposa, 29–33
antipasto, 348, 359
Apicius, 400
appetizers:
　antipasto, 348, 359
　broccoli Roman style, 349
　canapés, 210, 301, 304–5
　caponata, 375–79
　deep-fried spinach croquettes, 391–92
　pasticcio as, 331
　polenta as, 209, 210
　sardines in style of Alghero, 300–301
apple *tortelli* for Christmas Eve, 171–172
apricot nuts, 67
apricots with wine syrup, 56, 59
Arborio rice, 69, 199
arrocchiato di vitella, 269, 285–87
artichokes, 350–54, 355
　cleaning of, 350–52
　cooking of, 77, 350, 352–53
　in parsley sauce, 354
　selection of, 350
　stuffed with spinach and chard, 352–53
　trenette with, 149–50
artichoke sauce, veal scaloppine with, 271
Art of Carving (Cervio), 23
asparagi, 343–47
　alla Cornaro, 346–47
　alla fiorentina, 343
　in salsa, 345–46

asparagus, 343–47
　cannelloni stuffed with, 156–57
　cooking of, 343, 344–45
　"Cornaro," 346–47
　in egg-lemon sauce, 345–46
　"steamed" tips of, 345
　thickness of, 343
asparagus sauce:
　scaloppine with, 274–75
　tagliatelle with, 133–34
aspic, 431–50
　orange or lemon dessert, 56, 443–444
　preparation of, 432–34
　rolled chicken breast in, 96, 431, 435–37
　stuffed whole carp with, 313, 318–322

babà alla crema, 56, 425–28
bagnomaria, 70
　preparation of, 442
bain-marie, 70
Baldini, 496
balsamella, 332
　preparation of, 334–35
balsamic vinegar, 67
　veal in, 269, 290
barbabietola, 347
barley flour polenta, 199
barrels, wine-vinegar, 78
basil, 67
　sauce, 87
Bastone, Signor, 180
batters:
　for crêpes, 103, 105–7
　for deep-fried sage leaves, 112–13
batticarne, 70
battuto, 390
bavarese, 431, 444–48
　green pepper, 447–48
　Marsala-flavored, 444–46
　orange cream, 446–47
　preparation of, 444
bavarese, 431, 444–48
　all' arancia, 446–47
　al Marsala, 444–46
　di peperoni, 447–48
bay leaves, 67
　deep-fried, 113
　potatoes with, 381
beans, *see* legumes; string beans
beef:
　boiled lasagne with sauce of, 160–161

　braised rump of, Milan style, 226, 228–29
　braised rump of, Parma style, 226–227
　broth, 67
　flavored schiacciata, 417
　with seven flavors, 226, 230
　in U.S. vs. Italy, 268
beef sauce:
　boiled lasagne with, 160–61
　tagliatelle with, 132–33
beef shank, cubes of, in carrot-wine sauce, 230–31
beets, 347
beverages, sirups as, 56
bietole, 347–48
　all' agro, 347
　saltate, 347
blanching:
　of nuts, 87–88
　of vegetables, 352–53
bocca di dama, 476–79
boiled course, 375
Boletus edulis, 64
Bologna, 68
bomboloni, 423–24
bongo, 486–87
Borgotaro, mushrooms in, 64, 65
bottigliaria, 21
bowls:
　copper, 72
　terra-cotta, 71
bracioline, 268–69
　all' empolese, 271
brains, veal, in lemon sauce, 269, 298
brain sauce, 96–97, 257
braising, 226–31
bread crumbs, 67
breads, 402–24
　beef-flavored schiacciata, 417
　cheese dough pizza, 418
　cotechino sausage baked in a crust, 51, 54, 422–24
　from Ferrara, 402–6
　pillows, 415–16
　sage, 414
　schiacciata with coarse salt, 416
　"sponge," 402, 403–5
　stuffed focaccia, 419–21
　Tuscan, 402, 407–13
brick ovens, improvised, 402, 406
brioche, 423–24
broccoli, 341, 348–50, 359, 361
　Roman style, 349
　spaghetti with, 183

broccoli (cont.)
  in white wine sauce, 349–50
broccoli, 348–50
  alla romana, 349
  spaghetti con, 183
  al vino bianco, 349–50
broccolirab, 93, 348
  orecchiette with, 153–54
broccoletti, 348
broth, 67
  chicken ravioli in, 93
  kale simmered in, 362
budino, 431
  di pollo, 70, 440–43
Buontalenti, 20, 495
butter, 67
  sculpture, 19, 23

cabbage:
  black, *see* kale
  stuffed, 363
cabbage, savoy, 363–65
  cutting of, 363
  potato stew, 363–64
  Sardinia style, 365
  with sausages, 364–65
caciotte, 68
cafés, 495
cakes:
  almond, 87–89, 93
  baba layer, 56, 425–28
  chestnut torte, 100–101
  chocolate, 137
  Christmas fruit and nut roll, 55, 66,
    429
  Genoese pastry, 487–88
  Neapolitan Easter, 466–68
  panettone, 430
  panforte, 86
  polenta cheesecake, 211
  spongecakes, 476–79, 487–88
  walnut, 83–85
calamari, 301, 304–5, 306–7
canapés:
  polenta, 210
  rustic seafood, 301, 304–5
cannellini beans, 67, 71, 399
  baked, 213
  with celery and carrots, 401
  soup Sienese style, 99–100
cannelloni, 75, 104, 154–59
  cutting and preparing pasta for,
    154–55
  stuffed with asparagus, 156–57
  stuffed with tongue and chicken,
    156, 158–59
cannelloni, 75, 104, 154–59
  con lingua salmistrata, 156, 158–59
  con punte di asparagi, 156–57
cannoli, 66, 480–83
cannoli molds, 71
capelli d'angelo, 138
caper-anchovy sauce, fennel with,
    371–72
capers, 67, 82

fish with, 232
  tomato sauce, 99
capitoni, 307
caponata, 373, 375–79
  Genoese version, 377–79
  seafood, 375, 377–79
  Sicilian, 375, 376
  Tuscan, 375, 377
cappelletti, 176–78
  baked, Bolognese style, 177–78
  preparation of, 176–77
cappelletti alla bolognese, 177–78
cappone, 375
cappon magro, 377–79
capsicum annuum, 382
carciofi, 350–54
  alla fiorentina, 352–53
  ritti, 352
  in umido o in salsa, 354
cardi, 355–57
  bagna cauda, 355
  al forno, 356–57
  in pinzimonio, 355
  trippati, 356
cardoons, 352, 355–57, 361
  baked, 356–57
  cleaning of, 355
  cooking of, 353
carne ai sette sapori, 226, 230
carote, 357–59
  alla crema, 358
  al prezzemolo, 354, 358–59
carp, stuffed whole, with aspic, 313,
    318–22
carrots, 357–59
  boiling of, 357
  in cream sauce, 358
  in parsley sauce, 354, 358–59
carving and presentation, 19–37
  etiquette of, 23–29
  of fish, 25
  of fruit, 23, 24–25, 66
  in historical perspective, 19–37
  implements used for, 24, 25–28
  of stuffed fowl, 29–37
casseroles:
  enamel, 72
  flameproof, 72, 77
  terra-cotta, 77
Castiglione, Baldassare, 23
Caswell-Massey, 40*n*
catino, 71
cauliflower, 359–61
  as broccoli, 348, 359
  cleaning and boiling of, 360
  green, 359
  "Milan" variety of, 359
  purple, 348, 359
  steamed in wine, 360–61
cavolfiore, 359–61
  affogato, 360–61
cavolo alla Sarda, 365
cavolo nero, 361–62
  in umido, 362
cavolo verzotto (verza), 363–65

cecina, 400
celery, 352, 390–91
  "stir-sautéed," 391
cervello al limone, 269, 298
Cervio, Vincenzo, 23
champignons, 64
cheese:
  Gorgonzola, 67
  gramigna with, 142–43
  grating of, 27
  mozzarella, 38, 68, 272
  Pecorino, 39, 68
  sorbet of, 496, 499–500
  tart, 473
  see also mascarpone; ricotta
cheesecake, polenta, 211
chefs, as artists, 20
chestnuts:
  molded purée of, 100, 448–50
  peeling of, 449
  tart, 459, 463–64
  torte, 100–101
chicken:
  baked marinated, with peppers,
    240–41
  boned, tied "like a salami," 247–49
  boned whole stuffed, 261, 313, 323
  boning of, 233–36, 323–27
  broth, 67
  budino, 70, 440–43
  as cannelloni stuffing, 158–59
  cooked covered with salt, 224–25
  cutting of, into pieces with bone,
    238–40
  fenneled, 238
  fricassee, 238
  galantine, 261, 313, 323–30
  oregano, baked with potatoes and
    tomatoes, 242
  ravioli in broth, 93
  sautéed with mushrooms, 241
  with vinegar sauce, 242–43
  whole, cooked between terra-cotta,
    71, 213
  wrapped in prosciutto, 214, 217–19
chicken breasts:
  boning of, from whole chicken,
    233–34
  butterflying of, 237
  cooked on a plate, 222–24, 233
  grilled, 232
  rolled, in aspic, 96, 431, 435–37
  whole, boning of, 235–36
chicken drumsticks:
  boning of, 244
  stuffed, 243–45
chicken necks, boning of, 246
chick-peas, 399
  pizza, 400
  soup, taglierini in, 138–39
Chinese cooking, 59, 68, 341–42, 348,
    369
chitarra, 71
  how to cut pasta with, 143–44
  maccheroni alla, 93, 144–45

chocolate cream puff mound, 486–87
chocolate pasta, 118, 119
    in sweet and spicy sauce, 136–38
choppers, half-moon, *see* mezzaluna
chopping, 79–86
chopping boards, 77
Christmas recipes:
    fruit and nut roll, 55, 66, 429
    panettone, 430
    panforte, 86
    Sienese almond cookies, 89–90
    zampone, 51–54, 400
cialde, 103, 104
cilantro, 68
cima alla genovese, 60, 249–54, 269,
    285, 297
cime di rape, *see* broccolirab
cipolline, 366–67
    in agrodolce, 366–67
citrons:
    carving and presentation of, 25, 66
    whole glazed, 66
clay, cooking in, 212–13
clay vessels and pots, *see* terra-cotta
    vessels
Clement VII, Pope, 390
Cleofa, Maria de, 70
"Cleopatra's Feast," 19–20
coffee, 495
colla di pesce, 432–34
collo di tacchino ripieno, 245–47
Coltelli, Procopio, 495
coltelli per battere, 26
coniglio ripieno arrocchiato, 261–67
contrafiletto, 269
cookies:
    amaretti, 67
    Sienese almond, 89–90
cooking:
    of dried pasta, 181–82, 195–96
    of fresh pasta, 131
    of vegetables, 77, 343, 344–45, 353,
        357, 360
cooking, special methods of, 212–32
    braising meat, 226–31
    in clay, 212–13
    in a paper bag, 214–21
    on range-top grills, 231–32
    in salt, 224–25
    steaming on a covered plate, 222–
        224
coppe di crema zabaione alla
    parmigiana, 489, 491–94
copper:
    bowls, 72
    pans, 76, 102
Cornaro, Caterina, 346
cornmeal, *see* polenta
corn oil, 68
cornstarch, 489
Corrado, 61, 180, 182
Cortegiano, Il (Castiglione), 23
cosce di pollo ripiene, 243–45
coscia di agnello, 96
    in salsa di menta, 255–57

Cosimo I, grand duke of Tuscany,
    304
costine al "vecchio Molinetto," 214,
    219–21
cotechino, 400
    preparation of, 54
    sausage baked in a crust, 51, 54,
        422–24
cotechino, 400
    in camicia, 51, 54, 422–24
Courtier, The (Castiglione), 23
cream:
    pastry, 72, 76, 489–91, 494–95
    whipping of, 72, 493
cream-hazelnut sauce, string beans
    with, 368
cream puff pastry, 484–87
    chocolate cream puff mound, 486–
        487
    preparation of, 484–85
cream sauce, carrots in, 358
credenza, 21
crema di funghi, 64, 65–66
crema pasticceria, 489–91
crème caramel, 61
crêpe pans, 102
crêpes, 102–12
    Florentine style, 104, 110
    Grand Duke Ferdinand's snacks,
        104, 112
    potato flour, 104, 111
    stuffed handkerchiefs, 104, 107–9
crespelle, 102–12
    alla fiorentina, 104, 110
croquettes, deep-fried spinach, 391–
    392
crostini, 81, 82, 209
    caldi di mare, 301, 304–5
    di polenta, 210
custard cream, 489–91
cuttlefish, *see* inksquid
Cynara cardunculus, 355

De' Sorbetti (Baldini), 496
desserts:
    apricots with wine syrup, 56, 59
    brandied mascarpone, 43–44
    cups of *crema zabaione*, Parma
        style, 489, 491–94
    figs "nectared" with fig-flavored
        pastry cream, 494–95
    Marsala-flavored bavarese, 444–45
    molds, 431, 444–47
    orange cream bavarese, 446–47
    orange or lemon aspic, 56, 443–44
    pears Corrado style, 61–62
    tiramisù ("lift me up"), 44
    yeast doughs for, 402, 425–30
    see also cakes; cookies; ice cream;
        pastry
dill, 189–90
double boilers, 72, 491
doughs:
    pasta, 119–25, 127–29
    stretching of, 76, 123–25, 127–29

yeast, 402–30
dragoncello, *see* tarragon
duck:
    with green peppercorns, 29–33
    pasticcio, 332, 337–38
dumplings, 93–94, 391–92

eels:
    cleaning of, 307–8
    tart, 307, 474–76
egg-lemon sauce, asparagus in, 345–
    346
eggplant, 341, 373–79
    baked in batter, 379
    cutting of, 373–74
    lasagne with, 163–64
    pulp removed from, 78
    stuffed, Puglia style, 374–75
    see also caponata
eggs, *see* batters; crêpes;
    omelets
egg whites, beating of, 72
enamel:
    casseroles, 72
    pots, 350, 353
equipment, 15, 70–78
    bowls, 71, 72
    for carving, 24, 25–28
    casseroles, 72, 77
    knives, 24, 26, 27, 74, 79
    pans, 76, 102
    for truffles, 63–64
erbette filling, 347
Etruscans, 68, 212, 348

fagiano ripieno, 34–37
fagioli:
    al forno, 213
    con sedano e carote, 401
fagioliera, 213
fagiolini, 367–69
    alla genovese, 368–69
    alle nocciole, 368
faraona al cartoccio, 214–17
farcia, 313, 327–28
fazzoletti ripieni, 104, 107–9
fennel, 67, 189–90, 369–72
    "bulbs" Parma style, 370–71
    with caper-anchovy sauce, 371–72
    cutting of, 369–70
    Florence or sweet, 369
Ferdinand II, grand duke of
    Tuscany, 104
fero da pasta (ferra per pasta), 26
fichi giulebbati con crema di fichi,
    494–95
figs "nectared" with fig-flavored
    pastry cream, 494–95
filetti di sogliola fritti, 312
Fine Art of Italian Cooking, The
    (Bugialli), 11, 51, 61, 67, 82, 87,
        94, 239, 323, 373
    pasta in, 123, 149, 155
    seafood in, 302, 306
    vegetables in, 343, 347, 360

finocchi, 369–72
    alla parmigiana con salsicce, 370–371
    con salsa di capperi e acciughe, 371–72
finocchiona, 67
fiori di zucca ripieni, 398–99
fish:
    anchovies, 55, 196–97, 299
    with capers, 232
    carving and presentation of, 25
    cooking in clay of, 212
    galantine, 313, 314–18
    gelatin, 431, 432–34
    grilled, 232
    pike, 161–62
    sardines, 189–90, 299, 300–301, 369
    scaling and boning of, 314–16, 319–20
    sole fillets, 309–12
    steamed on a plate, 222
    stuffed whole carp with aspic, 313, 318–22
    trout, 141, 212, 222, 232
    tuna, 46, 197, 269, 287–89
    vegetable pasticcio, 332, 338–40
fish roe, spaghetti with, 186–87
fish sauce, Genoese, with spaghetti, 184–85
fish scalers, 72
flame-tamers, 73
flour:
    barley, 199
    potato, crêpes, 104, 111
    semolina, 118, 152–54, 199
    sifting of, 77, 104–5
flouring, technique for, 283
focaccia, stuffed, 419–21
focaccia farcita, 419–21
Foeniculum vulgare, 369
food mills, 73, 97–101
    how to pass food through, 98
fracassare, 295
French cooking:
    ice cream in, 495
    Nouvelle Cuisine in, 341
    vegetables in, 341
fricassea, 295
    de pollo, 238
    di vitella, 269, 295–97
frittata, 102, 113–17
    made in the manner of tripe, 113–114, 117
    with mixed fresh herbs, 113, 116
    pasta, 114, 116–17
    preparation of, 114–15
    with ricotta, 113, 115
frittata, 102, 113–17
    di pasta, 114, 116–17
    profumata, 113, 116
    con la ricotta, 113, 115
    trippata, 113–14, 117
frittatini ripieni, 104, 111
fruit:
    apple tortelli for Christmas Eve, 171–72

apricots with wine syrup, 56, 59
carving and presentation of, 23, 24–25, 66
figs "nectared" with fig-flavored pastry cream, 494–95
gelatina, 431, 443–44
glacéed, 58, 66, 67
ice creams, 495–98, 500–501
and nut roll, Christmas, 55, 66, 429
orange cream bavarese, 446–47
orange or lemon aspic, 56, 443–44
orange sirup, 56, 57–58
pears Corrado style, 61–62
pear tart, 468, 472
pheasant stuffed with, 34–37
relish of Cremona, 46, 59–60
servito, 19
stuffed peach tart, 465–66
Fusoritto de Narni, Reale, 23

galantina, 313–30
    pesce in, 314–18
    di pollo, 261, 323–30
galantines, 313–30
    chicken, 261, 313, 323–30
    fish, 313, 314–18
    stuffed whole carp with aspic, 313, 318–22
Galbreath, Betty, 171
gallo d'India, 28
gambi di bietola in padella, 348
gelatin:
    fish, 431, 432–34
    unflavored, 431
gelatina dolce di frutta, 56, 431, 443–444
gelato, 489–501
    di frutta fresca, 496–98
    di riso, 499
Giambologna, 20
giardiniera, 46
Giegher, Matteo, 21
ginepro, 80
giri, 451, 455–56
gnocchi, 93, 391
goose:
    preserved, tagliatelle with sauce of, 134
    preserved in its own fat, 27, 49–51
goose neck, boning of, 246
Gorgonzola, 67
gramigna ai quattro formaggi, 142–43
gran bollito misto, 51
granita di limone, 496, 500–501
gratella, 73, 231–32
graters, 27, 68
    hand, 73
gratta cascio, 27
grattugia, 73
green beans, *see* string beans
green sauce, 82
grills, range-top, 73
grinding, 87–97
    of herbs, 87
    of meat, 87, 92–93
    of nuts, 75, 88, 93

guinea hen cooked in a paper bag, 214–17
guitars, *see chitarra*

ham, *see* prosciutto
Hapsburg, Maria Luigia, 83
hare, pasticcio of, 331, 332–36
hen, guinea, cooked in a paper bag, 214–17
Henry III, king of France, 20–23
Henry IV, king of France, 20
herbs:
    grinding of, 87
    preserved aromatic, 48
    see also specific herbs

ice, lemon, 496, 500–501
ice cream, 489–501
    fresh Italian fruit, 496–98
    fruit, 495–98, 500–501
    history of, 495
    lemon ice, 496, 500–501
    preparation of, 497–98
    rice, 499
    sorbet of Parmigiano cheese, 496, 499–500
    types of, 495–96
    in U.S. vs. Italy, 495
ice sculptures, 19, 20
ingredients, 15, 38–69
    basic, glossary of, 38, 67–69
inksquid, 301
    cleaning of, 302–3
    Leghorn style, 301, 304
    in salad, 301, 306–7
insalata:
    composta, 347, 357
    mista, 357
    di pasta, 195–98
    di pomodori, 386–87
"*insalata*" *di riso estiva*, 205–6
"*insalata*" *di seppie, calamari e gamberi*, 301, 306–7
involtini, 268–69
    flouring of, 283
    preparation, rolling, and tying of, 282
    ripieni di rognone, 269, 280–84
    di vitella, 284–85
iron:
    in glazed terra-cotta pots, 77
    pots, cast, 350, 353
isinglass, 431, 432–34
Italian terms, glossary of, 504

Japanese cooking, 341–42
Jarro, 97
Jewish recipes:
    asparagus in egg-lemon sauce, 345–46
    fresh chestnut torte, 100–101
    stuffed whole carp with aspic, 313, 318–22
juniper berries, 67, 80

kale, 361–62
  cutting of, 362
  simmered in broth, 362
kidney, veal, rolled veal scaloppine
  stuffed with, 269
kidney beans, white, *see* cannellini
  beans
kidney sauce, 81–82, 93
knives, 24, 26, 27, 74, 79

ladyfingers, homemade Italian, 480
lamb:
  boning and stuffing of, 254–61
  grilled chops, 231
  in U.S. vs. Italy, 254, 258
lamb, leg of, 96
  boned, with fresh mint sauce, 255–
    257
  boning of, 255–57
lamb sauce, maccheroni cut with the
  "guitar" in, 93, 144–45
lamb shoulder:
  boning of, 258–59
  stuffed, 258–61
larding needles, 74
Larousse Gastronomique, 93, 495
lasagne, 75, 159–64
  boiled, with beef sauce, 160–61
  cutting and preparing pasta for,
    154–55
  with eggplant, 163–64
  with pesto, 159–60
  with pike, 161–62
lasagne, 75, 159–64
  alla genovese, 160–61
  con melanzane, 163–64
  al pesto, 159–60
latte all' portuguese, 61
lattuga, 372–73
la Varenne, 295, 313
leeks, 388–90
  cleaning of, 388
  in pork sauce, 390
  potato torte, 389
legumes, 67, 71, 399–401
  baked cannellini beans, 213
  bean soup Sienese style, 99–100
  cannellini beans with celery and
    carrots, 401
  chick-pea "pizza," 400
  lentils in rosemary-sage sauce,
    400–401
  taglierini in chick-pea soup, 138–39
legumi, 399–401
lemons:
  in bagnomaria, 70
  citron compared to, 66
  dessert aspic, 56, 443–44
  grating of, 55–56
  ice, 496, 500–501
  sirup, 56, 58
lemon sauce, veal brains in, 269, 298
lenticchie in umido, 400–401
lentils, 399
  in rosemary-sage sauce, 400–401

lepre, 331
  pasticcio di, 331, 332–36
lettuce, 372–73
  soup, 372–73
  types of, 372
linguine, 139, 179
liver, grilled veal, 232
lobster, spaghetti with, 186
Lorenzo the Magnificent, 104
Louis XIV, king of France, 23

macaroni:
  cut with the "guitar" in lamb sauce,
    93, 144–45
  tomatoes stuffed with, 387
maccheroni, 71
  alla chitarra, 93, 144–45
  alla napoletana, 182–83
McCully, Helen, 444
maionese, 195
  mold, 46, 431, 438–39
  tuna flavored, 287–88
mandolins, 26, 74
  cutting savoy cabbage with, 363
marinating, 232
marronata, 459, 463–64
Marsala, 61, 274, 332
  flavored bavarese, 444–46
Martino, Maestro, 20, 25
marzapane, 90–91
marzipan, 19, 90
mascarpone, 40–44, 70
  brandied, 43–44
mascarpone in coppa, 43–44
mayonnaise, 195
  mold, 46, 431, 438–39
  tuna flavored, 287–88
meat, 247–98
  boning and stuffing of, 247–67
  braising of, 226–31
  fat added to, 67, 74
  grilled, 231–32
  grinding of, 87, 92–93
  roasting of, 28
  tied "like a salami," 247–49
  vegetables vs., 341
  see also beef; lamb; pork; veal
meat pounders, 70
Medici, caterina de', 20, 495
Medici, Maria de', 20
melanzane, 373–79
  al forno, 379
  alla parmigiana, 379
  ripiene, 374–75
menus, suggested, 15, 512–16
merendine del Granduca, 104, 112
Messiburgo, Cristoforo di, 20
mezzaluna, 26, 64, 74, 79–86
  techniques for use of, 79–80
Michelangelo, 19, 167–68, 187,
  301
minestre, 363
  di lasagna con luccio, 161–62
  di lattuga, 372–73
minestrone, 361, 363

mint, 65, 67–68, 306
  sauce, 96, 255–57
molds, 431–50
  cannoli, 71
  in historical perspective, 431
  mayonnaise, 46, 431, 438–39
  purée of fresh chestnuts, 100, 448–
    450
mollusks, 301–7
Monte Bianco, 100, 448–50
mortadella, 68
mortars, 27
  china or ceramic, 74
  marble, 75, 87, 91
  stone, 87
mostarda di Cremona, 46, 59–60
"mothers," in wine vinegar, 44, 78,
  290
mozzarella, 38, 68, 272
mushrooms, 64–66
  chicken sautéed with, 241
  scaloppine with wild, 273
  soup, 64, 65–66
mustard, 59
mustard greens, 59

napkin folding, 21–23
needles, larding, 74
nepitella (mentuccia), 65, 68
noce moscade, *see* nutmeg
nodini, 285
Nouvelle Cuisine, 341
Nuovo Trattato de' Vini (Scarlino),
  21
nutmeg, 68, 392
nuts:
  apricot, 67
  blanching of, 87–88
  grinding of, 75, 88, 93
  see also almonds; chestnuts;
    walnuts

oca in pignatto, 27, 49–51
octopus, 301
oils, 68
olio di semi, 68
olive oil, 68
omelet pans, seasoning of, 102
omelets, 102, 113–17
  frittata made in the manner of
    tripe, 113–14, 117
  frittata with mixed fresh herbs, 113,
    116
  frittata with ricotta, 113, 115
  pasta frittata, 114, 116–17
  preparation of, 114–15
onions, 68
onions, button, 366–67
  cleaning of, 366
  sweet-and-sour, 366–67
Opera (Scappi), 21, 25
oranges:
  cream bavarese, 446–47
  decoration of, 24
  dessert aspic, 56, 443–44
  glacéed rind of, 58

oranges (cont.)
  grating of, 55–56
  sirup, 56, 57–58
orecchiette, 118, 152–54
  with broccolirab, 153–54
  preparation of, 152–53
orecchiette, 118, 152–54
  con cime di rape, 153–54
oregano, 68
  chicken baked with potatoes and
    tomatoes, 242
  potatoes, 382
ossobuco, 269, 290–95
  cutting veal shank into, 292
  from Novara, 291, 293–94
  turkey, 269, 291, 294
ossobuco, 269, 290–95
  alla novese, 291, 293–94
  di tacchino, 294–95
ovens, brick, improvising of, 402, 406

paintings, food in, 19–20
pancetta, 68, 74, 96
  zucchini with, 395–96
pane:
  ferrarese, 402–6
  alla salvia, 414
panettone, 430
panforte, 86
Panonto, 249
pans:
  copper, 76, 102
  for crêpes and omelets, 102
  seasoning of, 102
panzarotti, 415–16
pappardelle, 150–51
  allo spezzatino di coniglio, 150–51
parfaits, 496
"Parmesan" cheese, 68
Parmigiano, 68
  sorbet of, 496, 499–500
parsley, 68
parsley sauce:
  artichokes in, 354
  carrots in, 354, 358–59
passato di ceci con taglierini, 138–39
passing, 97–101
pasta:
  derivation of, 331
  with vegetables, 341
pasta, dried, 138, 179–98
  baked mold of, 193–95
  in cold dishes, 195–98
  cooking of, 181–82, 195–96
  with fresh sardines, 189–90, 299,
    369
  in hot dishes, 181–95
  "in the latest style Naples 1841,"
    182–83
  shapes of, 179
  see also pasta salads; penne;
    spaghetti
pasta, fresh, 118–78
  baked tortellini or cappelletti
    Bolognese style, 177–78

basic egg, 119
chitarra in cutting of, 143–44
chocolate, 118, 119
chocolate, in sweet and spicy
  sauce, 136–38
commercial, 119
cooking of, 131
drying of, 131
egg, 118–19
egg, without oil, 118, 120
without eggs, 118, 149–50
gramigne with four cheeses, 142–
  143
green, 118, 119
hand cutting of, 126, 148–49, 150,
  154
maccheroni cut with the "guitar"
  in lamb sauce, 93, 144–45
machine cutting of, 129–30, 139
orecchiette with broccolirab, 153–
  154
pappardelle with stewed rabbit
  sauce, 150–51
pinci Montalcino style, 147–48
preparation and kneading of dough
  for, 120–22
red, 118, 119
semolina, 118, 152–54
shaping of, 145–47, 152–53, 164–
  166, 175–77
storage of, 131
stretching of dough for, 123–25,
  127–29
trenette with artichoke, 148, 149–
  150
see also cannelloni; lasagne;
  spaghetti; tagliatelle; taglierini;
  tortelli
pasta boards, 77
pasta briciolata, 468–73
pasta con le sarde, 189–90, 299, 369
pasta cutters, 71, 75, 76
pasta frittata, 114, 116–17
pasta frolla, 459–68
  fragile, 459–63
pasta genovese, 487–88
pasta machines, 75
  cutting of pasta made with, 129–
    130, 139
  dough stretched with, 127–29
pasta mezza frolla, 474–76
pasta salads, 131, 195–98
  cooking pasta for, 195–96
  with peppers and anchovies, 196–
    197
  with swordfish, 197–98
  with tuna, 197
pastasciutta, 94
pasta sfoglia, 451–59
pasta soffiata, 484–87
pasticcio, 331–40
  duck, 332, 337–38
  fish-vegetable, 332, 338–40
  of hare, 331, 332–36
  hot vs. cold, 331

pasticcio, 331–40
  di anitra, 332, 337–38
  alla bolognese, 177–78
  di lepre, 331, 332–36
  di magro, 332, 338–40
  di pasta, 193–95
  di tortellini, 177–78
pasticium, 331
pastiera, 466–68
pastries, 451–88
  brioche, 423–24
  cannoli, 66, 480–83
  cheese tart, 473
  chestnut tart, 459, 463–64
  chocolate cream puff mound, 486–
    487
  cream puff, 484–87
  eel tart, 474–76
  equipment for, 26, 27, 75, 76
  Genoese, 487–88
  homemade Italian ladyfingers, 480
  homemade zuccotto, 67, 477–79
  Neapolitan Easter cake, 466–68
  pâte brisée, 468–73
  pear tart, 468, 472
  preparation of large turbante, 456–
    458
  puff, 451–59
  short, with hard-cooked egg yolks,
    459–64
  short, without hard-cooked egg
    yolks, 465–68
  short, with milk, 474–76
  spongecake, 476–79, 487–88
  stuffed peach tart, 465–66
pastry cream, 72, 76, 489–91
  fig-flavored, figs "nectared" with,
    494–95
pastry cutters, 75
pastry jaggers, 27
pastry scrapers, 76
patate, 380–82
  con alloro, 381
  all' olio o con maionese, 380–81
  "ragante," 382
paté, 331
pâte à chou, 484–87
pâte brisée, 468–73
  cheese tart, 473
  pear tart, 468, 472
  preparation of, 469–71
pavone, 28
peach tart, stuffed, 465–66
peacocks, 28
pears:
  carving of, 24
  Corrado style, 61–62
  tart, 468, 472
Pecorino, 39, 68
penne, 142, 190–93
  stir-sautéed in meat, 192–93
  stir-sautéed in veal sauce, 191–92
  with tripe sauce, 190–91
penne, 142, 190–93
  strascicate alla fiorentina, 192–93

strascicate al sugo di vitella, 191–192
trippate, 190–91
peperoni, 382–84
  bavarese di, 447–48
  ripieni, 384
peppercorns, 68, 96
  green, duck with, 29–33
  types of, 30
pepper plants, 29, 30
peppers, 382–84
  baked marinated chicken with, 240–41
  bavarese, 447–48
  cleaning and cutting of, 383
  pasta salad with anchovies and, 196–97
  stuffed with veal and ricotta, 384
  types of, 382–83
pere alla Corrado, 61–62
pesce:
  ai capperi, 232
  colla di, 432–34
  farcito, 313, 318–22
  in galantina, 314–18
  d'uovo, 113
pestles:
  china or ceramic, 74
  marble, 91
  wooden, 75, 87, 91
pesto, 87
  lasagne with, 159–60
petti di pollo allo specchio, 96, 431, 435–37
petto di pollo al piatto, 222–24, 233
pheasant:
  "in a paper bag," 214
  stuffed with fruits, 34–37
piatto di mezzo, 341, 352, 370, 379, 444
piccatine, 268–69
  in carpione, 275–76
piccoli crostini fritti, 373
pickles, 46–47
pignatto (pignatta), 27, 49, 71
  oca in, 27, 49–51
pike, lasagne with, 161–62
pinci, 118, 145–48
  di Montalcino, 145, 147–48
  shaping of, 145–47
Piper nigrum, 30
pistachios (*pistacchi*), 254
pizza:
  cheese dough, 418
  chick-pea, 400
  stuffed, 419–21
pizza al formaggio crescia, 418
plates, half-moon, 341
Platina, 20
polenta, 76, 199–200, 206–11
  canapés, 210
  from Casentino, 208–9
  cheesecake, 211
  cutting of, 209
  preparation of, 206–7

with sausages and quail in the style of Pistoia, 207–8
  types of, 199
polenta, 76, 199–200, 206–11
  del casentino, 208–9
  alla pistoiese, 207–8
pollo:
  all' aceto, 242–43
  affinocchiato, 238
  budino di, 70, 440–43
  alla cacciatora, 242
  disossato ripieno, 261, 313, 323
  in forno, 242
  al mattone, 71, 213
  ai peperoni, 240–41
  al prosciutto, 214, 217–19
  al sale, 224–25
  alla toscana, 241
polpo, 301
pomodori, 385–87
  insalata di, 386–87
  ripieni di pasta, 387
Pontormo, 113
ponzonetto, 76
porcini mushrooms, 64–66
  preparation of, 65
  scaloppine with, 273
  in soup, 64, 65–66
pork, 232
  cotechino sausage baked in a crust, 51, 54
  mortadella, 68
  pancetta, 68, 74, 96, 395–96
  prosciutto, 69, 214, 217–19
  Siena sausages, 93
  spareribs "Molinetto" style, 214, 219–21
  U.S. restrictions on importation of, 51, 69
  zampone, 51–54, 400
pork sauce, leeks in, 390
porri, 388–90
  al sugo di maiale, 390
  torta di, 389
potatoes, 380–82
  with bay leaves, 381
  oregano, 382
  salad, escalloped, 380–81
  shredding of, 380
potato flour crêpes, 104, 111
potato starch, 69, 489
pots, for cooking artichokes, 350, 353
pottaccio di vitello in fracasso, 295
poultry:
  boning of, 233–49
  carving and presentation of, 29–37
  duck pasticcio, 332, 337–38
  duck with green peppercorns, 29–33
  goose, 27, 49–51, 134, 246
  how to tie, 32
  pheasant stuffed with fruits, 34–37
  stuffed, how to carve, 29, 33
  stuffed turkey neck, 245–47
  turkey ossobuco, 269, 291, 294–95

see also chicken
poultry shears, 29
presentation:
  defined, 19n
  see also carving and presentation
prosciutto, 69
  chicken wrapped in, 214, 217–19
puff pastry, 451–59
  "stuffed" turbante, 269, 451, 458–459
puls, 118

quaglie:
  in foglie, 221–22
  nel nido di un pane toscano, 402, 407–13
quail:
  in the nest of Tuscan bread, 402, 407–13
  risotto with, 199, 200–201
  wrapped in grape leaves, 221–22
quinquinelle, 391

rabbit, 261–67
  boned whole, rolled and stuffed, 261–67
  boning of, 262–65
  pappardelle with sauce of, 150–51
rabiola, 93
ravioli, 93–95
  chicken, in broth, 93, 94–95
  naked, 391
ravioli, 93–95
  nudi, 391
  "*nudi*" *alla fiorentina*, 94
  di pollo in broda, 93, 94–95
ravioli cutters, 76
recipe list, by courses of meal, 15, 506–11
ricciarelli, 89–90
rice, 69
  Arborio, 69, 199
  ice cream, 499
  timballo stuffed with squab, 204–5
  see also risotto
rice salad, summer, 199, 205–6
ricotta, 38–40
  frittata with, 113, 115
  peppers stuffed with veal and, 384
  salata, 39, 69
  as substitute for mascarpone, 44
  in walnut sauce, 91
riso:
  in bianco, 199
  bollito, 199
  gelato di, 499
risotto, 69, 199–206
  preparation of, 200–201
  with quail, 199, 200–201
  rice timballo stuffed with squab, 199, 204–5
  with rosemary, 199, 203
  in the style of Parma, 202
risotto, 69, 199–206
  nero, 187

risotto (cont.)
  alla parmigiana, 202
  alle quaglie, 199, 200–201
  al ramerino, 199, 203
rolling pins:
  American type, 76, 123
  Italian type, 76, 123–35
  pasta dough stretched with, 123–25
Romano, 68
rooster of India, 28
Root, Waverley, 369
rosemary, 69, 203
  risotto with, 199, 203
rosemary-sage sauce, lentils in, 400–401
rotolo di natale, 55, 56, 429

sage, 69
  bread, 414
  deep-fried leaves of, 112–13
  veal scaloppine with, 272
salads, 342, 369
  composed, 347, 357
  of cuttlefish, squid, and shrimp, 301, 306–7
  escalloped potato, 380–81
  mixed, 357
  pasta, 131, 195–98
  summer rice, 199, 205–6
salami:
  finocchiona, 67
  mortadella, 68
salcicce di Siena, 96
salsa:
  asparagi in, 345–46
  di cervello, 96–97, 257
  di noci, 91, 136
  di pomodori ai capperi, 99
  di rognone, 81–82, 93
  rossa del Chianti, 82
  rustica, 82–83
  verde, 82
  verde del Chianti, 82
salt, 69
  anchovies in, 55
  chicken cooked covered with, 224–225
  copper bowls cleaned with, 72
  herbs preserved in, 48
  schiacciata with, 416
salvia fritta, 112–13
sardine, 299
  di Alghero, 299, 300–301
sardines, 299
  filleting of, 300
  fresh, pasta with, 189–90, 299, 369
  in style of Alghero, 299, 300–301
Sardo, 68
sauces:
  artichoke, veal scaloppine with, 271
  asparagus, scaloppine with, 274–75
  asparagus, tagliatelle with, 133–34
  avoiding conflicts of, 341

beef, tagliatelle with, 132–33
brain, 96–97, 257
caper-anchovy, fennel with, 371–372
cream, carrots in, 358
cream-hazelnut, string beans with, 368
egg-lemon, asparagus in, 345–46
Genoese fish, with spaghetti, 184–185
kidney, 81–82, 93
lamb, maccheroni cut with the "guitar" in, 93, 144–45
lemon, veal brains in, 269, 298
mint, boned leg of lamb with, 96, 255–57
parsley, artichokes, in, 354
parsley, carrots in, 354, 358–59
pork, leeks in, 390
preserved goose, tagliatelle with, 134
rabbit, pappardelle with, 150–51
rosemary-sage, lentils in, 400–401
tripe, penne with, 190–91
trout-black truffle, fresh spaghetti in, 141
Tuscan country, 82–83
veal, penne stir-sautéed in, 191–92
veal, stuffed zucchini in, 396–97
vinegar, chicken with, 242–43
walnut, 91
walnut, tagliatelle in, 136
white wine, broccoli in, 349–350
sausages, 49, 69
  baked in a crust, 51, 54, 422–24
  cotechino, 51, 54, 400, 422–24
  rolled veal scaloppine stuffed with, 284–85
  savoy cabbage with, 364–65
  Siena, 93
  zampone, 51–54, 400
savoiardi, 480
savori, 375
savoy cabbage, *see* cabbage, savoy
scaloppine, 268–69, 271–85
  with asparagus sauce, 274–75
  cold, in piquant sauce, 275–76
  "mock" game birds, 269, 276–79
  with puréed artichoke sauce, 271
  rolled, stuffed with kidney, 269, 280–84
  rolled, stuffed with sausage, 284–285
  with sage, 272
  with Vin Santo, 273–74
  with wild mushrooms, 273
scaloppine, 268–69, 271–85
  agli asparagi, 274–75
  all' empolese, 271
  ai funghi porcini, 273
  alla senese, 272
  al vin santo, 273–74
  di vitella alla salvia, 272
Scappi, 20, 21, 25, 28
Scarlino, 21

schiacciata, 400, 416–17
  beef-flavored, 417
  with coarse salt, 416
schiacciata, 400, 416–17
  al sale grosso, 416
  unta alla fiorentina, 417
schienali, 297
sciroppo di arancia, 57–58
sciroppo e sugo, 56–62
scorze di arancia candite, 58
seafood, 299–312
  canapés, 301, 304–5
  caponata, 375, 377–79
  cleaning of, 302–3, 305, 307–8
  eel tart, 474–76
  mollusks, 301–7
  salad of cuttlefish, squid, and shrimp, 301, 306–7
  spaghetti with lobster, 186
  see also fish; inksquid; squid
sedani, 390–91
  saltati, 391
semolina:
  in fresh pasta, 118, 152–54
  in polenta, 199
senape, 59
seppie, 301, 302–4, 306–7
  in umido, 301, 304
servito, 19
setaccio, 77, 92, 97
sfingione di San Vito, 419–21
sflogliata, 451–59
sformato, 341
  dolce di polenta, 211
  di maionese, 46, 431, 438–39
  di pollo, 70, 440–43
short pastry, 459–68
  chestnut tart, 459, 463–64
  eel tart, 474–76
  with hard-cooked egg yolks, 459–64
  without hard-cooked egg yolks, 465–68
  with milk, 474–76
  Neapolitan Easter cake, 466–68
  preparation of, 460–63, 474–75
  stuffed peach tart, 465–66
shrimp:
  cleaning of, 305
  in salad, 301, 306–7
sieves, 27, 77, 92, 97
sifters, 77
siringa, 26
sirups, syrups, 56–62
  glacéed orange rind, 58
  lemon, 56, 58
  mostarda of Cremona, 59–60
  orange, 56, 57–58
  pears Corrado style, 61–62
  wine, apricots with, 56, 59
skewers, 28
snow peas, 59
sole fillets, 309–12
  deep-fried, 312
  "how to" technique for, 309–11
sorbet, 495

of Parmigiano cheese, 496, 499–500

sorbetto, 495, 496
  di parmigiano, 496, 499–500

sottoaceti, 46–47, 366

soups, 359
  bean, Sienese style, 99–100
  chick-pea, taglierini in, 138–39
  kale in, 361
  lettuce, 372–73
  wild mushroom, 64, 65–66

spaghetti (dry):
  with broccoli, 183
  with fresh fish roe, 186–87
  Genoese fish sauce with, 184–85
  with lobster, 186
  thin, with aromatic herbs and vegetables, 184

spaghetti (dry):
  all' aragosta, 186
  con broccoli, 183
  con caviale di tonno, 186–87
  con passato di pesce alla genovese, 97, 184–85
  neri, 167, 187–88

spaghetti (fresh), 139–41
  cutting of, 139
  with the ink of the squid, 187–88
  in sauce with baked tomatoes, 140
  with trout-black truffle sauce, 63, 141

spaghetti (fresh):
  al pomodoro al forno, 140
  di scheggino, 63, 141

spaghettini dell' ortolano, 184

spareribs, "Molinetto" style, 214, 219–21

spearmint, 67–68

spezzare, 295

spezzatino, 238, 240, 258
  alle carote, 230–31
  veal, 269, 295–97

spianatoia, 77

spices, grinding of, 27, 74, 87, 91–92

spinach, 391–93
  artichokes stuffed with, 352–53
  deep-fried croquettes, 391–92
  Genoese style, 393

spinaci, 391–93
  alla genovese, 393
  polpettine di, 391–92

"sponge" bread, 402
  preparation of, 403–5

spuma, 496

squab:
  rice timballo stuffed with, 204–5
  tortelli stuffed with, 169–70

squid, 301
  cleaning of, 302–3
  rustic seafood canapés, 301, 304–5
  in salad, 301, 306–7
  spaghetti with ink of, 187–88

steaming, 222–24, 343, 345, 360–61

stew, cabbage-potato, 363–64

stracotto alla parmigiana, 226–27

string beans, 367–69
  cleaning of, 367
  with cream-hazelnut sauce, 368
  Genoese style, 368–69

stufato di Milano, 226, 228–29

stuffed handkerchiefs, 104, 107–9

sugar:
  caramelized, 61–62, 76
  sculptures, 19, 20–23

sunflower oil, 68

sweetbreads, "stuffed" turbante, 269

Swiss chard, 347–48
  artichokes stuffed with, 352–53
  with olive oil and lemon, 347
  sautéed stems of, 348
  "stir-sautéed," 347

swordfish, pasta salad with, 197–98

Tacca, 20

tagliatelle, 132–36
  with asparagus sauce, 133–34
  with beef sauce, 132–33
  hand cutting of, 126
  machine cutting of, 129–30
  red pepper, 91, 119, 135
  with sauce of preserved goose, 49, 134
  in walnut sauce, 91, 136

tagliatelle, 51, 132–36
  al peperoncino, 91, 119, 135
  con salsa di noci, 91, 136
  al sugo di asparagi, 133–34
  al sugo di manzo, 132–33
  con sugo di oca conservato, 49, 134

tagliere, 77

taglierini:
  in chick-pea soup, 138–39
  hand cutting of, 126
  machine cutting of, 129–30

Taillevent, 341

tarragon, 98, 99
  veal scaloppine Siena style with, 272

tartaric acid, 40*n*

tartufi, 62–64

tarts:
  cheese, 473
  chestnut, 459, 463–64
  eel, 474–76
  pear, 468, 472
  stuffed peach, 465–66
  zucchini, 55

technique, emphasis on, 15

tegamaccio di verdure, 343, 373

temperatures, 505

terra-cotta bowls, 71

terra-cotta jars, oil stored in, 68

terra-cotta tiles, 402, 406

terra-cotta vessels, 27, 49, 71
  for cooking artichokes, 350, 353
  glazed, 73, 77, 350, 353
  stovetop use of, 73, 77
  unglazed, 71, 73

Three Treatises (Giegher), 21

thyme, 99

tiles, unglazed terra-cotta, 402, 406

timballo (or *bomba*) *di riso alla parmigiana*, 199, 204–5

tiramisù ("lift me up"), 44

tomatoes, 69, 385–87
  Neapolitan salad, 386–87
  removing skin from, 384
  slicing of, for salad, 386
  spaghetti in sauce with, 140
  stuffed with macaroni, 387
  stuffing of, 385–86

tomato paste, 69, 291

tomato sauce, with capers, 99

tongue, as cannelloni stuffing, 158–159

tordimatti, 269, 276–79

torta:
  di anguille, 307, 474–76
  di castagne, 100
  al formaggio, 473
  genovese, 487–88
  di mandorle, 87–89, 93
  di noci, 83–85
  di pere, 468, 472
  di pesche alla crema, 465–66
  di porri, 389
  di zucchini, 55, 397

tortelli, 93, 164–74
  apple, for Christmas Eve, 171–72
  baked giant, 63, 172–74
  erbette filling for, 347
  preparation of, 164–66
  stuffed with squab, 169–70

tortelli, 93, 164–74
  di mele, 171–72
  di Michelangelo, 167–68
  di piccione, 169–70

tortelli cutters, 75, 76

tortellini:
  baked, Bolognese style, 177–78
  preparation of, 175–76

tortelloni, 164
  alla casentinese, 168–69

trenette, 118, 148–50
  cutting of, 148–49
  con salsa di carciofi, 148, 149–50

Tre Trattati (Giegher), 21

Trinciante, Il (Cervio), 23, 28, 249

tripe sauce, penne with, 190–91

trofie, 118

trout:
  cooked in clay, 212
  grilled, 232
  steaming of, 222

trout-black truffle sauce, spaghetti in, 141

truffle cutters, 77

truffles, 62–64, 141
  cleaning of, 63
  slicing of, 62–63

tuna:
  pasta salad with, 197
  veal with, 46, 269, 287–89

turbante, 451
  preparation of, 456–58

turbante (cont.)
  ripieno, 269, 451, 458–59
turkey, "ossobuco," 269, 291, 294
turkey neck:
  boning of, 246
  stuffed, 245–47
turnip, round, 93, 153–54
turnip greens, see broccolirab
Tuscan beans, see cannellini beans

uova alla fornaia, 63, 172–74

veal, 81, 268–98
  in balsamic vinegar, 269, 290
  brains in lemon sauce, 269, 298
  cuts of, 268–69
  fricassee of, 269, 295–97
  grilled chops, 231
  grilled liver, 232
  ossobuco, 269, 290–95
  peppers stuffed with ricotta and,
    384
  scaloppine, see scaloppine
  spinal marrow, 297–98
  "stuffed" turbante, 269
  sweetbreads, 269, 297
  with tuna sauce, 46, 269, 287–89
  in U.S. vs. Italy, 268
veal breasts:
  boning of, 250–51
  stuffed pressed, 60, 249–54, 269,
    285, 297
veal cutlets, cutting and pounding of,
  269–70
veal kidneys, 269
  cleaning and cutting of, 280–81
  rolled veal scaloppine stuffed with,
    269, 280–84
  sauce, 81–82
veal loins:
  butterflying of, 286
  Italian cut for, 285
  roast, laced with green
    peppercorns and sage, 269, 285–
    287
  rolling of, 287

veal sauce:
  penne stir-sautéed in, 191–92
  stuffed zucchini in, 396–97
Vecchio Molinetto restaurant, 214
vegetable oil, 68
vegetables, 26, 341–99
  bavarese, 444, 447–48
  compote of baked, 343, 373
  cooking of, 77, 343, 344–45, 353,
    357, 360
  cooking times for, 342
  fish-vegetable pasticcio, 332, 338–
    340
  food mills for, 73
  importance of, 341
  in Middle Ages and Renaissance,
    59
  piatto di mezzo, 341, 352, 370, 379,
    444
  pickled, 46–47, 366
  sauces for, 341, 345–46, 349–50,
    354, 358–59, 368, 371–72
  serving style for, 341
  steaming of, 222, 343, 345, 360–61
  types of, 342
  washing or soaking of, 71
  see also specific vegetables
vegetable shortening, 68
vermicelli, 26
Veronese, Paolo, 19
verza, 363–65
  e patate, 363–64
  con salsicce, 364–65
vinegar:
  copper bowls cleaned with, 72
  wine, see wine vinegar
vinegar sauce, chicken with, 242–43
Vin Santo, scaloppine with, 273–74
vitella, 268
  all' aceto balsamico, 269, 290
  arrocchiato di, 269, 285–87
  fricassea di, 269, 295–97
  involtini di, 284–85
  zucchini ripieni in sugo di, 396–97
vitello, 268
  tonnato, 46, 269, 287–89

vol-au-vent, 451, 456–58

walnuts:
  cake, 83–85
  sauce, 91, 136
weights and measures, 505
whisks, 71, 72
wines, 15, 502–3
  cauliflower steamed in, 360–61
  menu suggestions for, 512–16
  table used for, 21
  Vin Santo, 273–74
wine syrup, apricots with, 56, 59
wine vinegar, 45–47
  balsamic, 67, 269, 290
  barrels, 78
  "mothers" in, 44, 78, 290
  in pickles, 46–47

yeast, 45
yeast doughs, 402–30
  for bread, 402–24
  for desserts, 402, 425–30

zabaione, 72, 76
  preparation of, 492
zampone, 51–54, 400
zucchini, 393–99
  cutting of, 393–95
  with pancetta, 395–96
  stuffed, in veal sauce, 396–97
  torte, 55, 397
zucchini, 393–99
  alla pancetta, 395–96
  ripieni in sugo di vitella, 396–97
zucchini blossoms:
  preparation of, 398
  stuffed, 398–99
zucchini corers, 78
zuccotto, 67, 477–79
zuppa, 401
  di cavolo nero, 361
  alla senese, 99–100

Arrocchiato di vitella (*Roast Loin of Veal Laced with Green Peppercorns and Sage*), 285

A TASTE

Ossobuco alla novese (*Ossobuco from Novara*), 293

Polenta alla pistoiese (*Polenta with Sausages and Quail*), 207

Carciofi in umido o in salsa (*Artichokes in Parsley Sauce*), 354